# Evaluating Websites and Web Services:

## Interdisciplinary Perspectives on User Satisfaction

Denis Yannacopoulos
*Technological Educational Institute of Piraeus, Greece*

Panagiotis Manolitzas
*Technical University of Crete, Greece*

Nikolaos Matsatsinis
*Technical University of Crete, Greece*

Evangelos Grigoroudis
*Technical University of Crete, Greece*

A volume in the Advances in Web
Technologies and Engineering (AWTE)
Book Series

| Managing Director: | Lindsay Johnston |
| Production Manager: | Jennifer Yoder |
| Development Editor: | Austin DeMarco |
| Acquisitions Editor: | Kayla Wolfe |
| Typesetter: | Christina Barkanic |
| Cover Design: | Jason Mull |

Published in the United States of America by
Information Science Reference (an imprint of IGI Global)
701 E. Chocolate Avenue
Hershey PA 17033
Tel: 717-533-8845
Fax: 717-533-8661
E-mail: cust@igi-global.com
Web site: http://www.igi-global.com

Library of Congress Cataloging-in-Publication Data

Evaluating websites and web services : interdisciplinary perspectives on user satisfaction / Denis Yannacopoulos, Panagiotis Manolitzas, Nikolaos Matsatsinis, and Evangelos Grigoroudis, editors.
    pages cm
 Includes bibliographical references and index.
   ISBN 978-1-4666-5129-6 (hardcover) -- ISBN 978-1-4666-5130-2 (ebook) -- ISBN 978-1-4666-5132-6 (print & perpetual access) 1. Web sites--Design--Evaluation. 2. Web services--Evaluation. 3. Internet users. I. Yannacopoulos, Denis, 1949-
 TK5105.888.E926 2014
 006.7--dc23
                                        2013046354

This book is published in the IGI Global book series Advances in Web Technologies and Engineering (AWTE) (ISSN: Pending; eISSN: pending)

British Cataloguing in Publication Data
A Cataloguing in Publication record for this book is available from the British Library.

All work contributed to this book is new, previously-unpublished material. The views expressed in this book are those of the authors, but not necessarily of the publisher.

For electronic access to this publication, please contact: eresources@igi-global.com.

# Advances in Web Technologies and Engineering (AWTE) Book Series

ISSN: Pending
EISSN: pending

## MISSION

The **Advances in Web Technologies and Engineering (AWTE) Book Series** aims to provide a platform for research in the area of Information Technology (IT) concepts, tools, methodologies, and ethnography, in the contexts of global communication systems and Web engineered applications. Organizations are continuously overwhelmed by a variety of new information technologies, many are Web based. These new technologies are capitalizing on the widespread use of network and communication technologies for seamless integration of various issues in information and knowledge sharing within and among organizations. This emphasis on integrated approaches is unique to this book series and dictates cross platform and multidisciplinary strategy to research and practice.

The **Advances in Web Technologies and Engineering (AWTE) Book Series** seeks to create a stage where comprehensive publications are distributed for the objective of bettering and expanding the field of web systems, knowledge capture, and communication technologies. The series will provide researchers and practitioners with solutions for improving how technology is utilized for the purpose of a growing awareness of the importance of web applications and engineering.

## COVERAGE

- Case Studies Validating Web-Based IT Solutions
- Data Analytics for Business and Government Organizations
- Human Factors and Cultural Impact of IT-Based Systems
- Knowledge Structure, Classification and Search Algorithms or Engines
- Mobile, Location-Aware, and Ubiquitous Computing
- Ontology and Semantic Web Studies
- Security, Integrity, Privacy and Policy Issues
- Software Agent-Based Applications
- Strategies for Linking Business Needs and IT
- Web Systems Engineering Design

IGI Global is currently accepting manuscripts for publication within this series. To submit a proposal for a volume in this series, please contact our Acquisition Editors at Acquisitions@igi-global.com or visit: http://www.igi-global.com/publish/.

# Titles in this Series

*For a list of additional titles in this series, please visit: www.igi-global.com*

*Evaluating Websites and Web Services Interdisciplinary Perspectives on User Satisfaction*
Denis Yannacopoulos (Technological Educational Institute of Piraeus, Greece) Panagiotis Manolitzas (Technical University of Crete, Greece) Nikolaos Matsatsinis (Technical University of Crete, Greece) and Evangelos Grigoroudis (Technical University of Crete, Greece)
Information Science Reference • copyright 2014 • 328pp • H/C (ISBN: 9781466651296) • US $215.00 (our price)

*Solutions for Sustaining Scalability in Internet Growth*
Mohamed Boucadair (France Telecom-Orange Labs, France) and David Binet (France Telecom, France)
Information Science Reference • copyright 2014 • 288pp • H/C (ISBN: 9781466643055) • US $190.00 (our price)

*Adaptive Web Services for Modular and Reusable Software Development Tactics and Solutions*
Guadalupe Ortiz (University of Cádiz, Spain) and Javier Cubo (University of Málaga, Spain)
Information Science Reference • copyright 2013 • 415pp • H/C (ISBN: 9781466620896) • US $195.00 (our price)

*Public Service, Governance and Web 2.0 Technologies Future Trends in Social Media*
Ed Downey (State University of New York, College at Brockport, USA) and Matthew A. Jones (Portland State University, USA)
Information Science Reference • copyright 2012 • 369pp • H/C (ISBN: 9781466600713) • US $190.00 (our price)

*Performance and Dependability in Service Computing Concepts, Techniques and Research Directions*
Valeria Cardellini (Universita di Roma, Italy) Emiliano Casalicchio (Universita di Roma, Italy) Kalinka Regina Lucas Jaquie Castelo Branco (Universidade de São Paulo, Brazil) Júlio Cezar Estrella (Universidade de São Paulo, Brazil) and Francisco José Monaco (Universidade de São Paulo, Brazil)
Information Science Reference • copyright 2012 • 477pp • H/C (ISBN: 9781609607944) • US $195.00 (our price)

*E-Activity and Intelligent Web Construction Effects of Social Design*
Tokuro Matsuo (Yamagata University, Japan) and Takayuki Fujimoto (Toyo University, Japan)
Information Science Reference • copyright 2011 • 284pp • H/C (ISBN: 9781615208715) • US $180.00 (our price)

*Engineering Reliable Service Oriented Architecture Managing Complexity and Service Level Agreements*
Nikola Milanovic (Model Labs - Berlin, Germany)
Information Science Reference • copyright 2011 • 420pp • H/C (ISBN: 9781609604936) • US $180.00 (our price)

DISSEMINATOR OF KNOWLEDGE

www.igi-global.com

701 E. Chocolate Ave., Hershey, PA 17033
Order online at www.igi-global.com or call 717-533-8845 x100
To place a standing order for titles released in this series, contact: cust@igi-global.com
Mon-Fri 8:00 am - 5:00 pm (est) or fax 24 hours a day 717-533-8661

# Table of Contents

**Section 1**
**E-Government**

## Section 2
## Websites Evaluation

## Section 3
## E-Customer Satisfaction

# Detailed Table of Contents

## Section 1
## E-Government

Over the past few years, e-government growth has resulted in the development of many state and local e-government initiatives in both developing and industrialised countries. In most cases, e-government programs incorporate the implementation and operation of Web portals and Websites, putting information online, transforming processes to Web-based transactions, interacting with citizens and companies. While e-government Websites are evolving, evaluation and effectiveness assessments are emerging processes in order to optimise digital services and enhance the engagement of citizens and companies to government administrative processes for their own benefit. So far, many different measures of governmental Website effectiveness have been developed to address strategic, marketing, and design issues. This chapter aims to provide an insight on the theory and application of evaluation and effectiveness approaches with regards to Web portals and Websites implemented to operate under central or local government authorities. Both quantitative and qualitative aspects are analysed, addressing operational and functional tactics.

# Chapter 2

With the transition from government to e-government, greater transparency in government accountability has occurred. However, state government budgets and performance reports are voluminous and difficult to understand by the average citizen. There is a need for government Websites to promote public trust while providing understandable, meaningful, and usable government accountability information. The public needs to have access to information that links the outcome of government spending so that government can be accountable for their spending. There are three fundamental functions for government: accountability, budgeting, and policy-making. The chapter discusses literature specifically relating to government accountability resulting in a checklist being developed to provide a mechanism for evaluation of government Websites from a technical and usability perspective. Therefore, it is not only important for a Website to have the government accountability information but to also display it in a useful and meaningful format understandable by citizens accessing the Website.

**Chapter 3**

*Rimantas Gatautis, Kaunas University of Technology, Lithuania*
*Elena Vitkauskaite, Kaunas University of Technology, Lithuania*

Adoption of ICT in the public sector has rapidly progressed over the last decade. Many national and local governmental institutions move towards more sophisticated public electronic services aiming to increase service provision efficiency and effectiveness as well as develop services attractive for citizens. However, such digitalization represents supply-driven approach while governmental institutions and software development companies move public services online. Demand side user satisfaction and acceptance usually is ignored supposing ICT-based services pretend to be modern services. Public electronic services' acceptance heavily depends on citizens' attitudes. In this context, citizens' understanding of public electronic service quality plays an important role. The current chapter's propose is to show public electronic service quality assessment model considering three perspectives – environment quality, delivery quality, and outcome quality. The proposed model is verified empirically assessing three different public electronic services in Lithuania.

**Chapter 4**

*Sandra Kalidien, Ministry of Security and Justice, The Netherlands*
*Richard van Witzenburg, Ministry of Security and Justice, The Netherlands*
*Sunil Choenni, Ministry of Security and Justice, The Netherlands*

For the purpose of good and trustworthy management of information for the government, responsible for the justice domain, the research institute was requested to build a monitor that makes it possible to periodically monitor data flows within as well as between organizations of the justice domain. The aim of this monitor is to get insight into the performance and possible bottlenecks in the criminal justice domain. An important component of the monitor is a Web interface. The Web interface should be user friendly and, more importantly, facilitate policy makers to interpret the data flows in the justice domain. To meet with this facilitation, the authors created a fixed set of variables for the interface that minimizes misinterpretation of the data. In this chapter, they describe how they managed to develop and implement the Web interface. Additionally, the authors illustrate how the Web interface works in practice and describe how they managed to evaluate the Web interface on usefulness and satisfaction.

## Section 2
## Websites Evaluation

### Chapter 5

*Drosopoulou Charoula, University of Macedonia, Greece*
*Malama Eleonora-Ioulia, University of Macedonia, Greece*
*Patsioura Fotini, University of Macedonia, Greece*
*Vlachopoulou Maro, University of Macedonia, Greece*

Developing their e-marketing strategy, Destination Marketing Organizations (DMOs) invest in the establishment of their Websites to provide extended accessibility, real-time information/services, and personalization capabilities. This chapter aims to review prior tourism studies that refer to Website evaluation by taking DMOs' Websites as the focus of the investigation. A comprehensive literature review on theories, models, and surveys on evaluating tourism Websites is presented and analyzed. The major benefit of this study is the digest of multiple approaches regarding DMOs' Website evaluation within the tourism sector. The chapter gives an integrated overview of the historical development of Website evaluation studies in the tourism field in order to draw conclusions about the dimensions and key factors that drive Website success. Furthermore, the effectiveness of the DMOs' Websites of five Mediterranean countries are assessed through content analysis in terms of information, communication, transaction, relationship, and technical merit dimensions based on a modified approach of the ICTRT model (Li & Wang, 2010). The research findings should be of interest to DMOs as the findings shed light on the effectiveness of their Websites over a period of time facilitating continuous improvements and comparisons between competitive tourism destinations/countries.

### Chapter 6

*Athanassios Vozikis, University of Piraeus, Greece*

In the context of intensified business competition and globalization of markets, the strategic use of the Internet in e-commerce can provide a business advantage. The research scope was the evaluation and benchmarking of pharmaceutical companies' Websites in Greece, in order to draw conclusions about the level of Information and Communication Technologies (ICT) use and specifically the ways they become active in e-business. For the evaluation of the Websites, the authors used scientifically accept-able criteria suited to the business sector of our research. From the survey, it was unveiled that phar-maceutical companies operating in Greece have a rather limited Web presence. Specifically, out of the 112 pharmaceutical companies, only 60 have developed their own Website with the multinationals to be more active. In addition, the majority of the pharmaceutical companies' Websites provide business information but limited additional information and interactive features to potential users. In conclusion, the pharmaceutical industry in Greece must undergo critical steps to further obtain an anthropocentric approach that the global pharmaceuticals sector has already begun to adopt.

**Chapter 7**

*Leo Lentz, Utrecht University, The Netherlands*

*Sanne Elling, firMM Information + Service Design, The Netherlands*

Websites increasingly encourage users to provide comments on the quality of specific pages by clicking on a feedback button and filling out a feedback form. The authors investigate users' (N=153) abilities to provide such feedback and the kind of feedback that is the result. They compare the results of these so called user page review methods with the concurrent think-aloud method, applied on the same websites. Results show that it is important to keep feedback tools both simple and attractive so that users will be able and willing to provide feedback. The authors also find that the number of problem detections is higher in the review condition, but the two methods seem to be highly complementary. An analysis of the detections from a practice-oriented perspective reveals that the overlap between the two methods is rather high and that reviewing participants seem capable of signalling important problems that are also exposed in a think-aloud study.

## Section 3
## E-Customer Satisfaction

**Chapter 8**

*Dimitrios Drosos, Technological Education Institute of Piraeus, Greece*

*Nikolaos Tsotsolas, Technological Education Institute of Piraeus, Greece*

The rapid development of tourist supply and demand makes Information Technologies (IT) significant, and thus, they increasingly play a more critical role in tourism marketing, distribution, promotion, and coordination. IT influences the strategic management and marketing of contemporary organisations as a paradigm-shift is experienced, transforming the best business practices globally. IT is one of the main key influences of competitiveness in the tourism/travel industry. The original purpose for adopting IT systems was simply to provide an automatic means of store and manage data (e.g. on flights and accommodation). At the same time, IT in the tourist sector enables an increased volume of transactions to be handled rapidly and effectively. This chapter presents an original customer satisfaction survey in the Greek Online Travel Agencies. For the collection of the data, a Website questionnaire was used in order to better record the customers' views on the service overall as well as their satisfaction levels on particular aspects of the service. The survey was conducted within the period September – November 2012. Final input data consists of 510 questionnaires.

**Chapter 9**

*Luc Honore Petnji Yaya, Universitat Internacional de Catalunya, Spain*

*Frederic Marimon, Universitat Internacional de Catalunya, Spain*

*Marti Casadesus, Universitat de Girona, Spain*

This chapter proposes a model that (1) analyzes the direct and indirect effects of e-service quality on satisfaction and value with the moderating/mediating role of value as well as (2) analyzes the positive impact of gender, age, education, and income on quality, satisafaction, and value. The overall results show service quality is a major predictor of perceived value, which in turn is positively related to customer satisfaction. The mediating/moderating role of perceived value on the relationship between service quality and satisfaction is confirmed. Contrary to the proposed hypothesis, no relationships and no differences in the various subgroups categories of age, education, and income are detected in terms of service quality, value, and satisfaction. Consequently, customers' demographic characteristics limitation on the adoption of online banking is now a past history. However, the authors recommend that managers always consider each segment of the customers' demographic profiles individually while making their decisions.

*Evangelos Grigoroudis, Technical University of Crete, Greece*
*Vassilios Fortsas, Technical University of Crete, Greece*
*Petros Pallis, Technical University of Crete, Greece*
*Nikolaos Matsatsinis, Technical University of Crete, Greece*

In the last few years, customer loyalty for products and services has become an object of extensive studies from researchers of various scientific fields. Its importance is justified from the fact that, in many cases, particularly in strong competition conditions, measuring customer satisfaction does not provide a reliable quality performance indicator for business organizations. According to recent research, loyalty is defined as a positive level of customers' commitment, which should not be based only in previous purchases (repeated or not) of a product/service. This chapter presents the development of a multicriteria methodology aiming at measuring user loyalty in social networking services and estimating the importance of influencing factors. In this context, a multicriteria analysis approach is adopted in order to measure user loyalty, assuming that the overall commitment depends on a number of criteria. The applied multicriteria approach is based on the UTADIS method, and the presented results confirm the strong relation between user satisfaction and loyalty. The results, however, reveal also that satisfaction is a necessary but not a sufficient condition for customer loyalty.

*Gabriella Spinelli, Brunel University, UK*
*Seema Jain, Brunel University, UK & Age UK, UK*

With the unprecedented changes in demographic structure, the ageing population is becoming a more powerful and attractive audience for Web-based services. To provide this group with satisfying user experiences, it is necessary to understand the impact that the ageing process has on abilities, needs, and expectations. While researchers and practitioners can apply inclusive design and methods to centre the development of Internet-based services around the lifestyle and behaviours of the ageing population, it is also important to consider what innovations can be introduced to online services to make them more attractive and sustainably adopted among older people. The chapter is centred on issues affecting the online experience of users in later life: physical and cognitive abilities, aspirations, and constraints. It then provides an overview of the methods inspired by User-Centred Design. Finally, it considers challenges that go beyond the remit of design but still powerfully affect the Web experience of older users.

## Section 4
## Special Topics in E-Services

### Chapter 12

*Constantinos K. Coursaris, Michigan State University, USA*

*Sarah J. Swierenga, Michigan State University, USA*

*Pamela Whitten, Michigan State University, USA*

This chapter describes a multi-group research study of the usability evaluation and consequent results from participants' experiences with the MyPryamidTracker.gov Website application. The authors report on a study of a sample consisting of 25 low-income participants with varied levels of vision (i.e., sighted, low vision, and blind Internet users). Usability was assessed via both objective and subjective measures. Overall, participants had significant difficulty understanding how to use the MyPyramidTracker.gov Website. The chapter concludes with major recommendations pertaining to the implementation of Website design elements including pathway/navigation, search, links, text chunking, and frames layout. An extensive set of actionable Website design recommendations and a usability questionnaire are also provided that can be used by researchers in their future evaluations of Websites and Web services.

### Chapter 13

*Georgia Kyriakaki, Technical University of Crete, Greece*

*Nikolaos Matsatsinis, Technical University of Crete, Greece*

E-learning has known a large expansion in the past decades due to the advent of the Internet as a major communication medium and the WWW as a technology that provides enormous capabilities for information exchange anytime, anywhere, anyhow. Few studies exist on the evaluation of e-learning Websites in terms of their pedagogical quality that is, on their success in helping learners learn through specific pedagogical principles. Pedagogical evaluation, however, is very important in e-learning as it can improve the quality of the system greatly and help the decision maker choose the most appropriate among different systems or designs. This chapter proposes a multi-criteria evaluation model for e-learning websites based on well-known pedagogical principles, namely Bloom's taxonomy of six cognitive objectives, Knowledge, Comprehension, Application, Analysis, Synthesis, and Evaluation.

### Chapter 14

*Hanna Jochmann-Mannak, University of Twente, The Netherlands*

*Leo Lentz, Utrecht University, The Netherlands*

*Theo Huibers, University of Twente, The Netherlands*

*Ted Sanders, Utrecht University, The Netherlands*

This chapter presents an experiment with 158 children, aged 10 to 12, in which search performance and attitudes towards an informational Website are investigated. The same Website was designed in 3 different types of interface design varying in playfulness of navigation structure and in playfulness of visual design. The type of interface design did not have an effect on children's search performance, but it did influence children's feelings of emotional valence and their evaluation of "goodness." Children felt most positive about the Website with a classical navigation structure and playful aesthetics. They found the playful image map Website least good. More importantly, children's search performance was much more effective and efficient when using the search engine than when browsing the menu. Furthermore, this chapter explores the challenge of measuring affective responses towards digital interfaces with children by presenting an elaborate evaluation of different methods.

**Chapter 15**
*S. Zimeras, University of the Aegean, Greece*

Information system users, administrators, and designers are all interested in performance evaluation since their goal is to obtain or provide the highest performance at the lowest cost. This goal has resulted in continuing evolution of higher performance and lower cost systems leading to today's proliferation of workstations and personal computers, many of which have better performance than earlier supercomputers. As the variety of Web services applications (Websites) increases, it gets more important to have a set of evaluation criteria that should evaluate the performance of their effectiveness. Based on those criteria, the quality of the services that the Web applications are providing could be analysed. This work represents software metrics that could (or need) be used to quantify the quality of the information that the Web services are providing. These measures could be useful to understand problematic frameworks during the implementation of the Websites and could lead to solutions preventing those problems.

# Preface

Internet plays a vital role for the development of global economy. Using Websites, people have broad access to information and products. Given the fast growth of Internet and e-services, significant research focuses on the evaluation of Websites and Web services using very different methodological approaches and tools. The main objective of these research efforts is the improvement of services provided to users and, thus, the quality and efficiency of Websites and Web services. Taking into account the rapidly evolving technological and business environment, current research gives emphasis on the quality evaluation of e-services, studying the factors that may affect user satisfaction.

The main aim of this book is to present original methodological approaches for Websites and Web services evaluation. In particular, this edited volume aims at presenting the different interdisciplinary perspectives on the problem and illustrating successful real-world applications from different areas, like governance, banking, tourism, health, and education.

The book is organized into 4 sections, including 15 chapters that cover all these topics in a comprehensive manner. The first 4 chapters refer to the evaluation of e-government services. In particular, the first chapter by Patsioura presents an overview of evaluation approaches regarding Web portals and Websites implemented to operate central or local government authorities. The chapter discusses both quantitative and qualitative aspects, addressing operational and functional tactics.

In the 2nd chapter, Carstens, Kies, and Stockman emphasize the need for government Websites to promote public trust, while providing understandable, meaningful, and usable government accountability information. They discuss literature helpful in the evaluation of government accountability and transparency Websites and provide a mechanism for evaluation of government Websites from a technical and usability perspective. The chapter pinpoints the importance for a Website not only to have the government accountability information but also to display it in a useful and meaningful format understandable by citizens.

Chapter 3 by Gautatis and Vitkauskaite proposes a new methodology for the evaluation of the e-government sites based on a public electronic service quality assessment model that considers 3 perspectives: environment quality, delivery quality, and outcome quality. The proposed model is verified empirically, assessing 3 different public electronic services in Lithuania.

In chapter 4 by Kalidien, van Witzenburg, and Choenni, a successful implementation of an e-government Web site is presented. In particular, for the purpose of good and trustworthy management information for the government, responsible for the justice domain, a monitor has been developed that makes it possible to periodically monitor data flows within as well as between organizations of the justice domain. The aim of this monitor is to get insight into the performance and possible bottlenecks in the criminal justice domain.

The following 3 chapters cover alternative approaches in Website evaluation based on user preferences, usability tests, and empirical research. In particular, chapter 5, by Drosopoulou, Malama, Patsioura, and Vlachopoulou, reviews prior tourism studies referring to the evaluation of Destination Marketing Organizations' (DMOs) Websites. The authors discuss alternative theories, models, and surveys on evaluating tourism Websites, giving emphasis on the key factors that play an important role for the success of these particular Websites. In addition, they present an evaluation of 5 Mediterranean DMOs' Websites using content analysis in terms of information, communication, transaction, relationship, and technical merit dimensions based on a modified approach of the Information, Communication, Transaction, Relationship, and Technical (ICTRT) merit model.

The next chapter, by Vozikis, focuses on the evaluation and benchmarking of Greek pharmaceutical companies' Websites in order to draw conclusions about the level of Information and Communication Technology (ICT) use and, specifically, the ways they become active in e-business. The presented results show that Greek pharmaceutical companies have a rather limited Web presence, while they provide limited additional information and interactive features to potential users.

In Chapter 7, Lentz and Elling study users' comments on the quality of specific Webpages and investigate the users' abilities to provide such feedback, as well as the kind of feedback that is obtained. To this end, they compare the results of the, so-called, user page review methods with the concurrent think-aloud method, applied on the same Websites, and they show that it is important to keep feedback tools both simple and attractive so that users will be able and willing to provide feedback.

Chapters 8-11 refer to research in the field of user or e-customer satisfaction. In this context, Drosos and Tsotsolas present an original customer satisfaction survey in Greek Online Travel Agencies. In addition, the authors present a literature review regarding information technology in the tourism industry and customer satisfaction on online tourist services, and discuss the user satisfaction levels on particular aspects of the service.

In the following chapter, Yaya, Marimon, and Casadesus propose a model that analyzes the direct and indirect effects of e-service quality on satisfaction and value with the moderating/mediating role of value. In addition, they study the positive impact of gender, age, education, and income on quality, satisfaction, and value. The presented results show that service quality is a major predictor of perceived value, which in turn is positively related to customer satisfaction.

Chapter 10, by Grigoroudis, Fortsas, Pallis, and Matsatsinis, presents the development of a multi-criteria methodology aiming at measuring user loyalty in social networking services and estimating the importance of influencing factors. In the proposed approach, a multi-criteria analysis model is adopted in order to measure user loyalty, assuming that the overall commitment depends on a number of criteria. The applied multi-criteria approach is based on the UTADIS method, and the presented results confirm the strong relation between user satisfaction and loyalty. The results, however, also reveal that satisfaction is a necessary but not a sufficient condition for customer loyalty.

The next chapter, by Spinelli and Jain, focuses on issues affecting the online experience of users in later life, like physical and cognitive abilities, aspirations and constraints, etc. The chapter provides an overview of the methods inspired by User-Centered Design and presents challenges that go beyond the remit of design but still powerfully affect the Web experience of older users.

The last 4 chapters of the book refer to special topics on Websites evaluation, Web services, and e-services. In particular, Chapter 12, by Coursaris, Swierenga, and Whitten, presents a multi-group research study of the usability evaluation and consequent results from participants' experiences with the MyPryamidTracker.gov Website application. The chapter concludes with major recommendations pertaining to the implementation of Website design elements, including pathway/navigation, search, links, text chunking, and frames layout. An extensive set of actionable Website design recommendations and a usability questionnaire are also provided that can be used by researchers in their future evaluations of Websites and Web services.

In the following chapter, Kyriakaki and Matsatsinis propose a multi-criteria evaluation model for e-learning Websites based on well-known pedagogical principles, namely Bloom's Taxonomy of 6 cognitive objectives: Knowledge, Comprehension, Application, Analysis, Synthesis, and Evaluation. The aim of the proposed approach is to serve as preference model for a decision maker (e.g., educator, educational organization, learner) wishing to employ an appropriate Web-based learning environment to meet his/her needs. In this context, the decision makers' attitudes towards the pedagogical characteristics of the system are related to a specific set of Web-based learning services and criteria that can enhance the decision process.

In chapter 14, Jochmann-Mannak, Lentz, Huibers, and Sanders present an experiment in a sample of children, aged 10 to 12, in which search performance and attitudes towards an informational Website are investigated. The authors analyze the effects of different design approaches of an informational Website on children's interaction with these interfaces and on children's affective responses towards these interfaces. They also explore the effects of children's use of a search engine on search performance and affective responses.

The book closes with a chapter by Zimeras, who presents software metrics that may be used to quantify the quality of the information provided by Web services. These measures are based on probabilistic models and may be useful to understand problematic frameworks during the implementation of the Websites and lead to solutions preventing those problems.

This edited book may be used as a textbook for courses covering topics like information management, e-government, information technology, as well as Website evaluation methodologies and tools. In addition, the book aims at providing a comprehensive overview of the recent developments, from different scientific perspectives, in the area of user-oriented Website and Web services evaluation. We hope that this book will provide a useful resource of ideas, techniques, and methods for additional research on this topic.

*Denis Yannacopoulos*
*Technological Educational Institute of Piraeus, Greece*

*Panagiotis Manolitzas*
*Technical University of Crete, Greece*

*Nikolaos Matsatsinis*
*Technical University of Crete, Greece*

*Evangelos Grigoroudis*
*Technical University of Crete, Greece*

# Acknowledgment

The editors of the book would like to express their sincere thanks to all the authors who have devoted considerable time and effort for their comprehensive contributions. We also thank IGI Global and the publishing team for their encouragement and support during the preparation of the book.

*Denis Yannacopoulos*
*Technological Educational Institute of Piraeus, Greece*

*Panagiotis Manolitzas*
*Technical University of Crete, Greece*

*Nikolaos Matsatsinis*
*Technical University of Crete, Greece*

*Evangelos Grigoroudis*
*Technical University of Crete, Greece*

# Section 1
# E-Government

# Chapter 1
# Evaluating E-Government

**Fotini Patsioura**
*University of Macedonia, Greece*

## ABSTRACT

*Over the past few years, e-government growth has resulted in the development of many state and local e-government initiatives in both developing and industrialised countries. In most cases, e-government programs incorporate the implementation and operation of Web portals and Websites, putting information online, transforming processes to Web-based transactions, interacting with citizens and companies. While e-government Websites are evolving, evaluation and effectiveness assessments are emerging processes in order to optimise digital services and enhance the engagement of citizens and companies to government administrative processes for their own benefit. So far, many different measures of governmental Website effectiveness have been developed to address strategic, marketing, and design issues. This chapter aims to provide an insight on the theory and application of evaluation and effectiveness approaches with regards to Web portals and Websites implemented to operate under central or local government authorities. Both quantitative and qualitative aspects are analysed, addressing operational and functional tactics.*

## INTRODUCTION

E-Government is the use of Information and Communication Technology (ICT) and particularly Internet-based and web-based telecommunication practices to facilitate connections within and between the authorities and agencies of the Public Sector and also deliver government critical information and digital services to both citizens and companies. Various e-Government business models have been implemented and matured to enhance the efficiency of public sector organisational processes by supporting transactions between the employees in government agencies and also

transactions with private individuals, businesses and other stakeholders in the e-government environment.

So far, e-government web sites remain the main critical information resource and service delivery medium. Because of the diversity and range of e-government web sites, a typology of them is required to address issues with regards to business models' analysis, strategic design, management and evolution. With most e-government projects in the maturity phase of their life cycle, effectiveness assessment is becoming vital for the optimisation of their performance. Particularly in the e-government area, evaluation and effective-

DOI: 10.4018/978-1-4666-5129-6.ch001

ness measures of public sector web portals and sites are both quantitative and qualitative. While quantitative measures examine the level of adoption and impact of the web sites in question with the use of e-metrics and user-satisfaction indices, qualitative measures have a different dual purpose: firstly, to investigate and assess the government web sites performance in terms of functionality and usability and secondly to identify information and system qualitative factors in evaluating e-services delivered by the web sites in question.

The European Commission of the European Union and the U.S.A E-Government Resource Centre have provided guidelines and standards for effective federal, state and local government web sites addressing analysis, design and evaluation issues. However, in many cases governmental web portals and sites have failed to meet their objectives. In this context, the implementation of evaluation frameworks is vital as it will contribute to the identification of the key performance factors and indicators for better and further e-government development.

It is a common belief among academics and practitioners that e-government is now growing in a fast manner. Government web sites are transforming, from basic online presence providing mainly information and a medium level of interactivity to fully transactional channels. Meanwhile, Web 2.0 government has strengthened the relationship between governments and the citizens or companies. For public and government administration authorities that have already stepped in the digital era proving information, communication and services through the operation web portals and web sites, web site evaluation should be a continuous process to achieve efficiency of their performance.

## DEFINING E-GOVERNMENT

## What is E-Government

The e-government idea was introduced by a former U.S vice president and includes two concepts: firstly the governments' obligation to provide a link to citizens for getting services from various government agencies in an automatic way and secondly the governments' need to reduce cost and improve performance with the use of information and communication networks among its authorities (Almarabeh & AbuAli, 2010). Despite its short history (e-government emerged in the late 90's), the e-government concept has been well defined by academics and researchers. Different definitions of e-government focus on different elements and dimensions of government or governance emphasizing on its strategic role. However, in most definitions, the use of Information and Communication Technology (ICT) is described as the key enabler for all e-government projects.

It is clear, that each definition describes the environment formed in that particular period of time by the advances and applications of ICT and the e-government initiatives in progress. Table 1 includes definitions to capture the evolution of e-government over the past ten years.

Bannister's (2007) definition of e-government as the "delivery of government services over the internet in general and the Web in particular" describes best the e-government evolution with most e-government projects implementing and supporting web-based applications through the development and exploitation of public portals and web sites. As ICT advances, e-government portals and web sites are becoming more complex in architecture and structure supporting multiple business models.

*Table 1. E-government definitions*

| Year | Definition | Author |
|------|------------|--------|
| 2000 | E-government is the continuous optimization of service delivery, constituency participation and governance by transforming internal and external relationships through technology, the Internet and new media. | Gartner Group (Baum & Di Maio) |
| 2001 | A government's use of technology, such as the Internet, to aid the delivery of information and services to citizens, employees, business partners, other agencies and other government entities. | Layne & Lee |
| 2004 | The use of ICT in public administrations combined with organisational change and new skills in order to improve public services, democratic processes and strengthen support to the public policies. | European Information Society |
| 2004 | E-Government refers to the use by government agencies of information technologies that have the ability to transform relations with citizens, businesses, and other arms of government. These technologies can serve a variety of different ends: better delivery of government services to citizens, improved interactions with business and industry, citizen empowerment through access to information, or more efficient government management. | World Bank |
| 2007 | electronic Government' (or in short 'e-Government') essentially refers to 'The utilization of Information Technology (IT), Information and Communication Technologies (ICTs), and other web-based telecommunication technologies to improve and/or enhance on the efficiency and effectiveness of service delivery in the public sector. | Jeong |
| 2011 | E-government refers to the use of information and communication technologies (ICT) - such as Wide Area Networks, the Internet, and mobile computing - by government agencies. | The United Nations |

## E-Government Business and Service Delivery Models

The scientific field of e-government is almost 20 years old with official governmental web sites first appearing in the mid 1990's (Coursey & Norris, 2008). However, several business models were formed and analysed in literature. An e-government business model identifies the key stakeholders in the e-government environment and their interrelationships and specifies the key business processes that represent the integration of governmental information and services.

Figure 1 presents the main business models of e-government with regards to outside and inside the government stakeholders based on the academic literature (Holmes, 2001; Fang, 2002; Beyon - Davies, 2007; Palvia & Shalma, 2007; Albarabeh et al, 2010):

- G2G (Government to Government) refers to ICT applications (information systems, intranets, data & communication networks, Internet services) providing a common communication and information exchange base to accomplish and optimise coordination and cooperation between local, departmental and national authorities

- G2E (Government to Employee) is the employment of basically information and other back office systems to support the main stakeholder of internal governmental body, the employee

- G2B (Government to Business) describes all online interactions and transactions between the government agencies and private sector companies. Two of its main forms are e-procurement and auctioning of government oversupplies

- B2G (Business to Government) refers to public sector businesses selling services and products to government agencies with the use of Internet and ICTs

- G2C (Government to Citizen) remains the business model of most e-government initiatives in which the government provides online access to information and digital services to its main outside stakeholders (the citizen)

*Figure1. E-government business models*

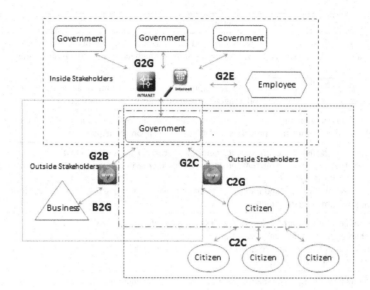

- C2G (Citizen to Government) refers to the two –way communication activities which allows citizens to interact online with their government requesting answers and solutions or providing feedback with regards to the government agencies' performance
- C2C (Citizen to Citizen) describes a future perspective of e-government with citizens interacting with each other forming an online community to address governmental issues

In recent times, web based software platforms such as public portals, web sites and digital services remain a common place for the implementation of e-government policies with outside stakeholders. The establishment of local, regional and national web sites is the main outlet to integrate G2B and G2C activities. Companies and citizens interacting with government web sites have convenient access to textual and multimedia information and digital services outside of office hours avoiding long waits in queues to have a face to face meeting with civil servants (Fairweather & Rogerson, 2006). In addition, C2C interactions as a result of

the e-government evolution require more advanced web based applications to enable the citizens' e-participation and therefore support consultative and participatory activities (Reddick, 2011).

## E-Government and E-Commerce: Similarities and Differences

E-commerce and e-government are subsets of e-business adopting technological innovations to transform their internal and external relations for their own and their stakeholders benefit. E-commerce proceeds e-government and this is why early e-government initiatives have adopted concepts, technologies and processes already applied online in the private sector. Therefore, the comparison between e-government and e-commerce could be considered justified and constructive uncovering the deficiencies and benefits of the two concepts correlation in theory and practice.

Similar to e-commerce companies that use ICT to conduct business with other companies (B2B), engage customers (B2C) and support the work of their employees (B2E), organisations with e-government activities enable the optimisation of interagency coordination and cooperation (G2G), improve communication and transactions with citizens (G2C) or organizations (G2B) and provide public servants with the appropriate technical tools to increase their productivity (G2E) (Fang, 2002; Scholl et al, 2010) (Figure2).

It is evident that e-government business models have been influenced by commercial business models on the Internet as they share the same social and technological environment (Carter & Belanger, 2004). However, the drivers and priorities of e-government affected by its political concept formed different to commercial online relationships (Warkentin, 2002).

Comparative analyses between e-commerce and e-government outlets are limited in literature review. Table 2 summarises differences and similarities of the two concepts identified in previous research (Jorgenson & Cable, 2002; AL-Shehry et al, 2006; Stahl, 2008; Scholl et al, 2009).

On the other hand, many state that a comparison between e-commerce and e-government web sites is irrelevant since payment transaction is the main interaction format of commercial web-sites. In addition, the political nature of e-government policies is also an important distinguishing factor between commercial and government web sites (Warkentin et al, 2002). In this context, Morgeson III and Mithas (2009) per-

formed a comparative analysis between e-government and e-business web sites (the main objective of these sites is the dissemination of information similar to e-government web sites). Outcomes of their research support the idea that e-government can learn from the private sector but should take under consideration the differences of their target group's needs and expectations.

## E-Government Web Sites Typology

So far, in the area of e-government there is not an accepted government web site classification or typology. This is due to the diversity in scope and range of the implemented e-government projects. However, a categorisation of government portals and web sites is necessary in order to understand their strategic and organisational objectives.

Two criteria are used to classify current e-government web sites (Figure 3):

- Level of e-government: based on this criterion, government web sites could be local, state/provincial, regional, national or international (Albarabeh and Abuali, 2010).
- Level of growth (maturity)/service development: A lot of growth and maturity models were implemented to conceptualise the steps or stages of the government

*Figure 2. E-Commerce and e-government business models*

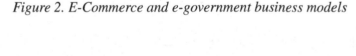

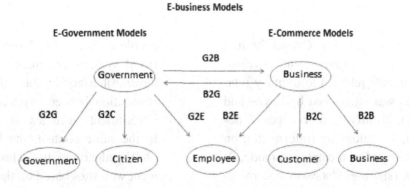

*Table 2.Similarities and differences between e-commerce and e-government*

| Elements of Comparison | E-Commerce | E-Government | Similar | Different |
|---|---|---|---|---|
| **Motivation** | Make profit | Maximise social utility, create e-participation | | *a* |
| | Cost reduction of service delivery | Cost reduction of service delivery | *a* | |
| | Automation of internal processes | Automation of internal processes | *a* | |
| **Objectives** | Sale of products and services | Optimisation of service quality to citizens | | *a* |
| | Information provision | Information provision | *a* | |
| | Online Customer service | Online services to citizens | | *a* |
| **Priority** | Safe & secure transactions | Minimise digital divide | | *a* |
| **Technology** | Internet, Web Based Platforms, Back Office Systems | Internet, Web based platforms, back office systems | *a* | |
| **Decision Making Authority** | Centralised | Dispersion of authority | | *a* |
| **Target Group** | customers, potential customers | Any Citizen | | *a* |
| **Legislation** | Freedom | laws and regulations restrictions and complexity | | *a* |
| **Services** | Primarily transactional | Primarily informational | | *a* |

*Figure 3. E-government websites typology*

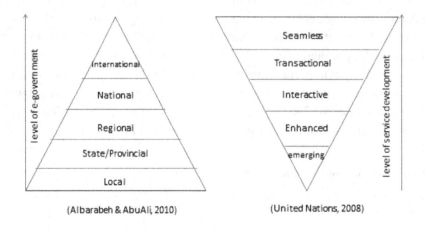

(Albarabeh & AbuAli, 2010)       (United Nations, 2008)

web sites implementation. One of the first classification of e-government development, commonly referred to in many relative studies was introduced by Layne and Lee (2001), identifying four stages of development, 1)cataloguing (information on site are presented in a catalogue mode, 2) transaction (site uses database systems to enable transactions, 3)vertical integration (local systems are linked to higher lever ones) 4)horizontal integration (an interconnection between systems across sever government agencies is accomplished). In the same context, the United Nations (2002) identified five classes of government web sites based on the service development 1)emerging (simple online presence), 2)enhanced (information on the web site becomes more dynamic) 3) interactive (the web site enable two-way interactive communication through the web site) 4) transactional (several transactions are conducted) 4) seamless (the site provides fully integrated digital services).

Based on the above classification, a local site (i.e. a Municipality's web site) could be a transactional web site, whereas a national site (i.e. a Ministry's portal) could be an enhanced site because of the differences in the organisational objectives or the differences in the technological requirements with regards to the services provided by the government authorities.

## EVALUATING E-GOVERNMENT WEB SITES

Web site evaluation refers to the assessment of a web site's performance towards specific criteria. The importance of e-government web sites' evaluation due to the vast investments of countries and agencies and the raised requirements and expectations of citizens for better online services, resulted in a variety of models, methods and practices. With e-government web sites including a wide range of materials from simple information publications to databases and digital services available online, the evaluation of governmental Internet performance has become a complex and demanding process, yet vital (Gupta & Jana, 2003).

Despite the importance of the evaluation procedure and the attention given by academics and practitioners, the evaluation of e-government initiatives is considered to be immature with reference to management and development tools (Alshawi et al, 2007). In addition, because of the diversity in design and implementation of the e-government web-based projects (Middleton, 2007), it is difficult to summarise the different

perspectives and methodologies developed by academics and practitioners with regards to their measurement and assessment.

This sections attempts to categorise both quantitative and qualitative methodologies of governmental web sites' evaluation. The concept of G2C and G2B web sites as web-based information systems is adopted in order to present the different dimensions and aspects of their evaluation. Figure 4, illustrates the identified approaches of e-government web sites' evaluation towards the basic elements and aspects of an integrated web-based information system delivering information and services to both business and citizens. In that context, governmental web site evaluation and effectiveness measurements attempt to investigate and assess its performance towards the strategic and organisation objectives of the government authority or agency operating the web site and the end users' needs and requirements using the web site, in that case the outside stakeholders (citizens and business interacting with the web site).

Specifically based on a literature review, the following approaches and methodologies were identified:

- Conceptual evaluation frameworks' implementation which identify the effectiveness variables towards the web site's objectives.
- Usability measurements to examine the user interface effectiveness.
- E-services' qualitative measurements to assess the web site's performance towards the delivery of digital services.
- User-satisfaction models to measure up the overall positive or negative web site's impact to its end users.

The evaluation measurement of e-government web sites will provide meaningful feedback to improve design, content and management features. The selection of the appropriate evaluation methods could create a scientific basis for governmental administration decisions (Luo & Shi, 2010). Both

*Figure 4. Evaluation approaches of e-government web sites*

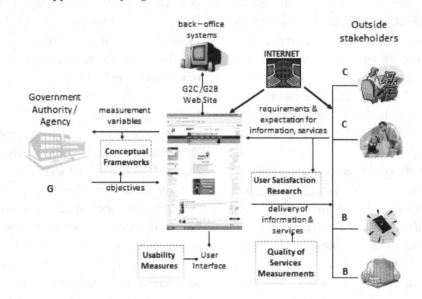

subjective perceptions of the end users and web site consumers and measures based on objective criteria are necessary to complete an overall analysis of the web site's performance (Morgeson III & Mithas, 2009).

## Conceptual Evaluation Frameworks

Conceptual frameworks in web site evaluation research identify the quality factors and their interrelationships in order to investigate their importance in terms of efficiency and effectiveness. With Regards to e-government, several evaluation frameworks have been implemented and tested by academics.

Table 3 presents some of the related research presenting the criteria examined and the methodologies used for their implementation or empirical testing.

An analysis of the conceptual evaluation frameworks reveals that there is no identification or consistency with regards to their theoretical approach or the methodologies of assessment. Each evaluation framework focuses on different aspects and elements of e-government web sites' development and operation.

An early attempt to address the e-government evaluation in terms of citizens' adoption by Carter and Belanger (2004) was based on constructs established in the area B2C e-commerce like Technology Acceptance Model (TAM) and Diffusion of Innovation Theory (DOI), but also introduced the perception of trustworthiness to encompass the trust to Government dimension.

It is evident that many e-government evaluation studies are influenced by research in the area of Information Systems (IS) conceptualising e-government web sites as integrated information systems delivering services to different stakeholders in a complicated social and technical context. This approach led to the study and analysis of qualitative factors closely related to the IS theory like information, system and service quality (Wang et al, 2008) and the analysis of qualitative variables to address the social and financial aspects of the e-government environment (Alshawi, 2007).

Other approaches focus on the specific characteristics of the web site as the main medium to deliver information and services to citizens. Wang et al (2005) incorporated to their evaluation framework web site features based on the main citizens' activities on government web sites,

*Table 3. Conceptual evaluation frameworks for e-government web sites*

| Authors | Concept | Evaluation Criteria | Methodologies |
|---|---|---|---|
| Carter and Belanger, 2004 | Provide a framework from the integration of constructs from the technology acceptance model (TAM), diffusions of innovation theory (DOI) and Web trust model to investigate the adoption of e-government initiatives by the citizens. | • DOI (compatibility, relative advantage, image, complexity.) <br> • TAM (perceived ease of use, perceived usefulness.) <br> • Trustworthiness (trust of Internet, trust of Government.) | Data collected from users. |
| Wang et al, 2005 | Web site evaluation is based on the transaction between the individual & the web site. | Three clusters of variables: <br> • Site characteristic. <br> • Task characteristics. <br> • Individual characteristics. | Case Study (web site development.) |
| Eschenfelder & Miller, 2005 | Openness of e-government portals should be evaluated in a social-technical context. | • Internal website/information characteristics. <br> • Elements to capture the social and political context of the information. <br> • Assumptions about the roles of citizens and government information. | Comparative Case study of U.S state web sites. |
| Melitski et al, 2005 | Provide an evaluation framework to be applied national and international e-government web sites. | • Security & privacy. <br> • Usability. <br> • Content. <br> • Services. <br> • Citizen participation. | Applied to several e-government web sites. |
| Alshawi et al, 2007 | Identify evaluating factors that influence citizens' utilisation of e-government web sites. | • Technical issues (performance, accessibility.) <br> • Economical issues (cost saving.) <br> • Social issues (openness, trust, perceived ease of use and perceived usefulness. | Literature analysis |
| Liu et al, 2008 | Provide Key Performance Indicators for different e-government stakeholders. | Value Categories: <br> • Strategic. <br> • Operational. <br> • Social. <br> • Financial. | Comparative analysis of previous public value frameworks and Case Study. |
| Wang and Liao, 2008 | An adaption of an IS success model in the e-government context. | • Information quality. <br> • System quality. <br> • Service quality. <br> • Use. <br> • User satisfaction. <br> • Perceived net benefit. | Data collected from users. |

while Eschenfelder and Miller (2005) introduced objective and subjective measures of the web site and its information to assess the openness of government web sites and portals. In the same concept, Melitski et al (2005) proposed factors that influence the quality of government web sites approach in a five-step framework addressing usability, security, content, services and citizens participation issues.

Liu et al, (Liu, Derzsi, Raus & Kipp, 2008) were the first to provide Key Performance Area and Key Performance Indicators for government projects. Their work based on a comparative analysis of previous value framework was empirical tested and provided four value categories to assess the success of governmental web sites with reference to their strategic role and objectives addressing financial and social implications of their environment.

On the whole, despite the limited and in some ways unclear conceptual e-government evaluation research, the proposed frameworks introduced several key variables focusing on different aspects and perspectives, providing guidance for the development of both qualitative and quantitative evaluation indices.

## Usability Measures

Web usability measures examine how useful, user-friendly and accessible is a web site with respect to the needs and expectations of its target audience. Simple, clear and consistent web site design enables users to perform their tasks and activities effortlessly during their navigation (Cappel & Juan, 2007). Nielsen (2000) created the acronym HOME (High quality – Often updated – Minimum Download time – Ease of use) to introduce the basic principles of usability that enhances the loyalty of a web site's users. Also, the International ISO/IEC standard 9241-11 identifies three main attributes to define usability:

- Effectiveness
- Efficiency
- Satisfaction

These attributes are further analysed to create specific usability metrics. Different approaches led to different sub criteria. Usability metrics are quality components that assess the site's effectiveness and efficiency in terms of information transparency, interactivity, design layout, aesthetics, accessibility, transactions (Casalo et al, 2005).

Kappel et al (Kappel, Proll, Reiche & Retschitzegger) categorize usability measures in two classes:

- User-based methods (i.e. user testing) are based in the involvement and participation of end users in the evaluation process.
- Expert methods (i.e. heuristics evaluation) which require the experience of experts.

Usability measures apply to both commercial and government web portals and sites and in most cases combine both classes of measures (Wood, 2003). Specifically, for e-government projects, usability evaluation is of great significance due to the heterogeneous Internet skills and the nature and the variety of the information and the digital services delivered through the web site (Huang & Brooks, 2011). Good usability enhances user satisfaction and improves users' trust in e-government (Youngblood & Mackiewicz, 2012).

There are several usability evaluation measures of e-government web sites and portals. Different approaches identify and examine different usability attributes and criteria. The following table presents related usability studies (Table 4).

In most usability measures, the main evaluation criteria are further analysed to specific guidelines with the use of usability heuristics which are either used by experts to perform an overall investigation of the web site or transformed to tasks or typical scenarios executed by end-users (user testing) (Huang, 2003; Huang & Brooks, 2011; Youngblodd & Mackiwicz, 2012).

A significant subarea of usability measures is accessibility (Brajnik, 2000) which "means that people with disabilities can perceive, understand, navigate, and interact with the Web, and that they can contribute to the Web" (Wolrd Wide Web Consortium). Especially for government web sites, accessibility is a quality component that should be considered as a requirement by ethics or in some countries by law and not an option like in commercial web sites. For government organisations operating web sites it is essential to provide equal opportunities to all citizens obtaining information. Therefore, a lot of research in e-government evaluation has been focused on the accessibility aspect applying specific guidelines produced by the World Wide Web Consortium (W3C) (Huang, 2003; Abanumy, 2005; Baowaly et al, 2012). WCAG 1.0 is an internationally accepted standard including a set of 14 guidelines. Accessibility evaluations are conducted with the

*Table 4. Usability studies for e-government web sites*

| Authors | Criteria / Guidelines | Evaluation object | methodology |
|---|---|---|---|
| Katre & Gupta, 2011 | • Accessibility<br>• Navigation<br>• Visual Design<br>• Information Content<br>• Branding<br>• Interactivity<br>• Ownership | State Government Web Portals | Expert method |
| Asiimwe & Lim, 2010 | • Design Layout<br>• Navigation<br>• Legal Policies | Ministries' Web sites | Expert method |
| Soufi & Maguire, 2007 | • Information Architecture<br>• Page Layout<br>• Design<br>• Accessibility | Local Government Web sites | User based method |
| Baker, 2009 | • Information Architecture<br>• User Help<br>• Legitimacy<br>• Navigation<br>• Accessibility accommodations<br>• Online services | | Content analysis |

help of expert evaluators, the participation of humans with disabilities or the use of specific software tools and automated systems (Abanumy, 2005; Youngblood & Mackiwicz, 2012).

Scott (2005) identifies usability as one of the basic components that enhance the quality and ease of use of government web sites. Usability measures should be a continuous process in order to identify mistakes in design and improve user interface. Site's usability could influence the adoption and engagement of citizens to government web sites and services. Government organisation operating web sites should invest time and money to improve their usefulness and quality.

## Quality Evaluation of E-Government Digital Services

E-services in government web sites can be defined as the electronic delivery of information and services. Specifically, services through government web sites describe the provision of information, interactive communication and transactions Ser-

vice quality has been well researched in the private sector and several models have been implemented to address the issue of service quality measurement. Research in the public sector has been clearly affected by the conceptual approaches in the private sector, but the ''multiplicity'' of the objectives and drivers of e-government organisations requires the investigation of different dimensions (Buckley, 2003).

Based on literature review, qualitative measures of e-government services can be categorised in two classes:

- The investigation of various qualitative variables that influence the efficiency and effectiveness of the provided services in terms of information, communication and transaction.
- The development of customer satisfaction models which measure the perceived quality of services towards the users' expectations.

## E-Services Quality Evaluation

E-government services evaluation is based on the identification and testing of quality variables. Kašubienė and Vanagas (2007) classified the various quality criteria for e-services systems into three groups in order to point out the impact of related research in the private sector to the e-government area:

- Criteria related to web sites (i.e. use, content, structure, complexity.)
- Criteria related to features of traditional services (i.e. reliability, credibility, access, ease of use, security.)
- Mixed criteria systems (i.e. web interaction, web interface, aesthetics.)

Also, with respect to e-government, they also divided e-service quality into information quality and process quality taking into account the different stages of e-government systems' maturity. On the whole, models in this class focuses on three core quality features information quality, process quality and service quality based on the main activities of citizens within the government web sites which is obtaining information, interact and proceed to transactions.

Research in this area led to the implementation of several frameworks with reference to models already introduced in the e-commerce area. Parasuraman (1988, 1991) theoretical model SERVQUAL on traditional services was a great contribution to the development of e-government service quality models. In this context, Viscusi (2009) introduced eGovQual which incorporates organisational, technical, social and juridical perspectives to address issues like the diversity of the e-government stakeholders. Wang and Liao (2008) proposed an IS success model in the e-government context identifying information quality, system quality, service quality, use, user satisfaction and perceived net benefit as significant quality dimensions.

Papadomichelaki et al (2006) propose four key quality dimensions for e-government service quality evaluation:

- The service key area to assess the web sites ability to deliver services accurately, consistently and in time and facilitate interaction between the sites' stakeholders.
- The content key area which involves quality dimensions relative to information and presentation aspects.
- The system key area which includes quality variables availability, accessibility, system integrity, performance, reliability, interoperability, regulatory and security.
- The organisation key area to address organisational perspectives.

E-service quality in e-government has recently begun to receive increasing attention because of the significant progress made in the development and implementation of digital services in government portal and web sites. The huge amounts invested in e-government projects and the uniqueness of the services provided by local, regional and national government web sites by citizens raises the importance of the theoretical grounding and the empirical research of e-government service quality.

## User Satisfaction Models

User satisfaction Index methodologies attempt to quantify qualitative variables. Specifically, quality dimensions of satisfaction are identified, weighted with regards to their impact on the overall satisfaction and produce a final result – index. Data from users are required to select the variables and investigate their relationship to the overall consumer satisfaction. User satisfaction models are cause-and-effect models which enable to predict the effects of web sites' changes and enhancements to the overall satisfaction (Papadomichelaki, 2006) and project future behaviour based on satisfaction.

Such methodologies are commonly and widely used in the e-commerce area. In the e-government research field, user/citizen satisfaction indices have been developed and used in comparative analyses and benchmarking researches to measure the impact of e-government web sites. According to Halaris et al (2007) customer satisfaction index ''is affected both from perceived by citizens quality and from their expectations about the service'.'

The American Satisfaction Index (ACSI) is a leading and well established customer satisfaction model to evaluate both traditional and online services. It was developed by the National Quality Research Centre and has served as basis for the development of customer satisfaction index models in other countries. It is composed of six factors: perceived quality, customer expectations, perceived value, overall customer satisfaction, customer complaints, and customer loyalty. More than 90 U.S. government web sites are evaluated and rated quarterly by the ACSI. Results of each survey are announced to the public including information on the top rated e-government web sites, an overall satisfaction rate with e-government services, suggestions on priorities to improve government web sites and comparative analysis between satisfaction for the private and public sector. The European Consumer Satisfaction Index (EUSI) is another variation of the ACSI than can be applied to companies in several industries and public organisations as well.

Halaris et al (2007) identifies the following principles/criteria of customer satisfaction models:

- Service reliability
- Personalisation
- Navigation/accessibility
- Information/content
- Customer service

Customer satisfaction index could be a significant evaluation tool for countries to assess the efficiency and effectiveness of the implemented e-government web sites and portal. Improvements on measurement methodologies are necessary (Abdelgawad and Snaprud, 2011). The quantitative satisfaction metrics provide insight on the citizens' perceptions towards specific quality dimensions of government e-services and identifies usability, functional or organisational problems and suggest improvements in this area. In an ideal world each government would implement a national customer satisfaction model to address the special characteristics of e-government services consumers.

## DESIGN AND EVALUATION QUIDELINES AND STANDARDS BY THE U.S.A GOVERNMENT, THE EUROPEAN UNION AND THE UNITED NATIONS ORGANISATION

Due to the advanced progress and significance of e-government, evaluation procedures take place in national and international level. Several assessment models were implemented to enhance current e-government initiatives and provide design guidelines for future e-government projects.

E-government Act of 2002 was the first attempt to provide an e-government framework at a national level by the government of the U.S.A. It's objective was "to enhance the management and promotion of electronic Government services and processes by establishing a Federal Chief Information Officer within the Office of Management and Budget, and by establishing a broad framework of measures that require using Internet-based information technology to enhance citizen access to Government information and services, and for other purposes" (U.S. Government Printing Office). Under this act federal agencies were obligated to utilise Internet in order to provide access to information and services to the public. In addition, standards were established to organise, preserve government information and make it accessible to citizens through federal web portals. E-government Act of 2002, remains a prototype of an e-government framework and was used as a basis for other similar models by other countries or international organisations.

The United Nations (http://unpan3.un.org) introduced a comparative e-government evaluation framework to support sustainable e-government development and also monitor the progress of current e-government initiatives. The United Nations annual global survey report presents "a systematic evaluation of the use and potential of ICT to transform the public sector by enhancing efficiency, effectiveness, transparency, accountability, access to public services and citizen participation in the all Member States of the United Nations, and at all levels of development" (The United Nations, 2013). The main features reviewed by The United Nations survey are information dissemination/outreach, access/usability, service delivery capability, citizen participation/ interconnectedness. Some of the evaluation indices adopted in The United Nations assessment model measure e-government readiness, e-service delivery, telecommunication infrastructure index, e-participation indices. The United Nations vision for e-government is Connected Governance which will enhance public administration efficiency and public service delivery.

Similarly, the European Union and specifically the European Commission investigates the progress of e-government initiatives in the European Countries. Multiple surveys with the use of benchmarking methodologies are conducted to provide an insight on the development and use of ICT for interacting with public administrations in the European Union. Currently, the i2010 framework which follows previous action plans of the European Union (e-Europe 2003 and e-Europe 2005) sets three political priorities for e-government:

- To facilitate citizens and businesses mobility in the single market.
- Create a legitimate eUnion and gaining high trust.
- Reduce administrative costs for citizens and business.

Some of the indices introduced by this new framework are developments of broadband, advanced services, security, impact and investment in ICT research (Fitsilis et al, 2010). The European Union announced already the new European e-government action plan 2011-2015 (ec.europe. eu). The objective of this new action plan is to provide guidelines for more flexible, open and cooperative e-government services and at the same time increase the use of e-government services by 50% on households and 80% on businesses by the year 2015.

Over the last years, the United Nations and the European Commission evaluation frameworks provide suggestions for improvements in designing web-based government services and present case studies of successful e-government strategies.

## CONCLUSION

E-government progresses vastly in many countries. Web portals and web sites remain the main and most significant component of e-government construction. Enormous amounts of money are invested for their implementation by local, regional and national agencies and authorities. In most cases, governmental web sites integrate G2C and G2B policies. With their development being a continuous process, evaluation measurements are vital for their optimisation in delivering critical information and unique services. A thorough literature review identified several measurement approaches focusing on different dimensions and features of the government web sites design and functionality. Based on the concept that a government web site is an integrated web-based information system, with citizens and enterprises being its end-users, evaluation measurements are categorised in four classes: 1) conceptual evaluation frameworks, 2) usability measurements, 3) e-services' quality measurements and 4) customer satisfaction models.

So far, the empirical testing of the several e-government evaluation models revealed a gap between theory and practice. In most cases, government web sites are in their early maturity phases (simple online presence or interactive web sites) or having major usability and accessibility problems. Improvements are required to meet the raised expectations of citizens and businesses.

Little attention has been given by governments on the evaluation stage of a web sites life cycle. However, a lot of surveys conducted in an international or supranational level by the United Nations and the European Union, provide guidance and suggestions for better services design and web-based system's implementation.

E-government is now facing a new era. Web 2.0 provides new opportunities for governments (Chua et al, 2012) and will cause a profound change on the delivery of information and services. Governments should be devoted to utilise and measure effective use of Internet enabled technologies. A thorough investigation and evaluation of an e-government web site should be considered an investment to achieve efficiency and effectiveness.

# REFERENCES

W3C. (2013). *Accessibility — W3C*. Retrieved April 20, 2013, from, http://www.w3.org/standards/webdesign/accessibility

Abanumy, A., Al-Badi, A., & Mayhew, P. (2005). e-Government website accessibility: In-depth evaluation of Saudi Arabia and Oman. *The Electronic. Journal of E-Government, 3*(3), 99–106.

Al-adawi, Z., Yousafzai, S., & Pallister, J. (2005). Conceptual model of citizen adoption of e-government. In *Proceedings of the Second International Conference on Innovations in Information Technology*. Retrieved April 10, 2013, from http://www.it-innovations.ae/iit005/proceedings/articles/G_6_IIT05-Al-Adawi.pdf

Almarabeh, T., & Abu Ali, A. (2010). A general framework for e-government: Definition, maturity, challenges, opportunities and success. *European Journal of Scientific Research, 39*, 29–42.

Asiimwe, E. N., & Lim, N. (2010). Usability of government websites in Uganda. *Electronic. Journal of E-Government, 8*(1), 1–12.

Baker, D. L. (2009). Advancing e-government performance in the United States through enhanced usability benchmarks. *Government Information Quarterly, 26*(1), 82–88. doi:10.1016/j.giq.2008.01.004

Bannister, F. (2007). The curse of the benchmark: An assessment of the validity and value of e-government comparisons. *International Review of Administrative Sciences, 73*(2), 171–188. doi:10.1177/0020852307077959

Baowaly, M., Hossain, M., & Bhuiyan, M. (2012). Accessibility analysis and evaluation for government-websites in developing countries: Case study Bangladesh. *Computer Engineering and Intelligent Systems, 3*(4).

Baum, C., & Di Maio, A. (2000). *Gartner's four phases of e-government model*. Retrieved April 15, 2013, from http://www.gartner.com

Beynon-Davies, P. (2007). Models for e-government. *Transforming Government: People. Process and Policy, 1*(1), 7–28.

Brajnik, G. (2000). Automatic web usability evaluation: What needs to be done? In *Proceedings of the 6th Conference on Human Factors & the Web*. IEEE.

Cappel, J., & Huang, Z. (2007). A usability analysis of company websites. *Journal of Computer Information Systems, 48*(1), 117–123.

Carter, L., & Belanger, F. (2004). Citizen adoption of electronic government initiatives. In *Proceedings of 37th Annual Hawaii International Conference on System Sciences.* IEEE.

Carter, L., & Belanger, F. (2005). The utilization of e-government services: Citizen trust, innovation and acceptance factors. *Information Systems Journal, 15*(1), 5–25. doi:10.1111/j.1365-2575.2005.00183.x

Casaló, L., Flavián, C., & Guinaliú, M. (2005). The role of accessibility and commitment in the development of an e-government strategy. In *Proceedings of eGovernment Workshop '05 (eGOV05).* Brunel University.

Chua, A., Goh, D., & Ang, R. (2012). Web 2.0 applications in government websites: Prevalence, use and correlations with perceived web site quality. *Online Information Review, 36*(2), 175–195. doi:10.1108/14684521211229020

Coursey, D., & Norris, D. F. (2008). Models of e-government: Are they correct? An empirical assessment. *Public Administration Review, 68*(3), 523–536. doi:10.1111/j.1540-6210.2008.00888.x

Eschenfelder, K. R., & Miller, C. (2005). *The openness of government websites: Toward a socio-technical government website evaluation toolkit.* Seattle, WA: MacArthur Foundation/ALA Office of Information Technology Policy Internet Credibility and the User Symposium.

Fairweather, N., & Rogerson, S. (2006). Towards morally defensible e-government interactions with citizens. *Journal of Information. Communication and Ethics in Society, 4*(4), 173–180. doi:10.1108/14779960680000290

Fang, Z. (2002). E-government in the digital era: Concept, practice and development. *International Journal of The computer. The Internet and Management, 10*(20), 1–22.

Gupta, M. P., & Jana, D. (2003). E-government evaluation: A framework and case study. *Government Information Quarterly, 20*, 365–387. doi:10.1016/j.giq.2003.08.002

Halaris, C., Magoutas, B., Papadomichelaki, X., & Mentzas, G. (2007). Classification and synthesis of quality approaches in e-government services. *Internet Research: Electronic Networking Applications and Policy, 17*(4), 378–401. doi:10.1108/10662240710828058

Holmes, D. (2001). *E-gov: E-business strategies for government.* London: Nicholas Brealey Publishing.

Huang, J. C. (2003). Usability of e-government web-sites for people with disabilities. In *Proceedings of the 36th Hawaii International Conference on System Sciences.* IEEE.

Huang, Z., & Brooks, L. (2011). Credibility and usability evaluation of e-governments: Heuristic evaluation approach. In *Proceedings of tGov 2011.* Brunel University.

Jansen, A., & Ines, S. (2004). Quality assessment and benchmarking of Norwegian public web sites. In *Proceeding from European Conference on E-Government.* Retrieved March 15, 2013, from http://www.afin.uio.no/english/research/ arild/QualityAssessment.pdf

Jeong Chun Hai @Ibrahim. (2007). *Fundamental of development administration.* Selangor: Scholar Press.

Jorgenson, D., & Cable, S. (2002, Summer). Facing the challenges of e-government: A case study of the city of Corpus Christi, Texas. *SAM Advanced Management Journal.*

Kappel, G., Proll, B., Reich, S., & Retschitzeger, W. (2006). *Web engineering: The discipline of systematic development of web applications.* London: John Wiley & Sons Ltd.

Kašubienė, L., & Vanagas, P. (2007). Assumptions of e-government services quality evaluation. *The Engineering Economist, 5*(55), 68–74.

Katre, D. S., & Gupta, M. (2011). Expert usability evaluation of 28 state government web portals of India. *International Journal of Public Information Systems,* (3), 115-130.

Layne, K., & Lee, J. (2001). Developing fully functional e-government: A four stage model. *Government Information Quarterly, 18*(2), 122–136. doi:10.1016/S0740-624X(01)00066-1

Liu, J., Derzsi, Z., Raus, M., & Kipp, A. (2008). eGovernment project evaluation: An integrated framework. *Lecture Notes in Computer Science, 5184,* 85–97. doi:10.1007/978-3-540-85204-9_8

Melitski, J., Holzer, M., Kim, S.-T., Kim, C.-G., & Rho, S.-Y. (2005). Digital government worldwide: An e-government assessment of municipal web sites. *International Journal of Electronic Government Research, 1*(1), 1–19. doi:10.4018/jegr.2005010101

Middleton, M. R. (2007). Approaches to evaluation of websites for public sector services. In *Proceedings IADIS Conference on e-Society,* (pp. 279-284). Lisbon, Portugal: IADIS.

Morgeson, F. V. III, & Mithas, S. (2009). Does e-government measure up to e-business? Comparing end-user perceptions of U.S. federal government and e-business websites. *Public Administration Review, 69,* 740–752. doi:10.1111/j.1540-6210.2009.02021.x

Nielsen, J. (2000). *Designing web usability: The practice of simplicity.* New Riders Publishing.

Palvia, S. C. J., & Sharma, S. S. (2007). E-government and e-governance: Definitions/domain framework and status around the world. In *Foundation of e-government.* ICEG.

Papadomichelaki, X., Magoutas, B., Halaris, C., Apostolou, D., & Mentzas, G. (2006). A review of quality dimensions in e-government services. In M. Wimmer et al. (Eds.), *EGOV 2006 (LNCS)* (Vol. 4084, pp. 128–138). Berlin: Springer. doi:10.1007/11823100_12

Parasuraman, A., Berry, L. L., & Zeithaml, V. A. (1988). SERVQUAL: A multiple-item scale for measuring customer perceptions of service quality. *Journal of Retailing, 64*(1), 12–40.

Parasuraman, A., Berry, L. L., & Zeithaml, V. A. (1991). Refinement and reassessment of the SERVQUAL scale. *Journal of Retailing, 67*(4), 420–450.

Reddick, C. (2011). Citizen interaction and e-government: Evidence for the managerial, consultative, and participatory models. *Transforming Government: People. Process and Policy, 5*(2), 167–184.

Scholl, H. J., Barzilai-Nahon, K., Jin-Hyuk, A., Popova, O. H., & Re, B. (2009). E-commerce and e-government: How do they compare? What can they learn from each other? In *Proceedings of System Sciences, 42nd Hawaii International Conference on system Sciences.* IEEE.

Scott, J. K. (2005). Assessing the quality of municipal government websites. *State & Local Government Review, 37*(2), 151–165. doi:10.1177/0160323X0503700206

Soufi, B., & Maguire, B. (2007). Achieving usability within e-government web sites illustrated by a case study evaluation. In *Human interface and the management of information: Interacting in information environments (LNCS)* (Vol. 4558, pp. 777–784). Berlin: Springer. doi:10.1007/978-3-540-73354-6_85

Stahl, B.C. (2005). The paradigm of e-commerce in e-government and e-democracy. *Electronic Government Strategies and Implementation, 1*-19.

United Nations. (2008). *UN e-government survey 2008: From e-government to connected governance.* Retrieved May 12, 2013, from http://www. ansa-africa.net/uploads/documents/publications/ UN_e-government_survey_2008.pdf

United Nations. (2011). *E-government.* Retrieved March 10, 2013, from http://unpan1.un.org

Viscusi, G. (2009). The eGovQual methodology: Information systems planning as research intervention. *Working Papers on Information Systems, 9*(15).

Wang, L., Bretschneider, S., & Gant, J. (2005). Evaluating web-based e-government services with a citizen-centric approach. In *Proceedings of the 38th Hawaii International Conference on System Sciences,* (pp. 129-137). IEEE.

Wang, Y. S., & Liao, Y. W. (2008). Assessing egovernment systems success: A validation of the DeLone and McLean model of information systems success. *Government Information Quarterly, 25*(4), 717–733. doi:10.1016/j.giq.2007.06.002

Warkentin, M., Gefen, D., Pavlou, P. A., & Rose, G. M. (2002). Encouraging citizen adoption of e-governement by building trust. *Electronic Markets, 72*(3), 157–162. doi:10.1080/101967802320245929

Wood, F. B., Siegel, E. R., LaCroix, E., & Lyon, B. (2003). A practical approach to e-government web evaluation. In *IT professional human interface and the management of information: Interacting in information environments (LNCS)* (Vol. 4558, pp. 777–784). Berlin: Springer. doi:10.1109/ MITP.2003.1202231

World Bank. (2013). *Defining e-government.* Retrieved March 10, 2013 from http://web. worldbank.org

Youngblood, N., & Mackiewicz, J. (2012, June). A usability analysis of municipal government website home pages in Alabama. *Government Information Quarterly,* 582–588. doi:10.1016/j. giq.2011.12.010

## KEY TERMS AND DEFINITIONS

**E-Government:** The use of Information and Communication Technology (ICT) and particularly Internet-based and Web-based telecommunication practices to facilitate connections within the authorities and also deliver digital services to citizens and companies.

**E-Government Business Models:** Identify the key stakeholders in the e-government environment and their interrelationships and specify the key business processes that represent the integration of governmental information and services.

**E-Government Web Site Evaluation:** Is the assessment of a governmental web site towards specific criteria.

**E-Government Web Site Typology:** A categorisation of governmental portals and web sites based on the level of e-government and their level of growth (maturity)/service development.

**E-Services Quality Evaluation:** Is the identification and testing of quality variables for e-services systems.

**Usability Measures:** Examine how useful, user-friendly and accessible is a governmental web site with respect to the needs and expectations of its target audience.

**User Satisfaction Models:** Are cause-effect models which enable the prediction of effects to governmental web sites' changes to the overall citizen satisfaction.

# Chapter 2
# Achieving Useful Government Accountability and Transparency Websites

**Deborah S. Carstens**
*Florida Institute of Technology, USA*

**Stephen Kies**
*Florida Institute of Technology, USA*

**Randy Stockman**
*Florida Institute of Technology, USA*

## ABSTRACT

*With the transition from government to e-government, greater transparency in government accountability has occurred. However, state government budgets and performance reports are voluminous and difficult to understand by the average citizen. There is a need for government Websites to promote public trust while providing understandable, meaningful, and usable government accountability information. The public needs to have access to information that links the outcome of government spending so that government can be accountable for their spending. There are three fundamental functions for government: accountability, budgeting, and policy-making. The chapter discusses literature specifically relating to government accountability resulting in a checklist being developed to provide a mechanism for evaluation of government Websites from a technical and usability perspective. Therefore, it is not only important for a Website to have the government accountability information but to also display it in a useful and meaningful format understandable by citizens accessing the Website.*

## INTRODUCTION

There is a need for government Websites to promote public trust while providing understandable, meaningful and usable government accountability information (Posey, 2006). With the transition from government to e-government, greater transparency in government accountability has occurred. However, state government budgets and performance reports are voluminous and difficult to understand by the average citizen. The public needs to have access to information that links the outcome of government spending so that government can be accountable for their spending. The

DOI: 10.4018/978-1-4666-5129-6.ch002

chapter discusses literature specifically relating to government accountability resulting in a checklist being developed to provide a mechanism for evaluation of government Websites from a technical and usability perspective. Therefore, it is not only important for a Website to have the government accountability information but to also display it in a useful and meaningful format understandable by citizens accessing the Website.

The chapter discusses literature helpful in the evaluation of government accountability and transparency Websites. The background section consists of a discussion on how government has transformed to e-government with the topic of transparency in government accountability emerging. The main focus of the chapter discusses literature that addresses the current issues, controversies and problems of transparency in government accountability as it specifically relates to budgeting, performance measures, social media, usability, accessibility, supportability, navigation and readability. Then, solutions are presented focused on the topics of citizen engagement, government citizen relationships and customer, or rather citizen, satisfaction is discussed. Furthermore, a checklist is provided to provide guidance to those that evaluate or develop transparency Websites. Conclusions are discussed leading to future research within the topic of transparency in government accountability.

There are three fundamental functions for government which are accountability, budgeting and Policy-making. Accountability is enhanced through providing improved visibility into what government does, and how much it costs; a common managerial framework; connection of all costs to specific measurable activities. Budgeting is addressed through providing increased visibility into performance budgeting by displaying individual activities and reconciling total costs to budget. Lastly, Policy-making is more effective through providing a basis for prioritizing spending and ensures alignment with legislative priorities; identification of areas for program/process im-

provement; a foundation for establishing realistic performance targets, benchmarks for government activities/agencies.

## BACKGROUND

Thornton and Thornton (2013) discuss the increasing demand by the public for government fiscal transparency by the public. There has been a rising demand to the economic slowdown, exposed government fraud and fiscal mismanagement. As the public's pure trust in the fiscal responsibility of their state and federal government has declined, individual states have stepped up to provide more insight into government transparency and fiscal reporting. The primary way this has been done is through government transparency websites. Traditionally, detailed state government spending data was not available online. However, recently states have begun to release this information via government transparency websites, also known as e-government. Exploration of the topics of e-government, transition from government to e-government and accountability will lead into a discussion in the main section of the chapter regarding why transparency in government accountability is necessary.

### E-Government

E-government is merely the conversion of government services, information, transactions and relationships to an electronic form (Harris, Coles & Davis, 2003). Silcock (2001) defines it as "the use of technology to enhance the access to and delivery of government services to benefit citizens, business partners, and employees". Thornton and Thornton (2013) define it as "the use of information technology to enable and improve the efficiency with which government services (and information) are provided to citizens, employees, businesses and agencies." Does this mean that it merely takes an existing activity and just offers it in a new electronic format or does it discontinue old activities being transformed by new ones? Sometimes it is just taking an old activity and offering it in a new format such as renewing driver licenses online or submitting taxes electronically. However, new activities transform such as various accountability and transparency Websites that have been created where there is public access to review state agencies' financial data or government performance data on a Website. Information that was not readily available in the past is now just a few mouse clicks away. For instance, a person can find crime rates for a state or even for a city and use this knowledge for their own decision-making such as which city is best to purchase a house.

Government has followed business to Web 2.0 which provides citizens access to information twenty-four hours a day and seven days a week. It has improved the efficiency and greatly increased public access to information (Dadashzadeh, 2010). "eGovernment is not just about putting forms and services online. It provides the opportunity to rethink how the government provides services and how it links them in a way that is tailored to the users' needs" (Burn & Robins, 2003).

## Transition from Government to E-Government

Chandler (1998) discusses the recent move towards a more open government and information, such as government financial data being put online. Over the 1990's, governments have made the move toward public accountability and accessibility of official information. In the early nineties, fifteen state governments were actively publishing (in print) financial information for counties and other municipalities within the state (Thornton & Thornton 2013). By the early 2000's, many Websites existed for government but most were not used for publishing financial reports. By 2012, it has been found that forty-three out of fifty state governments had and maintained fiscal transpar-

ency websites, although out of the states without a website, four had websites that were created by other groups who wished to increase public awareness about fiscal responsibility. Of the remaining, two planned to launch one in the near future, and the third (California) had removed its site in a measure to ironically cut cost. As Thornton and Thornton, (2013) discuss, there is not a standard that exists for transparency sites as each of them have differences with regard to their layout and functionality. This shows that the website designs are driven by the states individually and not by the federal government. On average, four years of spending data were available on government transparency websites and one website offered up to 18 years of historical data (Vermont). The varying level of history available is just one of the indicators that it is not only the design requirements that are not mandated, content requirements are not uniform as well.

Governments are traditionally slower to change their operations and slower to reform; but there has been a recent shift towards e-government. Davison, Wagner, & Ma (2005) describe the shift as a great potential for governments to transition into a better more efficient system. "The government to e-government transition process offers governments a unique opportunity to enhance not only their operational transparency, clarity of purpose and responsiveness to citizens, but also their own internal efficiency and effectiveness" (Marche & McNiven, 2003).

## Accountability

E-government has provided a way for Websites to provide insight into fiscal transparency of respective state governments (Thornton & Thornton, 2013). First, fiscal transparency must be defined. Fiscal transparency is defined by the International Monetary Fund as entailing "being open to the public about the government's fiscal activities and about the structure and functions of government that determine fiscal policies and outcomes" Thornton and Thornton (2013) identify three questions that citizens may be interested in knowing regarding how their tax dollars are being spent. The first question is, "which state programs consume the largest amount of resources?" Second, "what are the largest sources of state revenues?" Third, "what are the largest sources of state expenditures?" In theory, the answers to these questions should be readily available to anyone searching on government transparency Websites.

In 2006, the European Commission developed the i2010 eGovernment Action Plan. This plan sets goals for their e-government to: leave no citizen behind, be efficient and effective, have key services available online, assure convenient, secure services, and have citizen participation and democratic decision making enhanced. Governments all around the world are increasingly moving towards this new online approach. Let's take a look at the transition process.

There are obstacles to implementing e-government. Some of the biggest challenges are citizen privacy and security as well as the issue of accessibility, which is later addressed under "Supportability" and "Accessibility", respectively. Other barriers include the tendency for e-government to simply replicate a traditional government style, the lack of inter-departmental cooperation, and the need for government employee training (Marche & McNiven, 2003). "Considerable strategic planning is essential if a fully (-) fledged e-government is to be achieved" (Davison, Wagner, & Ma, 2005). There have been a few models developed for governments to transition their services online. One example is Accenture's (2003) process consisting of the five stages listed below:

1. Establish an online presence.
2. Provide basic capability.
3. Make services available.
4. Mature delivery.
5. Service transformation.

Luftman (2000) proposed a strategic alignment maturity model with five levels (initial startup -> commitment -> establishment and focus -> improvement/management -> and optimization) that focuses on core criteria such as communication, value measurement, governance, partnership, scope, and architecture. Another model developed by Hodgkinson (2002), uses an S-curve to show the transition process. These stages are: initiation, contagion, control, interoperability, data management, and lastly, maturity.

Alt, Lassen and Skilling (2008) explore the effects of the transparency of fiscal institutions in government on the scale of government and gubernatorial approval using a formal model of accountability. It is suggested that fiscal transparency increases both the scale of government and gubernatorial approval. It was interesting to see that having a more transparent government actually increased the size of government. This may be attributed to the fact that more transparent financial institutions are the result of higher effort by politicians, which in turn voters approve of more. If voters approve more of the politicians in place, the voters in turn allow the politicians more power due to increased trust. A theory on Transparency and Political Accountability is discussed which is a principal-agent model of retrospective voting in which political agents can make their actions more transparent to voters in order to attract more money and support. In this model, the principles (voters) allocate resources to the agent (the politician) who is expected to turn tax revenue into a pure public good. They discuss how basically the government is only as transparent as the documents they provide. Governments are only really transparent if their financial statements provide "comprehensive, verifiable information." This is because no matter how much data is provided, the data is only useful if it can be interpreted by the target audience, which in this case is the citizen. The study findings suggest that in states where there is an initiative for government transparency, there is indeed less corruption, all else being equal. Also, institutions that define the transparency of the budget process usually affect the job performance, and approval ratings of state governors.

## TRANSPARENCY IN GOVERNMENT ACCOUNTABILITY

### Issues, Controversies, Problems

This section addresses the current issues, controversies and problems of government accountability as it specifically relates to budgeting, performance measures, social media, usability, accessibility, supportability, navigation and readability.

## BUDGETING

When examining the data reports of a Website such as a budget, it is important to note that reports varies as sometimes year to year comparisons, agency comparisons, and information on top vendors exist. However, a report alone doesn't provide transparency. It is far more valuable to the citizen if there are comparisons shown. Users of Websites want to see how the report has fluctuated since the previous year and why, as well as how one agency compares to another. Some reports contain graphics capabilities and others displayed textual information without the use of charts. For maximum transparency to the citizen, it is important to explain the purposes of the expenditures and have budget and revenue overviews that describe the processes. The Government Financial Officers Association (2003) identified five benefits of disclosing budget documents on government websites: 1) increased awareness; 2) increased usage; 3) application of analytical tools; 4) avoidance of disclosure redundancy; and 5) savings. It is important not only for the site to show the budget and how much an agency

or program was appropriated, but also the actual expenditure of that agency or program. Looking at a past budget with no comparison is useless, as the citizen does not know if the budget was exceeded or not. The budget must also break down the information by agencies and programs (or departments and projects) to be transparent. Big broad budgets are a great way to lose citizen trust.

Chase, Taylor & Phillips (2008) discuss the operational accountability of government financial statements. Operational accountability is defined as "governments' responsibility to report the extent to which they have me their operating objectives efficiently and effectively, using all resources available for that purpose, and whether they can continue to meet their objectives for the foreseeable future." Financial data is now being made available to the public; this offers new opportunities to test the operational accountability of states, as well as drill down further into the meta layer and test individual cities in the state, that is what this study decided to do. The study performed a test of two government-wide financial statements for ten cities in Virginia. The first government-wide financial statement was the Statement of Net Assets, A statement of net assets reports assets, liabilities and the net difference between the two, which is net assets. This attempts to accurately show the financial position of the government by showing the amount of net assets of the government. The second government-wide financial statement tested was the Statement of Activities. This statement shows the results of operations for the year in question by reporting revenues, expenses and changes in net assets. It was explained that it is the equivalent to an income statement for businesses. Third, the test used a few ratios to more accurately measure the financial performance of each city. One of the ratios used was the Change in Net Assets/Expenses ration. "Because it is expressed in terms of total expenses, it provides a relative measure in change in the financial position for the year." The study concludes that "operational accountability is the extent to which a government has met its operating objectives efficiently and effectively, using all resources available for that purpose. Citizens' groups, policymakers and government officials can use information in the government-wide statements to better evaluate operational accountability." Due to the fact that now much of this data is online, there are many more checks and balances placed on the government, since now anyone can access and interpret the data at any time. This in turn should improve the operational accountability of the respective governments and should allow citizens to feel a bit more secure that their money is being used efficiently and effectively.

## PERFORMANCE MEASURES

Tracking performance is very important internally as well as externally. The government needs to know if they are performing according to plan and relay that information, good or bad, to the citizens to maintain transparency. Measuring performance is popular and common for state and local governments to do. However, Harris, McKenzie and Rentfro (2011) suggest, "Having a performance measurement system does not guarantee that results are shared with the citizenry". The study conducted was to evaluate the accessibility of such reports and found that many governments' performance information is difficult to find. Ho (2002) used six search processes to locate performance reports on e-government websites. The basis of the study developed was from what Ho (2002) had earlier described as two approaches for reporting information; the e-government model and the traditional bureaucratic model. Two search processes represented the e-government model, and four represented the bureaucratic. The e-government model is one that organizes information based on the user's viewpoint and interests. There are two ways to display this model when it comes to

locating targeted information such as a performance report. The first is to have a direct link to the report on the main webpage. The second is to have an effective internal search tool on the main webpage that can just as easily locate the report.

With regards to performance measures, the bureaucratic model for performance measures focuses on the department, and often requires an inside understanding of the government to find the targeted information (Ho, 2002; Harris et al., 2011). In this case, the information is placed inside the respective department's page that produces the information. This requires the citizen to know which department is responsible for what functions; and often the citizen does not have knowledge of this information. Therefore, four search processes that the citizen might use to locate a performance report on a bureaucratic modeled site were identified. These consist of a) the government services page, b) the governor's website, c) the budget office's page, and d) the state's audit information page. Each state's performance report was searched for in these six ways. Using scores of 3 = highly effective, 2 = somewhat effective, and 1 = not effective, the search methods were ranked and averaged. The results revealed that the most effective way to find the report was to search the budget office's page (2.28 mean score), followed by the main page search function (1.98 mean score) and searching the government services page (1.68 mean score (Harris, McKenzie, & Rentfro, 2011). The most user accessible method of finding the report (displaying a link to it on the home page) scored the least effective (1.24 mean score). This shows how much more widely used the bureaucratic method is compared to the e-government and how little of a factor accessibility plays in placing information on a site. Performance reports are valuable as they can highlight the accomplishments and be proof to citizens that their money is actually being used responsibly.

## SOCIAL MEDIA

Governments have started to jump onto the social media train, and why shouldn't they? Social media is a very powerful tool to reach citizens. Presidential candidates have increasingly used social media to campaign. The presence of social media applications has been found to correlate with better overall website and service quality (Chua, Goh, & Ang, 2012). There are different types of social media primarily used by governments such as blogs, wikis, social networking, media sharing,microblogging and mashups (Bertot, Jaeger & Grimes, 2012). The goal of these social media sites is to create a more inclusive environment and a better look into the governmental process resulting in enhanced transparency. The main opportunities for revolutionizing government consist of promoting democratic participation and engagement, facilitating co-production of materials between governments and the public and crowdsourcing solutions and innovations.

Some of the most used forms of social media in government, found by Chua, Goh, & Ang (2012), are: RSS feeds, photo and video sharing services, blogs, forums, social tagging, social networking and wikis. Blogs are used to have open public conversations, allowing anyone to voice their opinions and enable government to respond informally. Wikis are great as they allow public collaboration and input. RSS feeds provide automated notifications of regularly updated content of interest to citizens who sign up. Bertot, Jaeger & Grimes (2012) describe how social media is currently used in e-government which includes offering information via the internet through multiple dynamic interactive channels, interacting with members of the public addressing interests and concerns, reaching populations who might not otherwise encounter government, serving as information and communication outlets for whistleblowers, supplementing incorrect information with citizen journalism to better inform members of the public

of conditions and crowdsourcing the monitoring of government corruption. Rudall and Mann (2007) discuss how computing has shifted into combining both social and technological aspects. Duarte and Snyder (1999) identified how different modes of communication such as audio, video or data assist with different types of tasks thereby social media is a significant contribution for interaction but also for learning to occur through this different interaction.

Photo and video sharing are increasingly growing in popularity. Video sharing websites like YouTube are one of the biggest growing communication channels. Social networking is being used by millions of users each day. New networks and uses are constantly being developed, even for government use. Microblogging is similar to Twitter, it is only for brief instant messages to broadcast messages in emergencies. Bertot, Jaeger and Grimes (2012) seek to examine the ways that governments use and build social media and information and communication technologies into e-government transparency initiatives to connect to the public and promote a more open government. In recent years, there has been a movement towards a more open government not just in the United States, but worldwide. More than thirty countries have established a national –level, centralized anti-corruption agency. The public has demanded more accountability. A lack of transparency can make corruption less risky and more attractive, prevent the use of public incentives to make public officials act responsibly and in the public interest, create informational advantages to privileged groups, instill and perpetuate control over resources, incentivize opportunism and undermine cooperation, limit the ability to select for honesty and efficiency in public sector positions and contract partners, and it can hinder social trust, and therefore development. The authors highlight corruption as a large hindrance to socio-economic development, especially in developing countries. Information and communication technology

(ICT) is a way for the government to reduce corruption by promoting improved governance and strengthening reform initiatives. ICT's are also a way to supply efficiency and transparency simultaneously.

## USABILITY

Usability is the cornerstone for website evaluations. No matter how much technical content a site has, without successful usability features, the technical information will not be usable. "If a user finds a site difficult to use, the user will typically leave that site" (Nielsen, 2003). It is recommended that sites spend ten percent of their development budgets on usability features. To prove why, a study with forty-two different organizations was conducted. Nielson (2003) had the organizations redesign their sites with usability as a primary concern. The result – website traffic increased 150% and sales conversion rates increased by 135%. Nielson (2003) suggests: "It is more important for design to meet the needs of the customer rather than be attractive and fun. If the customer finds the site too difficult to use, there will not be a return visit".

Even if a site has the information needed, if the user has too much difficulty accomplishing their task– they will leave the site (McKinney, Yoon, & Zahedi, 2002). Download speed is also important, if users become impatient waiting too long to access information, they will leave (Tarafdar & Zhang, 2005). Thornton and Thornton (2013) discuss that even though state governments are attempting to provide increased transparency, little has been done in enabling citizens to better understand the information that is being provided. Citizens are still finding the information confusing and lengthy. Another fact that the study uncovered is that the emergence of E-Government is expanding the role of librarians. The article attributes this to the "inherent ambiguity" of the fiscal data that

is being published by the state governments. The article says that with transparency websites, the librarian's role has shifted from access, to navigation and interpretation. In order to meet these upcoming challenges, brought on by the greater access to state government fiscal records, librarians must be able to able to explain the data, in ways people can comprehend, this requires expanding their skill set. "E-government services should be designed so as to help citizens get in, find their information, and then get out as efficiently as possible" (Davison, Wagner, & Ma, 2005). Too much personalization can also overwhelm the user and trigger a user to leave (Liang, Lai, & Ku, 2006-2007). Bose (2002) suggests that there must be an understanding of how, when and where the system will be interacting with user and the type of decision processes involved so that the interface serves the user properly.

Thornton and Thornton (2013) offer four key areas that state governments should focus on, to be able to better serve citizens.

1. Expand content displaying detailed expenditures, budget and comparisons of budgeted to actual expenditures. Comparative data provides the most transparency as opposed to data listed on a Website that doesn't provide data on past performance.

2. Enhance navigation so users can view the level of granularity desired. Adding features that allow a user to drill-down or to customize reports also provides enhanced navigation and information. Furthermore, the use of interactive graphs, charts and tables displaying trends are further desirable.

3. Incorporate teaching tools such as tutorials and documentation relating to information literacy skills on the budgeting process. Government accountability data is only useful if it is data that is understood.

4. Engage users by providing tools for user feedback. Designers of Government ac-

countability Websites need to try and get users engaged so that there can be an agile, iterative process to improving these sites and keeping government accountable and transparent.

## ACCESSABILITY

Accessibility is essentially making information available to the largest amount of users possible, including people with disabilities (Nielsen, 1996). It is defined as "the usability of a product, service, environment, or facility by people with the widest range of capabilities" (International Standards Organisation, 2008). The World-Wide Web was founded on the principle of accessibility; the goal was for users to be able to access information regardless of their hardware/software, network infrastructure, language, location, culture, or impairment whether it be mental or physical (Paris, 2006). "E-government web sites should aim to facilitate usage by all citizens and businesses independent of circumstances, such as age, origin, disability, and social status" (Panopoulou, Tambouris, & Tarabanis, 2008).

The issue of accessibility is complex. There are still gaps in the U.S. when it comes to citizen education and connection. "Many of the people who might stand to gain (the) most from e-government are the least connected, least educated, and least aware of how to do so" (Accenture, 2001). A way to counteract this is for the government to provide free public accessible internet facilities as well as educational programs (Davison, Wagner, & Ma, 2005).

There are also many challenges with accessibility for the disabled. Impairment could be visual, mental, physical, or auditory. "Disabled people are less likely to have access to the Internet in the first instance, and where they do have access; they may face the additional problem of inaccessible websites" (Paris, 2006). It is important for websites to provide the necessary accommodations to us-

ers with disabilities, as they may not have access to other forms of communication (The Equality Commission for Northern Ireland, 2004).

There are many tools and ways for websites to combat disabilities. As sites are mainly visual, text-only versions of pages can be implemented, allowing users to use screen readers (either text-to-speech or text-to-Braille). Larger font size also benefits users who are not completely blind. To have visual and auditory be equivalent, alternative text for images and summaries of tables must be provided (Paris, 2006).

Panopoulou *et al.* (2008) developed three metrics to assess a website's accessibility. The first measures the site's technical accessibility by testing the sites download time through a public switched telephone network connection. The second metric checks to see if the site meets the basic accessibility standards in the guidelines set by the World Wide Web consortium. The third metric looks for the site's availability of download links to free software that is needed to view the site's content.

## SUPPORTABILITY

Contact information, online help documentation, and feedback options are a key part of getting the citizens engaged and building better citizen to government relationships. With that comes the importance of quickly addressing the citizen's questions/requests once they submit them. Live online help is ideal as it provides the quickest response time. Panopoulou *et al.* (2008) used four metrics of "public outreach" to assess a site's contact information in their study. They looked for basic information such as addresses, phone numbers, and emails for both the organization and the webmaster; for ways to submit requests/complaints (feedback); and lastly, they sent an email to the webmaster to test the response time.

Privacy and security is very important to citizens when using a government website, especially one that allows them to pay taxes and complete other online transactions (Panopoulou, Tambouris, & Tarabanis, 2008). It is so important that research findings show "citizens place security and a desire for greater accountability above convenience or the expansion of services and information" (Moon & Welch, 2005). Citizens are already concerned for their information safety as PublicTechnology.net (2007) explains in their survey results: "85 percent of users of online government services believe that their local authority's IT systems have probably already suffered a security breach at the hands of cyber criminals, and, in such circumstances, 86 percent of users would hold the local authority itself responsible, rather than the hackers".

"Government organizations have a moral responsibility to protect the privacy of citizens" (Arnesen & Danielsson, 2007). Panopoulou *et al.* (2008) conclude that "although municipal web sites place emphasis on content and communication features, they seem to overlook privacy and security features". These privacy/security policies explain the way the site uses the information gained and how it is protected. Similarly, the accessibility policy identifies how users with disabilities can access the web site thereby ensuring equal access to electronic and information technologies.

## NAVIGATION

Navigation is an important design component that makes information easier to find for users (Calero & Piattini, 2005). Navigation includes topics such as breadcrumb trails and table of contents or site maps to help orient a user on a Website. Websites when using a link that brings a user to a different Website can cause confusion for a user especially in trying to navigate back to the original site. This can be corrected through the use of pop-up windows that lead to external sites thereby providing the original site to still display on the computer screen. Use of images with labels is also an important navigational feature as then

the image can be described to those with visual impairments that are using a screen reader. Less than three clicks are recommended to access desired information as users tend to stray from sites that are too complex to use (Carstens & Patterson, 2005; Carstens & Becker, 2009; Becker, Carstens & Linton, 2009).

Useful navigation devices include: sitemaps, search engines, breadcrumb trails, friendly printing, and a "back to the homepage" option. Literature has time and time again outlined that navigation menus, site maps, search tools, and help documentation should always be present (Bonson-Ponte, Escobar-Rodriguez, & Flores-Munoz, 2008). Search engines are very popular and are the most common starting point for a user looking for information. It is important for sites, especially ones with large amounts of information, to have an internal search engine tool. Average users are likely to abandon a search if their efforts do not find what they are looking for in a relatively short period of time (Harris, McKenzie, & Rentfro, 2011). Some e-businesses try to keep their consumers on their site as long as possible, in anticipation that they will buy something as e-government sites should not follow this (Davison, Wagner, & Ma, 2005). Panopoulou *et al.* (2008) used eight metrics to assess a site's navigation features. These included having an internal search engine, having a site map or index, and placement consistency of navigation menus on each page. They also evaluated the availability of links back to the home page and if the site showed the navigational path, breadcrumb trails, of where the user is on the site.

## READABILITY

Readability consists of how easy it is for Website content to be seen. Readability looks at font size to see if the site used 12 point font size or larger. Text resizing can be tested to see if text can be increased in size. Images on Websites need to not be overlaid with text as it disrupts the readability of the content. Another readability aspect is whether translation options exist. The Flesch Reading Ease Score is also a great tool to measure a text's readability. It can be added to Microsoft Word's spelling & grammar tool by going to File -> Options -> Proofing -> When Correcting Spelling and Grammar Mistakes in Word -> Show Readability Statistics. It rates text on a 100 point scale based on the average number of syllables per word and words per sentence. The higher the Flesch Reading Ease Score, the easier it is to understand the text. For standard documents, it is recommended to have a score of at least 60.

As the world increasingly gets more flat, people are no longer limited to live in their origin country. Diversity abounds in the U.S., and there is a need for the government to be accessible in multiple languages. To reach a larger targeted citizen audience, sites should provide translation of information and services.

## Solutions and Recommendations

The solution to the issues, controversies and problems presented on transparency in government accountability is focused around citizen engagement, government citizen relationships and customer satisfaction. Citizen engagement refers to the degree to which citizens participate in government accountability activities such as the use of the information available. Government citizen relationships views government and citizens not as separate entities but as being in a relationship where there would be mutual trust and information sharing. Customer satisfaction focuses on how pleased customers or rather citizens are with the level of transparency that exists with regards to government accountability information. A recommendation is for government to use a checklist to evaluate transparency Websites to identify how much improvement is needed. It also provides a mechanism for which government agencies can strive for in providing content that is technical, useful and meaningful.

## CITIZEN ENGAGEMENT

"E-participation refers to the ability of citizens to have access to information and to the promotion of participation in public decision-making" (Panopoulou, Tambouris, & Tarabanis, 2008). There are three levels of participation according to OECD (2001): information, consultation, and active participation. Information simply informs; a one way message from government to the citizen. Consultation refers to a two-way medium where both parties can communicate but is limited. Lastly, active participation is improved, allowing the citizens to actively speculate and contribute input to government processes such as policy-making.

Layne and Lee (2001) also refer to a similar fully functional e-government stage they term the Horizontal Integration stage. To reach this level of active participation, the site must be accessible and transparent. "Inadequate or poor access to information contributes to the lack of citizen engagement in democratic processes..." (Harris, McKenzie, & Rentfro, 2011) "If citizens trust in their government, they will eagerly participate in the transparency and the accountability... And, in a circular fashion, such transparency and accountability make the foundation upon which the public trust is built" (Devaney, 2009). "Not only elected representatives, but also citizens need to be educated in exploiting the potentially valuable online tools in a way that enhances their status and influence in state-citizen relations" (Kolsaker & Lee-Kelley, 2008).

## GOVERNMENT CITIZEN RELATIONSHIPS

There is often a poor relationship between the government and the citizens due to mistrust and misunderstanding. "Numerous recent studies suggest that citizens in established democracies feel disconnected from the institutions and processes that are supposed to represent them" (Coleman, 2005). States can improve their government-to-citizen (G2C) relationships by making information more easily accessible and understandable. Berman (1997) suggests that the government can improve G2C relations by: 1) showing citizens how actions are benefitting them, 2) let the citizens give input in the decision making, and 3) perform well and communicate that performance to the citizens. Everyone is affected by official information, since it spans many topics, both personal and local (Chandler, 1998). Official information ranges from how to deal with noisy neighbors to international measures such as environmental issues. For much of the twentieth century, and for all time before, access to official publications has been very restricted. The goal is to make citizens informed of government. The United Kingdom has Websites for citizens to access official information. These Websites have expanded over the last few years and now include most of the government branches as well as features such as the ability to translate into 10 languages. However, there is still far to go to have a completely "open" government, but the government websites have definitely been improving over the last few years. Since this article was written, we have come a long way with open government. Many governments, not just western governments have accountability and transparency initiatives and much information is available online, at the citizens' fingertips

## CUSTOMER SATISFACTION

This section pertains to the treatment of citizens as customers. E-government is constantly being compared to E-business. "Local government is much like any for-profit or not-for-profit service provider, Citizens (customers) exchange money (taxes and fees) for products (services such as street cleaning, garbage collection, and disposal, and even childcare)" (Adam & Featherstone, 2007). Osbourne and Gaebler (1992) recommend that citizens be treated like customers, and that government services be re-designed focus on the customer. Citizens are looking for a one-stop service, and will be more likely to use the site if it is designed to address their needs (Davison, Wagner, & Ma, 2005). Services should be designed around the needs of the citizens, not the organization, in ways that will improve quality, effectiveness, and response (Northern Ireland Assembly, 2001).

"A completely satisfied customer believes that the supplier excels in understanding and addressing his or her personal preferences, values, needs, or problems" (Jones & Sasser, 1995). Curtin (2010) suggests that the federal government is still failing to meet the financial reporting needs of taxpayers and falling short of expectations. This is negatively impacting the trust between taxpayers and their government. Curtin (2010) further suggests that "75% of Americans believe that the availability of government financial management information is very important." The survey administered was called "Public Attitudes toward Government Accountability and Transparency." It measured attitudes and opinions toward governmental fiscal reporting and transparency issues. The findings suggest that the public heavily believes that there is an obligation to report and explain exactly what government money is used for since it is taxpayer's money. Also, the survey found that the public generally believes that governments, at the state and local levels are "significantly under-delivering in terms of practicing open, honest spending." This is causing trust issues between the public and the government entities. The survey findings also suggest that there is a 67 percentage point gap between what taxpayers expect from the government, and what taxpayers believe is received. The survey was given to 1,024 adults aged 18 and over in the United States. Hopefully through more transparency initiatives, the government will be able to make the gap narrower between expectations and reality.

## CHECKLIST

The checklist developed provides guidance to web developers in developing a website interface with high usability making it easy for the public to use as well as to provide meaningful fiscal data with an explanatory context, narrative statements explaining the data and programs that agencies use the money to support and performance information on how well these programs are operating. The checklist is displayed in Table 1. It is divided between both usability and technical content both of importance to the public. The technical content is needed as it provides the public with the accountability and transparency of state spending. However, without successful usability content to a Website, the technical information would not be usable if it is displayed in a format not easily readable or understood by the Website user.

## FUTURE RESEARCH DIRECTIONS

Transparency in government accountability is continuously evolving with slow moving progress. However, any progress in this area is truly considered successful. Additional research should be conducted to identify the essential goals to be achieved in the e-government setting and spe-

cifically transparency Websites (Saxena, 2005). Therefore, planning to include research is necessary to establishing commitment and governance procedures, identifying stakeholders, defining the mission and value, identifying governance issues such as with efficiency or effectiveness, and determining the scope of transparency Websites. This includes a thorough understanding of the users of these Websites to make certain that the information of interest is displayed as well as the proper navigation and especially usability needs of users are met. Furthermore, research needs to be conducted to understand the influence of animations on interaction with web pages to measure the effectiveness of these interface features (Schaik and Ling, 2004; Lee & Benbasat, 2003).

Alt, Lassen and Skilling (2008) describe potential future research, investigating whether fiscal transparency also assists voters in assigning responsibility and thereby strengthening electoral accountability. The public can definitely put to use social media and ICT's that the government has now created to keep government more transparent and accountable creating more trust in citizens with regard to their government (Bertot, Jaeger & Grimes 2012). Other roles for the government in social media will definitely develop as the use of ICT's and social media increase, but this is a good start in the era of transparency and governmental social responsibility. Carstens (2005) discussed the importance of research in the identification of guidelines that could be developed to design out cultural barriers to ICT or in this case transparency Websites. This is of increasing importance as the world is much more global today as well as different cultures present within each country (Luckin 2003).

The checklist identified in this chapter needs to be further researched and tested to enhance the value of it in both serving as an evaluation tool of Websites but also as a tool used by developers of transparency Websites. Similarly, mobile web research needs to be identified as more individuals are conducting their computing tasks using

*Table 1. Technical and usability checklist*

| State = Grade | | |
|---|---|---|
| **Link** | | |
| **Points Received** | **Supportability** | **Yes/No** |
| 1 | Has Contact information | |
| 1 | Has Live online help | |
| 1 | Has Feedback option(s) | |
| 1 | Has Privacy policy | |
| 1 | Has accessibility policy | |
| **Total (out of 5):** | | |
| **Points Received** | **Navigation** | **Yes/No** |
| 2 | Uses breadcrumb trails | |
| 2 | Internal links are primarily used (does not lead to an external site) | |
| 2 | Uses Table of Contents | |
| 2 | Uses Images with labels | |
| 2 | Less than 3 clicks are needed to access information | |
| **Total (out of 10): 0, 3 or 5** | | |
| **Points ReceivedTotal (out of 5):** | **Flesch Reading Ease Score** | **Flesch-Kincaid Grade Level** |
| **Points Received** | **Readability** | **Yes/No** |
| 1 | Uses 12 point font size or larger | |
| 1 | Text resizing works | |
| 1 | Images overlaid with text | |
| 1 | Font was readable | |
| 1 | Has option to translate text | |
| **Total (out of 5):** | | |
| **Points Received** | **Data content** | **Yes/No** |
| 3 | Shows Agency appropriations | |
| 3 | Shows program appropriations | |
| 3 | Shows Agency expenditures | |
| 2 | Shows Program expenditures | |
| 1 | Expenditure funding source available | |
| 2 | Shows Payee information | |
| 1 | Shows Expenditure document # | |
| 2 | Performance measures – output listed | |
| 2 | Performance measures – outcome listed | |
| 2 | Relevant audits and evaluations available | |
| **Total (out of 21):** | | |
| **Points Received** | **Search Capability (Can you search by:?)** | **Yes/No** |
| 1 | Expenditure type | |
| 1 | Vendor | |
| 1 | Employee | |

*continued on following page*

*Table 1. Continued*

| State = Grade | | |
|---|---|---|
| **Link** | | |
| **Points Received** | **Supportability** | **Yes/No** |
| 1 | Contract | |
| 1 | Keyword | |
| 1 | Agency | |
| 1 | Program | |
| 1 | Dollar threshold | |
| 1 | Grant or earmark | |
| **Total (out of 9):** | | |
| **Points Received** | **Download Capability** | **Yes/No** |
| 5 | To Excel | |
| 5 | To other applications | |
| **Total (out of 10):** | | |
| **Points Received** | **Report Functionality** | **Yes/No** |
| 4 | Has year to year comparisons | |
| 4 | Has Agency comparisons | |
| 2 | Shows Top vendors | |
| **Total (out of 10):** | | |
| **Points Received** | **Graphics Capabilities** | **Yes/No** |
| 5 | Uses YTD bar or pie charts | |
| 5 | Has Year to year comparisons | |
| **Total (out of 10):** | | |
| **Points Received** | **Contextual Information** | **Yes/No** |
| 4 | Shows Purpose of Expenditures | |
| 3 | Displays Budget overview | |
| 3 | Displays Revenue overview | |
| **Total (out of 10):** | | |
| **Points Received** | **Supportability via Social Media** | **Yes/No** |
| 0 or 4 | Has Social Media Links displayed anywhere on the site | |
| 0 or 5 | Has Social Media Links on the main page | |
| **Types of Social Networks Found:** | | |
| **Total (out of 5):** | | |
| **Total (out of 100):** | | |
| **Resulting Grade:** | | |

mobile devices. Websites do not always display properly from mobile devices. Therefore, government or rather e-government will need to produce mobile friendly Websites. Earlier discussions in the chapter discussed the importance of graphics in displaying information which further becomes complex when faced with users pulling up Website information on smaller devices. Readability continues to be an area of concern on larger screens and will further need to be evaluated when faced with the reality of small numbers or charts displayed on smaller screens such as those affiliated with smart phones. Future research in these areas will only positively impact the transparency in government accountability.

## CONCLUSION

Wagner, Cheung, Lee and Ip (2003) suggest that e-governments must focus on how to bridge relationships with the public, as well as those interactions within and between governmental departments. Essentially, transactions with the public, whether they are about a payment or a question about a regulation, must focus efforts on how to better provide information to its users. Government has been innovative in providing greater access to government content through connecting people to information sources. This has resulted in the emergence of e-government which is defining forces by replacing traditional means of accessing public services. However, Ray and Mukherjee (2007) report that national e-government must also address social challenges that are ever present within every country. These common problems are not limited to any one social concern but include several such as varying levels of education, training and support needed for current and potential users of e-government systems. Bean, Carstens and Barlow (2008) noted several key social paradoxes in creating e-government systems that directly apply to transparency Websites as well. These social paradoxes that must not be ignored in the creation of transparency Websites are that: (1) Websites can not only cater to a population of literate individuals only, (2) Websites must consider other communication issues such as language barriers or other impairments (Ray & Mukherjee, 2007; Gasson & Shelfer, 2007).

E-Government poses many opportunities, but also poses many challenges that designers and government will have to face (Thornton & Thornton 2013). The chapter authors' hope is that we can successfully overcome these challenges, and all future challenges, to successfully accomplish our goal, which is the best government accountability and the most government transparency we can achieve. Many governments, not just western governments have accountability and transparency initiatives and much information is available online, at the citizens' fingertips (Chandler,1998). Zwick and Dholakia (2004) discusses that adoption of any technology such as a Website brings about multiple issues to consider regarding social, political, economic, and cultural implications. Therefore, Websites are adopted generally to solve a business need but there are always new challenges that arrive before achieving full resolution of addressing the original problem such as transparency in government. We still have a long way to go, but the improvement is still advancing forward, and hopefully will continue to do so.

## REFERENCES

Alt, J. E., Lassen, D. D., & Skilling, D. (2008, Fall). Fiscal transparency, gubernatorial approval, and the scale of government: Evidence from the states. *State Politics & Policy Quarterly*, 230.

Accenture. (2001, April). *eGovernment leadership: Rhetoric vs. reality - Closing the gap.* Retrieved from http://www.epractice.eu/files/media/media_846.pdf

Accenture. (2003). *eGovernment leadership: Engaging the customer.* Retrieved from http://www.accenture.com/us-en/Pages/insight-egovernment-2003-summary.aspx

Adam, S., & Featherstone, M. D. (2007). A comparison of web use in marketing by local government in the United States and Australia. *Database Marketing & Customer Strategy Management, 14*(4), 297–310. doi:10.1057/palgrave. dbm.3250057

Arnesen & Danielsson. (2007). *Protecting citizen privacy in digital government.* Hershey, PA: Idea Group Reference.

Becker, S. A., Carstens, D. S., & Linton, T. M. (2010). Heuristic evaluation of state electronic government to promote usability for citizens of all age. *Journal of Management & Engineering Integration, 3*(2), 24–31.

Berman, E. (1997). Dealing with cynical citizens. *Public Administration Review, 57*(2), 105–112. doi:10.2307/977058

Bertot, J. C., Jaeger, P. T., & Grimes, J. M. (2012). Promoting transparency and accountability through ITC's, social media, and collaborative e-government. *Transforming Government: People. Process and Policy, 6*(1), 78–91.

Bonson-Ponte, E., Escobar-Rodriguez, T., & Flores-Munoz, F. (2008). Navigation quality as a key value for the webpage of a financial entity. *Online Information Review, 32*(5), 623–634. doi:10.1108/14684520810914007

Bose, R. (2002). Customer relationship management: Key components for IT success. *Industrial Management & Data Systems, 102*(2), 89–97. doi:10.1108/02635570210419636

Burn, J., & Robins, G. (2003). Moving towards egovernment: A case study of organisational change processes. *Logistics Information Management, 16*(1), 25–35. doi:10.1108/09576050310453714

Calero, R. C., & Piattini, M. (2005). Classifying web metrics using the web quality model. *Online Information Review, 29*(3), 227–248. doi:10.1108/14684520510607560

Bean, L., Carstens, D., & Barlow, J. (2008). E-government knowledge management (KM) and data mining challenges: Past, present and future. In H. Rahman (Ed.), *Social and political implications of data mining: Knowledge management in e-government.* Hershey, PA: IGI Global.

Carstens, D. S. (2005). Cultural barriers to human-computer interaction. In S. Marshall, W. Taylor, & X. Yu (Eds.), *Encyclopedia of developing regional communities with information and communication technology.* Hershey, PA: IDEA Group Inc. doi:10.4018/978-1-59140-575-7.ch026

Carstens, D. S., & Becker, S. A. (2009). A heuristic study on the usability of state government performance data web sites. *Issues in Innovation, 4*(1), 15–44.

Carstens, D. S., & Patterson, P. (2005). Usability study of travel websites. *Journal of Usability Studies, 1*(1), 47–61.

Chandler, H. E. (1998). Towards opend government: Official information on the web. *New Library World, 99*, 230–237. doi:10.1108/03074809810236784

Chase, B. W., Taylor, R. L., & Phillips, R. H. (2008). Government-wide information and operational accountability. *The Journal of Government Financial Management, 57*(3), 48.

Chua, A., Goh, D., & Ang, R. (2012). Web 2.0 applications in government websites: Prevalence, use and correlations with perceived website quality. *Online Information Review, 36.*

Coleman, S. (2005). The lonely citizen: Indirect representation in an age of networks. *Political Communication, 22*(2), 197–214. doi:10.1080/10584600590933197

Curtin, J. I. (2010, February 17). Current government financial reporting leaves taxpayers dissatisfied and distrustful. *Business Wire.*

Dadashzadeh, M. (2010). Social media in government: From egovernment to egovernance. *Journal of Business & Economics Research, 8*(11), 81–86.

Davison, R. M., Wagner, C., & Ma, L. C. (2005). From government to e-government: A transition model. *Information Technology & People, 18*(3), 280–299. doi:10.1108/09593840510615888

Devaney, E. E. (2009, May 5). *Testimony of the honorable Earl E. Devaney.* Retrieved from http://gop.science.house.gov/media/hearings/oversight09/may5/devaney.pdf

Duarte, D. L., & Snyder, N. T. (1999). *Mastering virtual teams.* San Francisco: Jossey-Bass.

Gasson, S., & Shelfer, K. M. (2007). IT-based knowledge management to support organizational learning Visa application screening at the INS. *Information Technology & People, 20*(4), 376–399. doi:10.1108/09593840710839806

Government Financial Officers Association. (2003). *Using websites to improve access to budget documents and financial reports.* Retrieved from http://www.gfoa.org/downloads/caafr-budgets-to-websites.pdf

Harris, J. A., McKenzie, K. S., & Rentfro, R. W. (2011). Performance reporting: Assessing citizen access to performance measures on state government websites. *Journal of Public Budgeting, Accounting &. Financial Management, 23*(1), 117–138.

Ho, A. T.-K. (2002). Reinventing local governments and the e-government initiative. *Public Administration Review, 62*(4), 434–444. doi:10.1111/0033-3352.00197

Hodgkinson, S. (2002). Managing an e-government transformation program. In *Proceedings of Working Towards Whole-of-Government Online Conference.* Canberra, Australia: Academic Press.

Hong, S., Katerattanakul, P., & Lee, D.-H. (2008). Evaluating government website accessibility. *Management Research News, 31*(1), 27–40. doi:10.1108/01409170810845930

International Standards Organisation. (2008). *Ergonomics of human-system interaction -- Part 171: Guidance on software accessibility.* Retrieved from http://www.iso.org/iso/home/store/catalogue_ics/catalogue_detail_ics.htm?csnumber=39080

Jones, T., & Sasser, E. Jr. (1995). Why satisfied customers defect. *Harvard Business Review, 73*(6), 88–91.

Kolsaker, A., & Lee-Kelley, L. (2008). Citizens' attitudes towards e-government and e-governance: A UK study. *International Journal of Public Sector, 21*(7), 723–738. doi:10.1108/09513550810904532

Kumar, A., & Kumar, P. (2010). Managing privacy of user generated information in a web 2.0 world. *Journal of Information Privacy & Security,* 3-16.

Layne, K., & Lee, J. (2001). Developing fully functional e-government: A four stage model. *Government Information Quarterly, 18,* 122–136. doi:10.1016/S0740-624X(01)00066-1

Lee, W., & Benbasat, I. (2003). Designing an electronic commerce interface: Attention and product memory as elicited by web design. *Electronic Commerce Research and Applications, 2*(3), 240–253. doi:10.1016/S1567-4223(03)00026-7

Liang, T., Lai, H., & Ku, Y. (2006-2007). Personalization content recommendation and user satisfaction: Theoretical synthesis and empirical findings. *Journal of Management Information Systems, 23*(3), 45–70. doi:10.2753/MIS0742-1222230303

Luckin, R. (2003). Between the lines: Documenting the multiple dimensions of computer-supported collaborations. *Computers & Education, 41,* 379–396. doi:10.1016/j.compedu.2003.06.002

Luftman, J. (2000). Addressing business-IT alignment maturity. *Communications of the Association for Information Systems, 4*(14), 1–51.

Marche, S., & McNiven, J. (2003). E-government and e-governance: The future isn't what it used to be. *Canadian Journal of Administrative Sciences, 20*(1), 74–86. doi:10.1111/j.1936-4490.2003.tb00306.x

McKinney, V., Yoon, K., & Zahedi, F. (2002). The measurement of web-customer satisfaction: An expectation and disconfirmation approach. *Information Systems Research, 13*(3), 296–315. doi:10.1287/isre.13.3.296.76

Moon, M., & Welch, E. (2005). Same bed, different dreams? A comparative analysis of citizen and bureaucrat perspectives on e-government. *Review of Public Personnel Administration, 25*(3), 243–264. doi:10.1177/0734371X05275508

Nielsen, J. (1996, October 1). *Accessible design for users with disabilities.* Retrieved from http://www.nngroup.com/articles/accessible-design-for-users-with-disabilities/

Nielsen, J. (2003, August 25). *Usability 101: Introduction to usability.* Retrieved from http://www.nngroup.com/articles/usability-101-introduction-to-usability/

Northern Ireland Assembly. (2001, September 20). *E-government.* Retrieved from http://archive.ni-assembly.gov.uk/research_papers/research/0901.pdf

OECD. (2001). *Citizens as partners OECD handbook on information, consultation, and public participation in policy-making.* Paris: OECD Publishing.

Osbourne, D., & Gaebler, T. (1992). *Reinventing government: How the entrepreneurial spirit is transforming the public sector.* Reading, MA: Addison Wesley.

Panopoulou, E., Tambouris, E., & Tarabanis, K. (2008). A framework for evaluating web sites of public authorities. *ASLIB Proceedings: New Information Perspectives, 60*(5), 517-546.

Paris, M. (2006). Website accessibility: A survey of local e-government websites and legislation in Northern Ireland. Universal Access in the Information Society, 292-299.

Pearson, J., Pearson, A., & Green, D. (2007). Determining the importance of key criteria in web usability. *Management Research News, 30*(11), 816–828. doi:10.1108/01409170710832250

Posey, W. J. (2006). *Activity based total accountability.* Retrieved from http://billposey.com/abta/

PublicTechnology.net. (2007, November 22). *HMRC fallout: 85 per cent of public now lack confidence in council web services.* Retrieved from http://www.publictechnology.net/sector/hmrc-fallout-85-cent-public-now-lack-confidence-council-web-services

Ray, S., & Mukherjee, A. (2007). Development of a framework towards successful implementation of e-governance initiatives in health sector in India. *International Journal of Health Care Quality Assurance, 20*(6), 464–483. doi:10.1108/09526860710819413 PMID:18030965

Rudall, B. H., & Mann, C. J. H. (2007). Smart systems and environments. *Kybernetes*, 36.

Saxena, K. B. C. (2005). Towards excellence in e-governance. *International Journal of Public Sector Management, 18*(6), 498–513. doi:10.1108/09513550510616733

Schaik, P. V., & Ling, J. (2004). The effects of graphical display and screen ratio on information retrieval in web pages. *Computers in Human Behavior.* PMID:14983895

Silcock, R. (2001). What is e-government? *Parliamentary Affairs*, *54*, 88–101. doi:10.1093/pa/54.1.88

Tarafdar, M., & Zhang, J. (2005). Analyzing the influence of web site design parameters on web site usability. *Information Resources Management Journal*, *18*(4), 62–80. doi:10.4018/irmj.2005100104

Equality Commission for Northern Ireland. (2004). *Disability discrimination law in Northern Ireland - A short guide*. Retrieved from http://www.equalityni.org/archive/pdf/disabilitysgfinal04.pdf

Thornton, J. B., & Thornton, E. (2013). *Assessing state government financial transparency websites* (Vol. 41). London: Emerald Group Publishing Limited.

Wagner, C., Cheung, K., Lee, F., & Ip, R. (2003). Enhancing e-government in developing countries: Managing knowledge through virtual communities. *The Electronic Journal on Information Systems in Developing Countries*, *14*(4), 1–20.

Zwick, D., & Dholakia, N. (2004). Consumer subjectivity in the age of internet: The radical concept of marketing control through customer relationship management. *Information and Organization*. doi:10.1016/j.infoandorg.2004.01.002

## ADDITIONAL READING

Ardichvilli, A., Page, V., & Wentling, T. (2003). Motivation and barriers to participation in virtual knowledge-sharing communities of practice. *Journal of Knowledge Management*, *7*(1), 64–77. doi:10.1108/13673270310463626

Cannon, J. P., & Homburg, C. (2001). Buyer-seller relationships and customer firm costs. *Journal of Marketing*, *65*, 29–43. doi:10.1509/jmkg.65.1.29.18136

Carstens, D. S. (2005, July) *Human Factors in Medicine: Task and Error Analysis*, Proceedings of the Human Computer Interaction International 2005, Las Vegas, NV. CD-ROM

Carstens, D. S., Bell, P., Malone, L., & DeMara, R. (2004). Evaluation of the human impact of password authentication practices on information security. *Informing Science Journal*, *7*, 67–85.

Carstens, D. S., & McCauley-Bell, P. (2000). *Importance of human error on logistics information security*. Proceedings of the International Society of Logistics Engineer Congress, USA, 2000, 18-30.

Carstens, D. S., McCauley-Bell, P. R., & Malone, L. C. (2000). *Development of a model for determining the impact of password authentication practices on information security*. Proceedings of the XIVth Triennial Congress of the International Ergonomics Association and 44th Annual Meeting of the Human Factors and Ergonomics Society, USA, 2000, 342-345.

Cowan, N. (2001). The magical number 4 in short-term memory: A reconsideration of mental storage capacity. *The Behavioral and Brain Sciences*, *24*(1), 87–185. doi:10.1017/S0140525X01003922 PMID:11515286

Dumas, J. S., & Redish, J. C. (1999). *A practical guide to usability testing*. Portland, OR: Intellect.

Ebrahim, Z., & Irani, Z. (2005). E-government adoption: architecture and barriers. *Business Process Management Journal*, *11*(5), 58–611. doi:10.1108/14637150510619902

Eden, S. (2007). Vendors jump on e-discovery bandwagon. *Intelligent Enterprise*, *10*(1), 9.

Federal Accounting Standards Advisory Board. (1995). Statement of Federal Financial Accounting Standards (SFFAS no. 30).

Gaffney, S., & Tabin-Berger, B. (2009). Accountability and Transparency in the American Recovery and Reinvestment Act. *Government Finance Review, 25*(3), 78–82.

Gao, F., Li, M., & Nakamori, Y. (2002). Systems thinking on knowledge and its management: systems methodology for knowledge management. *Journal of Knowledge Management, 6*(1), 7–17. doi:10.1108/13673270210417646

Gibson, S. (2006). The urgent need for e-data management at the enterprise level: the impending implosion of electronic stored information. *Computer and Internet Lawyer, 23*(8), 5–8.

Hazzan, O., Impagliazzo, J., Lister, R., & Schocken, S. (2005). *Using history of computing to address problems and opportunities.* Proceedings of the 36th SIGCSE technical symposium on Computer science education, 126-127.

Heldal, F., Sjøvold, E., & Heldal, A. F. (2004). Success on the internet – optimizing relationships through the corporate site. *International Journal of Information Management, 24*(2), 115–129. doi:10.1016/j.ijinfomgt.2003.12.010

Himma, K. E. (2007). Foundational issues in information ethics. *Library Hi Tech, 25*(1), 79–94. doi:10.1108/07378830710735876

Jantsch, J. (2010). *Let's talk social media for small business, Version 2.* E-book, Duct Tape Marketing.

Kaplan, A. M., & Haentein, M. (2010). Users of the world, unite! The challenges and opportunities of social media. *Business Horizons, 53*(1), 59–68. doi:10.1016/j.bushor.2009.09.003

Kassel, D. S. (2008). Performance, Accountability, and the Debate over Rules. *Public Administration Review, 68*(2), 241–252. doi:10.1111/j.1540-6210.2007.00859.x

Kidwell, L. A., Ho, S. K., Blake, J., Wraith, P., Roubi, R., & Richardson, A. W. (2002). New Management Techniques: An International Comparison. *The CPA Journal, 72*(2), 63–66.

Kim, Y. J., Kishore, R., & Sanders, G. L. (2005). From DQ to EQ: Understanding data quality in the context of e-business systems. *Communications of the ACM, 48*(10), 75–81. doi:10.1145/1089107.1089108

Lawson, C. (2008). Re-invigorating the Accountability and Transparency of the Australian Government's Expenditure. *Melbourne University Law Review, 32*(3), 79–921.

Lund, J., & McLuckie, J. (2007). Labor Organization Financial Transparency and Accountability: A Comparative Analysis. *Labor Law Journal, 58*(4), 251–266.

Madden, M. (2010). Older adults and social media. Pew Research Center. Retrieved March 19, 2013, from, http://pewinternet.org/ Reports/2010/ Older-Adults-and-Social-Media.aspx.

Mead, D. M. (2008). SEA Performance Reporting. *The CPA Journal, 78*(1), 6–12.

Koh, C. E., Ryan, S., & Prybutok, V. R. (2005). Creating value through managing knowledge in an e-government to constituency environment. *Journal of Computer Information Systems, 45*(4), 32–42.

Lahaie, D. (2005). The impact of corporate memory loss. *Leadership in Health Services, 18*, 35–48. doi:10.1108/13660750510611198 PMID:16167654

Malhotra, Y., & Galletta, F. D. (2003). *Role of commitment and motivation in knowledge management systems implementation: theory, conceptualization, and measurement of antecedents of success.* IEEE Computer Society Proceedings of the 36th Annual Hawaii International Conference on System Sciences (HICSS'03), Track 4, Volume 4, page 115.1.

McLure, W., & Faraj, S. (2000). It is what one does': why people participate and help others in electronic communities of practice. *The Journal of Strategic Information Systems, 9*(2/3), 155–173. doi:10.1016/S0963-8687(00)00045-7

Moffett, S., McAdam, R., & Parkinson, S. (2003). An empirical analysis of knowledge management applications. *Journal of Knowledge Management, 7*(3), 6–26. doi:10.1108/13673270310485596

National Association of State Chief Information Officers (NASCIO). (2010). *A national survey of social media in state government.* Retrieved March 19, 2013, from, www.nascio.org/ publications/ documents/NASCIO-SocialMedia.pdf.1

Nielsen, J. (1993). *Usability Engineering.* San Diego, CA: Morgan Kaufmann.

Norman, D. A. (1999). *The invisible computer.* Cambridge, MA: The MIT Press.

O'Donnell, S. (1994). *Programming for the world: A guide to internationalization.* Engelwood Cliffs, NJ: Prentice-Hall.

Office of Management and Budget. (2008). *Financial Reporting Requirements (Circular NO. A-136 Revised).* Washington, DC: U.S. Government Printing Office.

O'Reilly, T. (2005). *What is Web 2.0: Design Patterns and Business Models for the Next Generation of Software.* O'Reilly Media, Inc. Retrieved March 19, 2013, from, http://oreilly.com/pub/a/web2/archive/what-is-web-20.html?page=2.

Perlman, E. (2009). See-Thru Government. *Governing, 22*(8), 34–37.

Pollach, I. (2007). What's wrong with online privacy policies? *Communications of the ACM, 50*(9), 103–108. doi:10.1145/1284621.1284627

Posey, W. J. (2006). *Activity Based Total Accountability.* Rockledge, FL: Posey & Co.

Riege, A., & Lindsay, N. (2006). Knowledge management in the public sector: stakeholder partnerships in the public policy development. *Journal of Knowledge Management, 10*(3), 24–39. doi:10.1108/13673270610670830

Sears, A., Jacko, J. A., & Dubach, E. M. (2000). International Aspects of World wide web usability and the role of high-end graphical enhancements. *International Journal of Human-Computer Interaction, 12*(2), 241–261. doi:10.1207/S15327590IJHC1202_5

Siala, H., O'Keefe, R. M., & Hone, K. S. (2004). The impact of religious affiliation on trust in the context of electronic commerce. [from Science Direct database.]. *Interacting with Computers, 16*(1), 7–27. Retrieved March 30, 2013 doi:10.1016/j.intcom.2003.11.002

Smith, A. (2004). Global human-computer systems: cultural determinants of usability. [from Science Direct database.]. *Interacting with Computers, 16*(1), 1–5. Retrieved April 13, 2013 doi:10.1016/j.intcom.2003.11.001

Smith, A., Dunckley, L., French, T., Minocha, S., & Chang, Y. (2004). A process model for developing usable cross-cultural websites. [from Science Direct database.]. *Interacting with Computers, 16*(1), 63–91. Retrieved April 13, 2013 doi:10.1016/j.intcom.2003.11.005

Taipale, K. (2003). Data mining and domestic security: connecting the dots to make sense of data. *Columbia Science & Technology Law Review, 5*(2). Retrieved March 24, 2013 from http://www.stlr.org/html/volume5/taipaleintro.php

U.S. Government Accountability Office (GAO). 1999. Standards for Internal Control in the Federal Government. Washington, DC: Government Printing Office. GAO/AIMD-00-21.3.1.

Yang, K., & Hsieh, J. Y. (2007). Managerial Effectiveness of Government Performance Measurement: Testing a Middle-Range Model. *Public Administration Review*, *67*(5), 861–879. doi:10.1111/j.1540-6210.2007.00774.x

Zhang, P., von Dran, G.M., Blake, P., & Pipithsuksunt, V. (2001). Important design features in different web site domains. *e-Service Journal*, 1(1), 77-92.

Zhang, P., & von Dran, G. M. (2001-2002). User expectations and rankings of quality factors in different web site domains. *International Journal of Electronic Commerce*, 6(2), 9–33.

## KEY TERMS AND DEFINITIONS

**Accessibility:** Providing electronic access of government services, information, transactions and relationships in a format where anyone with or without any impairment is able to have access to the content displayed.

**Accountability:** Requiring government agencies to be held responsible for the spending incurred from operations.

**E-Marketing:** Marketing of government services, information, transactions and relationships in an electronic format to make the public aware of what can be accessible electronically.

**E-Government:** The conversion of government services, information, transactions and relationships to an electronic form to enhance public access.

**G2C-Government-to-Citizens (G2C):** Is the relationship between government and citizens and specifically relates to the sharing of information between government to citizens.

**Navigation:** The ability for a user of a Website to be able to easily find information displayed.

**Performance Measures:** Information or graphics presented to display the outcome of government spending such as crime rates, state testing results for K-12, etc.

**Readability:** Information provided on a Website should be written in a format that is understandable by the average citizen and is presented in a clear manner such as not having hard to see wording overlaid on graphics.

**Transparency:** Providing citizens with access to government agency spending data so that taxpayers, policy-makers and government can track how and when funding is used.

**Usability:** Providing access to information in a form that is meaningful and easy to navigate.

# Chapter 3
# E–Government Services:
## Creating Value Through Services' Quality

**Rimantas Gatautis**
*Kaunas University of Technology, Lithuania*

**Elena Vitkauskaite**
*Kaunas University of Technology, Lithuania*

## ABSTRACT

*Adoption of ICT in the public sector has rapidly progressed over the last decade. Many national and local governmental institutions move towards more sophisticated public electronic services aiming to increase service provision efficiency and effectiveness as well as develop services attractive for citizens. However, such digitalization represents supply-driven approach while governmental institutions and software development companies move public services online. Demand side user satisfaction and acceptance usually is ignored supposing ICT-based services pretend to be modern services. Public electronic services' acceptance heavily depends on citizens' attitudes. In this context, citizens' understanding of public electronic service quality plays an important role. The current chapter's propose is to show public electronic service quality assessment model considering three perspectives – environment quality, delivery quality, and outcome quality. The proposed model is verified empirically assessing three different public electronic services in Lithuania.*

## INTRODUCTION

E-Government strategies across the European Union (EU) display great diversity and various degrees of success. Diversity is a function of the different historical and sociopolitical contexts in which these strategies are implemented. Relative degrees of success are related to the coexistence of sets of factors within strategic frameworks that ensure not only continuity and coherence of implementation but also the creation of conditions of demand of e-Government services on the part of civil society. One of the key factors of successful development of e-Government services is quality of services. From the user perspective quality is one of the key factors assuring value of service.

The services in the virtual environment or electronic services contain a wide spectrum of operations starting from pure sales via internet to the pure services – free or as the part of service agreement. The share of public institutions' services provided through virtual environment

DOI: 10.4018/978-1-4666-5129-6.ch003

is constantly increasing worldwide. Electronic services are relatively new kind of activity from theoretical and practical point of view. In that context a question arises – what methods should be applied in estimation of public electronic services' quality and what dimensions should be treated as critical.

The development of public electronic services is rather supply driven process – governmental organizations and software development companies are dedicating effort to digitize public services. However researchers (Codagnone, et al. 2006; Millard, 2008) outline importance of citizen perspective or demand perspective – services will not be accepted by user if they are not seen as high quality services. In this case citizens rather continue using physical services instead of electronic ones.

The issue of electronic service quality is addressed in research, but research focused towards public electronic service quality is insufficient. Considering this, the goal of this chapter is to propose the public electronic service quality assessment framework taking into consideration the latest state of art of electronic services and public electronic services quality assessment research and provide empirical evidences of framework validity.

## QUALITY OF E-SERVICES AND ITS PECULIARITIES

### Electronic Service

Electronic service (hereinafter – e-Service) is widely recognized term among scientists and practitioners. E-Service can be defined as a service in virtual environment (Rust & Lemon, 2001). According to Reynolds (2000), e-Services are web-based services provided via internet. De Ruyter, Wetzels & Kleijnen (2000) claim that an e-Service is an interactive, content-centered and Internet-based customer services, driven by the customer and integrated with related organizational customer support processes and technologies with the goal of strengthening customer-service provider relationship. According to Rahman (2004) e-Service is a service delivered via internet by using advanced telecommunications, information, and multimedia technologies. Besides, Surjadjaja, Ghosh & Antony (2003) claim that electronic service is not simply a combination of terms "electronic" and "service". Electronic service is transaction between service provider and customer performed via internet. In case of pure electronic services entire process happens in virtual environment, i.e. purchase of a ticket online. Therefore, electronic service within this chapter is perceived as delivery of services between a service provider and a customer of a service in virtual marketplace.

It should be noted that e-Services vary from pure e-Services to extra services next to sales of tangible goods. According to Surjadjaja et al. (2003) e-Services can be provided as stand-alone offer to customer, or it can supplement goods sold online (pure electronic commerce).

King, Lee & Viehland (2004) identified following list of main e-Services:

- Tourism and travel services.
- Recruitment and other labour market services.
- Realty, insurance and stock exchange services.
- Banking and personal finance services.
- Services of digital goods provision.
- Ordering and delivery of some food products.

King et al. (2004) listed those electronic services without distinction between pure electronic services and pure electronic commerce.

In order to make a service accessible and attractive to customer, it should be considered that service is made not only of core service, but from supplementing services as well. All these services combined together make service offer, which could be also understood as service package. Van Riel, Liljander & Jurriens (2001) identified following five elements of e-Services: (1) the core service; (2) facilitating services; (3) supporting services; (4) complementary services; and (5) the user interface – through which customer accesses the services. The core service enables the company to enter the market. Company can provide several core services. In order to use the service supplementing services are often needed for customers (e.g. facilitating service which helps in using the core service). Supporting services are used for increasing value or in order to distinguish the core service among services provided by competitors.

The core service is closely connected to supplementing services and user interface. Error in any of these elements impacts entire e-Service offer and final result as well. It should be noted that loyal consumers are especially important in e-Service market. First of all, they spend more that new customers, and less costs are needed for their customer service. Besides, they convey positive attitude towards the service to their peers. Though loyal consumers and trust are important in offline market as well, they are way more important in virtual environment as search and change costs of service providers online are very low and customers are able to compare offers of many competing service providers in little time. Van Riel et al. (2001) claim that trust and security are more important for e-Services than price.

However not all services might be digitalized. Rahman (2004) presented model which enables to identify which services might be digitalized and offered online. This model is based on two key questions–towards whom service is oriented; and what is the scale of service? Such approach identifies four types of services.

*The first type* of services is characterised through high level service application and services' actions are directed towards the people. These services do not necessarily require direct contact between the service provider and the user. Provision of the service requires user trust, because these services can not be described accurately before delivery. One example is the Internet as a media channel. This type of services is appropriate to the digitalization and provision over the Internet and has good development perspectives.

*The second type* represents services whose activities are focused on people, and level of service application is low. These services are intended to be delivered as cheaply as possible, because their individual adaptation level is low. Therefore the same service satisfies a lot of users. However, over the Internet is possible to offer the user to customize the service, because the Internet is like an interactive space. This allows the service provider to communicate with each customer individually, so they can amend the offer in response to user needs. However, the services of this type have limited capabilities in virtual environment.

*The third type* service's actions are directed towards objects, and application of services is high. In this case, the direct recipient of the service is the user's assets. Also in this case, there is a need of contact between the service provider and the user, since the recipient is the object to be identified by the service provider to provide the service. These services can not be provided online, but they can be supported through websites.

*The fourth type* service's actions are directed towards objects, and application of services is low. These services can not be customized and are standardized for all users. Service delivery online is not possible. The internet can only give the user the opportunity to select and subscribe to the service without leaving home.

The services might have low demand if the user has to visit a specific organization or location of service delivery. By offering services through multiple sales channels company aims to increase demand for services. In some cases, companies are coming to the consumer, but in this case, it is too expensive to transport necessary staff and equipment. In many cases, direct contact between the service provider and the user is not required, so in this case the Internet and other information technologies might be very useful. Many service companies can bring services closer to consumers by using these technologies and save money by operating in one physical location.

For analyzing electronic service quality, it is important to consider the fact that these services are different from traditional services. The importance of direct customer's interaction with the service provider decreases in the electronic service provision process, because such interaction almost doesn't exist. Instead of direct communication two different types of communication appear during electronic services provision (Cai & Jun, 2003):

- Customer and service provider Internet based communication through various means such as e-mail, chat rooms, forums or traditional communications means.
- Customer communication with a website of a service provider, where customers can browse for information, receive the information and make order goods or services.

As communication with a website of a service provider increases, as a consequence electronic service quality is highly dependent on website characteristics such as design, graphic attractiveness, information provision, etc.

Aspects important in quality measurement of traditional services such as positive or negative feelings are not that important in evaluation of e-Service quality. According to Bressolles & Nantel (2004) it is difficult to apply a method of calculating the difference between customer expectations and perceived value in case of e-Service quality assessment as customers can not clearly define expectations related to electronic services quality.

## Electronic Service Quality

According to van Riel et al. (2001), research in the field of electronic service quality is still in an early stage. Two main attitudes to e-Service quality research are identified at this time. The first one is focused on the technological interface, through which e-Services are provided (Dabholkar, Shepherd & Thorpe 2000; Lociacono, Watson & Goodhue, 2000; Webb & Webb, 2004). Based on another attitude, scientists study e-Service quality from the perspective of existing traditional service quality theories (Grönroos et al., 2000; Parasuraman, Zeithaml & Malhotra, 2005; Santos, 2003).

One of the first definitions of electronic service quality was suggested by Zeithaml, Parasuraman & Malhotra (2002). This definition states that service quality in the Internet is the scope, to which an Internet site facilitates an effective and efficient shopping, and product/service purchase and delivery. Scientist (Gummerus et al., 2004; Fassnacht & Koese, 2006) criticized this definition, stating that it encompasses a too narrow field of electronic services, i.e., only the online shopping. Also, only the importance of a website in electronic service provision is identified in the definition. Certainly, a website is important, as it is a visible user interface of electronic services. However, technical infrastructure and aspects of electronic service provision invisible for the customer are also important. Their importance particularly increases, when the time for service fulfillment comes.

Santos (2003) defined electronic service quality as a general customers' evaluation and opinions about the expertise of electronic service provision in the virtual market. According to Fassnacht & Koese (2006) electronic service quality is the degree to which electronic services can meet most significant needs of the customer effectively and efficiently (this is a modification of the definition presented by Zeithaml, Parasuraman & Malhotra (2002)).

## Dimensions of Electronic Service Quality

Traditional service quality models SERVQUAL (Parasuraman, Zeithaml & Berry, 1985; 1988) and SERVPERF (Cronin & Taylor, 1992) assess service quality according to the five dimensions of tangibles, responsiveness, reliability, assurance, and empathy. These dimensions were suitable for evaluation of traditional service quality, but not e-Service quality, as electronic services have unique features (e.g. server problems, outages for backing up information, and connectivity problems), which are not relevant in case of traditional services and might impact perception of service quality.

Early research oriented to conceptualization of e-Service quality was focused on user communication with the website. Loiacono et al. (2000) created an e-Service quality scale, which they called WEBQUAL. Scale was divided into 12 dimensions which can improve user communication with website of service provider (see Table 1). Yoo & Donthu (2001) developed SITEQUAL model for evaluation of e-Service quality. Authors identified four dimensions – ease of use, aesthetic design, processing speed, and security. Other authors, namely Webb & Webb (2004), developed another model which they also named SiteQual. Model combines criteria for two main dimensions – service quality (based on SERVQUAL model: reliability, responsiveness, assurance, empathy, and tangibility) and information quality (accessibility quality, contextual quality, representational quality, and intrinsic quality).

Later research provided insight on e-Service quality from a wider perspective. Yang & Fang (2004) identified six e-Service quality dimensions: reliability, access, ease of use, personalization, security, and credibility. These dimensions help online shoppers to evaluate e-Service quality. These authors also revealed that traditional service quality dimensions such as competency, politeness, cleanliness, comfort and friendliness are inapplicable for evaluation of e-Service quality.

Madu & Madu (2002) identified 15 dimensions of e-Service quality: performance, features, structure, aesthetics, reliability, storage capacity, serviceability, security and system integrity, trust, responsiveness, product/service differentiation and customization, web store policies, reputation, assurance, and empathy.

Parasuraman, Zeithaml & Malhotra (2005) proposed two models for evaluation of e-Service quality, namely E-S-QUAL and E-RecS-QUAL (these models will be discussed in detail further in this chapter).

*Table 1. Dimensions of electronic service quality*

| Model and / or Authors | Dimensions of Electronic Service Quality |
|---|---|
| WEBQUAL (Loiacono, Watson & Goodhue, 2000) | Informational fit to task, Trust, Design appeal, Visual appeal, Flow (emotional appeal), Business process, Interactivity, Response time, Intuitiveness, Innovativeness, Integrated communication, and Substitutability |
| SITEQUAL (Yoo & Donthu, 2001) | Ease of use, Aesthetic design, Processing speed, and Security |
| Madu & Madu (2002) | Performance, Features, Structure, Aesthetics, Reliability, Storage Capacity, Serviceability, Security and system integrity, Trust, Responsiveness, Product/service differentiation and customization, Web store policies, Reputation, Assurance, and Empathy |
| SiteQual (Webb & Webb, 2004) | Service quality: Reliability, Responsiveness, Assurance, Empathy, and Tangibility Information quality: Accessibility quality, Contextual quality, Representational quality, and Intrinsic quality |
| Yang & Fang (2004) | Reliability, Access, Ease of use, Personalization, Security, and Credibility |
| E-S-QUAL and E-RecS-QUAL (Parasuraman, Zeithaml & Malhotra, 2005) | E-S-QUAL: efficiency, fulfilment, system availability, and privacy E-RecS-QUAL: responsiveness, compensation, and contact |
| eTransQual (Bauer, Falk, & Hammerschmidt, 2006) | Functionality/design, Enjoyment, Process, Reliability, and Responsiveness |
| Perceived e-Service Quality (PeSQ) (Cristobal, Flavián & Guinalíu, 2007) | Web design, Customer service, Assurance, and Order management |

Santos (2003) proposed a model of e-Service quality. According to the author, dimensions can be divided into active and passive ones. Dimensions in both of these categories can be further ranked according to importance in regards to e-Service quality to very important ones and less important ones. Model is unique because it provides a scheme of weights or importance of e-Service quality dimensions which was not approached by previous research. Author also pointed out that it is not necessary to improve all aspects of e-Service quality. First of all importance of aspects of given e-Service should be identified and focus most efforts to improvement of most important dimensions first. Unfortunately this model does not provide an instrument for evaluation of the e-Service quality.

Analysis of e-Service quality dimensions allows to claim that there is no unanimous opinion regarding the dimensions, which are most important for e-Service quality evaluation. Though dimensions mentioned most often include ease of use, visual/ graphic quality, information quality, privacy/ security, reliability, speed/ reaction and content. This set of dimensions should be considered by researchers attempting to research e-Service quality and to develop a model for e-Service quality evaluation.

## Models of Electronic Service Quality Evaluation

Academia's interest in evaluation of e-Service quality started not long ago, though scientists proposed few models already. Early models similarly to dimensions of e-Service quality were focused on quality of websites rather than on quality of e-Services (e.g. WEBQUAL (Loiacono, et al., 2000), SITEQUAL (Yoo & Donthu, 2001), etc.). Models, which were developed later, cover wider aspects of e-Service quality by including such dimensions as order fulfilment (e.g. eTailQ (Wolfinbarger & Gilly, 2003), E-S-Qual (Parasuraman et al., 2005), etc.). Some researchers seek to identify important

aspects and significant dimensions of e-Service quality rather than to create a model which could be practically applied for evaluation of e-Service quality (e.g. Grönroos et al. (2000), Madu & Madu (2002), Santos (2003), Webb & Webb (2004), etc.). Further on descriptions of few models, which can be applied practically for evaluation of e-Service quality, are provided.

*SITEQUAL Model:* Of e-Service quality evaluation was proposed by Yoo & Donthy in 2001. E-Service quality is evaluated based on 9 statements which represent four dimensions: ease of use (This site is convenient to use; It is easy to search for information), aesthetic design (This site is colourful; This site is creative; This site shows good pictures of the products), processing speed (It is easy to access the results; This site has quick process), and security (This site ensures me of security; I am confident of security with this site). Data for empirical validation of the model was gathered by survey of marketing area students, who were asked to visit, browse and then evaluate three online shops of their own choice. Parasuraman et al. (2005) criticize this model arguing that it does not cover all aspects of purchase process and therefore can not be suitable for evaluation of quality of services provided via website. However Bressolles & Nantel (2004) compared SITEQUAL, Webqual (Barnes & Vidgen, 2003) and eTailQ (Wolfinbarger & Gilly, 2003) models and found that SITEQUAL model is the best of three for measuring perceived quality of e-Services.

*eTailQ Model:* Was developed by Wolfinbarger & Gilly (2003) after performing a study with traditional focus groups and survey of users via internet. They created a scale of 14 statements which represent four dimensions: design, customer service, reliability/compliance with commitments and security/privacy. Parasuraman et al. (2005) think highly of efforts to develop a model for perceived quality of online retail as well as attitudes of authors of the model. However they have few reservations regarding the model: dimensions of design and customer service are less compatible and stand out more than other two dimensions. First two dimensions, as other dimensions of the model, that are not validated can be significant to users while evaluating the quality of services on websites therefore the model should be developed further. Bressolles & Nantel (2004) in their study did not find this model significantly useful for evaluation of e-Service quality.

*E-S-QUAL and E-RecS-QUAL Models:* Parasuraman et al. (2005) point out that there are different perceptions of e-Service quality. Researchers in general focus their attention to technical quality of the website but not to studies of e-Service quality. Therefore authors attempted to develop a model for e-Service quality evaluation based on SERVQUAL model they developed earlier. Parasuraman et al. (2005) chose earlier studies on e-Service quality for their own research. They analysed studies on e-Service quality within retail, web design, travel agencies as variety of areas enables wider reflection of e-Service quality.

Researchers identified 5 main criteria based on which users evaluate quality of e-Services: (1) information availability and content, (2) ease of use or usability, (3) privacy/security, (4) graphic style, and (5) reliability/fulfilment. Building on these criteria, results of previous research, grouping of perceived attributes of websites and target groups of e-Service users, Parasuraman et al. (2005) developed E-S-QUAL model of e-Service quality evaluation, accompanied by instrument for practical application of the model. Instrument is applied by figuring out minimum and maximum requirements of users for quality, i.e. user grades limits of quality he is comfortable with, and later he assesses quality of service he experienced after he used it.

Four dimensions are used for evaluation of e-Service quality: efficiency, fulfilment, system availability, and privacy. Other three dimensions (responsiveness, compensation, and contact) are used for evaluation of e-Service quality if user faces some problems.

This model is useful because users are indicating the limits of service quality they would be comfortable with which is useful to know for service provider and evaluation results show what should be changed in order to improve quality of e-Service.

*Hierarchical Model:* Fassnacht & Koese (2006) developed their model for e-Service evaluation basing on service quality model offered by Rust & Oliver (1994) which considers service environment (related to physical ambiance of the service encounter), service delivery (process of interaction between employees and customers) and service product (the core benefit that customers receive after service delivery, that is, the outcome of the service exchange) to be three most important dimensions in regards of service quality. Other concept they used for model development was hierarchical structure developed during research of Brady & Cronin (2001) (cited by Fassnacht & Koese, 2006). As a result of combining those two separate concepts, authors developed a concept of three-dimensional hierarchical service quality. Hierarchical structure means that subdimensions are factors or parts of main three dimensions (environment quality, delivery quality and outcome quality). Fassnacht & Koese (2006) identified nine subdimensions based on extensive scientific literature analysis and empirical validation.

As the environment quality dimension is related to the visual appearance of the user interface, it is assigned with two subdimensions (Fassnacht & Koese, 2006): graphic quality (defines "how well represented are the various elements of the user interface (e.g., text, icons, digital images, or backgrounds)", p. 26) and clarity of layout ("the degree to which the design structure of the user interface helps users to find their way", p. 26).

Delivery quality is related to the customer–website interaction during usage of the service, thus four related subdimensions are assigned (Fassnacht & Koese, 2006). The first, attractiveness of selection defines "the extent to which the available range of offerings appeals to the customer" (p. 26). Information quality subdimension covers "the extent to which complete, accurate, and timely information is provided for the customer during the interaction process with the user interface (e.g., product descriptions, payment information, or frequently asked questions)" (p. 26). Ease of use subdimension defines "the degree to which the functionality of the user interface facilitates the customer's retrieval of the electronic service" (p. 26). The fourth subdimension, technical quality, reflects "the goodness of data transfer and data processing during the delivery of the e-Service" (p. 27).

In the model, outcome quality is viewed as what the customer is left with after service delivery. Three subdimensions represent this dimension (Fassnacht & Koese, 2006): reliability ("the extent to which the provider keeps its service promise" (p. 27), though it does not cover reliable functioning of the provider's technical infrastructure during service delivery), functional benefit ("the extent to which the service serves its actual purpose"; p. 27) and emotional benefit ("the degree to which using the service arouses positive feelings", p. 27).

Practical application of the model for e-Service quality evaluation is enabled by accompanying instrument which is composed of 39 statements, which, assessed by users, provides numerical values of nine subdimensions and general quality of e-Service.

Analysis of models for e-Service quality evaluation reveals evolution of models from ones being focused mainly on quality of websites to ones covering wider aspects of e-Services including such dimensions as order fulfilment. Hierarchical Model developed by Fassnacht & Koese (2006) stands out because of comprehensive details and broad possibilities to apply the model in practice.

## CONCEPTUAL MODEL FOR THE EVALUATION OF QUALITY OF PUBLIC ELECTRONIC SERVICES

After an analysis of scientific literature the Hierarchical model of Fassnacht & Koese (2006) was selected in this work, as the basis of conceptual model for the evaluation of quality of public electronic services. The selection was conditioned by the fact that earlier evaluation models encompass only a narrow part of electronic service evaluation, i.e., only user interface (service provider's website) quality evaluation, whereas this model encompasses quality of the user interface, service and its provision process, as well as quality of service purchasing process.

Another advantage of this model is the fact that it is intended for an evaluation of quality of various electronic services. This model has already been tested in cases of three different business-to-customer electronic services: personal website creation and support service (pure service), sport news provision service (information provision), and an electronic shop of electronic equipment (product selling).

However, suitability of the model for the quality evaluation in cases of business-to-business or public electronic services is not known, though studies performed by authors supported the model's suitability for the evaluation of quality of analyzed services. According to authors' view, a universal adoption of the model can be also limited by the fact that the model has been tested only in one country, namely Germany.

The model's review reveals that two of nine subdimensions suggested by the Fassnacht & Koese (2006) Hierarchical model are not relevant in the evaluation of quality of public electronic services, namely, attractiveness of selection (determines the level, to which the available variety of selection attracts and appeals the customer) and functional benefit (the scope of service conformity with itself). Public electronic services mean provision or reception of information and documents to citizens and organizations, determined in legal acts issued by state or municipal institutions. Variety of selection enabling the customer (whether a citizen of organization) to choose if one needs a particular service or not does not exist in the case of these services. The only thing one can choose is using the service online or offline. It is impossible for these services to not conform to their purpose; therefore, an evaluation of the functional benefit subdimension loses its meaning.

The conceptual model for the evaluation of quality of public electronic services is presented in Figure 1.

Statements (33 statements are left, because 6 statements related to attractiveness of selection and functional benefit dimensions have been removed from the original instrument developed by Fassnacht & Koese (2006)), dedicated to obtain numerical values of 7 subdimensions and a total value of the electronic public service quality evaluation. The design of the model has been based on results obtained in the analysis of scientific literature. Therefore, the model is theoretical and its suitability for practical application should be validated.

## USE OF PUBLIC ELECTRONIC SERVICES IN LITHUANIA

The "Exemplary list of public services that should be provided by municipal institutions and agencies by means of digital technologies" approved by the order No. 1V-148, 30 April 2004, of the Minister of Interior of the Republic of Lithuania containing very comprehensive list of public services to be provided online by municipalities – it identifies 27 groups of services. Some groups of services include even up to 36 services (e.g., services related to the Order of trade and other service delivery in markets and public places, permit (license) issuing in cases determined by laws and the order). In total, this list includes 148 services. Also, it must be noted that services included into this list are related to particular institutions belonging to a municipality; however, usually these services are transferred to virtual environment by an adequate institution, not a municipality itself (e.g. Primary personal and public healthcare – these services are provided by polyclinics or clinics belonging for a municipality, which take care about transferring these services to virtual environment). It should be noted that there are no other documents regulating a classification and a list of public services provided by governmental institutions in Lithuania. Though the list of 20 public services benchmarked in EU

*Figure 1. Conceptual model for the evaluation of quality of electronic public services (adopted from Fassnacht & Koese, 2006)*

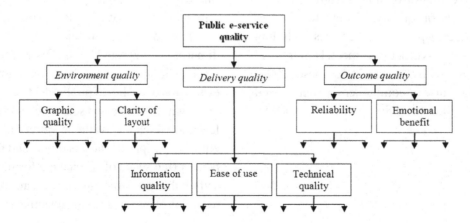

is also evaluated in Lithuania. The list consists of 12 Citizen and 8 Business services. Services for citizens include: Income taxes, Job search services, Social security benefits (Unemployment benefits, Child allowances, Medical costs, and Student grants), Personal documents (Passports, and Driver's license), Car registration, Application for a building permission, Declaration to the police, Public libraries (catalogues, search tools), (Birth and marriage) Certificates, Enrolment in higher education, Announcement of moving, and Health-related services. Services for business include: Social contribution for employees, Corporate tax, VAT, Registration of a new company, Submission of data to statistical offices, Customs declaration, Environment-related permits, and Public procurement (Capgemini, 2010).

One of most important criteria applied when assessing digitization of public service a level of maturity of electronic service is measured. 5-stage maturity model developed by Capgemini (2010) is used for evaluation of sophistication and availability of public electronic services in Lithuania. This model reveals how organizations and citizens can interact with governmental institutions. Governments' service delivery processes are described according to five following stages: (i) information, (ii) one-way interaction, (iii) two-way interaction, (iv) transaction, and (v) targetisation/automation.

According to (Information Society Development Committee under the Ministry of Transport and Communications of the Republic of Lithuania (2012a) 39 percent of citizens were looking for information about public services over the last 12 months online. It is even seven percent more than at the end of 2011. The most popular public electronic services between citizens – Tax Returns and health-related services.

According to Kalinauskas (2012), director of the Information Society Development Committee under the Ministry of Transport and Communications of the Republic of Lithuania, "information retrieval on the Internet and the use of public electronic services and administrative growth is a natural process. These trends are driven by two factors: the population is increasingly using the Internet and more and more the most necessary public and administrative services moved to the Internet. Residents evaluate simplicity and benefits of the services which are received electronically so that they are becoming more relevant to more people."

By age groups, the public authorities' websites are mainly visited by 25-34 year old age group - 62.9%, as well as the 16-24 year age group – 47.1%.

The main reason to visit public institution website is search for information – 48% of citizens search info about institution and its activities. Employees usually are looking for contact information (40%, November 2011 - 24%). 41% is looking for electronic applications and forms necessary for public service (November 2011 – 38%).

The most citizens use the income tax declaration service – 20% of Lithuania population (in November 2011 – 16%), health-related services (information services in different institutions, to register with the health care professionals) – 20% (November 2011 – 11%), job search services – 16% (November 2011 – 5%), social security and social services – 14% (November 2011 – 6%).

## EMPIRICAL VALIDATION OF THE MODEL IN LITHUANIA

### Research Methodology

The developed conceptual model was used to evaluate public services in Lithuania. The empirical research was oriented towards three services.

*Research Problem*: Can the designed conceptual model for the evaluation of quality of electronic public services be applied in practice?

*Research Purpose*: To perform an empirical research of possibilities for an application of the conceptual electronic public service model in cases of public electronic services characterized by three different maturity levels.

*Research Object*: Evaluation of quality of electronic public services characterized by three different maturity levels.

Three different services provided by Lithuanian public institutions were selected for the empirical investigation:

- Issue of a passport of a citizen of the Republic of Lithuania. Customers can receive information about terms and places where they can get a passport, and about required documents, using electronic means. It is possible to find out status of passport issue online. This is an electronic service of the first maturity level (Information Society Development Committee under the Ministry of Transport and Communications of the Republic of Lithuania, 2012b). Service available at: http://www.dokumentai.lt/

- Services of public libraries. Search of issues present in archives of large Lithuanian cities can be performed in Internet at this time. Also, desired books can be ordered. One just have to arrive to the library later and receive ordered books, presenting a reader's certificate, for reading in the reading-room or at home (if selected books are allowed to take way from the library). If a requested book is electronic, it can be received via electronic means. This is an electronic service of the fourth maturity level (Information Society Development Committee under the Ministry of Transport and Communications of the Republic of Lithuania, 2012b). Service available at: http://www.libis.lt/

- Delivery of the annual income declaration for the State Tax Inspectorate. Declarations are accepted by the Inspectorate in electronic form through EDS (Electronic declaration system) since 2004. With a help of this systems, customers can deliver their declarations without a need to walk away from their computers. This is an electronic service of the fifth maturity level (Information Society Development Committee under the Ministry of Transport and Communications of the Republic of Lithuania, 2012b). Service available at: http://deklaravimas.vmi.lt/

## Research Hypotheses

**H1:** Respondents will give quite low scores for the graphical quality, but they will evaluate the clarity quality better, therefore, total evaluations of environment quality will not be low (public institutions creating their Internet sites pay more attention to site functionality, not attractiveness and beauty)

**H2:** Presentation quality in different maturity levels is evaluated differently (customers of electronic services sometimes don't understand that value of provided services is not always equal, if levels of their transfer to the electronic media are different, and they want equal ease of use and simplicity)

**H3:** The emotional benefit subdimension of the result quality dimension is the element of electronic public services receiving lowest scores (the use of electronic services by customers is more stimulated by necessity than by willingness. In case of electronic services, customer experiences positive feelings, knowing that he has avoided the necessity to visit a public institution, or at least has reduced the visit duration and has saved some time. However, the using a service does not cause many positive feelings on its turn).

*Research Method Selection*: A quantitative method was selected for the research. This method enables to select particular research aspects and motives beforehand. Besides, data of a quantitative research enable comparison of relative significance of investigated aspects, in this case – different quality aspects. Obtained data can be processed statistically.

*Data Collection Method Selection*: Considering the fact that customers are going to evaluate service quality, when the model is applied, as they fill their questionnaires, questionnaires with analogical structure have been chosen for the survey. Survey questionnaires were presented in the Internet site www.apklausa.lt. The decision to present questionnaires in the Internet was determined by the fact that the evaluation of quality of electronic services, i.e., services provided in the virtual environment was studied. Customers who use Internet were surveyed this way, and there was no need to waste time with answers of customers who don't use Internet.

*Respondent Selection*: Internet addresses of questionnaires were not promoted purposefully and were not sent to any particular potential respondents; consequently, they were filled by interested visitors of the site www.apklausa.lt.

*Questionnaire Composition*: A separate questionnaire was designed for each case of evaluation of quality of public electronic services. Questionnaire composition was based on the conceptual model for the evaluation of quality of electronic public services presented in the theoretical part of this work. The questionnaire consisted of 33 statements, which were grouped according to subdimensions:

- **Graphic Quality:** 5 statements.
- **Clarity of Layout:** 3 statements.
- **Information Quality:** 4 statements.
- **Ease of Use:** 6 statements.
- **Technical Quality:** 5 statements.
- **Reliability:** 4 statements.
- **Emotional Benefit:** 3 statements.
- And 3 statements assigned for evaluation of general quality.

Short descriptions of services investigated by a particular questionnaire were presented in the preamble of each questionnaire, and Internet sites to reach these electronic public services were presented. Formulation of statements in each questionnaire was adapted for particular services.

Respondents were asked to give 1 to 9 points for statements, where 1 is the lowest score, and 9 is the highest score. Respondents could just select the score, not to write it (for questionnaires were not spoiled, writing higher or not whole numbers).

MS Excel program was used for obtained data processing, which is a popular tool enabling presentation of analysis results in the form of various diagrams.

## Research Results

Response rate in two weeks, when questionnaires were presented in the Internet site www.apklausa. lt, was as following: 123 respondents completed the questionnaire on the service of Lithuanian citizen passport issuing, 145 - the questionnaire on e-Services of public libraries, 108 - the questionnaire on annual income declaration delivery through RDS system. Totally, data from 376 questionnaires is analyzed.

*Environment Quality Dimension:* This dimension is related to the visual appearance of the user interface, it is assigned with two subdimensions: *graphic quality*, which defines "how well represented are the various elements of the user interface (e.g., text, icons, digital images, or backgrounds)", and *clarity of layout*, which defines "the degree to which the design structure of the user interface helps users to find their way" (Fassnacht & Koese, 2006)). After calculation of respondents' evaluations results were presented graphically in Figure 2.

The Figure 2 reveals that respondents evaluated *graphic quality* of all services lower than clarity of layout. As it is seen after the review of all sub dimensions, only emotional benefit sub

*Figure 2. Values of subdimensions of Environment quality dimension and their average (points, in the scale 1 to 9)*

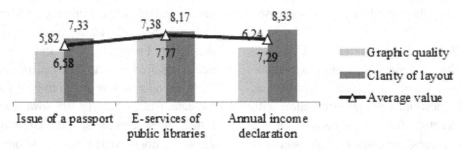

dimension is scored lower. Graphic quality of the public service related to Lithuanian citizen's passport issue received the lowest score among all three services from respondents – 5.82 points. Likely, respondents, most of which are men, didn't pay much attention to the appearance and attraction and they are not inclined to score these graphic quality aspects high. Respondents gave highest scores for graphic quality of electronic services provided by public libraries, among three evaluated electronic services–7.38 points. Such a high score can be influenced by the fact that libraries are objects of culture and they care about visual expression of websites more than other public institutions, therefore, respondents grade graphic quality aspects of these services higher than respondents evaluating quality of other services.

Clarity of layout was scored higher than graphical quality. Among all three evaluated services, respondents who evaluated quality of electronic services related to Lithuanian citizen's service issue gave lowest scores for clarity of layout, same as in the case of graphic quality evaluation. However, the score is higher than the score given by respondents for service quality in general. This shows that respondents grade clarity of layout in the case of this service higher than general quality. Declaration submission clarity of layout was graded higher (8.33 points). This shows that, though the e-Service created by the State Tax Inspectorate for the EDS system through which the mentioned

service is delivered is not attractive, everything is presented clearly in it. Values obtained after calculation of average values of graphical quality and clarity quality sub dimensions are presented in Figure 2 as well. These values express total value of the environment quality dimension. Environment quality of electronic services provided by libraries has scored highest, and quality of electronic services related to Lithuanian citizen's passport issue has scored lowest.

*Delivery Quality Dimension:* Delivery quality is related to the customer–website interaction during usage of the service, thus three related subdimensions are assigned. The first, *information quality* subdimension covers "the extent to which complete, accurate, and timely information is provided for the customer during the interaction process with the user interface (e.g., product descriptions, payment information, or frequently asked questions)". *Ease of use* subdimension defines "the degree to which the functionality of the user interface facilitates the customer's retrieval of the electronic service". The fourth subdimension, *technical quality*, reflects "the goodness of data transfer and data processing during the delivery of the e-Service" (Fassnacht & Koese, 2006). Values of these subdimensions calculated according to respondents' answers are presented in Figure 3.

As Figure 3 shows, respondents of the survey have given highest scores for the *information quality* sub dimension in all cases – all average scores are higher than 8 points (of 9 possible).

*Figure 3. Values of subdimensions of delivery quality dimension and their average (points, in scale 1 to 9)*

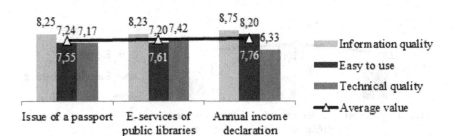

This shows that providers of electronic services evaluated in this work take care of novelty, clarity, comprehensiveness, and accuracy. As it was in the case of clarity of layout subdimension, respondents gave highest scores for annual income declaration delivery quality (8.75 points). This affirms that concern of the State Tax Inspectorate that has created the site for EDS system, through which the mentioned service is provided, about provision comprehensive, accurate and clear provision of information for system users is valued by customers.

Another sub dimension, *ease of use*, is scored a little lower than the general average of delivery quality dimension quality. This means that service providers should find the way to make using services easier for customers. Respondents graded this sub dimension lowest in the case of annual income declaration electronic service (6.33 points). The score is very low, because respondents don't think that using this service is easy. This sub dimension was scored highest (average – 7.42) by respondents using electronic services of public libraries. It is likely that most respondents use these services often, and they are used to the system, therefore, using services seems easy to them. However, there was no question in the questionnaire about service usage frequency of respondents, therefore, it is impossible to prove this assumption.

*Technical quality* sub dimension was scored highest in the case of annual income declaration delivering electronically (8.20 points). This can be

caused by the belief of EDS system users that data transmission is secure, because service provider is the State Tax Inspectorate. Also, customers of this service graded data transmission security higher. They evaluated other statements almost the same, as respondents who evaluated quality of two other services.

*Outcome Quality Dimension*: In the model, *outcome quality* is viewed as what the customer is left with after service delivery. Two subdimensions represent this dimension: *reliability*, which defines "the extent to which the provider keeps its service promise", though it does not cover reliable functioning of the provider's technical infrastructure during service delivery, and *emotional benefit*, which defines "the degree to which using the service arouses positive feelings" (Fassnacht & Koese, 2006). Values of these subdimensions calculated according to respondents' answers are presented in Figure 4.

Data presented in Figure 4 reveals that, according to the respondents' opinion, reliability of Lithuanian public electronic services is high. They gave highest scores for annual income declaration delivering service *reliability*. This is likely more related to customers' belief that the State Tax Inspectorate has to fulfill services it provides fast and reliably than to reality. Among all three evaluated electronic services, respondents scored reliability of electronic services related to Lithuanian citizen's passport issue lowest. This result was conditioned by especially low scores of the statement "service provision is such as you want".

*Figure 4. Values of subdimensions of outcome quality dimension and their average (points, in scale 1 to 9)*

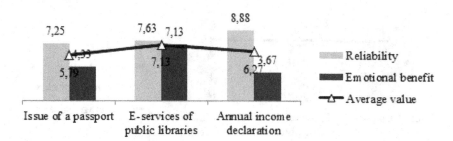

It can be assumed that customers of this service expect more than just information, therefore, they feel disappointed when their expectations are not met.

*Emotional benefit* in all cases, as it was mentioned before, received lowest scores from respondents. Lowest scores were given in the case of annual income declaration delivery – 3.67 points. This shows that usage of this service does not cause many positive emotions for customers. Emotional benefit of electronic services provided by public libraries had highest scores – 7.38 points. This is understandable, because usage of library services is caused by necessity only in very rare cases, customers use these services voluntarily, and their usage on Internet causes positive feelings.

## FUTURE RESEARCH DIRECTIONS

The evaluation of public electronic services remains important challenge for scholars and public servants. The evaluation usually have 2 different perspectives – supply driven approach (reflecting position of public institutions and software developers) and demand driven approach (reflecting user perspectives on public electronic services). Public electronic services quality assessment represents demand driven approach considering qualitative aspect of services use presuming more subjective assessment perspective.

The future research might be extended within several directions. First of all we concentrated this research analyzing services dedicated to citizens. The proposed model might be adapted considering peculiarities of G2G and G2B services and verified empirically identifying another segment approaches towards public electronic services quality. Another perspective relates to growing social citizen and policy-making 2.0 issues. This implies analysis how social aspect should be considered and demonstrated in public electronic service delivery and how users assess social aspects of service delivery as a dimension of service quality.

## CONCLUSION

The public electronic service adoption is growing all over the world. As citizens are spending more time online, public administration institutions are keen to digitize services they are offering. Looking from the institutions perspective this is supply driven approach driven mainly by technologies and software development companies.

The paper represents demand driven approach analyzing services acceptance through citizens perspective in services quality context. Electronic services quality is widely analyzed however public electronic services require adoption and modification of such models considering peculiarities of such services.

The proposed approach aims to evaluate public electronic services through environment quality, delivery quality and outcome quality perspectives indicating in total 7 subdimensions. The proposed model empirically validates on three different maturity level public electronic services in Lithuania – annual income declaration, passport issue and public libraries services.

Empirical investigation of proposed conceptual model of public electronic services quality evaluation demonstrated this model is suitable for the evaluation of public e-Services. The arguable aspect might be only formulation of statements reflecting different subdimensions because these statements' evaluations conducted during the investigation seem to be quite biased.

# REFERENCES

Barnes, S. J., & Vidgen, R. T. (2003). An integrative approach to the assessment of e-commerce quality. *Journal of Electronic Commerce Research*, *3*(3), 114–127.

Bauer, H. H., Falk, T., & Hammerschmidt, M. (2006). eTransQual: A transaction process-based approach for capturing service quality in online shopping. *Journal of Business Research*, *59*(7), 866–875. doi:10.1016/j.jbusres.2006.01.021

Bressolles, G., & Nantel, J. (2004). Electronic service quality: A comparison of three measurement scales. In *Proceedings of the 33th EMAC Conference* (pp. 1–7). Murcia: EMAC.

Cai, S., & Jun, M. (2003). Internet users' perceptions of online service quality: A comparison of online buyers and information searchers. *Managing Service Quality*, *13*(6), 504–519. doi:10.1108/09604520310506568

Capgemini. (2010). *Digitizing public services in Europe: Putting ambition into action - 9th benchmark measurement* (Technical Report by European Commission). Directorate General for Information Society and Media. Retrieved April 12, 2013, from http://ec.europa.eu/information_society/newsroom/cf/document.cfm?action=display&doc_id=747

Cristobal, E., Flavián, C., & Guinalíu, M. (2007). Perceived e-service quality (PeSQ): Measurement validation and effects on consumer satisfaction and web site loyalty. *Managing Service Quality*, *17*(3), 317–340. doi:10.1108/09604520710744326

Cronin, J. J., & Taylor, S. A. (1992). Measuring service quality: a re-examination and extension. *Journal of Marketing*, *56*(3), 125–131. doi:10.2307/1252296

Dabholkar, P. A., Shepherd, C. D., & Thorpe, D. I. (2000). A comprehensive framework for service quality: An investigation of critical conceptual and measurement issues through a longitudinal study. *Journal of Retailing*, *76*(2), 131–139. doi:10.1016/S0022-4359(00)00029-4

De Ruyter, K., Wetzels, M., & Kleijnen, M. (2000). Customer adoption of e-service: An experimental study. *International Journal of Service Industry Management*, *12*(2), 184–207. doi:10.1108/09564230110387542

Fassnacht, M., & Koese, I. (2006). Quality of electronic services: Conceptualizing and testing a hierarchical model. *Journal of Service Research*, *9*(1), 19–37. doi:10.1177/1094670506289531

Grönroos, C., Heinonen, F., Isoniemi, K., & Lindholm, M. (2000). The NetOffer model: A case example from the virtual marketspace. *Management Decision*, *38*(4), 243–252. doi:10.1108/00251740010326252

Gummerus, J., Liljander, V., Pura, M., & Van Riel, A. (2004). Customer loyalty to content-based websites: The case of an online health-care service. *Journal of Services Marketing, 18*(3), 175–186. doi:10.1108/08876040410536486

Information Society Development Committee under the Ministry of Transport of the Republic of Lithuania (2012). *Pagrindinių elektroninių viešųjų ir administracinių paslaugų vertinimas: 2011 m. tyrimo ataskaita.* Retrieved February 11, 2013, from http://www.ivpk.lt/uploads/Leidiniai/Pagrindiniu%20ePaslaugu%20vertinimas_2012%20tyrimo%20ataskaita.pdf

King, D., Lee, J., & Viehland, D. (2004). *Electronic commerce: A managerial perspective.* Upper Saddle River, NJ: Prentice Hall.

Loiacono, E., Watson, R. T., & Goodhue, D. (2000). *WebQual: A web site quality instrument* (Working Paper). Worcester Polytechnic Institute.

Madu, C. N., & Madu, A. A. (2002). Dimensions of e-quality. *International Journal of Quality & Reliability Management, 19*(3), 246–258. doi:10.1108/02656710210415668

Parasuraman, A., Zeithaml, V. A., & Berry, L. L. (1985). A conceptual model of service quality and its implications for future research. *Journal of Marketing, 49*(4), 41–50. doi:10.2307/1251430

Parasuraman, A., Zeithaml, V. A., & Berry, L. L. (1988). SERVQUAL: A multiple-item scale for measuring consumer perceptions of service quality. *Journal of Retailing, 64*(1), 12–40.

Parasuraman, A., Zeithaml, V. A., & Malhotra, A. (2005). E-S-QUAL: A multiple-item scale for assessing electronic service quality. *Journal of Service Research, 7*(3), 213–233. doi:10.1177/1094670504271156

Rahman, Z. (2004). E-commerce solution for services. *European Business Review, 16*(6), 564–576. doi:10.1108/09555340410565396

Reynolds, J. (2000). e-Commerce: A critical review. *International Journal of Retail and Distribution Management, 28*(10), 417–444. doi:10.1108/09590550010349253

Rust, R. T., & Lemon, K. N. (2001). E-service and the consumer. *International Journal of Electronic Commerce, 5*(3), 85–101.

Rust, R. T., & Oliver, R. L. (1994). Service quality – Insights and managerial implications from the frontier. In *Service quality: New directions in theory and practice.* Thousand Oaks, CA: Sage. doi:10.4135/9781452229102.n1

Santos, J. (2003). E-service quality: A model of virtual service quality dimensions. *Managing Service Quality, 13*(3), 233–246. doi:10.1108/09604520310476490

Surjadjaja, H., Ghosh, S., & Antony, F. (2003). Determining and assessing the determinants of e-service operations. *Managing Service Quality, 13*(1), 39–53. doi:10.1108/09604520310456708

van Riel, A. C. R., Liljander, V., & Jurriens, P. (2001). Exploring consumer evaluations of e-services: A portal site. *International Journal of Service Industry Management, 12*(4), 359–377. doi:10.1108/09564230110405280

Webb, H. W., & Webb, L. A. (2004). SiteQual: An integrated measure of web site quality. *Journal of Enterprise Information Management, 17*(6), 430–440. doi:10.1108/17410390410566724

Yang, Z., & Fang, X. (2004). Online service quality dimensions and their relationships with satisfaction: A content analysis of customer reviews of securities brokerage services. *International Journal of Service Industry Management, 15*(3), 302–326. doi:10.1108/09564230410540953

Yoo, B., & Donthu, N. (2001). Developing a scale to measure the perceived quality of an internet shopping site (sitequal). *Quarterly Journal of Electronic Commerce, 2*(1), 31–46.

Zeithaml, V. A., Parasuraman, A., & Malhotra, A. (2002). Service quality delivery through web sites: A critical review of extant knowledge. *Journal of the Academy of Marketing Science*, *30*(4), 362–375. doi:10.1177/009207002236911

## KEY TERMS AND DEFINITIONS

**Delivery Quality:** Dimension of e-Service quality related to the customer–website interaction during usage of the service.

**Electronic Service:** Delivery of services between a service provider and a customer of a service in virtual marketplace.

**Electronic Service Quality:** Is the degree, to which electronic services can meet most significant needs of the customer effectively and efficiently (Fassnacht & Koese, 2006).

**Environment Quality:** Dimension of e-Service quality related to the visual appearance of the user interface.

**Outcome Quality:** Dimension of e-Service quality defining what the customer is left with after service delivery.

# Chapter 4
# Developing, Implementing, and Evaluating a Web Interface in the Field of E-Government

**Sandra Kalidien**
*Ministry of Security and Justice, The Netherlands*

**Richard van Witzenburg**
*Ministry of Security and Justice, The Netherlands*

**Sunil Choenni**
*Ministry of Security and Justice, The Netherlands*

## ABSTRACT

*For the purpose of good and trustworthy management of information for the government, responsible for the justice domain, the research institute was requested to build a monitor that makes it possible to periodically monitor data flows within as well as between organizations of the justice domain. The aim of this monitor is to get insight into the performance and possible bottlenecks in the criminal justice domain. An important component of the monitor is a Web interface. The Web interface should be user friendly and, more importantly, facilitate policy makers to interpret the data flows in the justice domain. To meet with this facilitation, the authors created a fixed set of variables for the interface that minimizes misinterpretation of the data. In this chapter, they describe how they managed to develop and implement the Web interface. Additionally, the authors illustrate how the Web interface works in practice and describe how they managed to evaluate the Web interface on usefulness and satisfaction.*

## INTRODUCTION

In the field of the government responsible for the criminal justice domain, many organizations are involved that can be considered partners in a chain of events (i.e. criminal cases or offenders or victims). This implies that the input of one or-ganization is dependent on the output of another organization in the chain (e.g. Kalidien et al., 2009, 2010). From the perspective of the government responsible for this domain, it is desirable to have a good and reliable understanding of the flows within as well as between the organizations in this domain (Choenni et al., 2011). Having a good

DOI: 10.4018/978-1-4666-5129-6.ch004

understanding of these flows may give insight into the performance and possible bottlenecks in the justice domain. This way, the government can actively stimulate organizations to solve potential problems at an early stage, which in turn may lead to a system that acts more efficiently.

Current means, such as statistical yearbooks may help the government to get insight in the criminal justice chain. For instance, the Dutch publication 'Crime and Law enforcement' describes developments of crimes experienced by victims, crimes registered by the police and the reaction of the criminal justice system on crime (Rosmalen et al., 2012). The book is updated annually and is valuable to a broad audience, such as policy makers, criminologists and media. However, for the means of monitoring data flows within and between organizations the book is less practical, as it is not easy to compare and combine the data of different organizations (Kalidien et al., 2009).

Furthermore, the information need of the government is dependent on the policy that is applicable a certain moment in time. For instance, the current Dutch government's policy on the justice domain is to reduce crimes such as street robberies, burglaries and violent crime in general (Rutte II, 2012). Detailed information for specifically these types of crimes are of interest to the government at this time. So, the information need of the government is in some sense 'ad hoc', depending on the topics in daily politics. Yearbooks often have static information available, with limited possibilities to drill down information. Moreover, to be able to act on the criminal justice system on possible bottlenecks at an early stage, the government requires information rather quickly and as recent as possible. So updates more frequent than on a yearly basis are a must.

But books are not only less practical. Until recently, policy makers and experts from the justice domain periodically discussed developments of data flows in the justice domain through meetings with some organizations in the justice domain, assisted by a manually composed collection of written reports describing main indicators for each of these organizations. The effectiveness at these meetings can be improved, since the focus often remained on one organization (in particular the Public Prosecution, having a central role in the Dutch Criminal Justice System), and a clear understanding of what happens with data flows between organizations was missing. If there was a comparison between organizations this happened in an unstructured way. Furthermore, only a few organizations were involved in these meetings.

To improve the management information in the justice domain, the government recently requested our research institute to develop and implement a monitor that could provide reliable and valid management information on the criminal justice domain. The monitor should, among other things, be able to monitor flows within and between organizations, and periodically show the data in a way that makes it easy for experts to draw conclusions and have the possibility to produce graphs and reports. In other words, the monitor should include capabilities to facilitate the interpretation of the data in a structured way. An important component of the monitor should be a web interface that makes the data digitally available in a user friendly way and offers the end users the possibility to drill down information. Having such a web interface should make it easier for officials of the government and related partners to monitor the functioning of the entire Dutch criminal justice domain.

In this chapter we focus on the development and implementation of the web interface part of the monitor. We describe how we managed to build a web interface that meets the information need and requirements of the government. For the development of the monitor we used the concept of *data space* (Kalidien et al, 2009, 2010; Choenni et al., 2011). There are three layers in this concept, a data space layer, a space manager layer and a user interface layer. In this chapter we focus on the latter.

The remainder of this chapter is organized as follows: first, we describe the background of the characteristics of the information flows in the criminal justice domain. Second, we describe how we developed and implemented the web interface (section 3). In section 4, we illustrate how the web interface works in practice. In section 5, we describe how we evaluated the web interface on user satisfaction and usefulness. In the last section, we make some concluding remarks and give future research directions of the web interface.

## BACKGROUND: CHARACTERISTICS OF THE INFORMATION FLOWS WITHIN THE CRIMINAL JUSTICE DOMAIN

In the criminal justice domain many organizations are involved, such as the police, the public prosecution and organizations involved in the execution of penalties, for example the correctional institute of the ministry of Security and Justice. Each organization has its own information system and its own definitions of variables (Kalidien et al., 2009). As the output of one organization is the input of another organization in the justice domain, the data of the organizations are related to each other.

To get a good insight into the efficiency of the criminal justice domain a good understanding of flows within as well as between organizations is needed. Figure 1 shows an example of a simplified schema of flows in a specific part of the criminal justice system. The schema shows the number of crimes registered by the police and how the police act on these crimes. After a suspect is found, the police have several ways of dealing with a suspect, for instance by imposing a fine. This means that the suspect has to pay a sum of money. In case of a police transaction, the police send a notification to the organization responsible for the execution of transactions ('CJIB' in Dutch). The police may also decide to give a warning and to dismiss a sus-

pect. In case of minors, the police may decide to send a suspect to HALT. This bureau gives minors the opportunity to prevent getting a crime record. Also, the police may decide to send a suspect to the Public Prosecution ('OM' in Dutch). Note that from the police there are also connections to several other organizations, for instance to the National Forensic Institute ('NFI' in Dutch) and the bureau for victims ('SHN' in Dutch). So, the criminal justice domain is not necessarily a linear process, as there are different flows to and from several organizations possible.

There is a huge amount of data available from all the organizations together. To have a good understanding of how the criminal justice system performs, the government is not only interested in information of the organizations separately, but also in flows between organizations. Having information about flows within as well as between organizations may give the government insight into, for instance, workloads of organizations and the time needed to handle a case compared to the elapsed time.

As the criminal justice domain can be considered a chain, one can imagine that what goes out from one organization, goes into another. For instance, the police send 100 suspects to the prosecution, then one may expect the input of the prosecution to be a 100 as well. Although this seems logical, in practice this is not the case. In reality, out of these 100 suspects there may remain 50 cases in the input for the prosecution. This 'loss' of suspects has several reasons. First, there is a definition issue, namely, the police register *suspects*, while the prosecution registers *cases*. So the unit changes from person to cases. A person may have more than one case. Secondly, due to a new information system at the public prosecution, not all input from the police is registered automatically. The prosecution may calculate beforehand that a case will be dropped for reasons of feasibility and therefore decide not to register the input. So the output of the police does not necessary reflect the whole input at the

*Figure 1. Schema of flows in a part of the criminal justice system. Note that exact numbers are hidden, because it concerns non-public information.*

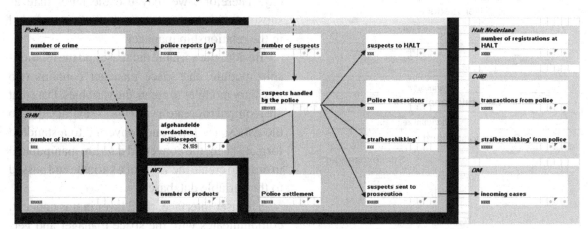

prosecution. Moreover, in practice it seems there is also an unexplainable 'loss' of suspects (Court of Audit, 2012). In other words, there is no 'one to one' connection between organizations in the criminal justice domain.

Since, organizations have several means to handle cases, the data reflects a hierarchy. For example, if we consider the prosecution, then an officer has the possibility to handle a case in different ways, for instance by means of a transaction, a settlement or he can sent the case to court. A transaction in turn can be a community service or the payment of a sum of money. Furthermore, a community service can be on probation or not etc. (see Figure 2). So there is a clear hierarchy in the data of the criminal justice domain that we have to take into account. Presenting this hierarchy may facilitate the interpretation of the data flows.

*Figure 2. Example of the hierarchy of the data*

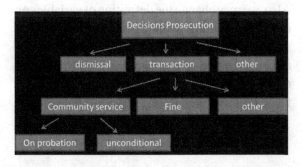

# DEVELOPMENT AND IMPLEMENTATION: FROM PROTOTYPE TO WEB INTERFACE

In this section we describe how we developed and implemented the web interface given the information need of the government and the requirements of the web interface. First, we describe the architecture of the monitor (3.1). In section 3.2 we focus on the challenges and solutions by developing the web interface and in section 3.3. we describe how we implemented the web interface.

## Architecture of the Monitor

For the development and implementation of the monitor we used the data space concept. In this concept, we distinguish three layers: a data space layer, a space manager and an interface layer (Kalidien et al. 2009, 2010; Choenni, 2011). The data space layer consists of a set of databases. The space manager handles the information need of users and communicates the results. The interface layer consists of a set of user interfaces, which communicates on the one side with the space manager and on the other side with its users. We have elaborated these layers for the monitor. In Figure 3, the architecture of the monitor is depicted.

*Figure 3. Architecture of the monitor*

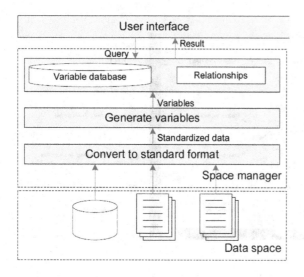

The data space contains data sources of different types, ranging from comma-separated files containing aggregated data to a data warehouse with detailed information about a part of the justice system. The space manager consists of different components. An important component is the variable database, containing a large set of variables. A variable is defined as a meaningful notion to the end users, which is obtained by manipulation of a set of attributes. Attributes are fields/records that can be found in a database that is stored in the data space. For example, the elapsed time of a case is a variable that is obtained by looking up the date that a case enters and the date that the case exits the system. Subtracting the latter date from the former results in the elapsed time of a case.

To ensure the quality of the data, a set of rules are implemented in a relationship module. These rules are based on domain knowledge available from experts who are working for many years in the field. Most of the rules pertain to the handling of missing values and rules for imputation (Choenni et al., 2011). Suppose that we need the date that a crime is committed but for some reasons this date is not available or unreliable. We know that in practice the date that a crime is committed,

this crime is usually also reported at the same day. Therefore, we may use the latter date as substitute for the former. Such a rule is included in the relationship manager.

Besides the variable database and the relationship module, the space manager contains two auxiliary modules to create the variables. Data that are required to create a variable are extracted from the data space layer and converted to a standard format. Then, the converted data are manipulated in order to create the value of a variable and passed to the variable database.

The user interface, third layer in this concept, communicates with the space manager and gets it variables directly from there. The interface layer is responsible for the presentation of the data to end users. It returns the information to the user visualised in the form of a table or, when requested, a graph. Since the user interface communicates with the data spacelayer through the space manager, users can generate the information needed by means of this interface without seeing the data spacelayer.

Our architecture has two major advantages. First, the architecture is flexible and extendable. New data sources can be included in the data space without changing existing data sources. Also, new variables can be defined on the basis of, amongst others, the new data sources and passed onto the interface layer. Whenever new relationships between databases are made explicit, they can be included in the relationship manager. Secondly, our architecture supports the independency of layers. The way that variables are presented to the end user may be changed without changing anything in the space manager and the data space layer. Also, we may change the definition of variables or including/deleting/updating rules in the relationship module in the space manager, while leaving the organization of the data space as it is. In the next section, we will focus on the challenges we faced building the interface layer of the monitor.

## Development of the Web Interface

As there was neither a clear predefined model of the information need nor any requirements for the web interface, besides that the government wanted to monitor flows in the criminal justice domain and get insight in possible bottlenecks in this domain, we started by building a prototype of the web interface first. We evaluated the prototype on usability and user satisfaction by asking the end users in person if it met with their expectations. In this way a few prototypes were built. Functionalities of the web interface were built and added incrementally.

As mentioned earlier, the main goal of the web interface was to present the information flows in the criminal justice domain in a visually pleasant and user friendly manner. Moreover, the way of presentation should facilitate policy makers to interpret the data flows in the criminal justice domain. To meet these goals we ran into several challenges.

First, as the criminal justice domain is quite complex given different flows and a lot of heterogeneous data, we faced the challenge to present the data in such a way that misinterpretations of the data flows are minimized. To prevent misinterpretation we created a fixed set of variables that reflects the hierarchy of the data and is visible in the user interface. So end users do not have the possibility to create variables by means of mash ups themselves. From this fixed set of variables end users are able to drill down to the data in several dimensions. These dimensions are region, sex, crime type and age.

To visualize the variables in a user friendly manner and facilitate the interpretations of data flows, the easiest way to get a first glance on the variables would be with tables and charts. The question would then be what range does one show the user, and how can the table be visualised in a way that clearly shows trends within the data. Furthermore, the user interface needs to deal with regular updates in changes in requirements and variables. How does one keep a consistent visualisation experience for the user in both tables and charts? For now, a choice has been made to show the data for the last 7 periods with the possibility to switch between 12 months and 3 months periods. The table is automatically refreshed when a new update is added.

We solved the visualization of the data and its hierarchy by creating a main results table where links indicate the existence of a next level of information. Clicking on them would get the user to a yet deeper level of the data, while the table shown would not change its visible structure. A breadcrumbs trail of links right above the table gives the user both an indication of the present level, and the opportunity to move back to the previous level.

To drill down to the desired dimensions a separate selection panel was added to the interface, on the left side of the main results table. Filtering the initial results of the main results table on dimensions can be seen by selecting one or more items from the left dimension panel, and then by pushing the Select-button to initiate the filtering. After this selection, only figures are shown that correspond to the selected dimensions.

To show the user unexpected deviations in the data, a special feature had to be developed that is easily noticeable and traceable to its origins. While no clear definition of 'unexpected deviations' where available, we had to consult domain experts in order to build this alert function. In a few meetings with the organizations and government we discussed the norm for this alert feature. It became clear that the alert should not be too sensitive but sensitive enough to capture possible bottlenecks. These meetings with experts from the field and the government led to a decision to build the alert feature in the form of a traffic light, showing a green light with deviations of 5 percent and lower, orange between 5 and 10 percent, and a red light for deviations of 10 percent and more, where the red and orange "traffic lights" alert the user to unexpected fluctuations in trends. In the

*Figure 4. Example of the alert feature in the web interface*

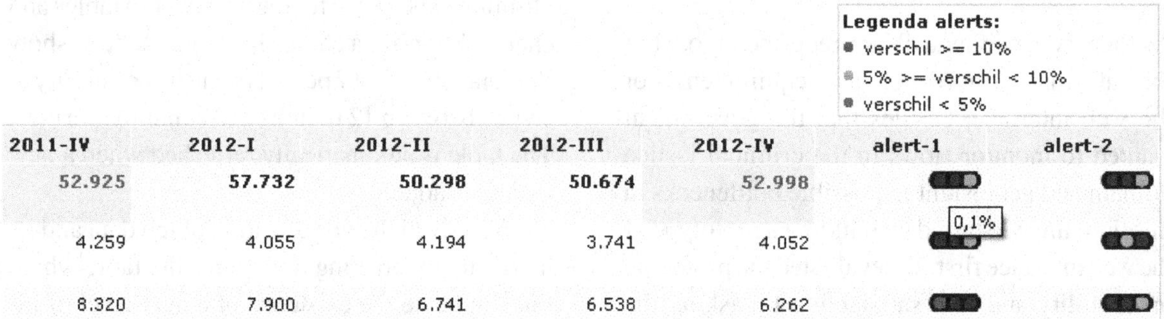

**Legenda alerts:**
- verschil >= 10%
- 5% >= verschil < 10%
- verschil < 5%

| 2011-IV | 2012-I | 2012-II | 2012-III | 2012-IV | alert-1 | alert-2 |
|---|---|---|---|---|---|---|
| 52.925 | 57.732 | 50.298 | 50.674 | 52.998 | | |
| 4.259 | 4.055 | 4.194 | 3.741 | 4.052 | 0,1% | |
| 8.320 | 7.900 | 6.741 | 6.538 | 6.262 | | |

web interface, users have the ability to analyse the cause of an unexpected fluctuation by using the drill down functionality. Two types of alerts were developed, as the interest was to take into account seasonal effect or not. Figure 4 shows an example of these alerts. The first alert compares the last 12 month period with the year before (2012 IV versus 2011 –IV), while the second alert compares the last period with 3 months earlier (2012 IV versus 2012 III). The alert feature is developed for each level and dimension in the web interface as well as for 12 month and 3 month periods. In this example the third row of data shows a red light for the first alert, while the first two rows have green lights on the first alert. The second alert shows an orange light for the second row of data.

To select data flows between or within organizations we added an option in the main navigation menu. Here, the user can select from a list of external interfaces ('Externe koppelvlakken' in Dutch) or internal interfaces ('Interne koppelvlakken' in Dutch), the latter being the list of data flows inside organizations and the former the flows between two organizations After selection of one of these options, a table of results is shown with again the same layout and possibilities of seeing more details within the chosen selection.

## Implementation of the Web Interface

The implementation of the web interface was done on a Microsoft.Net platform, as this is a well-known and powerful technology for developing complicated websites that deal with high data traffic. Usage of this specific platform was requested by the government. The data are stored in a Oracle database. The database contains the data from the variables database, and is optimized for web usage before building webpages with ASP.Net. For now, only organizations who are connected to the internal web environment of the Justice department will be granted access to the web interface, but only if they are authorized by the government.

Every quarter there is an update of the monitor. However, a factor complicating the regular updates of the monitor is that we are dependent on the ICT organization of the government called GDI. GDI controls the server where the website is running. Updates to both the code of the web interface and the data have to be sent to GDI, where they will update both website and database. Our institute is responsible for the functional management.

Recently, we managed to release a first version of the web interface that is used by authorized officials of the government and related partners responsible for the criminal justice domain. Currently, about 21 data sources from 18 different organizations are used and the web interface contains more than 500 variables.

## THE WEB INTERFACE IN PRACTICE: AN EXAMPLE

Figure 5 shows a screenshot of the web interface. In this screenshot, the output of the Court in first instance is presented for seven time periods. The total number of output of the Court is presented in bold. This output is built from three other variables, from bottom to top respectively: "acquittals", "convictions", and "other verdicts". Note that only this middle variable is clickable,

and by clicking it the user asks the interface to descend in the variable hierarchy and show the child variables of this parent variable. Note that in this example only court region is available (the option for police region is disabled, as the there is no data available). Note that in this figure the police region ('Politie regio' in Dutch) cannot be selected as this selection option was disabled, which means there is no data available for police region. Only the prosecution region can be selected ('Arrondissement' in Dutch), as only data of this region is available.

As the total output of the Court is green for the second alert, there is no reason to think there is a problem in the total output at the Court, but as the first alert is orange (deviation between 5 and 10%), policy makers may decide to drill down

*Figure 5. Screenshot from the web interface. Note that exact numbers are hidden, because it concerns non-public information.*

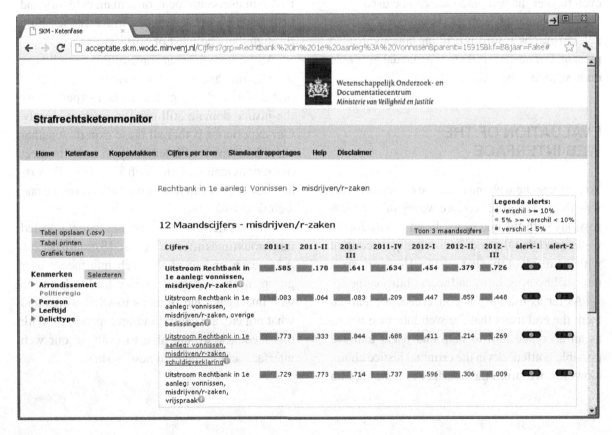

to several levels and dimensions to see whether there is a possible bottleneck somewhere. We stress that the web interface serves as a tool to help a policy maker to visualize where there may be possible bottlenecks and facilitate the interpretation of the data. The actual interpretation of the data by experts is still necessary.

Besides ways to view the information need at different levels, the web interface also has the possibility to print (standardized) PDF reports. These reports are the basis for periodical meetings with experts who interpret the developments. They contain a selection of the main variables of the web interface. In the reports no drill-down situations are available, but for some main variables a dimensional subset of the parent variable ('split variables') is presented. For instance, for the variable 'total prison population' the split variables 'total prison population [males]' and 'total prison population [females]' are presented as well. If during the meetings there is a need to drill down even further the web interface can be used.

Functionalities such as presentation of variables in graphs as well as printing options are also present. For new users there is a manual available on how to use the web interface.

## EVALUATION OF THE WEB INTERFACE

To evaluate the web interface we closely interact with the end users. Therefore we organized a few sessions with the end users. From the feedback, we learned that the end users were quite content with the result of the first release. However, soon new wishes on usability and accessibility came up.

As far as usability is concerned, we learned from the end users that the web interface works as an adequate tool to help end users indicate possible bottlenecks in the criminal justice chain. However, we stress the interface is not a tool on

its own. Getting insight by means of the interface into the criminal justice domain is one thing, for the interpretation of the data flows experts from the criminal justice domain are still needed given their knowledge and expertise. The web interface serves to facilitate the interpretation of data flows by means of a fixed set of variables that reflects the data flows and its hierarchy and minimizes misinterpretation, and also visualizes possible bottlenecks by using traffic lights. The actual interpretation of the data flows is done in so called Early Warning meetings in which experts in the criminal justice domain and the government participate. The web interface is used as a tool to visualize possible bottlenecks in the chain in these meetings.

Where accessibility is concerned, new wishes came up soon. For instance, one wish was to narrow down the crime type dimension to a few main categories, as this dimension existed of over 30 different crime types. By concentrating this dimension users can focus on a main category and drill down from this category, instead of scrolling through the whole list of crime types.

As the new wishes are on usability as well as on accessibility and new information need, we stress that different developers and data experts from the justice domain still need to interact closely. Our experience is that all these experts together should be involved intensively in order to meet the requirements of the web interface. Experts and developers can indicate what is possible and technically feasible.

Meanwhile, the monitor has been updated numerous times after each passed 3 month period. After each update of the web interface a user group meets in person to give feedback on the web interface. Questions as to what works and what not etc. are central in these meetings. With this feedback we are able to evaluate our web interface and implement new wishes.

## CONCLUSION AND FUTURE RESEARCH DIRECTIONS

In this chapter we have described how we developed and implemented a web interface to monitor data flows in the Dutch criminal justice domain. The web interface appears to be a handy tool to give the government insight in the flows in this domain. By presenting a fixed set of variables at the user interface in the form of tables that also reflects the hierarchy of the data, the risk of misinterpretation of data flows is minimized. However, the interface is not a tool on its own as we stress that experts still need to interpret the data themselves given their domain knowledge.

Moreover, as the information need of the government is subject to change, the web interface is also subject to change, therefore an evaluation of the web interface is necessary after each update. As new wishes appear to be on usability and accessibility, as well as on new information need, it is important that developers of the web interface, domain experts and end users interact closely. To acquire and accomplish the implementation of new wishes we installed a group with these experts, that comes together after each update.

Currently, we keep on developing and improving the web interface. In future releases, the interface will be more customized to the individual needs of the users, based on their roles. Each user will therefore get its own authorization and one or more roles.

## REFERENCES

Choenni, R., Kalidien, S. N., Ariel, A., & Moolenaar, D. E. G. (2011). A framework to monitor public safety based on a data space approach. In *Electronic government and electronic participation: Joint proceedings of ongoing research and projects, EGOV and ePart 2011* (pp. 196–202). Linz, Germany: Trauner Verlag.

Court of Audit. (2012). *Prestaties in de strafrechtsketen*. The Hague, The Netherlands: Author.

Dutch Government. (2012, October). *Rutte II: Coalition agreement: Building bridges*. The Hague, The Netherlands: Author.

Kalidien, S. N., Choenni, R., & Meijer, R. (2009). Towards a monitoring tool for crime and law enforcement. In *Proceedings of ECIME 2009, 3rd European Conf. on Information Management and Evaluation*. Gothenburg, Sweden: Academic Publishing Limited.

Kalidien, S. N., Choenni, R., & Meijer, R. F. (2010). Crime statistics online: potentials and challenges. In *Proceedings of 11th Annual International Digital Government Research Conference on Public Administration Online: Challenges and Opportunities* (pp. 131-137). Puebla, Mexico: Digital Government Society of North America.

van Rosmalen, M. M., Kalidien, S. N., & de Heer-de Lange, N. E. (Eds.). (2010). Criminaliteit en rechtshandhaving 2010: Ontwikkelingen en samenhangen. Justitie in Statistiek, 1.

## ADDITONAL READING

Jehle, J.-M., & Wade, M. (Eds.). (2006). *Coping with Overloaded Criminal Justice Systems, The Rise of Prosecutorial Power Across Europe* (pp. 237–256). Berlin, Heidelberg: Springer.

Martine Blom &Paul Smit. The Prosecution Service Function within the Dutch Criminal Justice System

Paul, R. Smit. The Netherlands. In Graeme Newman, Marcelo F. Aebi, Veronique Jaquier (eds.). Crime and Punishment around the world, Volume 4: Europe, pp. 240-249.ABC-CLIO, 2010.

Tak, P. J. P. (2008). *The Dutch Criminal Justice domain*. Nijmegen: Wolf Legal Publishers.

## KEY TERMS AND DEFINITIONS

**Criminal Justice System:** System that is responsible for the enforcement of legal rules and regulations in a country.

**Data Hierarchy:** The organization of data in a specific way, namely as parent-child relations.

**Data/Information Flow:** The exchange of data/information between organizations.

**E-Government:** Exploiting government information by digital means.

**User Satisfaction:** The extent to which users are satisfied by the ease and usefulness of the interface.

**Web Interface:** User friendly access to information (in a visualized way) via the Web.

# Section 2
# Websites Evaluation

# Chapter 5
# Evaluating Destination Marketing Organizations' Websites:
## Conceptual and Empirical Review

**Drosopoulou Charoula**
*University of Macedonia, Greece*

**Malama Eleonora-Ioulia**
*University of Macedonia, Greece*

**Patsioura Fotini**
*University of Macedonia, Greece*

**Vlachopoulou Maro**
*University of Macedonia, Greece*

## ABSTRACT

*Developing their e-marketing strategy, Destination Marketing Organizations (DMOs) invest in the establishment of their Websites to provide extended accessibility, real-time information/services, and personalization capabilities. This chapter aims to review prior tourism studies that refer to Website evaluation by taking DMOs' Websites as the focus of the investigation. A comprehensive literature review on theories, models, and surveys on evaluating tourism Websites is presented and analyzed. The major benefit of this study is the digest of multiple approaches regarding DMOs' Website evaluation within the tourism sector. The chapter gives an integrated overview of the historical development of Website evaluation studies in the tourism field in order to draw conclusions about the dimensions and key factors that drive Website success. Furthermore, the effectiveness of the DMOs' Websites of five Mediterranean countries are assessed through content analysis in terms of information, communication, transaction, relationship, and technical merit dimensions based on a modified approach of the ICTRT model (Li & Wang, 2010). The research findings should be of interest to DMOs as the findings shed light on the effectiveness of their Websites over a period of time facilitating continuous improvements and comparisons between competitive tourism destinations/countries.*

DOI: 10.4018/978-1-4666-5129-6.ch005

## INTRODUCTION

Web-based marketing strategies have become more widely adopted by the tourism industry, since more and more travelers use the Internet in order to select a destination or organize their overall travelling experience. The Information and Communication Technologies (ICTs) have increased the efficiency of tourism industry and enhanced competitiveness of tourism organizations and destinations (Buhalis, 2003). The interaction between the two fields started from 1970s with the establishment of Computer Reservation Systems and due to the development of the internet and the services that it provides to consumers - travellers, they no longer are not only able to obtain information and make reservation at lower time and monetary costs, but also share their travelling experience, change opinions and make a relationship with people from different destinations (Buhalis and Law, 2008). The interactive ability of the internet has made it an important marketing tool to communicate with travellers (Wang, 2008a).

Since today's consumers become highly educated, tourism organizations face the marketing challenge of how to impact consumers through effective messages (Yeoman and McMahon-Beattie, 2006). Website evaluation can help organizations track the performance of their websites over a period of time, and thereby facilitate continuous improvements through comparison of site performance against competitors and industry peers (Morrison et al., 2004).

Destination Marketing Organizations (DMOs') are defined as organizations that have been established to promote a specific destination to potential travelers. In terms of geography, DMOs can be categorized into three main categories included 1) national tourism authorities/organizations 2) regional, provisional or state and 3) local, based on a smaller geographic area or city/town (Li & Wang, 2010).

Destination marketing organizations invest considerable amounts of money in the development of Web sites as part of their overall marketing strategy (Park & Gretzel, 2007). Web based destination marketing constitute a great opportunity and a great challenge for DMOs'. Within this terms web evaluation has become a critical process in DMOs' performance measurement efforts. However, it is fair to say that DMOs' websites evaluation is still in its early stages of development. As yet there are no standardized models, dimensions, and items for evaluating tourism websites.

The study attempts to provide an updated and comprehensive overview of prior research on DMOs' website evaluation. Relevant theories and methods along to empirical studies would provide a significant trustworthy resource to researchers and scholars in the tourism academic discipline. The findings are expected to offer researchers insights into research gap which indicate future research on tourism website evaluation and practitioners an index in judging the performance of their websites against competitors, so that they have useful information to facilitate continuous improvement.

A comprehensive literature review on theories, models and surveys on evaluating tourism destination portals is presented and analyzed. Furthermore, the chapter utilized a modified approach of the ICTRT model (Li &Wang, 2010) which is described below with the scope to measure the importance, complexity and the overall effectiveness of five Mediterranean countries. The chapter concludes with a discussion of empirical implications and future research.

## CONCEPTUAL REVIEW

The importance of website evaluation has been addressed by many scholars (e.g. Law et al. 2010, Morrison et al., 2004). Therefore, several models have been developed for the evaluation of tourism websites and measurement of their overall effectiveness, e.g. modified balanced Score Card - BSC (Feng et al., 2003; Ismail, Labropoulos, Mills, & Morrison, 2002; Morrison, Taylor, Morrison, & Morrison, 1999; Myung, Morrison, & Taylor, 2005; So & Morrison, 2004), the extended Model of Internet Commerce Adoption - eMICA, (Doolin, Burgess, & Cooper, 2002), the ICTR (Information, Communication, Transaction and Relationship) model (Wang, 2008a; Wang, 2008b; Wang & Russo, 2007). Nevertheless, a widely- accepted evaluation standard specifically for the tourism industry and DMOs' websites has not yet been proposed or established.

Based on the specific type of evaluation methods which have been used, two broad categories can be detected (Corigliano, Baggio, 2006): 1) automated methods and 2) heuristic usability methods, with the second one the most used class. On the one hand there are automated tools that capture mainly technical characteristics such as response times or structural coherence, whereas the actual evaluation is carried out using software systems. The advantages of an automated method include consistency in evaluation and a relatively faster process, compared to human-based evaluation. On the other hand, there are casual or expert users who judge whether each element of a web interface follows specially determined usability and aesthetics rules. Respondents can be any combinations of academic researchers, industrial practitioners and consumers.

Prior studies on website evaluation fall into two broad categories: qualitative and quantitative. In qualitative studies, the researchers assessed website quality without generating indices or scores. Their main concern was to examine users' and experts' opinion regarding specific features or functions of tourism websites. Quantitative studies usually generate performance scores to capture the overall quality of a website. (Law, Qi, Buhalis, 2010). To date, several studies are integrating qualitative and quantitative methodologies in the tourism website evaluation process.

Table 1 lists the related literature on DMOs tourism website evaluation studies in chronological order in terms of publication year with an additional indication of the "what, how and where" terms. Thus, the table briefly presents the author/s and publication year, the focus of the DMOs' website evaluation, the methodology/model used and the geographical area of the research/implementation.

The main attempts of the studies in order to evaluate DMOs websites are further presented.

Jung and Baker (1998) attempted to develop a framework to evaluate the market effectiveness of the World Wide Web in National Tourism Organizations (NTOs) from the perspective of suppliers using quantitative and qualitative methods. A questionnaire was used to collect the views of NTO suppliers, and a qualitative method was adopted to collect the views of researchers. The findings of this study indicated that most NTO professionals considered a website to be an effective marketing medium. Several factors that should be included in website design were identified, including ease of use, joy of use, content, interactivity, transaction support, added value, appearance, and clear navigation paths.

Frew (1999) established a list of success factors for DMSs and used the list to evaluate destination websites in several European countries. The author then combined the attribute importance ratings to generate a score for each website. For their evaluation of destination websites, Benckendorff and Black (2000) conducted content analysis of data collected from the Australian Regional Tourism Authorities (RTAs) to assess four major dimensions – planning, site management, site design, and site content – of the selected websites. Buhalis and Spada (2000) developed a comprehensive list of success factors of destination management systems (DMSs) by collecting the views of researchers, suppliers, and consumers..

Doolin, Burgess, and Cooper (2002) presented an extended model of Internet Commerce Adoption (eMICA) based on a benchmarking process

*Table 1. DMOs tourism website evaluation studies*

| Author, Year | Where | What | How |
|---|---|---|---|
| Jung and Baker, 1998 | Worldwide | The views of websites users regarding NTOs focusing on the importance and percentage of website design | Web design factors, success factors, marketing value determination |
| Frew, 1999 | Austria; England; Ireland; Scotland | Counting the appearances and rating the importance of the DMO implementation characteristics | Database, distribution, management, and operation |
| Tierney, 2000 | US | Gather consumers' point of view on e-search (usage of an online survey) | Taking under consideration consumers' point of view in Initial prophase; Post; Second Prophase to test website effectiveness |
| Buhalis and Spada, 2000 | World-wide | Implementation of an integrated mehtod to analyse needs and wants of stakeholders | Development of success criteria from consumers/tourism sectors/public sectors/ investors/tour operators/travel agents' point of view |
| Oertel, Thio, and Feil, 2001 | Europe | External benchmarking analysis | Destination website in search engine, content, and functions |
| Doolin, Burgess and Cooper, 2002 | New Zealand | Level of website development | Use of eMICA to measure the level of website development |
| Feng et al, 2003 | China and US | Content analysis to identify critical success factors and evaluate hotel websites | Modified Balanced scorecard model: Marketing information and strategies; Technical quality |
| Aaberge et al., 2004 | Norway | Benchmarking process | The scope and correctness of the description of the object in order to test technical functionality |
| Larson and Ankomah, 2004 | USA | Degree of sophistication of the websites | Adoption of eMICA to evaluate the features of the sites |
| So and Morrison, 2004 | East Asia | Website effectiveness from customers' perspective | Modified BSCmodel: Technical; Marketing; Customer perspective; Content analysis |
| Kaplanidou and Vogt, 2004 | USA | Website quality and design. Discover consumers' perception regarding website' importance and performance | Evaluation of the importance and performance of DMO website features. Website usage and satisfaction in terms of navigation, content, accessibility performance |
| Author, Year | Where | What | How |
| Gupta, Jones and Coleman, 2004 | Wales, UK | The extent of Welsh tourism SME websites | Modification of Nassar's model |
| Douglas and Mills, 2005 | Caribbean (USA) | Website retention examining technical features, users friendliness, site attractiveness and marketing effectiveness | Used Balanced scorecard model to examine the extent of NTOs in Web advertising and technologies (content analysis) |
| Hellemans and Govers, 2005 | Europe | Comparison the content between ETC website and corresponding NTO website | Investigation of the pictorial and textual information between ETC and NTO websites |
| Han and Mills, 2005 | USA. | Online consumer travel purchase behaviors | Use of problematic integration theory to determine customers' travel purchase behavior |
| Han and Mills, 2006 | World–wide | Marketing effectiveness of websites | Use of grounded theory technique to determine online promotional efforts of websites. Aesthetics features; Informative features; and interactive features |

*continued on following page*

*Table 1. Continued*

| Author, Year | Where | What | How |
|---|---|---|---|
| Beldona and Cai, 2006 | US | Content analysis | Content, interactivity promotional value |
| Park and Gretzel, 2007 | Worldwide | Website effectiveness in terms of Ease of use; Information quality; visual appearance; Fulfillment; responsiveness | Categorization of review studies by meta analysis |
| Qi, Buhalis and Law, 2007 | China | Usability hazard indices | Using a modifi ed heuristic evaluation methodology to evaluate the usability of websites |
| Bauernfeind and Mitsche, 2008 | Europe | Benchmarking combining with Data Envelopment Analysis | Data envelopment analysis, linguistic offer, interactivity, and tourism content |
| Qi, Law, et al. (2008) | China | Consumers and professionals' evaluation results: Numerical calculation process | User interface and navigation, language, layout and graphics, information architecture |

and counting method to evaluate the level of website development in New Zealand's regional tourism organizations. The eMICA model has three distinct stages that incorporate three levels of the business process: web based promotion, provision of information and services, and transaction processing.

Morrison, Taylor, Morrison, and Morrison (1999) applied the Balanced Scorecard (BSC) approach in the tourism context to evaluate 16 hotel websites in Scotland. The model includes multiple critical success factors based on four perspectives: technical, marketing, internal critical, and customer critical. The researchers also marked website performance based on the error rate and three levels of download speed. Each hotel website received a total score that represented the site's performance. This was the first tourism study to use the BSC in website evaluation. The approach was then modified by different researchers to match the specific needs of different industrial sectors or geographical regions.

Morrison, Taylor, and Douglas (2004) reviewed the application of a quantitative method named "Balanced Scorecard (BSC)" in tourism website evaluation studies and also predicted that benchmarking will be a major approach in future

research in this area. A benchmarking approach combines user perceptions with website performance to help owners identify the strengths and weaknesses of their own websites and in comparison with those of their competitors and the best practical examples in the industry.

Li & Wang (2010, 2011) points out that information technology usage and utilization differentiate Internet marketing from traditional marketing. Therefore, an effective DMO portal depends on an integration of technology and marketing principles and could be evaluated on five dimensions, including Information, Communication, Transaction, Relationship and Technical merit (ICTRT model) (Figure 1). The information dimension includes all the up-to-date and accurate information about the destination, while the communication dimension involves all aspects of promotion that enable the immediate communication with the consumer contributing to future relationships. Moreover, the transaction component of the model enables STOs to generate revenue for internal use and external stakeholders. The forth dimension of the proposed model is the most difficult to implement, because of the required technological expertise and lack of knowledge in the area. As far as the technical merit dimension is concerned, it affects the ef-

*Figure 1. ICTRT model. (Adapted from [Li & Wang, 2010]).*

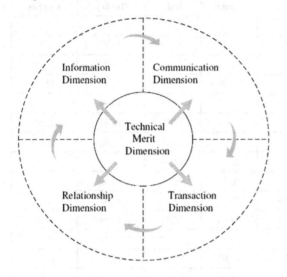

fectiveness of the four above dimensions. The ability to maintain current users while attracting new ones is a difficult procedure for a website and it needs continuous effort in all five dimensions through incessant upgrade of its services in order to increase the effectiveness of a tourism website.

## EMPIRICAL REVIEW

Compared to the above models and theories in evaluation of a tourism website, the ICTRT model is chosen to evaluate the official DMOs' portals of Mediterranean Countries because this model applies the Technical Merit dimension which is related to the other four dimensions of the model, something that lacks in the other models and lists of criteria that until now have been developed. Additionally, it is a recent model that has been applied and tested in America and China, but now the authors try to apply a modified version of it to Mediterranean Countries.

The model has been reviewed empirically in order to evaluate the effectiveness of official state destination portals regarding the tourism appeal of the Mediterranean Countries, due to the fact that

these countries are widely known as highly tourist destinations, especially in summer period and are highly competitive among themselves as far as the visitor's options for travelling is concerned. This survey applies a slightly modified version of the ICTRT model (adapted from Li &Wang, 2010) as far as few attributes are concerned, in order to measure the effectiveness of five DMOs' portals of Mediterranean Countries which are Greece, Spain, Italy, Turkey and Cyprus. This modified version of the model resulted from a pre-test that was conducted from the experts' evaluators of the research in order to apply a more appropriate evaluation model for the countries of the Mediterranean region. This research identified 46 attributes consisting of 18 attributes for Information dimension, 10 attributes for the Communication dimension, 5 attributes for the Transaction dimension, 6 attributes for the Relationship dimension and 7 attributes for the Technical merit dimension (Table 2).

The research used content analysis of the five official STOs' portals from a functional perceptive and was conducted in January 2012. The evaluators were thirty four undergraduate and postgraduate students who study Applied Informatics, Business Administration and Information Systems. During the semester, they took classes on tourism and information technology and were trained on how to evaluate a website. They evaluated the importance of all the attributes regarding the 5 functional dimensions for a STO portal on a 5-point Likert scale (1=not important at all, 5=very important), as well as the performance of all the examined STOs' portals on a 5-point Likert scale (1=very poor, 5=very good, 0 if the attribute does not exist). Due to the fact that the complexity of each attribute requires more expertise in technology theory and practice, an expert panel composed of two information technology professors and five STOs' technology practitioners who rated the complexity of implementing each of the attributes in a STO's website. The complexity of all 46 attributes for the four

*Table 2. Effectiveness scores of the 5 DMOs portals of Mediterranean Countries*

| Website Attributes | Greece | Spain | Italy | Turkey | Cyprus |
|---|---|---|---|---|---|
| **Information Dimension** | | | | | |
| Activities information | 26,98 | 28,12 | 25,66 | 21,70 | 25,66 |
| Accommodation information | 18,28 | 31,08 | 21,13 | 23,97 | 29,26 |
| Attraction information | 26,63 | 27,00 | 25,33 | 24,40 | 24,21 |
| Events calendar | 19,70 | 21,87 | 11,85 | 10,85 | 21,54 |
| Entertainment information | 21,70 | 25,31 | 17,18 | 16,81 | 23,50 |
| Maps & directions | 29,49 | 29,27 | 27,71 | 27,93 | 28,60 |
| Restaurant information | 12,75 | 22,87 | 14,84 | 10,65 | 18,86 |
| Travel packages | 6,77 | 10,53 | 6,77 | 15,79 | 19,36 |
| Travel guides/brochures | 19,40 | 20,79 | 14,73 | 17,85 | 18,71 |
| Transportation information | 21,80 | 24,86 | 24,45 | 15,69 | 24,05 |
| Photo gallery | 17,50 | 16,70 | 20,87 | 15,41 | 16,86 |
| Links to regional/city/area pages | 17,57 | 18,02 | 21,12 | 17,28 | 16,24 |
| Shopping information | 10,75 | 14,88 | 7,85 | 8,54 | 8,41 |
| Information by market segment | 11,45 | 14,75 | 15,09 | 9,72 | 14,40 |
| Travel tips | 19,78 | 22,42 | 18,96 | 16,65 | 18,63 |
| State facts | 17,60 | 17,73 | 13,43 | 16,56 | 17,08 |
| Local weather information | 18,31 | 25,80 | 25,63 | 14,48 | 22,97 |
| Virtual tours | 18,60 | 14,62 | 30,78 | 19,04 | 19,49 |
| **Average Effectiveness of Information Dimension** | **18,62** | **21,48** | **19,08** | **16,85** | **20,43** |
| **Communication Dimension** | | | | | |
| Search function | 26,78 | 28,21 | 25,77 | 25,36 | 24,55 |
| Contact information | 24,52 | 21,80 | 18,22 | 24,18 | 18,22 |
| Brochure request capabilities | 13,89 | 18,52 | 5,87 | 12,19 | 11,88 |
| Nation Brand (logo, slogan, etc.) | 21,86 | 23,34 | 19,89 | 19,72 | 18,57 |
| Multiple language versions | 11,06 | 33,19 | 23,79 | 22,75 | 30,68 |
| E-mail newsletter | 20,69 | 21,74 | 9,14 | 10,19 | 14,09 |
| Links to social media (youtube, facebook, etc.) | 21,69 | 18,07 | 20,30 | 12,93 | 15,71 |
| Feedback forms | 13,80 | 12,61 | 17,55 | 7,16 | 6,65 |
| Surveys | 5,35 | 7,89 | 3,10 | 6,62 | 5,78 |
| Frequently asked questions | 12,56 | 11,26 | 17,75 | 18,04 | 8,80 |
| **Average Effectiveness of Communication Dimension** | **17,22** | **19,66** | **16,14** | **15,92** | **15,49** |
| **Transactions Dimension** | | | | | |
| Online reservation | 7,96 | 34,39 | 6,16 | 32,34 | 32,08 |
| Event tickets | 2,62 | 4,99 | 4,52 | 4,52 | 7,13 |
| Attraction tickets | 3,75 | 3,52 | 1,88 | 2,81 | 5,63 |
| Shopping carts | 0,64 | 4,93 | 1,07 | 1,50 | 1,29 |
| Web seal certification | 5,87 | 20,67 | 6,89 | 17,35 | 13,78 |
| **Average Effectiveness of Transaction Dimension** | **4,17** | **13,70** | **4,10** | **11,71** | **11,98** |

*continued on following page*

*Table 2. Continued*

| Website Attributes | Greece | Spain | Italy | Turkey | Cyprus |
|---|---|---|---|---|---|
| **Relationships Dimension** | | | | | |
| Privacy policy | 15,96 | 22,31 | 18,27 | 17,31 | 20,77 |
| Deals & discounts | 4,33 | 5,12 | 1,77 | 10,23 | 12,98 |
| Personalization | 13,06 | 14,93 | 9,95 | 12,65 | 15,35 |
| Cross-selling opportunities | 3,82 | 7,64 | 2,81 | 8,24 | 4,42 |
| Incentive programs/contests | 11,12 | 7,57 | 3,06 | 12,25 | 6,12 |
| Customer loyalty programs | 4,66 | 4,27 | 3,10 | 5,04 | 2,72 |
| **Average Effectiveness of Relationship Dimension** | **8,82** | **10,30** | **6,50** | **10,95** | **10,39** |
| **Technical Merit Dimension** | | | | | |
| Link workability | 19,67 | 20,63 | 19,39 | 16,92 | 18,84 |
| Load time | 18,75 | 17,77 | 18,33 | 16,64 | 18,47 |
| Search engine recognition | 17,41 | 18,94 | 16,57 | 17,69 | 15,74 |
| Visual appearance | 16,57 | 19,07 | 16,96 | 14,86 | 14,73 |
| Navigation | 17,14 | 19,30 | 16,87 | 14,57 | 17,27 |
| Webpage design | 17,03 | 20,25 | 15,55 | 14,48 | 15,96 |
| Sitemap | 17,94 | 17,07 | 15,70 | 9,34 | 16,57 |
| **Average Effectiveness of Technical Merit Dimension** | **17,79** | **19,00** | **17,05** | **14,93** | **16,80** |
| **TOTAL** | **66,61** | **84,15** | **62,87** | **70,35** | **75,10** |

marketing dimensions (information, communication, transaction and relationship) was rated on 5 point Likert scale (1=not complex at all, 5=very complex). The attributes of the technical merit dimension are not measured in terms of complexity. The effectiveness score was calculated by using the product of the rated performance value and the weight {i.e. effectiveness = performance * (importance + complexity)}.

In order to aggregate the performance results and measure the overall effectiveness of the tourism websites it would be problematic if it is not be taken into consideration the fact that some attributes would be more important than others. Furthermore the degree of complexity varies among the attributes of the four marketing dimensions. The more important attributes with more complex functions should be given more weight compared with their less important and complex counterparts (Li & Wang, 2010).

As a solution, in order to measure the effectiveness of the 5 DMOs' portals, the importance and complexity of the each attribute is analyzed. Figure 2 shows that the transaction dimension should be given more weight due to the high importance and complexity scores. In addition, regarding the relationship dimension the score of complexity is similar to the importance score amplifying the weightiness of this dimension.

Considering the above two parameters of the modified ICTRT model it would be crucial to report the performance of all the criteria of the 5 dimensions in relationship with the scores of importance and complexity (see Figure 2). Measuring the average score of the performance of the information dimension Turkey has the lowest score of 2.78, Spain has 3.58 out of 5 and Greece comes fourth with a score of 3.10. The scores are generally good but due to the low complexity of the dimension they should have better scores.

*Figure 2. Significance and complexity*

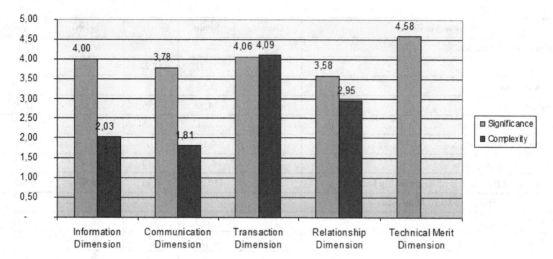

Further regarding the communication dimension the lowest score is 2.69 for Cyprus and the highest is 3.44 for Spain. Greece comes after Spain with a score of 3.09. The importance and complexity of the transaction dimension are much higher than those of the information and communication dimension but it seems that the scores of the 5 Mediterranean countries abstain a lot from 5 with Greece and Italy to concentrate 0.49 each, Cyprus 1.41, Turkey 1.36 and finally Spain 1.61. In the Relationship level the importance and complexity remain very important factors for the web development of all the criteria. The scores also remain low with Turkey to concentrate 1.70 out of 5 and Italy 0.99 which is the lowest score comparatively with the other countries. Finally the technical merit dimension is measured only taking in consideration the importance. Spain's score reaches 4.15 and Greece follows with 3.89. The rest of the Mediterranean countries fluctuate at the same levels with a score between 3.24 and 3.67.

An assessment of the effectiveness of all attributes in each of the five dimensions of DMOs' websites is presented in Table 2. The results revealed that Spain DMO's portal is the most effective with a total score of 84,15 and Italy DMO's portal is the least effective with a total score of 62,87. The highest effectiveness scores for the five Mediterranean DMOs are indicated in the attributes of Information dimension, whereas the lowest effectiveness scores are highlighted for the 5 DMOs in the Transaction dimension, demonstrating their focus in the dissemination of information to consumers, rather than their engagement in the development of relationships and transactions. With regard to individual dimensions there are differences between the five Mediterranean DMOs with Spain to concentrate the highest score in 4 of the 5 dimensions.

Table 2 shows the effectiveness results regarding each of the five dimensions explored: i.e information, communication, transaction, relationship and technical merit. Regarding the Information dimension, the portal of Spain is the most effective, while Turkey's portal is the least effective. All the examined DMOs' portals provide extensive information on activities, attractions, maps & directions, transportation and local weather. On the other side limited information is provided related to travel packages and shopping attributes.

With regards to communication dimension, search function and contact information where the most effective attributes for the five DMOs' portals. Spain's portal has been evaluated with the highest effectiveness score (19,66). For the five Mediterranean DMOs the 'Surveys' attribute is neglected, while 'FAQs' and 'Feedback forms' reveal lower effectiveness scores. The results indicate multiple variations among the examined portals in terms of 'Email Newsletter' and 'Multiple language versions'.

The weakest effectiveness scores are presented in the transaction dimension. A significant deviation is highlighted between Spain (13, 70), Greece (4, 17) and Italy (4, 10). The opportunity of consumers to buy events and attraction tickets is extremely limited in all portals, while the use of a shopping cart is ignored. As far as the Online reservation' and 'Web Seal Certification' attributes are concerned, Greece and Italy's scores are remarkably low, which reveals the overall weakness of their portals in the development of e-commerce transactions. This result indicates that the utilisation of this function is very complicated and requires both internal technology and support from industry and business.

For the relationship dimension, the results raised also some issues of concern. Most attributes in this category do not concentrate high scores for all the Mediterranean DMOs, especially 'Cross-selling Opportunities' and 'Customer Loyalty Programs'. Turkey's and Cyprus's portals offer some 'Deals & Discounts'. The DMO portals of Turkey ranks first in this dimension (10, 95), whereas Cyprus and Spain follow with (10, 39) and (10, 30) scores respectively. Greece's and Italy's scores are much lower. Even though building strong and long-term relationships with customers is a very important function of a DMO, the majority of the examined portals do not perform well.

As for the technical merit dimension, all the Mediterranean portals obtained generally high effectiveness scores. The attribute 'Link Workability' ranked the most effective for Spain's portal and 'Sitemap' score was lower for Turkey's website. By observing the results it is obvious that even if these DMOs are aware of the importance of technology for developing and maintaining their

websites, there is a gap between the importance of the criteria of this category and the performance of each country. Concluding, the survey results show that there is still room for enhancement both in the technological and marketing field.

## CONCLUSION AND IMPLICATIONS

Summarising, it is fair to say that DMOs' portals evaluation is still in its early stages of development. As yet there are no standardized models, dimensions, and items for evaluating tourism portals. The results of this chapter can provide the tourism industry with a conceptual and empirical review of the website evaluation models and help professionals understand the current importance, complexity and performance of DMOs' portals, identify major problems in future website development and built well-structured and effective tourism websites.

The proposed modified ICTRT model has its merits and limitation, that is, it evaluates a portal regarding its marketing effectiveness viewing it both, from the user's perspective and from an expert's perspective. Moreover, it doesn't incorporate a ROI calculation, since DMOs' portals do not always incorporate online sales and booking features, but only affiliate models in cooperation with private sector's websites, providing these services.

Online communication strategy is considered a very important element for DMOs' to compete effectively in the global tourism market. The portals of DMOs' are an efficient marketing tool in order to attract potential visitors, satisfy their needs, promote the transaction process and enhance the relationship with them. Mediterranean countries are considered to be very popular tourist destinations, so the services that are provided through their national DMOs' portals are very crucial for visitors. The current study applied the ICTRT model in order to evaluate five competitive Mediterranean DMOs' portals, aiming to compare them from the information, communication, transaction, relationship and technical merit dimensions.

Overall, the results revealed that Mediterranean DMOs are not using their portals effectively. It is highlighted that their websites are focusing mostly in the dissemination of information to tourists rather than engaging them in online transaction, social networks and relationships development. Of the five dimensions, the information as well as the technical merit dimensions has the highest effectiveness scores while there are significant efforts within the communication dimension. Considering the scores of each portal, Spain's slightly predominates comparatively to the others. The results of this research could assist DMOs managers in judging the performance of their national official tourism portal against competitors, so that they have useful information to facilitate continuous improvement. The model is used as a benchmarking tool to compare DMOs' portals and provide insight for official tourism organizations in their web marketing efforts. The limitation of the research is that only Greek evaluators took part in the evaluation process of the examined websites. The research could be expanded by using more evaluators from other Mediterranean countries in order to make a more integrated survey, taking into consideration possible cultural differences between the users. Also, further qualitative or quantitative approaches or models could be applied in order to measure the effectiveness of several Mediterranean DMOs' or city's websites. In conclusion, it must be pointed out that no single perspective or set of measures of a Website can produce a full assessment of its effectiveness. A combined qualitative and quantitative approach, focusing on a specific tourism website type (national DMOs, rural destination, city tourism website, etc.), enabling the incorporation/alteration of dimensions or criteria according to the changes of users' needs, should enhance the tourism website evaluation process.

# REFERENCES

Aaberge, T., Grøtte, I. P., Haugen, O., Skogseid, I., & Ølnes, S. (2004). Evaluation of tourism websites: A theoretical framework. In A. Frew (Ed.), *Information and communication technologies in tourism 2004* (pp. 305–317). New York: Springer-Wien. doi:10.1007/978-3-7091-0594-8_29

Bauernfeind, U., & Mitsche, N. (2008). The application of the data envelopment analysis for tourism website evaluation. *Information Technology & Tourism*, *10*(3), 245–257. doi:10.3727/109830508787157317

Beldona, S., & Cai, L. A. (2006). An exploratory evaluation of rural tourism websites. *Journal of Convention & Event Tourism*, *8*(1), 69–80. doi:10.1300/J452v08n01_04

Buhalis, D., & Spada, A. (2000). Destination management systems: Criteria for success – An exploratory research. In D. R. Fesenmaier, S. Klein, & D. Buhalis (Eds.), *Information and communication technologies in tourism 2000* (pp. 473–484). New York: Springer-Wien. doi:10.1007/978-3-7091-6291-0_43

Buhalis, & Schertler. (Eds.). (1999). *Information and communication technologies in tourism 1999*. New York: Springer-Wien.

Doolin, B., Burgess, L., & Cooper, J. (2002). Evaluating the use of the web for tourism marketing: A case study from New Zealand. *Tourism Management*, *23*(5), 557–561. doi:10.1016/S0261-5177(02)00014-6

Douglas, A., & Mills, J. E. (2005). Staying afloat in the tropics: Applying a structural equation model approach to evaluating national tourism organization websites in the Caribbean. *Journal of Travel & Tourism Marketing*, *17*(2), 269–293.

Feng, R., Morrison, A. M., & Ismail, J. A. (2003). East versus west: A comparison of online destination marketing in China and the U.S. *Journal of Vacation Marketing, 10*(1), 43–56. doi:10.1177/135676670301000105

Frew, D. A. (1999). Destination marketing system strategies: Refining and extending an assessment framework. In D. Buhalis, & W. Schertler (Eds.), *Information and communication technologies in tourism 1999* (pp. 398–407). New York: Springer-Wien. doi:10.1007/978-3-7091-6373-3_39

Gupta, H., Jones, E., & Coleman, P. (2004). How do Welsh tourism-SME websites approach customer relationship management? In *Information and communication technologies in tourism 2004*. New York: Springer-Wien. doi:10.1007/978-3-7091-0594-8_49

Han, J. H., & Mills, J. E. (2005). Use of problematic integration theory in destination online promotional activities: The case of Australia. com in the United States market. In *Information and communication technologies in tourism*. New York: Springer-Verlag. doi:10.1007/3-211-27283-6_23

Han, J.-H., & Mills, J. E. (2006). Zero acquaintance benchmarking at travel destination websites: What is the first impression that national tourism organizations try to make? *International Journal of Tourism Research, 8*(6), 405–430. doi:10.1002/jtr.581

Hellemans, K., & Govers, R. (2005). European tourism online: Comparative content analysis of the ETC website and corresponding national NTO websites. In *Information and communication technologies in tourism 2005*. New York: Springer-Verlag. doi:10.1007/3-211-27283-6_19

Jung, H.-S., & Baker, M. (1998). Assessing the market effectiveness of the world wide web in national tourism offices. In D. Buhalis, A. M. Tjoa, & J. Jafari (Eds.), *Information and communication technologies in tourism 1998* (pp. 93–102). New York: Springer-Wien. doi:10.1007/978-3-7091-7504-0_11

Kaplanidou, K., & Vogt, C. (2004). Destination marketing organization websites (DMOs). In *Evaluation and design: What you need to know.* Retrieved from http://www.travelmichigannews.org/research.htm

Larson, T., & Ankomah, P. (2004). Evaluating tourism web site complexity: The case of international tourism in the U.S. *Services Marketing Quarterly, 26*(2), 23–37. doi:10.1300/J396v26n02_02

Law, R., Qi, S., & Buhalis, D. (2010). Progress in tourism management: A review of website evaluation in tourism research. *Tourism Management, 31*(3), 297–313. doi:10.1016/j.tourman.2009.11.007

Oertel, B., Thio, S. L., & Feil, T. (2001). Benchmarking tourism destinations in the European Union. In P. J. Sheldon, K. W. Wober, & D. R. Fesenmaier (Eds.), *Information and communication technologies in tourism 2001* (pp. 473–484). New York: Springer-Wien. doi:10.1007/978-3-7091-6177-7_25

Park, Y. A., & Gretzel, U. (2007). Success factors for destination marketing web sites: A qualitative meta-analysis. *Journal of Travel Research, 46*(1), 46–63. doi:10.1177/0047287507302381

Qi, S. S., Buhalis, D., & Law, R. (2007). Evaluation of the usability on Chinese destination management organisation websites. In *Information and communication technologies in tourism 2007*. New York: Springer-Verlag.

Qi, S. S., Law, R., & Buhalis, D. (2008). Usability of Chinese destination management organization websites. *Journal of Travel & Tourism Marketing*, *25*(2), 182–198. doi:10.1080/10548400802402933

Qi, S. S., Leung, R., Law, R., & Buhalis, D. (2008). A study of information richness and downloading time for hotel websites in Hong Kong. In P. O'Connor, H. Wolfram, & G. Ulrike (Eds.), *Information and communication technologies 2008* (pp. 256–267). New York: Springer-Wien. doi:10.1007/978-3-211-77280-5_24

So, S. I., & Morrison, A. M. (2004). Internet marketing in tourism in Asia: An evaluation of the performance of East Asian national tourism organization websites. *Journal of Hospitality & Leisure Marketing*, *11*(4), 93–118. doi:10.1300/J150v11n04_07

Tierney, P. (2000). Internet-based evaluation of tourism web site effectiveness: Methodological issues and survey results. *Journal of Travel Research*, *39*(2), 212–219. doi:10.1177/004728750003900211

## KEY TERMS AND DEFINITIONS

**Destination Marketing Organizations:** Organizations that have been established to promote a specific destination to potential travelers. In terms of geography, DMOs can be categorized into three main categories included 1) national tourism authorities/organizations 2) regional, provisional or state and 3) local, based on a smaller geographic area or city/town.

**ICTRT Model:** A model that evaluates a website on five dimensions: Information, Communication, Transaction, Relationship and Technical merit.

**Website Evaluation:** The act of determining a correct and comprehensive set of user requirements, ensuring that a website provides useful content that meets user expectations and setting usability goals. Website evaluation can help organizations track the performance of their websites over a period of time, and thereby facilitate continuous improvements through comparison of site performance against competitors and industry peers.

# Chapter 6
# Pharma in the Web:
## Evaluation and Benchmarking of Pharmaceutical Companies' Websites in Greece

**Athanassios Vozikis**
*University of Piraeus, Greece*

## ABSTRACT

*In the context of intensified business competition and globalization of markets, the strategic use of the Internet in e-commerce can provide a business advantage. The research scope was the evaluation and benchmarking of pharmaceutical companies' Websites in Greece, in order to draw conclusions about the level of Information and Communication Technologies (ICT) use and specifically the ways they become active in e-business. For the evaluation of the Websites, the authors used scientifically acceptable criteria suited to the business sector of our research. From the survey, it was unveiled that pharmaceutical companies operating in Greece have a rather limited Web presence. Specifically, out of the 112 pharmaceutical companies, only 60 have developed their own Website with the multinationals to be more active. In addition, the majority of the pharmaceutical companies' Websites provide business information but limited additional information and interactive features to potential users. In conclusion, the pharmaceutical industry in Greece must undergo critical steps to further obtain an anthropocentric approach that the global pharmaceuticals sector has already begun to adopt.*

## INTRODUCTION

The necessity of using the Internet nowadays is obvious even for people who have no direct or indirect relationship with computing. The wealth of information provided, the immediacy update, the offered services and tools, make up the concept that we call total internet impress. Many even talk about technological exclusion and illiteracy for those cannot adapt and incorporate this new reality in the way of life and work (Dimitriadis, Baltas, 2005).

In this ever-changing and competitive environment trying to adapt all companies large and small if they want to survive, let alone grow. Inevitably, the Internet has changed a lot in recent years and the landscape of the global pharmaceuticals sector. More and more pharmaceutical companies are

DOI: 10.4018/978-1-4666-5129-6.ch006

making use of the possibilities offered by these new technologies and have an active and strong Internet presence, designed to meet their business goals, but also public information.

## BACKGROUND

### The Market of Pharmaceuticals in Greece

In Greece, pharmaceutical expenditure per capita accounted for 677$ PPP while 462$ PPP as the per capita average of EU-OECD countries during 2007. In 2000, pharmaceutical spending per capita in Greece was 275$ PPP and the average in EU-OECD was 292$ PPP. Between 2000 and 2007, the pharmaceutical spending in Greece augmented by 146% whiles the corresponding average increase in the EU-OECD countries was only 58%. Figure 1 presents the details of pharmaceutical expenditure for 2000-2010:

The supply of pharmaceuticals in Greece is determined by the pharmaceutical companies in the sector (production and marketing) and chain

of storage, distribution-handling and disposal to the public (IOBE, 2005). On the supply side, growth in sales of pharmaceutical products has halved within five years as from 22% in 2001 fell to 10.2% in 2005 (Koussoulakou, 2006).

Pharmaceutical sales in 2005, according to data from the Hellenic Association of Pharmaceutical Companies (SFEE, 2003), were 89% of brand medicines and 11% off-patent, while the first-selling therapeutic class were medicines for cardiovascular diseases (24% of total sales) followed by those for the central nervous system (15.7%) and digestive tract and metabolism (13%).

For the presentation of the financial picture of the pharmaceutical companies in the industry, a sample 112 companies was selected, representing more than 90% of the Greek pharmaceutical market in terms of total sales (Horngren, Sundem, Elliot, Philbrick, 2009). Key statistics of the Greek pharmaceutical market is shown in Table 1(SFEE, 2012):

The ranking of the first 25 companies in the industry based on the turnover of 2005 is presented in Table 4 (IOBE, 2007):

*Figure 1. Pharmaceutical spending per capita US $ PPP in Greece and in EU-OECD countries between 2000-2010*
*Source: OECD Health Data 2012*

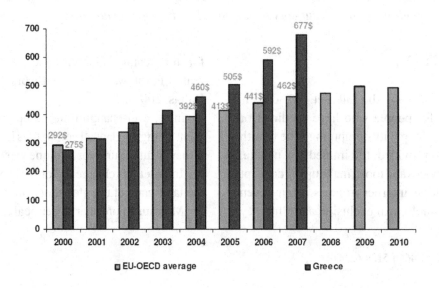

*Table 1. The Greek pharmaceutical market in figures*

| Number of companies | Manufacturers and Importers | ~100 |
|---|---|---|
| | Wholesalers (2011) | 135 |
| | Pharmacy cooperatives (2011) | 27 |
| Pharmaceutical sales | To wholesalers/pharmacies/ (at retail prices) | €5,558 mil. |
| | To hospitals (at hospital prices) | €1,200 mil. |
| | Total sales (2011) | €6,759 mil. |
| | Change 2010/2011 | -7.9% |
| Domestic production | At ex-factory prices (2011) | €846 mil. |
| Exports | Value (2011) | €859 mil. |
| Imports | Value (2011) | €3,003 mil. |
| Parallel exports | % of total sales (in value terms) (2011) | 7.1% |
| Employment | Number of employees (2011) | 13.600 |
| Public pharmaceutical expenditure | Expenditure 2011 | €3,729 mil. |
| | Expenditure 2012 | €2,880 mil. |
| | Change 2012/2009 | -43% |
| | % of GDP (2012) | 1.4% |
| | Net public pharmaceutical expenditure per capita (2012) | €253 |
| | % of public health expenditure (2011) | 17.7% |
| Price structure | Ratio of ex-factory price to retail price (2012) | 67.6% |
| Price change | Medicines Price Index 2005/2011 | -17.8% |
| | Medicines Price Index 2010/2011 | -10.7% |
| Generics | % of total sales (in value terms) (2011) | 18% |
| Generics and off-patent | % of total sales (in value terms) (2011) | 60% |
| R&D expenditure | EFPIA (2012) | €84 mil. |

## Technologies of Information and Communication Technologies (ICT) in the Pharmaceutical Industry

On a daily basis, millions of people use the Internet for communication, access to information in various subject areas, research and education. Almost every organization wants its presence on the Web to promote itself and distribute the content and activities through the Internet (Dimitriadis, Baltas, 2005). Unfortunately, there are no restrictions on the disposal of information via the Internet, resulting in a large number of websites may not yet have the required quality level (Kalakota, Robinson, 1999) & (Rajput, 2000).

Although today there are a plethora of books and published material relating to information about what should be followed and what should be avoided during the design, development or maintenance of a website (Lynch & Horton, 1999), it is proven that this information is extremely educational and useful, but it's not satisfactory. So in order to improve the quality of a website requires a more comprehensive treatment of the issue (Microsoft, 1999).

Overall, the quality is a broad and general sense, and the quality of a website is completely subjective. This is a property that is difficult to determine, although everyone perceives when extinguished. In fact, a website can be many aspects of its quality (Brajnik, 2001) & (Brajnik, 2002), just as many are the uses.

According to ISO 9126, the quality of a software product is defined as:

*The totality of features and characteristics of a software product on its ability to satisfy stated or implied needs.*

*Table 2. Ranking pharmaceutical companies in terms of turnover, 2005, (in thousands €)*

| | Name | Total Sales | % |
|---|---|---|---|
| 1 | PFIZER | 400,186 | 8.5% |
| 2 | BOEHRINGER INGELHEIM | 329,486 | 7.0% |
| 3 | GSK | 267,681 | 5.7% |
| 4 | NOVARTIS | 254,869 | 5.4% |
| 5 | VIANEX | 249,707 | 5.3% |
| 6 | ROCHE | 227,485 | 4.8% |
| 7 | JANSSEN - CILAG | 206,073 | 4.4% |
| 8 | ASTRA ZENECA | 203,500 | 4.3% |
| 9 | SANOFI-SYNTHELABO | 168,202 | 3.6% |
| 10 | AVENTIS | 151,892 | 3.2% |
| 11 | BAYER | 147,924 | 3.1% |
| 12 | PHARMASERVE LILLY | 144,812 | 3.1% |
| 13 | ABBOTT | 130,749 | 2.8% |
| 14 | GENESIS | 130,486 | 2.8% |
| 15 | BRISTOL MYERS SQUIBB | 123,137 | 2.6% |
| 16 | WYETH | 100,137 | 2.1% |
| 17 | ΓΕΡΟΛΥΜΑΤΟΣ | 100,080 | 2.1% |
| 18 | SCHERING-PLOUGH | 92,705 | 2.0% |
| 19 | ELPEN | 74,401 | 1.6% |
| 20 | DEMO | 70,373 | 1.5% |
| 21 | FAMAR | 67,056 | 1.4% |
| 22 | ΙΦΕΤ | 46,217 | 1.0% |
| 23 | CANA | 44,314 | 0.9% |
| 24 | BAXTER | 43,405 | 0.9% |
| 25 | SERVIER | 37,709 | 0.8% |

Quality, therefore, is defined as a complex property that includes a set of interdependent factors (Kalogerou, 2007).

First, the quality of a website depends on factors related to its objectives, such as (Karagiorgoudi, 2004):

- The quality of presentation and sensation that causes the website to the user.
- Completeness of the content and of its functions.
- The navigability.

Also, the quality of a website depends on factors related to performance. These factors include:

- Response time.
- Throughput in the execution of the various processes.
- The reliability of the content.
- The robustness of site.

Finally, the quality of a website depends on factors related to the development process. These include:

- The complexity of the code.
- The readability of code.
- The flexibility of the code.
- The portability of the website in other environments.
- The connection of the website pages.

It can therefore be seen that the quality of a website is determined by processes involving the analysis, design, implementation and maintenance and ensuring that involves diverse individuals, resources, methods and tools. When these procedures are not based on well-defined frameworks, it is likely that there will be neither effective nor efficient, leading to low quality products (Chaffey, 2004). Therefore a comprehensive treatment of the issue of quality is required, which makes it necessary to have a model quality.

The need for a comprehensive treatment of the issue of quality of Web sites emerged strongly and in harmonized European efforts in the field of digitization (Ashurst Morris Crisp, Executive Perspective SA, 1999). These efforts begin from the great interest of the E.U. to optimize the value of European cultural content and to develop and promote the principles and best practices (Papadakis, 2006) & (Syrros, 2005).

## Research Purpose, Methodology and findings

The scope of our research was the evaluation and benchmarking of websites of Greek pharmaceutical companies in order to draw conclusions about how the Greek pharmaceutical companies make use of Information and Communication Technologies (ICT) and specifically what is their presence on the Internet.

For this purpose, we make use of the official list of the members of Hellenic Association of Pharmaceutical Companies (SFEE) to access their websites.

Today in our country operate 112 pharmaceutical enterprises, of which, according to the Association of Pharmaceutical Companies, of which the 64 covers virtually all pharmaceutical research and 90% of the Greek pharmaceutical market. Unfortunately only 64 of these companies appear to have a presence on the Internet through an active and accessible website.

Our research was conducted by visited the 112 websites of the pharmaceutical companies and assessed them against the evaluation criteria and their weighting as detailed in Table 3:

The following Table 4 shows the total pharmaceutical companies' evaluation, the overall rating and the average thereof, the ranking of each company based on the total score and the degree of readiness achieved, ie the score obtained by the each pharmaceutical company as a percentage of the maximum total score that could succeed and its grade. Note that the maximum possible score, that a website pharmaceutical company based on the scale of rating categories could succeed, was 51 points.

The criteria we used included 27 criteria in four major categories, with particular interest in their analysis and significant differences in the ranking of companies in several of them.

## Solutions and Recommendations

The development of ICT in the current era set the imperative for large, medium and small companies to be active in the Internet (Turban, King, Lee & Viehland, 2006). The use of technology involves a human-centric service system, focusing on the citizen-user. So, more and more companies in the pharmaceuticals sector also followed the pace by seeking to create greater value for the customer.

Pharmaceutical companies are now facing increased demand, as they operate in a promising market characterized by significant magnitudes and small consumer mobility between competing firms. So, the prospects seem to be great in long term because of the growing demand for services through the Internet and the existence of a need to modernize the global pharmaceutical market as technology capabilities allow significant improvements in their operation.

The research on the web presence of the pharmaceutical companies in Greece revealed that of the total 112 pharmaceuticals that exist, only 60 appear to have a web presence via some active and accessible website (53.6%).

Therefore, all the pharmaceutical companies high ranked, are the pharmaceutical AstraZeneca SA, achieving an objective rate 84.31%, while runners-coming companies Genzyme Hellas EPE and Abbott Laboratories Hellas SA achieved 80.39% of the target. We observe that the pharmaceutical companies with the highest percentage achieved target are large and multinational companies. Meaning, companies with high-selling medicines. This may be due mainly due to the large costs required to implement the development site with such content elements and also due to the growing interest for information on pharmaceuticals with wide circulation.

From our research findings, all pharmaceutical companies have a rather good image in terms of providing general information. We found that a large percentage of pharmaceutical offers via their website general information (history, goals,

*Table 3. Categories of assessment - Scale - Content*

|  | Categories of Assessment | Scale | Content | Max Score |
|---|---|---|---|---|
| **Presentation** | | | | |
| 1 | Statement of Purpose - Objective | (Scale 0-1) | No information = 0, any information = 1 | 1 |
| 2 | General Information - History | (Scale 0-1) | No information = 0, any information = 1 | 1 |
| 3 | Company-Group Structure | (Scale 0-1) | No information = 0, any information = 1 | 1 |
| 4 | E – mail | (Scale 0-1) | No information = 0, any information = 1 | 1 |
| 5 | Data Management and Communication-Access | (Scale 0-3) | Mailing address & phone, area map, general location description | 3 |
| **Content** | | | | |
| 6 | List of Medicines | (Scale 0-1) | No list = 0, any list = 1, information about prescription of drugs | 1 |
| 7 | List of complementary products | (Scale 0-1) | No list = 0, any list = 1, information about complimentary products | 1 |
| 8 | Contents of medicine package | (Scale 0-1) | No information = 0, any information = 1, number of tablets | 1 |
| 9 | Drug dosages | (Scale 0-3) | Information about the dosage of medication | 3 |
| 10 | Available Provision of Services | (Scale 0-3) | Information about the therapeutic classes | 3 |
| 11 | General Information of Diseases | (Scale 0-3) | Information on the definition, how to deal with the symptoms | 3 |
| 12 | Social Responsibility | (Scale 0-1) | No information = 0, any information = 1, implementing SR activities | 1 |
| 13 | Career Opportunities | (Scale 0-3) | About the working environment, job profile, hiring procedures, CV form or e-mail address | 3 |
| 14 | Financial Information | (Scale 0-2) | Financial information of the company (shareholders, financial results, balance sheet) No information = 0, basic information = 1, full resolution = 2 | 2 |
| 15 | Usefulness of the website | (Scale 0-3) | Meeting the users' needs, acquisition of new knowledge. | 3 |
| 16 | Comprehensibility of Text | (Scale 0-3) | Complexity of language, lean texts | 3 |
| 17 | Site Organization | (Scale 0-3) | Topics, headings use, TOC | 3 |
| 18 | Content renewal Date | (Scale 0-1) | No date = 0, any date = 1 | 1 |
| **Policy** | | | | |
| 19 | Clearly distinguish advertising - Informative Material | (Scale 0-2) | No discrimination = 0, moderate = 1, comprehensive = 2 | 2 |
| **Design & Usability** | | | | |
| 20 | Language Selection | (Scale 0-1) | No foreign language version = 0, any foreign language version = 1 | 1 |
| 21 | Response Rate | (Scale 0-3) | Speed of website access | 3 |
| 22 | Visibility of page without scrolling | (Scale 0-1) | scrolling = 0, no scrolling = 1 | 1 |
| 23 | broken links –Web pages under construction | (Scale 0-1) | exist = 0, non exist = 1 | 1 |
| 24 | Connection with databases | (Scale 0-3) | For example: Any article relating to the company, articles, white papers, reports etc | 3 |
| 25 | Search tools | (Scale 0-1) | No search option = 0, any search option = 1 | 1 |

*continued on following page*

*Table 3. Continued*

|  | Categories of Assessment | Scale | Content | Max Score |
|---|---|---|---|---|
| **Presentation** | | | | |
| 26 | Usability of the website | (Scale 0-3) | Easiness for the visitor to navigate in the website | 3 |
| **Interaction- Feedback** | | | | |
| 27 | Complaints - Questions | (Scale 0-1) | No information = 0, any information = 1 | 1 |
| *TOTAL* | | | | *51* |

*Table 4. Readiness rating and ranking of all pharmaceutical companies*

|  | Name | Total | Rank | Readiness Rate % |
|---|---|---|---|---|
| 1 | AstraZeneca S.A. | 43 | 1 | 84.31 |
| 2 | Genzyme Hellas ΕΠΕ | 41 | 2 | 80.39 |
| 3 | Abbott Laboratories Hellas S.A. | 41 | 2 | 80.39 |
| 4 | Janssen-Cilag Pharmaceutical S.A.C.I. | 39 | 3 | 76.47 |
| 5 | Roche (Hellas) S.A. | 36 | 4 | 70.59 |
| 6 | Octapharma Hellas SA | 36 | 4 | 70.59 |
| 7 | Lundbeck Hellas S.A. | 36 | 4 | 70.59 |
| 8 | Lavipharm S.A. | 36 | 4 | 70.59 |
| 9 | Alcon Laboratories Hellas S.A. | 35 | 5 | 68.63 |
| 10 | Pfizer Hellas S.A. | 33 | 6 | 64.71 |
| 11 | Alapis Pharma ABEE | 33 | 6 | 64.71 |
| 12 | Bayer Hellas A.G. | 32 | 7 | 62.75 |
| 13 | Merck E.P.E. | 31 | 8 | 60.78 |
| 14 | Ferring Ελλάς S.A. | 31 | 8 | 60.78 |
| 15 | Bristol Myers Squibb A.E. | 31 | 8 | 60.78 |
| 16 | Serono Hellas S.A. An Affiliate Of Merk Serono | 30 | 9 | 58.82 |
| 17 | Pharmaserve Lilly S.A.C.I. | 30 | 9 | 58.82 |
| 18 | Gilead Sciences Hellas M.EPE. | 30 | 9 | 58.82 |
| 19 | Faran S.A. | 30 | 9 | 58.82 |
| 20 | Wyeth Hellas S.A. | 29 | 10 | 56.86 |
| 21 | Schering Plough S.A. | 29 | 10 | 56.86 |
| 22 | Menarini Hellas S.A. | 29 | 10 | 56.86 |
| 23 | Baxter Hellas Ltd | 29 | 10 | 56.86 |
| 24 | Novartis Hellas S.A. | 28 | 11 | 54.90 |
| 25 | I.T.F. Hellas S.A. | 28 | 11 | 54.90 |
| 26 | Genesis Pharma S.A. | 28 | 11 | 54.90 |

*continued on following page*

*Table 4. Continued*

| | Name | Total | Rank | Readiness Rate % |
|---|---|---|---|---|
| 27 | Astellas Pharmaceuticals S.A | 28 | 11 | **54.90** |
| 28 | Organon Hellas S.A. | 27 | 12 | **52.94** |
| 29 | Novo Nordisk Hellas Ltd | 27 | 12 | **52.94** |
| 30 | GlaxoSmithKline S.A. | 27 | 12 | **52.94** |
| 31 | GE Healthcare S.A. | 27 | 12 | **52.94** |
| 32 | Galderma Hellas S.A. | 27 | 12 | **52.94** |
| 33 | CSL Behring Hellas M.EPE. | 27 | 12 | **52.94** |
| 34 | Servier Hellas Ltd | 26 | 13 | **50.98** |
| 35 | Omega Pharma Hellas S.A. | 26 | 13 | **50.98** |
| 36 | Leo Pharmaceutical Products Hellas Ltd | 26 | 13 | **50.98** |
| 37 | UCB A.E. | 25 | 14 | **49.02** |
| 38 | PNG Gerolymatos S.A | 25 | 14 | **49.02** |
| 39 | Pharmanel Pharmaceuticals S.A. | 25 | 14 | **49.02** |
| 40 | Sambrook Pharmaceutical S.A | 23 | 15 | **45.10** |
| 41 | Nycomed Hellas S.A. | 23 | 15 | **45.10** |
| 42 | Chiesi Hellas S.A. | 23 | 15 | **45.10** |
| 43 | Solvay Pharma LTD | 22 | 16 | **43.14** |
| 44 | Pierre Fabre S.A. | 22 | 16 | **43.14** |
| 45 | Boehringer Ingelheim Ellas S.A. | 22 | 16 | **43.14** |
| 46 | Allertec Hellas A.E. | 22 | 16 | **43.14** |
| 47 | Arriani Pharmaceuticals S.A. | 21 | 17 | **41.18** |
| 48 | Sanofi Aventis A.E.B.E. | 20 | 18 | **39.22** |
| 49 | Pharmex S.A. | 20 | 18 | **39.22** |
| 50 | Minerva Pharmaceutical S.A. | 20 | 18 | **39.22** |
| 51 | Vioser S.A. | 19 | 19 | **37.25** |
| 52 | Galenica S.A. | 19 | 19 | **37.25** |
| 53 | Fresenius Kabi Hellas S.A. | 19 | 19 | **37.25** |
| 54 | Famar ABE | 19 | 19 | **37.25** |
| 55 | Elpen Pharmaceutical Co.Inc. | 19 | 19 | **37.25** |
| 56 | Adelco S.A. | 17 | 20 | **33.33** |
| 57 | Help S.A. | 16 | 21 | **31.37** |
| 58 | Lapapharm Inc. | 11 | 22 | **21.57** |
| 59 | Cana S.A. | 3 | 23 | **5.88** |
| 60 | Vian S.A. | 0 | 24 | **0.00** |

objectives), data management and communication system (almost all evaluated pharmaceutical companies also provided the opportunity for online communication and feedback), a list of medicines and complementary products that each company produces.

At the same time, the image of the pharmaceutical websites in Greece is assessed as moderate, with regard to data about the contents of the medicine package, the services offered, the language selection and the organization of the website.

Finally, despite the provision of the above information to a greater or lesser degree, the image of the websites of pharmaceutical companies is assessed as poor, in terms of providing information about the dosage of medicines, reference information for the conditions treatment as well as the existence of a link where users can ask questions.

## CONCLUSION

It is evident, then, from all the above that pharmaceutical companies in Greece do not provide adequate information considered necessary for the user. This finding shows that they have adopted in a very small extent the anthropocentric philosophy by which it must be creating the greatest possible value for the user through the best possible service and information.

## REFERENCES

Brajnik, G. (2001). Towards valid quality models for websites. In *Proceedings of Human Factors and the Web*. Retrieved from www.dimi.uniud.it/~giorgio/papers/hfweb01.html

Brajnik, G. (2002). *Quality models based on automatic webtesting*. Paper presented at CHI2002 Workshop - Automatically Evaluating Usability of Web Sites. Minneapolis, MN. Retrieved from http://www.dimi.uniud.it/~giorgio/papers/quality-models.html

Chaffey, D. (2004). *E-business and e-commerce management* (2nd ed.). Upper Saddle River, NJ: Prentice Hall.

Crisp, A. M., & Executive, P. S. A. (1999). *Impact of electronic commerce on the european pharmaceutical sector*. Efpia.

Dimitriadis, S., & Baltas, G. (2005). *E-business and marketing*. Athens, Greece: Rosili Publications.

Horngren, C., Sundem, G., Elliot, J., & Philbrick, D. (2009). *Introduction to financial accounting* (9th ed.). Upper Saddle River, NJ: Pearson Education International.

IOBE. (2007). *The pharmaceutical market in Greece*. Athens, Greece: IOBE.

Kalakota, R., & Robinson, M. (1999). e-Business, roadmap for success. Reading, MA: Addison-Wesley.

Kalogerou, V. (2007). *Communicational evaluation of websites, national & capodestrian*. Athens, Greece: University of Athens.

Karagiorgoudi, S. (2004). *Systems of websites quality assessment*. Patras, Greece: University of Patras.

Koussoulakou, H. (2006). *The pharmaceutical market in Greece*. Athens, Greece: IOBE.

Lynch, P., & Horton, S. (1999). *Web style guide*. New Haven, CT: Yale University.

Microsoft Corporation. (1999). e-Commerce development: Business to consumer. Microsoft Corporation.

OECD. (2012). *Health data 2012*. Paris: OECD.

Papadakis, M. (2006). Applications of informatics in services. In *Health policy and economics*. Athens, Greece: Papazisis Publications.

Rajput, W. E. (2000). *E-commerce, systems, architecture and applications*. Artech House.

SFEE. (2003). *The pharmaceutical market in Greece: Facts and figures*. Athens, Greece: SFEE.

SFEE. (2012). *The pharmaceutical market in Greece: Facts and figures*. Athens, Greece: SFEE.

Syrros, J. (2005). *ICT projects implementation in health sector: Success factors*. Athens, Greece: SEPE.

Turban, E., King, D., Lee, J. K., & Viehland, D. (2006). *Electronic commerce: A managerial perspective* (4th ed.). Upper Saddle River, NJ: Prentice Hall.

## KEY TERMS AND DEFINITIONS

**E-Business:** Electronic Business, commonly referred to as "eBusiness" or "e-Business", may be defined as the utilisation of information and communication technologies in support of all the activities of business.

**EHealth:** Is the transfer of health resources and health care by electronic means.

**Pharmaceutical Companies:** A pharmaceutical company, or drug company, is a commercial business whose focus is to research, develop, market and/or distribute drugs, mostly in the context of healthcare.

**Pharma CRM:** A business strategy directed to understand, anticipate and respond to the needs of a Pharmaceutical Company's current and potential customers in order to grow the relationship value.

**Websites Evaluation:** Actually, the techniques for evaluating the authority and reliability of web sites.

# Chapter 7
# User Page Reviews in Usability Testing

**Leo Lentz**
*Utrecht University, The Netherlands*

**Sanne Elling**
*firMM Information + Service Design, The Netherlands*

## ABSTRACT

*Websites increasingly encourage users to provide comments on the quality of specific pages by clicking on a feedback button and filling out a feedback form. The authors investigate users' (N=153) abilities to provide such feedback and the kind of feedback that is the result. They compare the results of these so called user page review methods with the concurrent think-aloud method, applied on the same websites. Results show that it is important to keep feedback tools both simple and attractive so that users will be able and willing to provide feedback. The authors also find that the number of problem detections is higher in the review condition, but the two methods seem to be highly complementary. An analysis of the detections from a practice-oriented perspective reveals that the overlap between the two methods is rather high and that reviewing participants seem capable of signalling important problems that are also exposed in a think-aloud study.*

## INTRODUCTION

Organizations increasingly recognize the importance of giving the user a voice, and many websites contain a feedback option that invites users to comment on various aspects of the website. In this chapter, we focus on evaluation methods that enable users to give feedback on specific pages of a website. Such methods have received little attention in the literature about website evaluation methods, and there is no generally accepted term for this type of method yet. These methods, however, can be categorized as self-reported metrics (Tullis & Albert, 2008) because, as in surveys, users are asked about their experiences on the website. But unlike surveys, the methods we focus on ask for page-level feedback and allow for open comments, sometimes combined with an overall rating or some scale questions. We propose to call these methods *user page reviews* (UPR) because they invite users to review a website by clicking on a button that appears on selected pages. In such reviews, users evaluate a website in much the same way as experts do (Welle Donker-Kuijer,

DOI: 10.4018/978-1-4666-5129-6.ch007

De Jong, & Lentz, 2008). Of course, users cannot be expected to have professional expertise about Web design, but they may be able to provide useful feedback from their own user perspective about their attitudes and experiences with the website. These comments might shed light on user problems that experts fail to diagnose because of their curse of expertise (De Jong & Lentz, 1996).

Tools that can be used for gathering user feedback on website pages include Opinionlab, Kampyle, Usabilla, and Infocus. These instruments enable website visitors to share their opinions on everything they consider important. Selected website pages (or sometimes all pages) contain a button that users can click on if they want to react to something. These buttons can be small icons (e.g., a thumb or a plus–minus icon with the word feedback) or longer text links that invite reactions to the page. Users click on the link to open a screen on which they can provide their comments. Users can give open-ended comments, but the instruments often also ask users to choose a feedback category, provide ratings, or answer questions about page-specific topics.

Figures 1-4 show screen shots of feedback forms from Opinionlab, Kampyle, Infocus, and Usabilla, respectively.

The Opinionlab form in Figure 1 looks rather dense and asks users to complete several tasks: to choose a topic from predefined categories, enter an open comment, rate the page on three aspects as well as overall, enter an e-mail address (which is optional), and indicate whether or not their comment is about the website. The Kampyle form in Figure 2 uses icons that users select to express their feelings and categorize their feedback. It asks users to rate the site by choosing an emoticon, to select a feedback topic (under the topics that are visible in the figure are rows with subtopics), and to fill in an open comment. The Infocus form (see Figure 3) includes a list of predefined categories, a place to formulate comments, and three options for marking specific elements or segments: Users can underline, point an arrow at, or draw a frame around a relevant section that they want to comment on. This marking function is different from most other tools, in which users have to describe the exact location

*Figure 1. Opionlab feedback form*

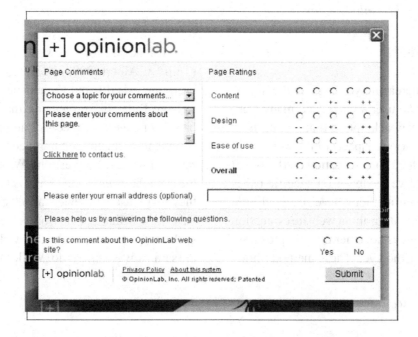

*Figure 2. Kampyle feedback form*

*Figure 3. Infocus feedback form*

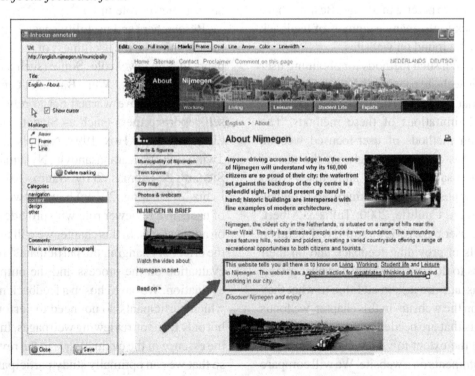

*Figure 4. Usabilla add-note option and invitation to users to click on elements they like*

of the object of their feedback. Only Usabilla (see Figure 4) offers a form of marking that enables users to add a note on the web page. But it is not possible to mark the exact size of the selection or to use other more precise markings. Besides these four feedback tools, many examples of feedback buttons can be found on websites.

Even though such methods for obtaining user feedback on website pages have become more and more popular in practice, little is known about the merits and limitations of these methods. The literature on methods of user-focused website evaluation has focused strongly on the use of think-aloud usability testing and surveys and neglected the possibilities of asking users to review a website (e.g., Cunliffe, 2000; Tullis & Albert, 2008). The user page reviews strongly depend on users' skills in providing feedback and on their willingness to do so. Users may consider giving feedback as an extra task in addition to what they are doing on the website. In this chapter, we focus on the skills that are needed to provide feedback, examining the extent to which users are able to provide comments on a website. We will compare

the output with a more traditional usability method: the concurrent think aloud method (CTA). The main difference between both methods is the role assigned to the participant: a user role in CTA and a reviewer role in UPR.

Researchers and usability specialists differ in their opinion on the usefulness of putting participants in a reviewer role. Some (such as Nielsen, 2001; Spyridakis, Wei, Barrick, Cuddihy, & Maust, 2005) have warned not to rely on users' self-reports; others (such as Sienot, 1997; Castillo, Hartson, & Hox, 1998; Nichols, McKay, & Twidale, 2003; Karahasanovíc, Nyhamar Hinkel, Sjøberg, & Thomas, 2009; Sauro, 2010; Elling, Lentz, & De Jong, 2012a) have shown the value of users in a reviewer role who provide feedback on applications. In this chapter we will investigate the effect of changing the participants' role in the evaluation on the process and the output of the evaluation. We have chosen a feedback method in which participants do not need to perform tasks, but only focus on reviewing web pages. In this way, the essence of the evaluation is in the review task, so that we can optimally study participants in the reviewer role, and the contrast with CTA where participants perform user tasks while thinking aloud is most significant. Are participants in the reviewer role able to produce useful feedback? And what are the differences in the output between the user page review and a concurrent think aloud evaluation? We will compare the output of both methods on different websites and analyse the problems found on a single web page more in detail. In the next section we will further explore relevant theoretical notions of cognitive demands that different roles impose on participants. Then we will discuss the design of this research project and the procedures we used in analysing the results. Academic readers will want to read these sections. Usability professionals might prefer to skip these three sections and continue reading the 'Results' paragraph.

## BACKGROUND

Although it may be important to give users the opportunity to provide feedback on specific pages, they must be able to express that feedback. Users need some critical capacity to signal the problems they are experiencing with a specific page before they can report these problems. They need to be able to monitor their thinking processes and behaviour. This critical skill is closely related to the concept of metacognition, which has been described as "one's knowledge and beliefs about one's own cognitive processes and one's resulting attempts to regulate those cognitive processes to maximize learning and memory" (Ormrod, 2006). Literature on metacognition and comprehension monitoring (e.g., Baker, 1989) shows that readers with higher verbal abilities have greater awareness and control of their own cognitive activities while reading than do readers with lower verbal abilities. Readers with higher verbal abilities also appear to use a greater diversity of evaluation standards in their assessment of text quality.

Once users are able to signal their own problems with a web page, the next step is that they attribute these problems to the website. The self-serving bias predicts that users tend to blame the website when they fail to reach their goals (Moon, 2003; Serenko, 2007). But several studies have shown that users sometimes blame themselves for problems they encounter. Schriver (1997) concluded that users of manuals for complicated home electronics predominantly blamed themselves for their problems with the described products. In a follow-up study, Jansen and Balijon (2002) found that a high percentage of the respondents (more than 50%) reported blaming themselves and not the manual when something went wrong. And Serenko (2007), who studied "interface agents" (software systems that support users on the computer), found that users may attribute their success to an interface agent and hold themselves responsible for task failure. Thus, users who experience problems and signal these problems may not attribute them to the website and therefore may not report them with the feedback option.

The final step in the feedback process is to submit the feedback by formulating the problem on a feedback form. Besides describing their feedback, users are often asked for additional information, such as the category of the comment or answers to scaled questions. In certain contexts, user feedback might be very useful. Nichols, McKay, and Twidale (2003) advocated empowering end users to proactively contribute to usability activities with end-user reporting tools. Karahasanovíc, Nyhamar Hinkel, Sjøberg, and Thomas (2009) described a feedback-collection method that asked for written feedback at different times during an experiment. They compared this method with concurrent and retrospective think-aloud protocols and concluded that the feedback method revealed more difficulties than did the concurrent and retrospective think-aloud protocols and that the feedback method seemed better at identifying difficulties that prevented progress or caused significant delay. Castillo, Hartson, and

Hix (1998) found that users are able to identify and report their own critical incidents, but these studies involved highly educated participants. Earlier research on the evaluation of documents has shown that highly educated people provide more comments and more diverse feedback than do people who are less educated (De Jong & Schellens, 2001). If less educated or inexperienced users are indeed less able to formulate their feedback, user page reviews will probably fail to uncover some relevant problems.

All these steps in the feedback process require that users perform two tasks at the same time: finding and using the information while reviewing a web page. Switching between these tasks is difficult for users because it requires a configuration of mental resources. Monsell (2003) provided an overview of studies on task switching, which show that task switching leads to longer response times and a higher error rate. Users are inclined to concentrate on one task and to neglect other tasks, a phenomenon that is called ''cognitive lockup'' (Neerincx, Lindenberg, & Pemberton, 2001). Older people especially seem to have trouble switching between tasks (Kramer, Hahn, & Gopher, 1999). A study by Barkas-Avila, Oberholzer, Schmutz, De Vito, and Opwis (2007) of error messages for users who fill out a form online shows practical consequences of problems with task switching. Their results show that error feedback should be provided only after users have completed the whole form because providing error feedback immediately negatively affects users' performance. This study also underlines that trying to perform additional tasks while completing the primary task may cause users to expend too many additional cognitive resources, resulting in cognitive overload. This difficulty of having to switch between two different tasks is likely present in both user page reviews and think aloud methods. Users may stop verbalizing thoughts when they encounter difficulties during their task completion (Boren & Ramey, 2000). In one of our recent eye tracking studies (Elling,

Lentz & De Jong 2012b), we demonstrated that users stop verbalizing thoughts at moments they start scanning web pages, which seems a cognitive demanding task.

As we said, we compared the results of user page reviews with the output of a study using Concurrent Think Aloud on the same website. Although CTA can provide useful insights into users' processes and problems, the method also has its limitations, such as participants' incapability of verbalizing all the thoughts they have. Many processes take place rather quickly, and people are not conscious of everything in their minds. This results in many verbalizations in which participants simply read things from the screen, use fillers such as 'okay', or describe what they are doing at a particular moment (Cooke, 2010; Elling, Lentz & De Jong, 2012b). Another limitation concerns the naturalness of the user role. To what extent does the think-aloud task interfere with the task performance, the so called reactivity? Several studies (e.g. Van den Haak, De Jong & Schellens, 2003; Ummelen & Neutelings, 2000; Hertzum, Hansen & Andersen, 2009; Krahmer & Ummelen, 2004; Olmsted-Hawala, Murphy, Hawala & Ashenfelter, 2010) show that thinking aloud may influence task performance, which means that in CTA evaluations the participant is also not really in a natural user role. The extent to which participants' thinking aloud affects task performance may depend on the settings of the study, such as the frequency and style of probing and interfering during the study.

Some studies have compared methods with participants in a reviewer role and in a user role. Sienot (1997) compared the think-aloud method and the plus-minus method, with respect to their suitability for the measurement of website quality. The plus-minus method is a feedback method in which participants are asked to assign plus and minus marks to parts of the document they consider good or bad, and after that account for all pluses and minuses in an individual interview (De Jong, 1998). Sienot found no differences between the methods in the average number of problems per participant and the types of problems they revealed. Only the number of appreciation problems was higher in the plus-minus condition. Further, a larger number of distinctive problems were found in the plus-minus method. Finally, participants in the plus-minus condition provided a diagnosis or a suggested revision in their comments more often than participants in the other condition, which Sienot attributes to their reviewer role.

Lentz & Pander Maat (2007) compared a reading-aloud method with the plus-minus method and Focus (De Jong & Lentz, 2001), a feedback method which enables participants to provide written feedback on texts. These three methods were used for the evaluation of patient information leaflets on medicines. They found that the number of problems was higher in the reading-aloud condition than in both the reviewer methods. A comparison of types of problems only revealed a difference regarding comprehension problems, from which more were detected with reading-aloud than with the other two methods.

These studies show mixed results on the numbers of problems found through reviewer methods compared to think-aloud methods. They vary from equal numbers for both methods, to more problems found with reviewer methods, to more problems found with think-aloud protocols. However, the studies are difficult to compare, as they all used other variants of feedback methods and think-aloud methods. In Sienot's (1997) study, for example, the think-aloud participants had a posttest interview that also revealed problems. These problems were also included in the results section, which deviates from other studies that only reported problems found during task performance. Lentz and Pander Maat (2007) used reading-aloud and let participants read out a whole text, which is different from the common think-aloud procedure. Besides differences between the methods used, the objects to be evaluated differed as well: a website in Sienot's study and patient information leaflets in Lentz & Pander Maat.

## AN EMPIRICAL STUDY: DESIGN OF THE EVALUATIONS

In this study, we focus on the extent to which users are able to productively formulate review comments on websites and we compare the results with a more widely used concurrent think aloud method. We conducted the study in a controlled context in which users with various background characteristics provided feedback. In the UPR study, 93 participants provided feedback on three websites. Two websites were evaluated by 30 participants each and one website was evaluated by 33 participants. The think-aloud study (CTA) was conducted with 60 participants, 20 on each of the same three websites. All participants of both studies were selected by a specialized agency, from an extensive database of potential candidates with different characteristics. They received financial compensation for taking part in the study. The participants were selected in such a way that for each method and website there was an equal distribution of educational levels (low, medium, and high), age-categories (18-29, 30-39, 40-54, and 55 and older) and gender. This chapter is based on a research project financed by the Dutch Organization for Scientific Research (NWO) which has resulted in two earlier studies on the same data published by Elling (2012) and Elling, Lentz and De Jong (2012a). More details about the participant groups and the design of these studies can be found in both publications.

The participants evaluated three websites of medium to large Dutch municipalities: www.apeldoorn.nl (website 1), www.dordrecht.nl (website 2), and www.nijmegen.nl (website 3). Municipal websites provide information and services to citizens and to other interested users, such as tourists and businesses. These websites invariably contain a variety of information because they are designed to satisfy the informational needs of a broad target group. The three websites cover similar types of information, but this information is structured and presented in different ways.

In both studies the participants evaluated the websites based on scenario tasks (De Jong & Lentz, 2006). The content of the tasks differed per website, but they resembled each other in difficulty and length of navigation path. Moreover, all the tasks (a) covered realistic activities that correspond to those that users usually perform on municipal websites; (b) included searching for information, as well as reading, understanding, and applying the relevant information to the described scenario; and (c) applied to different domains of the website. For example, a task pertaining to information on a government subsidy supporting people who are buying a house for the first time asked participants to search for answers to three questions: (1) What is the name of this subsidy? (2) Do you meet the requirements for this subsidy? (3) What should you do to make a request for this subsidy? The shortest navigation path to this information consisted of six links, the last of which was a link to a pdf file containing information about all kinds of subsidies available for buying or renovating a house.

In the *user page review* evaluations participants worked individually in group sessions with approximately ten participants. They used the tool *Infocus* to provide their comments using two scenario tasks. In the *think-aloud* evaluations participants performed three sets of tasks, one of which was analyzed for the comparative study. They worked individually in sessions of approximately 25 minutes in which they completed these tasks. They were asked to verbalize all their thoughts during task performance. When they fell silent the facilitator asked them to keep verbalizing in short non obtrusive probes, such as 'please keep thinking aloud' or 'what are you thinking at this moment?'.

The development of the *Infocus* tool was based on research on the plus-minus method (De Jong, 1998) and Focus (De Jong & Lentz, 2001). With this tool, users can surf through a website and click on a comments button whenever they want to give positive or negative feedback. The tool enables participants to select and comment on any element on a web screen, ranging from specific words, sentences, paragraphs, chapters, illustrations, and navigational aids to the entire web page. After clicking the comments button, participants see a screen shot of the web page. They have several options for marking the specific element that they want to comment on: They can point to it by drawing an arrow, underline it, or add a frame around it. On the left side of the screen, participants can choose one of the predefined comment categories and type in their feedback. Users' feedback is saved in a database together with images and URLs of the marked web screen and some log data such as the navigational path and a time outline.

Like many other tools for user page reviews, *Infocus* is able to ask users to categorize their feedback. In this study, we used four categories: (a) navigation (easy or difficult to find), (b) content (clear or unclear information), (c) design (does or does not look good), and (d) other. This categorization has three potential benefits. First, the availability of comment categories may remind participants of their reviewing task. The comment categories emphasize that we are asking participants to provide feedback on the website and not, for example, answers on tasks. Second, the specific categories chosen may guide the kinds of feedback participants provide. By explaining the categories and including them on the feedback screen, we are underlining which aspects of website quality we consider important to evaluate. Third, the comment categories may serve as clues to help us to interpret unclear comments when we analyze the data.

As we said, the participants were guided through the website following a scenario. They were asked to look at pages from the perspective of the scenario questions and they provided feedback by clicking on the *Infocus* feedback link. After clicking on this link, a screen appeared with a screenshot on which they could mark the object that they wanted to comment on (see Figure 3).

They could also formulate their feedback and choose a category that best fitted their comment. In earlier evaluations we noticed that it was difficult for participants to perform tasks and provide feedback at the same time. Therefore, we chose this guided evaluation design, because we wanted to make providing feedback easier for participants. In the *think aloud* evaluation participants were not guided while performing the scenarios. Thus, we realized an optimal contrast between the reviewer and the user role of participants.

## RESEARCH QUESTIONS AND ANALYSIS PROCEDURES

Our first research question was: To what extent are participants able to provide comments on the relevant issues for informational websites? To answer this question, we determined the number of comments made per participant, the proportion of positive versus negative comments, and the number of unclear comments. We also categorized the comments using the four feedback categories (navigation, content, design, and other). The first author and an independent rater coded all the comments, achieving a satisfactory Cohen's k (.81). Next, we analyzed the negative feedback. As Hornbæk (2010) argued, the matching of comments into a list of user problems is not straightforward and can be done in different ways. In our matching procedure, we used a four-step analysis. First, we gathered the comments that were made on the same page; second, we divided the feedback into comments on different parts of the page (menu, illustration, text block, etc.); third, we analyzed these groups of comments using the categories; and fourth, we analyzed these comments using the participants' exact description. The description of the cause of the problem was decisive for merging two comments into one user problem. If, for example, two comments were about the bad legibility of the text, we would consider them to be two different problems if one comment criticized the small font and the other the color of the text. This rather strict and fine-grained method of matching resulted in a large list of different user problems with relatively little overlap.

The second question was: Are there any age or education-related differences between participants' user page reviews? We analyzed the comments for differences between the four age categories and the three education levels using analysis of variance. We used four dependent variables: overall number of comments, number of positive comments, number of negative comments, and number of unclear comments.

The last question is about the comparison of the output of user page reviews with the results of think aloud protocols. For this analysis we merged two sets from the *user page review* evaluation and the CTA evaluation – both for one and the same task on the same website - into one large set, in order to determine the numbers of problems found with each distinctive method and with both methods. In order to analyze the mean number of problem detections per participant, we also made a dataset which included all participant characteristics, the evaluation condition, the website, and the total number of problem detections. Next, we categorized all the problems into the same three categories: *navigation*, *content*, and *design*. The second author and an independent rater categorized all problems on one of the websites. Cohen's Kappa was satisfactory (.82).

## RESULTS

We will first concentrate on the results of the 93 UPR participants working in the review role and at the end of this section we will compare the results with the CTA evaluation where participants worked in a user role.

All UPR evaluation sessions took place in a positive atmosphere. Participants seemed to feel motivated to evaluate the website. As we expected, the sessions with participants who were 55 years of age and older took more time because these participants needed more help and instructions than did younger participants. Overall, the participants judged their experiences and their review abilities positively. They reported that the review task was easy to do (mean score on a 5-point scale: 4.03, SD = 0.80) and that they enjoyed the process of giving comments on web pages (mean score: 4.15, SD = 0.82).

To what extent are participants able to provide comments on the relevant issues for informational websites?

On average, each of the participants provided 16.1 comments during a session with two scenario tasks (SD = 6.1). Of these comments, an average of 0.8 (SD = 1.3) were judged to be unclear (5%). Of the clear comments, an average of 9.5 (SD = 5.6) were negative (62%). If we consider the negative comments to be the core of the evaluation, the net result of the user page-review evaluation is 9.5 potential user problems per participant. Because many of the negative comments may point to the same potential user problem, we also looked at the number of different potential problems per website. This analysis resulted in, respectively, 107, 110, and 156 potential user problems for the three websites.

Table 1 gives an overview of the categories of the total set of negative comments on the three municipal websites (based on the two coders' categorization). Navigation appears to be an important aspect of the participants' feedback, but many comments were also made about content and design. Whereas the proportion of navigation-related comments was nearly stable across the three websites, the proportion of content and design comments varied between the three sites, with relatively more comments about content in websites 1 and 3 and design in website 2. That website had a lot of comments on the inconvenient arrangement of the home page and on poor legibility due to the size and colour of the fonts. The other websites had more content comments, such as long texts with complicated and vaguely formulated information. The category other included feedback on technical problems (e.g., a picture that did not appear correctly), redundant information (e.g., an item on the home page with detailed information about clearing away leaves in autumn), or missing functionalities (e.g., a form that was not available online). In all, we can conclude that users were able to report many comments and that they succeeded in addressing navigation, content, and design issues.

Are there any age- or education-related differences between participants' user page reviews?

Differences between the four age categories and the three education levels were analysed in regard to four dependent variables: total number of comments, number of positive comments, number of negative comments, and number of unclear comments. The results are shown in Tables 2 and 3.

Regarding the total number of comments made, we found no significant differences between the four age groups and between the three education levels. Also, no significant interaction effect was found. The same applied to the number of positive comments. For the other two dependent variables, however, significant education-related differences were found, for the number of negative comments and for the number of unclear comments. Post hoc analyses showed that participants with a high education level produced more negative comments than did participants with a low or medium education level and that the participants with a higher level of education produced fewer unclear comments than did participants with a lower level of education. ($F (2, 90) = 6.818$, $p < .01$; $F (2, 90) = 5.725$, $p < .01$)

In all, the user page review appeared to be usable for all age groups and all education levels included in our study. When we focus on quality of feedback, however, higher educated participants were better able to provide feedback, producing more negative comments (which could serve as clues to improve the website) and fewer unclear comments.

*Table 1. Number of negative comments per dimension for each of the three websites*

|  | Website 1 | Website 2 | Website 3 | Total |
|---|---|---|---|---|
| Navigation | 132 (43%) | 132 (45%) | 127 (46%) | 391 (44%) |
| Content | 116 (38%) | 57 (19%) | 91 (33%) | 264 (30%) |
| Design | 30 (10%) | 92 (31%) | 37 (13%) | 159 (18%) |
| Other | 27 (9%) | 15 (5%) | 24 (9%) | 66 (8%) |
| Total | 305 | 296 | 279 | 880 |

*Table 2. Mean number of all comments, positive comments, negative comments and unclear comments for the three educational levels (SD). *p<.05*

|  | Lower Education | Middle Education | Higher Education | Total Mean Number |
|---|---|---|---|---|
| All comments | 15.0 (3.9) | 15.0 (4.9) | 18.0 (7.9) | 16.1 (6.1) |
| Positive comments | 6.5 (4.1) | 5.5. (4.2) | 5.8 (4.1) | 5.9 (4.1) |
| Negative comments * | 7.1 (3.2) | 8.7 (4.8) | 11.9 (6.7) | 9.5 (5.6) |
| Unclear comments * | 1.4 (1.9) | 0.8 (1.1) | 0.3 (0.5) | 0.8 (1.3) |

*Table 3. Mean number of all comments, positive comments, negative comments and unclear comments for the four age groups (SD)*

| Age | 18-29 | 30-39 | 40-54 | >55 | Total |
|---|---|---|---|---|---|
| All comments | 15.9 (5.5) | 17.0 (5.9) | 16.6 (6.7) | 15.0 (6.0) | 16.1 (6.1) |
| Positive comments | 5.2 (3.9) | 6.5 (4.8) | 6.2 (3.9) | 5.4 (4.2) | 5.9 (4.1) |
| Negative comments | 10.2 (5.6) | 10.1 (5.2) | 9.1 (6.3) | 8.8 (5.4) | 9.5 (5.6) |
| Unclear comments | 0.5 (1.2) | 0.3 (0.6) | 1.2 (1.4) | 0.8 (1.6) | 0.8 (1.3) |

How do participants formulate their comments on a website?

Looking at the participants' comments in more detail, we made some interesting observations about the content of these comments. First, participants differed in the ways they formulated their comments, which could be written in the form of reporting a problem's cause, effect, or solution. For example, on one of the web pages, participants had difficulty navigating back to the home page due to the small size of the home icon. Several participants reported this problem by describing its effect ("I can't find my way back to the home page"). Others reported its cause ("The icon of the homepage is too small and inconspicuous")

or a possible solution ("This icon should get more attention"). Individual participants sometimes reported both the cause and the effect and occasionally a solution. These differences in style of reporting sometimes made it difficult to categorize the comments. In the preceding example, the cause of the reported problem was a design issue, but the effect concerns navigation: not finding the way back to the home page. We systematically categorized on the cause of the problem unless the cause was not mentioned by the participant.

Second, the participants sometimes used the comment button to provide an answer on the scenario task. Participants who used the feedback option to comment on the scenario or to formulate answers to scenario questions did not understand, or forgot, the reviewing task at hand. We did not find differences in the number of scenario-related comments between the education levels. On average, participants in all the groups entered between 0.4 and 1.0 scenario-related comment. There was, however, a significant difference between the age groups, $F(3, 89) = 2.794$, $p < .05$: older participants made significantly more scenario-related comments (1.0, SD = 1.4) than did younger participants (0.29, SD = 0.7). Older participants perhaps experience more trouble understanding the task of reviewing a website and separating this task from searching for information and answering scenario questions.

Third, some participants repeated the same comment several times. For example, one participant reported that the website did not fill the whole screen. He repeated this comment in nearly the same wording on several web pages. Perhaps, the structure of the guided review procedure pressures participants to comment even when they are uncertain of what to say. Repeating the same comment could be a reaction to this pressure. Other participants wrote down a positive remark (e.g., ''This is clear to me'') when they did not see any problem.

Fourth, participants sometimes made more than one comment in one feedback screen. In the instructions, we asked participants to make a new annotation for every comment they wanted to report. Nevertheless, they sometimes combined two comments, often a positive and a negative statement (e.g., ''The home page looks up to date, but it is difficult to find what you look for on this page''). In doing so, participants may have been trying to soften their negative feedback by saying something nice about the web page as well. Giving negative feedback can be seen as a ''face threatening act'' (Brown & Levinson, 1987) that people want to compensate for by showing appreciation and respect.

Finally, the older participants often referred to using another medium in their feedback (e.g., ''I would have used the telephone by now / It is a lot easier to go and ask for the information''). They seemed to feel less familiar with the Internet than the younger participants did and, as a result, seemed to prefer other media, such as the telephone or face-to-face contact. This observation corresponds with the research finding that people need time to get accustomed to new media (Van Dijk, Pieterson, Van Deursen, & Ebbers, 2007).

To what extent do participants use the problem-marking function?

The marking function was introduced to help users adequately indicate the object of their feedback. A verbal description of the location of an object on the screen is far less specific and effective than a picture of the specific page with, for example, an arrow pointing at that object. Of all the participants' negative comments, 51% were accompanied by some form of marking - a reasonably good result, considering that most of the participants were introduced to this functionality for the first time. So participants seem to be able to mark the object of their feedback, which makes this marking functionality a useful innovation for the user page reviews. Of course, for some comments, the absence of a marking could be explained by the nature of the comment. In three situations, marking an object was impossible. First, some comments were about the whole web page (e.g., ''It's strange that the design of this page deviates from the design of the other parts of the website''). Second, some comments were about items that were missing on the page or that could not be found (e.g., ''I don't know what link I should choose here''). And third, some comments did not even pertain to any object on the Web page (e.g., ''I had to click too much to reach this information'').

How well are participants able to categorize their feedback?

Participants categorized all their feedback into the four categories (i.e., content, navigation, design, and other). Also, one of the authors and an independent coder categorized all the participants' feedback. This categorization resulted in a Cohen's κ of .81, indicating a high agreement between the two expert coders. But the agreement between the participants and the expert coders was considerably lower, with a κ of .26. We categorized 51% of the comments differently than the participants had.

Content was the most problematic category. Participants tended to put not only comments about content in this category but also comments about unclear labels for links and other navigational problems. We transferred as many as 191 of these comments into the navigation category. These differences in coding choices do not mean that the participants did not thoughtfully categorize their problems. The categories had rather open and broad formulations, so many different comments fit into these categories. This result raises questions about users' ability to categorize their feedback. In our study, we explained the categories to the participants, providing examples, and they could ask questions if they did not understand the categories. In an online remote setting, users would not have these opportunities, which would probably result in users' having even more difficulty categorizing comments than what they would have in a laboratory setting.

## Comparison UPR–CTA

To what extent did the different user roles result in differences in the number of problem detections per participant? In order to answer this question, we analysed the results of one of the scenario tasks for both methods. Table 4 shows the mean number of problem detections per participant for participants with a reviewer role (*user page reviews*) and a user role (*concurrent think-aloud*).

Table 4 shows that participants in the *user page review* evaluations reported a higher number of problem detections on each of the three websites. Overall, the mean number of problem detections was significantly higher in the *user page review* evaluation ($t(151)=3.211, p<.01$). The difference between the conditions was also significant for website 3, with a mean number of 5.90 problem detections in the reviewer condition and a mean number of 2.70 detections in the think-aloud condition ($t(48)=3.170, p<.01$). For websites 1 and 2 the differences were not significant.

Individual problem detections might refer to the same problem. In the matching procedure we compared the problem detections and derived a set with unique problems. In this way, we were able to determine the extent to which the two methods show overlap in the problems they yield. A total number of 240 different problems were found with the two evaluation methods combined: 72 problems on website 1, 66 on website 2, and 102 on website 3. Of these problems, only 10% were detected with both methods. A percentage of 70%

*Table 4. Mean number of problem detections in one scenario task (standard deviation) per participant for each website and method (* indicates significant difference)*

|  | User Page Reviews (N=93) | Concurrent Think-Aloud (N=60) |
|---|---|---|
| Website 1 | 3.97 (2.68) | 3.50 (2.35) |
| Website 2 | 4.60 (3.54) | 3.20 (2.57) |
| Website 3* | 5.90 (4.26) | 2.70 (1.78) |
| Overall* | 4.80 (3.58) | 3.13 (2.24) |

was found only in the *user page review* condition, and 20% only in the think-aloud condition[1]. This would mean that the overlap between the two methods is very small. We will elaborate on this further on, when we compare the results of both methods for one specific web page.

To what extent do the two methods generate different types of problem detections? Table 5 shows the distribution of the problems over the categories *navigation*, *content*, and *design*.

Looking at Table 5, some interesting observations can be made. First, we see that the think-aloud evaluation hardly generated any problems that directly point to design issues. Participants in a user role seem to focus on task processing and do not pay attention to design issues. The reviewing participants, on the other hand, report many design issues. They seem to focus not only on the pragmatic quality, whether the website provides effective and efficient ways to achieve the users' goals, but also on the hedonic quality, the extent to which users experience pleasure (Hassenzahl, 2004; Van Schaik & Ling, 2008). This does not mean, however, that the many design issues reported by reviewing participants are not related to pragmatic quality issues. Design issues can be the cause of problems experienced during navigation or comprehension of relevant information. For example, an inconveniently arranged homepage can lead to more difficulties finding the right link, or a small font size can prevent participants from thoroughly reading an important piece of text, leading to content problems. Second, most think-aloud problem detections were related to navigational issues. Participants verbalized many doubts, expectations, and frustrations on their search process, while searching for information. And the facilitator observed the most problems during this navigation stage, such as clicks on wrong links that do not lead to the required information. Third, in the think-aloud evaluation only a few problem detections were related to the content of the information. As mentioned earlier, when think-aloud participants reached the requested information they often focused primarily on providing the right answers, and less on verbalizing the problems they encountered on the target pages. But the participants in the reviewer role took a critical attitude and provided much more feedback on those same pages.

These results show a rather small overlap between the two methods, only 10% of the problems on the websites were found with both methods. This percentage of overlap, however, only shows one aspect of the comparison between the two methods, influenced by underlying choices related to matching. Let us have a look at the problem descriptions from both methods on one web page of website 2 in more detail. How do the descriptions differ from each other, and what are the consequences for the matching procedure? To what extent does the overlap between the methods vary, depending on choices related to matching? Figure 5 shows the schematic outline of the web page.

The web page in Figure 5 was part of the navigation click path to information about school holidays for children. The top of the page comprises the website's logo, a poem, the secondary links (such as the *sitemap*, and *contact*), and the search box of the internal search engine. Below, a 'breadcrumb-trail' is shown with the pages that the participant clicked on and the user's current

*Table 5. Distribution types of problem detections found with user page reviews (UPR) and with concurrent think-aloud (CTA): percentages of all detections and numbers of problem detections*

| Method | Navigation | Content | Design |
|---|---|---|---|
| UPR (N=93) | 32% (143) | 36% (162) | 32% (141) |
| CTA (N=60) | 69% (130) | 28% (52) | 3% (6) |

*Figure 5. Schematic outline of the web page 'Education' on website 2*

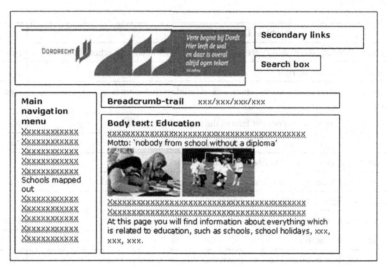

location. It allows users to navigate back easily to a page visited earlier. On the left side is the main navigation menu, in which the users should choose the link '*schools mapped out*' to find school holidays. The middle of the website contains the body text with information on education related topics. We have made visible some parts of the text that are relevant for understanding the problems on this page. Table 6 shows all problems that were reported on this web page, the categories of these problems, and the number of times they were detected with *user page reviews* (UPR) and the concurrent think-aloud method (CTA).

We will first look at the first three problems in Table 6, which were all found with both methods. What are the underlying problem detections, how are they formulated, and how do they differ from each other[2]?

The first problem concerns the link 'schools mapped out' which is not associated by participants with school holidays. In the *user page review* condition 28 participants commented on this link, which means that they massively pointed to an important problem on this page. Note that these participants were guided through the website, so they had been told that this link should be clicked

on to find information about school holidays. Although all 28 comments were formulated differently, we can distinguish three main types of comments. Most participants describe the cause of the problem, as in "the link label schools 'mapped out' does not clearly point to school holidays' or 'I would expect that this link leads to a map which shows addresses of schools and not to school holidays." Also, some comments describe the effect 'this is very confusing' or 'this label makes it difficult to find the information about school holidays'. The third group of comments provides a solution of the problem, for example the suggestion "it would be better to change this label into school holidays." There were also comments that contained combinations of cause, effect, and solution. Although the reviewing participants may take a different perspective, the problems that they signal here are closely related. The three problem detections of think-aloud participants all concern observations from the facilitator combined with verbalizations that explicitly address the problematic link. One participant read aloud all the links in the navigation menu, and verbalized '*schools mapped out... that is also not the right one*' and after that continued reading other links.

*Table 6. Overview of problems found with user page reviews and concurrent think-aloud on the web page presented in Figure 5*

| | Problem Description | | UPR | CTA |
|---|---|---|---|---|
| 1 | Participants reject 'schools mapped out' as an adequate link that is associated with school holidays. | Nav | 28 | 3 |
| 2 | Participants find it difficult to find the right link to information about school holidays | Nav | 11 | 3 |
| 3 | The body text in segment 2 refers to information about school holidays, but there is no link with the label school holidays | Con | 2 | 2 |
| 4 | Participant clicks on a wrong link which does not lead to the required information | Nav | 0 | 11 |
| 5 | It is difficult to find the right link to information about compulsory education | Nav | 0 | 1 |
| 6 | Participant thinks this is not the right page to find information about school holidays | Nav | 0 | 1 |
| 7 | Participant clicks on the link 'education' while he is already on the web page 'education' | Nav | 0 | 1 |
| 8 | The main menu contains several links with unclear labels | Nav | 2 | 0 |
| 9 | The information on this page is unclear | Con | 2 | 0 |
| 10 | The photos are not related to education | Des | 2 | 0 |
| 11 | Labels in the menu do not show a comprehensive overview of education related topics | Nav | 1 | 0 |
| 12 | The photo quality is poor | Des | 1 | 0 |
| 13 | The motto 'nobody from school without a diploma' is not eye-catching | Des | 1 | 0 |

Legenda: Nav = Navigation, Con = Content, Des = Design

Another participant read aloud "schools mapped out," did not click on it and continued with "no, I have not a clue where I should search now." The third participant also read aloud the link, and did not click on it. Only after many other clicks, he tried 'schools mapped out' and verbalized "this is not very logical, I would have expected schools and environments here." These CTA detections combine cause and effect, and are combinations of observations and verbalizations. Problem detections 1 and 2 reflect the mental processes of the navigating participants. Detection 3 is formulated as a critical comment that resembles the reviewer comments. After having experienced some major problems, this participant seems to switch to a reviewer role and provides an analysis of the cause of the problem. In sum, in the detections of problem 1 we see differences in the perspective, which can be a cause, an effect, or a solution. The think-aloud problem detections are combinations of observations and verbalizations, while in the *user page review* condition the same problem is signalled in critical comments.

Problem 2 is reported by 11 participants in the user page review evaluation (see Table 6). They all report that it is difficult to find the right information from here, without explicitly addressing the link label 'schools mapped out'. Examples of comments are "school holidays cannot be found here" or "it is difficult to find the information, it takes too much time to reach your goal." The three think-aloud participants also verbalized they found it difficult: "difficult to find," or "it is difficult to find the school holidays." In the comments above, we signalled a difference in the level of abstraction. Some comments are rather global and only express that something is difficult. Other comments are more specific and explain what exactly is difficult and why this is the case. The global comments could refer to the unclear link described in problem 1, but we cannot be sure about that. They can also be related to the third problem or to other potential problems in this page.

The third problem, mentioned in Table 6, is that the body text refers to information about school holidays that can be found 'here', but there is no (embedded) link with the label school holidays. Two user page review participants explicitly formulated the advice to make this item clickable, as in "When I read the word 'here' I expect that I can click on this right away, also on the other choices in this sentence. Make these items links." In the think-aloud condition two participants read the text and verbalized a comment. One of the participants read aloud the body text and said: "strange that there is no link here to school holidays." This verbalization corresponds to the feedback of participants in a reviewer role. The other participant said after having read the text "where?" and after having searched for a while "there is no link." This verbalization reflects the navigation process and is therefore more related to the user perspective.

The analysis of these three problems that were found with both methods shows that the underlying problem detections can differ from each other in three ways. First, they can differ in the perspective taken, which can be a cause, an effect, or a solution. Second, the way in which problems are detected can differ: through a verbalization, an observation, or a review comment. Third, the level of abstraction differs, varying from global to detailed specific comments. Participants in the user role experience problems that become apparent in observations and verbalizations of cognitive processes. However, these participants sometimes also take a reviewer perspective and verbalize comments that resemble the comments made by reviewing participants.

These differences between problem detections make it difficult to determine to what extent problem detections are related. Can each click on a wrong link, for example, be related to the problem of the unclear link label? This question relates directly to the matching procedure. During the analysis of the data we applied a rather strict matching procedure in which we were cautious when merging problem descriptions. We only combined problems if we had clear evidence that they referred to the same object and the same problem related to this object. As a result, we analyzed many problems separately that might be related with each other. Look for example at the first four problem descriptions in Table 6. Problem 1 shows the comments in which participants explicitly rejected the link "schools mapped out" as an appropriate option for finding school holidays. Problem 2 shows the comments in which participants expressed their difficulty finding the right link on this page, and problem 4 refers to clicks on wrong links that did not lead to the desired information. Problem 3 shows comments on a missing embedded link. Although these four problems are very closely related, we did not merge them in our dataset. The experienced difficulty (problem 2) and the wrong link clicks (problem 4) are probably effects of the unclear labels (problem 1), and the unclickable reference to school holidays (problem 3). Other problem detections, which were found through only one of the methods, more specifically the problem detections 8, 9, 11 from user page review participants, and problems 6 and 7 from think-aloud participants, might also be related to the problems explained above. However, we cannot be sure of the relations between the detections above, as there might be other reasons why participants experience difficulties or click on wrong links.

For academic research into differences in evaluation methods these reflections are most relevant, but if we look at the results of the evaluations from the perspective of a practitioner who wishes to optimize this web page, these different problem descriptions would be taken together. Participants obviously have trouble finding their way to information regarding school holidays on this web page. It would help them if the vague link label was rephrased into a clearer label, and if an embedded link was added in the body text that referred directly to school holidays. Of course, more substantial adjustments, which address the whole design of the page, could also be made, and thus also solve other issues raised by the participants. In sum: in our academic approach differences in the formulation make it difficult to decide whether detections refer to the same underlying problem. However, from a professional usability perspective several problem detections would probably lead to the same diagnosis. Taking that perspective the overlap between both methods is substantial.

Finally, we will take a closer look at the problems in Table 6 that were only found with one of the two methods. The problems 4 to 7 were detected by think-aloud participants. These are all navigational issues: two problems (4 and 7) concern wrong link clicks, and in the other two cases participants express confusion about what to choose on the web page. The problems 8 to 13 are provided by the reviewing participants. In 8 and 11 we see navigational feedback on unclear labels and on the comprehensibility of the menu. Problem 9 is a content problem, which refers to the body text which is considered to be unclear. The other three problems are design issues, which criticize the photos and the visibility of the motto. These are the more hedonic design issues that are not directly related to optimal task performance.

We can conclude from this detailed page level analysis that all think-aloud problems also seem to be indicated in one way or another by the user page review method. Furthermore, the reviewing participants detect four extra problems that are related to the content of the body text and to design issues that do not match think-aloud problems.

## CONCLUSION

In this study we compared a *user page review* evaluation and a *think-aloud evaluation*, with which we aimed to get a better understanding of differences between participants in a reviewer role and in a user role. The results of our study showed that the two methods seem to be highly complementary. Only 10% of the problems were found with both methods. Further, the *user page review* participants reported a higher number of problems, which is in line with Karahasanovíc, Nyhamar Hinkel, Sjøberg, and Thomas (2009).

The higher number of review problems can be explained by the participants' roles that resulted in different evaluation processes. The reviewing participants experienced less cognitive load, had a stronger desire to produce comments, they also reported problems that were outside their task domain, and they seemed less hindered by self blaming in their problem attribution.

The participants' roles not only influenced the number of problems, but also the types of problems detected. The *user page review* participants took a more hedonic perspective and reported many problems concerning design issues. The think-aloud participants focused on task performance and on the achievement of goals. This led to a more pragmatic view on quality, in which navigational issues in particular played an important role. The think-aloud participants performed a substantial navigation task during which many problems were verbalized and observed. On target pages these participants were mainly occupied with answering the questions, while the review participants took the opportunity to comment on the content and the design of these pages.

The detailed analysis of the problem detections on one specific web page shows that detections can have different representations. Participants in a user role mainly frame their verbalizations in terms of effects, as they experience the effects of website problems themselves. And the facilitator observes effects of problematic choices, which further contributes to the detection of problems that are framed as effects. During the verbalization of thoughts, think-aloud participants often do not provide solutions. On the contrary, reviewing participants are in a stronger position to provide feedback, and they often describe a solution in their comments. Furthermore, in both methods the level of abstraction of the problem detections can differ. These differences between detections make it difficult to decide whether two descriptions refer to the same problem. We applied a rather strict matching procedure, and chose to consider problems as separate, unless there was clear evidence that they were of the same type. From a professional usability perspective, however, many more problems will be considered to be related to each other. When taking this perspective, we also see that the reviewing participants are able to detect the important problems that the participants in a user role experience. At the same time, participants in a user role sometimes take a reviewer perspective in their verbalizations. Hence, the two participant roles we distinguished might in reality be less distinct from each other than we initially have expected them to be.

In this comparison, we used specific representations of the reviewer and user methods. In our reviewer condition the participants were guided through the website using a step by step procedure following a scenario. Other review methods might generate other results. Also, the concurrent think-aloud method we used, is just one variant of the many approaches that might be used. Yet, we think that this study sheds light on important underlying processes during evaluation which are influenced by the role that is assigned to participants. These processes have a considerable influence on the numbers of problems, types of problems, representations of problems, and the way in which these problems are detected.

This study shows that users are able to provide useful feedback in situations in which they concentrate on the review task. The limitation of this study is that it shows only one way of evaluating a website with the user page review method: a step-by-step laboratory procedure with the *Infocus* tool. We chose this procedure to contrast the results with the task oriented think aloud protocols. In our procedure, then, we chose to reduce the participants' cognitive load by allowing them to focus on one task: reporting problems with the feedback option. In this way, we could optimally study the abilities of users to provide feedback and contrast the results with the CTA output.

We have gained more knowledge about users' abilities to provide feedback on website pages in such a controlled context. Although our study

showed that most users have the ability to provide feedback, evaluators in an online context should carefully interpret the results of the user page-review tools. Less educated users have more trouble reporting their problems and are possibly less inclined to share their feedback. Tools should have a clear and uncomplicated design. Also, to stimulate users to share their feedback, these tools need to be eye-catching, attractive, fast, and easy to use. Extra options, such as a categorization, scales, or ratings, should be used with reserve.

Our study indicates that methods that put participants in a review position should be taken seriously. They are able to generate useful feedback which points to obstacles that are experienced by participants in a user role. Moreover, these *user page review* evaluations can be conducted with relatively little costs and effort. We expect that technical developments will further increase the possibilities for gathering participants' feedback and the ease with which this can be done. The think-aloud method also generates useful insights, but the costs are high and the yield appears to be more limited.

## FUTURE RESEARCH DIRECTIONS

The results of our study cannot easily be generalized to contexts in which usability professionals generally organize evaluation studies. In such studies users often conduct more than one task, which imposes a higher cognitive load on them. We did several other studies using *Infocus* for the evaluation of websites without the strong guidance of the present UPR study. These studies also revealed large numbers of problem detections, which indicates that participants seem to be able to work with *Infocus* for User Page Reviews. But we do think that further research is needed into participant roles and the production of feedback under different extents of cognitive load. Such studies should test user page reviews in more natural circumstances and compare the outcomes of the evaluation to those of observational methods, such as the think-aloud method, in order to obtain more information about the merits and restrictions of user page reviews.

The literature about problems with task switching raises questions about the online feedback tools. To what extent are online users able to provide adequate feedback? What are the characteristics of the users who provide feedback with online tools? Perhaps especially highly educated and experienced users are triggered to provide their feedback while other users need all their cognitive energy just to realize their primary goals on the website. It would be useful, then, to have more knowledge about the personal characteristics of the online respondents. Also, comparisons should be made between the feedback that users give with the online tools and in the laboratory: To what extent do these comments correspond with each other?

The participants in this study varied in educational levels, ages, and gender. Our study differs in this respect from other studies that compared methods with user and review roles (Karahasanovíc et al., 2009; Lentz & Pander Maat, 2007; Sienot, 1997), which only included higher educated participants. We have not yet analyzed whether one of the participant roles is more beneficial for specific participants. We observed that some participants in the think-aloud evaluation who performed their tasks without problems, hardly contributed to the detection of problems. In the review condition, we observed that lower educated participants sometimes had trouble providing useful feedback, which is in line with earlier research by De Jong & Schellens (2001), who found that highly educated participants provided more comments and more diverse feedback. In future research these differences between participants and methods should be further explored, in order to provide advice on optimal combinations of methods and participants.

In this study we did not analyze the effort that both methods take. Karahasanovíc et al. (2009) performed a detailed analysis which indicated that feedback collection was far less expensive than think-aloud. Our experiences confirm this. The *user page review* evaluations took less time because they were done in sessions with ten participants, and yielded written comments that were automatically transported to a database. The *think-aloud sessions* took place individually, and much time was needed afterwards to transcribe the protocols and analyze them. Future research could analyze the costs involved more precisely, and relate these to the yield of both methods.

## REFERENCES

Baker, L. (1989). Metacognition, comprehension monitoring, and the adult reader. *Educational Psychology Review*, *1*, 3–38. doi:10.1007/BF01326548

Barkas-Avila, J. A., Oberholzer, G., Schmutz, G., de Vito, M., & Opwis, K. (2007). Usable error message presentation in the world wide web: Do not show errors right away. *Interacting with Computers*, *19*, 330–341. doi:10.1016/j.intcom.2007.01.003

Boren, M. T., & Ramey, J. (2000). Thinking aloud: Reconciling theory and practice. *IEEE Transactions on Professional Communication*, *43*, 261–278. doi:10.1109/47.867942

Castillo, J. C., Hartson, H. R., & Hix, D. (1998). Remote usability evaluation: Can users report their own critical incidents? In *Proceedings of the Conference on Human Factors on Computing Systems* (CHI '98), (pp. 253-254). New York: ACM Press.

Cooke, L. (2010). Assessing concurrent think-aloud protocol as a usability test method: A technical communication approach. *IEEE Transactions on Professional Communication*, *35*, 202–215. doi:10.1109/TPC.2010.2052859

Cunliffe, D. (2000). Developing usable web sites: A review and model. *Internet Research, 10*, 295–307. doi:10.1108/10662240010342577

De Jong, M. (1998). *Reader feedback in text design: Validity of the plus-minus method for the pretesting of public information brochures.* Atlanta, GA: Rodopi.

De Jong, M., & Lentz, L. (1996). Expert judgments versus reader feedback: A comparison of text evaluation techniques. *Journal of Technical Writing and Communication, 26*, 507–519.

De Jong, M., & Lentz, L. (2001). Focus: Design and evaluation of a software tool for collecting reader feedback. *Technical Communication Quarterly, 10*, 387–401. doi:10.1207/s15427625tcq1004_2

De Jong, M., & Lentz, L. (2006). Scenario evaluation of municipal web sites: Development and use of an expert-focused evaluation tool. *Government Information Quarterly, 23*, 191–206. doi:10.1016/j.giq.2005.11.007

De Jong, M., & Schellens, P. J. (2001). Readers' background characteristics and their feedback on documents: The influence of gender and educational level on evaluation results. *Journal of Technical Writing and Communication, 31*, 267–281. doi:10.2190/0XJ7-4044-G7LC-AT8Y

Elling, S. (2012). *Evaluating website quality: Five studies on user-focused evaluation methods.* (Dissertation). Utrecht University, Utrecht, The Netherlands.

Elling, S., Lentz, L., & De Jong, M. (2012a). Users' abilities to review website pages. *Journal of Business and Technical Communication, 26*, 171–201. doi:10.1177/1050651911429920

Elling, S., Lentz, L., & De Jong, M. (2012b). Combining concurrent think-aloud protocols and eye tracking observations: An analysis of verbalizations and silences. *IEEE Transactions on Professional Communication, 55*, 206–220. doi:10.1109/TPC.2012.2206190

Hassenzahl, M. (2000). Prioritizing usability problems: Data-driven and judgement-driven severity estimates. *Behaviour & Information Technology, 19*, 29–42. doi:10.1080/014492900118777

Hertzum, M., Hansen, K. D., & Andersen, H. H. K. (2009). Scrutinising usability evaluation: Does thinking aloud affect behaviour and mental workload? *Behaviour & Information Technology, 28*, 165–181. doi:10.1080/01449290701773842

Hornbæk, K. (2010). Dogmas in the assessment of usability evaluation methods. *Behaviour & Information Technology, 29*, 97–111. doi:10.1080/01449290801939400

Jansen, C., & Balijon, S. (2002). How do people use instruction guides? Confirming and disconfirming patterns of use. *Document Design (Amsterdam), 3*, 195–204. doi:10.1075/dd.3.3.01jan

Karahasanovíc, A., & Nyhamar Hinkel, U., Sjøberg, D. I. K., & Thomas, R. (2009). Comparing of feedback-collection and think-aloud methods in program comprehension studies. *Behaviour & Information Technology, 28*, 139–164. doi:10.1080/01449290701682761

Krahmer, E., & Ummelen, N. (2004). Thinking about thinking aloud: A comparison of two verbal protocols for usability testing. *IEEE Transactions on Professional Communication, 47*, 105–117. doi:10.1109/TPC.2004.828205

Kramer, A. F., Hahn, S., & Gopher, D. (1999). Task coordination and aging: Explorations of executive control processes in the task switching paradigm. *Acta Psychologica, 101*, 339–378. doi:10.1016/S0001-6918(99)00011-6 PMID:10344190

Lentz, L., & Pander Maat, H. (2007). Reading aloud and the delay of feedback: Explanations for the effectiveness of reader protocols. *Information Design Journal, 15*, 266–281. doi:10.1075/idj.15.3.09len

Monsell, S. (2003). Task switching. *Trends in Cognitive Sciences, 7,* 134–140. doi:10.1016/S1364-6613(03)00028-7 PMID:12639695

Moon, Y. (2003). Don't blame the computer: When self-disclosure moderates the self-serving bias. *Journal of Consumer Psychology, 13,* 125–137.

Neerincx, M. A., Lindenberg, J., & Pemberton, S. (2001). Support concepts for web navigation: A cognitive engineering approach. In *Proceedings of the 10ᵗʰ International Conference on World Wide Web,* (pp. 119-128). Hong Kong: ACM.

Nichols, D. M., McKay, D., & Twidale, M. B. (2003). Participatory usability: Supporting pro-active users. In *Proceedings of 4ᵗʰ ACM SIGCHI NZ, Symposium on Computer-Human Interaction* (CHINZ '03), (pp. 63-68). Dunedin, New Zealand: ACM.

Nielsen, J. (2001). *Alertbox: First rule of usability? Don't listen to users.* Retrieved September 13, 2012, from http://www.useit.com/alertbox/20010805.html

Olmsted-Hawala, E. L., Murphy, E. D., Hawala, S., & Ashenfelter, K. T. (2010). Think-aloud protocols: A comparison of three think-aloud protocols for use in testing data-dissemination web sites for usability. In *Proceedings of the 28th International Conference on Human Factors in Computing Systems,* (pp. 2381-2390). ACM.

Ormrod, J. E. (2006). *Educational psychology: Developing learners* (5th ed.). Upper Saddle River, NJ: Pearson Education.

Sauro, J. (2010). *Can users self-report usability problems?* Retrieved September 13, 2012, from http://www.measuringusability.com/blog/self-reporting.php

Schriver, K. A. (1997). *Dynamics in document design: Creating text for readers.* New York, NY: Wiley.

Serenko, A. (2007). Are interface agents scapegoats? Attributions of responsibility in human-agent interaction. *Interacting with Computers, 19,* 293–303. doi:10.1016/j.intcom.2006.07.005

Sienot, M. (1997). Pretesting web sites: A comparison between the plus-minus method and the think-aloud method for the world wide web. *Journal of Business and Technical Communication, 11,* 469–482. doi:10.1177/1050651997011004006

Spyridakis, J. H., Wei, C., Barrick, J., Cuddihy, E., & Maust, B. (2005). Internet-based research: Providing a foundation for web design guidelines. *IEEE Transactions on Professional Communication, 48,* 242–260. doi:10.1109/TPC.2005.853927

Tullis, T., & Albert, B. (2008). *Measuring the user experience: Collecting, analyzing, and presenting usability metrics.* San Francisco, CA: Morgan Kaufmann Publishers Inc.

Ummelen, N., & Neutelings, R. (2002). Measuring reading behavior in policy documents: A comparison of two instruments. *IEEE Transactions on Professional Communication, 43,* 292–301. doi:10.1109/47.867945

Van den Haak, M. J., De Jong, M. D. T., & Schellens, P. J. (2003). Retrospective vs. concurrent think-aloud protocols: Testing the usability of an online library catalogue. *Behaviour & Information Technology, 22,* 339–251. doi:10.1080/0044929031000

Van Dijk, J., Pieterson, W., Van Deursen, A., & Ebbers, W. (2007). E-services for citizens: The Dutch usage case. *Lecture Notes in Computer Science, 4656,* 155–166. doi:10.1007/978-3-540-74444-3_14

Van Schaik, P., & Ling, J. (2008). Modelling user experience with web sites: Usability, hedonic value, beauty and goodness. *Interacting with Computers, 20,* 419–432. doi:10.1016/j.intcom.2008.03.001

Welle Donker-Kuijer, M., De Jong, M., & Lentz, L. (2008). Heuristic web site evaluation: Exploring the effects of guidelines on experts' detection of usability problems. *Technical Communication*, *55*, 392–404.

## ADDITIONAL READING

Boren, M. T., & Ramey, J. (2000). Thinking aloud: Reconciling theory and practice. *IEEE Transactions on Professional Communication*, *43*, 261–278. doi:10.1109/47.867942

Cooke, L. (2010). Assessing concurrent think-aloud protocol as a usability test method: a technical communication approach. *IEEE Transactions on Professional Communication*, *35*, 202–215. doi:10.1109/TPC.2010.2052859

Hornbæk, K. (2010). Dogmas in the assessment of usability evaluation methods. *Behaviour & Information Technology*, *29*, 97–111. doi:10.1080/01449290801939400

Tullis, T., & Albert, B. (2008). *Measuring the user experience. Collecting, analyzing, and presenting usability metrics*. San Francisco, CA: Morgan Kaufmann Publishers Inc.

## KEY TERMS AND DEFINITIONS

**Cognitive Lockup:** The inclination of users to concentrate on one task and to neglect other tasks; this explains why participants stop thinking aloud when much energy is needed for task performance.

**Concurrent Think Aloud Protocols:** A method that stimulates participants to think aloud while performing specific tasks on a web site.

**Matching:** The procedure to merge different problem detections into a set of user problems

**Problem Detection:** Any obstacle in navigation or comprehension and any negative attitude towards the website that the evaluator finds in the data.

**Reviewer Role:** The participant is invited to review (parts of) a website and provide comments.

**Scenario Task:** A short story introducing a main character who needs some information for a specific goal which leads to specific questions that must be answered. A scenario helps participants to imagine a task that corresponds to those that people usually perform on websites, such as searching for information, reading, understanding, and applying the relevant information.

**User Page Review:** A method that enables website users to review a website by clicking on a button that appears on selected pages and to provide written comments on these pages.

**User Role:** The participant is invited to perform a task and report experiences and reflections on task performance.

## ENDNOTES

[1] Note that the *user page review* evaluation involved 30-33 participants per website, and the think-aloud condition 20 participants per website. These different group sizes further increase the difference between the number of *user page review* problems and think-aloud problems.

[2] The interpretation of the UPR comments was not only based on the formulations, but also on the marking of these problems by the participants. Sometimes a comment could be interpreted in different ways, depending on the object that the participant underlined or pointed to.

# Section 3
# E–Customer Satisfaction

# Chapter 8
# Customer Satisfaction Evaluation for Greek Online Travel Agencies

**Dimitrios Drosos**
*Technological Education Institute of Piraeus, Greece*

**Nikolaos Tsotsolas**
*Technological Education Institute of Piraeus, Greece*

## ABSTRACT

*The rapid development of tourist supply and demand makes Information Technologies (IT) significant, and thus, they increasingly play a more critical role in tourism marketing, distribution, promotion, and coordination. IT influences the strategic management and marketing of contemporary organisations as a paradigm-shift is experienced, transforming the best business practices globally. IT is one of the main key influences of competitiveness in the tourism/travel industry. The original purpose for adopting IT systems was simply to provide an automatic means of store and manage data (e.g. on flights and accommodation). At the same time, IT in the tourist sector enables an increased volume of transactions to be handled rapidly and effectively. This chapter presents an original customer satisfaction survey in the Greek Online Travel Agencies. For the collection of the data, a Website questionnaire was used in order to better record the customers' views on the service overall as well as their satisfaction levels on particular aspects of the service. The survey was conducted within the period September – November 2012. Final input data consists of 510 questionnaires.*

## INTRODUCTION

In the digital era that we live in, IT has a major role in every organisational aspect. Practically, every company and institution is considering the new opportunities offered by innovative technology. Kekre et al (1995) clearly states that IT is one of the most important issues discussed in manage-

ment nowadays, and that there is high chance of improving the performance of organisations by adopting the appropriate information system.

In addition, Colier et al (2003) become more specific and describe the immense expansion of the web technology, claiming that internet infrastructures and practices are the mean for organisational development. Enterprises proceed

DOI: 10.4018/978-1-4666-5129-6.ch008

in the adoption of information systems in order to achieve reduced costs, higher production and high quality services to their customers (Legris et al, 2003). In fact, IT is *"just and an enabler"* (Malhotra, 2005) in using this invisible force of knowledge which finally allows organisations to stay strong in business. In contrast to this view, IT, along with competition and globalisation, can be considered as environmental factors that keep pressuring organisations in adopting strategies (Zack, 1999).

Two decades later, the most popular technology which appears to have significant impacts on business is the Internet. The web technology allows the establishment of networks which enable vast amount of information to be transferred around the globe. Considering that the capacity of computers is growing rapidly, Collier et al (2003) state that almost all enterprises have been influenced and searched for opportunities provided by the use of internet and information technology.

Benbya et al (2004) also note that the use of IT enables organisations to store, and exchange vast amount of information allowing the generation and the sharing of useful knowledge. Thus while, the business world is transforming around technology, the e-business appears to be steadily expanding and the use of knowledge is becoming important for organisations that are looking for extensive information technology opportunities in order to adapt more quickly in the knowledge – based global economy.

The tourism industry is one of the largest users of IT and has some of the largest computer installations in the business world. IT provides both opportunities and challenges for the tourist industry. (Buhalis, 1994). The development of new technologies is making the tourism world a much smaller place. The communication between tourism organisation and the customers is now faster and more flexible. Tourist organisation is already taking big advantages of the new technologies to increase the scope of their products.

According to D. Buhalis (2003) IT, is one of the most dynamic motivators of global economy. IT is a powerful tool for economic growth for the industry to continue being competitive and to provide strategic opportunities. Information technology can reduce costs, enhance operational efficiency, and most importantly improve service quality and customer experience. Technology in this case has been described as a profit and efficiency maximisation tool that revolutionises the way business is conducted and removes all geographical boundaries.

The aim of this chapter book is to present an original customer satisfaction survey in Greek Online Travel Agencies. This chapter book is organized into 6 sections. Section 2, presents the literature review, regarding tourism as an industrial sector, information technology in tourism industry and customer satisfaction on online tourist services. Section 3 presents the MUSA (Multicriteria Satisfaction Analysis) method, which is the Decision Support System that was used in order to measure the customer satisfaction. Section 4 presents the methodological frame and section 5 the results of our research. Finally, section 6 presents some concluding remarks, as well as future research in the context of the proposed method.

## LITERATURE REVIEW

### Tourism as an Industrial Sector

The subject of tourism – travel is exciting and fascinating. Tourism as a whole is one of the fastest growing industries in Europe and worldwide. In recent years, growth rates in tourism have been higher than those of the overall world economy. (E-Business Watch, 2006). Human beings have been moving from place to place for about 1 million years. Since the time of wanderings of ancient people, we have been travelling in ever-widening patterns around the earth.

From the days of such early explorers as Marco Polo, Christopher Columbus, there has been a steady growth in travel. Tourism is a composite of activities, services, and industries that delivers a travel experience: transportation, accommodations, eating and drinking establishments, shops, entertainment, activity facilities, and other hospitality services available for individuals or groups who have been travelling away from home. It encompasses all providers of visitor and visitor-related services.

Tourism is usually defined as services provided for people travelling and staying outside their usual environment for less than one consecutive year, for leisure or for business purposes. (E-Business Watch, 2004b). Tourism is the entire world industry of travel, hotels, transportation, and all other components, including promotion that serves the needs and wants of travelers. According to another approach, tourism is the sum total of tourist expenditures within the borders of a nation or a political subdivision or a transportation-centred economic area of contiguous states or nations. (Mcintosh et all, 1995)

The World Tourism Organization defines tourists as people "traveling to and staying in places outside their usual environment for not more than one consecutive year for leisure, business and other purposes" (UNWTO Technical Manual, 1995). In the Manila Declaration on World Tourism (1980) tourism was defined as "an activity essential to the life of nations because of its direct effects on the social, cultural, educational, and economic sectors of national societies and on their international relations"

Tourism is a special type of product and it needs to be analysed into two dimensions (Witt and Moutinho, 1995). First into the overall tourist product, the combination of all the service elements that visitors consume from the time they leave home, to the time they come back.

The overall tourism product consists of five main components: Destination, attractions, destination facilities, accessibility, images and price.

And second the commercial products, which are components of the overall tourism product such as accommodation, transport. For a number of countries (e.g. Greece) tourism is the largest commodity in international trade. In many others it ranks among the top three or four industries. Tourism has grown rapidly to become a major social and economic force in the world. The tourism industry has the potential to generate foreign exchange earnings, create employment, promote development in various parts of the country, reduce income and employment disparities among regions, strengthen linkages among many sectors of the national economy and help to alleviate poverty. (Azhar Harun, 2012)

International tourist arrivals (overnight visitors) grew by 4% in 2012 surpassing a record 1 billion tourists globally for the first time in history. Asia and the Pacific saw the highest growth of all regions with 7% more international tourists. With an additional 39 million tourists, international arrivals reached 1,035 million, up from 996 million in 2011.

Demand held well throughout the year, with a stronger than expected fourth quarter. Despite ongoing economic challenges, the growth of international arrivals worldwide is expected to continue in 2013 at a similar to slightly slower pace (+3% to +4%) and in line with UNWTO's long-term outlook Tourism Towards 2030, which projects an average growth of 3.8% per year between 2010 and 2020. (World Tourism Barometer, 2013)

## Information Technology in Tourism Industry

During recent years the IT related tourism innovations have led to dramatic changes in the tourism sector. IT in the tourist sector enables an increased volume of transactions to be handled rapidly and effectively.

The tourism industry in general is ideally suited for computer technology. It requires a system of registering availability of transport and accommodation at short notice; of making immediate reservations, amendments and cancellations on such facilities, of quoting complex fares and conditions of travel, of rapidly processing documents such as tickets, invoices, vouchers and itineraries, and of providing accounting and management information (Holloway, 1998).

Usage of IT can result in a positive effect to the level of quality provided to the customer. With the use of IT higher living standards result for the customer. IT improves the service quality and contributes to higher quest/traveler satisfaction. Customer satisfaction depends highly on the assurance and comprehensiveness of specific information on destinations' accessibility, facilities and activities. IT enables customer to communicate directly with tourism organisation in order to request information and purchase products. IT increases a number of intra-organisational processes by supporting a certain level of integration between different functions within tourist organisations.

A lot of the manual works is reduced in leading with the tasks of payroll, inventory control, and general ledger. This saves time and releases staff to provide a better personal service to the customers.

Three main waves of technological developments established IT in tourism enterprises. In the 1970s Computer Reservation System's (CRSs), in the 1980s Global Distribution System's (GDSs) and in 1990s Internet. Although these technologies emerged of about 10 years each other. These systems currently operate both separately and jointly controlling different and target tourist markets. (Buhalis, 2003)

CRSs became central to the distribution mix and strategy of airlines. CRSs are widely regarded as the critical initiators of the electronic age, as they formulated a new travel marketing and distribution system. A CRS is essentially a database which manages the inventory of a tourism enterprise, whilst it distributes it electronically to remote sales offices and external partners. (Buhalis, 1998). Single access information system offered

information in the first years on the product of the airlines companies. The first use of the systems was just a mere adaptation of general databank technology to meet the needs of the airlines. It has indeed been both of a stipulation and a consequence of deregulation and liberalisation.

Since the mid 1980s, airlines CRSs have emerged into Global Distribution Systems (GDSs). (Buhalis, 1998) The range of functions of the GDSs do not only include the airlines mode with information on tariff and seat availability, reservations, automatic prising, ticketing, accounting travel information and internal links with the airlines flight operations, but also provide the agencies and tourism intermediaries with booking facilities for the tour operators for the whole range of tourism products like hotel, rail travel. Car ferries, cruises, travel insurance, car rentals and ticket for culture and events.

It is apparent that IT can transform the nature of tourism and hospitality products, processes, businesses, and competition. Major changes came along for the entire industry with the introduction of online travel agents through the evolution of the internet. Internet is one of the latest IT applications. It is a network of computers around the world, which link via telephone lines and satellite links.

The Internet convergence media, telecommunications and IT increase the interactivity between consumer and suppliers. The Internet, by general consent, is the way ahead for an increasing number of tourist companies/organisations, especially those who need to do business across international borders or in market where computer lines are not always easily accessible. And while the acceptance of the Internet gathers pace around the world, the variations of its possible application are also multiplying at incredible speed.

Since the early 1990s the World Wide Web (www) has emerged as the fastest growing area from internet enabling distribution of multimedia information. Information via Internet presented by a combination of speech, music, animation, video and graphics. The development of World

Wide Web (www) is making the tourism world a much smaller place. The communication between tourism organisation and the customers is now faster and more flexible. Tourist organisation is already taking big advantages of the new technologies to increase the scope of their products. (Buhalis, 1998, 2000),

A tourist organisation can achieve strategic benefit by using World Wide Web namely: establishing entry barriers, affecting switching cost, differentiating products/services, limiting access to distribution channels, ensuring competitive pricing, decreasing supply cost and easing supply, increasing cost efficiency, using information as a product itself, and building closer relationships with suppliers and customers. (Buhalis, 1998)

Tourism providers have been using the internet to communicate, distribute and market their products to potential customers worldwide in a cost- and time-efficient way. In fact, the individual company website had become the most important platform for e commerce, followed by electronic marketplaces (E-Business Watch, 2004a). A serious relevant effect of the advent of the Internet is the birth of new players in the sector. Besides online agencies, the role of new e-intermediaries such as travel portals and regional and local tourist portals is quite important. Travel portals have been established with the specific mission of offering tourist products via the web. (E-Business Watch, 2003b)

Last years the use of online travel services is now the most popular way consumers purchase their travel tickets and other related conveniences, resulting in traditional travel agencies being ranked last in customer usage. Online travel agencies function as traditional agencies in that they deliver travel-related products/services and provide travel-related information and various services to customers. Traditional travel agents can provide much more customized information by gathering and organizing information unique to their customers' travel needs. (Kaynama and Black, 2000, Clemons et al, 2002).

Tourists are expected to increasingly arrange their own package tours directly via the web through dynamic packaging. But despite the fact that the number of offline travel agents will decrease, they will not disappear. In the future, travel agents will have to provide both internet applications, as well as individual and qualified customer advice at physical information points (Buhalis and Costa, 2006).

The online travel agencies collect information from the customer (e.g., departure and arrival destinations, number of travelers). This information is submitted to a Computerized Reservation System (CRS), which searches for relevant flights from the compilation of offerings from participating airlines. (Clemons et al, 2002). According to a report by Mintel Group 48,9% of Europeans are internet users which comes to prove that there is still potential for growth. (Mintel Group 2009).

While researching the impact of technology on the Tourism industry, one discovers that: (Law and Jogaratnam, 2005)

- From a strategic point of view technology is gradually reshaping the fundamental structure of the Tourism industry.
- The consumer is more and more in control through the use of personal computers with greater ability to compare prices and products.
- Tourism and hospitality organisations that will fail to master the right IT systems will find it difficult to direct and manage their information-intensive businesses and will damage their competitiveness

## Assessment of Customer Satisfaction on Online Tourism Services

During the last decade, an increasing interest in measuring patient satisfaction levels has been noticed, and is certified by a number of studies. Customer satisfaction is central to the marketing concept, with evidence of strategic links between satisfaction and overall service performance (Truch, 2006). According to Bartikowski and Llosa (2004) "customer satisfaction is typically defined as an overall assessment of the performance of various attributes that constitute a service".

Another definition that has been proposed for the satisfaction of customer is the following: "Satisfaction is the result of purchase and use of a product or service, which derives from the customer's comparison between the remuneration and the cost of purchase, taking into consideration the expected result" (Churchill and Suprenant, 1982).

Satisfaction is the reaction of consumers in the evaluation process, which examines the discrepancies between prior expectations and actual performance level of the product as perceived by the consumer after use (Tse and Wilton, 1988). As explained by Oliver (1996), Gerson (1993) and Vavra (1997), satisfaction is a measure of how the total offered product or service fulfills customer expectations.

The worldwide interest on measuring patient satisfaction levels has been empowered by the need for evaluation and improvement on the quality of online tourist services. Last years an increasing number of researchers around the world have focused on line customer satisfaction. According to Flavian et al., (2006) customer satisfaction plays a major role in the online business because it helps to build customer trust.

Anderson and Srinivasan (2003) in their study with title "e-Satisfaction and e-loyalty: A contingency framework" defined e-satisfaction as "the contentment of the customer with respect to his or her prior purchasing experience with a given electronic commerce firm". Lin (2010) investigated the impact of three factors (relevance of information content, information quality, and functionality needs services) of e-travel sites on consumers' perceived ease of use and usefulness, which influenced behavioural intention towards these sites.

Last years an increasing number of researchers have focused on online customer satisfaction and e–service quality. To better understand online customer satisfaction, many models were developed. Szymanski and Hise (2000) developed a simple model which was limited only four web dimensions, namely convenience, merchandizing, site design, and financial security. Lee (2001) developed a sophisticate model with many interrelated constructs and hence it was not able to provide further understanding on customer satisfaction.

Parasuraman et al. (2005) in their study with title "E-S-Qual: A Multiple-Item Scale for Assessing Electronic Service Quality" acted on a wide view of e-service quality when they published two scales for assessing e-services both adapted from the well-known SERVQUAL scale. The first of the two scales was termed E-S-QUAL and included 22 items arranged in four dimensions: Efficiency, Fulfilment, System availability and Privacy The second scale was termed the E-RecS-QUAL; it was designed for conditions where customers had non-routine encounters with a site, such as attempted service recovery. Including 11 items arranged in three dimensions of: Responsiveness, Compensation and Contact.

Au Yeung and Law (2006) developed a model with five dimensions for usability of travel and hotel websites (language, layout and graphics, information architecture, user interface and navigation). Mills and Morrison (2003) in their study with title "Measuring customer ssatisfaction with online travel" developed an e-satisfaction model for travel website evaluation, which consisted of three main dimensions: interface, perceived quality, and value. Lu et al. (2002) used a model for travel website evaluation, with seven functions: general tourism service information publicity, advertising tourism product/service, advertising with price information, email enquiry, online booking, on-line payment, and tourism website registration with user ID.

Kim et al (2007) developed nine rating criteria to evaluate online travel agency: Finding low fares, security, ease of use, booking flexibility, sorting options, speed of the website, useful and relevant content, ability to book all travel services in one transaction, design and presentation of the website. According to Szymanski and Hise (2000), the most important factors which illustrate e-tourism satisfaction have been summarized as convenience, site design, financial security and product information.

## MUSA METHOD

The MUSA (Multicriteria Satisfaction Analysis) method of Grigoroudis and Siskos (Grigoroudis and Siskos, 2002; Siskos and Grigoroudis, 2002) has been chosen to be used in order to measure customer satisfaction in this research. The basic principle of MUSA is the aggregation of individual judgements into a collective value function, assuming that customer's global satisfaction depends on a set of criteria representing service characteristic dimensions.

The global satisfaction is denoted as a variable Y and the set of criteria is denoted as a vector $X=(X_1, X_2, ..., X_n)$. MUSA was chosen over other statistical, econometrical methods because it gives reliable answers to the following criticism of other methods, namely:

1. Most of the statistical models that are used to analyze consumers' behavior cannot deal with qualitative variables, and whenever this happens, the variables are a priori encoded which results to a loss of the information provided by the consumer.
2. In several methods strong hypotheses are concerned which is difficult to be proved. These hypotheses may refer either to consumer behavior or to the estimation model (e.g. satisfaction assessment using a specific probability function).
3. Many methods focus mostly on the description of the characteristics which affect customer's satisfaction and not on the synthesis of these characteristics to a global satisfaction index.
4. Finally, several methods need information which is difficult to be collected (e.g.: customers' expected utility, tradeoffs, etc.)

This preference disaggregation methodology is implemented through an ordinal regression based approach in the field of multicriteria analysis used for the assessment of a set of a marginal satisfaction functions in such a way, that the global satisfaction criterion becomes as consisted as possible with customer's judgments (Jacquet-Lagreze and Siskos, 1982; Siskos, and Yannacopoulos, 1985).

According to the survey, each customer is asked to express his/her own judgements, namely his/her global satisfaction and his/her satisfaction with regard to a set of discrete criteria, representing characteristics of the provided products and services. Based on these assumptions, the problem is approached as a problem of qualitative regression and solved via special linear programming formulations where the sum of deviations between global satisfaction evaluation expressed by customers and the one resulting from their multicriteria satisfaction evaluations is minimized. The main results from the aforementioned preference disaggregation approach are focused on global and partial explanatory analysis.

Global explanatory analysis lays emphasis on customers' global satisfaction and its primary dimensions, while partial explanatory analysis focuses on each criterion and their relevant parameters separately. Satisfaction analysis results, in more detail, consist of:

- **Global Satisfaction Index:** It shows in a range of 0-100% the level of global satisfaction of the customers; it may be considered as the basic average performance indicator for the organisation.

- **Global Demanding Index:** It shows in a range of -100%-100% the demanding level of customers according to the following:
    - **Demanding Index 100%:** Extremely demanding customers.
    - **Demanding Index 0%:** "Normal" customers.
    - **Demanding Index 100%:** Non-demanding customers.
- **Criteria/Sub-Criteria Satisfaction Indices:** They show in a range of 0-100% the level of partial satisfaction of the customers according to the specific criterion/sub-criterion, similarly to the global satisfaction index.
- **Weights of Criteria/Sub-Criteria:** They show the relative importance within a set of criteria or sub-criteria.
- **Demanding Indices:** They show in a range of -100%-100% the demanding level of customers according to the specific criterion/sub-criterion, similarly to the global demanding index.

Combining weights and satisfaction indices, a series of "Performance/Importance" diagrams (called also Action Diagrams) can be developed (Figure 1). Each of these diagrams is divided into quadrants according to performance (high/low), and importance (high/low), that may be used to classify actions:

- **Status Quo (Low Performance And Low Importance):** Generally, no action is required.
- **Leverage Opportunity (High Performance/High Importance):** These areas can be used as advantage against competition.
- **Transfer Resources (High Performance/ Low Importance):** Organisation's resources may be better used elsewhere.
- **Action Opportunity (Low Performance/ High Importance):** These are the criteria/ sub-criteria that needs attention.

The above methodology has been successfully implemented in many customer satisfaction surveys. Moreover, it has been used in similar research related to customer satisfaction (Siskos and Grigoroudis, 2002).

*Figure 1. Performance/importance diagram*

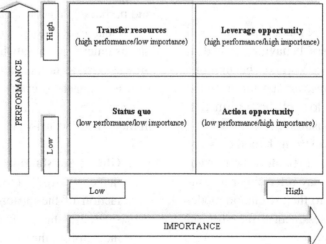

## RESEARCH METHODOLOGICAL FRAME

This research process consists of the steps below (Hayes, B.E., 1992. Measuring Customer Satisfaction: Development and Use of Questionnaire, ASQC Quality Press, Milwaukee, WI.Hayes, 1992):

- **Preliminary Analysis:** Customer satisfaction research objectives should be specified in this stage; preliminary market and customer behavioural analysis should be conducted in order to assess satisfaction dimensions (customers' consistent family of criteria).
- **Questionnaire Design and Conducting Survey:** Using results from the previous step, this stage refers to the development of the questionnaire, the determination of survey parameters (sample size, collection data form, etc.) and the survey conduction.
- **Analysis:** The implementation of the model is included in this stage providing several results as described in the previous paragraph. Analysis is performed into the total set of customers, as well as into distinctive customer segments. Provided results involve basic descriptive statistical models, as well as the multicriteria preference disaggregation MUSA model.
- **Results:** Using the results from the analysis stage, final proposals for organization's improvement strategy can be formulated; a reliability testing process for the results of the model is also included in this stage.

## Survey Conduction

The results which presented in this paper come from a satisfaction survey. For the implementation of this survey a structure questionnaire was developed. For the purposes of this research a web site was constructed. Through the web site the customer had the opportunity to answer a web based questionnaire. The survey was conducted within the period September – November 2012. Final input data consist of 510 questionnaires.

## Satisfaction Criteria

The assessment of a consistent family of criteria representing customers' satisfaction dimensions is one of most important stages of the implemented methodology, as mentioned in the previous section. This assessment can be achieved through an extensive interactive procedure between the analyst and the decision-maker (company). In any case, the reliability of the set of criteria/subcriteria has to be tested in a small indicative set of customers. (Mihelis et al, 2001). The main satisfaction criteria for the survey consist of:

- **Content:** This criterion includes all the characteristics concerning the web site contents (Completeness of Information, Content Reliability, Content Writing, and Usefulness of Content.
- **Navigation:** This criterion reflects the provided to users when moving in and around the web site. It includes Ease of Finding Website Link, Website Loading Speed, Browser Compatibility, Easy to Navigate, Structure Information, and Instructions.
- **Appearance:** This criterion captures aspects related to website's "look and feel". It includes Multimedia, Aesthetic Design, and Site Components.
- **E–Services:** This criterion refers to the E- service offered to the customers; it includes the Online Availability, Online Reservation, Online Buy & Payment, Transaction Security, and Technical Support.

*Figure 2. Hierarchical structure of customers satisfaction dimensions*

Users were asked to evaluate their satisfaction level on each one of these criteria, as well as to express their overall judgement using a 5-point qualitative scale of the form: very satisfied, satisfied, moderately satisfied, dissatisfied, very dissatisfied.

## RESULTS

### Sample

The sample selected with random sampling and constituted customers whose make reservation thought Online travel agency. In order to formulate a customer profile, user's characteristics were studied. The sample was almost equally distributed between males and females (male 52%, female 48%). All the information about our sample presented in Table 1.

### Satisfaction Analysis Results

The results given by MUSA method show that customers seem to be totally satisfied from the quality of the services that are offered by Greek Online Travel Agencies. More specifically, the average total satisfaction indicator amounts to 88.10% (Figure.3). Additionally, the concave form of total satisfaction function values in combination with the size of the estimated demand indicators, which are -40.80%, indicate that customers are

*Table 1. Sample information*

| | | Percent (%) |
|---|---|---|
| **Gender** | Male | 52% |
| | Female | 48% |
| **Age** | <24 Years | 13% |
| | Between 25 and 34 Years | 31% |
| | Between 35 and 44 Years | 26% |
| | Between 45 and 54 Years | 20% |
| | >55 Years | 10% |
| **Educational Level** | Lower Secondary School | 1% |
| | Upper Secondary School | 27% |
| | Vocational Training | 23% |
| | Graduate | 20% |
| | Postgraduate/Doctorate | 29% |
| **Family Status** | Single | 48% |
| | Married | 13% |
| | Married with children | 36% |
| | Divorce | 3% |
| **Income Level** | <1000 € | 32% |
| | Between 1001 and 2000 € | 37% |
| | Between 2001 and 3000 € | 20% |
| | Between 3001 and 4000 € | 5% |
| | >4000 € | 6% |

not particularly demanding, which means that they are easily satisfied even if only a part of their expectations is fulfilled.

Regarding the customers' partial satisfaction from the quality of provided services it is shown in Figure 4 that the highest satisfaction level is assigned to *Content* (90.98%) and the lowest to *Appearance* (77.80%). The other two dimensions show relative high degree of satisfaction (>80%).

The weight of each criterion shows the degree of importance that given by the total number of customers in each of the dimensions of satisfaction. Thus is determined the level of importance of each criterion in the formulation of global satisfaction. Figure 5 shows that the most important criterion is *Content* (39%) and that the least important one is the *Appearance* (18.34%). It shall be mentioned that the most important criterion is also the one with the highest satisfaction index.

Figure 6 is coming to confirm the initial results regarding the demanding level of customers on the basis of the form of the global satisfaction function and the degree of the average total demand index. In particular, customers are less demanding regarding the *Content*, which is the criterion with the highest level of importance.

MUSA results regarding the basic criteria can also help in the formulation of an action diagram through the combination of weights of satisfaction criteria with the average satisfaction indicators. Thus, the strengths and the weaknesses of the customers' satisfaction can be determined and also where any improvement efforts should be focused.

According to the action diagram (Figure 7) none of the criteria fall in the action area (high

*Figure 3. Global satisfaction index*

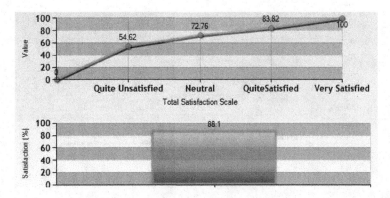

*Figure 4. Partial satisfaction indices*

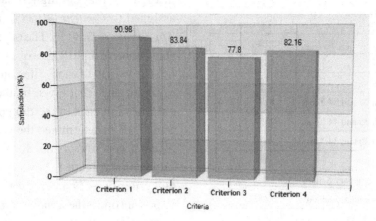

*Figure 5. Criteria weights*

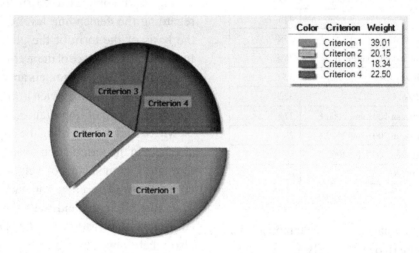

*Figure 6. Average demanding indices*

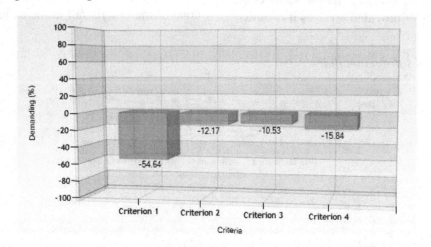

importance-low performance). This means that there were no important criteria in which patients are dissatisfied. Furthermore, the criterion of *Content* falls in the leverage opportunity area, so this criterion may be considered as the competitive advantage of online travel agencies in Greece which should be further improved and promoted.

## Relationship between Satisfaction, Frequency of Use and Loyalty

Trying to examine the relationship between the satisfaction, frequency of use and loyalty, we investigated the extent to which the customers' satisfaction level (overall, as well as partial on the criteria) is related to the level frequency of use of the services and/or to the loyalty of the customers as this loyalty is expressed in three questions ([i. willingness to continue the use the online services], [ii. proposing the on-line travel agency to other customers] and ([iii. willingness to continue the use the online services in case of prices rising]). For the evaluation of the aforementioned correlation we chose to use Spearman's correlation coefficient given the fact that all variables under question are ordinal.

From the performed Spearman's rank-order correlation analysis, which was conducted, it was concluded that global satisfaction as well as partial satisfaction concerning all four criteria are strongly positively correlated with the customers' loyalty level (see Table 2) regarding the three different loyalty questions.

Furthermore, a significant positive correlation is observed between the question concerning the frequency of use of online travel agencies services on one side and global satisfaction and satisfaction per criteria on the other side. A much weaker correlation is observed between both question concerning the frequency of use of travel agencies services in general (offline & on line) and the customers' satisfaction.

## CONCLUDING REMARKS AND FUTURE RESEARCH

The findings reported here suggest that overall customer satisfaction is real and so the service quality is very good for the majority of customers. The original study presented in this paper illustrates the implementation of a preference dissagregation methodology for measuring the

*Figure 7. Action diagram*

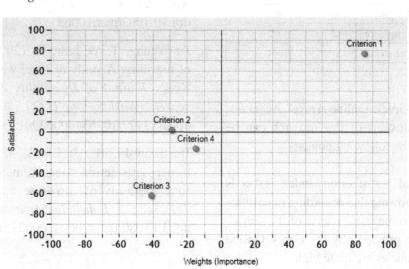

*Table 2. Spearman's rho*

| | Criteria | Spearman's Rho | Significance |
|---|---|---|---|
| **Loyalty [question i]** | Global Satisfaction | .539** | .000 |
| | 1. Content | .413** | .000 |
| | 2. Navigation | .318** | .000 |
| | 3. Appearance | .210** | .000 |
| | 4. E - Services | .456** | .000 |
| **Loyalty [question ii]** | Global Satisfaction | .529** | .000 |
| | 1. Content | .401** | .000 |
| | 2. Navigation | .329** | .000 |
| | 3. Appearance | .207** | .000 |
| | 4. E - Services | .467** | .000 |
| **Loyalty 3** | Global Satisfaction | .329** | .000 |
| | 1. Content | .260** | .000 |
| | 2. Navigation | .199** | .000 |
| | 3. Appearance | .327** | .000 |
| | 4. E - Services | .370** | .000 |
| **Frequency of use concerning travel agencies in general** | Global Satisfaction | .145** | .002 |
| | 1. Content | .083 | .077 |
| | 2. Navigation | .081 | .086 |
| | 3. Appearance | .029 | .539 |
| | 4. E - Services | .096* | .040 |
| **Frequency of use concerning online travel agencies** | Global Satisfaction | .206** | .000 |
| | 1. Content | .139** | .003 |
| | 2. Navigation | .099* | .035 |
| | 3. Appearance | .042 | .372 |
| | 4. E - Services | .153** | .001 |

satisfaction of Greek Online Travel Agencies. The basic conclusions of this research can be summarised in the following points:

- The global satisfaction index exceeds 88.10%, showing that according to costumers' opinion the quality level of the services that are provided by the Greek Online Travel Agencies are quite high.

- The highest satisfaction level is assigned to Content (90.98%) and the lowest to Appearance (77.80%).
- Customers are not particularly demanding, which means that they are easily satisfied even if only a part of their expectations is fulfilled.

In any case it should be pointed out the necessity of repetition of the survey on a regular basis (creation of a permanent satisfaction barometer) in order to observe the Online Travel Agencies needs that may alter. This mainly happens as a result of the rapid development of technology, the creation and the development of new services and finally the changes in the competitive field. A permanent customer satisfaction barometer can assist Total Quality Management and Continuous Improvement concepts in every business organisation (Edosomwan, 1993). Moreover, the focus on total customer satisfaction should be integrated into the accepted management process and the Online Travel Agencies's culture.

## REFERENCES

Anderson, R. E., & Srinivasan, S. S. (2003). E-satisfaction and e-loyalty: A contingency framework. *Psychology and Marketing, 20*(2), 123–138. doi:10.1002/mar.10063

Au Yeung, T., & Law, R. (2006). Evaluation of usability: A study of hotel websites in Hong Kong. *Journal of Hospitality & Tourism Research (Washington, D.C.), 30*(4), 452–473. doi:10.1177/1096348006290115

Bartikowski, B., & Llosa, S. (2004). Customer satisfaction measurement: Comparing four methods of attribute categorizations. *The Service Industries Journal, 24*, 67–72. doi:10.1080/0264206042000275190

Benbya, H., Passiante, G., & Belbaly, N. A. (2004). Corporate portal: A tool for knowledge management synchronization. *International Journal of Information Management*, *24*(3), 201–220. doi:10.1016/j.ijinfomgt.2003.12.012

Buhalis, D. (1994). Information and telecommunications technologies as a strategic tool for small and medium tourism enterprises in the contemporary business environment. In *Tourism--The state of the art*. London: J. Wiley and Sons.

Buhalis, D. (1998). Strategic use of information technologies in the tourism industry. *Tourism Management*, *19*(5), 409–421. doi:10.1016/S0261-5177(98)00038-7

Buhalis, D. (2000). Distribution channels in the changing travel industry. *International Journal of Tourism Research*, *2*(5), 357–359. doi:10.1002/1522-1970(200009/10)2:5<357::AID-JTR233>3.0.CO;2-B

Buhalis, D. (2003). *eTourism: Information technology for strategic tourism management*. Upper Saddle River, NJ: Pearson - Financial Times/Prentice-Hall.

Buhalis, D., & Costa, C. (2006). *Tourism business frontiers*. Oxford, UK: Elsevier.

Churchill, G. A., & Surprenant. (1982). An investigation into the determinants of customer satisfaction. *JMR, Journal of Marketing Research*, *19*(4), 491–504. doi:10.2307/3151722

Clemons, E., Hann, I., & Hitt, L. (2002). The nature of competition in electronic markets: An empirical investigation of on-line travel agent offerings. *Management Science*, *48*(4), 534–549. doi:10.1287/mnsc.48.4.534

Clemons, E.K., Hann, I., & Hitt, L.M. (2002). Price dispersion and differentiation in online travel: An empirical investigation management science, *48*(4), 534–549.

Collier, G., Norris, D. M., Mason, J., Robson, R., & Lefrere, P. (2003). A revolution in knowledge sharing. *EDUCAUSE Review*, *38*(5).

E-Business Watch / European Commission. (2003b). *ICT & e-business in the tourism sector*. No.13 II/July 2003.

E-Business Watch / European Commission. (2004a). *Electronic business in tourism - The quantitative picture: Diffusion of ICT and e-business in 2003/04*. Sector Report No. 07-I, May 2004.

E-Business Watch / European Commission. (2004b). *Electronic business in tourism - Key issues, case studies, conclusions*. Sector Report No. 07-II, August 2004.

E-Business Watch / European Commission. (2006). *ICT & e-business in the tourism sector - ICT adoption and e-business activity in 2006*. Sector Report No. 8, July 2006.

Earl, M. (1996). *Information management: The organizational dimension*. Oxford, UK: Oxford University Press.

Edosomwan, J. A. (1993). *Customer and market-driven quality management*. Milwaukee, WI: ASQC Quality Press.

Flavian, C., Guinaliu, M., & Gurrea, R. (2006). The role played by perceived usability, satisfaction and consumer trust on website loyalty. *Information & Management*, *43*, 1–14. doi:10.1016/j.im.2005.01.002

Gerson, R. F. (1993). *Measuring customer satisfaction: A guide to managing quality service*. Menlo Park, CA: Crisp Publications.

Grigoroudis, E., & Siskos, Y. (2002). Preference disaggregation for measuring and analysing customer satisfaction: The MUSA method. *European Journal of Operational Research*, *143*, 148–170. doi:10.1016/S0377-2217(01)00332-0

Harun, A. (2012). Thailand tourism industry: The impact of tourism sector to Thai's gross domestic product (GDP). In *Proceedings of 2nd International Conference on Business, Economics, Management and Behavioral Sciences* (BEMBS'2012). BEMBS.

Hayes, B. E. (1992). *Measuring customer satisfaction: Development and use of questionnaire.* Milwaukee, WI: ASQC Quality Press.

Holloway, C. (1998). *The business of tourism* (5th ed.). London: Addison Wesley Longman.

Jacquet-Lagreze, E., & Siskos, J. (1982). Assessing a set of additive utility functions for multicriteria decision-making: The UTA method. *Journal of Operational Research, 10*(2), 151–164. doi:10.1016/0377-2217(82)90155-2

Kaynama, S. A., & Black, C. I. (2000). A proposal to assess the service quality of online travel agencies: An exploratory study. *Journal of Professional Services Marketing, 21*(1), 63–88. doi:10.1300/J090v21n01_05

Kekre, S., Mukhopadhyay, T., & Kalathur, S. (1995). Business value of information technology: A study of electronic data interchange. *Management Information Systems Quarterly, 19*(2), 137–156. doi:10.2307/249685

Kim, D., Kim, & Han. (2007). A perceptual mapping of online travel agencies and preference attributes. *Tourism Management, 28*(2), 591–603. doi:10.1016/j.tourman.2006.04.022

Kim, H. (2005). Developing an index of online customer satisfaction. *Journal of Financial Services Marketing, 10*, 49–64. doi:10.1057/palgrave.fsm.4770173

Law, R., & Jogaratnam, G. (2005). A study of hotel information technology applications. *International Journal of Contemporary Hospitality Management, 17*(2), 170–180. doi:10.1108/09596110510582369

Lee, M. (2001). *Comprehensive model of internet satisfaction.* Kowloon, Hong Kong: City University of Hong Kong.

Legris, P., Ingham, J., & Collerette, P. (2003). Why do people use information technology? A critical review of the technology acceptance model. *Information & Management, 40*(3), 191–204. doi:10.1016/S0378-7206(01)00143-4

Lin, Ch.-T. (2010). Examining e-travel sites: An empirical study in Taiwan. *Online Information Review, 34*(2), 205–228. doi:10.1108/14684521011036954

Lu, Z., Lu, J., & Zhang, J. C. (2002). Website development and evaluation in the Chinese tourism industry. *Networks and Communication Studies, 16*(3/4), 191–208.

Malhotra, Y. (2005). Integrating knowledge management technologies in organizational business processes: Getting real time enterprises to deliver real business performance. *Journal of Knowledge Management, 9*(1), 7–28. doi:10.1108/13673270510582938

*Manila Declaration on World Tourism.* (1980). World tourism conference. Retrieved 2013-04-09, from http://www.univeur.org

McIntosh, R. W., Goeldner, C. R., & Ritchie, J. R. (1995). *Tourism principles, practices, philosophies* (7th ed.). New York: Wiley.

Mihelis, G., Grigoroudis, Siskos, Politis, & Malandrakis. (2001). Customer satisfaction measurement in the private bank sector. *European Journal of Operational Research, 130*(2), 347–360. doi:10.1016/S0377-2217(00)00036-9

Mills, J. E., & Morrison, A. M. (2003). Measuring customer satisfaction with online travel. In A. J. Frew, M. Hitz, & P. O'Connor (Eds.), *Information and communication technologies in tourism* (pp. 11–28). New York: Springer-Wien.

Mintel Group. (2009). *European leisure travel industry - Europe - September 2009*. Online Travel Groups.

Oliver, R. L. (1996). *Satisfaction: A behavioural perspective on the customer*. New York: McGraw-Hill.

Parasuraman, A., Zeithaml, V., & Malhotra, A. (2005). E-S-qual: A multiple-item scale for assessing electronic service quality. *Journal of Service Research, 7*(3), 213–233. doi:10.1177/1094670504271156

Poon, A. (1993). *Tourism, technology and competitive strategies*. Oxford, UK: CAB.

Siskos, J., & Yannacopoulos, D. (1985). Utastar: An ordinal regression method for building additive value functions. *Investigacao Operacional, 5*(1), 39–53.

Siskos, Y., & Grigoroudis, E. (2002). Measuring customer satisfaction for various services using multicriteria analysis. In *Aiding decisions with multiple criteria: Essays in honor of Bernard Roy*. Dordrecht, The Netherlands: Kluwer Academic Publishers. doi:10.1007/978-1-4615-0843-4_20

Szymanski, D., & Hise. (2000). E-satisfaction: An initial examination. *International Journal of Retailing, 3*(76), 309-322.

Szymanski, D., & Hise, R. (2000). E-satisfaction: An initial examination. *Journal of Retailing, 76*(3), 309–322. doi:10.1016/S0022-4359(00)00035-X

Truch, E. (2006). Lean consumption and its influence on brand. *Journal of Consumer Behaviour, 5*, 157–165. doi:10.1002/cb.42

Tse, D. K., & Wilton, P. C. (1988). Models of consumer satisfaction: An extension. *JMR, Journal of Marketing Research, 25*(2), 204–212. doi:10.2307/3172652

UNWTO Technical Manual. (1995). *Collection of tourism expenditure statistics*. World Tourism Organization. Retrieved 2013-04-09, from http://www2.unwto.org

*UNWTO World Tourism Barometer*. (2013). Retrieved 2013-04-09 from http://www2.unwto.org

Vavra, T. G. (1997). *Improving your measurement of customer satisfaction: A guide to creating, conducting, analyzing, and reporting customer satisfaction measurement programs*. Milwaukee, WI: ASQC Quality Press.

Witt, S. F., & Moutinho, L. (Eds.). (1995). *Tourism marketing and management handbook*. London: Prentice Hall.

Zack, M. (1999). Developing a knowledge strategy. *California Management Review, 41*(3), 125–145. doi:10.2307/41166000

## ADDITIONAL READING

Applegate, A., Austin, R., & McFarlan, F. (2003). *Corporate Information Strategy and Management: Text and Cases*. New York: McGraw-Hill.

Bai, B., Law, R., & Wen, I. (2008). The impact of website quality on customer satisfaction and purchase intentions: Evidence from Chinese online visitors. *International Journal of Hospitality Management, 27*, 391–402. doi:10.1016/j.ijhm.2007.10.008

Bennett, M. M., & Lai, C. W. K. (2005). The impact of the internet on travel agencies in Taiwan. *Tourism and Hospitality Research, 6*(1), 8–23. doi:10.1057/palgrave.thr.6040041

Buhalis, D., & Deimezi, O. (2004). E-Tourism developments in Greece: Information communication technologies adoption for the strategic management of the Greek tourism industry. *Tourism and Hospitality Research, 5*(2), 103–130. doi:10.1057/palgrave.thr.6040011

Buhalis, D., & Kaldis, K. (2008). eEnabled internet distribution for small and medium sized hotels: the case of Athens. *Tourism Recreation Research*, *33*(1), 67–81.

Buhalis, D., & Law, R. (2008). Progress in information technology and tourism management: 20 years on and 10 years after the internet — The state of the eTourism research. *Tourism Management*, *29*(4), 609–623. doi:10.1016/j.tourman.2008.01.005

Buswell, D. (1983). Measuring the Quality of In-branch Customer Service. *International Journal of Bank Marketing*, *1*(1), 26–41. doi:10.1108/eb010718

Cai, S., & Jun, M. (2003). Internet users' perceptions of online service quality: a comparison of online buyers and information searchers. *Managing Service Quality*, *13*(6), 504–519. doi:10.1108/09604520310506568

Dwyer, L., Forsyth, P., & Dwyer, W. (2010). *Tourism economics and policy*. Cheltenham: Channel View Publications.

Eklöf, J., & Westlund, A. H. (2002). The pan European customer satisfaction index program. *Total Quality Management*, *13*(8), 1099–1106. doi:10.1080/09544120200000005

Frew, A. J. (Ed.). (2005). Information and Communication Technologies in Tourism. *Proceedings of the International Conference in Innsbruck*. Vienna.

Gronroos, C. (2000). *Service Management and Marketing: A Customer Relationship Management Approach*. England: John and Sons Ltd.

Hashim, N. H., Murphy, J., & Law, R. (2007). A Review of Hospitality Website Design Frameworks. In Proceedings of the International Conference in Ljubljana, Slovenia.

Kao, Y., Louvieris, P., Powell-Perry, J., & Buhalis, D. (2005). E-Satisfaction of NTO's Website Case Study: Singapore Tourism Board's Taiwan Website. In A. Frew (Ed.) *Information and Communication Technologies in Tourism* 2005 — Proceedings of the International Conference in Innsbruck. 227–237. Wien.

Kim, W. G., Ma, X. J., & Kim, D. J. (2006). Determinants of Chinese hotel customers' e-satisfaction and purchase intentions. *Tourism Management*, *27*(5), 890–900. doi:10.1016/j.tourman.2005.05.010

Law, R., Leung, K., & Wong, J. (2004). The impact of the internet on travel agencies. *International Journal of Contemporary Hospitality Management*, *16*(2), 100–107. doi:10.1108/09596110410519982

Mills, J., & Law, R. (Eds.). (2005). *Handbook of Consumer Behaviour, Tourism and the Internet*. Harworth.

Mills, J. E., & Morrison, A. M. (2003). Measuring Customer Satisfaction with Online Travel. *International Federation of Information and Communication Technologies in Tourism 2003 Conference Proceedings*. Helsinki.

O'Connor, P. (1999). *Electronic Information Distribution in Tourism and Hospitality*. Wallingford, CT/Oxford, UK: CAB International.

Papathanassis, A., & Buhalis, D. (2007). Exploring the Information & Communication Technologies Revolution and Visioning the Future of Tourism, Travel and Hospitality Industries. *International Journal of Tourism Research*, *9*(5), 385–387. doi:10.1002/jtr.624

Rayman-Bacchus, L., & Molina, A. (2001). Internet-Based Tourism Services: Business Issues and Trends. *Futures*, *33*(7), 589–605. doi:10.1016/S0016-3287(01)00003-9

Riemenschneider, C., Harrison, D., & Mykytyn, P. (2003). Understanding IT adoption decisions in small business: integrating current theories. *Information & Management*, *40*(4), 233–349. doi:10.1016/S0378-7206(02)00010-1

Vrana, V., & Zafiropoulos, C. (2006). Tourism agents' attitudes on internet adoption: An analysis from Greece. *International Journal of Contemporary Hospitality Management*, *18*(7), 601–608. doi:10.1108/09596110610703039

Watson, R. T., Berthon, P., Pitt, L. F., & Zinkhan, G. M. (2000). *Electronic Commerce The Strategic Perspective*. Fort Worth, TX: Dryden Press.

World Tourism Organization. WTO (2001). E-Business for Tourism — Practical Guidelines for Tourism Destinations and Businesses. Madrid, Spain: The World Tourism Organisation.

World Tourism Organization. WTO. (2012). World tourism barometer. Madrid: UNWTO, Tourism Trends and Marketing Strategies.

Zeithaml, V. A., Parasuraman, A., & Malhotra, A. (2002). Service quality delivery through web sites: A critical review of extant knowledge. *Journal of the Academy of Marketing Science*, *30*(4), 362–375. doi:10.1177/009207002236911

Zhou, Z. (2004). *E-commerce and information technology in hospitality and tourism*. Canada: Delmar.

## KEY TERMS AND DEFINITIONS

**Computer Reservation System's (CRSs):** A computerized system used to store and retrieve information and conduct transactions related to a travel agency.

**Customer Satisfaction:** The degree of satisfaction provided by the goods or services of a company as measured by the number of repeat customers.

**Global Distribution System's (GDSs):** A worldwide computerized reservation network used as a single point of access for reserving airline seats, hotel rooms, rental cars, and other travel related items by travel agents, online reservation sites, and large corporations.

**Information Technology:** The application of computers and telecommunications equipment to store, retrieve, transmit and manipulate data, often in the context of a business or other enterprise.

**Internet:** A global system of interconnected computer networks. It is a network of networks that consists of millions of private, public, academic, business, and government networks.

**On Line Travel Agency:** A web site which specializes in offering planning sources and booking capabilities

**Tourism:** A composite of activities, services, and industries that delivers a travel experience.

# Chapter 9
# Customer Satisfaction and the Role of Demographic Characteristics in Online Banking

**Luc Honore Petnji Yaya**
*Universitat Internacional de Catalunya, Spain*

**Frederic Marimon**
*Universitat Internacional de Catalunya, Spain*

**Marti Casadesus**
*Universitat de Girona, Spain*

## ABSTRACT

*This chapter proposes a model that (1) analyzes the direct and indirect effects of e-service quality on satisfaction and value with the moderating/mediating role of value as well as (2) analyzes the positive impact of gender, age, education, and income on quality, satisafaction, and value. The overall results show service quality is a major predictor of perceived value, which in turn is positively related to customer satisfaction. The mediating/moderating role of perceived value on the relationship between service quality and satisfaction is confirmed. Contrary to the proposed hypothesis, no relationships and no differences in the various subgroups categories of age, education, and income are detected in terms of service quality, value, and satisfaction. Consequently, customers' demographic characteristics limitation on the adoption of online banking is now a past history. However, the authors recommend that managers always consider each segment of the customers' demographic profiles individually while making their decisions.*

## INTRODUCTION

In the increasingly competitive and changing world of online services, customer satisfaction management has emerged as a strategic imperative for most companies. It is extremely important that online service providers know how to improve customer satisfaction. Since, it was shown that managers who aim at merely satisfying rather than completely satisfying customers run the

DOI: 10.4018/978-1-4666-5129-6.ch009

risk of undermining customer retention (Mittal and Kamakura, 2001). Moreover, it is costly to recruit new customers and between 65% and 85% of existing customers who defect to a competitor confesses to being either satisfied or very satified with the product or service they left (Reichheld and Schefter, 2000). Drawing on that, some authors have frequently emphasized the need to examine ways to increase customers satisfaction levels and the internet consumer acquisition decision (Parasuraman et al., 2005; Al-Hawari & Ward, 2006; Herington and Weaven, 2009). Obviously, understanding these antecedents can help online service provider to gain competitive advantages by implementing specific strategies to increase customer satisfaction. Given that higher levels of customer satisfaction reduces customers' perceptions of the potential benefits of alternative suppliers and enhances repurchase intentions with the present supplier (Ribbink et 2004; Petnji et al., 2011).

Moreover, previous research also evidenced that customer satisfaction is crucial in realizing desired outcomes such as customer loyalty and customer retention which in turn enhance business profitability (Oliver, 2010, Kotler & Armstrong, 2010). However, online service providers are particularly alarmed about achieving customer satisfaction to make their business tactics successful. They tend to search for resources and capacities on which to based their competitive strategies while taking into account their customers´satisfaction and needs (Martinez-Ruiz, 2012).

Furthermore, the concepts of service quality and customer perceived value are fundamental to successful business because they are crucial to costumers' decisions making. Particularly in the context where online service consumers are becoming more and more knowledgeable and are willing to share their experiences through social media (Petnji et al., 2012) and online competitors are only a mouse click away (Marimon et al., 2012). Yet, Day, (2002) argued that the theoretical

relationship between value and other key marketing constructs such as consumer satisfaction are not fully understood. This is perhaps because related research on the issue in the field remains largely speculative. Therefore, the question that then arises for online service provider is the extent to which satisafction depends on antecedents such as customer online service quality and perceived value. Particularly while considering the moderating/mediating effects of customer perceived value

In addition, it was reported that early internet users were primarily middle-aged or younger and had less purchasing power than those who were older (e.g Bigne et al., 2005 and Zhou et al., 2007). Moreover, early researchers such as Donthu and Garcia (1999) argued that there is no significant age difference among online shoppers and that online shoppers were older than traditional store shoppers. Likewise, Zhou et al., (2007) did a review of litterature on online shopping acceptance and concluded that the age gap between online and non-online consumers is diminishing, but the effect of age and education on consumers' intention to purchase online remains unclear. Thus, it was also apparent the necessity to ascertain or not that some demographic characteristics such as gender, age, education and income are factors that may influences customer satisafaction and perception of service offer in online banking. Against this backgrounds, the main objectives of this study were two folds:

- To propose and empirically analyse an integrated model that may shed some light to the direct and indirect effects of e-service quality on satisfaction with customer perceived value as a modiator/mediator.
- To examine both the positive impact and any segment differences of customer demographic characteristics in terms of customer service quality, custome satisfaction and perceive value.

The remainder of this chapter is organized as follows. The next section start with some brief literature review on the topic and the development of the study hypotheses. Thereafter, the methodology used are described followed by the study results. The paper closed with the conclusions and some managerial implications.

## BACKGROUND AND MAIN FOCUS OF THE CHAPTER

### Relatioship between Customer Service Quality and Satisafction

According to (Marimon et al., 2012) online service quality in an online banking setting can be defined as the extent to which a web site facilitates efficient and effective online operation/transaction and delivery of product and services. Conversely, customer satisfaction is generally understood as a process of evaluating a product or service after consumption to discover whether customer's expectations have been met or even exceeded. In that sens Oliver, (2010) defined customer satisfaction as customer reaction to the state of fulfilment, and customer judgment of the fulfilled state. Meaning that when customer's expectations are exceeded, they are highly satisfied. On the other hand, if the customer's expectations are not met, then they will feel dissatisfied with the service (Kotler & Armstrong, 2010).

Thus far, a thorough understanding of service quality and its role as antecedent of customer satisfaction in the banking sector has remained elusive. For example, Saurina and Coenders (2002), argued that satisfaction and quality are the same construct in the context of traditional banking services in Spain. Since, customers seem not to perceive the minor differences between the conceptual definitions of both concepts as given by marketing theoreticians. In this respect, the authors concluded that discussion regarding whether satisfaction precedes quality or the other way around seems to be meaningless. On the other hand, Herington and Weaven, 2009, Petnji et al., (2011) found e-service quality to be predictor of overall customer satisfaction with banking performance. Moreover, Al-Hawari & Ward (2006) investigated the automated banking service quality dimensions and the results of the study revealed the positive effects of e-service quality on customer satisfaction and that customer satisfaction contributed towards improved financial performance of banks.

Although the precise nature of the interaction between service quality and customer satisfaction is notoriously elusive in the banking sector, several studies indicate an emerging consensus that service quality is a key determinant of customer satisfaction (Petnji et al., 2011; Al-Hawari and Ward, 2006). This has also been established in other online environment. For example where Ribbink et al., (2004) confirmed a direct link between service quality and satisfaction of actual consumers of online books and CD stores.

Furthermore, according to Cronin and Taylor, (1992), customers do not principally purchase the superior quality service, but may also take into account situational factors such as price, convenience, and availability that may directly impact on satisfaction while not having an influence on customers perceived service quality. Consequently, satisfaction appears to be a broader and more inclusive concept that is based upon perceived service quality and other factors (Oliver, 2010). Moreover, banks products or services offered to customers are in general relatively standardized in nature. As matter of this fact, banks are feeling an increasing need to differentiate themselves from the competitors on criteria such as perceived service quality that can positively affect customer satisfaction, loyalty and consequently bank performance. Therefore, it was anticipated that:

**H1:** Online service qaulity positively and directly affect customer satisfaction.

## Relationship between Customer Perceived Quality and Perceived Value

According to Woodruff and Flint (2006), customer perceived value is a customer´s judgement about the goodness or badness of an expereince, a perceptual state of being. Quite likely, customers could hold multiple judgement of value regarding a product or service offering simultaneously. The litterature recognizes this possibility by refering to value as the trade-offs that customers makes between positive (e.g. benefits) versus negative (e.g. sacrifices) value judgement (Day, 2002). In that sens, Zeithaml (1988) conceptualized perceived value as the consumer's overall assessment of the utility of a product based on the perceptions of what is received and what is given. The competitive advantage of successful service providers and retailers is often explained with a logic. Wherein service quality contributes to customer value, resulting from an increase customer satisfaction and behavioral intentions. Eventually creating loyalty that manifests itself and enhance profitability (Rintamaki et al., 2007). In general, most scholars regard quality as antecedent to perceived value and as a significant variable with strong influence on customers' natural behavior. For example, Parasuraman and Grewal (2000) argued that service quality is a logical driver of perceived value and even in instances where the buyer-seller exchange involves a physical product, superior pre-sale and post-sale service rendered by the seller can add to the perceived value.

More recently, Fuentes-Blasco (2010) and Petnji et al., (2013) found in their research that value is largely defined by perceptions of service quality. According to their studies, service consumers place greater importance on the quality of the service than they do on the costs associated. Besides, Akinci et al., (2010) appraised the electronic service quality offered by 13 banks in Turkey, providing a refined and more stable version of the E-S-QUAL scale for the internet banks. They found that service quality have a strong direct effects with the overall perceived value construct. In the same vein (Marimon et al., 2012) indicated as well that service quality has an important role in the development of perceived value in the online environment. According to the authors, e-consumers expect equal or higher levels of service quality than customers in traditional brick-and-mortar. Hence, when online shoppers perceive high e-service quality, they will exhibit high customer perceived value and become a loyal customer. Therefore, this study posited that:

**H2:** Service quality direcly and positively affects customer perceived value.

## Relationship between Perceived Value and Satisafction

The concept of value is fundamental to successful business because value is believed to be essential to consumer decision making. According to Day (2002), customers viewed value somewhat differently depending on whether a purchase involved a product or service and on the type of product or service. In addition, the author argued that assessing service value is more difficult than assessing product value. Since value is not always considered in consummers' choices and consumers' expectations greatly influence value assessments. However, as we explained before, customer value can be considered a cognition based construct capturing any discrepancy between benefits and sacrifices, whereas customer satisfaction is primarily an affective and evaluative response (Oliver, 2010). Moreover, the social science literature specifies that cognitive thought processes trigger affective responses, suggesting that customer value judgments affect perceptions of satisfaction (Lam et al., 2004).

According to Spiteri and Dion (2004), perceived value is an antecedent of overall satisfaction and that management can improve customer value rating by increasing the effectiveness of appropriate antecedents. Moreover, based on the American Customer Satisfaction Model, Bontis et al., (2007) showed that perceived value had a positive direct effect on customer satisfaction which in turn was positively related to loyalty, reputation, and recommendation in the North American banks. Furthermore, Oliver and DeSarbo (1988), proposed an equity model of satisafaction that considers the ratio of the customers' perceived outcome to input to that of the service provider's outcome to input. They argued that satisafction results when customers faith they are being treated fairly in an exchange and that costumers perceives that the outcome-to input ratio is fair and equitable. This outcome-to input ratio perspective is equivalent to the costs versus benefits definition of value by Zeithaml, (1988), which further suggests that value is an antecedent of costumer satisfaction. Therefore, we anticipated that

**H3:** Perceived service value directly and positively affects customer satisfaction.
**H4:** Perceived value mediate/moderate the effects of service quality on customer satisfaction.

## Demographic Characteristics

According to Ganesan-Lim et al., (2008) study in the traditional services, women were more in favor of shopping activities because they were usually in charge of the household shopping and hold more positive attitudes towards the traditional store in addition to catalogue shopping than their male counterparts. Moreover, based on the same level of the average satisfacction Mittal and Kamakura (2001) argued that subjects with higher education tend to have lower levels of retention than those with a high school education or less. The authors further agued that the probability of repurchase among women was uniformaly higher than among men and that older customers repurchase probality is higher. In addition, they may have stable preferences than younger consumers.

However, the new shopping channel provided by the internet seems to result in a different, if not opposite pattern. E.g. early researches such as Donthu and Garcia (1999) showed that men were found to make more purchases and spend more money online than women. Furthermore, they indicated that there were no significant difference of age among online shoppers. Besides, online shoppers were older than traditional store shoppers and tend to earn more money. In addition, Zhou et al., (2007) conducted a review of the existing litterature on online shopping and argued that nowadays the age gap between online and non-online consumers is fading, and that the effect of age on consumers' intention to purchase online remains unclear. Their findings further show that income is positively related to online shopping tendency. However, they argued that education level produces mixed effects ranging from no effect to a positive effect.

Furthermore, Ganesan-Lim et al., (2008) argued that it is of paramount importance to understand the relationship between the customer's perception of service quality and demographic information such as age, gender, education and income level. Obviously, this information may be useful for safeguarding that there are suitable products and services a vailable for the target market. According to Kotler & Armstrong (2010) demographic characteristics are an acceptable basis of segmenting customers and markets. Since, there has been an increase in educated people which may lead to an increase in the demand for quality products. Moreover, Meng et al (2009) argued that customers with different demographic characteristics such as income level shop at different stores which further indicate that they might be differences in the perception of service quality, customer satisfaction and value based on income level. Based on these backgrounds, we hypothesized that

**H5:** Demographic characteristics such as gender, age, education, income are positively related to service quality, customer satisfaction and value.

In order to find evidence from the survey study to support the literature review and the hypotheses, a model that identified the key constructs included in this research was proposed (see Figure 1). The framework presents customer satisfaction as a consequence of direct/ indirect relationships with service quality and perceived value, as well as the direct effects of demographic characteristics on all the constructs.

## METHODOLOGY

### Questionnaire Design

To examine the associations between the constructs and to test the hypotheses mentioned above a structured questionnaire was specially designed for the study. The construct of e-SQ was measured using an adapted version of the original E-S-QUAL proposed by Parasuraman et al., (2005). Three items FUL2, FUL4, and FUL5 from the fulfilment dimension were deleted as they

referred to the physical delivery of goods deemed not relevant in the present case of online banking. Also, this study adopted the construct of perceived value from Parasuraman et al., (2005) and the the construct of satisfaction was evaluated using four items borrowed from Ribbink et al. (2004) with minor alterations. All the items were assessed on a five-point Likert-type scale (1 = 'strongly disagree'; 5 = 'strongly agree').

## Sample and Data Collection

The online banking users sample was drawn from a database maintained by Spanish banks. We first set a random starting point, thereafter, we selected every fiftieth individual customer in succession. Based on that technique, 1600 potential respondents were selected. An e-mail invitation was then send to each potential respondent and those agreeing to participate were directed to a specific website containing the structured questionnaire, which they then self-administered. The data collection was completed from March to May 2010. After deleting some incomplete or invalid questionnaires, a total of 428 usable responses representing a response rate of 26.75% were reatined.

*Figure1. Satisfaction model*

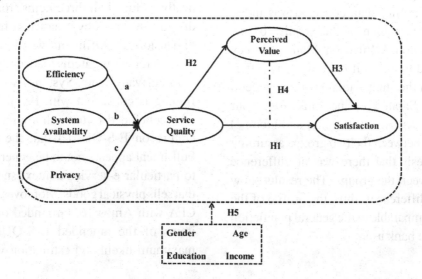

*Table 1. Summary of the demographic characteristics sample*

| Demographic Profiles | | n | % |
|---|---|---|---|
| Gender | Female | 225 | 52,6 |
| | Male | 203 | 47,4 |
| Age | 17-24 | 106 | 24,8 |
| | 25-34 | 150 | 35,0 |
| | 35-44 | 102 | 23,8 |
| | 45 and above | 70 | 16,4 |
| Education | College or institute diploma and below | 102 | 23,8 |
| | University degree | 196 | 45,8 |
| | Master degree and above | 91 | 21,3 |
| | Others | 39 | 9,1 |
| Annual income (€) | Less than 12,000 | 134 | 31,3 |
| | 12,001-24,000 | 148 | 34,6 |
| | 24,001 and above | 146 | 34,1 |

A summary of the demographic characteristics of the respondents is presented in Table 1. The results show no gender bias was detected and two-thirds of the respondents were aged less than 34 years. The educational level of the sample was high, with more than two-thirds of the sample having at least a university degree. A large majority (65.9%) of the respondents earned an annual income of less than €24,000. Evidently to meet external validity conditions, it was essential to verified that the final data collected was indisputably a representation of the Spanish online banking population. A Wilcoxon–Mann–Whitney tests were used to assess if there was any differences between the study sample and the general population of Sapnish online bank user. Four contrasts (Gender, Age, Education and Income) were assessed between the two groups assuming a null hypothesis that there was no difference of means between the groups. The results show no statistical differences, thus, the profile of the sample was comparable to the general population Spanish online bank users.

# RESULTS

## Scale to Assess E-Service Quality

In this study, identification of underlying factors was done through both Exploratory Factor Analysis (EFA) and Confirmatory Factor Analysis (CFA). Because the E-S-QUAL scales adopted in this study was originally developed to evaluate service quality of e-retailing that sales physical goods different from those offering pure services and principally e-banking. This study first performed EFA to determine the sets of items that hang together using SPSS 19 software package. The study adopted the normalised varimax as the rotation method (Hair et al., 1998) and the Kaiser criteria of eigenvalues greater than 1 to determine the initial number of factors to retain. The overall results showed the Kaiser-Meyer-Olkin (KMO) measure was 0.935 and Bartlett's sphericity test was 5,125.3 with $Df = 171$ and $P < 0.001$. Only three dimensions, which accounted for 64.11% of the variance (see Table 2).

The first factor was labelled "Efficiency" and it gathered seven out of eight original items from efficiency. The second factor was labelled "system availability" and it was composed of the original four items of system availability, one item of efficiency and two items of fulfilment dimension. The final factor was labelled "Privacy" and it neatly included all three items from the original dimension of privacy. Please note that the original dimension of "Fulfilment" was discarded because the two remaining items loaded poorly an equally in "Privacy" and "System Availability". This finding is consistent with Petnji et al., (2012), who concluded (after a thorough review of literature on E-S-QUAL) that the dimension of Fulfilment appears not to be generic but specific to particular e-service context such as web site that sells physical goods. Moreover, we performed CFA with Amos 16. Grounded on the retained items of the amended E-S-QUAL, a robust maximum-likelihood estimation was used. The

*Table 2. Measurement items in their corresponding factors*

| Factors | CFA Loadings [a] | | EFA Loadings [b] | | |
|---|---|---|---|---|---|
| | Loadings | t-value [c] | 1 | 2 | 3 |
| **Efficiency (α = 0.91, AVE= 0.64)** | | | | | |
| EFF1: It is easy to find what I need | 0.81 | 41.69 | .78 | | |
| EFF2:It is easy to get anywhere | 0.81 | 44.51 | .77 | | |
| EFF3:It enables me to complete a transaction quickly | 0.72 | 25.68 | .60 | | |
| EFF4:Information at this site is well organized | 0.83 | 52.87 | .77 | | |
| EFF6:This site is simple to use | 0.81 | 39.12 | .74 | | |
| EFF7:This site enables me to get on to it quickly | 0.76 | 35.71 | .61 | | |
| EFF8:This site is well organized | 0.87 | 67.93 | .80 | | |
| **System Availability (α = 0.89, AVE= 0.60)** | | | | | |
| SAV1: This site is always available for business | 0.73 | 25.17 | | .74 | |
| SAV2: This site launches and runs right away | 0.86 | 56.27 | | .78 | |
| SAV3: This site does not crash | 0.79 | 30.59 | | .82 | |
| SAV4: The pages site does not freeze | 0.78 | 31.53 | | .64 | |
| FUL1: This performs orders when promised | 0.76 | 34.83 | | .55 | |
| FUL2: It quickly delivers what I order | 0.83 | 54.39 | | .64 | |
| EFF5: This site loads its pages faster | 0.68 | 17.62 | | .55 | |
| **Privacy (α = 0.89, AVE= 0.82)** | | | | | |
| PRI1: It protect information and my online behaviour | 0.89 | 65.54 | | | .834 |
| PRI2: It does not share my personal information | 0.90 | 63.05 | | | .857 |
| PRI3: It protects my credit and debit information | 0.92 | 105.25 | | | .845 |
| **Satisfaction(α = 0.92, AVE= 0.80)** | | | | | |
| ESA1: I am generally pleased with the site | 0.89 | 76.55 | | | |
| ESA2: The site is enjoyable | 0.84 | 45.98 | | | |
| ESA3: I am very satisfied with this site services | 0.93 | 112.72 | | | |
| ESA4: I am happy with this site | 0.92 | 118.86 | | | |
| **Perceived Value(α = 0.83, AVE= 0.67)** | | | | | |
| PVA1: The prices and services are economical | 0.75 | 32.06 | | | |
| PVA2: Overall, this site is convenient to use | 0.87 | 74.12 | | | |
| PVA3: This site gives me a feeling of being in control | 0.75 | 26.87 | | | |
| PVA4: This site provides value for money and effort | 0.88 | 80.62 | | | |

*continued on following page*

*Table 2. Continued*

| Factors | CFA Loadings [a] | | EFA Loadings [b] | | |
|---|---|---|---|---|---|
| | Loadings | t-value [c] | 1 | 2 | 3 |
| **Goodness of Fit Indices [d]** | | | | | |
| | Service Quality Model | | Satisfaction Model | | |
| χ2/df | 2.56 | | 2.16 | | |
| GFI | 0.92 | | 0.90 | | |
| NFI | 0.93 | | 0.92 | | |
| CFI | 0.96 | | 0.95 | | |
| RMSEA | 0.60 | | 0.50 | | |

Note: CFA=Confirmatory Factor Analysis; EFA= Exploratory Factor Analysis; GFI= Goodness-of-Fit Index CFI= Comparative Fit Index; NFI= Non-normed Fit Index; RMSEA= Root Mean Square Error of Approximation; a: The CFA are the PLS output loadings; b: EFA are the SPSS output loadings. Total variance extracted by the three factors equal 64.11%; Rotation: Varimax normalized; The Kaiser-Meyer-Olkin (KMO) measure = 0.935; Bartlett's sphericity test = 5,125.3; df = 171 with a significance of $p < 0.001$; c: all t-value are significant at $P < 0.001$; d: the model fit was computed based on AMOS software package

results of the quality model presented at the bottom of the Table 2 indicated that global fit indices were within the acceptable level (Hu & Bentler, 1999).

## Structural Equation Modelling (SEM)

Before checking the causal model, it was necessary to check their validity in the current context by performing tests of internal consistency, convergent validity, and discriminant validity. First, we computed the internal consistency of the dimensions. The results evidenced a considerable degree of internal consistency for all the dimensions. Since, the Cronbach's alpha for the constructs ranged from 0.83 "Perceived Value" to 0.91 "Efficiency" (see Table 3), which exceeded

the generally accepted minimum level of 0.7 (Nunnally & Bernstein, 1994).

Moreover, the average variance extracted (AVE) for every scale (see Table 2 and 3) was greater than the recommended value of 0.5 (Fornell and Larcker, 1981) and each individual item's coefficient was more than double the value of its standard error, reflecting that the items represent their underlying construct . Therefore, the measurement scales were considered to possess high-internal consistency and reliability among the items.

We further assessed the satisfactoriness of the measurement scales by evaluating the reliability of the individual items with PLS software package. As shown in Table 2, the loadings of items on their respective constructs confirmed the three dimen-

*Table 3. Hypotheses results for the structural model*

| | AVE | Composite Reliability | R Square | Cronbach's Alpha | Communality | Redundancy |
|---|---|---|---|---|---|---|
| Efficiency | 0.64 | 0.93 | | 0.91 | 0.64 | |
| Perceived Value | 0.67 | 0.89 | 0.52 | 0.83 | 0.67 | 0.22 |
| Privacy | 0.82 | 0.93 | | 0.89 | 0.82 | |
| Satisfaction | 0.80 | 0.94 | 0.72 | 0.92 | 0.80 | 0.27 |
| System Availability | 0.60 | 0.91 | | 0.89 | 0.60 | |

sions of the modified E-S-QUAL and revealed a high degree of individual item reliability. Since all the items have loadings greater than 0.5 in their respective constructs (Sanzo et al., 2003). Moreover, the validity of individual items in relation to the relevant factors was confirmed by load values greater than 0.707 (Carmines & Zeller, 1979), with the exception of item 'EFF 5', which was slightly lower (0.68). However, because it was so close to the threshold, it was decided to retain this item. Besides, each factor loadings of the confirmatory model were found to be statistically significant (P< 0.001) and greater than 0.5 (Sanzo et al., 2003). The evidence of the EFA and CFA, taken together, supported the convergent validity of the component dimensions of the proposed scales.

Additionally, discriminant validity, which confirms that every factor represents a distinct dimension, was examined through linear correlations or standardized covariance between latent factors by examining whether inter factor correlations are less than the square root of the average variance extracted (Fornell and Larker, 1981). Table 4 shows that the square root of the AVE, emphasized in bold italic, was greater than the correlations presented by each construct with other constructs. Besides, the correlation coefficients were less than 1 by an amount greater than twice their respective standard errors (Ribbink et al., 2004). Taken as a whole, these evidences supported the discriminant validity of the items as measures of their respective underlying constructs.

## Causal Estimates of the Relationship between Factors

After screening the distribution of the data for normality it was evidenced that most variables were slightly off-centre. Thus, this study proposed structural model was estimated by means of Partial Least Squares (PLS version 2.0). Since, PLS makes no assumptions regarding the distribution of the variables and ensure optimal prediction accuracy (Fornell and Cha., 1994). Moreover, it has superior capabilities that brand it more suitable than other methods when examining small sample sizes and it was shown to be very robust against multicollinearity (Cassel et al., 2000).

We computed the goodness-of-fit index by taking into account both the explained variances for the latent dependent variables and their commonalities. The results showed a superior fit (GoF = 0.68) as proposed by Tenenhaus et al. (2004). Moreover, a simple routine test of the fit indices of the satisfaction model based on AMOS software package (see Table 2) further confirmed decent goodness of fit indices according to Hu & Bentler, (1999) benchmarks. Furthermore, PLS analysis showed the model explained between 52 and 72% of the variance of each independent variable (see Table 3). In addition, the index of variance for endogenous variables explained by the path was more than 0.015 (see Table 5). Based on the model performance statistics, it can be concluded that the suggested model demonstrated an acceptable fit to the data and the hypothesized relationships were tested.

*Table 4. Correlation matrix and square root of the average variance extracted*

|  | Mean | SD | 1 | 2 | 3 | 4 | 5 |
|---|---|---|---|---|---|---|---|
| 1. Efficiency | 3.93 | 0.70 | *0.80* | | | | |
| 2. Perceived Value | 3.72 | 0.74 | 0.64 | *0.82* | | | |
| 3. Privacy | 4.21 | 0.80 | 0.48 | 0.56 | *0.91* | | |
| 4. Satisfaction | 3.95 | 0.76 | 0.72 | 0.73 | 0.66 | *0.89* | |
| 5. System Availability | 3.99 | 0.67 | 0.69 | 0.62 | 0.53 | 0.69 | *0.77* |

**Notes:** Square Root of AVE are in **bold italic font style** on the main diagonal and correlations between latent variables follow below; all correlations were significant at the P<0.01 level (two-tailed)

*Table 5. Hypotheses results for the first and second order structural model*

| | Hypothesis | Path coefficient | SE[a] | t-value | P-value | Conclusion |
|---|---|---|---|---|---|---|
| H2a | Efficiency -> Perceived value | 0.35 | 0.05 | 7.69 | 0.000 | Accepted*** |
| H1a | Efficiency -> Satisfaction | 0.28 | 0.04 | 7.30 | 0.000 | Accepted*** |
| H3 | Perceived value -> Satisfaction | 0.29 | 0.04 | 7.39 | 0.000 | Accepted*** |
| H2c | Privacy -> Perceived value | 0.26 | 0.04 | 7.23 | 0.000 | Accepted*** |
| H1c | Privacy -> Satisfaction | 0.26 | 0.03 | 7.62 | 0.000 | Accepted*** |
| H2b | System Availabili -> Perceived value | 0.22 | 0.05 | 5.00 | 0.000 | Accepted*** |
| H1b | System Availability -> Satisfaction | 0.17 | 0.04 | 4.53 | 0.000 | Accepted*** |
| H2 | Service Quality -> Perceived Value | 0.71 | 0.03 | 27.36 | 0.000 | Accepted*** |
| H1 | Service Quality ->Satisfaction | 0.58 | 0.02 | 14.30 | 0.000 | Accepted*** |

a: Standard Error; Significant at two tail: (*) P-value < 0.05; (* *) P-value <0.01and (***) P-value < 0.001

The significance of the paths of the inner model was computed by using bootstrapping based on 2,000 re-samples to ascertain the steadiness and the statistical significance of the parameter estimates. Table 5 summarizes the results of the hypothesis testing. The overall results showed that all the hypotheses were totally supported. As expected, hypothesis H3 predicting the positive impact of perceived value on satisfaction was significantly supported. Furthermore hypotheses H1 and H2, predicting a positive influence of perceived online service quality on value and satisfaction were unambiguously supported. Since, all three online service quality dimensions loaded as first order constructs and overall service quality as second order were significantly related to customer satisfaction and value. Moreover, efficiency and privacy were the strongest predictor of both value and satisfaction.

To test H4, we first analysed the moderation interaction of service quality and perceived value on customer satisfaction. The overall results of the PLS analysis confirmed the moderating role of perceived value (P-value < 0.001). Consequently, an increase of service quality perception will positively increase the relationship potency of value on satisfaction.

In addition Table 3 showed a squared multiple coefficient for online perceived value was 52% (p <.000), indicating that a large segment of variation in online satisfaction is accounted for by online service quality. As we hypothesized, then, we tested the indirect effects of service quality to satisfaction through value based on Sobel tests. Since, the Sobel tests of the direct effects can address mediation more directly than a series of separate significance tests not directly involving the indirect effect found in the mediation model (Preacher and Hayes, 2004).The results showed the t-static was equal to 199.47 corresponding to P < 0.001. Hence, indicating that value mediate the effect of service quality on customer satisfaction. However, although the direct effects of service quality on satisfaction has decreased in strength, it was still significant indicating that there was only partial mediation.

To test hypothesis H5 we first set service quality, customer satisfaction and perceived value factors as dependent variables and the manifest variables of gender, age, education and income as independent variables. Thereafter, we did multi-regression analysis to identify if there were any relationships between the independent and the dependent variables. The overall results show only gender was positively related to service quality

($R^2 = 0.17$; $P < 0.01$) and satisfaction ($R^2 = 0.23$; $P < 0.05$). In addition, independently of the multi-regression results, the sample was also subjected to the T-student and Kruskall-Wallis tests to detect any interaction effects between variables, as well as identifying among the subcategories if there were any mean differences (see Table 6).

The overall results further confirmed that age, education and income are not factors that can influence customers' perception of service quality, customer satisfaction and perceived value in an online banking setting. The results also confirmed that gender was positively related to quality and satisfaction. However, an in-depth analysis shows only 12% of female have different view on EFF7 and PRI1 variables than men, and 16% have different view on PRI3 variable. More specifically, the small group of female who caused the gender differences were generally pleased with their online bank website as they do not shows their online banking behaviour as well as protecting information about their credit and debit cards.

These findings were consistent with the study of Bigne et al. (2005) who found that men and women did not significantly show different behaviours in shopping purchasing decision through the mobile technology in Spain. According to the review of literature in online shopping acceptance model, Zhou et al., (2007) established that women have a higher-level of web apprehensiveness and are more sceptical of e-business than men. Nevertheless, they concluded that the effect of age on consumers' intention to purchase online remains unclear. Likewise, Ganesan-Lim et al., (2008) also found no differences in the perception of service quality based on gender.

However, the extant literature indicates that some studies found different results. For example, according to Mittal and Kamakura (2001), consumers with higher education have greater ability to search and are aware of superior alternative in the market. Moreover, Spathis et al., (2004) argued that male customer of Greek banks have a more positive perception of the quality of service they receive than women. Also in contrast to this

*Table 6. The effects of demographic characteristics subcategories on latent factors*

| | | Mean | SD [a] | chi | Df | P-value[b] |
|---|---|---|---|---|---|---|
| **Kruskall-Wallis Tests** | | | | | | |
| Income | Service Quality | 4.04 | 0.62 | 2.38 | 4 | 0.66 |
| | Satisfaction | 3.95 | 0.76 | 3.25 | 4 | 0.51 |
| | Perceived Value | 3.72 | 0.74 | 1.93 | 4 | 0.74 |
| Education | Service Quality | 4.04 | 0.62 | 6.32 | 4 | 0.17 |
| | Satisfaction | 3.95 | 0.76 | 4.46 | 4 | 0.34 |
| | Perceived Value | 3.72 | 0.74 | 8.77 | 4 | 0.06 |
| Age | Service Quality | 4.04 | 0.62 | 4.09 | 5 | 0.53 |
| | Satisfaction | 3.95 | 0.76 | 4.47 | 5 | 0.48 |
| | Perceived Value | 3.72 | 0.74 | 3.03 | 5 | 0.69 |
| **T-student Tests** | | Mean | SD | F-value | MD[c] | P-value |
| Gender | Service Quality | 4.04 | 0.62 | 5.64 | 0.15 | 0.01 |
| | Satisfaction | 3.95 | 0.76 | 0.89 | 0.15 | 0.03 |
| | Perceived Value | 3.72 | 0.74 | 5.36 | 0.06 | 0.37 |

a: Standard Deviation; b: P-value < 0.05 is significant; c: Mean Difference study, Sum & Hui, (2009) argued that customers with high income might favour traditional retailers with high levels of service quality while customers with low incomes might be more tolerant to lower levels of service quality in Hong-Kong. This view was further emphasized by Meng et al., (2009) who found that Chinese consumers shop at different stores based on their income level. Thus, implicating that income level might be a source of discrepancies in the perception of service quality, value and satisfaction in China. In the same vein, Homburg and Giering (2001) found income has a relationship with purchasing decisions and that high income customers gather information prior to buying a product which may have an influence on satisfaction. The author further argued that age and income are found to be important moderators of the satisfaction–loyalty relationship.

## CONCLUSION AND RECOMMENDATIONS

This study proposed a satisfaction model that analysed the direct effects of online service quality and perceived value on customer satisfaction, as well as, assessed the indirect effects of quality on satisfaction with value as a mediator/moderator. In addition, this study also analysed the impact of demographic characteristics such as gender, age, education and income on customer perceived service quality, value and satisfaction. The overall results showed that perceived service quality is major predictor of both customer satisfaction and perceived value. However, the relationship strength between the online perceived service quality and perceived value was as twice as stronger than with satisfaction. Moreover, all the three service quality dimensions of efficiency, system availability and privacy have direct positive effects on both satisfaction and value. In addition, the pattern of the relationships between the three service quality dimensions on both customer satisfaction and value were similar. Efficiency was

the strongest predictors followed by privacy and system availability. These findings were consistent with (Ribbink et al., 2004, Parasuraman et al., 2005, Herington and Weaven, 2009; Petnji et al., 2011; Marimon et al., 2012) who also find service quality was directly and positively related to value and satisfaction.

This study also found that customer perceived value is positively related to customer satisfaction, in addition to moderating the effects of service quality on satisfaction. Consequently, an increase of service quality perception will positively increase the relationship strength of customer perceived value on satisfaction. Moreover, based on the Sobel tests, this study also show that value partially mediates the effects of quality on satisfaction. The direct effects of value on satisfaction are consistent with Spiteri and Dion (2004) and Bontis et al., (2007) who also found a positive relationship.

Finally, this study examined whether the demographic characteristics of gender, age, education and income have any influences on the relationships between service quality, value and satisfaction. Contrary to the proposed hypotheses, no relationships and no differences in the various subgroups categories of age, education and income were detected in terms of quality, value and satisfaction. However, the demographic characteristic of gender was positively related to both customer satisfaction and service quality. Nonetheless, a thorough analysis showed that less than 16% of female were among those creating the differences. In order words there were no significant differences for the majority of 84% of the overall sample. These findings agreed with Bigne et al., (2005) and Petnji et al., (2012) who argued that the use of internet is becoming growingly widespread and online consumers are becoming more and more knowledgeable.

The findings of this study can be used as a basis for planning efforts to increase customer satisfaction. For example, to optimize customers' satisfaction, we advise managers to maximize performance on attributes such as efficiency, privacy and value that have the strongest strength in determining satisfaction in online banking. Moreover, contrary to the general thought and previous studies who argued that online banking was limited to middle aged customers, require higher education and/or higher income. The outcomes of this study evidenced that online banking is now a relatively easy task for customers. Since, customers' demographic characteristics limitation on the adoption of online banking is now a past history. However, we advised managers to consider each segment of the customers' demographic profiles individually. Because firms may segment customers according to the value potential they represent for the company and allocate more resources where necessary to improve satisfaction and avoid any potential defection.

## ACKNOWLEDGMENT

This article was written as part of a research project entitled "Comparative study between English and Spanish e-banking consumers (ref: TIN2011-13075-E)" financed by the Ministry of Economy and Competitiveness within the aid subprogram of complementary actions to research no orientated.

## REFERENCES

Akinci, S., Atilgan-Ina, E., & Aksoy, S. (2010). Reassessment of E-S-Qual and E-RecS-QUAL in a pure service setting. *Journal of Business Research*, *63*, 232–240. doi:10.1016/j.jbusres.2009.02.018

Al-Hawari, M., & Ward, T. (2006). The effect of automated service quality on Australian banks' financial performance and the mediating role of customer satisfaction. *Marketing Intelligence & Planning*, *24*(2), 127–147. doi:10.1108/02634500610653991

Bigné, E., Ruiz, C., & Sanz, S. (2005). The impact of internet user shopping patterns and demographics on consumer mobile buying behaviour. *Journal of Electronic Commerce Research*, *6*(3).

Bontis, N., Booker, L. D., & Serenko, A. (2007). The mediating effect of organizational reputation on customer loyalty and service recommendation in the banking industry. *Management Decision*, *45*(9), 1426–1445. doi:10.1108/00251740710828681

Carme, S., & Germà, C. (2002). *Predicting overall service quality: A structural equation modelling approach*. in Ferligoj, A. and Mrvar, A. (Eds), Developments in Social Science Methodology, Metodolos ki Zvezki, FDV, Ljubljana, pp. 217-38.

Carmines, E. G., & Zeller, R. A. (1979). *Reliability and validity assessment (Stage university paper series on quantitative applications in the social sciences, no. 7010)*. Beverly Hills, CA: Sage.

Cassel, C. M., Hackl, P., & Westlund, A. H. (2000). On measurement of intangible assets: A study of robustness of partial least squares. *Total Quality Management*, *11*(7), S897–S907. doi:10.1080/09544120050135443

Cronin, J. J., & Taylor, S. A. (1992). Measuring service quality: A re-examination and extension. *Journal of Marketing*, *56*, 55–68. doi:10.2307/1252296

Day, E. (2002). The role of value in consumer satisfaction. *Journal of Consumer Satisfaction. Dissatisfaction and Complaining Behavior*, *15*, 22–32.

Donthu, N., & Garcia, A. (1999). The internet shopper. *Journal of Advertising Research*, *39*(3), 52–58.

Fornell, C., & Cha, J. (1994). Partial least squares. In *Advanced methods of marketing research*. Oxford, UK: Blackwell.

Fornell, C., & Larcker, D. F. (1981). Evaluating structural equation models with unobservable variables and measurement error. *JMR, Journal of Marketing Research, 28*(1), 39–50. doi:10.2307/3151312

Fuentes-Blasco, M., Gil-Saura, I., Berenguer-Contrí, G., & Moliner-Velázquez, B. (2010). Measuring the antecedents of e-loyalty and the effect of switching costs on website. *The Service Industries Journal, 30*(11), 1837–1852. doi:10.1080/02642060802626774

Ganesan-Lim, C., Russell-Bennett, R., & Dagger, T. (2008). The impact of service contact type and demographic characteristics on service quality perceptions. *Journal of Services Marketing, 22*(7). doi:10.1108/08876040810909677

Hair, J. F., Anderson, R. E., Tatham, R. L., & Black, W. C. (1998). *Multivariate data analysis* (5th ed.). Upper Saddle River, NJ: Prentice Hall International, Inc.

Herington, C., & Weaven, S. (2009). E-retailing by banks: E-service quality and its importance to customer satisfaction. *European Journal of Marketing, 43*(9/10), 1220–1231. doi:10.1108/03090560910976456

Homburg, C., & Giering, A. (2001). Personal characteristics as moderators of the relationship between customer satisfaction and loyalty—An empirical analysis. *Psychology and Marketing, 18*(1), 43–66. doi:10.1002/1520-6793(200101)18:1<43::AID-MAR3>3.0.CO;2-I

Hu, L., & Bentler, P. (1999). Cut-off criteria for fit indexes in covariance structure analysis: Conventional criteria versus new alternatives. *Structural Equation Modeling, 6*(1), 1–55. doi:10.1080/10705519909540118

Kotler, P., & Armstrong, G. (2010). *Principles of marketing* (13th ed.). London: Pearson.

Lam, S. Y., Shankar, V., Erramilli, M. K., & Murthy, B. (2004). Customer value, satisfaction, loyalty, and switching costs: An illustration from a business-to-business service context. *Journal of the Academy of Marketing Science, 32*(3), 293–311. doi:10.1177/0092070304263330

Marimon, F., Petnji, Y. L. H., & Casadesus, M. (2012). Impact of e-quality and service recovery on loyalty: A study of e-banking in Spain. *Total Quality Management & Business Excellence, 23*(7), 769–787. doi:10.1080/14783363.2011.637795

Martınez-Ruiz, M. P., Jimenez-Zarco, A. I., & Izquierdo-Yusta, A. (2012). The effects of the current economic situation on customer satisfaction and retail patronage behaviour. *Total Quality Management & Business Excellence, 23*(11), 1207–1225. doi:10.1080/14783363.2012.661133

Meng, J., Summey, J., Herndon, N., & Kwong, K. (2009). Some retail service quality expectations of Chinese shoppers. *International Journal of Market Research, 51*(6), 773–796. doi:10.2501/S1470785309200967

Mittal, V., & Kamakura, W. A. (2001). Satisfaction, repurchase intent, and repurchase behavior: Investigating the moderating effect of customer characteristics. *JMR, Journal of Marketing Research, 38*(1), 131–142. doi:10.1509/jmkr.38.1.131.18832

Nunnally, J. C., & Bernstein, I. H. (1994). *Psychometric theory*. New York: McGraw-Hill.

Oliver, R. L. (2010). *Satisfaction: A behavioral perspective on the consumer* (2nd ed.). Armonk, NY: M.E. Shape.

Oliver, R. L., & DeSarbo, W. S. (1988). Response determinants in satisfaction judgments. *The Journal of Consumer Research, 14*(4), 495–507. doi:10.1086/209131

Parasuraman, A., & Grewal, D. (2000). The impact of technology on the quality-value-loyalty chain: A research agenda. *Journal of the Academy of Marketing Science*, 28(1), 168–174. doi:10.1177/0092070300281015

Parasuraman, A., Zeithaml, V. A., & Malhotra, A. (2005). A multiple-item scale for assessing electronic service quality. *Journal of Service Research*, 7(3), 213–233. doi:10.1177/1094670504271156

Petnji Yaya, L. H., Marimon, F., & Casadesus, M. (2011). Customer's loyalty and perception of ISO 9001 in online banking. *Industrial Management & Data Systems*, 111(8), 1194–1213. doi:10.1108/02635571111170767

Petnji Yaya, L. H., Marimon, F., & Casadesus, M. (2013). Can ISO 9001 improve service recovery. *Industrial Management & Data Systems*, 113(8), 1206-1221.

Petnji Yaya, L. H., Marimon, F., & Casadesus Fa, M. (2012). Assessing e-service quality: The current state of E-S-QUAL. *Total Quality Management & Business Excellence*, 23(12), 1363–1378. doi:10.1080/14783363.2012.728850

Preacher, K. J., & Hayes, A. F. (2004). SPSS and SAS procedures for estimating indirect effects in simple mediation models. *Behavior Research Methods, Instruments, & Computers*, 36, 717–731. doi:10.3758/BF03206553 PMID:15641418

Reichheld, F. F., & Schefter, P. (2000). E-loyalty: Your secret weapon on the web. *Harvard Business Review*, 87(4), 105–113.

Ribbink, D., van Riel, A., Liljander, V., & Streukens, S. (2004). Comfort your online customer: Quality, trust and loyalty on the internet. *Managing Service Quality*, 14(6), 446–456. doi:10.1108/09604520410569784

Rintamaki, T., Kuusela, H., & Mitronen, L. (2007). Identifying competitive customer value propositions in retailing. *Managing Service Quality*, 17(6), 621–634. doi:10.1108/09604520710834975

Sanzo, M.J., Santos, M.L., & Va'zquez, R., & A´lvarez, L.I. (2003). The effect of market orientation on buyer–seller relationship satisfaction. *Industrial Marketing Management*, 32(4), 327–345. doi:10.1016/S0019-8501(01)00200-0

Spathis, C., Petridou, E., & Glaveli, N. (2004). Managing service quality in banks: customers' gender effects. *Managing Service Quality*, 14(1), 90–102. doi:10.1108/09604520410513695

Spiteri, J. M., & Dion, P. A. (2004). Customer value, overall satisfaction, end-user loyalty, and market performance in detail intensive industries. *Industrial Marketing Management*, 33(8), 675–687. doi:10.1016/j.indmarman.2004.03.005

Sum, C., & Hui, C. (2009). Academic paper sales persons' service quality and customer loyalty in fashion chain stores A study in Hong Kong retail stores. *Journal of Fashion Marketing and Management*, 13(1), 98–108. doi:10.1108/13612020910939905

Tenenhaus, M., Amato, S., & Esposito, V. (2004). A global goodness-of-fit index for PLS structural equation modeling. In *Proceedings of the XLII SIS Scientific Meeting*, (pp. 739-742). SIS.

Woodruff, R. B., & Flint, D. J. (2006). Marketing's service-dominant logic and customer value. In *The service-dominant logic of marketing: Dialog, debate, and directions* (pp. 183–195). Academic Press.

Zeithaml, V. A. (1988). Consumer perceptions of price, quality, and value: A means-end model and synthesis of evidence. *Journal of Marketing*, 2–22. doi:10.2307/1251446

Zhou, L., Dai, & Zhang. (2007). Online shopping acceptance model - A Critical survey of consumer factors in online shopping. *Journal of Electronic Commerce Research*, 8(1), 41–62.

## KEY TERMS AND DEFINITIONS

**Age:** Here refers to the length of time during which a being have existed.

**Annual Income:** Refers to how much an individuals earn in term of salary per year.

**Customer Perceived Service Quality:** Is The differences between what customer think a product or service might perform and how it actually perform.

**Customer Perceived Value:** Is the arbitrage judgement that customers makes between the payback of a product or service against his forgo.

**Customer Satisfaction:** It is a customer judgement of how good the actual performance of a product or service meet and exceed his/her expectations.

**Demographic Characteristics:** Are facts related to the composition of a population and may include the gender, age, education, annual income as well as race, religion, residence etc.

**Education:** Refers to the amount of knowledge acquired by an individual after attending school or university.

**Gender:** Refers to the human social attributes related to being male or female.

**Online Banking:** Refers to individuals who use internet to do their banking.

# Chapter 10
# Estimating User Loyalty in Social Networking Services

**Evangelos Grigoroudis**
*Technical University of Crete, Greece*

**Vassilios Fortsas**
*Technical University of Crete, Greece*

**Petros Pallis**
*Technical University of Crete, Greece*

**Nikolaos Matsatsinis**
*Technical University of Crete, Greece*

## ABSTRACT

*In the last few years, customer loyalty for products and services has become an object of extensive studies from researchers of various scientific fields. Its importance is justified from the fact that, in many cases, particularly in strong competition conditions, measuring customer satisfaction does not provide a reliable quality performance indicator for business organizations. According to recent research, loyalty is defined as a positive level of customers' commitment, which should not be based only in previous purchases (repeated or not) of a product/service. This chapter presents the development of a multicriteria methodology aiming at measuring user loyalty in social networking services and estimating the importance of influencing factors. In this context, a multicriteria analysis approach is adopted in order to measure user loyalty, assuming that the overall commitment depends on a number of criteria. The applied multicriteria approach is based on the UTADIS method, and the presented results confirm the strong relation between user satisfaction and loyalty. The results, however, reveal also that satisfaction is a necessary but not a sufficient condition for customer loyalty.*

## INTRODUCTION

Modern research considers customer loyalty as the main outcome of customer satisfaction, while the positive relationship between customer loyalty and profitability is emphasized in numerous studies.

This relationship is justified by the reduced marketing costs, the increased sales and the reduced operational costs. As noted by Reichheld & Sasser (1990), loyal customers are less likely to switch because of price and they make more purchases. In particular, loyal customers increase sales by

DOI: 10.4018/978-1-4666-5129-6.ch010

purchasing a wider variety of the products and by making more frequent purchases, while they also cost less to serve, in part because they know the product/service and require less information. In addition, loyal customers may promote the business organization, since they can provide strong word-of-mouth, create business referrals, provide references, and serve on advisory boards.

In this context, studying customer satisfaction and loyalty reveals that their relationship is not straightforward (Grigoroudis & Siskos, 2010). Several researchers urge that customer satisfaction is not able to provide a reliable measure for the performance or the quality level of a business organization, particularly in a highly competitive environment. Instead, they suggest that measuring customer loyalty may give a better understanding of consumer behavior in terms of repeated purchases, and thus improve corporate financial results (Stewart, 1995).

Although, customer loyalty and satisfaction are strongly related, they are not identical. Previous research efforts have found that (Griffin, 1995; Vandermerwe, 1996; Oliver, 1997; Hill & Alexander, 2006):

- Customer satisfaction and loyalty are strongly related; however their relation is rather nonlinear.
- Loyalty is considered as the main consequence of customer satisfaction.
- Satisfaction is a necessary but not a sufficient condition for customer loyalty.

On the other hand, social network services (SNSs), such as Facebook, Flickr, Google+, MySpace, and Twitter, are platforms offering connecting opportunities to people. A social network is used for people to get to know each other and to create new friends/connections, while they also use it to share things with others. According to Boyd and Ellison (2008), a SNS is a web-based service that allows individuals to:

1. Construct a public or semi-public profile within a bounded system.
2. Articulate a list of other users with whom they share a connection.
3. View and traverse their list of connections and those made by others within the system.

The nature and nomenclature of these connections may vary from site to site. Currently, however, there are hundreds of SNSs with various technological affordances, which support a wide range of interests and practices. These SNSs have attracted millions of users, many of whom have integrated these sites into their daily practices.

Based on the previous, the importance of SNSs in modern marketing management has been widely recognized by business organizations, since SNSs may easily offer a relatively reliable communication channel between a company and its customers (current and potential). For this reason, previous research efforts have focused on exploiting SNSs in order to increase customer satisfaction and loyalty. The most characteristic example is the incorporation of SNSs in customer loyalty programs offered by numerous companies. In addition, other studies have examined customer loyalty in various Internet contexts. However, only limited research efforts have studied user loyalty for SNSs, with most of them focusing on conceptualizing and empirically validating either theoretical customer loyalty models or the determinants of customer loyalty for SNSs (Gu et al., 2010).

The main of this chapter is to propose a multicriteria methodology, based on the UTADIS method, in order to evaluate user loyalty in SNSs and estimate the importance of influencing factors. The UTADIS method is a multicriteria classification technique that adopts the principles of ordinal regression analysis. Although the method has been widely used in real-world applications from business and finance, it has never been previously adopted in a customer loyalty classification problem.

This chapter is organized into 4 more sections. Section 2 presents the theoretical background of customer loyalty, giving emphasis on the assessment of different loyalty levels. The next section is devoted to the proposed methodological approach, presenting the applied research framework, the questionnaire development, and the UTADIS method. The empirical results of the multicriteria analysis and their implications are presented and discussed in section 4. Section 5, finally, presents some concluding remarks, the limitations of the study, as well as future research in the context of the proposed approach.

## CUSTOMER LOYALTY

### Definition and Principles

Until mid-1970s, customer loyalty measurement was mainly based on analyzing repurchase and brand choice data, using classical statistical methods and data analysis techniques (Newman & Werbel, 1973; Bass, 1974). Modern approaches are based on the works of Jacoby (1975), Jacoby & Chestnut (1978), Tarpey (1975), and Elrod (1988), in which the definition of loyalty depends on a positive commitment level by customers, instead of purchase (or repurchase) actions for a product or service. In particular, Oliver (1997) provides the following definition:

*…Customer loyalty is a deeply held commitment to rebuy or repatronize a preferred product or service consistently in the future, despite situational influences and marketing efforts having the potential to cause switching behavior…*

The critical factors that affect customer loyalty are the commitment to a brand and the repeated purchase rate. According to Dick & Basu (1994), customer loyalty may be examined by relating attitude and repeated purchasing (relative attitude is the degree to which the consumer's evaluation of one alternative brand is dominated by that of

another). In this context, true loyalty exists only when repeated patronage coexists with high relative attitude. This approach is also adopted by Griffin (1995), who distinguishes four types of loyalty (Figure 1):

1. **No Loyalty:** For several reasons some customers do not develop loyalty to certain products or services, since both repeated patronage and relative attachment are low. Some marketeers suggest that businesses should avoid targeting these buyers because they will never be loyal customers, while others believe that if a reasonably frequent need for a product/service exists, potential efforts may increase the relative attachment, and thus customers may switch to another loyalty segment.

2. **Inertia Loyalty:** A low level of attachment coupled with high repeated purchase produces inertia loyalty, which means that customers usually buy out of habit. The primary reasons for buying are based on non-attitudinal/situational factors (e.g., convenience). These customers feel some degree of satisfaction, or at least no real dissatisfaction. Thus, it is possible to turn inertia loyalty into a higher form of loyalty by courting the customer and increasing the product/service differentiation.

*Figure 1. Types of loyalty (Griffin, 1995)*

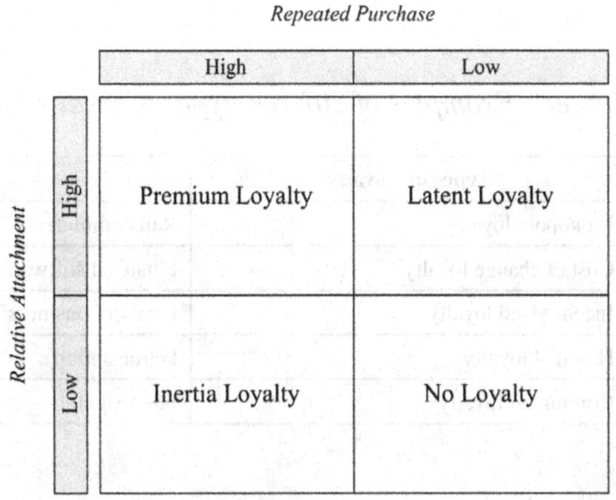

3.  **Latent Loyalty:** A high relative attitude combined with low repeated purchase signifies latent loyalty. In this case situational effects rather than attitudinal influences determine repeated purchase (e.g., inconvenient store locations, out-of-stock situations, influence of other people). Dick & Basu (1994) outline that managerial efforts are best focused on removing the obstacles to patronage, for example by extending the branch network.

4.  **Premium Loyalty:** Premium loyalty is produced when high level of attachment and repeated patronage coexists. It is the preferred type of loyalty for all customers and any business. Premium loyalty is achieved when the company has developed and communicated a proposition that clearly has long-term benefits for the customer, and when the customer modifies his/her behavior to remain loyal over time.

Although several alternative types of loyalty have been proposed, all of them follow the aforementioned framework and combine the different types of repurchase patterns with customer's attitude toward the company or brand, as presented in Table 1. However, all these categorizations of different types of loyalty are able to give a better understanding and provide alternative assessments for this concept.

Customer loyalty is not a constant and one-dimensional concept, but it is a rather dynamic process having different stages and evolving over time. The main customer loyalty stages are presented in Figure 2 and include (Griffin, 1995; Hill & Alexander, 2006):

1.  **Suspects:** Suspects include everyone who may buy the examined product/service. Suspects are either unaware of the offering or they have no inclination to buy it.

2.  **Prospects:** A prospect is someone who has the need for the examined product/service, as well as the ability to buy it. Prospects are potential customers who have some attraction toward the company, but they have not taken the step of purchase yet.

3.  **First-time customers:** These are the customers who have purchased the products or services offered (usually once, although the category may include some repeat buyers). First-time customers have no real feeling of affinity toward the company.

4.  **Repeat customers:** Repeat customers are people who have purchased the examined product/service two or more times. They have positive feelings of attachment toward the organization, but their support is rather passive, than active, apart from making purchases.

5.  **Clients:** Clients buy regularly all the product or services offered by a business organization, if they have the need for them. Usually, there is a strong relation between the organization and a client, positively affecting his/her switching behavior.

*Table 1. Examples of different types of loyalty (Hill & Alexander, 2006)*

| Types of Loyalty | Example | Degree of Allegiance |
|---|---|---|
| Monopoly loyalty | Rail commuters | Low |
| Cost of change loyalty | Financial software | Medium |
| Incentivized loyalty | Frequent business flyers | Low to medium |
| Habitual loyalty | Petrol station | Low |
| Committed loyalty | Football club | High |

*Figure 2. The customer development process (Griffin, 1995)*

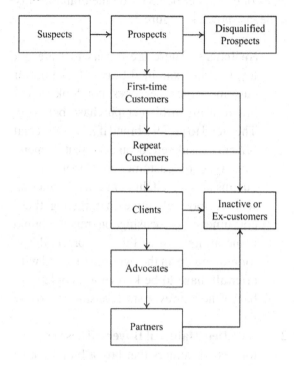

6. **Advocates:** Advocates are clients who additionally support the organization by talking about it and/or recommending it to others.
7. **Partners:** This is the strongest form of customer-supplier relationship, which is sustained because both parties see partnership as mutually beneficial.

Other alternative approaches for assessing the different levels of customer loyalty are proposed in the context of consumer behavioral analysis and social psychology (Crosby & Taylor, 1983; Kuhl, 1986; Reichheld, 1993).

A large number of research efforts focus on the measurement and analysis of customer loyalty, by applying different techniques and tools (Sproles & Kendall, 1986; Tranberg & Hansen, 1986; Czepiel & Gilmore, 1987; McDonald, 1993; Bawden, 1998). The most important approaches are based on the following:

- Repeated purchase data or patterns (e.g., purchase frequency and quantity).
- Ratio of brands in the region of acceptance to brands in the region of rejection (i.e., the ratio of the number of brands that a customer would definitely use to the number of brands that he/she would never use).
- Attitudinal scales (e.g., repurchase intention, recommendation to others).

An alternative interesting approach is presented by Oliva et al. (1992, 1995) who modeled the relation between customer loyalty and satisfaction using a catastrophe model (these models are used in order to describe nonlinear "jumps" once a threshold level of a critical variable is attained).

Taking into account the definition of customer loyalty, as well as the aforementioned measurement approaches, it is clear that since loyalty is a commitment from customers, it is not possible to directly measure it. Instead, it seems more appropriate to measure its consequences, in terms of customer repurchase behavior, and its drivers according to customer's attachment to the examined brand.

Satisfaction surveys may also be used in order to analyze customer loyalty by applying the following process (Hill, 1996):

1. Evaluate the level of customer satisfaction not only for the examined product/service, but also for the product/services of the main competitors.
2. Segment the total set of customers using a cross table that contains the results of the previous measurement.
3. Determine different strategies for each one of the previous segments (e.g., communicate with customers, develop an appropriate database, establish a loyalty club), taking into account the different levels of customer loyalty.

Other research efforts are focused on the determination of business strategies for improving customer retention, increasing purchase budget, evaluating customer trust, or studying further the relation between customer satisfaction and purchase intention (Howard, 1977; Beatty et al., 1988; McQuarrie, 1988; Morgan & Dev, 1994; Keaveney, 1995).

## Loyalty Levels

A first approach for the classification of customers taking into consideration their level of loyalty, is that of Brown (1952), according to whom the buyers can only be classified in the following four categories:

1. Hardcode loyals: those who continuously buy products of the same brand.
2. Split loyals: those who are devoted in two or three brand names.
3. Shifting loyals: those who are devoted to a brand for a time period but are easily turned to another brand because of the potential advantages it has to offer.
4. Switchers: those who have no loyalty.

A second approach, is that of David A. Aaker (1991) who defines brand loyalty as a measure of the attachment that a customer has to a brand. It reflects how likely a customer will be to switch to another brand, especially when that brand makes a change, either in price or in product features. In his Brand Loyalty pyramid, Aaker identifies five levels of brand loyalty, ranging from not loyal to very loyal (the lowest level is depicted at the bottom of the pyramid). He describes the customer behavior for each level, and pinpoints challenges faced by marketing professionals in their efforts to lift a customer/consumer to a higher level. The greater the number of customers/consumers in the higher sections of the pyramid, the more effective the pursued branding policy.

Aaker's Brand Loyalty pyramid describes five types of consumer behavior on the brand loyalty scale, as shown in Figure 3:

1. **Switchers:** These are buyers that are not loyal to the examined brand. This kind of customer/consumer does not look at the brand at all in his/her purchase behavior. They tend to prefer a brand if it is in a special offer or considered adequate by that moment. This type of customer/consumer has no qualms about switching brands. Marketing will be most effective in targeting these consumers by focusing on raising brand name awareness, as this is a precondition for moving up on the pyramid (a brand will, after all, have to be known to people first, before they can even start considering to buy it).

2. **Satisfied/Habitual Buyers:** These are customers/consumers that buy a brand out of habit. These tend to be reasonably satisfied customers, who basically do not see any reason to change their purchase behavior, and are therefore not on the lookout for alternatives. When such a customer gets into troubles, while looking for his usual brand, he/she will relatively easily buy another brand instead of going to another shop to get the brand he/she usually buys. Marketing

*Figure 3. Loyalty pyramid (Aaker, 1991)*

efforts will here have to raise the thresholds between the brand and other brands, which will create opportunities to make a customer more loyal to the brand.

3. **Satisfied Buyers with Switching Costs:** These are satisfied buyers that are reluctant to switch to a competing brand due to existing thresholds (switching costs). Such thresholds can come in the form of: expenses incurred in terms of time (the time it takes to go to another shop to find the usual brand), financial expenses (when switching costs money), and the feeling of making concessions to quality. If marketing efforts look to entice satisfied buyers of another brand into switching to a brand, the brand will have to offer major benefits compensating the switching costs (such as a free iPod when signing up for a credit card). Retaining buyers or attracting new ones at this level of brand loyalty requires a marketing strategy based on increasing perceived quality.

4. **Brand Likers:** These buyers can be typified as true bran enthusiasts. Their brand preference is mostly engendered by an experience of emotional benefits-alongside more rational benefits, such as price, time and quality. Emotional benefits can be pursued by linking certain associations (through TV ads) and/or experiences (such as the shopping experience) to a brand. This highly positive attitude towards a brand can be seen as a kind of friendship. This is further reflected by the fact that brand likers are generally unable to state why exactly they have such a strong preference for the brand in question (which is normal for people with an emotional bond with a brand).

5. **Committed Buyers:** These are the proud users of a brand, in whose (daily) lives the brand in question actually plays an important role. Committed buyers buy this brand because it closely ties in with their personal

values. Examples of committed buyers can be found in the customer bases of brands like Harley-Davidson and Apple. Retention of customers/consumers at this level of brand loyalty can best be realized by rewarding their loyalty. This can be done through loyalty cards, reward programs enabling customers to earn points, preferential treatment when issuing limited editions, etc.

## METHODOLOGY

### Methodological Framework

The presented study assumes that the overall loyalty level of a SNS user depends upon a number of criteria, and thus the problem of measuring user loyalty can be considered in the context of multicriteria analysis. More specifically, according to the proposed approach, the users are asked to provide their judgments in a set of loyalty criteria. Applying the UTADIS method on these evaluations, the users' loyalty level may be estimated and the users may be classified into predefined loyalty groups. In addition, the multicriteria analysis is able to estimate the importance of the influencing factors, i.e., the weights of the aforementioned loyalty criteria.

Planning is one of the most important stages of a customer survey that aims at avoiding potential errors and ensuring appropriate results by designing an effective research process. The general process applied in the presented study consists of the following main steps (Grigoroudis & Siskos, 2010):

1. **Determine Survey Objectives:** It is the most important step in this general process, since it may affect all the other steps when designing and conducting a customer survey. In this study, the main goal is the estimation

of the loyalty level of Facebook users by applying the UTADIS method.

2. **Determine Loyalty Dimensions:** In this step, the set of customer loyalty dimensions, as well as the related hierarchy should be determined (see below).

3. **Determine Measurement Process:** Based on the survey objectives, the detailed measurement process should be determined in this step. In addition it should be integrated with additional available information.

4. **Determine Sample Size and Survey Procedure:** This particular step concerns the determination of the sampling process (type of sampling process, sample size, etc.). Moreover, the type of survey and the communication procedures with customers should also be determined.

5. **Develop Questionnaire:** Based on the decisions made during the previous steps, the questionnaire is developed. The importance of this step is justified by the fact that the questionnaire is the main survey instrument.

6. **Test Questionnaire and Refine:** This final step refers mainly to the pilot survey, which aims at testing the effectiveness of the research methodology.

The assessment of the loyalty dimensions comprises a critical part of the preliminary user behavioral analysis and it is based on the general information of the market environment and a series of personal interviews with users. The term "loyalty dimensions" refers to the aforementioned loyalty criteria, i.e., the factors that influence the SNS user loyalty level.

There are two main approaches to developing a value hierarchy, which are based on whether or not sources of user loyalty are available (Grigoroudis & Siskos, 2010). If this information is available,

then a "bottom-up" approach may be appropriate. With this approach, users with different loyalty levels are examined to determine the ways in which they differ. In situations where this information is not available, a "top-down" approach starting with user's overall loyalty and successively subdividing objectives is more appropriate (Siskos et al., 2001).

The final assessment of the criteria is validated through an interactive continuous communication process with SNS users and consists of the following main dimensions (Figure 4):

1. **Satisfaction:** User satisfaction is considered as the main determinant of loyalty and it contains the confirmation of expectations and the overall user satisfaction. These criteria are justified by the relevant literature, and particularly the expectation confirmation theory (for a detailed discussion see Oliver, 1997).

2. **Image:** This dimension refers mostly to how the examined SNS is perceived by users. It consists of the following criteria: awareness, perceived image (compared to other competitors), and social influence.

3. **Behavior:** This loyalty dimension is related to the general user behavioral aspects and includes the reuse intention, the user involvement, the resistance to negative Word-Of-Mouth (WOM), the price elasticity (willingness to pay for using SNSs), the switching costs (difficulties to use a different SNS), and the user recommendations (intention to recommend SNS to others).

Finally, in order to apply the UTADIS multicriteria method, it is necessary to define the different classification groups, i.e., the user loyalty levels. These groups are chosen based on the 5 levels of the Aaker's Loyalty Pyramid.

*Figure 4. Hierarchical structure of loyalty criteria*

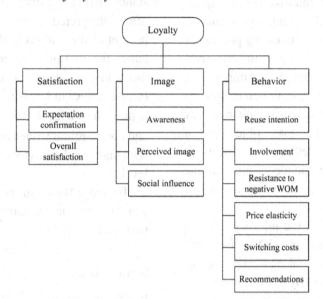

## Questionnaire Design

Questionnaire's content and structure are critical factors for the success of any marketing survey. In fact, it has been said that a survey is only as good as the questions it asks (Dutka, 1995). In any case, it should be emphasized that a questionnaire is a communication tool between an organization and its customers (Naumann & Giel, 1995). However, it is not a one-way communication device, whereby information is collected from customers, but rather an interactive communication tool.

Although there is no analytical methodological framework for questionnaire design in survey research, the major principles that should be respected are (Fowler, 1993):

- The questionnaire should be kept simple and comprehensive.
- The questions should be specific and single-minded.
- The structure of the questionnaire should help respondents to give their answers.

In this context, Vavra (1997) notes that the rule of thumb for successful question writing is to "keep it short, keep it simple, and single-minded", namely KIS[3]. Following these critical rules, a questionnaire helps in maximizing the participation of respondents and ensuring the reliability and validity of the collected information.

The final questionnaire of the presented study has been developed based on the aforementioned principles and the loyalty criteria hierarchy discussed in the previous section. The questionnaire consists of three main parts. The first part contains general questions for the usage of SNSs, as well as user characteristics (gender, age, education level, and occupation). The second part of the questionnaire refers to the loyalty criteria, where users are asked to give their judgments using a 5-point Likert type scale (strongly agree-agree-neither agree nor disagree-disagree-strongly disagree). In the last part of the questionnaire, the users are asked to self-assess their overall loyalty level using a set of five behavioral questions, which are used in order to classify users in one of the Aaker's Loyalty Pyramid levels.

Finally, it should be emphasized that the questionnaire has been tested through a pilot survey, which is the final step in the planning process of a customer survey aiming at testing the effectiveness of the research methodology. The importance of this step is justified, as mentioned earlier, by the fact that the questionnaire is the main survey instrument. Generally, the main objectives of pilot surveys are to test whether survey questions are fully understood by respondents and examine the effectiveness of the questionnaire in terms of structure, presentation, etc.

In the presented study, the pilot survey was conducted in a small number of SNSs users and it helped to improve several characteristics of the questionnaire, particularly its appearance and structure, as well as the wording of questions.

## UTADIS Method

The UTADIS method is a multicriteria classification approach that adopts the principles of preference disaggregation (Zopounidis & Doumpos, 1999; Doumpos & Zopounidis, 2002). The main aim of the method is the development of an additive value function that is used to estimate the loyalty level of each SNS user. The developed additive function has the following general form:

$$V(\mathbf{x}_i) = \sum_{j=1}^{n} w_j v_j(x_{ij}) \in [0, 1]$$

where $\mathbf{x}_i = (x_{i1}, x_{i2}, ..., x_{in})$ is the description of user $i$ on the set of $n$ evaluation criteria (i.e., the 11 factors of Figure 4), $w_j$ is the trade-off constant of criterion $j$ and $v_j(\cdot)$ is the marginal value function of criterion $j$. The trade-off constants are non-negative, they sum up to 1, and are often interpreted as proxies for the relative important of the criteria in the mode. On the other hand, the marginal value functions provide a mechanism for decomposing the aggregate result (global value) in terms of individual assessment at the criterion level. Both the global value $V(\mathbf{x}_i)$ and the marginal values are normalized in $[0, 1]$, with higher values associated with higher loyalty levels.

To avoid the estimation of both the criteria weights and the marginal value functions, it is possible to use the transformation $u_j(x_{ij}) = w_j v_j(x_{ij})$. Since $v_j(x_{ij})$ is normalized between 0 and 1, it is obvious that $u_j(x_{ij})$ ranges in the interval $[0, w_j]$. In this way, the additive value function is simplified to the following form:

$$V(\mathbf{x}_i) = \sum_{j=1}^{n} u_j(x_{ij})$$

The assignment of a user $i$ into one of the $k$ predefined loyalty classes, is determined by comparing its global value $V(\mathbf{x}_i)$ to $k-1$ thresholds $0 < t_1 < t_2 < \cdots < t_{k-1} < 1$, that distinguish the classes. Thus, a user $i$ is assigned to loyalty group $\ell$ if $t_\ell \leq V(\mathbf{x}_i) < t_{\ell-1}$.

The estimation process for the additive value function and the cut-off thresholds uses a set of data to fit the model using linear programming techniques. The objective of the method is to develop an optimal additive model that minimizes the classification error for the examined SNS users. This is achieved through the solution of the following optimization problem:

$$\min \sum_{i=1}^{m} (\sigma_i^+ + \sigma_i^-)$$

$$\text{s.t.} : \sum_{j=1}^{n} u_j(x_{ij}) + \sigma_i^+ - t_\ell \geq \delta$$

for each user i from class $\ell = 1,...,k-1$

$$\sum_{j=1}^{n} u_j(x_{ij}) - \sigma_i^- - t_{\ell-1} \leq -\delta$$

for each user i from class $\ell = 2,...,k$

$$u_j(x_{ij}) - u_j(x_{i'j}) \geq 0$$

for all $j = 1,...,n$ and user i, i' with $x_{ij} \geq x_{i'j}$

$$\sum_{j=1}^{n} u_j(x_{j*}) = 0, \quad \sum_{j=1}^{n} u_j(x_j^*) = 1 \qquad j = 1,...,n$$

$$t_\ell - t_{\ell+1} \geq \varepsilon \qquad \ell = 1,...,k-2$$

$$\sigma_i^+, \sigma_i^-, t_\ell \geq 0 \qquad i = 1,...,m, \ell = 1,..,k-1$$

where $\sigma_i^+$ ($\sigma_i^-$) is the classification error for user i from group $\ell$ with respect to the lower (upper) threshold of the group, $x_{j*}$ and $x_j^*$ denote the anti-ideal and ideal performances on criterion $j$, and $\varepsilon$, $\delta \geq 0$ are user defined constants. With a piece-wise modeling of the marginal value functions, the above optimization formulation can be expressed in linear programming form.

A detailed description the model and its properties can be found in the works of Zopounidis & Doumpos (1999) and Doumpos & Zopounidis (2002).

It should be noted that the aforementioned modeling shows that the UTADIS method is well-suited for the data of the examined problem. Although the UTADIS method has been successfully used in several fields, such as bankruptcy prediction, credit scoring, stock selection, auditing, environmental management, innovation management, etc., the presented application is the first research attempt in the field of customer management.

## RESULTS

### Sample Profile

The presented survey was conducted in December 2011 and the sample concerns Greek users of Facebook that is one of the most widely accepted SNS. For the purpose of the survey, an on-line questionnaire was developed and collected data were directly stored in a database. This type of data collection was preferred due to the familiarity of SNS users with electronic forms and questionnaires. In addition, the on-line survey was able to cover different regions in Greece. A total of 364 questionnaires were collected 33 out of which were rejected after the validation process. Thus the final sample consisted of 331 respondents.

The profile of the final sample is presented in Figures 5-9. As shown, the majority of the respondents is male (64%) in the age group of 25-29 years old (see Figures 5-6). However, the sample is able to cover both sexes (female 36%) and different age groups (21% young users below 25 years old, 15% of users between 30 and 34 years old, and 22% relatively older users above the age of 35).

As shown in Figure 7, the characteristic user holds a University degree (44%), while the percentage of the respondents having completed a post-graduate program is also significant (29%). The percentage of the respondents belonging to

*Figure 5. Gender of the sample*

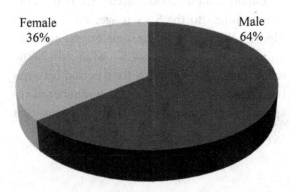

Female 36%

Male 64%

*Figure 6. Age distribution of the sample*

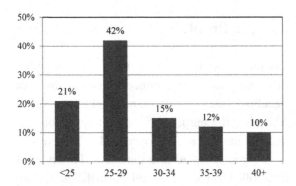

*Figure 7. Educational level of the sample*

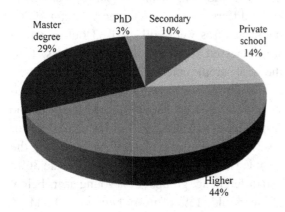

the other educational levels is relatively lower (3-14%).

Regarding the occupation, the majority of the sample is either studying (27%) or working in the private sector (42%), as shown in Figure 8. The rest of the sample refers to public servants, self-employees, unemployed, entrepreneurs, and others. (3-11%).

Finally, another important characteristic of the sample refers to the SNS usage. As shown in Figure 9, the majority of the sample uses Facebook for more than three years (48%), while 38% of the respondents uses this SNS for a period between two and three years. Only a small number of respondents refer to relatively new SNS users that

have been using this SNS for less than two years (14%). These figures justify the familiarity of the respondents with SNSs usage, and thus, collected loyalty can be considered reliable.

## Loyalty Analysis

The loyalty analysis presented in this section is based on the results of the UTADIS method and focuses on the estimation of users' loyalty level and the analysis of the influencing factors. As already noted, the aim of the UTADIS method is to develop an additive value model, which will be able to classify SNS users in predefined loyalty groups with the minimum classification errors.

The 11 criteria considered in the analysis are presented in Figure 4 and they are grouped in three main dimensions (i.e., satisfaction, image, and behavior), while the five loyalty groups are based on the Aaker's Loyalty Pyramid, as previously discussed in this chapter. These loyalty groups are:

- **First group ($C_1$):** Committed buyers.
- **Second group ($C_2$):** Brand likers.
- **Third group ($C_3$):** Satisfied buyers with switching costs.
- **Fourth group ($C_4$):** Satisfied/habitual buyers.
- **Fifth group ($C_5$):** Switchers.

According to the UTADIS method, the overall value $V(\mathbf{x}_i)$ for each user $i$ is calculated based on the marginal values $u_j(x_{ij})$ of every criterion $j$. The classification of users is achieved by comparing their global values with some thresholds that distinguish the loyalty classes. In the presented application, the SNS users are assigned to the aforementioned predefined loyalty groups according to the following rule:

*Figure 8. Occupation of the sample*

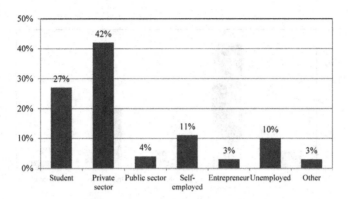

$$\begin{cases} V_i \geq t_1 & \text{then } i \in C_1 \\ t_2 \leq V_i < t_1 & \text{then } i \in C_2 \\ t_3 \leq V_i < t_2 & \text{then } i \in C_3 \\ t_4 \leq V_i < t_3 & \text{then } i \in C_4 \\ V_i < t_4 & \text{then } i \in C_5 \end{cases}$$

Figure 10 presents these estimated classification thresholds and the corresponding loyalty groups, where it should be noted that $V_i$ is normalized in [0, 1]. These results show that the estimated $t_\ell$ are able to effectively distinguish the examined loyalty groups. As observed, these classification groups are not proportional. This is justified by the nature of loyalty, which has been proven to be strongly non-linear according to the relevant literature.

Based on these UTADIS results, the respondents have been classified in the aforementioned loyalty groups. As shown in Figure 11, only 4% of the sample may be characterized as truly loyal users (i.e., committed buyers), while on the other hand a small number of users (8%) appears truly disloyal (i.e., switchers). The majority of the respondents seem to have a relatively lower loyalty level, belonging in the "satisfied/habitual buyers" group. These findings show that Facebook users are not truly loyal or disloyal to this particular SNS, but they seem to use Facebook out of habit, although they appear reasonably satisfied. As a result, Facebook users appear relatively

*Figure 10. Estimated loyalty classification thresholds*

*Figure 9. SNS usage*

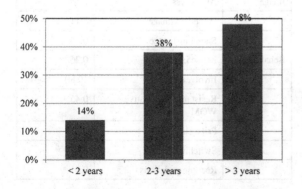

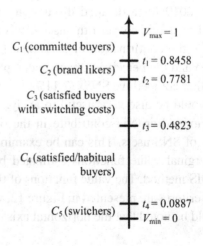

*Figure 11. Classification of users into loyalty groups*

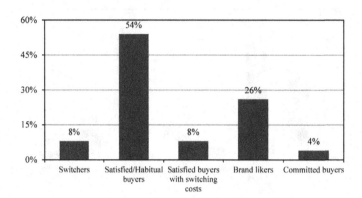

vulnerable, since they can easily switch to alternative SNSs if they have troubles with the service or receive a better offer.

The estimation of the loyalty criteria weights is another important result of the UTADIS method. These weights indicate the relative importance of the examined factors that influence user loyalty. As presented in Table 2, the most important loyalty dimension refers to user satisfaction (overall weight of 75.03%), while image and behavior seem to have lower importance levels (overall weights of 9.23% and 15.79%, respectively). Regarding the analytical factors, user overall satisfaction from the SNS is by far the most important evaluation criterion (65.3%). This is consistent with the relevant literature, where customer satisfaction is considered as the main determinant of loyalty (see Grigoroudis and Siskos, 2010 for a detailed discussion). Other important factors concern the user involvement (10.8%), the confirmation of user expectations (9.73%) and the perceived image in comparison with other competitive SNSs (7.11%).

It would be also very useful to analyze how the examined criteria contribute in the overall loyalty of SNS users. This can be examined by the marginal value functions estimated by the UTADIS method. The value functions of the assessed criteria are presented in Figure 12, where it should be noted that the horizontal axis corre-

sponds to the applied ordinal evaluation scale (i.e., the 5-point Likert scale, with SD: Strongly Disagree, D: Disagree, NAND: Neither Agree Nor Disagree, A: Agree, SA: Strongly Agree). The curve shape of the value functions indicates the demanding level of the examined criteria. In particular, a convex form shows a high demanding level, i.e., the contribution of this criterion to the loyalty level is not high, unless its performance is high. The opposite occurs in the case of a concave form, i.e., the contribution of this criterion to the loyalty level is high, even if its performance is not relatively high. Based on the results of

*Table 2. Estimated criteria weights*

| Dimension | Criterion | Weight (%) |
|---|---|---|
| Satisfaction | Expectation confirmation | 9.73 |
| | Overall satisfaction | 65.30 |
| Image | Awareness | 1.18 |
| | Perceived image | 7.11 |
| | Social influence | 0.94 |
| Behavior | Reuse intention | 0.26 |
| | Involvement | 10.80 |
| | Resistance to negative WOM | 0.45 |
| | Price elasticity | 0.41 |
| | Switching costs | 3.46 |
| | Recommendations | 0.41 |

*Figure 12. Normalized marginal value functions*

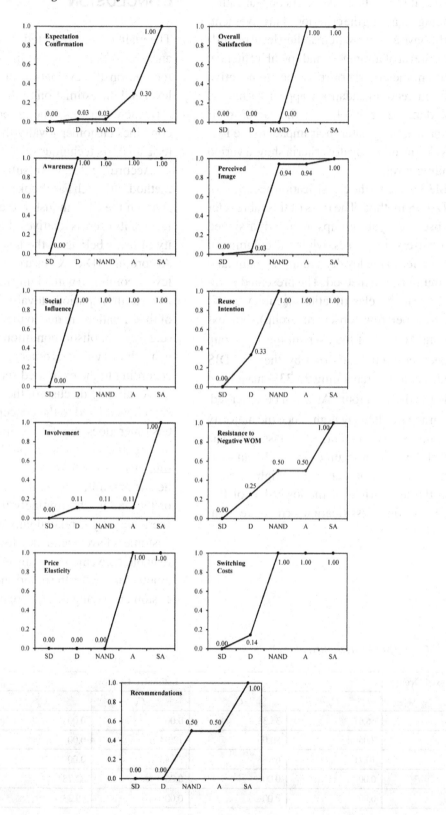

Figure 12, it seems that SNS users appear rather demanding regarding the criterion of involvement, while the have a very low demanding level regarding the criteria of awareness and social influence. In addition, the criteria of resistance to negative WOM and recommendations appear to have a neutral demanding level, i.e., the larger their performance, the greater their impact to the loyalty level. The other loyalty criteria show a varied demanding level.

Table 3 presents the classification accuracy of the UTADIS method. The rows of this table refer to the observed loyalty groups, as directly assigned based on users' responses, while the columns of the table refer to the loyalty groups, as estimated by the multicriteria method. The presented numbers concern the classification accuracy in %, normalized per row (observed group). For example, the 66.67% of the users in the $C_1$ group have been correctly classified by the UTADIS method, while the remaining 33.33% have been assigned to the $C_2$ group. As it can be observed, the accuracy is relatively high, since the majority of the sample has been correctly classified. The overall classification accuracy is 72.21% and it is important to note that there are no high percentages in the upper-right or the lower-left of this table. Thus, the classification errors are relatively low.

## CONCLUSION

The main of the presented survey is to study and analyze SNS user loyalty. In particular, the study focuses on the evaluation of the users' loyalty level and the estimation of the importance of the influencing factors. The proposed methodology combines customer loyalty theory and multicriteria analysis techniques.

According to the results of the UTADIS method, although Facebook has the largest market share in the SNS industry, the estimated loyalty level of its users is relatively low, since the majority of users belong to the lowest loyalty groups. According to Dick & Basu (1994), the low loyalty levels, combined with highly repeated usage, have as a result a spurious loyalty. The main reasons of this situation are due to the lack of alternatives (e.g., monopolistic conditions), the easiness of using the service, and other barriers that may vary according to the examined service.

As already discussed, the spurious loyalty is somehow related to the concept of inertia, as the customer does not find significant differences among the competitive products/services, and thus he/she tends to prefer the product/service he/she is familiar with, the one that is available, or the one he/she routinely used to buy or use. Inertia loyalty is related with the situation where customers have a tendency toward the brand due to habit, convenience or any other reason without emotional tie with the brand and social effect. The customers having this nature of loyalty can make

*Table 3. Classification accuracy (%)*

| Observed Group | Estimated Group | | | | |
|---|---|---|---|---|---|
| | $C_1$ | $C_2$ | $C_3$ | $C_4$ | $C_5$ |
| $C_1$ | 66.67 | 33.33 | 0.00 | 0.00 | 0.00 |
| $C_2$ | 7.06 | 80.00 | 12.94 | 0.00 | 0.00 |
| $C_3$ | 10.71 | 67.86 | 21.43 | 0.00 | 0.00 |
| $C_4$ | 0.00 | 0.00 | 0.00 | 82.78 | 17.22 |
| $C_5$ | 0.00 | 0.00 | 0.00 | 69.23 | 30.77 |

a systematic selection among other brands, but while this selection has a low level of emotional involvement and personal investment there is no devotion to the brand (Akin, 2012).

According to Solomon (2004), inertia is a situation where customers select the same brands because they need less effort to reach them. Since they do not have sufficient motivation to assess alternatives they make their decisions according to habits. The results of the presented study reveal such a situation. Facebook users appear somehow satisfied with the offered services or at least they do not seem to have a low satisfaction level. However, these users have a relatively low involvement with the SNS, and thus their attitude to use Facebook without considering other alternatives is a habit. As a result, these users may easily switch to other alternative SNSs, if a new service with specific characteristics (e.g., easiness of use, ability to transfer account data) succeeds to attract them.

The results of this study reveal also the strong relationship between customer satisfaction and loyalty, given that the estimated contribution of users' satisfaction to loyalty is extremely high. This is consistent with the existing literature, which suggests that satisfaction is the main determinant of customer loyalty (Newman & Werbel, 1973; Bearden & Teel, 1983; LaBarbera & Mazursky, 1983; Dick & Basu, 1994; Oliver, 1997). However, as already emphasized, satisfaction is a necessary but not a sufficient condition for customer loyalty. This is important given that the truly loyal customers are crucial or the long-term sustainability of a company.

The user involvement is another important determinant of loyalty, given the nature of SNSs which offer social networking opportunities. Therefore, the more the user is involved with the service, the strongest the developed connection is, which may increase loyalty. In other words, the higher the involvement of a SNS user, the higher his/her loyalty level is.

Furthermore, the importance of expectation confirmation is justified by the popularity of the examined SNS and the publicity it has attracted (TV, press, movies, etc.). On the other hand, the relatively high weight of expectations' confirmation is a result of the strong relation between satisfaction and loyalty, since confirmation of expectations is considered as one of the main drivers of customer satisfaction.

The proposed methodology applies the UTADIS multicriteria method in order to measure and analyze user loyalty. Given the relatively low estimation errors, the UTADIS method appears suitable in the examined problem. The main advantage of the method is its ability to handle qualitative (ordinal) data, while using linear programming techniques, the model is very flexible and powerful. Also, the methodology requires a rather simple and short questionnaire in order to collect input data.

Several extensions of the study may be proposed, focusing on the assessment of users' loyalty level. Currently, the loyalty level is estimated using a set of classification rules that depend on a set of behavioral questions. Thus, the observed loyalty level may be considered as a stated variable. Future research may develop additional classification procedures based on longitudinal behavioral data.

Other future research directions refer to the further analysis of user satisfaction, since it is the most important loyalty criterion. This may be achieved by integrating a user satisfaction measurement procedure that will analyze particular characteristics of the SNS (e.g., structure, design, navigation, personalization). As a result, the overall satisfaction may be more accurately estimated, while these results may indicate the strengths and weaknesses of the service. Finally, the proposed approach may be applied in other products/services, in order to study how market competition and barriers affect customer loyalty.

# REFERENCES

Aaker, D. A. (1991). *Managing brand equity: Capitalizing on the value of a brand name*. New York: The Free Press.

Akin, E. (2012). Literature review and discussion on customer loyalty and consciousness. *European Journal of Economics, Finance, and Administrative Sciences, 51*, 158–173.

Bass, F. M. (1974). The theory of stochastic preference and brand switching. *JMR, Journal of Marketing Research, 11*(1), 1–20. doi:10.2307/3150989

Bawden, P. (1998). Nortel's practical path to customer loyalty. *Measuring Business Excellence, 2*(1), 8–13. doi:10.1108/eb025513

Bearden, W. O., & Teel, J. E. (1983). Selected determinants of consumer satisfaction and complaint reports. *JMR, Journal of Marketing Research, 20*(1), 21–28. doi:10.2307/3151408

Beatty, S. E., Kahle, L. R., & Homer, P. (1988). The involvement-commitment model: Theory and implications. *Journal of Business Research, 16*(2), 149–167. doi:10.1016/0148-2963(88)90039-2

Boyd, D. M., & Ellison, N. B. (2008). Social network sites: Definition, history, and scholarship. *Journal of Computer-Mediated Communication, 13*(1), 210–230. doi:10.1111/j.1083-6101.2007.00393.x

Brown, G. H. (1952). Brand loyalty: Fact or fiction? *Advertising Age, 23*, 53–55.

Crosby, L. A., & Taylor, J. R. (1983). Psychological commitment and its effects on post-decision evaluation and preference stability among voters. *The Journal of Consumer Research, 9*(4), 413–431. doi:10.1086/208935

Czepiel, J. A., & Gilmore, R. (1987). Exploring the concept of loyalty in services. In J. A. Czepiel, C. Congram, & J. Shanahan (Eds.), *The services challenge: Integrating for competitive advantage* (pp. 91–94). Chicago: American Marketing Association.

Dick, A., & Basu, K. (1994). Customer loyalty: Toward an integrated conceptual framework. *Journal of the Academy of Marketing Science, 22*(2), 99–113. doi:10.1177/0092070394222001

Doumpos, M., & Zopounidis, C. (2002). *Multicriteria decision aid classification methods*. Dordrecht, The Netherlands: Kluwer Academic Publishers.

Dutka, A. (1995). *AMA handbook of customer satisfaction: A complete guide to research, planning and implementation*. Chicago: NTC Business Books.

Elrod, T. (1988). A management science assessment of a behavioral measure of brand loyalty. In M. J. Houston (Ed.), *Advances in consumer research* (pp. 481–486). Provo, UT: Association for Consumer Research.

Fowler, F. J. Jr. (1993). *Survey research methods*. Newbury Park, CA: Sage Publications.

Griffin, J. (1995). *Customer loyalty*. Lexington, MA: Lexington Books.

Grigoroudis, E., & Siskos, Y. (2010). *Customer satisfaction evaluation: Methods for measuring and implementing service quality*. New York: Springer. doi:10.1007/978-1-4419-1640-2

Gu, R., Oh, L., & Wang, K. (2010). Determinants of customer loyalty for social networking sites. In R. Sharman, T. S. Raghu, & H. R. Rao (Eds.), *Exploring the grand challenges for next generation e-business (LNBIP)* (Vol. 52, pp. 206–212). Berlin: Springer. doi:10.1007/978-3-642-17449-0_21

Hill, N. (1996). *Handbook of customer satisfaction measurement*. Hampshire, UK: Gower Publishing.

Hill, N., & Alexander, J. (2006). *Handbook of customer satisfaction and loyalty measurement*. Aldershot, UK: Gower.

Howard, J. A. (1977). *Consumer behavior: Application of theory*. New York: McGraw-Hill.

Jacoby, J. (1975). A brand loyalty concept: Comments on a comment. *JMR, Journal of Marketing Research*, *12*(4), 484–487. doi:10.2307/3151103

Jacoby, J., & Chestnut, R. W. (1978). *Brand loyalty: Measurement and management*. New York: Wiley.

Keaveney, S. M. (1995). Customer switching behavior in service industries: An exploratory study. *Journal of Marketing*, *59*(2), 71–82. doi:10.2307/1252074

Kuhl, J. (1986). Motivation and information processing. In R. M. Sorrentino, & E. T. Higgins (Eds.), *Handbook of motivation and cognition* (pp. 404–434). New York: Guilford Press.

LaBarbera, P. A., & Mazursky, D. (1983). A longitudinal assessment of consumer satisfaction dissatisfaction: The dynamic aspect of the cognitive process. *JMR, Journal of Marketing Research*, *20*(4), 393–404. doi:10.2307/3151443

McDonald, W. J. (1993). The roles of demographics, purchase histories, and shopper decision-making styles in predicting consumer catalog loyalty. *Journal of Direct Marketing*, *7*(3), 55–65. doi:10.1002/dir.4000070308

McQuarrie, E. F. (1988). An alternative to purchase intentions: The role of prior behaviour in consumer expenditures on computers. *Journal of the Market Research Society. Market Research Society*, *16*(3), 203–226.

Morgan, M. S., & Dev, C. S. (1994). An empirical study of brand switching for a retail service. *Journal of Retailing*, *70*(3), 267–282. doi:10.1016/0022-4359(94)90036-1

Morris, M. H., & Holman, J. L. (1988). Source loyalty in organizational markets: A dyadic perspective. *Journal of Business Research*, *16*(2), 117–131. doi:10.1016/0148-2963(88)90037-9

Naumann, E., & Giel, K. (1995). *Customer satisfaction measurement and management: Using the voice of the customer*. Cincinnati, OH: Thomson Executive Press.

Newman, J. W., & Werbel, R. A. (1973). Multivariate analysis of brand loyalty for major household appliances. *JMR, Journal of Marketing Research*, *10*(4), 404–409. doi:10.2307/3149388

Oliva, T. A., Oliver, P. L., & Bearden, W. O. (1995). The relationships among consumer satisfaction, involvement, and product performance: A catastrophe theory application. *Behavioral Science*, *40*, 104–132. doi:10.1002/bs.3830400203

Oliva, T. A., Oliver, P. L., & McMillan, I. C. (1992). A catastrophe model for developing service satisfaction strategies. *Journal of Marketing*, *56*(2), 83–95. doi:10.2307/1252298

Oliver, R. L. (1997). *Satisfaction: A behavioral perspective on the customer*. New York: McGraw-Hill.

Reichheld, F. F. (1993). Loyalty-based management. *Harvard Business Review*, *71*(2), 64–73. PMID:10124634

Reichheld, F. F., & Sasser, W. E. (1990). Zero defections: Quality comes to services. *Harvard Business Review*, *68*(5), 105–111. PMID:10107082

Solomon, M. R. (2004). *Consumer behavior*. Upper Saddle River, NJ: Prentice-Hall.

Sproles, G. B., & Kendall, E. L. (1986). A methodology for profiling consumers' decision-making styles. *The Journal of Consumer Affairs*, *20*(2), 267–279. doi:10.1111/j.1745-6606.1986.tb00382.x

Stewart, M. (1995). *Keep the right customers.* New York: McGraw Hill.

Tarpey, L. X. (1975). Brand loyalty revisited: A commentary. *JMR, Journal of Marketing Research*, *12*(4), 488–491. doi:10.2307/3151104

Tranberg, H., & Hansen, F. (1986). Patterns of brand loyalty: Their determinants and their role for leading brands. *European Journal of Marketing*, *20*(3), 81–109. doi:10.1108/EUM0000000004642

Vandermerwe, S. (1996). Becoming a customer owing corporation. *Long Range Planning*, *23*(6), 770–782. doi:10.1016/S0024-6301(97)82815-4

Vavra, T. G. (1997). *Improving your measurement of customer satisfaction: A guide to creating, conducting, analyzing, and reporting customer satisfaction measurement programs.* Milwaukee, WI: ASQC Quality Press.

Zopounidis, C., & Doumpos, M. (1999). A multicriteria decision aid methodology for sorting decision problems: The case of financial distress. *Computational Economics*, *14*(3), 197–218. doi:10.1023/A:1008713823812

## ADDITIONAL READING

Bagozzi, R. P. (1993). On the neglect of volition in consumer research: A critique and proposal. *Psychology and Marketing*, *10*(3), 215–223. doi:10.1002/mar.4220100305

Bagozzi, R. P., Baumgartner, H., & Yi, Y. (1992). State versus action orientation and the theory of reasoned action: An application to coupon usage. *The Journal of Consumer Research*, *18*(4), 505–518. doi:10.1086/209277

Bagozzi, R. P., & Warshaw, P. R. (1990). Trying to consume. *The Journal of Consumer Research*, *17*(2), 127–140. doi:10.1086/208543

Belch, G. E. (1981). An examination of comparative and noncomparative television commercials: The effects of claim variation and repetition on cognitive response and message acceptance. *JMR, Journal of Marketing Research*, *18*(3), 333–349. doi:10.2307/3150974

Cheong, K. J. (1993). Observations: Are cents-off coupons effective? *Journal of Advertising Research*, *33*(2), 73–78.

Jacoby, J. (1971). A model for multi-brand loyalty. *Journal of Advertising Research*, *11*(3), 25–31.

Jacoby, J., & Kyner, D. B. (1973). Brand loyalty versus repeat purchasing behavior. *JMR, Journal of Marketing Research*, *10*(1), 1–9. doi:10.2307/3149402

Jarvis, L. P., & Wilcox, J. B. (1976). Repeat purchasing behavior and attitudinal brand loyalty: Additional evidence. In K. L. Bernhardt (Ed.), *Marketing 1776-1976 and beyond* (pp. 151–152). Chicago: American Marketing Association.

Johnson, M. D., & Fornell, C. (1991). A framework for comparing customer satisfaction across individuals and product categories. *Journal of Economic Psychology*, *12*(2), 267–286. doi:10.1016/0167-4870(91)90016-M

Kasper, H. (1988). On problem perception, dissatisfaction, and brand loyalty. *Journal of Economic Psychology*, *9*(3), 387–397. doi:10.1016/0167-4870(88)90042-6

Kuhl, J. (1985). Volitional mediators of cognition-behavior consistency: Self-regulatory processes and action versus state orientation. In J. Kuhl, & J. Beckman (Eds.), *Action control: From cognition to behavior* (pp. 101–128). Berlin: Springer-Verlag. doi:10.1007/978-3-642-69746-3_6

Mazursky, D., & Geva, A. (1989). Temporal decay in satisfaction: Purchase intention relationship. *Psychology and Marketing*, 6(3), 211–227. doi:10.1002/mar.4220060305

Mazursky, D., LaBarbera, P., & Aiello, A. (1987). When consumers switch brands. *Psychology and Marketing*, 4(1), 17–30. doi:10.1002/mar.4220040104

Mittal, B., & Lee, M. S. (1989). A causal model of consumer involvement. *Journal of Economic Psychology*, 10(3), 363–389. doi:10.1016/0167-4870(89)90030-5

Oliver, R. L., & Linda, G. (1981). Effect of satisfaction and its antecedents on consumer preference and intention. *Advances in Consumer Research. Association for Consumer Research (U. S.)*, 8(1), 88–93.

Ping, R. A. Jr. (1994). Does satisfaction moderate the association between alternative attractiveness and exit intention in a marketing channel? *Journal of the Academy of Marketing Science*, 22(4), 364–371. doi:10.1177/0092070394224005

Raju, P. S. (1980). Optimal stimulation level: Its relationship to personality, demographics, and exploratory behavior. *The Journal of Consumer Research*, 7(3), 272–282. doi:10.1086/208815

Snyder, D. R. (1991). Demographic correlates to loyalty in frequently purchased consumer services. *Journal of Professional Services Marketing*, 8(1), 45–55. doi:10.1300/J090v08n01_04

Stum, D. L., & Thiry, A. (1991). Building customer loyalty. *Training and Development Journal*, 45(4), 34–36.

Tarpey, L. X. (1974). A brand loyalty concept: A comment. *JMR, Journal of Marketing Research*, 11(2), 214–217. doi:10.2307/3150565

Tellis, G. J. (1988). Advertising exposure, loyalty, and brand purchase: A two-stage model of choice. *JMR, Journal of Marketing Research*, 25(2), 134–144. doi:10.2307/3172645

Wernefelt, B. (1991). Brand loyalty and market equilibrium. *Marketing Science*, 10(3), 229–245. doi:10.1287/mksc.10.3.229

## KEY TERMS AND DEFINITIONS

**Customer Loyalty:** Commitment to rebuy or repatronize a preferred product or service consistently in the future, despite situational influences and marketing efforts having the potential to cause switching behavior.

**Customer Satisfaction:** The consumer's fulfillment response; it is a judgment that a product or service feature, or the product or service itself, provided (or is providing) a pleasurable level of consumption-related fulfillment, including levels of under- or over-fulfillment.

**Multicriteria Analysis:** Methods, models and approaches that aim to aid the decision-makers to handle semi-structured decision problems with multiple criteria; it handles problems where the rational solution does not preexist, but constitutes an objective of research usually through an interactive process.

**Social Networks Services:** Platforms offering connecting opportunities to people through a web-based service that allow individuals to: construct a public or semi-public profile within a bounded system, articulate a list of other users with whom they share a connection, and view and traverse their list of connections and those made by others within the system.

**UTADIS Method:** A multicriteria classification approach that adopts the principles of preference disaggregation, aiming at the development of an additive value function with the minimum classification errors.

# Chapter 11
# Designing and Evaluating Web Interaction for Older Users

**Gabriella Spinelli**
*Brunel University, UK*

**Seema Jain**
*Brunel University, UK & Age UK, UK*

## ABSTRACT

*With the unprecedented changes in demographic structure, the ageing population is becoming a more powerful and attractive audience for Web-based services. To provide this group with satisfying user experiences, it is necessary to understand the impact that the ageing process has on abilities, needs, and expectations. While researchers and practitioners can apply inclusive design and methods to centre the development of Internet-based services around the lifestyle and behaviours of the ageing population, it is also important to consider what innovations can be introduced to online services to make them more attractive and sustainably adopted among older people. The chapter is centred on issues affecting the online experience of users in later life: physical and cognitive abilities, aspirations, and constraints. It then provides an overview of the methods inspired by User-Centred Design. Finally, it considers challenges that go beyond the remit of design but still powerfully affect the Web experience of older users.*

## INTRODUCTION

The UK's population of the over 50's is projected to increase by 1.7 million over the next five years (ONS, 2012). With such growth, the commercial targeting of this age group has consequently increased (Coleman, 2004). The Internet and digital technologies are a huge part of most people's lives, with companies and the government moving more of their services online to reach a greater number of people and reducing costs. Choudrie, Weerakkody and Jones (2005) explain that gov-

ernments all over the world are aiming to make public sector services and products available online. Whilst moving services online can be considered a positive transition, it is also imperative to understand that access to the Internet is not universally available throughout the UK, both for the unavailability of fast internet connection in rural areas, the unfamiliarity with online services among certain social groups and the, although declining, cost of PCs. The Office of National Statistics –ONS- illustrates that socioeconomic background, geographical location, age and gender

DOI: 10.4018/978-1-4666-5129-6.ch011

characteristics are all determinants of Internet access (ONS, 2013). The older and disabled are identified as the groups who are less likely to have ever used the Internet, with approximately 6.3 million people in the UK aged over 55 having never used the Internet (ibid). Initiatives such as the Go On UK, aim to improve the skills of individuals, SMEs and charities to facilitate access to digital infrastructure and services online for all (Go On UK, 2013). It can be said that web-based services and applications are intuitive for younger users given the great exposure and familiarisation accumulated in their life-time. On the other hand, a successful user experience for the minority groups mentioned above is a challenge that needs more attention and careful planning.

To a great extent a satisfactory user experience of web-based services is determined by the usability of the designed system. A plethora of guidelines for web accessibility and usability are currently available to practitioners from bodies such as the British Standards Institute and the Web Accessibility Initiative (BSI, BS 8878.2010; WAI, 1998). One main lesson highlighted with the hope of aiding older Internet users' online experiences is the importance of not creating an information overload for online pages (Gao, Sato, Rau and Asano, 2007; BSI, BS 8878.2010; WAI, 1998; Coleman, 2004; ONS, 2012) as this confuses and disenfranchises the users, making online satisfaction a hard goal to achieve.

Although 6.3 million people in the UK aged 55 and over have never used the Internet, the number of older people taking up the Internet has increased over the past two years (Ofcom, 2012). From 2010 to 2012, broadband take-up increased from 46 per cent to 62 per cent amongst those aged 65 to 74 and from 21 per cent to 25 per cent for those aged 75 and over (Ofcom, 2012). The increase in the up-take of broadband services with the UK older population supports the case for online and multichannel services to adopt accessibility and usability guidelines to facilitate older users' experiences online. It is also imperative for busi-

nesses to offer online commerce channels that can attract and flexibly manage the demands and expectations of a broader user audience (Curran, Meuter, and Surprenant 2003). This, while it represents a benefit for users who can browse and shop ubiquitously, also helps the businesses in cutting down costs for physical retail outlets and personnel. Considering the rising uptake of Internet technologies and the fact that in the UK, the over 50s control approximately 80 per cent of the country's wealth, the silver surfers have certainly become a high priority target for many businesses (DWP, 2005). For this age group, the Internet should represent a viable channel for information, entertainment and retail.

This chapter aims to give an overview of the factors that impact the satisfaction of ageing users when interacting with web and online services. It also provides clear methodological guidance on evaluation protocols that can lead to effective design guidance. The chapter does so by firstly addressing the characteristics that make older users somehow different from the general population. The chapter then moves to discuss methodological considerations in the evaluation of web interactions among older users. Recommendations on how to design methodological protocols to evaluate the satisfaction of older users are presented. The discussion section broadens the final considerations to elements that go beyond design and that are equally important to consider when designing satisfactory online user experience for the silver surfers. This section highlights the challenges that academic and practitioners face and set the directions for future research.

## CAPABILITIES AND LIFESTYLE PREFERENCES AMONG THE AGEING POPULATION

This section reviews capabilities and lifestyle issues relevant to the ageing population. The aim is to highlight these capabilities and characteristics, which are crucial when designing web interactions. Studying ageing factors that can effect older peoples' interaction with the Internet is important to help researchers identify the characteristics that are age-specific from those that are due to the user's level of exposure to the Internet (Zajicek, 2006). The following section reviews two groups of issues:

- Those linked to the ageing process and their potential impact on reduced capabilities.
- Those associated with lifestyle and preferences among ageing users.

## Capabilities

The change in capabilities among the older population can include vision, motor skills and dexterity alongside cognition and memory skills. Seidel, Richardson, Crilly, Matthews, Clarkson and Brayne (2010) promote the importance of considering older people's capabilities in design with the aim to allow this age group to perform daily activities which are instrumental for independent living. This section reviews existing literature on the decline in capabilities experienced with age, paying attention to the impact these changes have in interacting with computers.

## Vision

Interaction with computers and the Internet can be problematic for older people, especially those with vision impairments as the information on screen is often small (Dickinson, Arnott and Prior, 2007). The decline in vision with age is well documented in academic research. Seidel et al. (2009:670) define vision as *"the ability to see objects and differentiate surfaces"*, explaining that this ability deteriorates with age and can result in the loss of visual field, blurry vision and reduced contrast sensitivity. All of the aforementioned

characteristics in the decline of vision undoubtedly impact older users' interaction with websites. Clarkson, Coleman, Hosking and Waller (2007) designed an online toolkit which allows users to simulate the different conditions which affect eyesight (www.inclusivedesigntoolkit.com). This is a very useful tool for both designers and businesses to understand the impact of these visual conditions on the usability of products, websites and interfaces.

Guidelines to improve website usability with older people experiencing vision decline have been proposed through research by Zaphiris, Kurniawan and Ghiawadwala (2007). Examples of these guidelines include suggestions to enlarge the spacing between hyperlinks and their click or 'hot' areas (ibid). This was proved to help older users distinguish between links and also allow the website to detect smaller, less accurate movements of the cursor (Hawthorn, 2000). The British Standard for Web Accessibility (BS 8878: 2010) details specific guidelines for older people which consider the use visually emphasized navigation features, taking into account text, contrast, colour and web page customisation and also providing trustworthy content which is accurate and reassures the user. Although we have only highlighted some examples of the varying range decline in the visual capabilities of older people, it is obvious that these changes with age are different for every user. For web interaction, vision is regarded as the most relied on sensory channel which is even more crucial when browsing an unfamiliar website with new layout, context and content. For example, using colour as a primary indicator of important information strongly goes against accessibility guidelines (Kuzma, 2010). With the ageing population being subjected to changes in visual acuity, colour sensitivity and glare sensitivity reliance on colour in website design does not support inclusively their capabilities (Becker, 2004).

## Motor Skills and Dexterity

Alongside decline in vision, motor skills and dexterity play a considerable role in the usability of technology through different input devices such as mice, track pads or touchscreens. Barry and Carson (2004) describe the degeneration of the motor system with age as resulting in the substantial decline in strength and steadiness. In addition hand dexterity, particularly grip and pinch strength, decrease with age due to hand structural changes, decreased neural control and heath conditions such as osteoporosis and arthritis (Carmeli, Patish, and Coleman, 2003). Interaction with the Internet requires accurate movements through the aforementioned input devices from users who may experience dexterity problems (Wood, Willoughby, Rushing, Bechtel and Gilbert, 2005; Dickinson, Eisma, Gregor, Syme and Milne, 2005; Czaja and Lee, 2003; Ellis and Kurniawan, 2000; Sayago and Blat, 2011). Bearing in mind the reduced dexterity and motor skills of the older user, Zaphiris et al. (2007) suggest the practice of not using double-clicking to perform functions. Although websites do not usually demand a great deal of double-clicking (as hyperlinks require single-clicks), the action is difficult to carry out for this age group as they can struggle to keep the mouse still enough (ibid). Rollover menus are another example of an Internet-based function which can be difficult to use especially for novice users. The quick movement of the cursor needed to keep the sub-menus visible can prove troublesome for users with dexterity problems (Hawthorn, 200). In addition, the unfamiliar action of rolling over a button or link is a computer-technology based function and therefore may cause confusion to those who are unfamiliar. Gao et al. (2007) investigated the effects of navigation tools with older Internet users. The research advises that the use of tab menus (with rollover functions) helps to reduce the effect of older users' decline in motor skills and dexterity when interacting with the Internet.

## Cognition and Memory

Human Computer Interaction (HCI) research suggests that older users' interaction with computers is affected by their age-related decline in memory and cognitive capabilities (Czaja and Lee, 2003). It is widely reported that older users take longer to retrieve information on the web than their younger counterparts (Stronge, Rodgers and Fisk, 2006; Wagner, Hassanein and Head, 2010). Chevalier, Dommes and Martins (2012) suggest that the decline in memory of older users results in their increased time required to search and retrieve information online. Specifically, in the comparative navigation study of younger and older web users searching for information on two different websites; one which met the stipulated ergonomic guidelines and one which violated them. Chevalier et al. (2005) found that older users, despite forgetting the information they had previously retrieved online, were still able to achieve task completion during both website information searching tasks albeit at a slower time than their younger counterparts. Ellis and Kurniawan (2000) support the finding that older users require more time to find information, explaining that the nature of web interaction demands work on the short-term memory to process the vast amount of information available (Sayago and Blat, 2011). Particularly with web interaction, the structure and complexity of information has a notable impact on older users. Structuring websites with flatter structures, e.g. with less sub-pages, have proved to be more usable for older people (Burmeister, 2010). Whereas flat structures in web design are not always suitable, Burnmeister's findings highlight the need to display information transparently in order to ease cognitive load. The heavy workload with web interaction stresses the importance of compensating for age-related changes, not only in the controlled environment of research, but also the more realistic scenario of everyday independent use.

In addition to their memory capabilities, the use of language online should also be studied carefully for older Internet users. In a web-based study carried out with older users, Aula (2005) found that older users experienced "confusion" and a feeling of "helplessness" when presented with Internet-specific terminology. Specifically, participants were found to experience confusion with pop-up security messages when using websites and immediately sought the help of facilitators to rectify their perceived error. It is therefore imperative for web content managers to deliver comprehensible information online, not only due to the complexity of the task, but the need and desire of this age group to source information (Gilroy, 2005). The standards and guidelines highlighted earlier on in this chapter from the BSI, WAI and WCAG, stress the importance of accessibility in web design (BSI, BS 8878.2010; WCAG, 2008; WAI, 1998). For older Internet users in particular, the criticality of web design guidelines can be explained by the mental representations of information that older users develop. Van der Veer and Meguizo (2003) explain that the confusion between a website organisation and the users' mental model of the website can lead to a fail in its design. Understanding users and designing online interaction for them means bridging the gap between the designers' model of the system and the users' model of the system. In achieving this insight, it is possible to map the users' online interactions more accurately and therefore achieving the effective retrieval of the information available. Pak and Price (2008) suggest the use of keywords when structuring the content of a website rather than the more commonly used taxonomical hierarchical structure. A comparative study testing older users with a "user friendly" and "non-user friendly" website, where the former was designed based on usability and accessibility standards and the former without this consideration (Chevalier and Kicka, 2006). The research found that older users were distracted by non-relevant information on the non-ergonomic website. The non-relevant information was found to distract users from their information search, resulting in an increase in cognitive load and longer times to complete tasks (ibid). Bearing in mind the cognitive changes associated with age that are discussed in this chapter, the need for usable (ergonomic) websites is key in easing the cognitive load of older users.

## Lifestyle and Preferences

Dickinson et al. (2007) remark how the over 50s are a heterogeneous age group due to several factors such as: different lifestyle characteristics, accumulated life experience, education levels, flexibility of free time and sensory, cognitive and mobility differences which are a result of ageing. Carmichael, Newell and Morgan (2007) have discussed the barriers that older people come across when interacting with computers and the Internet, with particular attention to older people's apprehension towards technology and their weary attitude towards unfamiliar environments. Although the aforementioned researchers discuss older people's negative attitude towards technology, there are also older people who appreciate the positive impact technology can have on their lives. In a survey carried out by Age UK (2012), nearly 40 per cent of respondents (from a sample of 485) explained that they like to learn about new technologies. In the same survey 85 per cent of respondents stated they currently owned a mobile phone and 57 per cent use the Internet (Age UK, 2012).

The research conducted by Age UK also reveals that over 60 per cent of the survey respondents send and receive emails more than once a week; this being their most common use of the Internet. The second most common activity is searching for information and news online (ibid). A recent survey by Ofcom (2012) confirms that older users' second most popular purpose of using the Internet is for accessing information. However, the same research also notes that the most popular site amongst older people in the UK aged 50 and over is Amazon.co.uk (ibid). Internet adoption by the older population is also increasing, therefore contradicting the research conducted by Carmichael et al. (2007). As mentioned in the introduction, broadband take-up has increased among the older population in the UK, lending further support to their interest in technology. Furthermore, older people not only have spendable wealth, but have more free time with the onset of retirement (DWP, 2005). Age UK's (2012) research found that the over 50s also choose to use the Internet in their leisure time with 33.7 percent booking holidays online and 36.7 percent using the Internet as an information source whilst shopping. These finding illustrate that the older population not only have an interest in technology but also more free time to explore the opportunities available through using the Internet. The confirmed usage of the Internet and willingness to learn about technology truly exemplify that older consumers are not a case apart when it comes to technology or online interactions.

## NAVIGATIONAL STRATEGIES AND BEHAVIOURS

This section reviews and discusses the online navigational strategies that are employed by older users. Together with an account of the pathways undertaken by older users, we also highlight the factors that mostly contribute to a successful web experience. We focus on factors affecting tasks representative of everyday use among ageing users such as seeking information, accessing entertainment and shopping online. In light of empirical findings obtained from first hand observations, this section aims to equip the reader with a comprehensive understanding of the factors affecting online navigation by older users. We have structured the following section in three core themes:

- Exposure to the Internet.
- Information processing.
- Website attributes.

## Participant Exposure to the Internet

The UK's older population is heterogeneous, with varying life experiences, demographic characteristics, lifestyle preferences and importantly varying exposure to the Internet. Charness and Czaja (2005) highlight the core contexts in which older people are exposed to the Internet and technology, these being work, home and public venues. The differences generated by belonging to different generations, such as general education level and consequent job roles, can dictate how much exposure to and knowledge of web technologies the older population may have accumulated throughout their lifetime while working. In detail, advances in technology and the Internet during the 1990s allowed the work force to grow accustomed to technological developments and adoption in organisations. The same is not applicable among people who by the 1990s were enjoying retirement and had less opportunity to familiarise with digital technology, and especially the web, through the work context (W3C, 2013). Technology is undoubtedly becoming a necessity in daily life today, however there is still a substantial digital divide between the younger and the older generations as shown in figure 1 (Ofcom, 2012).

Despite the divide in the use of the Internet between age groups, the up-take of the Internet is increasing in the UK year on year. From 2010 to 2012 there was a consistent increase in home Internet access for those aged 55-64, 65-74 and 75+ (ibid). The encouraging increase of Internet take-up somewhat contradicts the common misconception that older people are adverse to technology because they cannot or do not want to use it (Aula, 2005). Olson, O'Brien, Rodgers and Charness (2011) suggest that this misconception

*Figure 1. Home Internet access in the UK by age group. Data from the Ofcom Communications and Marketing Report (2012:243).*

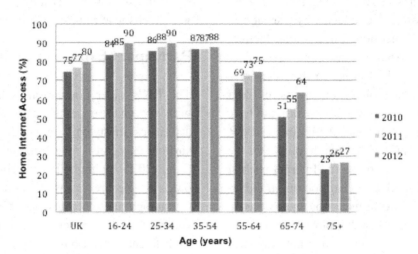

is due to the different usage patterns of older users, some being as frequent as younger users and others being using the Internet rarely.

As previously mentioned, older users' previous experience and exposure to the Internet can impact their interaction online. One of the observed challenges that older users experience is the interaction with hyperlinks. Chadwick-Dias, McNulty and Tullis (2003) found that older participants could not distinguish between links and non-links and therefore proceeded to click many times all over the webpages presented. Problems with hyperlinks can be explained in several ways. Firstly, older people are less likely to be familiar with the Internet than younger people and therefore their understanding of Internet-only components of web sites may be affected by this diminished experience (Docampo Rama, Ridder and Bouma, 2001). Secondly, the participants' inability to identify whether a hyperlink is present and active results in users unnecessarily clicking multiple times on hyperlinks or ignoring them (Chadwick-Dias et al., 2003; Jain, Spinelli, Garaj and Dong, 2012). Difficulties with hyperlinks can also be explained by older users' declining motor dexterity capabilities affecting their control over

input devices when interacting with the Internet (Blake, 1993). Researchers have highlighted that to allow for successful interactions with websites, it is important to compensate for the varying exposure and therefore familiarity that older users have with the Internet. Chisnell, Redish, and Lee (2006) carried out research into web usability with older people, highlighting the depth of consideration needed by designers to make websites usable and accessible to a diverse range of older people. The research tested a series of heuristics accounting for factors affecting older users' interaction with the web and users' expertise (ibid). For example, the researchers suggest minimizing the need for vertical scrolling and including a site map, with a link to it on all pages of a website. Where this heuristic recommendations were not met, the novice participants tested encountered more difficulties than those with more expertise (ibid). Unfortunately even today many websites still do not meet basic heuristic guidelines set out by Nielsen (1995) and adapted by Chisnell et al. (2006). Not considering these basic principles in the process of designing websites excludes a potentially profitable user group (Dickinson et al., 2007; Carmichael et al., 2007).

## Cognitive Processing of Information

In the previous section we have reviewed how lack of familiarity with the Internet and its language and components can hinder older users' online interaction. In this section we discuss how even partial exposure to unknown websites can be beneficial to develop a mental model of the Internet and facilitate effective cognitive processing of online information. Applying previous skills learnt whilst interacting with an unfamiliar website was found to be beneficial for older users. Reading or skimming information quickly and accurately helped users ascertain whether they were at the correct page they desired. Li, Rau, Fujimura, Gao, and Wang (2012) found that older people are the fastest growing group of Internet users. This can obviously be explained by their interest in learning, but also by their ability to transfer existing skills to new visited websites. By applying previous skills learnt outside the Internet domain, such as skim reading, older users in the aforementioned study were able to apply existing knowledge to their interaction with the Internet, despite the contexts were dissimilar. While cognitive processing can be facilitated with partial experience of online interactions, it is worth noting that younger users are still able to perform tasks quicker than their older counterparts (Hawthorn, 2000). Skim reading can be said to illustrate where the application of existing skills (distinct from the Internet and computer technologies) successfully support older participants' online experience.

Conversely, older users were found to experience problems in navigating online websites' menu when users' navigational strategies acquired from the real world could not be applied to the online interactions. In the case where a website's structure is not easy to understand by inexpert users, their navigation strategies can no longer be employed and therefore results in unsuccessful interactions. This phenomenon can be explained by the users' inability to relate the website to a real world convention and therefore, as Nielsen explains (1994),

frustration and failed interactions can occur. Van der Veer and Meguizo (2003) suggest that a measure to reduce such frustration is for the web designers to pay particular attention to the users' mental content structure so as to encapsulate it in the web site architecture and ultimately affording a more direct interaction. Older Internet users in particular should be provided with clear navigation as this allows them to visualise the structure of the information available on the website and therefore better understand how to navigate through it (Zaphiris et al., 2007). It has been observed that when a site hierarchy is flatter and broader, henceforth with fewer sub-sections, the resulting website structure is more transparent and easier to follow (Chisnell et al., 2006). Such suggestion is particularly pertinent for those users who have lower levels of exposure to the Internet. This is because, as demonstrated by Lidwell, Butler and Holden (2003) a flatter hierarchical navigation allows users to understand the organisation of a complicated site and visualise the connections between site pages.

Several studies have highlighted how website architecture and navigation seem to be two interdependent factors. However while a website architecture is somehow static the navigational style of online users is highly influenced by their preferences, abilities and past experience. Danielson (2002) for example discusses navigation in terms of the hierarchical levels users move through in order to find information. The research found that users use the 'back' button less when they have an understanding of the site structure and instead are able to make much larger jumps deeper into the website's hierarchy when they possess this knowledge (ibid). Danielson's (ibid) findings support the need to consider the way in which users navigate websites and find information. This is a constantly changing strategy and dependent upon individual preference, the website architecture and also the interface through which the search is being performed. From research conducted by Nilsson and Mayer (2002), the need for clear navigation to support humans' mental representation of information has also been stressed. The findings of this study demonstrate how special skills and the users' interpretations of the navigational pathways determine the usability of websites. Additional factors to consider in web site architecture for older users are information density, layout, organisation and the provision of a number of navigation options to encourage successful searches via different user's preferred navigation (Tedesco, Schade, Pernice and Nielsen, 2008).

## Website Attributes Independent of the Users' Expertise

In addition to encapsulating the user's mental model and designing website hierarchy so as to reflect their level of familiarisation with online information, website navigation can be aided by including shortcuts and quick links. Quick links on a website homepage can aid older users' by providing fast routes to information buried deeper in the site and also to frequently requested information, which users may desire to reach effectively. In order to design appropriate quick links the users patterns of information retrieval should be understood and the language used for labelling things such as short cuts should be unambiguous. For example, during a web usability study with older Internet users, it was found that keeping up to date quick links to popular content on a website can significantly aid both novice and expert users (Jain et al., 2012).

## METHODOLOGICAL CONSIDERATIONS

There have been many investigations into the ageing population, from different perspectives such as HCI, design, psychology, gerontology and medical sciences. All of the aforementioned disciplines have applied a variety of techniques to achieve an understanding of how older people differ from and compare to the population as a whole. In the last decades this multidisciplinary interest in ageing has been reflected in the application of several techniques providing a thesaurus of tools and recommendations researchers can now employ to study older participants. For example Dickinson et al. (2007) suggest factoring in additional time when including older people in research, especially those who are not experienced with using computers, to compensate for their decline in memory skills.

This section aims to focus on the methodological considerations needed when designing and evaluating the web with older people. The aim is to highlight successful techniques and how they can contribute to a more effective design of the ever-evolving Internet. The following part of the chapter reviews established research and it is structured around the following topics:

- User centred design techniques.
- Overall considerations when researching with older people as users.
- Controversies and trade-offs in the selection of methods.
- Emerging trends in web design.

## User-Centred Design Techniques

User-Centred design (UCD) or Human-Centred design (HCD) is defined by the British Standard as:

*[the] approach to systems design and development that aims to make interactive systems more usable by focusing on the use of the system and applying human factors/ergonomics and usability knowledge and techniques. (BS EN ISO 9241-210:2010:2)*

In addition to this definition, ISO 9241-210 goes further to explain the importance of usable products and systems not only in the economic and social contexts but specifically in meeting the needs of the users (BS, 2010). For example, the standard explains that through explicit understanding of users and context, a system is able to achieve high usability and therefore achieve technical and commercial success. The creation of a website or user interface involves many stakeholders ranging from board level sign-off to information designers and developers. In such a multidisciplinary team, it is crucial for the correct specification to be passed from one stage of the design and development process to the next, also including iterations where necessary. Throughout the stages of design and development, user involvement is paramount and results in a final product, which is more likely to meet the needs of the user. A user of a product or service is defined as a *"person who interacts with the product"* (British Standard ISO 9241-11:1998: 2).

Luostarinen, Manner, Määttä and Järvinen (2010) examined the process of UCD into the design of a graphical user interface (GUI). The research found that through user feedback, the GUI was made more usable by hiding the complexity of the system whilst still retaining all levels of functionality. Whilst arriving at the correct trade-off between complexity and usability proved successful in the aforementioned research, in industry various factors can impact the application of the UCD process. The constraints that can hinder the full application of UCD in industry might be lack

of time, resources, funds and buy-in from clients and management. Lately there has been a desire for more informal methods of gaining user insight in design practice that are not only cost effective but flexible to a variety of briefs and contexts (Goodman-Deane, Langdon and Clarkson 2009). The model presented in Figure 2 highlights the four main stages of the Interaction Design Model. The model is an adaptation from the Interaction Design Model presented by Preece, Rogers and Sharp (2002).

Using the blueprint identified in Preece et al. (2002) the following sections illustrate each of the four design stages and mention the techniques recommended to fulfil each stage's aim. In order to understand the use of each technique, they are classified as providing 'in-depth insight' -providing comprehensive detailed information (Oxford University Press, 2013)-, or 'shallow insight' -high level, non-detailed information (ibid)- or indeed both. A visual summary of such techniques is presented in Table 1.

## Stage 1: Identify Needs and Establish Requirements

Understanding the user group(s), the task(s) performed and the context(s) are all key factors in the identification of need and requirements for an interactive system. The first stage of the Interac-

*Figure 2. Interaction Design Model adapted from Preece, Rogers and Sharp (2002)*

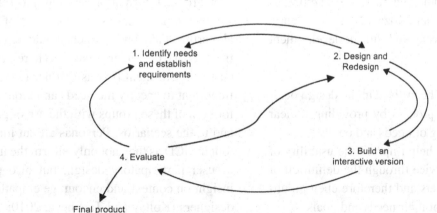

*Table 1. The design stages and relevant research techniques*

| Design Stage | Techniques | In-Depth Insight | Shallow Insight | Participant Number Required |
|---|---|---|---|---|
| 1. Identify Needs and Establish Requirements | Survey | ✓ | ✓ | 100s |
| | Focus Group | ✓ | | 6 – 8 per user group |
| | Interview | ✓ | | 4-6 per identified user group |
| | User Personas and Usage scenarios | ✓ | ✓ | Informed by survey, focus groups or interviews |
| | Competitor analysis | | ✓ | n/a |
| | Journey mapping | ✓ | ✓ | 4-6 per user group |
| 2. Design and Redesign | Card sort | | ✓ | 4-6 per user group |
| | Focus Group | ✓ | | 6 – 8 per user group |
| | Exploratory usability testing | ✓ | ✓ | 4-6 per user group |
| 3. Build an interactive model | Formative usability testing | ✓ | | 4-6 per user group |
| 4. Evaluate | Evaluative usability test | ✓ | | 4-6 per user group |
| | Benchmarking | | ✓ | n/a |
| | Customer feedback | | ✓ | 100s |

tion Design Model is required as the majority of design projects start with needs and requirements (Preece et al., 2002). By developing specific insights into the needs and requirements of the user and business, the end system can attempt to meet the needs of all the stakeholders involved. Miaskiewicz and Kozar (2011) agree that the creation of personas can aid the UCD process. Pruitt and Adline (2006) define a persona as a 'fictitious, specific, concrete representations of target users' (p.11). Furthermore, personas represent the user groups of a product or service and illustrate their common characterises and preferences. Miaskiewicz and Kozar (2011) catalogue a series of benefits associated with the development of Personas, such as:

- Personas can be utilised in the design decision-making process by providing a clear understanding of needs and context.
- Personas can help improve the usability of a product/service through the definition of users/customers and therefore elicit an understanding of their needs and goals.

- Persona research encourages innovation through the focus on user goals rather than the business.
- Personas help in making the identified requirements more tangible and are a reference point for all design and development team, even those without a design background.

In order to achieve the benefits outlines by Miaskiewicz and Kozar (2011), a Persona should provide data on a typical user from the targeted user group. Information such as job title, age, gender, skillset, interests and context of use are all pertinent attributes which should be included in a user and customer persona. Where a user and customer are identified as distinct groups, it is important to specify the needs and requirements for both of these groups with the use of personas and usage scenarios. Personas are an important tool in UCD as they not only inform the methods of user participatory design, but also provide insight on context and encourage empathy from designers (Koltay and Tancheva, 2010; Siddall,

Baibarac, Byrne, Byme, Deasy, Flood Goulding, O'Driscoll, Rabbitt, Sweeny, Wang and Dyer, 2011). This can be achieved by helping to bridge the gap between designers and users (Massanari, 2010). Koltay and Tancheva (2010) also remark on the importance of Personas as a tool to communicate user characteristics within an industry context, proving to be a useful tool throughout design and development.

Other tools useful at this stage of the design process are those which give insight to the system's context of use. Usage scenarios, workflows and storyboards are a suite of tools that provide the design team with a deep understanding of the context of use for an interactive system. The definition of usage scenarios, workflow and storyboards is informed by insight gathered during the creation of user and customer personas and therefore they consist of effective additional tools generated with relatively little effort. Understanding the context of use has become increasingly salient as accessing the Internet is no longer expected to take place on a single platform and therefore the contexts of use of the web can vary significantly (Wäljas, Segerståh, Väänänen-Vainio-Mattila and Oinas-Kukkonen, 2010). As the frequency of accessing the Internet through mobile, tablet, laptop and desktop platforms is growing exponentially, the web design industry is adapting to meet this trend (Joly, 2012) Usage scenarios are crucial in delivering the relevant information to the user on the correct platform. For instance they support responsive web design that, with the use of multiple style sheets, allows a single website to be accessed on multiple platforms (ibid). A practical example of the importance of usage scenarios is the adaptation of a web site designed for a desktop, to be suitable for a mobile phone. This might mean that certain aspects of the webpages will need to be sacrificed in order to deliver legible content on a smaller screen. Journey mapping is a method which can be used to illustrate a usage scenario for different platforms. Not only will it consider the context of use, but should also include all the

touchpoints users experience with the system (Stickdorn and Schneider, 2011). Understanding the user and their priorities in this context is where Personas and scenarios can maximise the usability of an interface. Qualitative research techniques including interviews and focus groups can by utilised to source user information to inform the creation of personas and usage scenarios. Interviews can provide in-depth information about users behaviours, preferences and characteristics whereas focus groups can explore potential ideas and users acceptance of them. Quantitative surveys can also be used here to provide vast amounts of information which may lack the qualitative detail but can still deliver representative data to create representative personas and scenarios.

Users have been discussed as core stakeholders who are at the centre of the UCD process. However, in order to achieve an end product, which meets the needs of all stakeholders, it also needs to meet the requirements of the client or business. For doing so, performance indicators need to be identified as they allow for the measurement of a success in a tangible way that business can relate to. Competitor analysis is another tool, which can inform a business on how to differentiate their offering within their target market whilst employing a UCD strategy (Brock 1984). As illustrated in Figure 1, the creation of user persona(s), customer Persona(s) and usage scenarios can be informed by a number of techniques.

## Stage 2: Design and Redesign

During this stage ideation, design and development is carried out applying information design (ID), visual design and information architecture (IA) design. In a UCD process the research and insights gathered at Stage 1 are instrumental for starting the design of the product/service iteratively. The design of interactive systems and online services requires attention to the content structure (information design), the system design (information architecture) and its visual design. A challenge that designers face at this stage is that of ensuring that the used language, taxonomies and labels are understandable by the intended users. Nielsen (2004) promotes the importance of IA research as a way of informing the content's structure from the users' perspective and not the business' or the designer's viewpoints. Additionally, carrying out IA research increases the likelihood of users experiencing successful interactions with the system, resulting in a more useable end-product (Duncan and Holliday, 2008). This in turn can result in more satisfying experiences through creating a system which closely meets the needs of the intended users. A research method, which informs the arrangement of IA is a card sort. In this technique users are able to arrange content by their own chosen categories or predetermined ones which can allow designers to gauge the users understanding of a system (Nielsen, 2000).

Iteration is a core characteristic of the Interaction Design Model presented in Figure 2. Although a design may strive to meet the identified user needs and requirements at a first attempt, further user testing can bring to light issues that were not previously understood, foreseen or articulated by the users. Nielsen (1993) goes further to explain that designers are not able to arrive at a perfect solution in a single attempt and therefore refining the design based on user participatory evaluation methods is necessary. At the design stage, exploratory usability testing or focus groups with low fidelity prototypes or wireframes can prove very effective (Mayhew and Tremaine, 2005). Low fidelity prototypes, while they do not demand a great deal of time from designers in their creation, can result in quick and valuable feedback from users. Making design alterations based on exploratory usability testing is feasible at this stage as the system architecture and its interface have not yet been built or coded.

## Stage 3: Build an Interactive Model

Once design decisions have been reached combining the users knowledge (Stage 1) with the design experience (Stage 2), resources can be committed to build an interactive model of the system. Here, the prototypes created are partially or mostly coded in order to allow realistic navigation behaviour to be observed. Formative usability testing allows the real representative users to perform actual tasks on interactive system (Mayhew and Tremaine, 2005). Similarly to Stage 2, the application of usability testing can help in identifying additional suggestions for the interactive model and for the overall accessibility of the system and its interface. A formative approach to usability testing is employed here to gather feedback from partially coded prototypes and also on IA, ID and visual design. This type of usability test gathers feedback on a partially functioning and interactive site, the finding of which can inform decisions before the system is fully coded.

## Stage 4: Evaluate

The final stage of the Interaction Design Model is split into two sub stages; the first consists of assessing the usability of the final, fully coded system (evaluative usability testing) and the second is gathering feedback after the system has gone 'live' and it has been used for some time (ibid). Collecting feedback from real users of the live system helps with the site maintenance and can bring to light potential ideas for future development. This customer feedback can be achieved through online surveys, be informed by customer feedback and by observation of real use. Lastly, learning competitors' best practices or processes can further improve a system through benchmarking. Benchmarking can aid the differentiation of the system designed by measuring its performance measures and its offering against competitors.

In Table 2 we summarise all the techniques that researchers and practitioners might wish to employ to successfully complete each stage of the Interaction Design Model. For each technique Table 2 illustrates the purpose, the pros and cons and reference to studies where such techniques have been applied.

## Overall Considerations when Researching Older People as Users

As discussed in section 2 of this chapter, older people experience a varying degree of change in their vision, motor and cognition skills. In addition, the diverse lifestyle characteristics, experiences and preferences of the older population make researching with this age group distinct. In research fields such as HCI and technology adoption, the study of older people as users of technology is a broadly covered topic highlighting the need to give particular consideration to this age group (Wagner et al., 2010; Zajicek, 2006; Dickinson et al, 2007; Blythe, Monk and Doughty, 2005; Kurniawan, 2008; Dickinson et al., 2005; Chevalier et al., 2012; Stronge, Rogers and Fisk, 2006). Through a review of previous studies and with a first-hand knowledge of this user group, a set of guidelines to consider when researching with older participants is presented below. The guidelines are organised following a logical sequence of steps that researchers will have to follow to conduct a user participatory study:

- Recruitment.
- Participant profiling.
- Computer expertise.
- Research design.

## Recruitment

Including participants with different levels of expertise with the Internet is recommended due to the fact that expertise can directly affect the task performance and participant feedback (Chadwick-

Dias, Tedesco and Tullis, 2004). Although it may be dependent on the aim of the research, attention to expertise is recommended ahead of the study design. Research carried out by Karavidas, Lim and Katsikas (2005) found that when older participants experience anxiety during research, this can affect self-efficacy. In order to minimise the likelihood of anxiety, full disclosure of the study motivation and the use of the findings is necessary throughout the recruitment and study process.

## Participant Profiling

As discussed in Stage 1 of the UCD process, understanding the user group(s) of a system is crucial in the creation of Personas and also in informing the recruitment of participants to study. It is recommended to segment the participants in accordance to their age, as well as the identified Personas (Miaskiewicz and Kozar 2011; Pruitt and Adlin, 2006). Although personas should take age into account, lifestyle characteristics and the level of exposure to the Internet can be diverse with the older population particularly (Dickinson, 2007). Furthermore, when deciding on the age range of participants in each persona, the W3C points out that older people's exposure to the Internet can depend upon its availability; the Internet only became widely used in the 1990s (W3C, 2013).

## Computer Expertise

Several HCI studies have measured participants' computer expertise as a pre-requisite to eligibility for research because the frequency of Internet use and the number of functions performed was found to influence task performance (Chadwick-Dias et al., 2004; Redish and Chisnell, 2004; Olson, O'Brien, Rogers and Charness, 2011). It is therefore recommended to measure participants' level of expertise with the Internet before the study takes place (e.g. pre-test questionnaire). Once participants' expertise has been gauged, we suggest normalising the minimum level of the participants'

*Table 2. Techniques for user centred design process*

| Research Technique | Purpose | Pros | Cons | Reference |
|---|---|---|---|---|
| User personas | Defines the characteristic and preferences of a representative target group of users | - Identifies and represents the different users of a system<br>- Strong foundation to inform design decisions<br>- Encourages innovation through focus on user goals rather than the business' | - Requires early buy-in into resources for research (which informs personas)<br>- Requires know-how from designer/researcher to construct | Miaskiewicz and Kozar, 2011; Pruitt and Adline, 2006 |
| Usage scenarios | Give insight to the system's context of use based on the personas identified | - Provides a clear understanding of context(s) of where the system is used<br>- Clarifies the different scenarios, objectives and behaviours for each user persona<br>- Can be referred to throughout the design process | - Sometimes many are required to meet the different user groups identified | Yannou, Yvars, Hoyle and Chen, 2013; Jong and Lentz, 2006 |
| Survey | To define and measure insights of the system or context being investigated alongside user characteristics | - Can be done remotely<br>- Reach large numbers<br>- Can be representative<br>- Cost-effective<br>- Can provide statistically significant data | - Correct survey design and wording is crucial in obtaining reliable results<br>- Difficult to ask the reasoning behind behaviours or answers | Miasiewicz and Kozar, 2011; Hessler, 1992; Turnbow, Kasianovitz, Snyder, Gilbert, Yamamoto, 2005; Siddall et al., 2011 |
| Focus group | Discuss and explore topics or concepts in a group format to collate qualitative feedback | - Explore potential and current attitudes<br>- Gather feedback on low fidelity prototypes in an informal setting | - Discussions can be digressive<br>- Influence from other participants | Küster and Vila, 2011; Belzile and Öberg, 2012; Barbour, 2005; Tremblay, Hevner and Berndt, 2010 |
| Interview | Discuss, in-depth, topics or system being explored. This is done on a one-to-one basis with a facilitator | - In-depth information<br>- Facilitator can probe further into interesting discussions<br>- Can be contextual | - Time-consuming<br>- Demanding on resources | Koltay and Kancheva, 2010; McCloskey, 2006 |
| Competitor analysis | Investigates and compares identified competitors offering, customers and the company itself | - Can define the value of the offering delivered by competitors<br>- Learn from competitors successes and failures<br>- Seek scope for gap in the market | - Competitors information is not always openly available<br>- It would be difficult to gather primary insights | Brock (1984) |
| Journey mapping | Provides a structured overview of the user experience. This user insight can be gathered from interviews or expert evaluations | - Ascertains all the touch points of a system<br>- Can be carried out by the user themselves<br>- Provides an overview of the whole system and interaction points | - Not as accurate or rich as a usability test | Stickdorn and Schneider (2011) |
| Card sort | Identifies or confirms the taxonomy and labelling used in the system from the users' perspective | - Useful in structuring and deciding the labels for menus<br>- Matches the users' mental model<br>- Can be done remotely<br>- Software such as TreeJack can also product dendrograms<br>- Quick and cost effective | - Requires software or expert knowledge to analyse the data | Nielsen (2000); Lewis and Hepburn (2010); Zaphiris et al., 2007 |

*continued on following page*

*Table 2. Continued*

| Research Technique | Purpose | Pros | Cons | Reference |
|---|---|---|---|---|
| Exploratory usability testing | Test low fidelity wireframes and sketches with users | - Wireframes are cheap and quick to make<br>- Fast results early on in the design stages | - Cannot test interaction at this stage<br>- Requires heavy involvement from facilitator | Prakash and Gopalakrishnan, 2011; McDonald, Edwards and Zhao, 2012 |
| Formative usability testing | Test low to medium fidelity prototypes with users | - Visual design feedback<br>- Some interaction can be tested<br>- Test whilst coding is still be refined | - Cannot test all interactions<br>- Changes can be implemented without hefty costs<br>- Not true to the end product | Craven and Booth, 2006; Neilsen and Landauer, 1993; Høegh, Nielsen, Overgaard, Pedersen and Stage, 2006 |
| Evaluative usability test | Test the final fully functioning system with users | - Able to test real usage and in context<br>- Ensures the usability of the system before going live. | - More time consuming to test all aspects of fully functioning system | Shackel, 2009 |
| Benchmarking | Comparing the processes, best practices and performance measures of one business to others in industry | - Learn from competitors in order to differentiate the system's offering | - Website benchmarking must take into account many factors such as attractiveness, accessibility, usability, structure and navigation | Kim, Shaw and Schneider, 2003 |
| Customer feedback | Gather feedback from real users of the final system | - Specific to the final system<br>- Can inform redesign<br>- Often low cost (e.g. online survey) | - Need to provide an incentive for customers to take part<br>- Customers may be more likely to report negative feedback than satisfactory | Caemmerer and Wilson, 2010 |

exposure to the Internet by conducting pre-test training exercise. This will help in ensuring that non-users of the Internet do not adversely affect the distribution of results, i.e. produce outliers, (Ellis and Kurniawan, 2000).

## Research Design

The design and set-up of the research can have several impacts on older participants. Firstly, attempting to create a more informal atmosphere during research is advised in order to minimise self-blame in task failure, which has been observed from research with older participants (Hawthorn, 2007). Secondly, as older people might experience a decline in their cognitive capabilities and varying expertise with the Internet, it is suggested to

allow more time for older participants to complete tasks than their younger counterparts (Chevalier et al., 2012; Sayago and Blat, 2011; Dickinson, et al., 2007). Furthermore, setting a number of simpler, shorter tasks are preferable to a few longer complex tasks. Li et al. (2012) found that with older participants, longer complex tasks are more demanding on cognitive load and results in more errors. Lastly, from our own research with older participants, we found that presenting printed task instructions in a short and succinct manner proved useful. This was found to reduce the participant's focus on remembering the task at hand and instead focusing on navigation through the website/interface that was being tested (Jain et al., 2012).

## Controversies and Trade-Offs in the Selection of Design Techniques

It is accepted that including usability throughout the design and development process can reduce costs and time (Nielsen, 2003). However as technology become more accessible and user-friendly and broadband connections more affordable, the profile of internet users also becomes broader and more diverse. In designing for Internet experiences, practitioners are faced by the challenge of engaging with users as soon as possible as well as selecting an inclusive sample of users who may represent the broader target user audience. This is not an easy task and requires careful considerations according to the applications, systems or sites one might be interested in developing. One of the trade-offs that designers are faced with is whether to have an inclusive, hence larger user groups involved in the design process, or keeping a modest core user groups that might only in part be representative of the needs of the final audience. In the former case the design process may be controversial and challenging, also resulting in extended timeframes. However it would iron out issues that once the site/application is launched, would hardly be discovered or mended as users would naturally avoid accessing the site if their experience with it is unpleasant. The latter case instead might be an easier option but might simply postpone the resolution of accessibility and usability issues, overall resulting in an initial less than adequate reputation for the site/service. To combine the business pressure of delivering on time with an appropriate inclusive design approach, practitioners may consider a mixture of user evaluation, heuristic methods and simulation tools that could help informing the design in the most comprehensive way. A heuristic evaluation, a terminology coined by Nielsen (1994), is a list of defined principles which should be applied by experts when evaluating interfaces, websites and systems at large. This involvement of experts to evaluate the system, eligibly help in bringing issues to light in a faster and more effective way. Practitioners can also consider using tools freely available online, which can simulate older peoples changing capabilities. Coleman et al. (2007) developed a very useful toolkit, which simulates varying degrees of visual impairments and offers a wealth of knowledge on designing for those with impairments. In essence, using the toolkit to quickly assess factors such as colour use can provide very quick and economically viable feedback throughout the design process.

## Emerging Trends in Web Design

Over recent years, user experience (UX) has become a more established topic in HCI and more notably in the design industry. UX refers to maximising the usability of a product, service or system by exploring *all* of the touch points associated with it (Hassenzahl and Tractinsky, 2006). UX aims to differentiate a product or service by offering a greater competitive insight on the users' experience (Pine and Gilmore, 2011). UX seems particularly relevant to Internet-based development where the experience is not always tangible, however satisfying the users is critical in securing their retention, referral and loyalty.

A specific attribute of Internet-based development is that the information provided must be up-to-date to be valuable to its users. Such attribute requires robust back-end processes that ensure the currency of the system, hence its success. This fast pace of change has recently led to Agile software development, a process which aims to deliver high quality tested units of a website or software with short iterations cycles (Wolkerstorfer, Tscheligi, Sefelin, Milchrahm, Hussain, Lechner and Shahzad, 2008). The process of Agile development is capable of handling the necessary continuous updates that an Internet-based application may require, and it does so by allowing the development and release of smaller sections of an overall system, rather than redesigning an entire system or its architecture (Agile Alliance, 2013).

Although this method is becoming very popular for its obvious business benefits, from a usability perspective there are still concerns regarding the segmented approach to design (Dingsøyra, Nerurc, Balijepally and Moea, 2012). Where an Agile and segmented approach to design takes place, the resulting lack of unification may hinder the UX and it may also impinge on the ability to gather user insights from the entire functioning system (as it is ever-changing). Hong, Thong, Chasalow, and Dhillon (2011) studied users' acceptance of Agile systems, highlighting that current literature mostly focuses on Agile system from the perspective of developers. Whilst the research recommends to constantly seeking to measure the users' acceptance of evolving Agile systems, it is also emerging that the need to consider the usefulness of the new releases is also pertinent (ibid). When considering the UCD methods previously discussed in this chapter, it seems that the trend in Agile development will not be incorporated within UCD cycle without challenges due to the quick turnaround in Agile development, i.e. a matter of weeks.

## DISCUSSION

So far we have discussed the conditions, needs and lifestyles of ageing individuals and how these may affect their online experience. We have also considered the challenges faced in the design process of web services for ageing users. This section explores items that have a strong impact on the online user satisfaction, but might not be resolved solely by good web design. Such perusal will start with three elements, namely confidence, motivation and trust, which have a deep impact on ageing users when dealing with the Internet. This section does not mean to be comprehensive about all issues of socio-economic nature that affect the adoption and use of Internet technologies, but rather aims to give a flavour of the inherent complexity of the topic under investigation.

While baby boomers, the generation born post World War II, is getting increasingly versed with the use of the Internet in everyday life, the technology gap with younger generation is bound to stay for some time. Practitioners and academics are faced with the dilemma of whether they should consider designing exclusively for targeted user groups, such as the elderly, or pursue inclusivity by creating adaptive interfaces that could fulfil the needs of diverse users. Although meaningful efforts are invested in creating more satisfactory experience for a broader user audience, there are concerns related to the adoption of web-based services that go beyond the successful design of a user interface.

Despite the good design of web services, the initial resistance to the use of technology can be the biggest barrier that could hinder the successful start of the user experience. Confidence, and the lack of it, impinges on the ability to feel stress-free when dealing with an unfamiliar context and initiate the need for continuous reassurance feedback that could itself deteriorate the navigational behaviour and the resulting user experience. Users may manifest lack of confidence in their abilities and this may be generated by unfamiliarity, previous bad experiences and fear of making irretrievable mistakes, demonstrating that technologies are beyond the users' abilities (Gatto and Tak, 2008). At times, lack of trust in the technology can also greatly discourage the initial interest and curiosity that ageing users may normally manifest towards online technologies and services (Dutton and Shepherd, 2006) leading to a tamed motivation that often translates in a 'I can do without it as I have done so for many years' type of attitude.

The mechanisms to relieve the above concerns vary from personal initiatives, e.g. attendance to computer courses for the elderly and *ad hoc* help from the friends and family circle, to organised practice especially in the commercial sectors, where elderly can rely on the support of specialised call centres' personnel or in-store demos to support their online experience, and often complete a purchase.

Confidence building can take place through a steady process during which the users can familiarise with the interface and its informational content, while also resetting higher expectations as the learning progresses. However a challenge arises when dealing with web-based services, both informational and transactional in nature, as the information is updated continuously to stay current. While the trade-off between current content and consistent informational structure may be hard to strike, navigational pathways and intuitive menus' hierarchy can provide the necessary anchor points for inexperienced users (Jain et al., 2012).

When confidence cannot be built through the mechanisms aforementioned, elderly users delegate, defer or at times dismiss the benefit that technology, and the Internet, can bring to their life, perpetuating a sense of dependence from other people (Roupa, Nikas, Gerasimou, Zafeiri, Giasyrani, Kazitori and Sotiropoulou, 2010). Delegation often occurs for tasks that are perceived as complex, e.g. setting up browser preferences, email account management, or in full whereby users would allocate a whole activity, e.g. retrieving specific information online, to someone else, while still benefitting from the search results. In some cases ageing users dismiss entirely the positive impact that Internet can bring to their life, rejecting their adoption. Such attitude could be attributed to the high cognitive and emotional costs that the initial setting up and familiarisation processes might demand (Age UK, 2012).

For those ageing users who enjoy the online experience and engage with internet technologies, a satisfactory user experience is a goalpost that changes with their abilities and their developing expectations. User satisfaction in this case is determined by the effective journey to complete the planned tasks, the usability and aesthetics of the sites they visit, and the joy of use. This group of users are generally equipped with favourable intentions towards using the Internet and such attitude is generally correlated with higher levels of education and income (Eastman and Iyer, 1984).

Access to and satisfactory experience with web-based services are determinant factors that can significantly enhance the quality of life in later years, contributing to independent living, emotional wellbeing and social exchange (Hugh, 2004). An overall increased sense of empowerment has also been measured among those who engage with the Internet (Shapira, Barak and Gal, 2007).

On the basis of the above considerations, a satisfactory user experience goes much beyond a good design, although it starts from it. The initial satisfactory access to web services and applications can determine a stronger sense of self-confidence, and contribute to an improved quality of life overall. With an increasingly ageing population, the Internet has become a channel of service delivery that while cutting costs for businesses, also provides those with hampered mobility, access that would be otherwise unfeasible. A satisfactory experience with inclusive web-based service is the token necessary to initiate a journey to stronger social participation, heightened health awareness and ultimately towards choice through the World Wide Web.

## FUTURE RESEARCH DIRECTIONS

The profound changes to the population structure and the advancement in technology, with resulting decrease of costs associated with its purchase and use, are making older people an ever more numerous group of Internet users. While older people's exposure to technology is increasing, it would be a mistake to consider these Internet users as a homogeneous group because factors such as gender, education, personal attitude and physical and cognitive characteristics make each individual different. The challenge for web services starts from this very point: how can we design satisfactory online experiences and services with requirements that can be so diverse?

While web design is making significant advancements in becoming more user-centred, we propose that to achieve a higher online inclusivity rate and satisfactory online experience a rethinking of the business models that underpin many web services should be taking place. While Agile software development becomes more popular and affords effective web design and update, similarly users should be supported by web services that could develop progressively with the skills and the needs of the user. Such modular approach could allow personalisation but would require resources accounted in the business model underpinning the service provision. The research in user satisfaction online should then be coupled with areas of investigation in the realm of innovation and business modelling that, to-date, are lagging behind. Web 2.0 technologies have changed dramatically Web services giving back to users more control of their online experience. We suggest that organisations and businesses interested in developing online relations with older users should consider dedicating resources to support the learning process of those who may not be familiar with technology. The allocation of control back in the hands of the users could results in simplified web services that could bring older people closer to the Internet and build up their confidence and independence to rip the full benefits of Web services.

## CONCLUSION

The growth of the ageing population grants the heightened attention dedicated to the development of web services that can fulfil this increasingly larger demographic segment worldwide. In making this case, we have brought to the foreground and discussed the physical and cognitive changes and the behavioural preferences experienced in later life and that may have impacts on the user experience of the web. Such changes ought to be considered in the design process to facilitate digital inclusion. Methods and techniques applicable in the different stages of the design process have been examined at length, portraying the strengths and relevance of each of them. While ageing related conditions and preferences are often at the centre of the debate for the design of more inclusive user experiences, in the discussion section of this chapter we have broaden the analysis to issues such as self-confidence and trust in the technology as important elements to consider to picture a better web for older people. We have concluded the chapter by pointing out that while technological innovations, e.g. Web 2.0 and Agile software development, are allowing a better user control of the web experience, similarly business models and consequent resource allocation, should be re-considered to customise web services and make them truly inclusive.

## REFERENCES

Age UK. (2012). *Aging consumers: Lifestyle and preferences in the current marketplace 2012.* Unpublished.

Agile Alliance. (2013). *Agile alliance: The alliance.* Retrieved April 10th, 2013 from http://www.agilealliance.org/

Aula, A. (2005). User study on older adults' use of the web and search engines. *Universal Access Information Society, 4,* 67–81. doi:10.1007/s10209-004-0097-7

Barbour, R. S. (2005). Making sense of focus groups. *Medical Education, 39,* 742–750. doi:10.1111/j.1365-2929.2005.02200.x PMID:15960795

Barry, B. K., & Carson, R. G. (2004). The consequences of resistance training for movement control in older adults. *Journal of Gerontology, 59*(7), 730–754. PMID:15304540

Becker, S. A. (2004). E-government visual accessibility for older adults users. *Social Science Computer Review, 22*(1), 11–23. doi:10.1177/0894439303259876

Belzile, J. A., & Öberg, G. (2012). Where to begin? Grappling with how to user participant interaction in focus group design. *Qualitative Research, 12*(4), 459–472. doi:10.1177/1468794111433089

Blake, M. (1993). Internet access for older people. *Aslib Proceedings, 50*(10), 308–315. doi:10.1108/eb051509

Blythe, M. A., Monk, A. F., & Doughty, K. (2005). Socially dependable design: The challenge of ageing populations for HCI. *Interacting with Computers, 17*, 672–689. doi:10.1016/j.intcom.2005.09.005

British Standards. (1998). *ISO 9241-11:1998 - Ergonomic requirements for office work with visual display terminals (VDTs) -- Part 11: Guidance on usability*. Retrieved April 1, 2013, from http://www.iso.org/iso/catalogue_detail.htm?csnumber=16883

British Standards. (2010). *EN ISO 9241-210:2010 - Ergonomics of human-system interaction -- Part 210: Human-centred design for interactive systems*. Retrieved March 28, 2013 from http://www.iso.org/iso/catalogue_detail.htm?csnumber=52075

British Standards Institute. (2010). *BS 8878.2010 - Web accessibility code of practice*. Retrieved April 3, 2013, from http://shop.bsigroup.com/en/ProductDetail/?pid=000000000030180388

Brock, J. J. (1984). Competitor analysis: Some practical approaches. *Industrial Marketing Management, 13*(4), 225–231. doi:10.1016/0019-8501(84)90017-8

Burmeister, O. K. (2010). Websites for seniors: Cognitive accessibility. *International Journal of Emerging Technologies and Society, 8*(2), 99–113.

Caemmerer, B., & Wilson, A. (2010). Customer feedback mechanisms and organisational learning in service operations. *International Journal of Operations & Production Management, 30*(3), 288–311. doi:10.1108/01443571011024638

Carmeli, E., Patish, H., & Coleman, R. (2003). The aging hand. *Journal of Gerontology: Medical Sciences, 58A*(2), 146–152. doi:10.1093/gerona/58.2.M146 PMID:12586852

Carmichael, A., Newell, A. F., & Morgan, M. (2007). The efficacy of narrative video for raising awareness in ICT designers about older users' requirements. *Interacting with Computers, 19*, 587–596. doi:10.1016/j.intcom.2007.06.001

Chadwick-Dias A., McNulty, & Tullis. (2003). Web usability and age: How design changes can improve performance. *CUU,* 30–37.

Chadwick-Dias, A., Tedesco, D., & Tullis, T. (2004). Older adults and web usability: Is web experience the same as web expertise? In *Proceedings of CHI 2004*, (pp. 1391-1394). ACM.

Charness, N., & Czaja, S. J. (2005). Adaptation to new technologies. In *The Cambridge handbook of age and ageing*. New York: Cambridge University Press.

Chevalier, A., Dommes, A., & Martins, D. (2012). The effects of ageing and website ergonomic quality on the internet information searching. *Ageing and Society,* 1–27.

Chevalier, A., & Kicka, M. (2006). Web designers and web users: Influence of the ergonomic quality of the web site on the information search. *International Journal of Human-Computer Studies*, *64*, 1031–1048. doi:10.1016/j.ijhcs.2006.06.002

Chisnell, D. E., Redish, J., & Lee, A. (2006). New heuristics for understanding older adults as web users. *Technical Communication*, *53*, 39–59.

Choudrie, J., Weerakkody, V., & Jones, S. (2005). Realising e-government in the UK: Rural and urban challenges. *The Journal of Enterprise Information Management*, *18*(5), 568–585. doi:10.1108/17410390510624016

Clarkson, J., Coleman, R., Hosking, I., & Waller, S. (Eds.). (2007). *Inclusive design toolkit*. Cambridge, UK: University of Cambridge.

Coleman, R. (2004). Foreword. In *Countering design exclusion: An introduction to inclusive design*. London: Springer-Verlag.

Craven, J., & Booth, H. (2006). Putting awareness into practice: Practical steps for conducting usability tests. *Library Review*, *55*(3), 179–194. doi:10.1108/00242530610655984

Curran, J. M., Meuter, M. L., & Surprenant, C. F. (2003). Intentions to use self-service technologies: A confluence of multiple attitudes. *Journal of Service Research*, *5*(3), 209–224. doi:10.1177/1094670502238916

Czaja, S. J., & Lee, C. C. (2003). Designing computer systems for older adults. In *The human-computer interaction handbook: Fundamentals, evolving technologies and emerging applications*. Hoboken, NJ: Lawrence Erlbaum Associates Publishers.

Danielson, D. R. (2002). Web navigation and the behavioural effects of constantly visible site maps. *Interacting with Computers*, *14*, 601–618. doi:10.1016/S0953-5438(02)00024-3

Department for Work and Pensions. (2005). Focus on older people. In *The freetirement generation*. SIRC. Retrieved on March 27, 2013 from http://www.sirc.org/publik/freetirement_generation.shtml

Dickenson, A., Eisma, R., & Gregor, P. (2011). The barriers that older novices encounter to computer use. *Universal Access Information Society*, *10*, 261–266. doi:10.1007/s10209-010-0208-6

Dickinson, A., Arnott, J., & Prior, S. (2007). Methods for human–computer interaction research with older people. *Behaviour & Information Technology*, *26*, 343–352. doi:10.1080/01449290601176948

Dingsøyra, T., Nerurc, S., Balijepally, V., & Moea, N. B. (2012). A decade of agile methodologies: Towards explaining agile software development. *Journal of Systems and Software*, *85*, 1213–1221. doi:10.1016/j.jss.2012.02.033

Docampo Rama, M., Ridder, H., & Bouma, H. (2001). Technology generation and age in using layered user interfaces. *Technology Generation*, *1*(1), 1–16.

Duncan, J., & Holliday, W. (2008). The role of information architecture in designing a third-generation library web site. *College & Research Libraries*, 301–318.

Dutton, W. H., & Shepherd, A. (2006). Trust in the Internet as an experience technology information. *Communicatio Socialis*, *9*(4), 433–451.

Eastman, J. K., & Iyer, R. (2004). The elderly's uses and attitudes towards the Internet. *Journal of Consumer Marketing*, *21*(3), 208–220. doi:10.1108/07363760410534759

Ellis, R. D., & Kurniawan, S. H. (2000). Increasing the usability of online information for older users: A case study in participatory design. *International Journal of Human-Computer Interaction*, *12*(2), 263–276. doi:10.1207/S15327590IJHC1202_6

Gao, Q., Sato, H., Rau, P.-L. P., & Asano, Y. (2007). Design effective navigation tools for older web users. *Human-Computer Interaction, 1*, 765–773.

Gatto, S. L., & Tak, S. H. (2008). Computer, internet, and e-mail use among older adults: Benefits and barriers. *Educational Gerontology, 34*(9), 800–811. doi:10.1080/03601270802243697

Gilroy, R. (2005). Meeting the information needs of older people: A challenge for local governance. *Local Government Studies, 31*(1), 39–51. doi:10.1080/0300393042000332846

Go On, U. K. (2013). *Go on UK – Improving digital skills in the UK for people & businesses.* Retrieved on March 3, 2013 from http://www.go-on.co.uk/

Goodman-Deane, J., Langdon, P., & Clarkson, J. (2009). Key influences on the user-centred design process. *Journal of Engineering Design, 21*(2-3), 345–373.

Hassenzahl, M., & Tractinsky, N. (2006). User experience – A research agenda. *Behaviour & Information Technology, 25*(2), 91–97. doi:10.1080/01449290500330331

Hawthorn, D. (2007). Interface design and engagement with older people. *Behaviour & Information Technology, 26*(4), 333–341. doi:10.1080/01449290601176930

Hessler, R. M. (1992). *Social research methods.* St. Paul, MN: West Publishing Company.

Høegh, R. T., Nielsen, C. M., Overgaard, M., Pedersen, M. B., & Stage, J. (2006). The impact of usability reports and user test observations on developers' understanding of usability data: An exploratory study. *International Journal of Human-Computer Interaction, 21*(2), 173–196. doi:10.1207/s15327590ijhc2102_4

Hong, W., Thong, J. Y. L., Chasalow, L. C., & Dhillon, G. (2011). User acceptance of agile information systems: A model and empirical test. *Journal of Management Information Systems, 28*(1), 235–272. doi:10.2753/MIS0742-1222280108

Hugh, M. G. (2004). Exploring elders interaction with information technology. *Journal of Business and Economic Research, 2*(6), 62–66.

Jain, S. K., Spinelli, G., Garaj, V., & Dong, H. (2012). *The use of the internet by older people: A behavioural study.* Paper presented at the Universal Design Conference 2012. Fukuoka, Japan.

Joly, K. (2012). One design to rule them all? Responsive web design in higher education. *Internet Technology,* 498-500.

Jong, M., & Lentz, L. (2006). Scenario evaluation of municipal web sites: Development and use of an expert-focused evaluation tool. *Government Information Quarterly, 23*, 191–206. doi:10.1016/j.giq.2005.11.007

Karavidas, M., Lim, N. K., & Katsikas, S. L. (2005). The effects of computers on older adult users. *Computers in Human Behavior, 21*, 697–711. doi:10.1016/j.chb.2004.03.012

Kim, S.-E., Shaw, T., & Schneider, H. (2003). Web site design benchmarking within industry groups. *Internet Research, 13*(1), 19–26. doi:10.1108/10662240310458341

Koltay, Z., & Tancheva, K. (2010). Personas and a user-centred visioning process. *Performance Measurement and Metrics, 11*(2), 172–183. doi:10.1108/14678041011064089

Kumza, J. M. (2010). Accessibility design issues with UK e-government sites. *Government Information Quarterly, 27*, 141–146. doi:10.1016/j.giq.2009.10.004

Küster, I., & Vila, N. (2011). Successful SME web design through consumer focus groups. *International Journal of Quality & Reliability Management, 28*(2), 132–154. doi:10.1108/02656711111101728

Lewis, K. M., & Hepburn, P. (2010). Open card sorting and factor analysis: A usability case study. *The Electronic Library, 28*(3), 401–416. doi:10.1108/02640471011051981

Li, H., Rau, P.-L. P., Fujimura, K., Gao, Q., & Wang, L. (2012). Designing effective web forums for older web users. *Educational Gerontology, 38,* 271–281. doi:10.1080/03601277.2010.544578

Lidwell, W., Holden, K., & Butler, J. (2003). *Universal principles of design: 125 ways to enhance usability, perception, increase appeal, make better design decisions and teach through design.* Rockport, MA: Rockport Publishers Inc.

Luostarinen, R., Manner, J., Määttä, J., & Järvinen, R. (2010). User-centered design of graphical user interfaces. In *Proceedings of the 2010 Military Communications Conference – Unclassified Program – Cyber Security and Network Management.* IEEE.

Massanari, A. L. (2010). Designing for imaginary friends: Information architecture, personas and the politics of user-centered design. *New Media & Society, 12*(3), 401–416.

Mayhew, D. J., & Tremaine, M. M. (2005). A basic framework. In *Cost-justifying usability: An update for the internet age.* San Francisco: Morgan Kaufmann Publishers. doi:10.1016/B978-012095811-5/50003-1

McCloskey, D. W. (2006). The importance of ease of use, usefulness, and trust to online consumers: An examination of the technology acceptance model with older consumers. *Journal of Organizational and End User Computing, 18*(3), 47–65. doi:10.4018/joeuc.2006070103

McDonald, S., Edwards, H. M., & Zhao, T. (2012). Exploring think-alouds in usability testing: An international survey. *IEEE Transactions on Professional Communication, 55*(1), 2–19. doi:10.1109/TPC.2011.2182569

Miaskiewicz, T., & Kozar, K. A. (2011). Personas and user-centered design: How can personas benefit the product design processes? *Design Studies, 32,* 417–430. doi:10.1016/j.destud.2011.03.003

Neilsen, J., & Landauer, T. K. (1993). A mathematical model of the finding of usability problems. In *Proceedings of INTERCHI '93.* ACM.

Nielsen, J. (1993). Iterative user-interface design. *Computer, 26*(11), 32–41. doi:10.1109/2.241424

Nielsen, J. (1994). Heuristic evaluation. In *Usability inspection methods.* New York: John Wiley & Sons.

Nielsen, J. (1995). *Ten usability heuristics.* Retrieved on March 26, 2013 from http://www.nngroup.com/articles/ten-usability-heuristics/

Nielsen, J. (2000). *Why you only need to test with 5 users.* Retrieved March 25, 2013 from http://www.nngroup.com/articles/why-you-only-need-to-test-with-5-users/

Nielsen, J. (2003). *Usability engineering.* Academic Press.

Nielsen, J. (2004). *Card sorting: How many users to test.* Retrieved on March 25, 2013 from http://www.nngroup.com/articles/card-sorting-how-many-users-to-test/

Nilsson, R. M., & Mayer, R. E. (2002). The effects of graphic organisers giving cues to the structure of a hypertext document on users' navigation, strategies and performance. *International Journal of Human-Computer Studies, 57,* 1–26. doi:10.1006/ijhc.2002.1011

Ofcom. (2012). *Communications market report.* Retrieved March 19th, 2013, from http://stakeholders.ofcom.org.uk/binaries/research/cmr/cmr12/CMR_UK_2012.pdf

Ofcom. (2012). *Communications market report.* Retrieved on March 21, 2013 from http://stakeholders.ofcom.org.uk/market-data-research/market-data/communications-market-reports/cmr12/downloads/

Olsen, K. E., O'Brien, M. A., Rodgers, W. A., & Charness, N. (2011). Diffusion of technology: Frequency of use for younger and older adults. *Ageing International, 36,* 123–145. doi:10.1007/s12126-010-9077-9 PMID:22685360

ONS. (2012). *Internet access quarterly update, Q4 2012.* Retrieved on March 19, 2013 from http://www.ons.gov.uk/ons/dcp171778_300874.pdf

Oxford University Press. (2013). *In-depth definition.* Retrieved on March 26, 2013 from http://oxforddictionaries.com/

Pak, R., & Price, M. M. (2008). Designing an information search interface for younger and older adults. *Human Factors: The Journal of the Human Factors and Ergonomics Society, 50*(4), 614–628. doi:10.1518/001872008X312314 PMID:18767521

Pine, J. B., & Gilmore, J. H. (2011). *The experience economy.* Cambridge, MA: Harvard Business Review Press.

Prakash, V., & Gopalakrishnan, S. (2011). Testing efficiency exploited: Scripted versus exploratory testing. *Electronics Computer Technology,* 168-172.

Preece, J., Rogers, Y., & Sharp, H. (2002). *Interaction design: Beyond human-computer interaction.* New York: John Wiley & Sons.

Pruitt, J., & Adline, T. (2006). *The persona lifecycle: Keeping people in mind throughout product design.* San Francisco: Morgan Kaufmann Publishers.

Redish, J., & Chisnell, D. (2004). *Designing web sites for older adults: A review of recent research.* Retrieved on April 8, 2013 from http://assets.aarp.org/www.aarp.org_/articles/research/oww/AARP-LitReview2004.pdf

Roupa, Z., Nikas, M., Gerasimou, E., Zafeiri, V., Giasyrani, L., Kazitori, E., & Sotiropoulou, P. (2010). The use of technology by the elderly. *Health Science Journal, 4*(2), 118–126.

Sayago, S., & Blat, J. (2011). An ethnographical study of the accessibility barriers in the everyday interaction of older people with the web. *Universal Access Information Society, 10*(4), 359–371. doi:10.1007/s10209-011-0221-4

Seidel, D., Richardson, K., Crilly, N., Matthews, F. E., Clarkson, J. P., & Brayne, C. (2010). Design for independent living: Activity demands and capabilities of older people. *Ageing and Society, 30*(7), 1239–1255. doi:10.1017/S0144686X10000310

Shackel, B. (2009). Usability – Context, framework, definition, design and evaluation. *Interacting with Computers, 21,* 339–345. doi:10.1016/j.intcom.2009.04.007

Shapira, A., Barak, A., & Gal, I. (2007). Promoting older adults' well-being through internet training and use. *Aging & Mental Health, 11*(5), 477–484. doi:10.1080/13607860601086546 PMID:17882585

Siddall, E., Baibarac, C., Byrne, A., Byme, N., Deasy, A., & Flood, N. et al. (2011). Personas as a user-centred design tool for the built environment. *Engineering Sustainability, 164*(ES1), 59–69. doi:10.1680/ensu.1000015

Stickdorn, M., & Schneider, J. (2011). *This is service design thinking: Basics-tools-cases*. Amsterdam: BIS Publishers.

Stronge, A. J., Rodgers, W. A., & Fisk, A. D. (2006). Web-based information search and retrieval: Effects of strategy use and age on search success. *The Journal of Human Factors and Ergonomic Society*, 48(3), 434–446. doi:10.1518/001872006778606804 PMID:17063960

Tedesco, D., Schade, A., Pernice, K., & Nielsen, J. (2008). *Site map usability: 47 guidelines based on usability studies with people using site maps*. Retrieved on April 12, 2013 from http://www.nngroup.com/reports/sitemaps/

Tremblay, M. C., Hevner, A. R., & Berndt, D. J. (2010). Focus groups for artifact refinement and evaluation in design research. *Communications of the Association for Information Systems*, 26(27), 599–618.

Turnbow, D., Kasianovitz, K., Snyder, L., Gilbert, D., & Yamamoto, D. (2005). Usability testing for web redesign: A UCLA case study. *OCLC Systems & Services*, 21(3), 226–234.

University of Cambridge. (2013). *Inclusive design toolkit*. Retrieved on April 8, 2013, from http://www.inclusivedesigntoolkit.com

van der Veer, G. C., & Meguizo, C. P. (2003). Mental models. In *The human–computer interaction handbook: Fundamentals, evolving technologies and emerging applications*. London: Lawrence Erlbaum Associates Publishers.

W3C. (2013). *A little history of the world wide web*. Retrieved on March 22, 2013 from http://www.w3.org/History.html

Wagner, N., Hassanein, K., & Head, M. (2010). Computer use by older adults: A multi-disciplinary review. *Computers in Human Behavior*, 26, 870–882. doi:10.1016/j.chb.2010.03.029

WAI. (1998). *Web accessibility initiative 2.0*. Retrieved on March 22, 2013 from http://www.w3.org/WAI/intro/wcag.php

Wäljas, M., Segerståh, K., Väänänen-Vainio-Mattila, K., & Oinas-Kukkonen, H. (2010). Cross-platform service user experience: A field study and an initial framework. In *Proceedings of Mobile HCI'10*. Lisboa, Portugal: HCI. doi:10.1145/1851600.1851637

WCAG. (2008). *Web content accessibility guidelines*. Retrieved on March 23, 2013 from http://www.w3.org/WAI/intro/wcag

Wolkerstorfer, P., Tscheligi, M., Sefelin, R., Milchrahm, H., Hussain, Z., Lechner, M., & Shahzad, S. (2008). Probing an agile usability process. In *Proceedings of CHI 2008*. Florence, Italy: ACM.

Wood, E., Willoughby, T., Rushing, A., Bechtel, L., & Gilbert, J. (2005). Use of computer input devices by older adults. *Journal of Applied Gerontology*, 24(5), 419–438. doi:10.1177/0733464805278378

Yannou, B., Yvars, P.-A., Hoyle, C., & Chen, W. (2013). Set-based design by simulation of usage scenario coverage. *Journal of Engineering Design*, 1–29.

Zajicek, M. (2006). Aspects of HCI research for older people. *Universal Access Information Society*, 5, 279–286. doi:10.1007/s10209-006-0046-8

Zaphiris, P., Kurniawan, S., & Ghiawadwala, M. (2007). A systematic approach to the development of research-based web design guidelines for older people. *Universal Access Information Society*, 6, 59–75. doi:10.1007/s10209-006-0054-8

## KEY TERMS AND DEFINITIONS

**Information Processing:** Is the cognitive process that allow humans to perceive and process information and to consequently choose a plan of action.

**Later Life:** Is that stage of life taking place just pre-retirement or at retirement and that continues until end of life. Although there is no agreement on when later life starts and when an individual can be considered elderly, the changes in the demographic structure have pushed such starting point later on in life, e.g. when people are 60 years old or older.

**Online Navigational Strategy:** Consists of the behaviour that users adopts in planned or unplanned ways to accomplish activities online.

**User Centred Design:** Is a design approach that puts the users at the centre of every stage of the design through iterations that allow the users to evaluate any design progress.

**User Experience (UX):** Is the complex mix of emotional, sensorial and cognitive aspects generated within the interaction a user has with a product, a service, a brand or a web site.

**User Requirements:** Are the needs and aspirations that drive the design process. User requirements can be elicited using a variety of techniques and also serve the purpose of evaluating the relevance and fit of the design outcomes.

**Web Services:** Are services that a user can access online. Web services encompass informational services (e.g. TV listings), business propositions (e.g. online shopping) or governmental and community based services (e.g. e-voting and volunteering schemes).

# Section 4
# Special Topics in E-Services

# Chapter 12

# Usability and Accessibility of E-Health Websites:
## Enabling Nutrition and Physical Activity Education for Blind and Low Vision Internet Users

**Constantinos K. Coursaris**
*Michigan State University, USA*

**Sarah J. Swierenga**
*Michigan State University, USA*

**Pamela Whitten**
*Michigan State University, USA*

## ABSTRACT

*This chapter describes a multi-group research study of the usability evaluation and consequent results from participants' experiences with the MyPryamidTracker.gov Website application. The authors report on a study of a sample consisting of 25 low-income participants with varied levels of vision (i.e., sighted, low vision, and blind Internet users). Usability was assessed via both objective and subjective measures. Overall, participants had significant difficulty understanding how to use the MyPyramidTracker. gov Website. The chapter concludes with major recommendations pertaining to the implementation of Website design elements including pathway/navigation, search, links, text chunking, and frames layout. An extensive set of actionable Website design recommendations and a usability questionnaire are also provided that can be used by researchers in their future evaluations of Websites and Web services.*

## INTRODUCTION

According to the U.S. Department of Agriculture – Food and Nutrition Service's report on the "Dietary Intake and Dietary Attitudes Among Food Stamp Participants (FSP) and Other Low-Income Indi-

viduals" (USDA-FNS, 2000), additional research is needed to address FSP participants' "moderate" levels of nutrition knowledge and lack of awareness of key pieces of nutritional information. Nutrition education aimed at helping participants make more informed food choices may provide participants

DOI: 10.4018/978-1-4666-5129-6.ch012

with the tools and strategies to improve their nutritional intake and dietary quality.

However, most websites have not been designed with accessibility in mind. In fact, an empirical study found that 98.24% of the websites representing all types of firms, large and small, B2B and B2C, and profit-seeking and not-for-profit, did not meet minimal website accessibility standards (Milliman, 2002; Souza et. al, 2001). Another study by the Disability Rights Commission (Centre for HCI Design, 2005) found that 81% of websites (1,000 websites were evaluated) failed to satisfy the most basic requirements, and that characteristics of the sites make it very difficult, if not impossible, for people with disabilities, especially blind users, to use the website's services. Sites with small fixed-size fonts and links, small button sizes, insufficient color contrast and color combinations, poorly coded data table layouts, mouse-based and/or dynamic scripting, and lack of audio captioning are usually inaccessible for people with various disabilities (Thatcher et. al, 2003; Slatin & Rush, 2003; Swierenga et. al, 2011). Recognizing that more information and business is being conducted over the Internet, Congress mandated that the digital presence of all Federal agencies must be fully accessible in Section 508 of the Rehabilitation Act. Furthermore, the Web Content Accessibility Guidelines (WCAG) 2.0 are now the recognized standard for accessible web design and is approved as an International Organization for Standardization (ISO) standard: ISO/IEC 40500:2012. Thus, ensuring accessibility is no longer a premium or optional feature when designing websites. The benefits of meeting the guidelines are not limited to persons with disabilities, as accessible design increases product usability for everyone. Hence, our overall research questions are:

**RQ1:** What is the usability of e-health (nutrition and physical activity) websites when used by low-income, disabled (i.e., low vision and blind) Internet users?

**RQ2:** What is the impact of e-health websites on disabled Internet users' nutrition and physical activity knowledge and behaviors following a longer term exposure?

This chapter describes a multi-group research study of the usability evaluation and consequent results from participants' experiences with the MyPryamidTracker.gov website application. Specifically, we report on a study of a sample consisting of 25 low-income participants with varied levels of vision (i.e., sighted, low vision, and blind Internet users).

## BACKGROUND

Usability studies have their roots as early as the 1970's with the work of "software psychology." "Software psychology dealt with the utility of a behavioural approach to understanding software design, programming, and the use of interactive systems, and to motivate and guide system developers to consider the characteristics of human beings" (Carroll, 1997). Evolving into the analysis of user requirements and the conception of Graphical User Interfaces (GUI), "usability engineering" arrived (Nielsen, 1993; Hermann & Heidmann, 2002). A later stage that would form a subset of usability engineering concentrated on interfaces and came to be known as "information visualization" (Hornbaek, et. al, 2003). The most recent exploration in the field of usability was coined "new usability" (Thomas & Macredie, 2002) or "ubiquitous usability" (Hassanein and Head, 2003). "Ubiquitous usability" is concerned with the context in which new products and services are being used. Varied situational contexts will result in emerging usability factors, making traditional approaches to usability evaluation inappropriate.

The corresponding research has produced extensive resources in the form of usability guidelines and standards for various domains. Still, research in the two areas of context of use and a user's evaluative process of usability has been limited (Venkatesh et al., 2003). The importance of these two areas emerges from their importance in yielding a reasonable analysis during a usability study (Thimbleby et al., 2001; Maguire, 2001). For example, a usability study would be of limited value if it were not to account for the following factors (Hassanein and Head, 2003), which were the core dimensions of Coursaris and Kim's (2008) contextual usability framework:

- User (e.g., prior relevant/computing experience, age, education, culture, state of motion.)
- Environment (e.g. lighting, noise – music, speech, white noise.)
- Task (e.g., complexity, interactivity.)
- Technology (e.g., network dependability, interface design – input/output modes, size, weight, actual device vs. emulator.)

The takeaway is that usability experiments need to consider both the product/artifact and the user, and be designed subject to those considerations in addition to the environmental and task-related constraints. In this study, we focus on the users' visual impairment and how it may affect website usability, as disability has received little attention: in the context of mobile usability studies, for example, only 2% of studies explored any form of user disability (Coursaris and Kim, 2008).

At a lower level of abstraction, i.e., more specifically regarding the measurement of usability, a number of approaches have been put forth by scholars (for a review, see Coursaris and Kim, 2008). For this study, usability will be measured according to standard ISO 9241 (1998), where usability is defined as, and measured in terms of:

- **Efficiency:** The level of resource consumed in performing tasks.
- **Effectiveness:** The ability of users to complete tasks using the technology, and the quality of output of those tasks.

- **Satisfaction:** Users' subjective satisfaction to using the technology.

The ISO definition of usability was chosen for this study in part because it is the international standard (ISO-9241, 1998) of measuring usability. The use of this standard allows for consistency with other studies in the measurement of efficiency, effectiveness, and satisfaction (Brereton, 2004). Furthermore, accessibility, which addresses whether the system supports users who are relying on assistive technology such as a screen reader to perform tasks, will be assessed by coupling usability metrics along with qualitative data obtained through our post-study questionnaire. Next, we will discuss our study in detail.

## METHODS

## Participants

A convenient sample was recruited by means of snowball sampling. Participants were given a $100 gift card from a local merchant and a parking pass as compensation for the 90-minute lab experiment session. There were a total of 25 participants, 9 male and 16 female. From the 25 participants, 16 were blind, 4 were low-vision and 5 sighted. Participants ranged in age from 19 to 63, had a variety of educational and employment backgrounds, and all except for one indicated that they own a computer. All but one participant indicated that they were at least "a little" interested in programs that focus on diet, exercise and smoking cessation, with 15 participants stating that they were either "very" or "extremely" interested in these types of programs. The most preferred delivery method for these programs was videotapes, either in the form of CDs or DVDs. 12 participants stated that their current health status was "excellent or very good." 10 characterized their current health status as "good," 2 indicated that their current health status was "fair," and 1 called her current health status "poor."

## Testing Room Setup and Equipment

The usability evaluations were conducted at the state-of-the-art Usability/Accessibility Research and Consulting space, within University Outreach and Engagement at Michigan State University, East Lansing, Michigan (see Figure 1). The facility incorporates cutting-edge technologies and multipurpose spaces within an aesthetically appealing and accessible business environment. All spaces protect the privacy of individuals and accommodate those with disabilities.

Specifically, the usability testing room is equipped with three computers; digital video, audio, and screen recording equipment; a document camera; Internet connectivity; and white boards. The space includes an adjustable height workstation, and all computers have Freedom Scientific's JAWS® for Windows and Ai Squared's ZoomText® assistive technologies for blind and low vision users. Mixing and other production equipment are used to create picture-in-a-picture output for live viewing, as well as for recording for later analysis and reporting. Clients can observe the test activities through live video and audio feeds to a projection screen.

The following describes the hardware and relevant settings during our study: Dell Optiplex computer running Windows XP with a 17" monitor. The default screen resolution was 1024X768. The site was displayed in Internet Explorer running over a T3 Internet connection. Additionally, a set of assistive technologies was employed during the study, as follows. The screen reader participants used JAWS for Windows. Low vision users used ZoomText. Participants adjusted the settings as needed.

## Procedure

The one-on-one lab experiment sessions lasted 90 minutes for each participant, and included several components:

- **Verbal Overview Description of Study:** Participants were given a description of the general nature of the study and the order of activities that were conducted in the session.
- **Informed Consent Form for Human Subjects:** Each participant was asked to sign the Consent Form before they participated in the study.
- **Demographic Questionnaire:** We administered a brief pre-test questionnaire to gather background information on participants' work experience and Internet experience.
- **Task Scenarios Performance:** Participants were asked to perform seven (7) task scenarios using the MyPyramid Tracker website interface. Participants were asked to think aloud and verbalize any confusion while performing tasks, in order to identify areas of difficulty, as well as patterns and types of participant errors when performing typical search tasks.
- **Post-Study Questionnaire:** A post-study questionnaire was administered to address specific aspects of the task scenarios and obtain satisfaction ratings.

*Figure 1. Michigan State University usability/accessibility research and consulting testing room setup*

- Participants were debriefed at the end of the session and given a hard copy of the information.

## Tasks

Participants were asked to complete seven tasks on the MyPyramid Tracker website:

1. Register on the MyPyramid Tracker website.
2. Add a bagel, an apple, and a cup of coffee to your daily food intake list.
3. Add the apple to your frequently used food list.
4. Find out how well your eating behavior meets the dietary guidelines.
5. Enter the following physical activities: walking for 10 minutes, doing some light housecleaning, and sitting and typing on a computer.
6. Set walking as a frequently performed activity.
7. Determine your physical activity score.

## Measurement

As abovementioned, key usability goals included effectiveness, which refers to how well a system does what it is supposed to do; efficiency, or the way a system supports users in carrying out their tasks; satisfaction, which relates to the subjective responses users have to the system; and accessibility, which addresses whether the system supports users who are relying on assistive technology, such as a screen reader, to perform the tasks.

User performance data were collected during each lab experiment session, and metrics included:

- Percentage of tasks completed successfully.
- Mean time to perform a particular task.
- Types of errors.

Qualitative measures, used both during the test and after the test, included:

- Verbal feedback during and after the session.
- Participant satisfaction ratings via the post-study questionnaires.
- Written feedback on the demographic and post-study questionnaires.

The complete post-study questionnaire, which shows all measures used, is found in the Appendix.

## RESULTS

### User Performance–Objective Data

Quantitative data collected in relevance to user performance are summarized in Table 1.

### User Performance–Subjective Data (Direct Observation)

In addition to the objective data collected for participants' performance, the two authors observed each participant and recorded qualitative data to offer richer insight into the users' experience. These are reported below for each task, along with a set of recommendations made by the authors.

### Task 1–Register on the MyPyramid Tracker Website

- Users had difficulty properly entering height information. Many were confused by the two separate fields and the lack of preceding labels.
  - Several screen reader users entered their entire height in the first field before realizing there was a second field for inches.
  - Several participants included units with their height information, or expressed confusion that different units than expected were being applied to the numbers they entered: "You've

*Table 1. User Performance – Objective data*

| | Tasks | User | Successful Task Completion** | Ratio of Users who "Gave Up" to "Unsuccessful Task Completion" | Mean Task Completion Time (mm:ss) |
|---|---|---|---|---|---|
| 1 | Sign-up | B* | 10/16 (63%) | 4/6 | 06:35 |
| | | L | 2/4 (50%) | 1/2 | 06:24 |
| | | S | 4/5 (80%) | 0/1 | 02:26 |
| | | O | 16/25 (64%) | 5/9 | 05:31 |
| 2 | Add food item consumed | B | 8/16 (50%) | 5/8 | 09:56 |
| | | L | 3/4 (75%) | 0/1 | 06:00 |
| | | S | 4/5 (80%) | 0/1 | 04:15 |
| | | O | 15/25 (60%) | 5/10 | 07:38 |
| 3 | Add food to Frequently Used Foods list | B | 12/16 (75%) | 2/4 | 03:55 |
| | | L | 3/4 (75%) | 1/1 | 00:41 |
| | | S | 2/5 (40%) | 2/3 | 00:13 |
| | | O | 16/24 (67%) | 5/8 | 03:04 |
| 4 | View Nutrition Evaluation | B | 13/16 (81%) | 2/3 | 08:28 |
| | | L | 2/4 (50%) | 1/2 | 10:30 |
| | | S | 4/5 (80%) | 1/1 | 03:06 |
| | | O | 19/25 (76%) | 4/6 | 07:33 |
| 5 | Add physical activity | B | 6/13 (48%) | 6/7 | 12:56 |
| | | L | 1/3 (33%) | 1/2 | 14:34 |
| | | S | 3/5 (60%) | 2/2 | 03:48 |
| | | O | 10/21 (48%) | 9/11 | 09:52 |
| 6 | Add activity to Frequently Performed Activities list | B | 7/12 (58%) | 4/5 | 03:37 |
| | | L | 1/3 (33%) | 1/2 | 03:43 |
| | | S | 3/5 (60%) | 1/2 | 01:46 |
| | | O | 11/20 (55%) | 6/9 | 03:07 |
| 7 | View Physical Exercise Evaluation | B | 10/12 (83%) | 1/2 | 03:55 |
| | | L | 1/3 (33%) | 1/2 | 05:22 |
| | | S | 4/5 (80%) | 0/1 | 01:47 |
| | | O | 15/20 (75%) | 2/5 | 03:31 |

\* Blind users = B; Low-vision users = L; Sighted users = S; Overall = O

\*\* Total n=25; Blind n=16; Low-vision n=4; Sighted n=5

got to make sure it tells you what the default is." "When we enter into an edit box the website should say how they want it entered."

- Screen reader users were unsure if the information at the top of the page, before registration, was necessary or relevant. As one user remarked, "I don't know whether to skip this."

- Due to ineffective feedback, several users were unaware that they had correctly completed the task, while others were unaware that they had made errors.
  ○ The screen reader did not read out the pop-ups explaining errors.

○ Having a pop-up indicating both successfully saved changes and unsuccessful attempts was confusing to screen reader users—they were not sure if they had made an error or not.

○ One user read over the whole form again, remarking that it "went back to the same form, so I didn't think I did it correctly. Usually it goes back to a different page, thank you for registering then go to next page or the homepage." Another noted simply: "It doesn't move you forward."

## Task 1–Recommendations

• On the homepage, the sign up and login functions were buried beneath large chunks of text, and users were accustomed to seeing these options without having to scroll. Place these options closer to the top of the page for simpler access in order to encourage users to explore, to make the page appear more interactive, and to allow blind/low vision users to more easily locate these options.

• Ensure that all fields are properly labeled and it is clear to assistive technology users what units will be used for height, weight, etc.

• The explanation provided for invalid input indicators (asterisks, in this case) was below the form in a place where screen reader users may not encounter it at all. Place this information at the top of the page; consider displaying it only when users are directed to correct the form in some way.

• Eliminate the use of pop-ups for non-error notifications and instead take users to a new page that informs them that their information has been saved, and displays a user profile with options to proceed.

## Task 2–Add a Bagel, an Apple, and a Cup of Coffee to your Daily Food Intake List

• Users had difficulty with the search tool for adding food to the daily intake list. (See Figure 1.)

○ Many users searched for "cup of coffee," rather than just the keyword, "coffee."

○ Several people searched for two or more items at once: "bagel coffee" etc., similar to most search tools.

○ One user asked "Does spelling count?" Several people misspelled items but did not realize it, and were not given relevant results.

• Screen reader users had difficulty with almost every aspect of the process, depending on their individual skill levels with assistive technology.

○ When the search term was not exact, the list of search results was irrelevant (i.e., "cup of coffee" returns several "cupcake" items at the top of the list).

○ When a food item was added, there was no notification; hence, users were often confused about whether or not the item had been added.

○ The graphical "add" button and linked text both had the same function.

○ Several users accidentally added foods to their Frequently Used Foods list, or remarked that they did not know what "Freq foods" meant.

○ Clicking the link for a food in the links list did not add it to the daily food intake.

○ Users were generally confused and often frustrated by the set up of the page, especially the side-by-side content areas which made it difficult to navigate between the search function and the list of added items: "It's just not very clear! How do you check it?" "Where can I hear [what I have]?" "I'm not getting where I want to be."

- Some users thought there should be a separate entry for beverages.
- Some users thought they had successfully added items when they had only heard/ seen them in the list.
- "Once you clicked 'Add' it would be nice if the search box erased itself."

## Task 2–Recommendations

- The instructions should be concise and complete. Furthermore, it should be specified that beverages are included.
- The search function should be improved. Users expect "Google" type search and results, e.g., no Boolean connectors between words, and results sorted by relevance of the search terms.
  - Search should provide more logical results for common words and variations (verb tenses, etc.).
  - Common units and connectors such as "cup of" should be ignored.
  - Search should be able to provide relevant results for basic misspellings.
  - Search field text box should automatically clear after each search.
- Users should be notified when a food has been successfully added to their daily intake list.
- Use buttons for adding to both daily intake and frequently used foods lists; eliminate hyperlink in food text.
- Consider allowing users to select a quantity immediately after selecting a food, or indicate that quantities will be selected later.

## Task 3–Add the Apple to your Frequently Used Food List

- Several participants thought that clicking "add" should allow them to add the food to the Frequently Used Foods list.
- Several users tried to add the apple from their daily intake list on the right side of the page. Some believed they had to remove the apple from the first list in order to complete the task; others were confused and accidentally removed the apple from the daily list.
- Many screen reader users missed the link to add to the Frequently Used Foods list and had to go through the page several times trying to find what they were looking for, even after reading the help for frequently used foods.
  - Participants often didn't know what "freq" meant.
  - One user finally closed in on the link by listening to it letter by letter.
  - Users would sometimes click the "Frequently Used Foods" link, which simply refreshed the frame. Users had to go through the entire page again just to hear the phrase "There are currently no foods in your Frequently Used Foods list."
- Some participants used the search function again and clicked the food link itself, adding it to the daily intake list instead of frequently used foods.
- Participants were often confused by vaguely worded links such as "Frequently Used Foods List" or "Frequently Used Foods," and thought clicking those would allow them to construct the list.

*Figure 2. MyPyramid Tracker – Enter food item page*

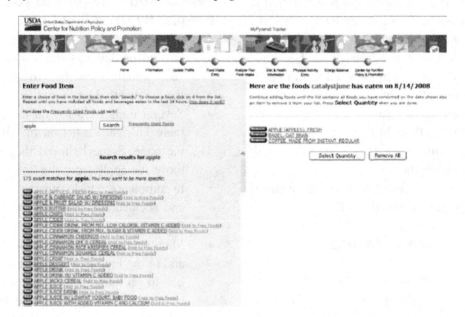

## Task 3–Recommendations

- Instructions and labels for the frequently used foods list should be explicit and integrated into the overall page architecture. There should be a landing page for the frequently used foods list that provides clear, concise instructions as well as a search field. A clear path to the "frequent" lists, as well as the lists themselves, should be evident to all users.
- The "freq" link must be replaced with a clear, logically-worded button that will make sense to screen reader users.
- Eliminate or clarify ambiguously worded links, e.g., use "How to make a Frequently Used Foods list," rather than "Frequently Used Foods list").

## Task 4–Find Out How Well your Eating Behavior Meets the Dietary Guidelines

- Several participants seemed unsure about how to begin the task.
  - Some looked for information on the dietary guidelines, not realizing that the guidelines would be provided as part of the sequence.
  - Participants did not associate the "add quantities" link with analyzing dietary intake. Several used the top navigation as opposed to the buttons in the content area.
  - Screen reader users had difficulty determining their location on the page and understanding when content in a frame had changed. Upon clicking the "Analyze your Food Intake" link from the global navigation, one user exclaimed: "That's what I clicked on, but it doesn't do anything!"

*Figure 3. MyPyramid Tracker – Frequently used food page*

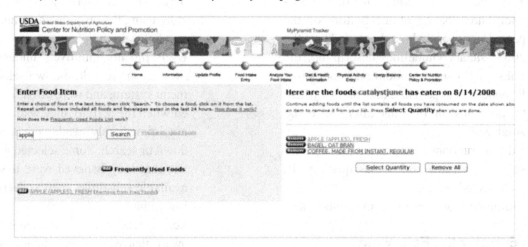

- Users were somewhat surprised to have to enter a quantity as part of the process: "[This] seems kind of silly – you should be able to put servings in when you select food."

- Several expressed uncertainty about the practicality of taking exact measurements in everyday life.

- A few screen reader users were confused by the abbreviations of serving units: "'Fl oz,' I wondered what that was."

- Participants were confused about the two editing fields on the quantities page: "I'm confused about what the extra edit field is. I would think the drop-down has all the serving sizes."

  ○ Several participants, especially screen reader users, entered information only in some or all of the drop-down menus.

  ○ One screen reader user skipped the drop-down menus altogether and only entered quantities.

  ○ One low vision participant using ZoomText scrolled over to see the second editing field and could not figure out how to indicate he drinks "way more" than 1 mug of coffee.

  ○ Most users who received an error message were able to determine their error and correctly enter the quantity, but several expressed confusion and/ or frustration, saying things like "I thought I already did [enter a valid serving size]," or "I don't know what I'm supposed to do."

- Reaction to the results table was mixed: Some screen reader users immediately interpreted it correctly, but others had trouble. One participant could not understand the headers and was confused about whether certain numbers were recommendations; one participant said, "I don't understand what it's reading me;" another simply called it "lousy."

- Many participants had a friendly reaction to the emoticons, pointing to them as a clear indicator of how their diets measured up to the dietary guidelines and even calling them "cute."

## Task 4–Recommendations

- Provide concise instructions for quantity selections, such as, "Select a serving size using the drop-down menu and then enter the number of servings in the text field."

- The links to the other nutrition evaluations are floating at the bottom of the page. For anyone who did not read past the 2005 Dietary Guidelines description, the links would seem random and confusing. Provide a clear path and indicator of where to move next on the page after "Save and Analyze."
- Add instructions to the error message for selecting serving size versus quantity for the selected serving size.
- Eliminate abbreviations from results tables.

## Task 5–Enter the Following Physical Activities: Walking for 10 Minutes, Doing Some Light Housecleaning, and Sitting and Typing on a Computer

- One user had difficulty changing the option from "standard" to "condensed" on the physical activity landing page.
- Users had difficulty with the search and selection option for adding physical activities. There was some confusion about whether they were supposed to use one or both, as with the food selection menu.
  - Participants would sometimes find the category of physical activity they wanted, but then move on without clicking the "Select" button.
  - Many users were confused by the presence of the Search field after they had already selected a category from the drop-down menu.
  - Several participants erroneously entered times in the search field, believing that once they selected an activity type they would logically enter the time.
  - Even after an activity was successfully added, some users did not remember the steps they had taken to get to that point.

  - Screen reader users often had difficulty using the drop-down menus and text fields on the page.
  - Users did not intuitively understand the dynamic drop-down/selection menu system, and were often frustrated when the activity they wanted was not immediately available via drop-down or search. Some selected activities that they believed were the best available substitute, such as "aerobic, low impact."
  - Screen reader users were caught unaware that when they selected an activity category from the drop-down, more specific choices would show up in the lower menu box. They did not realize that new information had appeared on the page.
  - Several users commented that "Activity Description" was a strange name, or believed that it meant they were supposed to enter a description. They tried to type in the area, since it looked like a text box.
- Some users selected Physical Activity Entry or Physical Activity Information from the main navigation when they were confused or did not know what to do next.
- Some screen reader users added physical activities without knowing it.

## Task 5–Recommendations

- Condensed option should be considered the default option and be featured as the first option. The standard option should be renamed "Detailed" or something similar.
- Users who want to change from "condensed" to "standard" or vice versa currently have to return to login and start over after changing the date and then changing it back. They should be able to make the switch within their current session.

- Fix the search method:
  - Until the search function can be greatly enhanced to better understand and infer a user's intent, we recommend using only the drop-down menu to sort and select physical activities.
  - Consider simplifying the categories and options available—categories like "Inactivity light" and "Inactivity quiet" or activities like "standing, talking in church" and "standing, singing in church, attending a ceremony" are too similar and could cause confusion.
  - Some choices may fit under more than one category ("meditating" should be listed under religion, but is only found under "Inactivity light").
  - Display search results similarly to food search results; eliminate text box.
- Change "Activity Description" label to "Choose from Activities List" or something similar.
- Eliminate the hyperlinked text from activities in the daily list; add a button for removal instead.

- Consider allowing users to add durations immediately after selecting an activity, or explicitly indicate that they will add durations later.

## Task 6–Set Walking as a Frequently Performed Activity

- Participants experienced many of the same issues with the search and menu functions as they did finding physical activities in Task 5.
- Some participants clicked on the link for information about frequently performed activities and expected to be able to construct a list that way.
- Many users did not know what "FPA" stood for.
- Some screen reader users accidentally or unknowingly removed activities from their daily list.
- Several participants noted the difference in the button labels for frequently performed activities and frequently used foods. They wondered why the signal for the frequently used foods was "freq" and for activities it was "FPA."

*Figure 4. MyPyramid Tracker – Enter activity type page*

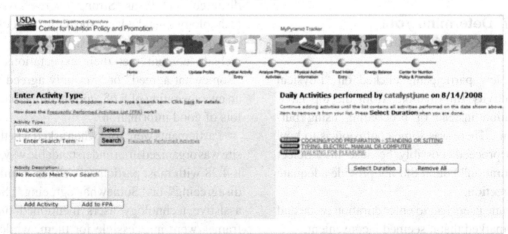

- Some users thought they had successfully added the activity to the FPA, but had only added it to their daily list of activities.
- One user noted that the "Select" button should be labeled as a button in its description.
- One user commented that removing items by accident seemed easier than adding items intentionally.

## Task 6–Recommendations

- "FPA" does not have meaning for users unless it is explained; we recommend using the entire text of "Frequently Performed Activity" whenever possible, or choosing another title such as "Frequent Activity" or "Favorite Activity."
- As with the Frequently Used Foods list, we suggest a landing page dedicated to constructing, maintaining, and viewing the FPA list. Users should be provided with, at least, a few clear pathways to access this list.
- Eliminate randomly-placed links to information about the FPA list.
- When users select a physical activity for their daily list that is not in the Frequently Performed Activities list, they should be prompted to add it to the FPA list at that point.

## Task 7–Determine your Physical Activity Score

- A few participants clicked on "Physical Activity Information" from the top navigation instead of proceeding using buttons. There was some confusion as to how to proceed, possibly because the "Select Duration" button did not provide adequate direction.
- Some users had to enter duration twice and remarked that it seemed inconvenient.

- One participant said she thought it would work like the nutrition analysis and give recommendations for improvement.
- One user did not know for sure if the duration fields referred to daily (as opposed to weekly) times.
- A few participants entered units with their durations or were not sure what units would be used.
- On the results page, one user questioned what "METs" was.

## Task 7–Recommendations

- Ensure that fields are properly labeled.
- Explain all acronyms/abbreviations.
- Entering duration should be part of selecting the activity, rather than the first step in analyzing levels of physical activity.
- On the overall process of selecting and analyzing physical activities, provide clear, concise instructions.

## User Assessment (Questionnaire)

In the post-study questionnaire (see Appendix), participants rated various aspects of the MyPyramid Tracker site as a whole. Overall, participants "slightly disagreed" that the MyPyramid Tracker website was easy to use, with an average rating of 3.8 on a scale from 1-7, where 1 was "Strongly disagree" and 7 was "Strongly agree." Assistive technology users had an especially difficult time moving through the process. When asked if the website content met their expectations, most "Somewhat agreed" or "Strongly agreed," with an average rating of 5.68, commenting that it had lots of good information.

Participants were split when asked whether the site was organized in an understandable way, rating it 4.28 with most participants either "Somewhat disagreeing" or "Somewhat agreeing." Several assistive technology users mentioned that the frames were inaccessible for them, while most people agreed that they understood the website structure better after some trial-and-error. Regarding how useful the participants found the site to be, participants overwhelming agreed that the site was either "Somewhat useful" or "Very useful," with an average rating of 4.4 on a scale of 1-5. Two participants were neutral, but no participants rated the site as "Not at all" useful or "Of little use;" however, many participants indicated that it would take time to learn the site before they would benefit from its use. And finally, when asked if they would recommend this site to colleagues and friends, most "Strongly agreed" that they would do so, with an average rating of 5.52 on a scale of 1-7.

Some participants gave recommendations for enhancing the accessibility of the site, noting that the Frequently Used Foods and Frequently Performed Activities lists were confusing, and the units and serving sizes were difficult for assistive technology users to understand. One participant recommended offering a text-only, plain HTML version of the site, while others recommended specific fixes, such as accurately labeling fields and the use of buttons instead of images. Participants also commented on the confusing nature of the search feature, and recommended something clearer for visually impaired users. Some additional comments and recommendations for the future included: "Avoid split screen" and "I would suggest updating the dietary guidelines to 2008."

These results show that while participants were enthusiastic about the MyPyramid Tracker site, they had difficulty actually using the system – especially assistive technology users. There is considerable opportunity for improvement, especially in organization and functionality.

## CONCLUSION AND RECOMMENDATIONS

This chapter describes the usability evaluation results involving participant reactions to the My-PryamidTracker.gov e-health website application. This evaluation was conducted at Michigan State University in one-on-one usability sessions with 25 food-stamp eligible (FSE) participants who were blind, low vision, and sighted Internet users.

Overall, participants had significant difficulty understanding how to use the MyPyramidTracker.gov website. The features of the MyPyramid Tracker website were meant to allow flexibility and specificity in order to deliver accurate healthy eating and physical activity recommendations to users. However, the complexity, design and functionality of the site present a steep learning curve and significant roadblocks for users, especially those using assistive technology. Participants had major difficulty using the search function and drop-down menus to add food or activities to their daily intake lists, and correctly using the Frequently Used Foods and Frequently Performed Activities features. They also had significant difficulty understanding and working within the dynamic, frames-based structure of the site. The most recurrent and significant problems were common across the vision spectrum, but in every case the task completion times for blind and low vision users were longer and their success rates lower than for sighted users.

## General Recommendations for All Users

### Layout

- Be conscious of category convention.
  - What people have experienced and will be expecting to see.
  - Identify opportunities for enhancing it.
- Remember eye-tracking results: The "F" shape, i.e., users look at the top and then the left for navigation menus.
- Make page elements hierarchical: Menus, navigation bars, content.
- Group related items together.

- For step-by-step processes, the buttons should be ordered in a logical fashion and should first include a "back" button. Any buttons relating to forms, such as "reset," should come next, followed by the option for saving and moving forward.
- Help create page order by respecting alignment.
- Minimize scrolling, create visual links when necessary.
- Use white space to frame content areas.

## Navigation

- Provide consistent global navigation across all pages.
  - Main navigation should not change from page to page.
  - Secondary navigation hierarchy should remain intact.
- Menu items that represent the process should be grouped together, and there should be some indication of what step the user is currently working on. Informational menu items that do not directly relate to the process should come after or be otherwise separated from the action-oriented items.
- Use link and label names that clearly and concisely indicate destination content.
- Use terms that your target audience will understand.
  - Keep dropdown menus short, and avoid multi-level dropdowns.
- Make links recognizable—color, underline, visited/non-visited.
  - Keep non-clickable text standard.
- Always warn users when a link will open a new window. Try to avoid secondary windows and pop-ups.

## Content

- Use language (terms and expressions) users expect and understand.
- Provide information based on their needs and expectations.
- Break large paragraphs into smaller chunks and cut out extraneous information and improve readability.
- Use headings to separate and identify topics.
- Fully spell out acronyms.
- Avoid italic type as it is more difficult to read.
- Anticipate accessibility elements.
  - Paragraph headings, meaningful link phrases (no "click here".)
  - Table formats (captions, concise/descriptive headings), Form formats (sections, concise/descriptive labels.)
  - Site map.

## Forms

- Use consistent format throughout page and site.
- Follow convention: Labels precede input fields, checkboxes and radio buttons precede labels.
- Imagine a conversation with person filling in form.
- Lead users through the form with logical steps.
- Ask only for what is needed.
- Use sensible labels to minimize explanations.
- Clearly indicate what is required.
- Include "key", i.e., "*" means required.
- Make accessible: Include * in label (all), describe as required or mandatory in tool tip (PDF)
- Provide help at point of input (with label, on focus).
- Use flexible input fields when possible.

## Interactive Components

- Decide if an interactive component is really necessary – no matter how helpful, it will add complexity.
- Simplify interactive components – have them perform only necessary tasks.
- Imagine
  - How should it work using only the keyboard?
  - How can I explain it to someone who can't see it?

## Additional Recommendations for Users who are Blind Using Screen Reader Adaptive Technology

- Ensure headings are used to identify sections and subsections so that screen reader users can easily scan pages that contain large amounts of information.
- Provide accurate and descriptive alternative text for all graphics and non-text content.
- Provide a link to the homepage at the top and bottom of all pages.
- Tag PDF files for accessibility so that they render properly with assistive technology.
- Provide a site map to help users understand site organization and content.
- Make sure that drop-down menus work with the "Enter" key, which is the expected behavior for screen reader users.
- Ensure that all form fields and radio buttons have labels that are descriptive and associated with input fields.

In summary, there are several areas in which MyPyramid Tracker could be improved based on the results of this study. Beyond these redesign recommendations, a major takeaway should be the promise MyPyramid Tracker offers to blind and low-vision SNAP eligible users to improve their nutrition and physical activity lifestyle choices. This outcome will be achieved once the system becomes easier to use, more useful in educating users in low-level information that can be easily implemented, and promote the continued use of the system by making the experience more personal.

## ACKNOWLEDGMENT

The research was funded by USDA Food and Nutrition Service through the Michigan Department of Human Services, grant number ADMIN-08-99009, to the Michigan Nutrition Network, to Usability/ Accessibility Research and Consulting at Michigan State University. We appreciate the contributions of JoDee Fortino and Hayley Roberts for providing technical support.

## REFERENCES

Brereton, E. (2005). Don't neglect usability in the total cost of ownership. *Communications of the ACM, 47*(7), 10–11.

Carroll, J. (1997). Human-computer interaction: Psychology as a science of design. *International Journal of Human-Computer Studies, 46,* 501–522.

Centre for HCI Design. (2005). *The web access and inclusion for disabled people: A formal investigation conducted by the disability rights commission.* Retrieved June 27, 2013, from http://hcid.soi.city.ac.uk/research/DRC_Report.pdf, http://hcid.soi.city.ac.uk/research/Drc.html

Coursaris, C. K., & Kim, D. J. (2011). A meta-analytical review of empirical mobile usability studies. *Journal of Usability Studies, 6*(3), 117–171.

Hassanein, K., & Head, M. (2003). Ubiquitous usability: Exploring mobile interfaces within the context of a theoretical model. In *Proceedings of the Ubiquitous Mobile Information and Collaboration Systems Workshop* (UMICS 2003). Velden, Austria: CAiSE.

Hornbaek, K., Bederson, B., & Plaisant, C. (2003). Navigation patterns & usability of zoomable user interfaces with and without an overview. *ACM Transactions on Computer-Human Interaction, 9*(4), 362–389.

ISO-9241. (1998). *Ergonomic requirements for office work with visual display terminals (VDTs) -- Part 11: Guidance on usability.*

ISO/IEC 40500. (2012). *Information technology – W3C web content accessibility guidelines (WCAG) 2.0.*

Milliman, R. E. (2002). Website accessibility and the private sector: Disability stakeholders cannot tolerate 2% access!. *Information Technology and Disabilities, 8*(1).

Nielsen, J. (1993). *Usability engineering*. Cambridge, MA: Academic Press.

Slatin, J., & Rush, S. (2003). *Maximum accessibility: Making your web site more usable for everyone*. Boston, MA: Addison-Wesley Longman.

Souza, R., Manning, H., & Dorsey, M. (2001). *Designing accessible sites now*. Forrester Research.

Swierenga, S. J., Sung, J. E., Pierce, G. L., & Propst, D. B. (2011). Website design and usability assessment implications from a usability study with visually impaired and sighted users. In *Universal access in HCI (LNCS)* (Vol. 6766, pp. 382–389). Berlin: Springer-Verlag.

Thatcher, J., Bohman, P., Burks, M., Henry, S. L., Regan, B., & Swierenga, S. J. … Waddell, C. D. (2003). Constructing accessible web sites. Birmingham, UK: Glasshaus.

Thomas, P., & Macredie, R. (2002). Introduction to the new usability. *ACM Transactions on Computer-Human Interaction, 9*(2), 69–73.

Thimbleby, H., Cairns, P., & Jones, M. (2001). Usability analysis with Markov models. *ACM Transactions on Computer-Human Interaction, 8*(2), 99–132.

USDA-FNS. (2000). *Dietary intake and dietary attitudes among food stamp participants and other low-income individuals*. U.S. Department of Agriculture – Food and Nutrition Services. Retrieved on June 27, 2013, from http://www.fns. usda.gov/fsp/nutrition_education/research.htm

Venkatesh, V., Morris, M. G., Davis, G. B., & Davis, F. D. (2003). User acceptance of information technology: Toward a unified view. *Management Information Systems Quarterly, 27*(3), 425–478.

## ADDITIONAL READING SECTION

Coursaris, C. K., Hassanein, K., Head, M., & Bontis, N. (2012). The impact of distractions on the usability and intention to use mobile devices for wireless data services. *Computers in Human Behavior, 28*(4), 1439–1449.

Coursaris, C. K., & Kripintiris, K. (2012). Web aesthetics and usability: An empirical study of the effects of white space. *International Journal of E-Business Research, 8*(1), 35–53.

Cyr, D. (2008). Modeling web site design across cultures: Relationships to trust, satisfaction, and e-loyalty. *Journal of Management Information Systems, 24*(4), 47–72.

Cyr, D., Head, M., & Ivanov, A. (2006). Design aesthetics leading to m-loyalty in mobile commerce. *Information & Management, 43*(8), 950–963.

Cyr, D., Head, M., & Ivanov, A. (2009). Perceived interactivity leading to e-loyalty: Development of a model for cognitive–affective user responses. *International Journal of Human-Computer Studies*, *67*(10), 850–869.

Cyr, D., Head, M., & Larios, H. (2010). Colour appeal in website design within and across cultures: A multi-method evaluation. *International Journal of Human-Computer Studies*, *68*(1-2), 1–21.

Diefenbach, S., & Hassenzahl, M. (2008). *Give me a reason: Hedonic product choice and justification. CHI'08 Extended Abstracts on Human Factors in Computing Systems* (pp. 3051–3056). Florence, Italy: ACM.

Frøkjær, E., Hertzum, M., & Hornbæk, K. (2000). Measuring usability: Are effectiveness, efficiency, and satisfaction really correlated? *Proceedings of the SIGCHI Conference on Human Factors in Computing Systems*, ACM, The Hague, The Netherlands, pp. 345-352.

Goodhue, D. L. (1995). Understanding user evaluations of information systems. *Management Science*, *41*(12), 1827–1844.

Gray, A. (2009). *Website aesthetics - what has it got to do with usability*. Webcredible.

Hassenzahl, M., & Tractinsky, N. (2006). User experience-a research agenda. *Behaviour & Information Technology*, *25*(2), 91–97.

Hermann, F., & Heidmann, F. (2002). User requirement analysis and interface conception for a mobile, location-based fair guide. *Proceedings from Mobile HCI 2002. LNCS*, *2411*, 388–392.

Lindgaard, G. (2007). Aesthetics, visual appeal, usability and user satisfaction: What do the user's eyes tell the user's brain? *Australian Journal of Emerging Technologies and Society*, *5*(1), 1–16.

Maguire, M. (2001). Context of use within usability activities. *International Journal of Human-Computer Studies*, *55*, 453–483.

Mbipom, G. (2009). Good visual aesthetics equals good web accessibility. *ACM SIGACCESS Accessibility and Computing*, *93*, 75–83.

Noiwan, J., & Norcio, A. F. (2006). Cultural differences on attention and perceived usability: Investigating color combinations of animated graphics. *International Journal of Human-Computer Studies*, *64*(2), 103–122.

O'Brien, H. L., & Toms, E. G. (2009). The development and evaluation of a survey to measure user engagement. *Journal of the American Society for Information Science and Technology*, *61*(1), 50–69.

Palmer, J. (2002). Designing for web site usability. *Information Systems Research*, *13*(2), 151–167.

Quesenbery, W. (2003). Dimensions of usability. In M. A. Albers, & B. Mazur (Eds.), *Content and complexity: Information design in software development and documentation technical communication* (pp. 81–102). Mahwah, NJ: Lawrence Erlbaum Associates.

Rubin, J. (1994). *Handbook of usability testing*. New York, NY: John Wiley and Sons.

Thüring, M., & Mahlke, S. (2007). Usability, aesthetics and emotions in human–technology interaction. *International Journal of Psychology*, *42*(4), 253–264.

Tractinsky, N., & Lowengart, O. (2007). Web-store aesthetics in e-retailing: A conceptual framework and some theoretical implications. *Academy of Marketing Science Review*, *11*(1), 1–18.

Van der Heijden, H. (2004). User acceptance of hedonic information systems. *Management Information Systems Quarterly*, *28*(4), 695–704.

van Schaik, P., & Ling, J. (2008). Modelling user experience with web sites: Usability, hedonic value, beauty and goodness. *Interacting with Computers*, *20*(3), 419–432.

Venkatesh, V., Morris, M. G., Davis, G. B., & Davis, F. D. (2003). User acceptance of information technology: Toward a unified view. *Management Information Systems Quarterly*, *27*(3), 425–478.

Webster, J., & Martocchio, J. J. (1992). Microcomputer playfulness: Development of a measure with workplace implications. *Management Information Systems Quarterly*, *16*(2), 201–226.

Zhang, P., & Li, N. (2005). The importance of affective quality. *Communications of the ACM*, *48*(9), 105–108.

## KEY TERMS AND DEFINITIONS

**Accessibility:** The degree to which the system supports users who are relying on assistive technology to perform tasks.

**Context of Use:** The user, task, technology, and environment characteristics in a specified use setting.

**Effectiveness:** The ability to complete a task, and the quality of that output.

**Efficiency:** The level of resources consumed during a specified task.

**Performance:** The efficiency and effectiveness associated with a user's interaction with a system.

**Satisfaction:** The subjective assessment of a user's experience with the system.

**Usability:** The efficiency, effectiveness, and user satisfaction with a system.

## APPENDIX–USABILITY STUDY QUESTIONNAIRE

This questionnaire contains items regarding your overall impressions of the MyPyramid Tracker website.

1.  Overall, the MyPyramid Tracker website was easy-to-use.

    | | | |
    |---|---|---|
    | Strongly Disagree | Somewhat Disagree | Slightly Disagree |
    | | Neither Agree nor Disagree | |
    | Slightly Agree | Somewhat Agree | Strongly Agree |

    Why? _____

2.  The content of the MyPyramid Tracker website met my expectations.

    | | | |
    |---|---|---|
    | Strongly Disagree | Somewhat Disagree | Slightly Disagree |
    | | Neither Agree nor Disagree | |
    | Slightly Agree | Somewhat Agree | Strongly Agree |

    Why? _____

3.  Overall, it was easy to understand the organization of the MyPyramid Tracker website screens, especially the menu levels and the flow of the screens.

    | | | |
    |---|---|---|
    | Strongly Disagree | Somewhat Disagree | Slightly Disagree |
    | | Neither Agree nor Disagree | |
    | Slightly Agree | Somewhat Agree | Strongly Agree |

    Why? _____

4.  How useful do you find the MyPyramid Tracker website to be?

    | | |
    |---|---|
    | Not at all | Of little use |
    | Neutral | |
    | Somewhat useful | Very useful |

    Why? _____

5.  I would recommend the MyPyramid Tracker website to my colleagues and friends.

    | | | |
    |---|---|---|
    | Strongly Disagree | Somewhat Disagree | Slightly Disagree |
    | | Neither Agree nor Disagree | |
    | Slightly Agree | Somewhat Agree | Strongly Agree |

    Why? _____

6.  What recommendations do you have for improving the *accessibility* of the site?

    _____

7.  Additional comments and/or recommendations for future enhancements:

    _____

# Chapter 13
# Pedagogical Evaluation of E–Learning Websites with Cognitive Objectives

**Georgia Kyriakaki**
*Technical University of Crete, Greece*

**Nikolaos Matsatsinis**
*Technical University of Crete, Greece*

## ABSTRACT

*E-learning has known a large expansion in the past decades due to the advent of the Internet as a major communication medium and the WWW as a technology that provides enormous capabilities for information exchange anytime, anywhere, anyhow. Few studies exist on the evaluation of e-learning Websites in terms of their pedagogical quality that is, on their success in helping learners learn through specific pedagogical principles. Pedagogical evaluation, however, is very important in e-learning as it can improve the quality of the system greatly and help the decision maker choose the most appropriate among different systems or designs. This chapter proposes a multi-criteria evaluation model for e-learning websites based on well-known pedagogical principles, namely Bloom's taxonomy of six cognitive objectives, Knowledge, Comprehension, Application, Analysis, Synthesis, and Evaluation.*

## INTRODUCTION

E-learning has known a large expansion in the past decades due to the advent of the Internet as a major communication medium and the WWW as a technology that provides enormous capabilities for information exchange anytime, anywhere, anyhow. E-learning is by its nature an interdisciplinary field as it combines domain knowledge, pedagogical knowledge and applied technological knowledge in a single environment that aims to cover specific needs of multiple user groups. Education providers employ e-learning systems in order to address problems such as the lack of educational resources: teachers, funds, space and other material resources. Teachers adopt e-learning in order to assist classroom-based learning and promote the active and personalized involvement of learners in the learning process.

However, e-learning systems are not a panacea and the decision for their adoption is very important especially in formal education. The decision for selecting the appropriate e-learning settings, systems, tools and processes is complicated and

DOI: 10.4018/978-1-4666-5129-6.ch013

involves criteria from multiple perspectives: the teacher's perspective, the learner's perspective and the organization's perspective. The primary criterion is certainly the ability of an e-learning system to improve the learners' knowledge and skills but that is a complicated question to be answered as well. It depends on a multitude of factors such as the quality of the system's scientific, pedagogical and technical characteristics.

Web-based learning environments are the most popular e-learning systems nowadays as they are easily delivered to end-users and furthermore they provide communication mechanisms among instructors and learners. Many research studies exist on the evaluation of web-based learning systems with the attention drawn primarily by the usability characteristics and usability performance of the system and secondly by the appropriateness of the web-based learning environment for meeting specific business-oriented criteria such as requirements, cost, quality assurance mechanism, etc. Very few studies exist on the evaluation of e-learning web sites in terms of their pedagogical quality that is, on their success in helping learners learn through specific pedagogical principles. Pedagogical evaluation however is very important in e-learning as it can improve the quality of the system greatly in terms of learner performance and satisfaction as well as in terms of instructor satisfaction.

This work proposes a multi-criteria evaluation model of e-learning web sites based on well-known pedagogical principles, namely Bloom's taxonomy (Bloom, 1971) of cognitive objectives, Knowledge, Comprehension, Application, Analysis, Synthesis and Evaluation. The goal of the model is to serve as a preference model for a decision maker who can be an educator, an educational organization or a learner wishing to employ an appropriate web-based learning environment to meet his needs. The decision maker's attitudes towards the pedagogical characteristics of the system are related to a specific set of web-based learning services and criteria that can enhance the decision process.

## BACKGROUND

Background knowledge on e-learning sites evaluation requires a thorough investigation of multiple dimensions and perspectives and therefore numerous studies exist on the field. As (Inglis, 2008) states, measuring quality in e-learning is not a unidimensional problem. Some of the desirable characteristics of e-learning systems emerge from the definition of e-learning. (Wheeler, 2012) defines e-learning (or "technology-enhanced learning" or "digital learning") as "*a set of technology-mediated methods that can be applied to support student learning and can include elements of assessment, tutoring, and instruction*" and as a synonym for web-based learning. The author therefore emphasizes the web and technological dimension of e-learning together with the existence of specific tools. (Khan, 2005) on the other hand implies the relationship of e-learning with the web since he defines e-learning as "*an innovative approach for delivering well-designed, learner-centered, interactive and facilitated learning environment to anyone, anyplace, anytime by utilizing the attributes and resources of various digital technologies along with other forms of learning materials suited for open, flexible and distributed learning environment*". Moreover the author identifies e-learning features such as interactivity, ease of use, support, search, accessibility, multiple expertise, collaborative learning, authenticity, learner-control etc., along eight dimensions of e-learning: "*Institutional, Management, Technological, Pedagogical, Ethical, Interface design, Resource support* and *Evaluation*". According to the authors, the pedagogical dimension addresses issues such as learning strategies and the analysis of goals, content and audience.

The quality of e-learning systems inherits the features of both software quality (quality of the technology) and quality in education. Through an e-learning system these features are connected with a relationship that holds the distinctive aspect of each field. Nevertheless, the evaluation should spread across the fields of users' satisfaction, teaching activities' effectiveness as well as of the software quality domain (Matsatsinis et al 2003, Delias 2007). Ehlers and Pawlowski (2006) define quality as a multidimensional space without a unique standard quality assurance solution. Ehlers and Goertz (2006) stress the importance of the evaluation of learning processes concerning quality, effect (acceptance and success in learning) and benefit. A differentiation between formative and summative evaluation is made, where formative evaluations addresses quality assurance in order to reveal process weaknesses. Summative evaluation is used to control the quality and the benefit of an educational offer, an e-learning system in the present context.

As part of the learning effectiveness, the specification of learning objectives has gained importance in ISO/IEC 19796-1 (ISO/IEC, 2005) standard on the quality for learning, education, and training. However, few studies exist on the specification of criteria and methods for the pedagogical evaluation of e-learning sites. The following sections present background knowledge on e-learning evaluation criteria with emphasis on methodologies that include pedagogical criteria. Three distinct user perspectives are proposed: the learners' perspective, the instructors' perspective and the organization's perspective, as well as combinations of them.

## E-Learning Quality Criteria and Evaluation

The ISO/IEC 19796-1 (ISO/IEC, 2005) aims to improve the quality of processes, products, and services of an educational organization and describes objectives as a quality criterion for the development of a learning process as the *"adequate selection of one or more didactic concepts according to learner preferences and learning styles"* (Pawlowski, 2007). The definition of objectives takes place during the requirement analysis process and the conceptual design process incorporates them into the overall model. According to Abdous

(2009), Quality Assurance in e-learning depends on the alignment of objectives with the content as a critical element.

We propose a description of quality evaluation criteria from different user perspectives: the leaners' perspective, the instructors' perspective and the organization's perspective. The three perspectives can serve as dimensions for measuring satisfaction of different user groups with respect to e-learning and web-based e-learning systems. For each perspective, an overall of six dimensions can be identified: Interface (I), Content (C), Functionality (F), Technology (T), Pedagogy (P) and Business (B). The first letter of each dimension is used as an abbreviation in order to enable the comparison of the various proposed methods. Table 1 presents a summary of the high-order criteria and sub-criteria that were investigated for the purpose of this chapter. The criteria presentation in Table 1 where indicated by a number in parentheses before the criterion name, shows the relative importance among the criteria, as was measured by the authors. It may depict calculated weights or influence in term of statistical analysis.

The related studies show that pedagogical quality is a dimension that applies along all three perspectives mentioned above. It can be evaluated through learners' cognitive achievements, the conformance of the e-learning system to instructors' goals and to the goals of the organization. The following sections present recent studies that prove this.

## The Learners' Perspective

Three evaluation criteria were proposed by Matsatsinis et al (2003) in order to measure user satisfaction from e-learning systems, namely: Interface, Contents and Functionality as ordinal criteria on top of fifteen corresponding measurable sub-criteria. The authors relied on multi-criteria methodology and specifically the MUSA (Grigoroudis & Siskos 2002) satisfaction evaluation

*Table 1. e-Learning Quality Criteria and evaluation methods (I=Interface, C=Content, F=Functionality, T=Technology, P=Pedagogy, B=Business)*

| Work | E-learning Quality Criteria | Evaluation Method |
|------|------------------------------|-------------------|
| Matsatsinis ea 2003, Delias ea 2007 | [1] Interface *(I)* (style, ease of use, customization, multimedia quality, communication), [2] Functionality *(F)* (response time, security, reliability, interoperability), [3] Content *(C)* (organization, up-to-dateness, assessment, sufficiency, format) | MUSA |
| Blass & Davis 2003 | Appropriateness *(B)*, Design *(I)*, Interaction *(I, F)*, Evaluation *(B)* | |
| Ehlers 2004 | Tutor Support *(F)*, Cooperation and Communication *(F)*, Technology *(T)*, Costs-Expectations-Benefits *(B)*, Information Transparency of Provider/Course *(F)*, Course structure *(C)*, Didactics *(P)* | |
| Hwang ea 2004 | User interface design *(I, F, C, T)* (Quality of web-page design, Suitableness of web-link design, Usability, Response time of the user interface, Quality of media presentation, Maintainability and extendibility, Quality of security mechanism, Quality of learning guidance and operational support), Quality of instructional contents *(C, P, T)* (Correctness, Structure, Completeness, Readability, Difficulty, Target fitting, Assistive content, Price, Portability, Digitization quality) | Fuzzy logic, AHP |
| Lanzilotti ea 2006 | Technology *(T)*, Interaction *(I,F)*, Content *(C)*, Services *(F)* | eLSE (Abstract Tasks inspection) |
| Gilbert ea 2007 | Synergy between theory and practice *(P)*, specific subject criteria *(C)*, discussion forums *(F)*, interaction *(I, F)*, learning support *(F)*, robustness *(F)*, usability *(I)*, access to resources *(F)*, currency of study Materials *(C)*, student work scheduling *(F)* | |
| Tzeng ea 2007 | Personal Characteristics and System Instruction *(F)*, Participant Motivation and System Interaction, Range of Instruction Materials and Accuracy *(C)*, Webpage Design and Display of Instruction Materials *(I)*, E-Learning Environment *(F)*, Webpage Connection *(F)*, Course Quality and Work Influence *(F)*, Learning Records *(F)*, Instruction Materials *(C)* | MCDM |
| Marques ea, 2008 | Content *(C)*, LMS Communication *(F)*, Management Processes *(B)*, Results (learners' performance, credibility, ROI, learners' satisfaction) *(B, F)* | Mean |
| Shee & Wang 2008 | Interface *(I)*, Learning Community *(F)*, Content *(C)*, Personalization *(F)* | MCDM |
| Sun ea 2009 | Instruction presentation *(I)*, student learning management *(B)* | |
| Büyüközkan ea. 2010 | [1] Complete Content *(C)*, [2] Right and Understandable Content *(C, P)*, [2] User Interface *(I)*, [3] Security *(T, B)*, [4] Personalization *(F)*, [4] Interactivity *(F)*, [5] Navigation *(T)* | Fuzzy AHP |
| Ertl ea 2010 | Cognition (prerequisites, strategies) *(P)*, Epistemology (content quality, content presentation, content acceptance) *(C)*, Society (facilitation/tutoring, sociability) *(B, F)*, Technology (usability, support) *(T, I, F)* | |
| Hogo 2010 | Learners' profile | |
| Huang & Huang 2010 | Usage data (viewing time, page view frequency, navigational path length) *(F)*, Questionnaire | Fuzzy clustering |
| Kurilovas & Diagene 2010 | General Criteria (architecture, interoperability, internationalization and localization, accessibility) *(F, T)*, Adaptation criteria (adaptability to organization's needs, personalization, extensibility and automatic adaptation to users' needs) *(B, F, T)* | Additive utility function |
| Lin 2010 | [1] Information quality (Accuracy, Currency, Completeness, Format) *(C)*, [2] System quality (Accessibility, Navigability, Response time, Learnability) *(F, P)*, [3] Service quality (Reliability, Responsiveness, Trust, Empathy) *(F, B)*, [4] Attractiveness (Multimedia capability, Webpage design, Course design) *(I)* | Fuzzy AHP |
| Lee 2010 | Perceived service quality (feedback, support) *(F)*, Perceived ease of use (clear, understandable, easy to use, goals' fitting) *(I, P)*, Perceived usefulness (learning speed, improvisation of accomplishment, productivity and effectiveness) *(F)*, Online learning acceptance and satisfaction | |

*continued on following page*

*Table 1. Continued*

| Work | E-learning Quality Criteria | Evaluation Method |
|------|------------------------------|-------------------|
| Alptekin ea 2011 | Customer needs (Completeness, Easy to understand, Credibility, Price, Ease of use, Visual attractiveness, Personalization) *(I, C, B, F)*, Product Characteristics (Links & references, Evaluation, Content organization, Attractive multimedia, Payment methods, Instructors' qualification, Personalized advisory, Credibility, Communication) *(C, B, I, F)* | Distance metric |
| Jung 2011 | [1] Staff Support *(B)*, [2] Institutional Quality Assurance Mechanism *(B)*, [2] Learning Tasks *(C, P)*, Interaction *(I)*, Institutional Credibility *(B)*, Learner Support *(F)*, Information and Publicity *(C, B)*, | |
| Kay 2011 | Learning *(P)*, Design *(I)*, Engagement *(I,F, B)* | |
| Liu & Hwang 2011 | web usability *(I)*, learning materials *(C)*, assisting functionality *(F)*, technology integration *(T)*, learner preferences *(F)* | |
| Jeong & Yeo 2013 | Multimedia content: [1] Learnability *(P, F)*, [2] User Friendliness *(C, I)*, [3] Enjoyment *(P, F)*, Media loss rates, Frame rates, Download time (Access time), File size, User control, Up-to-date. | |

model. The assessment of user satisfaction was based on an ordinal regression model while for the final grade of each alternative they used an aggregative function in order to handle non homogeneous information. Pedagogical evaluation has not been included has a distinct main criterion, as the focus on early evaluation studies was on more technical aspects of e-learning systems. In Delias et al. (2007) several questions arose regarding the purpose and the scope of the evaluation. In the same work, a web- based multiple criteria evaluation model was also proposed. In comparison to the authors' previous work some sub-criteria were dropped, namely personalization and quality of digitization - multimedia of the interface criterion, learning progress along the content dimension and security and interoperability in the functionality criterion. The proposed system was tested through a survey among nearly 300 students.

Lanzilotti et al (2006) and Costabile et al (2007) emphasize on the synergy between the learning process and the learner's interaction with the software and propose a new framework for evaluating the quality of e-learning systems, called TICS (Technology, Interaction, Content, Services). Usability is considered the prime criterion and secondly the fulfillment of the instructor's pedagogical objectives. The authors

develop an evaluation methodology, called eLSE (e-Learning Systematic Evaluation) that combines a specific inspection technique with user-testing. It is based on the use of evaluation patterns, called Abstract Tasks (ATs), which precisely describe the activities to be performed during inspection. (Gilbert ea 2007) investigate satisfaction and dissatisfaction criteria on e-learning that have been expressed by students and those criteria involve the synergy between theory and practice, specific subject themes, discussion forums and other student interaction, other learning support, as well as robustness, usability, access to resources, currency of study materials and student work scheduling. As was expected, the results of the study show that students do not have a clear expression of pedagogical issues within the (e-)learning context, however they acknowledge the importance of the synergy between theory and practice, thus intuitively discriminating between knowledge and application or knowledge and synthesis.

(Shee & Wang 2008) proposed a multi-criteria methodology from the perspective of learner satisfaction to support evaluation at the pre- and post-adoption phases of the web-based e-learning system life cycle. They proposed four high-level criteria, namely Learner Interface, Learning Community, System Content and Personalization and a total of thirteen sub-criteria. In addition, they empirically investigated learners' perceptions of the relative importance of the criteria and the collected data was then analyzed by analytic hierarchy process (AHP). They revealed that learners regarded the learner interface as the most important decision criteria.

Regarding web-specific learner-specific evaluation criteria, Web-Based Learning Tools (WBLTs) are defined as "online interactive tools that support the learning of specific concepts by enhancing, amplifying and/or guiding the cognitive processes of learners" (Kay 2011). The authors assess three key criteria of WBLTs, learning, design, and engagement with the Learning Object Evaluation Scale for students (LOES-S) methodology. Four learning objectives from the revised Bloom's taxonomy were also assessed (remembering - knowledge, understanding- comprehension, application, and analysis). Student perceptions of learning, design, and engagement of WBLTs were significantly correlated with positive gains in application and analysis, but not in knowledge or comprehension. In other words, higher scores on student perceptions of learning, WBLT design, and engagement were associated with higher scores in learning performance in two of the four learning performance categories assessed, although the magnitude of the correlation coefficients was relatively small.

In (Lee, 2010), the learners' perception towards online learning was surveyed in terms of ease of use, usefulness, service quality, technology acceptance and satisfaction. A survey among adult learners in (Jung 2011) followed by factor analysis identified seven main dimensions of learners' perspective regarding e-learning quality: interaction, staff support, institutional Quality Assurance Mechanism, institutional credibility, learner support, information and publicity and learning tasks. Learning Tasks was the second most influential dimension together with the in-

stitutional Quality Assurance Mechanism. (Jeong & Yeo 2013) evaluated multimedia e-learning content criteria with factor analysis and resulted in a group of 9 criteria from past studies: Media loss rates, Frame rates, Download time (Access time), File size, User control, Up-to-date, Enjoyment, Learnability and User Friendliness. The authors' statistical sample however was not a large one as it consisted of around 50 participants. The study of (Huang & Huang 2010) combines data mining with a questionnaire in order to study the importance of objective (observed human behavior) and subjective (opinion) criteria and perform fuzzy clustering along each dimension. The involved parameters are viewing time, page view frequency and navigational path length (objective).

## The Instructors' Perspective

Fewer evaluation studies exist from the instructor's perspective. (Sun ea 2009) identify from the instructors' perspective the most critical functional requirements (or criteria) of e-learning systems in two dimensions, instruction presentation and student learning management and in terms of functionalities (or sub-criteria), the electronic whiteboard and e-syllabus (instruction presentation), and online roll call, threaded discussions, assignment management, and online forum (learning management). (Hwang ea 2004) present a group-decision approach is proposed for evaluating educational web sites by employing several soft computing technologies such as fuzzy theory, grey system and AHP group decision. The proposed criteria involve user interface design and content quality divided in a total of 18 sub-criteria. A computer-assisted web site evaluation system, EWSE (Educational Web Site Evaluator) has been developed, for selecting the proper criteria for an individual web site from both experts and end-users.

## The Organization's Perspective

The organization's perspective involves criteria that relate to the appropriateness and the management of e-learning processes from the e-learning organization. (Blass & Davis 2003) have identified four high-order criteria for e-learning development in higher education, namely appropriateness (of staff, market, content and students), design (learning aspirations and cognitive ergonomics), interaction (faculty-student and student-student), and evaluation (reinforcement and achievement). The aspiration sub-criterion is shaped primarily by learning objectives. The e-QUAL model presented in (Marques ea, 2008) addresses e-learning quality from the organization's perspective by discussing issues such as content, communication tools, management processes and effects. In (Büyüközkan ea. 2010) seven criteria are chosen from the organization's perspective regarding systems' and services' quality: quality and comprehensibility of the content, completeness of the content, personalization/individualization, security, navigation, communication (interactivity) and user interface design.

## Multiple Perspectives

Several studies exist that combine different perspectives in one evaluation framework. (Tzeng ea 2007) propose a hybrid MCDM model that addresses the independent relations of evaluation criteria with the aid of factor analysis and the dependent relations of evaluation criteria with the aid of DEMATEL. The authors propose a non-additive multi-criteria evaluation technique with fuzzy measures and fuzzy integral, in order to cope for the assumption of independence between criteria. Empirical experimental results showed effective evaluation of e-learning programs when the evaluation criteria are numerous and intertwined. In the experiment a total of nine principal components were identified by e-learning experts or familiars, namely: Personal Characteristics and System Instruction, Participant Motivation and System Interaction, Range of Instruction Materials, and Accuracy, Webpage Design and Display of Instruction Materials, E-Learning Environment, Webpage Connection, Course Quality and Work Influence, Learning Records and Instruction Materials. The study of (Hogo, 2010) applies data mining techniques in order to incorporate the learner's profile in the evaluation by classifying learners into specific categories based on their profiles: regular, workers, casual, bad and absent. (Ertl ea 2010) discuss high-level quality dimensions for the evaluation of e-learning considering a cognitive, an epistemological, a social and a technical infrastructure. (Kurilovas & Dagiene, 2010) analyze the criteria of internal quality and quality in use of Learning Object Repositories as general and adaptation criteria synthesized in additive model.

(Lin 2010) studies the relative importance of e-learning web sites evaluation factors. Three main dimensions are chosen from the literature together with sub-criteria: System quality (Accessibility, Navigability, Response time, Learnability), Information quality (Accuracy, Currency, Completeness, Format), Service quality (Reliability, Responsiveness, Trust, Empathy) and Attractiveness (Multimedia capability, Webpage design, Course design). The study was carried out among two groups of users, high-experienced and low-experienced. Information quality was identified as the most important criterion by both groups. An important difference among the two groups was their perception on the weight of system quality as the low-experienced group put on it considerably less significance than the highly-experienced group.

(Alptekin ea 2011) suggest a quality decision framework for e-learning product selection. The target values for e-learning product characteristics that maximize overall customer satisfaction are determined and fuzzy regression is employed to determine the parameters of functional relationships between customer needs and e-learning product characteristics, and among e-learning product characteristics themselves. E-learning product alternatives are evaluated and ranked with respect to deviations from the target product characteristic values.

A multi-dimensional set of criteria to help learners and instructors evaluate the quality of English learning websites was proposed by (Liu & Hwang 2011). Five evaluation dimensions are identified, based on web usability, learning materials, assisting functionality, technology integration, and learner preferences. The set of sub-criteria was refined according to user preferences collected through a survey.

From the above analysis of proposed evaluation methods we conclude that pedagogy is either neglected or considered a sub-criterion of other main criteria in most of the studies. As the technology of e-learning systems has matured and reached new quality standards and their spread has expanded significantly, the issue of pedagogical value is becoming more and more important and influences the decision for the appropriate web-based e-learning system under a specific context. Therefore as an extension to previous works (Matsatsinis ea 2003) and (Delias ea 2007), we propose the addition of the dimension of pedagogical evaluation. The following section presents the concept of cognitive learning objectives and justifies their choice as the primary pedagogical dimension of e-learning systems.

## Learning Objectives

Objectives are a valuable tool for the development of learning, as they express what learners should achieve. ACM and AIS in (ACM 2008) and ACM and IEEE in (AIS 2010) have recently provided computer science curriculum guidelines in terms of learning objectives, in order to help the development of education in information technologies. Bloom's taxonomy (Krathwohl 2002) has been a very popular method for describing learning goals since 1956 when it was proposed. It identi-

fies three main categories of learning objectives: cognitive, affective and psychomotor, each one being divided into sub-categories. The cognitive level has been described in Bloom's taxonomy with 6 goals of scaling complexity, Knowledge, Comprehension, Application, Synthesis, Analysis and Evaluation. These goals are related to verbs that denote learning behavior. Knowledge refers to the recall of concepts while Comprehension refers to the understanding of problems. Application is related with the ability to apply knowledge and skills in new situations and problems and Analysis involves the separation of problem components and the creation of organizational structures from them. Synthesis is described as solving composite problems in order to create a whole solution and Evaluation is a learner's ability to judge solutions and concepts. Anderson and Krathwohl (Krathwohl 2002) revised Bloom's taxonomy by adding 4 dimensions, namely Factual, Conceptual, Procedural and Metacognitive and by changing the 6 Objectives into verbs: remember, understand, apply, analyze, evaluate and create. According to the revised taxonomy, factual knowledge includes 'the basic elements', while conceptual knowledge involves the 'interrelationships among the basic elements within larger structures'. Procedural knowledge is about knowing 'how to do something' and meta-cognitive knowledge is about cognition- awareness and self-awareness. The revised taxonomy has also been used extensively in educational research.

Pedagogical evaluation is limited compared to usability and appropriateness. (Ehlers 2004) distinguishes 3 dimensions of quality in e-learning, corresponding to different perspectives, meanings and levels. Learners' subjective preferences constitute 7 fields including didactics, course delivery, tutor support, collaboration, technology, the relationship of cost to expectations and benefits and information transparency of the provider which have been grouped in 4 learner profiles. Didactics in turn, in Ehlers' work, constitute 6 quality criteria: the presence of background material, the employment of multimedia, the structuring of the material in a goal-oriented way, the acquisition of lifelong learning skills, the presence of feedback during the learning process, and the personalization of tasks according to learners' needs. In our work, the evaluation of such criteria in a goal-oriented framework can offer a more thorough pedagogical evaluation, moreover if the evaluation is based on well-known pedagogical principles.

## METHODOLOGY

In this chapter we propose a methodology for multi-criteria pedagogical evaluation of e-learning web sites that can be used by decision-makers, mainly instructors and e-learning organizations. The methodology is multi-perspective and it is based on clear formal pedagogical goals, namely Bloom's taxonomy of Learning Objectives that are identifiable and measurable within web-based learning systems. We propose the use of the six cognitive levels from Bloom's taxonomy as the criteria for the pedagogical evaluation of an e-learning web site. We analyze below each one of the learning objectives (or pedagogical criteria) in terms of their implications to the characteristics of web-based learning systems. In order to provide an appropriate measurement mechanism, four dimensions of the pedagogical criteria are also proposed: Quantity, Pedagogical quality, Technical quality and Learners' satisfaction. Quantity can be defined as the number of items present in the web site, while pedagogical quality concerns instructors and their pedagogical preferences. Technical quality characteristics relate to the technical performance of a system, while Learners' satisfaction can be measured through a survey.

### Knowledge

The criterion of the Knowledge cognitive dimension in Bloom's taxonomy refers to the ability of a learner to memorize/remember/recall learned

information in a domain. Examples of verbs that can be used to describe the behavior of learners having achieved Knowledge are: *define, describe, identify, know, recall, state, label, list, match, name outline, recognize, reproduce* and *select*. The evaluation of an e-learning website in the Knowledge dimension, shall answer questions such as: *'Does the web site provide Knowledge items?', 'Does the web site help learners achieve Knowledge?', 'What is the pedagogical performance of the web-site regarding Knowledge?', 'What is the relative performance of a web site in Knowledge as opposed to other objectives?'* and so on. From the technical point of view, the question arises of how Knowledge can be evaluated or measured in an e-learning environment. An objective measure can be the quantity of Knowledge items presented to learners and the quantity of Knowledge tasks. A subjective measure that reflects the instructors' attitude is the pedagogical quality of the Knowledge items: correctness, completeness or range coverage, up-to-dateness or currency, appropriateness or target fitting, difficulty, structure and assessment. Technically, Knowledge items can be evaluated in terms of their usability characteristics: multimedia quality, presentation quality, ease of use, response time and navigation. Learners' satisfaction as a last measure, reflects the end-users' attitude towards Knowledge learning items present in web-site. As a further aid to instructors and evaluators, we propose specific types of Knowledge items and assessment tasks for measuring performance. Identifiable Knowledge content items involve definitions, axioms, theorems, statements, proofs, listings of characteristics and properties, hierarchical relationships and concept maps. Assessment items or assessment tasks can include close-ended questions such as true-false questions, multiple-choices, matching and the writing of definitions. Existing web-based learning systems perform relatively well in Knowledge as it is technically more feasible to achieve than other higher-level pedagogical characteristics.

## Comprehension

Understanding problems and situations in the learning domain is the next level to Knowledge in terms of cognitive achievement. A web site's pedagogical performance in terms of Comprehension can be measured by the existence of examples, explanations, interpretations, transformations, generalizations, extensions, summarizations and conclusions as content items or domain tasks, i.e. exercises. The pedagogical and technical quality as well as the learners' satisfaction has the same evaluation dimensions as Knowledge does: Quantity, Pedagogical Quality, Technical Quality and Learners' satisfaction.

## Application

The Application of Knowledge and Comprehension skills for solving new problems in a domain has been described as the ability to compute, solve, use, operate, demonstrate/show, etc, problems and tools. Problem-based learning is closely related to Application. Therefore web-based learning sites that include problem-based activities should be evaluated as having a high performance in Application, as long as measurements of quantity, quality, technology and learners' satisfaction are performed. From a technical point of view, application is at a high level in problem solving learning environments where the system can automatically assess the solutions of learners. Blended learning environments can also provide application learners' tasks at some extent.

## Analysis

The ability to analyze problems and solutions in distinct components as a cognitive skill can be measured by the quantity of relevant items and tasks, examples of which are the construction of diagrams and flowcharts.

## Synthesis

The production of composite solutions, plans and designs define the criterion of Synthesis as a pedagogical characteristic of web-based learning systems. Technically speaking, web-based Intelligent Tutoring Systems are the closest class of systems that can claim Synthesis as one of their pedagogical characteristics.

## Evaluation

Evaluating solutions and making decisions is proposed by Bloom's as the highest level skill in the cognitive dimension of learning. Relevant content items and tasks can assess a web site's performance along the specific criterion.

Table 2 summarizes the criteria description and provides examples for measuring the performance of each criterion in specific web sites.

As an example, when measuring the performance of a web site in terms of Knowledge, the number of content and assessment items targeting can be measured within the learning material. The pedagogical quality of Knowledge can be specified by an expert in pedagogy in an ordinal scale. The technical quality can be evaluated by experts of the organization while usability and user satisfaction require specific measures and methodologies such as usability tests and questionnaires.

The overall performance of a web-site along each criterion can be obtained by a weighted additive function fusing the decision's maker's preferences. For example, a decision maker with the intention to enhance the comprehension of learners in an online course through transformation material and activities as the most appropriate didactic method, can weigh the quantity of transformation examples and exercises with a higher importance than other types of material and/or exercises. As another example, from the point of view of specific pedagogy such as problem-based e-learning environments, application and synthesis learning objects will be weighed accordingly by the evaluator.

*Table 2. Pedagogical evaluation criteria from Bloom's taxonomy*

| Criterion | Description | Examples |
|---|---|---|
| Knowledge (*remember*) | Define, describe, identify, know, recall, state, label, list, match, name, outline, recognize, reproduce, select. | **Content items:** Definitions, Axioms, Theorems, Statements, Proofs, Lists, Hierarchies, Concept Maps. **Assessment items:** Write definitions, True/False questions, Multiple-choice questions, Close-ended questions, Matching questions. |
| Comprehension (*understand*) | Comprehend, convert, defend, distinguish, estimate, explain, extend, generalize, give examples, infer, interpret, paraphrase, predict, rewrite, summarize, and translate. | **Content items:** Examples, Transformations, Explanations, Interpretations, Inferences/ Conclusions, Extensions, Generalizations, Summaries. **Assessment items:** Comprehension questions, Transformation/ Conversion/ Translation/ Rewriting/ Summarization exercises, Extension/ Generalization exercises, Inference making exercises. |
| Application (*apply*) | Apply, change, compute, construct, demonstrate, discover, manipulate, modify, operate, predict, prepare, produce, relate, show, solve, use. | **Content items:** Solutions, Application examples, Operation examples, Demonstrations, Use cases. **Assessment items:** Problems |
| Analysis (*analyze*) | Analyze, break down, compare, contrast, diagram, deconstruct, differentiate, discriminate, distinguish, identify, illustrate, infer, outlines, relate, select, and separate. | **Content items:** Analyses, Decompositions/ Deconstructions, Flowcharts, Comparisons. **Assessment items:** Diagrams, Flowcharts. |
| Synthesis (*create*) | Categorize, combine, compile, compose, create, devise, design, explain, generate, modify, organize, plan, rearrange, reconstruct, relate, reorganize, revise, rewrite, summarize, tell, write. | **Content items:** Synthetic (composite) solutions, Complex Designs, Organizational plans, Summaries, Revisions, Essays, Workflows, Sequences. **Assessment items:** Projects |
| Evaluation (*evaluate*) | Appraise, compare, conclude, contrast, criticizes, critique, defend, describe, discriminate, evaluate, explain, interpret, justify, relate, summarize, support. | **Content items:** Comparisons, conclusions, critiques, defenses, evaluations. **Assessment items:** Solution evaluation and selection problems, decision and defense problems. |

## Additive Preference Aggregation Model

After identifying the six pedagogical criteria we deal of the problem of how to combine these criteria in a single evaluation model. Multicriteria decision analysis was chosen as an appropriate method for combining several antagonistic (conflicting) criteria. The antagonism among pedagogical criteria emerges from the technical and resource limitations underlying the development of web-based learning. A single system cannot perform well along the whole range of criteria. Concessions have to be decided among Knowledge, Comprehension, Application, Analysis, Synthesis and Evaluation. These concessions reflect the preferences of e-learning organizations and educators either in the design phase, or in the after-use phase. The proposed framework can be employed as tools for ranking solutions with specific design characteristics or existing systems. In the former case though, the dimension of learners' satisfaction is excluded from the discussion. Usability design issues also have to rely on existing studies that can be generalized in terms of their results. In the latter case of existing systems, a survey method regarding learners' satisfaction is necessary, as well as appropriate usability tests.

Thus, the pedagogical evaluation of different e-learning web sites (or designs) for decision making along the 6 pedagogical criteria, belongs to the 'a' type of multicriteria problematic, i.e. ranking of the alternatives. The formulation of the problem is as follows:

- The set of web-sites $S = \{s_j, j = 1..n\}$ that will be ranked according to their pedagogical performance (alternatives).
- The set of Learning Objectives (criteria) or learning goals that forms the set of pedagogical criteria along which web sites are evaluated, $O = \{o_k, k = 1..6\}$. They form a consistent family of criteria as they have the following characteristics (Roy 1996):
- **Monotonicity:** A web site $s$ is preferred to $s'$, if-and-only-if its performance is higher in the criterion $o$ given that their performance is the same in every other criterion, written as: $f_o(s) > f_o(s') \Leftrightarrow s \succ s'$ and $f_k(s) = f_k(s'), k \neq o$.
- **Exhaustivity:** If the performance of a web site in any two different Learning Objectives is the same, then the two sites are of an indifferent pedagogical state. For example, if a web site has the same performance in Knowledge and Comprehension, then the two web sites are indifferent.
- **Non-Redundancy:** If one of the learning objectives (criteria) is removed, the decision-maker cannot make a decision based on the rest of the learning objectives, as important information is missing. Given that every Learning Objective (criterion) is applied to all web sites, lack of knowledge regarding one of the criteria violates the property of exhaustivity as the decision maker cannot decide which web site is preferred to the other.
- The weights of the six criteria $w_k, k = 1..6, w_k \in (0,1)$

- The 5 dimensions (sub-criteria) of pedagogical performance along each criterion $D = \{d_i, i = 1..5\}$.
- The score of each web-site along each sub-criterion: $s_j = (g_{j1}, ..., g_{j5}), j = 1..n$
- The weights of each sub-criterion: $p_i, i = 1..5, p_i \in (0,1)$
- Marginal utility functions $u_i()$ for each sub-criterion. The marginal utility function of each criterion is defined as a monotonic function in the interval [0, 1], such that $u_i(g_{jl*}) = 0$, $u_i(g_{jl}^*) = 1$
- Additive global utility of each web site along the 5 sub-criteria:

$$U(s_j) = \sum_{i=1}^{5} p_i u_i(g_{ji}),$$ where $p_i$ is the weight of sub-criterion i, $i = 1..5, p_i \in (0,1)$ and $u_i()$ is the marginal utility function of sub-criterion i.

- Additive global utility of each web site along the six main criteria:

$$U'(s_j) = \sum_{k=1}^{6} w_k u'_k(U(s_j)),$$ where $w_k$ is the weight of criterion k and $k = 1..6, w_k \in (0,1)$.

Marginal utility functions $u_i()$ and $u'_k()$ are non-decreasing real valued functions normalized between 0 and 1 and have a piece-wise linear form (Doumpos & Zopounidis 2002), (Siskos et. al. 2005).

Since the six main criteria are of scaling complexity with Knowledge representing the lowest-level goal and Evaluation the highest-level goal, we propose the use of surrogate RS (Rank Sum) weights with $n = 6$, $n = 5$ and $n = 4$, as shown in the Table 3.

Rank Sum weights are proposed since they have better performance than other weight approximations such as ROC weights (Roberts &

*Table 3. RS weights for the 6 cognitive criteria*

| Criterion | RS Weight for 6 Goals | RS Weight for 5 Goals | RS Weight for 4 Goals |
|---|---|---|---|
| Knowledge | 0.0476 | 0.0667 | 0.1000 |
| Comprehension | 0.0952 | 0.1333 | 0.2000 |
| Application | 0.1429 | 0.2000 | 0.3000 |
| Analysis | 0.1905 | 0.2667 | 0.4000 |
| Synthesis | 0.2381 | 0.3333 | - |
| Evaluation | 0.2857 | - | |

Goodwin, 2002). RS weights take into account the pedagogical nature of Learning Objectives, rating Synthesis and Evaluation with higher weights than the other four goals. In cases were the e-learning site does not involve high-level goals such as Evaluation or/and Synthesis, RS weight approximations can be used for a smaller $n$.

## FUTURE RESEARCH AND DIRECTIONS

The main future research directions include the investigation of teachers' and students' attitudes towards Learning Objectives in web-based learning systems, as well as the evaluation of various weight approximations in case studies involving e-learning web sites currently in use in the authors' department for laboratory purposes.

## CONCLUSION

The advancement of e-learning technologies and the overcoming of the initial technical difficulties have shifted part of the research and development issues in web-based learning, towards pedagogy as a higher-level quality characteristic. However, pedagogical evaluation of web-based learning is not an easy task as it involves several dimensions and multiple users' perspectives. The merging of pedagogy with technology is the starting point for such an effort. Therefore we propose the use of formal educational objectives from Bloom's taxonomy as an evaluation mechanism of e-learning web sites' pedagogical performance. The six cognitive learning objectives form scaling complexity criteria and thus have different pedagogical importance.

In order to provide an adequate measurement mechanism, four dimensions of the pedagogical criteria are proposed: Quantity, Pedagogical quality, Technical quality and User satisfaction. A multicriteria analysis model is an appropriate mechanism for such a complex task. From the above discussion we conclude that most e-learning web sites constrain to Knowledge and Comprehension evaluation criteria. Therefore, for web-based learning to be pedagogically complete, along all the range of criteria, it takes considerably further technical effort. The present chapter aims to trigger a discussion that will bring together the technological and the pedagogical communities involved in e-learning and stress the critical issues to be considered thereafter.

## REFERENCES

Abdous, M. (2009). E-learning quality assurance: A process-oriented lifecycle model. *Quality Assurance in Education*, *17*(3), 281–295. doi:10.1108/09684880910970678

ACM. (2008). *ACM computer science curriculum 2008: An interim revision of CS 2001*. Retrieved from http://www.acm.org/education/curricula/ComputerScience2008.pdf/view

Alptekin, S. E., & Karsak, E. E. (2011). An integrated decision framework for evaluating and selecting e-learning products. *Applied Soft Computing*, *11*, 2990–2998. doi:10.1016/j.asoc.2010.11.023

Ardito, C., de Marsico, M., Lanzilotti, R., Levialdi, S., Roselli, T., Rossano, V., & Tersigni, M. (2004). Usability of e-learning tools. In *Proceedings of the Working Conference on Advanced Visual Interfaces*, (pp. 80-84). AVI.

Blass, E., & Davis, A. (2003). Building on solid foundations: Establishing criteria for e-learning development. *Journal of Further and Higher Education*, 27(3), 227–245. doi:10.1080/0309877032000098662

Büyüközkan, G., Arsenyan, J., & Ertek, G. (2010). Evaluation of e-learning web sites using fuzzy axiomatic design based approach. *International Journal of Computational Intelligence Systems*, 3(1), 28–42.

Cebi, S. (2013). Determining importance degrees of website design parameters based on interactions and types of websites. *Decision Support Systems*, 54, 1030–1043. doi:10.1016/j.dss.2012.10.036

Clark, D. R. (2009). *Bloom's taxonomy of learning domains - The three types of learning*. Retrieved from http://www.nwlink.com/~Donclark/hrd/bloom.html.

Costabile, M. F., Roselli, T., Lanzilotti, R., Ardito, C., & Rossano, V. (2007). A holistic approach to the evaluation of e-learning systems. In *Universal Access in Human-Computer Interaction (LNCS)* (Vol. 4556, pp. 530–538). Berlin: Springer. doi:10.1007/978-3-540-73283-9_59

Delias, P., Matsatsinis, N. F., & Karagounakis, A. (2007). Towards a multi-criterion web-based tool for evaluation of an e-learning system. In Innovations in E-learning, Instruction Technology, Assessment, and Engineering Education 2007, (pp. 289-293). IEEE.

Doumpos, M., & Zopounidis, C. (2002). *Multicriteria decision aid classification methods*. Dordrecht, The Netherlands: Kluwer.

Ehlers, U.-D. (2004). Quality in e-learning from a learner's perspective. *EURODL European Journal of Open, Distance and E-learning*. Retrieved from http://www.eurodl.org/index.php?tag=120&article=230&article=101

Ehlers, U.-D., & Goertz, L. (2006). Quality evaluation for e-learning in Europe. In *Handbook on quality and standardisation in e-learning 2006* (pp. 157–169). Berlin: Springer. doi:10.1007/3-540-32788-6_11

Ehlers, U.-D., & Pawlowski, J. (2006). Quality in European e-learning: An introduction. In *Handbook on quality and standardisation in e-learning* (pp. 1–13). Berlin: Springer. doi:10.1007/3-540-32788-6_1

Ertl, B., Ebner, K., & Kikis-Papadakis, K. (2010). An infrastructure approach for the evaluation of e-learning. *Communications in Computer and Information Science*, 111, 98–104. doi:10.1007/978-3-642-16318-0_11

Gilbert, J., Morton, S., & Rowley, J. (2007). e-Learning: The student experience. *British Journal of Educational Technology*, 38(4), 560–573. doi:10.1111/j.1467-8535.2007.00723.x

Gogus, A. (2012). Bloom's taxonomy of learning objectives. In Encyclopedia of the sciences of learning. Berlin: Springer Science+Business Media, LLC.

Grigoroudis, E., & Siskos, Y. (2002). Preference disaggregation for measuring and analyzing customer satisfaction: The MUSA method. *European Journal of Operational Research*, 143(1), 148–170. doi:10.1016/S0377-2217(01)00332-0

Hogo, M. A. (2010). Evaluation of e-learning systems based on fuzzy clustering models and statistical tools. *Expert Systems with Applications*, 37, 6891–6903. doi:10.1016/j.eswa.2010.03.032

Huang, C.-K., & Huang, C.-H. (2010). An integrated decision model for evaluating educational web sites from the fuzzy subjective and objective perspectives. *Computers & Education, 55*, 616–629. doi:10.1016/j.compedu.2010.02.022

Hwang, G.-J., Huang, T. C. K., & Tseng, J. C. R. (2004). A group-decision approach for evaluating educational web sites. *Computers & Education, 42*, 65–86. doi:10.1016/S0360-1315(03)00065-4

Inglis, A. (2008). Approaches to the validation of quality frameworks for e-learning. *Quality Assurance in Education, 16*(4), 347–362. doi:10.1108/09684880810906490

IS. (2010). Curriculum guidelines for undergraduate degree programs in information systems. New York: Association for Computing Machinery (ACM), Association for Information Systems (AIS).

Jeong, H.-Y., & Yeo, S.-S. (2013, April). The quality model for e-learning system with multimedia contents: A pairwise comparison approach. *Multimedia Tools and Applications.* doi:10.1007/s11042-013-1445-5

Jung, I. (2011). The dimensions of e-learning quality: from the learner's perspective. *Educational Technology Research and Development, 59*, 445–464. doi:10.1007/s11423-010-9171-4

Kay, R. (2011). Evaluating learning, design, and engagement in web-based learning tools (WBLTs): The WBLT evaluation scale. *Computers in Human Behavior, 27*, 1849–1856. doi:10.1016/j.chb.2011.04.007

Khan, B. (2005). *Managing e-learning strategies design, delivery, implementation and evaluation.* Hershey, PA: Information Science Publishing. doi:10.4018/978-1-59140-634-1

Krathwohl, D. R. (2002). A revision of Bloom's taxonomy: An overview. *Theory into Practice, 41*(4), 212–218. doi:10.1207/s15430421tip4104_2

Kurilovas, E., & Dagiene, V. (2010). Multiple criteria evaluation of quality and optimisation of e-learning system components. *Electronic Journal of e-Learning, 8*(2), 141 151.

Lanzilotti, R., Ardito, C., Costabile, M. F., & De Angeli, A. (2006). eLSE methodology: A systematic approach to the e-learning systems evaluation. *Journal of Educational Technology & Society, 9*(4), 42–53.

Lee, J.-W. (2010). Online support service quality, online learning acceptance, and student satisfaction. *The Internet and Higher Education, 13*, 277–283. doi:10.1016/j.iheduc.2010.08.002

Lin, H.-F. (2010). An application of fuzzy AHP for evaluating course website quality. *Computers & Education, 54*, 877–888. doi:10.1016/j.compedu.2009.09.017

Liu, G.-Z., Liu, Z.-H., & Hwang, G.-J. (2011). Developing multi-dimensional evaluation criteria for English learning websites with university students and professors. *Computers & Education, 56*, 65–79. doi:10.1016/j.compedu.2010.08.019

Marques, C. G., Noivo, J., & Veríssimo, M. (2008). e-QUAL: e-Learning with quality: Proposal for an evaluation model on the quality of e-learning courses. *Computers & Education*, 83–90. doi:10.1007/978-1-84628-929-3_9

Matsatsinis, N. F., Grigoroudis, E., & Delias, P. (2003). User satisfaction and e-learning systems: Towards a multi-criteria evaluation methodology. *Operations Research, 3*(3), 249–259.

Pawlowski, J. M. (2007). The quality adaptation model: Adaptation and adoption of the quality standard ISO/IEC 19796-1 for learning, education, and training. *Journal of Educational Technology & Society, 10*(2), 3–16.

Przybyszewski, K. (2006). A new evaluation method for e-learning systems. In *Artificial intelligence and soft computing (LNCS)* (Vol. 4029, pp. 1209–1216). Berlin: Springer. doi:10.1007/11785231_126

Roberts, R., & Goodwin, P. (2002). Weight approximations in multi-attribute decision models. *J. Multi-Crit. Decision Analysis*, *11*, 291–303. doi:10.1002/mcda.320

Roy, B. (1996). *Multicriteria methodology for decision aiding*. Dordrecht, The Netherlands: Kluwer. doi:10.1007/978-1-4757-2500-1

Shee, D. Y., & Wang, Y.-S. (2008). Multi-criteria evaluation of the web-based e-learning system: A methodology based on learner satisfaction and its applications. *Computers & Education*, *50*, 894–905. doi:10.1016/j.compedu.2006.09.005

Siskos, Y., Grigoroudis, E., & Matsatsinis, N. F. (2005). Outranking theory and the UTA methods. In J. Figueira, S. Greco, & M. Ehrgott (Eds.), *Multiple criteria decision analysis – State of the art – Surveys* (pp. 297–344). Berlin: Springer.

Sun, P.-C., Cheng, H.-K., & Finger, G. (2009). Critical functionalities of a successful e-learning system — An analysis from instructors' cognitive structure toward system usage. *Decision Support Systems*, *48*, 293–302. doi:10.1016/j.dss.2009.08.007

Tzeng, G.-H., Chiang, C.-H., & Li, C.-W. (2007). Evaluating intertwined effects in e-learning programs: A novel hybrid MCDM model based on factor analysis and DEMATEL. *Expert Systems with Applications*, *32*, 1028–1044. doi:10.1016/j.eswa.2006.02.004

Wheeler, S. (2012). E-learning. In *Encyclopedia of the sciences of learning 2012* (pp. 1108–1109). Berlin: Springer.

Yen, B., Hu, P. J.-H., & Wang, M. (2007). Toward an analytical approach for effective web site design: A framework for modeling, evaluation and enhancement. *Electronic Commerce Research and Applications*, *6*, 159–170. doi:10.1016/j.elerap.2006.11.004

## ADDITIONAL READING

Bloom, B. S. (1971). Learning for mastery. In B. S. Bloom, J. T. Hastings, & G. F. Madaus (Eds.), *Handbook on formative and summative evaluation of student learning*. New York: McGraw-Hill.

Bloom, B. S. (1974). Time and learning. *The American Psychologist*, *29*, 682–688. doi:10.1037/h0037632

Bloom, B. S. (1976). *Human characteristics and school learning*. New York: McGraw-Hill.

Clark, R. C., & Mayer, R. E. (2011). *E-learning and the science of instruction*. San Francisco, CA: Pfeiffer. doi:10.1002/9781118255971

Ehlers, U.-D., Goertz, L., Hildebrandt, B., & Pawlowski, J. M. (2005). *Quality in e-learning. Cedefop Panorama series, 116*. Luxembourg: Office for Official Publications of the European Communities.

Eom, S., & Arbaugh, J. B. (2011). *Student Satisfaction and Learning Outcomes in E-Learning: An Introduction to Empirical Research* (pp. 1-472). doi:10.4018/978-1-60960-615-2.

Figueira, J., Greco, S., Ehrgott, M. (Ed's) (2005). *Multiple Criteria Decision Analysis – State of the art – surveys*. Springer Science + Business Media, Inc.

Gillies, A. C. (1992). *Software Quality: Theory and Management*. London: Chapman & Hall, Ltd.

Pardalos, P., Siskos, Y., & Zopounidis, C. (Ed's) (1995). Advances in multicriteria analysis. Dordrecht: Kluwer Academic Publishers.

Pumilia-Gnarini, P., Favaron, E., Pacetti, E., Bishop, J., & Guerra, L. (2013). Handbook of Research on Didactic Strategies and Technologies for Education: Incorporating Advancements (2 Volumes) (pp. 1-1155). doi: doi:10.4018/978-1-4666-2122-0.

Seel, N. M. (Ed.). (2012). *Encyclopedia of the Sciences of Learning*. Springer. doi:10.1007/978-1-4419-1428-6

Stankov, S., Glavinic, V., & Rosic, M. (2011). *Intelligent Tutoring Systems in E-Learning Environments: Design* (pp. 1–446). Implementation and Evaluation.

Yang, H. H., & Wang, S. (2013). *Cases on Formal and Informal E-Learning Environments: Opportunities and Practices* (pp. 1-454). doi:10.4018/978-1-4666-1930-2.

## KEY TERMS AND DEFINITIONS

**Bloom's Taxonomy of Learning Objectives:** A classification of learning objectives, along the cognitive, affective and psych-motor domains proposed by Benjamin Bloom.

**Cognitive Domain of Bloom's Taxonomy:** A class of learning objectives referring to the development of knowledge and intellectual skills. It involves the six objective of Knowledge, Comprehension, Application, Analysis, synthesis and Evaluation.

**E-Learning:** The delivery of learning services through Information and Communication Technologies. Whereby learning services include tools, methods, processes, objects and systems that aim to provide, enhance or support learning.

**E-Learning Evaluation:** The process of assessing quality in e-learning. It involves the specification of the goal of the evaluation, the evaluation criteria and the methodology, as well as the procedures for assessing them.

**Learning Objectives:** What a learner is expected to achieve after the completion of a learning process.

**Multiple Criteria Decision Analysis (MCDA):** The field of Operations Research that involves the solution of decision problems based on multiple, usually conflicting criteria.

**Quality in E-Learning:** The degree of compliance of e-learning to a specific set of quality criteria.

**Web-Based Learning:** The delivery of learning services on the WWW.

# Chapter 14
# How Interface Design and Search Strategy Influence Children's Search Performance and Evaluation

**Hanna Jochmann-Mannak**
*University of Twente, The Netherlands*

**Leo Lentz**
*Utrecht University, The Netherlands*

**Theo Huibers**
*University of Twente, The Netherlands*

**Ted Sanders**
*Utrecht University, The Netherlands*

## ABSTRACT

*This chapter presents an experiment with 158 children, aged 10 to 12, in which search performance and attitudes towards an informational Website are investigated. The same Website was designed in 3 different types of interface design varying in playfulness of navigation structure and in playfulness of visual design. The type of interface design did not have an effect on children's search performance, but it did influence children's feelings of emotional valence and their evaluation of "goodness." Children felt most positive about the Website with a classical navigation structure and playful aesthetics. They found the playful image map Website least good. More importantly, children's search performance was much more effective and efficient when using the search engine than when browsing the menu. Furthermore, this chapter explores the challenge of measuring affective responses towards digital interfaces with children by presenting an elaborate evaluation of different methods.*

DOI: 10.4018/978-1-4666-5129-6.ch014

# INTRODUCTION

There is a trend in digital media for children to design digital products that are 'cool' and 'playful'. Part of taking a 'playful' approach in designing digital products for children is creating age-appropriate graphics, or graphics that children can relate to (Meloncon, Haynes, Varelmann & Groh, 2010). In a corpus study of 100 informational Websites for children, we recognized this playful design approach in many of the analyzed interfaces (Jochmann-Mannak, Lentz, Huibers & Sanders, 2012). More specifically, we identified three types of interface design for children, ranging from 1) classical interface design with a classical interaction style and without playful graphics, 2) interface design with playful graphics, but a classical interaction style and 3) playful interface design with playful graphics and a playful interaction style. In this study, we analyzed what the effects are of these different design approaches of an informational Website on children's interaction with these interfaces and on children's affective responses towards these interfaces.

The second important objective in this experiment, is to explore the effects of children's use of a search engine on children's search performance and affective responses. Conducting an experiment by letting children interact with digital interfaces is a big challenge. However, measuring children's affective responses towards these interfaces is an even greater challenge, as will be described in this chapter.

# THEORETICAL BACKGROUND

## Children's Informational Interface Design

Interactive products for children can be classified in entertainment, educational and enabling products (Markopoulos, Read, MacFarlane & Hoysniemi, 2008). Websites for children as a specific group of interactive products can also be classified in these three genres. Most Websites for children are aimed at entertaining children, for example by providing computer games. For our study with children's informational Websites, both educational and enabling Websites are relevant, because most informational Websites are educational and search engines that help children in finding relevant information, can be classified as enabling.

Researchers propose some guidelines for children's Web design (Nielsen & Gilutz, 2002; Meloncon, et al., 2010). Most of these guidelines were tested and validated with children, but many of the guidelines are not specifically aimed at children, and similar to standard Web design practices for adult Websites. In a large corpus study with children's informational Websites we identified current design conventions for children (Jochmann-Mannak et al., 2012). This study also showed that designers of children's Websites often follow general Web design guidelines. A closer look at the data in this study did reveal three categories of informational Websites especially designed for children. The first category is a Classic design type in which the layout of the pages is kept minimal and the design is aimed at simplicity, consistency and focus. We called the second category 'the Classical Play design type' in which a classic design approach for the navigation structure is combined with a playful, visual design approach. More effort is spent on the design of graphics, colors and games (Meloncon et al., 2010). The third category was called the 'Image Map design type' in which no classic Web design characteristics are used. The visual design and navigation structure on the Websites of this type are based on Image maps that incorporate objects or locations that children know from real life or from fiction. Children can explore this tableau of real life or fictional objects, which makes information-seeking a playful experience (Meloncon et al., 2010). This Image map web design can be compared to 'spatial metaphors', which can be employed to visually represent information, using the universe, the solar system, galaxies, and so on through which the user navigates to locate information (Chen, 2006).

In their study to develop a visual taxonomy for children, Large, Beheshti, Tabatabaei, and Nesset (2009) emphasized the importance of movement and color in any visualization designed for children. They argue that "such characteristics do not necessarily influence positively the effectiveness of a taxonomy, but the affective reaction of users, and especially of children, that should never be underestimated. If the presentation is not interesting and fails to catch the attention of users, it is unlikely to invite their repeat visits. It also might be argued that intrinsic to visualization schemes is the ability to provoke interest and even fun" (p. 1818).

## Two Search Strategies: Keyword Searching and Browsing

In the beginning of the Internet era a general assumption was made by researchers that browsing-oriented search tools, relying on recognition knowledge, were better suited to the abilities and skills of children than keyword search tools. The argument was that browsing imposes less cognitive load on children than searching, because more knowledge is needed to retrieve terms from memory when searching than simply to recognize offered terms when browsing (Bilal, 2000, 2001, 2002; Borgman, Hirsh, Walter & Gallagher, 1995; Large & Beheshti, 2000; Large, Beheshti, & Moukdad, 1999; Schacter, Chung & Dorr, 1998; Bilal & Watson, 1998).

Schacter et al. (1998) found that with both highly specific and vague search tasks, children sought information by using browsing strategies. In their research on children's internet searching on complex problems with thirty-two children in the age of 10 to 12 years, they reported: "Children

are reactive searchers who do not systematically plan or employ elaborated analytic search strategies" (p. 847).

Bilal (2000) found in her research on the use of the Yahooligans! Web Search Engine that most of the children (she observed twenty-two children in the age of 12 to 13 years) used keyword search. Only 36% of the searches were performed by browsing under subject categories. This finding may have been affected by the type of search task that was given in this research: a fact-driven query that automatically stimulated children to use keyword search instead of browsing the categories.

Revelle, Druin, Platner, Bederson, Hourcade and Sherman (2002) report on the development of a visual search interface to support children in their efforts to find animals in a hierarchical information structure. To examine searching and browsing behavior, 106 children (aged 5 through 10) participated in an experiment on this visual search interface. The researchers found that: "(…) even young children are capable of efficient and accurate searching. With the support of a visual query interface that includes scaffolding for Boolean concepts, children can use a hierarchical structure to perform searches and construct search queries that surpass their previously demonstrated abilities with the use of traditional search techniques" (p. 56).

By tracking the web logs of The International Children's Digital Library (ICDL), Druin (2003) found that, of 60,000 unique users between the ICDL's launch in November 2002 and September 2003, approximately 75% of the searches used category search (browsing), 15% used place search (by selecting a place using a world interface) and just over 10% of the searches used keyword search.

Hutchinson, Bederson and Druin (2006) found that children are capable of using both keyword search and category browsing, but generally they prefer and are more successful with category browsing. They explain this finding in relation to children's 'natural tendency to explore'. Young children tend not to plan out their searches, but simply react to the results they receive from the Information Retrieval system. Generally, their search strategies are not analytical and do not aim precisely at one goal. Instead, they make associations while browsing. This is a trial-and-error strategy.

It is clear that research results are very diverse when it comes to search strategies used by children. The results seem to depend on the type of interface used in the studies and the type of search task that was given to children. However, the trend in literature is that browsing is more suited for children than using a search engine.

## Difficulties with Keyword Searching and Browsing

Formulating a search query might be difficult for children, because they have little knowledge to base 'recall' on (Borgman et al., 1995; Hutchinson, Druin, Bederson, Reuter, Rose & Weeks, 2005). Besides, for searching relevant documents using keyword search, correct spelling, spacing and punctuation are needed. Children have difficulty with spelling and often make spelling errors (Borgman et al., 1995; Druin, Foss, Hatley, Golub, Leigh Guha, Fails, 2009). That is why an information retrieval system should be able to handle spelling errors, to help children find relevant documents using keyword search. Deciding on a single keyword is also difficult for a child, because children tend to use a full natural language query, especially with complex search tasks (Marchionini, 1989; Druin, et al., 2009). Thus, a system should also be able to handle natural language queries to find relevant information. In a comparison study between children and adults, Bilal and Kirby (2002) found that when children employed keyword search, most of their queries were single or multiple concepts, just like adults do. However, adults employed advanced search syntax, while children did not use this.

Browsing taxonomies may also be difficult for a child, because taxonomies in children's Web portals such as Kidsclick.org and Dibdabdoo.com use hierarchically structured taxonomies that may impose considerable cognitive load. Only a part of the hierarchy is displayed at any one time, and users must guess which route might eventually take them to the relevant term within the hierarchy (Large, Beheshti, Nesset & Bowler, 2006). With category search (i.e. browsing), children also have trouble finding the right category, because they have little domain-knowledge to decide which category is optimum. In addition, problems with browsing tools are mostly the result of a lack of vocabulary knowledge. Children often have difficulties understanding abstract, top-level headings, because their vocabulary knowledge is not yet sufficient to understand such terms (Hutchinson et al., 2006). Therefore, formulation of headings should be adjusted to children's vocabulary knowledge, using simple, concrete search terms.

Children may not think hierarchically like adults and may have trouble understanding the way in which hierarchically based categories are constructed. Knowing what their understanding of categories is, can therefore be of great value in designing browsing tools. Bar-Ilan and Belous (2007) tried to understand which browsable, hierarchical subject categories children create by conducting a card sorting experiment with twelve groups of four children in the age of 9 through 11 years. They suggested terms to the children through 61 cards. The children were free to add, delete or change terms. The researchers found that the majority of the category names used by existing directories were acceptable for the children and only a small minority of the terms caused confusion. Finally, often information in browsing systems is alphabetically displayed, requiring good alphabet skills. Many children have problems with alphabetizing and therefore have trouble finding information in such browsing systems (Borgman et al., 1995).

## Children's Search Behavior Characteristics

Bilal (2000) found in her research on the use of the *Yahooligans! Web Search Engine* that children were chaotic in their search performance: they switched frequently between types of searching (i.e. keyword search or browsing), they often looped their keyword searches and selected hyperlinks, and they frequently backtracked. These findings suggested that children want to combine different search strategies during one search task.

Bilal and Kirby (2002) also found that children were more chaotic in their search performance than adults. In their research, they compared search behavior between twenty-two children (aged 12 through 13) and twelve graduate students. Children made more web moves, they looped searches and hyperlinks more often, they backtracked more often, and they deviated more often from a designated target. The researchers concluded that adults adopted a "linear or systematic" browsing style whereas most children had a "loopy" style. They explain that this "loopy" style can be caused by children's lower cognitive recall, because the web imposes memory overload that reduces recall during navigation. They also found that children scrolled result pages less often than adults.

We should keep in mind however, that most of these studies were conducted in a time that children did not make use of computers and the Internet as much as they do anno 2013. Children nowadays are much more experienced users of digital interfaces because of iPads, Facebook, online gaming, etc., which makes it difficult to apply these research results to children's current information-seeking and navigation behavior on digital interfaces.

What we have learned so far from this theoretical background is that playful interface design emerges in the genre of children's informational Websites. Literature on children's search behavior and on problems and successes that children experience during information-seeking, especially dis-

cusses in pragmatic issues such as query handling and comprehensibility of taxonomies. However, the emergence of playful interface design asks for a broader focus than pragmatic issues. Also hedonic issues of playful interface design should be studied. It is assumed that product characters can be described by two attribute groups: pragmatic and hedonic attributes. Pragmatic attributes are connected to the users' need to achieve goals (e.g. finding information on an informational Website). Hedonic attributes are primarily related to the users' self. A product can be perceived by users as hedonic because it provides stimulation by its challenging character or identification by communicating personal values to relevant others (Hassenzahl, 2004). Hedonic issues of interface design will be discussed in the next part of the theoretical background.

## Fun and Engagement

From the beginning, research on interaction with digital interfaces is dominated by pragmatic issues such as the utility and usability of these systems (Thüring & Mahlke, (2007). This is the same for research on children's interaction with digital interfaces (Borgman et al., 1995; Bilal, 2000; Druin, 2003; Hutchinson, 2005). Usability, in particular, is a key concept for capturing the quality of use of digital products in which effectiveness and efficiency of system use is measured. The third component of the usability concept is 'user satisfaction'. Although this is measured using subjective judgments of users, these are mostly based on efficiency and effectiveness of interface usage.

In the field of Interaction Design for Children (IDC), there is a strong downplay in research about efficiency and task completion (Yarosh, Radu, Hunter & Rosenbaum, 2011). Instead of usability and satisfaction, that are goal related, desirability (being 'cool') has become very relevant in the community, which is not goal related. Malone (1980) pioneered the study of fun as an important aspect of software, and published guidelines designing for fun (Malone, 1984). According to his constructivist view, children acquire knowledge through experience. But for many years the study of fun in software was of marginal interest. In recent years there has been increasing interest in fun (Read, MacFarlane & Casey, 2002). Yarosh et al. (2011) report that 'enjoyment' and 'fun' are the most important values in 24% of the papers presented on the yearly Conference on Interaction Design & Children. They even claim that the values enjoyment and fun are that ubiquitous in the community, that they are no longer explicitly discussed, but that they became general assumptions when designing interactive products for children.

## User Experience

Also in the general field of Human Computer Interaction (HCI) researchers argue for a broader perspective on user experience (UX) (Hassenzahl & Tractinsky, 2006; Thüring & Mahlke, 2007) which can include, - besides perceived usability - beauty, overall quality and hedonic, affective and experiential aspects of the use of technology (van Schaik & Ling, 2008). Considering this broader perspective on UX, the reason for designing playful interfaces for children – as described in the Introduction of this chapter - becomes more clear. Playful design might have a positive effect on children's overall appraisal of a digital interface. This hypothesis is based on the idea that overall appraisal of a digital product is influenced by perception of both instrumental qualities (for example, effectiveness of a product) and non-instrumental qualities (for example, beauty of a product) as proposed by the Components of User Experience model (Thüring & Mahlke, 2007). Following this idea, playful design might have a positive effect on children's perception of hedonic quality, because children might feel stimulated by the creative and innovative interaction style or they might be able to easily identify with the playful environment. These are the hedonic attributes of stimulation and identification that are primarily related to the users'

self as described by Hassenzahl (2004). Thüring and Mahlke (2007) propose that both perception of instrumental and non-instrumental qualities have an influence on users' emotional reactions (such as subjective feelings, motor expressions or physiological reactions), which also has influence on overall appraisal of a system. For example, a slow working system (instrumental quality) may lead to frustration (negative emotion). At the same time, this slow working system might be presented with a creative interface design that may lead to enjoyment (positive emotion). Both experienced emotions have an influence on the overall appraisal of the system.

## The Interplay between Components of User Experience

What is interesting to know for designers of digital products is how the overall quality of an interactive product is formed. Evaluating interactive products is very complex, because many factors influence the quality of an interactive product: usability, beauty, overall quality, hedonic quality, and affective and experiential aspects of the use of a product.

Tractinsky, Katz and Ikar (2000), conducted an experiment to test the relationship between user's perceptions of computerized system's aesthetic beauty and usability. Perceptions were measured before and after actual use of the system. Both pre and post-use measures indicated strong correlations between perceived aesthetics and usability. Post-use usability ratings were not affected by actual usability (i.e. objective measured usability), which made Tractinsky et al. (2000) conclude that a product's beauty is a stronger indicator for its perceived usability than its actual usability. In other words, they claimed that "what is beautiful is usable". Tractinsky et al. (2000) propose the occurrence of a so-called *halo-effect*. The beauty of an interface overrules all other interface characteristics and therefore influences users' overall evaluation of the system.

Hassenzahl (2004) also studied the relation between perceived aesthetics and usability. He investigated the interplay between two product evaluations, beauty and goodness and the following perceptions of product attributes: pragmatic quality (i.e. usability as perceived by the user), hedonic quality of stimulation (personal) and hedonic quality of identification (social). He found that beauty as an evaluation was related to the hedonic quality of identification (e.g. a product is perceived as professional, valuable or presentable, etc.). Hassenzahl (2004) found that goodness was more closely related to attributes of pragmatic quality (e.g. a product is perceived as simple, practical, clear, predictable, etc.), especially when participants also interacted with the product under evaluation. These results of Hassenzahl (2004) contradict the results of Tractinsky et al. (2000), because Tractinsky et al. (2000) found no significant main effect of usability on post-use ratings of usability and beauty. In contrast, Hassenzahl (2004) did find an effect of actual usability on perceptions of usability. Hassenzahl (2004) explains this contradiction in results by the fact that Tractinsky's manipulation of usability was unlikely to induce stress for the participants, which makes any impact on post-use ratings of usability unlikely.

To study how the overall quality or goodness of an interactive product is formed, van Schaik and Ling (2008) also conducted an experiment on the interplay between components of UX. They found that all measures (i.e. evaluation of goodness, attributes of hedonic and pragmatic quality, task performance and mental effort) except evaluation of beauty, were sensitive to manipulation of web design. Evaluation of beauty was influenced by hedonic attributes (identification and stimulation), but evaluation of goodness was influenced by both hedonic and pragmatic attributes as well as task performance and mental effort. Attributes of hedonic quality were more stable with experience (i.e. using the interactive product) than attributes

of pragmatic quality. Evaluation of beauty was more stable than evaluation of goodness.

Hartmann, Sutcliffe, and DeAngeli (2008) found a link between aesthetics and usability. When users' usability experience was poor, positively perceived aesthetics could positively influence overall appraisal of a system, suggesting that "aesthetics could be an important determinant of user satisfaction and system acceptability, overcoming poor usability experience." (p. 176). Furthermore, they argued that the relative importance of aesthetics is related to the user's background and task. When the user's task is goal-oriented, then usability factors will weigh more than aesthetic considerations. When the user's task is action-oriented (the experience is more important than the goal), users choose designs based on a general impression of aesthetics and engagement.

Tuch, Roth, Hornbaek, Opwis and Bargas-Avila (2012) gave an overview of the current state of research on the aesthetics-usability relation. They made a distinction between correlative studies in which aesthetics and usability were not systematically manipulated as independent experimental factors and experimental studies in which these factors were systematically manipulated. The correlative studies showed some evidence for the relation between usability and aesthetics. However, there was only limited inference on the direction of any causality between aesthetics and usability. In the experimental studies, a pure "what is beautiful is usable" notion was only partially supported. Tuch et al. (2012) reported that there was also some evidence that in certain cases the relation is best described as "what is usable is beautiful" (p. 1598). Tuch et al. (2012) conducted an experiment on the aesthetics-usability relation and also found under certain conditions evidence for the relation "what is usable is beautiful". They found that the frustration of poor usability lowers ratings on perceived aesthetics.

Note that in none of the discussed studies so far children were involved. However, Hartmann et al. (2008) suggest that a metaphor-based interface style, such as an Image map Website type (considered more aesthetically pleasing and engaging), would be better for children than a menu-based style if they were interacting with it in their leisure time. They were undecided about this if the interface was to be used in the classroom within a formal educational context. Their reason for this assumption was that a metaphor-based style would likely prove more engaging but perhaps at the expense of usability.

In a study to validate the Fun Toolkit, a tool to evaluate technology with children, Sim, MacFarlane and Read (2005) did try to relate the constructs 'fun' and 'usability'. They report that children experience less fun when there were more usability problems. They conclude that it is not all about fun for children and that usability does matter to them.

We now learned that conducting research on hedonic issues such as fun and engagement became more important in the field of child-computer interaction in recent years. The study of pragmatic and hedonic issues of interface design with adult users from a subjective user-centered perspective on quality of use, is called 'user experience' (UX). An important topic in this field of research is the interplay between components of UX, such as usability, beauty and goodness. We think that this topic is also relevant for our research on children's informational Websites and especially concerning the emergence of playful interface design in this genre. However, methods used in studies with adults are mostly not suitable for studies with children. Current applied methods should be reflected on whether they are suited for children. Therefore, we will now discuss literature on the methods used in this field of research with adults and the methods used to measure hedonic components of UX with children.

## Methods to Measure the UX Components

As mentioned before, research on interaction with digital interfaces was dominated by pragmatic issues such as the utility and usability of these systems. Methods to measure usability are measuring effectiveness (the accuracy and completeness with which specified tasks can be conducted in a particular environment), efficiency (for example, the amount of time or digital events required to reach a specified goal) and satisfaction in using the system (based on instrumental qualities of the system). The same methods to measure these factors of usability that are validated in research with adults, can be used well in research with children, as we experienced in a prior explorative study on children's search behavior (Jochmann-Mannak, Huibers, Lentz and Sanders, 2010).

The evaluation of subjective aesthetic preferences and emotional experiences is more difficult to measure than objective usability scores. According to Laarni (2004), this is one of the reasons why these non-instrumental qualities have played a marginal role in human-computer interaction (HCI) research. Particularly with children, measuring subjective, non-instrumental qualities of a system, for example, with a survey method by asking children to rate product evaluations (such as fun, beauty and goodness) is very difficult, because of risks of satisficing, children's tendency to say yes irrespective of the question and children's tendency to indicate the highest score on the scale when scales are used to elicit opinions about software (Markopoulos et al., 2008).

Horton, Read and Sim (2011) report a study in which the reliability of children's responses on a pictoral questionnaire is tested by asking the same questions about children's technology twice one week after the other. None of the children produced the same results for a question after one week, which proves the difficulty of using survey questions with children and the issues with the validity and reliability of questionnaire answers given by children.

Read, MacFarlane and Casey (2002) developed the Fun Toolkit to measure children's opinions of technology which reduces the mentioned risks of evaluating products with children. The Fun Toolkit consists of four tools: a Funometer, a Smileyometer, a Fun Sorter and an Again-Again table. The Toolkit has been validated in several studies with children (Read & MacFarlane, 2006; Sim, MacFarlane & Read, 2006; Read, 2008).

Visual Analogue Scales (VAS) are often used in survey studies with children. With a VAS, children can identify and visualize their answers, feelings or opinions through pictorial representations instead of textual labels (Markopoulos, et al., 2008). The Smileyometer (Read et al., 2002) is an example of a VAS. But even with such a simple question-answering style as VAS, a child still needs to understand the question, needs to recall relevant information from memory, needs to decide what response is appropriate, needs to translate this response by deciding which pictogram from the VAS is relevant, and requires to physically act to make the selection. All of these steps put high cognitive load on children's working memory that can be problematic for a child.

An often used subjective method that uses VAS to measure emotional valence and arousal is the Self-Assessment Manikin (SAM) (see Figure 6 in the Method section), developed by Lang (1980). The SAM is a non-verbal pictorial assessment technique that measures the pleasure, arousal, and dominance associated with a person's affective reaction to a wide variety of stimuli (Bradley & Lang, 1994) which is based on the dimensions of valence, arousal and dominance (Russell, 1980). The use of SAM with children was validated by Greenbaum, Turner, Cook and Melamed (1990).

To measure users' perceptions of three product attributes (pragmatic quality, hedonic quality–identification and hedonic quality– stimulation) and two product evaluations (beauty and goodness), Hassenzahl, Burmester and Koller (2003) developed the AttracDiff 2 questionnaire. Each of the three product attributes is represented by seven 7-point semantic differential scales (e.g. professiona)– amateurish) and the two product evaluations by one 7-point semantic differential scale each (e.g. good– bad). To the best of our knowledge, the AttracDiff 2 questionnaire is not yet validated in survey studies with children.

## RESEARCH QUESTIONS

As we learned from the literature, there is a general assumption that digital products or systems for children should be fun and engaging (Yarosh et al., 2011). Non-instrumental product attributes - like beauty and fun- are expected to have an influence on overall appraisal of a digital product, just as instrumental product attributes such as effectiveness and learnability (Thüring & Mahlke, 2007; Van Schaik & Ling, 2008).

It seems that designers of children's interactive products make their products fun and engaging by adding playful design characteristics, both in visual design and in navigation design (Jochmann-Mannak et al., 2012). Therefore, we are interested whether the adding of playful design has a positive influence on children's perceptions of hedonic quality and on their overall appraisal of the system. We are also interested in the relation between children's perception of hedonic quality with their perception of usability and actual task performance.

In a previous explorative study, we did find a positive influence of playful interface design on children's perceptions of hedonic quality, measured by observing children's emotional expressions while working with informational Websites in a school setting (Jochmann-Mannak et al., 2010). However, most emotional expressions were based on pragmatic product attributes instead of hedonic product attributes. From this study, we concluded that playful design does not have a large influence on children's overall appraisal of informational interfaces. Usability seems much more important for children than non-pragmatic qualities, such as fun and beauty. However, that study was not set up as an experiment. Therefore, in this follow-up study, we want to test these initial results under controlled experimental conditions.

These are the research questions in our study:

1. What are the effects of different interface design types on...
   a. What are the effects of different design types of informational Websites on children's search behavior?
   b. What are the effects of different design types on children's attitude towards informational Websites (emotions, perceptions of pragmatic and hedonic quality and product evaluations, such as beauty, goodness and fun)?
   c. What is the relation between performance (objective usability) and attitude (subjective user-centered perspective on quality of use)?
   d. Is there an interaction between different interface design types with the chosen search strategy (searching with the search engine or browsing the main categories)?
2. If any, what problems and successes do children experience when searching with a search engine or when browsing main categories?
   a. Do these problems and successes relate to design characteristics of the different design types?

b. Do these problems and successes relate to the quality of the search engine?
   c. Do these problems and successes relate to characteristics of the children?
3. Are existing methods to measure feelings and perceptions of pragmatic and hedonic quality that are used in research with adults also suited for research with children?

## RESEARCH METHOD

### Experimental Design

The experiment used a 3 x 2 between groups design with two factors: interface design and use of the search engine. Three versions of the same Website varied in aesthetics and navigation style. We did not want to have an influence on children's natural search behavior by telling them to search by using the search engine or to browse by using the navigation to find information. Therefore, the use of the search engine was manipulated by presenting the Websites with or without a search engine. For each of the three Web design conditions, half of the children used the search engine and half of the children did not use the search engine.

Both independent variables were between-subjects; each child participant used one of the three interface designs and did (at least for one of the search tasks in the experimental session) or did not make use of the search engine at all. Outcome measures included perceptions of product attributes (pragmatic and hedonic quality), evaluations of the Websites (beauty, goodness and fun), objective performance measures, subjective emotion measures and objective emotion measures.

### Participants

There were 158 children in the age of 10 to 12 years old that took part in the experiment (70 boys and 88 girls, see Table 1a), with an average

age of 10.80 (SD = .65). From these children, 67 were in the fifth grade and 91 were in sixth grade. The children were tested on four different primary schools in the Netherlands. Children were randomly assigned to the three types of Websites concerning age, gender, school, grade and experience with the internet, based on randomization checks. The number of children that used the three different Website versions and the number of these children that did or did not use the search engine are presented in Table 1b.

## Materials and Equipment

For the manipulation of the interface design, an existing online encyclopedia for children was used (i.e. Junior Winkler Prins online encyclopedia). By using a fully working, existing Website, ecological validity is higher than by building a prototype Website for the experiment. The disadvantage of working with an existing Website is that the Website comes with real life flaws. For example, the search engine on the Website in our experiment did not provide query suggestions or spelling suggestions. Besides the existing version of the Website, two other fully working versions of this same Website were created; each of the three versions with a different interface design. Further, for each of the three versions, again there were two versions: one version with and one version without a search engine. In total, there were six different versions of the same Web site in the experiment.

The Classic version was presented with classical aesthetics and with a classical navigation style (see Figure 1). The Classical Play version (see Figure 2) was presented with expressive aesthetics, but with a classical navigation style. The Image Map version (see Figure 3) was presented with both expressive aesthetics and a playful navigation style. The three Website versions were identical concerning the main categories and subcategories,

*Table 1. (a) Age and gender of the participants. (b) Distribution of children over Website versions and use and non-use of the search engine*

| Age | Male | Female | Total |
|---|---|---|---|
| 9 | 1 | 0 | *1* |
| 10 | 15 | 34 | *49* |
| 11 | 44 | 44 | *88* |
| 12 | 10 | 10 | *20* |
| *Total* | *70* | *88* | *158* |

| Website Version | Number of Children that Used the Search Engine | Number of Children that did *not* Use the Search Engine | Total |
|---|---|---|---|
| Classic version | 26 | 25 | *51* |
| Classical play version | 26 | 26 | *52* |
| Image map version | 25 | 30 | *55* |
| *Total* | *77* | *81* | *158* |

the menu structure, the content and the logo, to control for effects of these factors. Also, on the deepest navigation level, all three Website versions referred to the same target pages with the same lay out for each of the three versions (see Figure 4).

The experiment ran on a laptop (Intel Core, 2,27 GHz, 4,0 GB RAM, Microsoft Windows 7 operating system) with a remote 20" monitor that the children worked on (Figure 5). The screen activities were recorded with Morae usability software (Techsmith) and video and audio recordings were made with a webcam. The children filled out an online questionnaire developed in PX Lab, an open source collection of Java classes and applications for running psychological experiments (Irtel, 2007). Childrens' electrodermal responses (physiological measure of emotional arousal) were measured with a Q Sensor (Affectiva) (Poh, Swenson, Picard, 2010).

*Figure 1. Classic Website version*

*Figure 2. Classical play Website version*

## Data Collection

### Measuring Performance

Each child conducted the same five fact-based tasks (see Appendix 1 for the full task descriptions). We tested ten tasks in a pilot test with a group of 14 children. Based on the results of this pilot test, we selected five tasks for the final experiment that varied in difficulty of conducting the task with the search engine or by browsing the categories. The task about Columbus, for example, was difficult to conduct both by using the search engine or by browsing the categories, because children had to find out which nation had discovered America 500 years before Columbus discovered America. The answer to this question was not mentioned on the content page about

*Figure 3. Image map Website version*

*Figure 4. Example of a target page that is identical for all three Website versions*

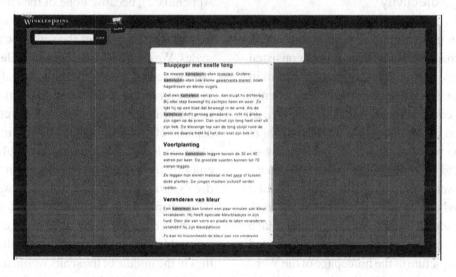

*Figure 5. Experimental setting*

'Christopher Columbus', but only on the content page about 'Discoveries' or at the content page about the 'Vikings'.

Task performance was measured by logging the amount of time and clicks needed to conduct the tasks. Also, per task was analyzed whether the relevant Web page was found and if and - if so - what type of help was offered. Recordings of the screen activities and video (see, for example, Figure 10) and audio recordings of the children were qualitatively analyzed, for example, to indicate what problems children experienced with particular design characteristics.

## Measuring Affectivity

The children gave responses to an online questionnaire to measure their feelings, that consisted of three parts: 1) the Self-Assessment Manikin (SAM) (Lang, 1985) to measure children's valence and arousal concerning the Website versions, 2) an adaptation of the AttracDiff 2 (Hassenzahl et al., 2003) to measure children's perceptions of pragmatic and hedonic quality and 3) a questionnaire to measure children's evaluations of beauty, goodness and fun by giving a report mark from 1 (= lowest score) to 10 (= highest score). Each of the items in the questionnaire was presented underneath a picture of the homepage of the Website version that the child had used to conduct the search tasks and that had to be evaluated by the child (for example, Figure 7). An added bonus to this study is that we can also evaluate whether this method is suited to measure product affectivity with children.

In the first part of our questionnaire, we used the same 5-point bipolar scale version of the SAM as used by Greenbaum et al. (1990) (see Figure 6) instead of the original 9-point bipolar scale (Lang, 1980). We decided to only measure the dimensions of valence and arousal and to leave out the dimension of dominance, as Thüring and Mahlke (2007) also did.

For the second part of our questionnaire, we developed Visual Analogue Scales (VAS) based on the AttracDiff 2 questionnaire (Hassenzahl et al., 2003). We translated 15 of the 21 bipolar verbal anchors for the product attribute groups from the AttracDiff 2 questionnaire in bipolar picture anchors as presented in Appendix B (for example, Figure 7: bipolar picture anchor of the semantic differential scale 'Clear – Confusing').[1] We used these 15 items in the pilot test and asked the children to explain the meaning of the pictures in the visual versions of the semantic differential scales. We decided to remove four of the items from the questionnaire (marked with an asterisk in Appendix 2), because none of the children could give a meaning to the pictures that was close to the original meaning of the semantic differential scales. We decided to use 5-point scales instead of 7-point scales. Younger children tend to respond in an extreme manner when asked to use Likert rating scales, whereas older children are more capable of providing graded ratings in the middle of the scale. As tasks become more subjective and emotion focused, as is the case in our study, children's extreme scores, regardless of age, increase (Chambers & Johnston, 2002). Therefore, although the children in our study were between 10 and 12 years old, providing them with more than three ratings in the middle of the scale, would not add value to the rating scales. For younger children, 3-point scales would probably be most suited, because of their tendency to give extreme ratings. However, children in the age of our study (i.e. 10-12 years old) are capable of differentiating between more and less extreme ratings on a 5-point scale. We did not use bipolar picture anchors for the product evaluations of beauty, goodness and fun. Instead of that, in the final part of the questionnaire we asked the children to give report marks for beauty, goodness and fun of the Websites.

Product experience is a multi-faceted phenomenon that involves feelings, behavioral reactions, expressive reactions, and physiological reactions

*Figure 6. SAM 5-point bipolar scales for valence (A) and arousal (B)*

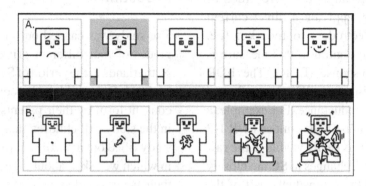

*Figure 7. Example of the bipolar picture version of the semantic differential scale 'Clear – Confusing' presented below the homepage of the Website version under evaluation. (The scores entered by placing the yellow cursor somewhere on the scale, were automatically recorded by the PX Lab software. The left end of the scale was scored as 1 and the right end of the scale as 5.)*

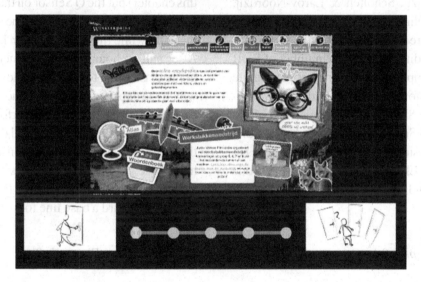

(Desmet & Hekkert, 2007). We measured feelings using the online questionnaire as described in the beginning of this section. We also made audio and video recordings of the children, through which behavioral and expressive reactions could be observed and analyzed[2].

However, because of risks of effects of satisficing (children's tendency to give superficial responses that generally appear reasonable or acceptable), suggestibility (the influence of the interviewer or evaluator on the children's question-and-answer process) and children's tendency to

give extreme scale ratings (Markopoulos et al., 2008), we also used a more objective method to measure product experience by measuring physiological reactions. We measured children's physiological emotional arousal with the Q Sensor.

The Q Sensor is a wearable, wireless biosensor that measures emotional arousal via skin conductance (SC), a form of electrodermal activity (EDA) that grows higher during states such as excitement, attention or anxiety and lower during states such as boredom or relaxation. The sensor also measures temperature and activity

(Affectiva.com). Typically EDA is recorded as skin conductance by applying a direct current (with two silver electrodes) to the skin (i.e. exosomatic method). Central to this measure is the electrodermal response (EDR). The EDR constitutes a sharp rise in the SC value, followed by a slower drop in conductance. For example, a sudden loud burst of noise will result an EDR 1-2 seconds later, and this is easily visible in the raw data signal. In general, changes in SC are closely linked to activity of the sympathetic part of the autonomic nervous system. Therefore, researchers and practitioners have taken EDA measurements as further operationalization for constructs such as attention, stress, anxiety, workload, pain, and arousal (Noordzij, Scholten & Laroy-Noordzij, 2012). When children emotionally react differently on the three types of Websites, this might be signaled by differences in the number of EDR and the total amplitude of these EDR per minute during task performance between the three Websites. In Figure 8 an example is presented of the output of the Q Sensor, in which can be seen that the device measures three physical properties at the same time: Electrodermal activity, Electrode Temperature and Acceleration.

## Procedure

The study was carried out in the fifth and sixth grades of four different primary schools in the Netherlands in the period of September – November 2011. Only children that could hand in a signed consent form by their parents, could co-operate in the study. All children that co-operated in our study filled out a profile survey in the class room in which we asked about their media use, such as their favorite video game, Website or television show, and the amount of time they spent on the Internet, on video games, or on watching television. Half an hour before a child contributed to our study, the test instructor (i.e. the first author of this chapter) put the Q Sensor on the child's wrist. In that way, the Q Sensor would be accustomed to the child while the child stayed in his class room. After half an hour, the test instructor came back in the class room to take the child to the room in which the experiment was conducted. Before the child started the actual task performance, first, the child was asked to run up and down the stairs three times to activate the Q Sensor. After that, half of the group of children was asked to watch a short animation film (Disney Pixar– "For the Birds") to record a base line for the Q sensor that

*Figure 8. Example of the Q-sensor's output for Electrodermal Activity, Electrode Temperature and Acceleration*

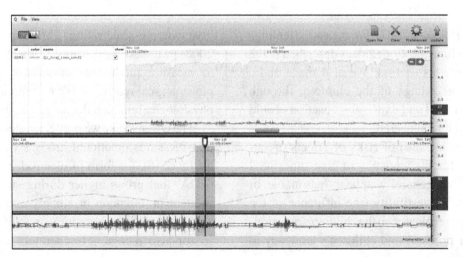

was the same for all 158 participants. The other half of the group of participants watched the film at the end of the session to control for a potential order effect of watching the film before or after task performance on the experimental Website.

Before the actual task performance started, the test instructor explained that the child would be asked to conduct five search tasks on a Website, because the designer of the Website wanted to know how children feel about the Website and if children can easily find information. The test instructor emphasized that "the child was not tested in this study, but that the Website was tested". The five search tasks were provided to the child in random order on separate sheets. When the child received the first search task, the test instructor started recording the screen activity and the video and audio recording of the child. The test instructor sat next to the child during the task performance and offered help when appropriate. Avoiding help and social interaction can make the child feel uncomfortable (Markopoulos et al., 2008). We listed the type of help that was offered for each conducted search task. Types of help were help in choosing the right category or sub-category, help in operating the navigation tools, help with spelling or formulation of a search query, or help in finding the right information on a particular content page. The effects of interface design on children's search performance were corrected for the help that was offered to the children. After the search tasks were completed, the test instructor started the online questionnaire and asked the child to read and answer the questions presented in the questionnaire.

## Data Analyses

To measure the effects of interface design and search engine use on children's Website performance and attitude towards the Website, a multilevel model was constructed. Independent variables were the type of interface design (Classic, Classical play and Image map) and the use (or non-use) of the search engine. Dependent variables were the percentage of children that were successful in finding the right answers to the search questions (i.e. the chance for success in our multilevel model), the time needed, and the number of clicks needed to find the right information. The model also estimates task variance (because one task can be more difficult than another task), between-children variance (because one child can be more or less skilled in searching information) and residual variance (for example, one child can have more difficulties with task 1, whereas another child can have more difficulties with task 2). By measuring these variances, we can estimate the extent to which we can generalize over tasks and children. When we do not take into account this task variance, between-children variance and residual variance, then the probability of falsely rejecting the null hypothesis is greater than 0.05 (Snijders & Bosker, 2012).

## RESULTS

### Reliability and Validity of the Affective Response Questionnaire

Before we report the results concerning the effects of interface design and search strategies on children's search performance and affectivity towards the interfaces, we will first report about the reliability and validity of the used methods.

We measured actual perceptions of hedonic and pragmatic quality using an instrument that was derived from the AttracDiff 2 questionnaire as composed by Hassenzahl et al. (2003). Cronbach's alphas for the two clusters of bipolar verbal anchors for the constructs of hedonic and pragmatic quality are shown in Table 2. A Cronbach's alpha of 0.6 is usually regarded as the lower bound of an acceptable reliability for experimental purposes. Both clusters measure the underlying constructs in a reliable way (see Table 2). However, the average scores and standard deviations show

*Table 2. Cronbach's alphas of the constructs of hedonic and pragmatic quality (using 5-point Likert scales from 1 to 5)*

| Cluster | Scale | N$_{semantic\ differentials}$ | Cronbach's Alpha |
|---------|-------|------------------------------|------------------|
| Hedonic quality | 5-point | 5 | .63 |
| Pragmatic quality | 5-point | 6 | .72 |
| All semantic differentials | 5-point | 11 | .80 |

that most children chose the center of the scales instead of the extreme scale ratings, which makes the reliability scores less meaningful. Apparently, children chose the safe, neutral ratings (the center) of the scales, for reasons that we will discuss in the following of this section.

The validity of the questionnaire was studied by a qualitative analysis of the recordings of all respondents that filled out the questionnaire.[3] In total, 2054 items were filled out by the 158 children and 151 of these children uttered a verbal or non-verbal interpretation of at least one of the 13 items from the questionnaire. These 151 children uttered 693 verbal or non-verbal interpretations of the items, which is 33.7% of the total items that were filled out in the experiment. The items from the questionnaire to measure beauty, goodness and fun were left out of this qualitative analysis, because none of the children indicated having problems with the meaning of these items. Of the 693 utterances in total, 224 utterances represented correct interpretations of the items (as intended by Hassenzahl et al., 2003) and 330 utterances represented incorrect interpretations of the items. For example, about the emotional arousal SAM-scale, many children gave the following incorrect interpretation: "I think this is about how easy or difficult the Website is". Another 84 utterances were verbal indications of incomprehension of the meaning of the items (e.g.

"I don't get it.") and 33 utterances were non-verbal indications of incomprehension (e.g. by frowning). While filling out the questionnaire, the test instructor helped the children when they asked for help, as discussed in the Method section. Most help was offered by asking a counter-question, for example: "What do you think the picture stands for?" Although, only a third of the items represent children's interpretations of these items, we think that these interpretations can be related to the entire set of items that were filled out in the experiment. The interpretations of the items will be discussed in the next section.

## Interpretations of the SAM-Scales for Emotional Valence and Arousal

Most children (138 of the 158 children) did not utter verbal or non-verbal interpretations of the valence scale (see Figure 6A). Children also did not ask many questions concerning this item. Most interpretations of this item were correct and were related to positive and negative emotional feelings, such as "The Website is kind of fun". Apparently, children understood the meaning of this valence scale with a more or less smiling manikin, which is related to the Smileyometer of the Fun Toolkit (Read et al., 2002). Therefore, we decided that the valence scale was a valid method to measure children's emotional valence towards a Website in our study.

The SAM scale for emotional arousal (see Figure 6B) caused many more problems than the scale for emotional valence. In total, 85 children uttered an incorrect interpretation or an indication of incomprehension concerning this scale and 32 children uttered a correct interpretation. Most conspicuous interpretations of the SAM-scale of arousal were: "I don't get it! Why is his belly exploding?" (while he points at the picture for highest arousal), or "I haven't got a clue. It looks like a fried egg on his belly, or something like that". Obviously, for most children the meaning of the SAM-scale for arousal was not clear at all and therefore, in our experiment, the arousal scale has proved to be an invalid method to measure children's emotional arousal towards a Website.

## Interpretations of the Bipolar Picture Anchors for Pragmatic Quality

The picture anchors for the semantic differential 'technical– human' were most problematic of all pragmatic semantic differential items for the children as can be seen in Table 3. Only one child gave the correct interpretation of the picture anchors. Many children associated the hearts and flowers with hedonic concepts of 'love' and 'fun', while it was intended as a pragmatic concept. Also, making a direct translation of these pictures to working with a Website was very difficult for the children. The reliability of the pragmatic scale items increased to .72 if this problematic item 'technical– human' was deleted from the list.

Almost half of the interpretations uttered on the picture anchors for the concept 'complicated-simple' were incorrect. Many children (27) asked for help interpreting these pictures, which also stresses the difficulty of these pictures. Some children gave a literal meaning to the pictures, such as 'neat or scratchy lines' and associated this with hedonic concepts. They could not make a translation to the pragmatic concepts of 'simple' and 'complicated'.

The same problem of literal translation of the pictures was the case with the picture anchors for 'impractical– practical'. Children asked what "tripping over a stone has to do with searching on a Website?" The interpretation 'easy– difficult' was often given to these picture anchors.

Although many children seemed to understand the meaning of the picture anchors for clear– confusing, they interpreted the meaning quite literally, by saying that the main and submenus offered many options to choose from. However, they did not give their opinion about whether these options were clear or confusing.

Most children gave a correct interpretation of the picture anchors for 'cumbersome– direct'. However, often help was asked from the test instructor and 25 children received help by giving them a counter-question or by explaining the meaning of the picture anchors. Many children gave the correct interpretation "whether you can find it directly or with a detour." However, most of them based their answer on their own performance instead of on the directness or cumbersomeness of the Website.

*Table 3. Frequency table of uttered interpretations of the pragmatic semantic differential items (N = absolute number of children that gave the interpretations)*

| | Technical-Human (N=158) | Complicated – Simple (N=158) | Impractical – Practical (N=158) | Confusing – Clear (N=158) | Cumbersome – Direct (N=158) | Unruly – Manage-Able (N=158) |
|---|---|---|---|---|---|---|
| Incorrect interpretations | 38 | 28 | 15 | 17 | 11 | 8 |
| Correct interpretations | 1 | 27 | 20 | 24 | 35 | 34 |
| Verbal indication of incomprehension | 18 | 2 | 2 | 2 | 1 | 0 |
| Non-verbal indication of incomprehension | 8 | 1 | 1 | 3 | 2 | 1 |
| No utterances | 90 | 98 | 118 | 112 | 106 | 118 |
| Missing values | 3 | 2 | 2 | 0 | 3 | 0 |

The pragmatic item that was least problematic for the children was the semantic differential 'unruly–manageable'. Most interpretations given for this item were correct and little help was offered by the test instructor. The reason for this is that a literal translation of the picture anchors can directly be related to a Website, because a Website can look neat or unruly.

## Interpretations of the bipolar picture anchors for perceived hedonic quality

The hedonic items were even more problematic than the pragmatic items (see Table 4), because the interpretations of these concepts were often even more difficult to translate to the use of a Website. The picture anchors 'easy–challenging' were given the most incorrect interpretations by the children, that is 'easy–difficult'. To strictly test the validity of the questionnaire, we decided to score these interpretations as incorrect, because 'easy–difficult' is a pragmatic concept as opposed to the hedonic concept 'easy–challenging'. The reliability of the hedonic scale items increased to .73 if this problematic item 'easy–challenging' was deleted from the list.

The picture anchors for 'cheap–valuable' caused a lot of problems for the children, because first of all, they did not understand the meaning of the paper hat versus the crown. When the test instructor asked: "What do you think is the difference between the two hats?" children gave the interpretation of 'poor versus rich'. However, they did not understand how a Website could be 'poor or rich'.

The children did not understand the picture anchors for 'amateurish–professional' at all. They often thought it was about 'a drilling machine versus a hammer' and they could not relate these concepts to a Website.

The picture anchors for 'presentable–unpresentable' evoked a lot of questions for the test instructor. When children gave the interpretation of an 'old or new present', or maybe even a 'beautiful or ugly present', they could not relate this 'present' to the Website.

Finally, also the picture anchors for 'lame–exciting' were problematic for the children. Again, the children had trouble understanding the meaning of the two types of 'cycling' to 'lame and exciting.' When the test instructor gave help with this first step, most of the time the children gave their opinion about whether searching for information is lame or exciting and not whether the Website was lame or exciting.

*Table 4. Frequency table of uttered interpretations of the hedonic semantic differential items*

|  | Easy – Challenging (N=158) | Cheap – Valuable (N=158) | Amateurish – Professional (N=158) | Unpresentable – Presentable (N=158) | Lame – Exiting (N=158) |
|---|---|---|---|---|---|
| Incorrect interpretations | 51 | 34 | 33 | 24 | 8 |
| Correct interpretations | 2 | 6 | 3 | 15 | 15 |
| Verbal indication of incomprehension | 7 | 16 | 5 | 2 | 2 |
| Non-verbal indication of incomprehension | 2 | 4 | 3 | 3 | 2 |
| No utterances | 95 | 97 | 113 | 113 | 127 |
| Missing values | 1 | 1 | 1 | 1 | 4 |

## Distinction between Perceptions of Pragmatic and Hedonic Quality

We also measured the reliability of all semantic differentials together and it turned out that Cronbach's alpha for all semantic differentials is .80 (see Table 2). It seems that the children perceived all items as the same construct, for example as the construct 'good or bad'. One child said: "It's all a bit the same to me" and often children asked for confirmation: "So this means good and this means bad, right?" In other words, the children did not make a distinction between hedonic and pragmatic constructs or between fun and usability.

And although children did not indicate having problems with the report marks for beauty, goodness and fun, it can be expected that these concepts were evaluated as the same construct. This was also reported by Read et al. (2002) concerning the Fun-Sorter in which children needed to sort products by concepts as 'worked the best', 'liked the most', 'most fun' and 'easiest to use'. They say: "This was quite difficult for the children with the result that some constructs turned out to be quite similar."

## Conclusion Validity Questionnaire Items

From the qualitative analysis of children's interpretations of the questionnaire items, we can conclude that, although the construct reliability of the questionnaire items is high, the questionnaire is not a valid method to measure children's perceptions of pragmatic and hedonic quality. The content validity cannot be guaranteed, because often children gave another explanation to the items than was intended by the designers of the questionnaire. Also, construct validity cannot be guaranteed, because items that should measure pragmatic quality, were associated with hedonic quality and vice versa. Besides that, it seems that children do not make a distinction between pragmatic and hedonic constructs at all. Also the SAM-scale for arousal has not proven to be a valid method to measure emotional arousal with children.

The most important problem that children experience with the questionnaire is that they have to interpret the picture anchors and to relate their meaning to using a Website. As children tend to take the picture anchors very literally, translating them to a more abstract concept is very difficult for them. The cognitive load of this task on children's working memory is too heavy for children to cope with. Furthermore, children tend to relate the picture anchors to their own performance or preferences instead of to the Website under evaluation. Finally, satisficing is a relevant problem in our experiment. Children are prone to satisficing as they find survey participation difficult (Markopoulos et al., 2008), as was the case in our study. From the recordings, we saw that children tend to ask questions about the first four or five items in the questionnaire, but after that fill out the questionnaire very quickly. It is clear that the children gave more or less superficial responses that generally appear acceptable, but without going through all the steps involved in the question-answer process.

Based on the validity analyses of the affective survey question, unfortunately, we can only work with a few items for further qualitative analysis of the affective data. We will work with the results from the SAM-scale for emotional valence, with the semantic differential scale for unruly-manageable and with the report marks for the product evaluations beauty, goodness and fun.

## Effects of Interface Design and Used Search Strategy

We will first report the pragmatic effects on children's search performance of differences in interface design (i.e. Classic, Classical Play and

Image map) and the used search strategy (i.e. keyword searching or browsing). After that, we will report the effects on children's emotional feelings, perceptions of hedonic quality and product evaluations of interface design and the used search strategy.

## What are the Effects on Task Performance of Playful Interface Design and Use of the Search Engine?

To establish whether there is a difference between task performance on the three different versions of the Website and between use and non-use of the search engine, the mean percentages for success were compared (see Table 5). Non-use of the search engine occurred in two situations; 1) when the search engine was not offered, children logically could not use the search engine and 2) when the search engine was offered, some children did not use it to search for information. We also compared the mean percentages of finding the right answer when help was offered and when no help was offered by the test instructor and we found significant effects of provided help (see * in Table 5). The following data analyses for the mean percentages for success are therefore corrected for help (mean percentages for help are grey colored in Tables 5, 6 & 7).

No main effect on task performance was observed for the design type of the Websites: there is no significant difference for the percentage of success in finding the right information between the three Website versions ($\chi^2 = 1.02$; df = 2; p = 0.31). However, a main effect was found for the use of the search engine ($\chi^2 = 43.19$; df = 2; p <.001): the percentage of success was much larger when the search engine was used than when the search engine was not offered ($\chi^2 = 27.33$; df = 1; p <.001) and when the search engine was not used ($\chi^2 = 40.63$; df = 1; p < .001). There is no significant difference between the percentage of success when the search engine was not offered and when the search engine was not used ($\chi^2 = 0.41$; df = 1; p = .52). No interaction-effect was found for the use of the search engine and the three Website versions ($\chi^2 \leq 3.04$; df = 2; p $\geq$ 0.080). In other words, the differences between use and non-use of the search engine for success are the same for the three Website versions.

## What are the Effects of Playful Interface Design and Use of the Search Engine on Time and Clicks Needed to Conduct the Tasks?

We also compared the mean amount of time and clicks children needed to conduct the tasks between the three Website versions and between the use

*Table 5. Percentages of success (logits between brackets) in using the different versions of the Website for use and non-use of the search engine and for help provided yes (grey colored) or no*

| Website Version | Search Engine Used | | Search Engine not Provided | | Search Engine Provided, but not Used | |
|---|---|---|---|---|---|---|
| | **No Help** | **Help** | **No Help** | **Help** | **No Help** | **Help** |
| **Classic** | .82 (1.53) | .83 (1.61) | .63 (.52) | .68 (.75) | .57 (.30) | .67 (.69) |
| **Classical play** | .84 (1.62) | .63 (.51)* | .63 (.54) | .58 (.32) | .49 (-.03) | .56 (.22) |
| **Image map** | .92 (2.42) | .76 (1.18)* | .52 (.10) | .25 (-1.10) | .61 (.44) | .54 (.17) |

Note. In all cases, a higher mean score represents a higher percentage for success in finding the right information for the search task. The answers for the binomial success-score (1= successful, 0= unsuccessful) are given in Logits that are used for the data analysis (between brackets).

* There is a significant effect of provided help on the mean percentage of success. The percentage of success in finding the right information was significantly lower for the children that used the search engine and received help from the test instructor for both the Classical play Website and the Image map Website (t $\geq$.2.01; p $\leq$ .04).

*Table 6. Mean time needed in seconds (ln between brackets) using the different versions of the Website, for use and non-use of the search engine and for help provided yes (grey colored) or no*

| Website Version | Search Engine Used | | Search Engine not Provided | | Search Engine Provided, but not Used | |
|---|---|---|---|---|---|---|
| | No help | Help | No help | Help | No help | Help |
| Classic | 139.9 (4.94) | 247.4 (5.51)* | 168.3 (5.13) | 264.4 (5.58)* | 157.9 (5.06) | 300.1 (5.70)* |
| Classical play | 149.7 (5.01) | 257.0 (5.55)* | 141.6 (4.95) | 283.9 (5.65)* | 142.7 (4.96) | 221.2 (5.40)* |
| Image map | 112.8 (4.73) | 236.0 (5.46)* | 170.4 (5.14) | 164.1 (5.10) | 148.5 (5.00) | 279.7 (5.63)* |

Note. The distribution of the raw data for time was not comparable to the normal distribution. Therefore, we took the natural log of the search times that did show a normal distribution.

* There is a significant effect of provided help on the mean amount of time needed. The amount of time needed to conduct the tasks was significantly higher for children that received help from the test instructor ($t \geq 3.73$; $p \leq .001$).

*Table 7. Mean number of clicks (ln between brackets) using the different versions of the Website, for use and non-use of the search engine and for help provided yes (grey colored) or no*

| Website Version | Search Engine Used | | Search Engine not Provided | | Search Engine Provided, but not Used | |
|---|---|---|---|---|---|---|
| | No Help | Help | No Help | Help | No Help | Help |
| Classic | 4.2 (1.44) | 7.4 (2.00)* | 9.8 (2.29) | 17.0 (2.83)* | 7.7 (2.04) | 17.6 (2.87)* |
| Classical play | 4.7 (1.55) | 8.1 (2.09)* | 7.7 (2.04) | 14.9 (2.70)* | 7.9 (2.07) | 8.5 (2.14)* |
| Image map | 3.3 (1.20) | 7.2 (1.97)* | 9.0 (2.20) | 8.3 (2.12) | 6.3 (1.85) | 14.4 (2.67)* |

Note. The distribution of the raw data for number of clicks was not comparable to the normal distribution. Therefore, we took the natural log of the number of clicks that did show a normal distribution.

* There is a significant effect of provided help on the mean number of clicks. The number of clicks needed to conduct the tasks was significantly higher for children that received help from the test instructor ($t \geq 2.85$; $p \leq .004$).

and non-use of the search engine (see Table 6 and 7). Because we also found significant effects of the provided help for these factors (see * in Table 6 and 7), we corrected the data for provided help.

No main effect was observed for the design of the Website versions: there is no significant difference in time needed to conduct the tasks between the three Website versions ($\chi^2 = 2.00$; df $= 2$; p $= 0.37$). However, a main effect was found for the use of the search engine ($\chi^2 = 8.10$; df $= 2$; p $=.017$): less time was needed when the search engine was used than when the search engine was not offered ($\chi^2 = 6.88$; df $= 1$; p $=.009$) and when the search engine was not used ($\chi^2 = 4.27$; df $= 1$; p $< .039$). There is no significant difference between the time needed when the search engine was not offered and when the search engine was not used ($\chi^2 = 0.88$; df $= 1$; p $= .35$).

No interaction effect was found for the use of the search engine and the three Website versions ($\chi^2 \leq 2.97$; df $= 1$; p $\geq 0.16$). In other words, the differences between use and non-use of the search engine for the time needed to conduct the search tasks are the same for the three Website versions.

No main effect on clicks was observed for the design of the Website versions: there is no significant difference in the number of clicks between the three Website versions ($\chi^2 = 4.08$; df $= 2$; p $= 0.13$). However, a main effect was found for the use of the search engine ($\chi^2 = 257.56$; df $= 2$; p $< .001$): the number of clicks needed when the search engine was used was lower than when the search engine was not offered ($\chi^2 = 80.27$; df $= 1$; p $< .001$) and when the search engine was not used ($\chi^2 = 66.52$; df $= 1$; p $< .001$). The number of clicks is also significantly higher when the search engine was not offered than when the search engine was not used ($\chi^2 = 212.78$; df = 1; p < .001). A reason for this could be that children in the condition without a search engine were normally used to working with a search engine and therefore, were less experienced and needed more clicks to find the information using the navigation structure.

No interaction effect was found for the use of the search engine and the three Website versions ($\chi^2 \leq 3.77$; df = 1; p = 0.052). In other words, the differences between use and non-use of the search engine for the clicks needed to conduct the search tasks are the same for the three Website versions.

In conclusion, children who used the search engine instead of browsing the categories, were more successful in finding the right information and they needed less time and clicks. There were no significant differences for task performance (i.e. success, time and clicks) between the three Website versions. Apparently, interface design of the search environments is less determinant for task performance than the search strategy (i.e. searching or browsing). The differences that we found between the conditions (independently of the used search method; searching or browsing) cannot be assigned to our manipulations of the interface design. These differences should be assigned to the differences between the children that participated in our experiment. In other words, differences in child characteristics, such

as their information skills, domain knowledge, operational skills, etcetera, cause more variance in children's search performance than variation in interface design.

## What is the Effect of Interface Design on Emotional Valence and on the Evaluation of Beauty, Goodness and Fun

To test whether there is an effect of design on children's affective responses, we computed both between groups and within groups analyses of variance. In that way, we took into account the "effect variation" and the "individual variation". Individual variation is the variation within condition differences called "error", because we cannot explain the fact that children who were in the same two conditions - who were all treated the same two ways – have different scores. In this way, we also took into account the "subject variation", which is the variation due to subject variability. For these tests on children's affective responses, we could only use a limited set of variables that proved to be valid (see Table 8).

There were significant differences for children's emotional valence and their evaluation of goodness between the three Website versions. The children judged their feeling with the Classical play Website as more positive than with the other two Websites (F $_{2,155}$ = 3.28; p = .040). Still,

*Table 8. Mean scores for emotional valence (5-point scale), the semantic differential 'unruly-manageable' (5-point scale) and the product evaluations for beauty, goodness and fun (report mark from 1-10) for the different versions of the Website (SD between brackets)*

| Website Version | Valence | Unruly-Manageable | Goodness | Fun | Beauty |
|---|---|---|---|---|---|
| **Classic** (N = 51) | 4.12 (.77) | 4.25 (.95) | 8.66 (1.31) | 8.29 (1.56) | 8.37 (1.42) |
| **Classical** play (N = 52) | 4.38 (.66)* | 4.10 (.79) | 8.71 (.84) | 8.50 (1.19) | 8.86 (1.05) |
| **Image map** (N = 55) | 4.05 (.68) | 3.90 (.91) | 8.22 (1.04)* | 8.13 (1.10) | 8.42 (1.03) |

* There is a significant effect of the type of design on the affective responses.

all scores are between 4 and 5 on a scale from 1 to 5, so the children are very positive about their feelings with all three types of Websites.

The children evaluated the Image map Website as least good ($F_{2,155} = 3.45$; $p = .034$) of the three Websites. We do not use the word 'worst', because with the 'least good' Image map Website, the children evaluated the goodness of the Image map Websites with an 8.2 on a scale from 1 to 10, which is still a very high score (see Table 8). There were no significant differences between the children's perceptions of hedonic quality (i.e. unruly-manageable) and between their evaluations of fun and beauty of the three Websites.

## What is the Effect of Playful Interface Design on Physiological Measurements of Emotional Arousal

We also used a more objective method to measure children's feelings towards the three Website types by measuring electrodermal activity (EDA). From the EDA-data, we computed the number of Electrodermal Responses (EDR) per minute and the total amplitude of the EDR per minute for the period of watching the film and the period of the actual task performance on the experimental Website. Watching the film served as a benchmark, because this was the same over all three conditions. To measure whether there is a difference in EDA between conditions, we computed the difference in number of EDR per minute between the task performance and watching the film for the three conditions. Unfortunately, the EDR data (both number of EDR per minute during the task performance and while watching the film, and the difference between these two variables) were not normally distributed. Therefore, we could not use a parametric test to compute the difference in EDA between conditions and we were constrained to using a non-parametric test.

First of all, we did not measure any EDA during the actual task performance with 47 children. We did not measure any EDA with 64 children

while they watched the film. Apparently, for many children, this type of scholarly tasks on a computer did not activate any electrodermal activity at all. Second, using a Wilcoxon signed rank test, there was no significant difference in EDA between task performance and watching the film.

According to an independent samples Kruskal-Wallis test, there was no significant difference in EDA between the three conditions. There was, however, a significant order effect in our study. According to an independent samples Kruskal-Wallis test, there was a significant difference in EDA between children that watched the film before or after performing the actual search tasks. Children that watched the film after the search task performance showed a higher number of EDR per minute during the task performance than children that watched the film before the search task performance. A regular univariate analysis of variance also showed no significant differences in EDA between the three conditions and it also did show a significant order-effect of watching the film before or after the search tasks ($F(1,135)=23.03$, $p < .05$). Apparently, children were less aroused by the use of the search interface when they first saw the film, than when they saw the film afterwards.

## What is the Effect of Playful Interface Design on Verbal Emotional Utterances?

Of the children that used the Image map Website, 25 video recordings were studied to collect the verbal emotional utterances about the pragmatic and hedonic quality of the Website. In total, 58 utterances were made. Of these utterances, 55 were related to pragmatic quality and 3 utterances were related to hedonic quality of the Image map Website (see Table 9).

As can be seen in Table 9, most verbal utterances were negative. These utterances were mostly related to the difficulty and inaccessibility of the Website for finding relevant information,

*Table 9. Number of positive and negative verbal utterances related to pragmatic and hedonic quality of the Image map Website*

| Quality | Number of Utterances | |
|---------|----------|----------|
|         | Positive | Negative |
| Pragmatic | 7 (12.1%) | 48 (82.8%) |
| Hedonic | 0 (0%) | 3 (5.2%) |

such as "I can't find it at all" or "I find it difficult to search on". There are only a few positive utterances, such as "This is not really difficult or anything" and "I found it quite fast". Verbal hedonic utterances are very rare and are more related to pictures on the Website than to the design of the Website itself, such as a child that says: "What an ugly man" (about Columbus). Apparently, children tend to say more about their search activities than about the design of the Website and verbal utterances are almost exclusively related to their perception of the Websites' pragmatic quality.

## Relation between Factors

### What is the Relation between Children's Performance on the Websites and their Attitude Towards these Websites?

To answer this question, we tested the difference for children's affective responses between tasks that were completed successfully and tasks that were not completed successfully. There was a significant difference between the successful and unsuccessful tasks for children's ratings of emotional valence (F = 5.07; df = 1; p = .025). Children expressed more positive feelings for tasks conducted on all three Website versions when the tasks were completed successfully than when the tasks were completed unsuccessfully (see Figure 9). There was no significant interaction effect between the Website version and whether the tasks were completed successfully or not for the ratings of emotional valence. Furthermore, there were no significant differences for children's product evaluations (beauty, goodness and fun) between tasks that were completed successfully and tasks that were not completed successfully.

*Figure 9. Estimated marginal means of valence (0 = negative feeling; 5 = positive feeling) plotted for the three Website versions with successful and unsuccessful tasks presented on separate lines*

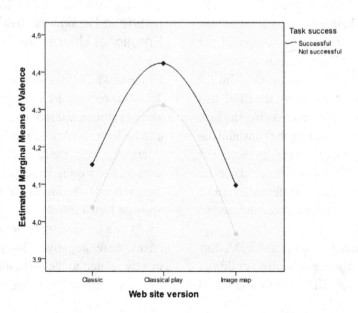

## Further Diagnosis of Children's Search Behavior

### Searching vs. Browsing in our Experiment

It is not clear from previous research results whether children in general use more searching or browsing strategies. However, most of the results suggest that children prefer to use search engines, but that they are more successful with browsing categories. Even recently, Meloncon et al. (2010) recommended not to include a search engine on a children's Website, because children have not yet fully developed the intellectual ability necessary to generate relevant search terms (Druin et al., 2009). In addition, giving children the option to search would undermine the process of having them read through the information and explore the Website (Meloncon et al., 2010). In other words, the search engine is seen as a distraction on a children's Website.

In our data, searching with the search engine scores better than browsing the main categories for almost all components of UX that we have measured. Children were more successful in finding the right content page when they had used the search engine. They also needed significantly less time and fewer clicks to find the information when they had used the search engine than when they had browsed the main categories.

These results are in contrast to results from previous studies on children's search behavior (Borgman et al., 1995; Schacter et al., 1998; Bilal, 2000). This difference might be caused by a better functioning search engine in our study, although we think that is hard to believe, because the search engine in our study did not work as well as Google, for example. The search engine in our study did not provide query suggestions or spelling corrections while typing a search query. Also, most natural language queries could not be processed by the search engine.

The main reason for the results in our study in comparison to previous research, is most likely caused by children's increased experience and skills in using a search engine with respect to a few years ago. Children now are members of the "Google generation" (Rowlands, 2008) and more familiar with the use of search engines. In the Netherlands, almost 80% of children ages 8-12 in 2008 used the Google search engine to find information on the Internet (Pijpers et al., 2008).

In our experiment, initially 115 children were offered a Website version with a search engine and 43 children without a search engine (see Table 10). This inequality was caused by the fact that many children that were offered a search engine, did not use the search engine at all. We offered children a version with a search engine as often as was necessary, to reach an equal number of children that used the search engine and children that browsed the main categories. In our research, we found it very important to compare searching with a search engine with browsing the main categories.

Therefore, we aimed at an equal distribution of children that did and did not use the search engine. We kept offering a Website version with a search engine until the distribution between use and non-use of the search engine was equal over the three Website versions (see Table 10). In total, 77 of the 115 children that were offered a search engine (67%), used the search engine for at least one of the five search tasks. The children that used a search engine, did not automatically use the search engine for all five tasks. Therefore, the percentage of search engine use per task that was conducted on a Website version with a search engine is lower. In total, 294 tasks were conducted by using a search engine, which is 51% of all tasks that were conducted on a Website version with a search engine.

As can be seen in Table 10, the search engine on the Image map was the least inviting to use for the children, because 25 of the 50 children that were offered a search engine on the Image map

*Table 10. Number of children that were offered a search engine and number of children that used the search engine*

| Website Version (N=158) | Presence of the Search Engine | | Use of the Search Engine | |
|---|---|---|---|---|
| Classic version | Present: | 32 | Used:<br>Not used: | 26<br>6 |
| | Not present: | 19 | | |
| Classical play version | Present: | 33 | Used:<br>Not used: | 26<br>7 |
| | Not present: | 19 | | |
| Image map version | Present: | 50 | Used:<br>Not used: | 25<br>25 |
| | Not present: | 5 | | |

Website, did not use it at all. The non-conventional visual design of the Image map version might have distracted the children's attention from the search engine as can be seen in Figure 3.

Another explanation for the low percentage of search engine use when a search engine was offered, can be children's infrequent use of search engines. We asked children how much time they spend using the Internet and most children used the internet less than one hour on both week days and weekend days. When we asked what type of activities they conducted on the Internet, than the activities can be ranked from most to least frequently conducted by most children as following:

1. Hyves (a Dutch social network).
2. Playing games.
3. Listening to music/watching video clips.
4. Watching you tube movies.
5. Searching information for myself.
6. Searching information for school work.

Internet activities for which a search engine is required (by searching information for themselves or for school work) are conducted least frequently according to children's self-reports. The children probably do not use a search engine for the Internet activities that are conducted most frequently, such as using Hyves or playing games. The fact that children do not use search engines frequently is a plausible cause for the fact that many children did not use a search engine in our study, even though a search engine was provided in many of these cases.

## Search Engine Strategies

In this section, we will analyze children's strategies and skills using a search engine. What makes keyword searching in our experiment successful? Do children experience the same problems or not with key word searching as reported in previous research? We will describe whether children are able to formulate a query and to select a search result that is coherent with the search task. For this qualitative study of submitted queries and selected search results, we have analyzed the submitted queries of the children that used the search engine on two of the three Website types: the Classical play Website (26 children) and the Image map Website (25 children).

For the qualitative data analysis of search engine use, we analyzed 190 search tasks conducted with the search engine[4]. These 190 search tasks consisted of 322 search attempts to formulate a query. Most search tasks (N = 117) consisted of one query attempt, but some children required more attempts to formulate a search query within one search task (40 * 2 attempts, 20 * 3 attempts, 7 * 4 attempts, 3 * 5 attempts, 2 * 6 attempts and 1 * 10 attempts).

*Quality of Query Attempts:* Most queries consisted of one word (117 query attempts) or more than one word (165 query attempts) and 40 queries existed of a whole sentence. Natural language querying is not as frequently applied by the children in our study as reported in previous studies (Marchionini, 1989; Druin, et al., 2009).

Most query attempts did not require any help with query formulation or spelling help from the test instructor (87% of all query attempts). The children had less problems with query formulation and spelling than expected from the literature (Borgman et al., 1995; Hutchinson, 2005). This was also shown by the fact that 79.5% of the query attempts were spelled correctly. An important reason was that the children in our study received the search tasks written on a task sheet, so they could use the correct spelling of words from the written task sheet. However, still spelling mistakes were made, although children could read the correct spelling from the task sheets.

Correct spelling does not automatically lead to finding the right content page, because almost half of the correctly spelled queries (44.5%) did not lead to a successful search result. Of course, the success of a search query also depends on the relevancy of the search query and the quality of the search engine.

One way to evaluate the quality of the search queries is to compute their latent semantic analysis (LSA) scores in comparison to the search task, following the example of Kitajima, Blackmon, and Polson (2000) that used LSA to simulate Web navigation. LSA is a technique in natural language processing, in particular in vectorial semantics, of analyzing semantic coherence between a set of documents and the terms they contain by producing a set of concepts related to the documents and terms. LSA assumes that words that are close in meaning will occur in similar pieces of text. Values close to 1 represent high semantic coherence while values close to 0 represent low semantic coherence. For the calculation of LSA-scores, spelling mistakes were corrected. We did not find an effect of high LSA-scores on task success. The mean LSA-score of the successful search queries was .26 and the mean LSA-score of the unsuccessful search queries was .24. LSA-scores do not predict the quality of search queries in our study very well. We will illustrate this with the task about Columbus (see Table 11). The query 'Columbus' had the highest LSA-score, but did not lead to success, because the answer to the search task was not mentioned on the content page about Christophorus Columbus, but on the content pages about 'Discoveries' or about 'Vikings'.

*Quality of Search Results' Selection:* When we look at the behavior of the children in selecting search results, we first of all see that most children tended to directly choose the first search result from the list. From the search attempts in which children actually selected a search result (N=216), 110 selected search results were the first result from the results list. Further, almost all selected search results (211) were selected from the first 10 results that were presented in the results list. This tendency to select the first search result or a search result from the first 10 search results presented was also reported in previous studies (Bilal, 2000; Druin et al., 2009).

The children were not inclined to select more than one search result from the search results that were presented for one search query. Most children only selected one search result (86%

*Table 11. LSA scores of the most frequently entered search queries for the search task about Columbus*

| Search Task | Frequent Search Queries (N) | LSA-Score | Successful? |
|---|---|---|---|
| "It is often said that Christopher Columbus discovered America. Some say that this is not true. They say that another nation discovered America 500 years before Columbus did. Can you find out what people discovered America before Columbus did at Junior Winkler Prins online?" | - America (19) | 0.27 | No |
| | - Discovery America (17) | 0.27 | Yes |
| | - Columbus (10) | 0.30 | No |
| | - Christopher Columbus (7) | 0.33 | No |
| | - Vikings (3) | 0.13 | Yes |

of the search attempts). Two search results were selected within 11% of the search attempts and more than two search results were selected within 3% of the search attempts.

Of all analyzed search tasks that were conducted with the search engine (N=190), 83% (after one or more unsuccessful search attempts) were successful and led to the right content page. Within 96% of the selected search results no help was provided by the test instructor. From our analysis it is not entirely clear what the main reason is for the unsuccessful search tasks. A possible explanation is the fact that often children chose high-scent incorrect links. However, our research was not concerned with the quality of the search engine and therefore we did not further analyze the relevancy of the provided search results by the search engine.

## Navigation and Browsing Categories

In this section, we will analyze children's navigation behavior. What makes browsing successful or unsuccessful? Do children experience the same problems or not with browsing as reported in previous research? For this qualitative study of selected main and subcategories and content pages, the navigation paths for the five search tasks of 46 children were analyzed that were either successful or unsuccessful in completing the search tasks by browsing the categories[5]. We will describe problems with the layout of the Websites, problems with the information structure of the Websites and operational navigation problems. The problems presented are not an exhaustive list of all problems, but give an illustration of the most important navigation problems.

*Problems with the Location of the Search Box:* The most important problem in our view with the layout of the Websites, and particularly with the Image map Website, is the location of the search box. Many children did not use the search engine when it was provided. We do not know for sure if these children were not familiar with using a

search engine or whether they did not notice the search box at all. The unconventional layout of the Image map Website and the unconventional location of the search box in the top left corner may have caused the search engine to have been unnoticed by many children (see Figure 10). In a corpus study of children's informational Websites Jochmann-Mannak et al. (2012) reported that 43% of the Websites with a search engine, presented the search engine in the top right corner of the page and 24% presented the search box in the top center of the page. Therefore, the top left corner is a non-conventional location for children's informational Websites. However, on the other two versions, the search box was also placed on the top left side, but on these two versions more children used the search engine when offered than on the Image map version.

*Problems with the Layout:* Most problems with the layout were experienced with the Image map Website, most likely because of the unconventional interface design. When parsing the homepage, children directly focused on a particular part (mostly on the main menu) of the Classic Website and the Classical play Website. This was in contrast to children's parsing behavior on the Image map. Most children parsed the entire homepage of the Image map and all main category links were looked at extensively. This was caused by the fact that the main menu covers the entire homepage of the Image map. There were many problems with the main category links on the Image map Website, because children had to 'mine sweep' the images to see the verbal link labels. However, many children did not directly recognize the main category links as such and did not notice their click ability, as can be seen in Figure 10.

*Problems with the Information Structure:* Problems with selecting the right main and sub categories occurred at all three type of Websites, but mostly at the Classic and the Image map Website. Especially choosing the right main category was problematic for many children, as was also reported

*Figure 10. The unconventional location of the search box and the main category links as images at the Image map Website*

by Hutchinson et al. (2006). Often, children had wrong expectations of the content behind main category links. For example, the main category link label 'human' was often selected for tasks about the first astronaut or about Columbus, because humans were mentioned in the task description. However, in fact the main category 'human' was about the human body.

Children did benefit from the addition of images with the main and subcategory link labels at the Classical play Website in comparison to the Classic Website (see Figures 11 and 12). The images helped children to choose the right main and sub categories and the children used more trial-and-error in choosing the right categories at the Classic Website.

The addition of images at the Image map Website often had an opposite effect on children's navigation behavior, because the images without the verbal link labels often did not speak for themselves (see Figure 10). In other words, addition of images to the category labels helps children in navigation, but corresponding text labels with the images are essential for quick understanding of the link labels.

*Operational Navigation Problems:* Children needed more assistance in operating the navigation tools on the Image map than on the other Website versions. The sub category link labels on the Image map appeared in a pop up layer across the homepage and often children did not know how to get out of this pop up layer (see Figure 13). There were no navigation tools provided to go back to the homepage, as was the case at the other two Website versions. Children had to find out for themselves that they had to click somewhere on the screen next to the popup layer to make the popup layer disappear.

*Children's Navigation Skills:* Many problems that children experienced on the Websites cannot be attributed to the design characteristics of the Websites, but are caused by children's own navigation and information skills. Differences between children's navigation and information skills are more determinant for differences in search performance than differences between Web design characteristics. We will illustrate this by describing differences between search behavior of children that were successful and unsuccessful in finding the right information on the Websites.

*Figure 11. The main and subcategory labels without addition of images at the Classic Website*

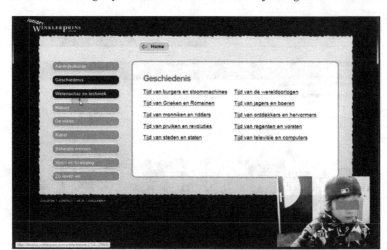

*Figure 12. The main and subcategory labels with addition of images at the Classical play Website*

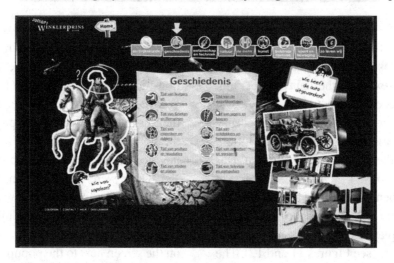

Where successful children showed a clear pattern in link selection, less successful children lacked such a clear pattern. Less successful children especially had problems with the interpretation of the main category link labels. They often selected high-scent incorrect links and they almost never selected low-scent correct links. They often lacked domain knowledge to select a relevant category link or did not keep the initial search task in mind. Also, less successful children often did not recognize when they selected the wrong main category link and got lost in the Website's menu structure.

Successful children did keep the initial search task in mind and had less problems with interpretation of the main category link labels. They were well aware when they had selected a wrong main category. They were often able to select low scent correct links and followed the optimum navigation path more often than unsuccessful children.

*Browsing Strategies:* Successful children used both a trial-and-error strategy and a 'think-than-act' strategy on the Classic Website. On the Classical play Website, successful children only used one strategy: the 'think-then-act' strategy. This might be explained by the fact that the link

*Figure 13. The sub category link labels at the Image map Website appear in a popup layer across the homepage*

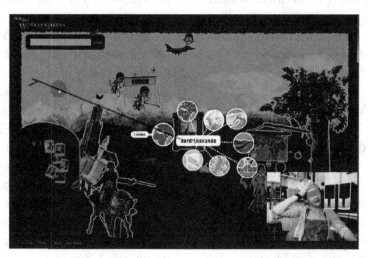

labels on the Classical play Website were presented with a picture that visually represented the textual link label, allowing children to make a better interpretation of the meaning of the link labels. This made the 'trial-and-error' strategy less necessary.

Less successful children exclusively used a trial-and-error strategy to find information on all three Website versions. They often only used one strategy and had no plan B, when plan A did not lead them to the right content page. They had trouble keeping the search task in mind and often applied a 'loopy' navigation style, which means that they selected the same incorrect main and sub category links again and again. This looping navigation behavior was also reported by Bilal (2000).

Another problem that occurred with some children while using the Image map Website was that they were hesitant to click on the main and sub category links. The playful lay out of the Image map Website made them insecure to click on the links.

*Processing the Content Page:* Successful children often asked for assistance in understanding the content. Less successful children did not ask for help, but just gave a wrong answer. Reasons for giving wrong answers were because of a wrong interpretation of the text, not recognizing internal hyperlinks to a relevant content page, because of low literacy skills, scanning the text too quickly or by not keeping the initial search task in mind. Successful children mostly had the capacity to reflect on the initial search task and made sure that they kept the search task in mind.

*Processing Problems:* It was noted that children experienced more problems on all areas of navigation on the Image map than on the other Website versions. Children even had trouble understanding the search tasks correctly when using the Image map Website, which did not occur with the other Website versions. This might be explained by the 'cognitive load theory' (Sweller, Merrienboer & Paas, 1998). Processing the Image map Website might have taken so much cognitive energy from the children, that there was too little cognitive energy left to interpret the search task.

*Game-Experience:* Finally, we found some clues that game-experience influences children's navigation behavior. Children with little game-experience (mostly girls according to the results of the profile survey) often think first before they act. Children with a lot of game-experience (mostly boys) use the trial-and-error search strategy. This trail-and-error strategy is provoked when children do not know exactly where to go, which is often the case on the Image map Website. Therefore, the use of the Image map seems more suited for children with a lot of game-experience.

## CONCLUSION AND DISCUSSION

### Validation of the Used Methods

In this section we will answer our research questions. The first question is about the suitability of existing methods for research with children to measure feelings and perceptions of pragmatic and hedonic quality that are used in research with adults. We experienced that methods such as the SAM-scale for emotional arousal and the AttracDiff 2 questionnaire are not valid methods in research with children. Unlike Greenbaum et al. (1990), we could not validate the use of the SAM-scale for emotional arousal with children. These opposite results might be caused by the different settings in which the method was used. The pictures in the SAM-scale for emotional arousal might be related easier to 'fear of the dentist' by children (which was the case in the research of Greenbaum et al., 1990) than the feeling experienced with using a Website. We could, however, validate the SAM-scale for emotional valence with children.

Almost all picture anchors for the semantic differential scales for the pragmatic and hedonic items could not be validated for use with children in our experiment (which we did not expect based on our pilot test of the semantic differential scales with 14 children). The children in the experiment did not interpret the picture anchors as intended by the developers of the AttracDiff 2 questionnaire (Hassenzahl et al., 2003). The children only made a clear distinction between which end of the scale was intended as positive and which end of the scale as negative in their opinion. The children were not able to make a distinction between

perceptions of hedonic and pragmatic quality of the Websites. The pragmatic and hedonic items were all seen as the same construct of valence (i.e. positive versus negative).

Although we did find differences in scores for the product evaluations beauty, goodness and fun, we doubt whether children were able to make a clear distinction between these concepts, as was also reported by Read et al. (2002). Fortunately, we were able to use an objective method to measure emotional arousal by using the Q-Sensor. This method turned out to be valid to measure emotional arousal with children in contrast to the subjective methods used in our experiment.

Based on this experiment, we cannot judge whether the UX models presented in research with adults (Hassenzahl, 2004; Thüring & Mahlke, 2007; van Schaik & Ling, 2008) can also be applied to children's UX. Although we could not entirely reproduce UX research concerning perceptions of pragmatic and hedonic quality in our experiment, we did show the difficulty of reproducing UX research with children. More research is needed to develop valid methods to measure children's perceptions of pragmatic and hedonic quality.

### Effects of Different Design Types

We did not find any effects on children's search performance on informational Websites of the different design types. The variation in design of the Websites did not have an effect on search success and efficiency. As opposed to the performance scores, there were differences in the subjective scores measured. Children were most positive about the Classical play Website according to their scores on the SAM-scales for valence. This positive score is most likely not based on pragmatic issues, because both children that were successful and unsuccessful in finding the right information on the Classical play Website, gave this Website higher scores than the other two Website versions. Apparently, their feelings about the Website is based on more hedonic issues, such as whether they are attracted to the interface design of the Website. Surprisingly, we saw the same pattern for children's evaluations of goodness: both successful and unsuccessful children evaluated the Image map version as less good than the other two Website versions. There were no significant differences between children that were successful and children that were unsuccessful in finding the right information. Apparently, search success was not determinant for children's evaluation of goodness.

## The Relation between Performance and Attitude

We did not find evidence for a strong relation between affectivity and usability in our study. Children's affective responses are not based on the effectiveness of search performance on the Websites. However, their affective responses could be based on pragmatic issues besides the final success in finding the information. For instance, their affective responses could be based on the ease of use while interacting with the interface, as was reported by Sim et al. (2006) who found that children appeared to have less fun when their interactions had more usability problems. However, in our study children's affective responses towards the search systems seem to be independent from their actual search behavior and most likely based on perceived hedonic quality and aesthetics of the interface. This could be best tested by a pre and post measure of affective responses, to see whether actual behavior changes children's attitude towards product evaluations such as beauty, goodness and fun (van Schaik & Ling, 2008). Because of time constraints it was not feasible in our experiment to conduct both pre and post tests to measure affective responses.

We did find some proof that the children's affective responses were based on the ease of use while interacting with the interface (i.e. pragmatic quality). An analysis of verbal utterances of 25 children that used the Image map Website, showed that most of the utterances were negative and related to the Websites' low pragmatic quality. This result supports the fact that the children's valence scores and evaluation scores for goodness were lowest for the Image map Website and that these scores are based on perception of pragmatic quality. The fact that almost no hedonic utterances were made, supports the fact that playfulness and expressive aesthetics do not have a large influence on children's attitude towards and evaluation of the Website.

The fact that we did not find a relation between beauty and usability in our experiment can also be caused by children's tendency to indicate the highest score on the scale (Markopoulos et al., 2008). Most children felt very positive about the three Websites and little frustration was uttered. Therefore, we did not find evidence that pragmatic frustrations lower children's perception of aesthetics as Tuch et al. (2012) found in their research with adults. This is most likely also caused by children's tendency to give socially desirable answers. Although they were often not successful at all in conducting a search task, children found it difficult to be negative about the system and tended to blame themselves instead of the system. This was also reported by Serenko (2007), who studied the self-serving biases of interface agent users. He found that adult users may attribute their success to an interface agent and hold themselves responsible for task failure, just like the children may have done in our experiment.

## Interaction with the Chosen Search Strategy

From this experiment we can conclude that the search strategy that is used by children is much more determinant for their search performance than the interface design of the search environment. Searching with a search engine proved to be much more effective and efficient than browsing the navigation structure. This was the case for all three types of Websites in our experiment.

We found that there was a significant difference in success scores when children received help from the test instructor. However, this difference meant that children were less successful. In other words, children did not become successful because of the help they received. These findings prove that help was only offered to motivate and reassure children during the search process (as recommended by Markopoulos et al., 2008) and offered help did not have a significant effect on children's success in finding the right information.

It turned out that searching with the search engine is more effective and efficient than browsing the categories. This is quite logical when considering the fact that children nowadays are members of the 'Google-generation' (Rowlands, 2008). However, we did not look at the long-term effects of the fact that children prefer and are better in searching than in browsing. Searching instead of browsing might, for example, have a negative effect on children's knowledge of information taxonomies. The search engine can be compared to a 'black box' that does not give insight in how information is related in a taxonomy. Future research is needed to study long-term effects on children's knowledge of information architectures of searching with a search engine in comparison to browsing categories.

Search and navigation behavior on the Web is constantly changing. Currently, traditional search engines as Google are loosing 'traffic', because people more and more use social media such as Facebook and Twitter as their primary Web entrance to find information (Xiang and Gretzel, 2010). This might also cause changes in children's search and navigation behavior.

## Children's Navigation and Information Skills

When studying children's search performance in more detail, we found that many problems that children experienced on the Websites cannot be attributed to the design characteristics of the Websites, but are caused by children's own lack of navigation and information skills. In other words, children's navigation and information skills are a better predictor of children's search success than the type of design characteristics of the search interface. Children with a lot of internet experience, encounter fewer problems with searching and browsing than children with little internet experience. Also, children with a lot of domain knowledge are more successful in formulating relevant search queries, selecting relevant search results, or selecting relevant main and subcategories. Children that are able to check and monitor their own activities, termed metacognition (i.e. the voluntary control an individual has over his own cognitive processes) (Brown & DeLoache, 1978) are more capable of keeping the initial search task in mind, or of recognizing when they select the wrong main or sub category link.

However, particular search characteristics might support particular groups of children. For example, our research provides indications that children with a lot of game experience are better off with the Image map Website, because this interface type is based on exploring and a trial-and-error strategy. Our research also provides clues that children with little internet experience are better off with the Classic Website, because there are not so many visual stimuli to distract these children from their navigation path.

An important lesson learned from this experiment is that the variance between children is much more determinant for differences in search success and performance than the variance between search interfaces. This makes the challenge for designers to design interfaces that support children in effective information-seeking even greater. It also stresses the importance of educating children in navigation and information skills. However, the most important lesson learned from this experiment is the fact that children's search success and search efficiency is much larger when they use a search engine, than when they browse the main categories of the Website.

## ACKNOWLEDGMENT

We would like to thank the children that cooperated in this study. We would also like to thank Matthijs Noordzij of the University of Twente for his help processing the data of the Q-sensor and MA students, Jiske Naber, Marjolein Makkinga, Aafke Ariaans, Yvonne Joosten and Amy Mooij, for their assistance in conducting the qualitative analyses of the experimental data. The research is funded by the Netherlands Institute for Public Libraries (SIOB) and the European Community's Seventh Framework Programme FP7/2007-2013 under grant agreement no. 231507, named 'PuppyIR'.

## REFERENCES

Bar-Ilan, J., & Belous, Y. (2007). Children as architects of web directories: An exploratory study. *Journal of the American Society for Information Science and Technology*, *58*(6), 895–907. doi:10.1002/asi.20566

Bilal, D. (2000). Children's use of the yahooligans web search engine: I. cognitive, physical, and affective behaviors on fact-based search tasks. *Journal of the American Society for Information Science American Society for Information Science*, *51*(7), 646–665. doi:10.1002/(SICI)1097-4571(2000)51:7<646::AID-ASI7>3.0.CO;2-A

Bilal, D. (2001). Children's use of the yahooligans! web search engine: II. cognitive and physical behaviors on research tasks. *Journal of the American Society for Information Science and Technology*, *52*(2), 118–136. doi:10.1002/1097-4571(2000)9999:9999<::AID-ASI1038>3.0.CO;2-R

Bilal, D. (2002). Children's use of the yahooligans! web search engine. III. cognitive and physical behaviors on fully self-generated search tasks. *Journal of the American Society for Information Science and Technology*, *53*(13), 1170–1183. doi:10.1002/asi.10145

Bilal, D., & Kirby, J. (2002). Differences and similarities in information seeking: Children and adults as web users. *Information Processing & Management*, *38*(5), 649–670. doi:10.1016/S0306-4573(01)00057-7

Bilal, D., & Watson, J. S. (1998). *Children's paperless projects: Inspiring research via the web.* Paper presented at the 64th General Conference of the International Federation of Library Associations & Institutions. Amsterdam, the Netherlands.

Borgman, C. L., Hirsh, S. G., Walter, V. A., & Gallagher, A. L. (1995). Children's searching behavior on browsing and keyword online catalogs: The science library catalog project. *Journal of the American Society for Information Science American Society for Information Science*, *46*(9), 663–684. doi:10.1002/(SICI)1097-4571(199510)46:9<663::AID-ASI4>3.0.CO;2-2

Bradley, M. M., & Lang, P. J. (1994). Measuring emotion: The self-assessment manikin and the semantic differential. *Journal of Behavior Therapy and Experimental Psychiatry*, *25*(1), 49–59. doi:10.1016/0005-7916(94)90063-9 PMID:7962581

Brown, A. L., & DeLoache, J. S. (1978). Skills, plans, and self-regulation. In R. S. Siegler (Ed.), *Children's thinking: What develops?* (pp. 3–35). Hillsdale, NJ: Erlbaum.

Chambers, C. T., & Johnston, C. (2002). Developmental differences in children's use of rating scales. *Journal of Pediatric Psychology*, *27*(1), 27–36. doi:10.1093/jpepsy/27.1.27 PMID:11726677

Chen, C. (2006). *Information visualization: Beyond the horizon.* London: Springer.

Druin, A. (2003). What children can teach us: Developing digital libraries for children with children. *The Library Quarterly*, *75*(1), 20–41. doi:10.1086/428691

Druin, A., Hutchinson, H., Foss, E., Hatley, L., Golub, E., Leigh Guha, M., & Fails, J. (2009). *How children search the internet with keyword interfaces*. Paper presented at the 8th International Conference on Interaction Design and Children. Como, Italy.

Greenbaum, P. E., Turner, C., Cook, E. W. III, & Melamed, B. G. (1990). Dentists' voice control: Effects on children's disruptive and affective behavior. *Health Psychology*, *9*(5), 546–558. doi:10.1037/0278-6133.9.5.546 PMID:2226384

Hartmann, J., Sutcliffe, A., & Angeli, A. D. (2008). Towards a theory of user judgment of aesthetics and user interface quality. *ACM Transactions on Computer-Human Interaction*, *15*(4), 15:1-15:30.

Hassenzahl, M. (2004). The interplay of beauty, goodness, and usability in interactive products. *Human-Computer Interaction*, *19*(4), 319–349. doi:10.1207/s15327051hci1904_2

Hassenzahl, M., Burmester, M., & Koller, F. (2003). AttrakDiff: Ein fragebogen zur messung wahrgenommener hedonischer und pragmatischer qualitat. In J. Ziegler, & G. Szwillus (Eds.), *Mensch & computer: Interaktion in bewegung* (pp. 187–196). Stuttgart, Germany: B.G. Teubner. doi:10.1007/978-3-322-80058-9_19

Hassenzahl, M., & Tractinsky, N. (2006). User experience–A research agenda. *Behaviour & Information Technology*, *25*(2), 91–97. doi:10.1080/01449290500330331

Horton, M., Read, J. C., & Sim, G. (2011). Making your mind up? The reliability of children's survey responses. In L. Little & L. Coventry (Eds.), *25th BCS Conference on Human-Computer Interaction* (pp. 437-438). Swinton, UK: British Computer Society.

Hutchinson, H., Druin, A., Bederson, B. B., Reuter, K., Rose, A., & Weeks, A. C. (2005). *How do I find blue books about dogs? The errors and frustrations of young digital library users*. Paper presented at the International Conference on Human-Computer Interaction (HCI). Las Vegas, NV.

Hutchinson, H. B., Bederson, B. B., & Druin, A. (2006). *The evolution of the international children's digital library searching and browsing interface*. Paper presented at the 2006 Conference on Interaction Design for Children. Tampere, Finland.

Irtel, H. (2007). PXLab: The psychological experiments laboratory (2.1.11 ed.). Mannheim, Germany: University of Mannheim.

Jochmann-Mannak, H., Huibers, T., Lentz, L., & Sanders, T. (2010). *Children searching information on the internet: Performance on children's interfaces compared to Google*. Paper presented at the 33rd Annual International ACM SIGIR Conference on Research and Development in Information Retrieval at the Workshop Towards Accessible Search Systems. Geneva, Switzerland.

Jochmann-Mannak, H., Lentz, L., Huibers, T., & Sanders, T. (2012). Three types of children's informational websites: An inventory of design conventions. *Technical Communication*, *59*(4), 302–323.

Kitajima, M., Blackmon, M. H., & Polson, P. G. (2000). *A comprehension-based model of web navigation and its application to web usability analysis*. Paper presented at the 14th Annual Conference of the British HCI Group (HCI 2000), People and Computers XIV: Usability Or Else! Sunderland, UK.

Laarni, J. (2004). *Aesthetic and emotional evaluations of computer interfaces*. Paper presented at the Nordi CHI 2004 Workshop: Aesthetic Approaches to Human–Computer Interaction. Aarhus, Denmark.

Lang, P. J. (1980). Behavioral treatment and bio-behavioral assessment: Computer applications. In J. B. Sidowski, J. H. Johnson, & T. A. Williams (Eds.), *Technology in mental health care delivery systems* (pp. 119–137). Norwood, NJ: Ablex Publishing.

Large, A., & Beheshti, J. (2000). The web as a classroom resource: Reactions from the users. *Journal of the American Society for Information Science American Society for Information Science*, 51(12), 1069–1080. doi:10.1002/1097-4571(2000)9999:9999<::AID-ASI1017>3.0.CO;2-W

Large, A., Beheshti, J., & Moukdad, H. (1999). *Information seeking on the web: Navigational skills of grade-six primary school students.* Paper presented at the ASIS Annual Meeting. Washington, DC.

Large, A., Beheshti, J., Tabatabaei, N., & Nesset, V. (2009). Developing a visual taxonomy: Children's views on aesthetics. *Journal of the American Society for Information Science and Technology*, 60(9), 1808–1822. doi:10.1002/asi.21095

Large, A., Nesset, V., Beheshti, J., & Bowler, L. (2006). Bonded design: A novel approach to the design of new technologies. *Library & Information Science Research*, 28(1), 64–82. doi:10.1016/j.lisr.2005.11.014

Malone, T. W. (1980). *What makes things fun to learn? A study of intrinsically motivating computer games* (Technical Report No. CIS-7 SSL-80-11). Palo Alto, CA: Xerox Palo Alto Research Center.

Malone, T. W. (1984). Heuristics for designing enjoyable user interfaces: Lessons from computer games. In J. C. Thomas, & M. L. Schneider (Eds.), *Human factors in computer systems* (pp. 1–12). Norwood, NJ: Ablex Publishing.

Marchionini, G. (1989). Information-seeking strategies of novices using a full-text electronic encyclopedia. *Journal of the American Society for Information Science American Society for Information Science*, 40(1), 54–66. doi:10.1002/(SICI)1097-4571(198901)40:1<54::AID-ASI6>3.0.CO;2-R

Markopoulos, P., Read, J., MacFarlane, S., & Hoysniemi, J. (2008). *Evaluating children's interactive products*. Burlington, UK: Elsevier.

Meloncon, L., Haynes, E., Varelmann, M., & Groh, L. (2010). Building a playground: General guidelines for creating educational websites for children. *Technical Communication*, 57(4), 398–415.

Nielsen, J., & Gilutz, S. (2002). *Usability of websites for children: 70 design guidelines based on usability studies with kids*. Nielsen Norman Group.

Noordzij, M., Scholten, P., & Laroy-Noordzij, M. (2012). *Measuring electrodermal activity of both individuals with severe mental disabilities and their caretakers during episodes of challenging behavior.* Paper presented at the 8th International Conference on Methods and Techniques in Behavioral Research: Measuring Behavior. Utrecht, The Netherlands.

Pijpers, R., Marteijn, T., Bosman, M., & Berg, V. D. W., & Dijkerman, E. (2008). Klik en klaar: Een onderzoek naar surfgedrag en usability bij kinderen (No. 111). Den Haag, The Netherlands: Stichting Mijn Kind Online.

Poh, M., Swenson, N. C., & Picard, R. W. (2010). A wearable sensor for unobtrusive, long-term assessment of electrodermal activity. *IEEE Transactions on Bio-Medical Engineering*, 1243–1252. PMID:20172811

Read, J. C. (2008). Validating the fun toolkit: An instrument for measuring children's opinions of technology. *Cognition Technology and Work*, 10(2), 119–128. doi:10.1007/s10111-007-0069-9

Read, J. C., & MacFarlane, S. (2006). *Using the fun toolkit and other survey methods to gather opinions in child computer interaction.* Paper presented at the International Conference on Interaction Design and Children. Tampere, Finland.

Read, J. C., MacFarlane, S. J., & Casey, C. (2002). *Endurability, engagement and expectations: Measuring children's fun.* Paper presented at the International Conference on Interaction Design and Children. Eindhoven, The Netherlands.

Revelle, G., Druin, A., Platner, M., Bederson, B. B., & Sherman, L. (2002). A visual search tool for early elementary science students. *Journal of Science Education and Technology, 11*(1), 49–57. doi:10.1023/A:1013947430933

Rowlands, I. (2008). *Information behaviour of the researcher of the future.* British Library JISC. doi:10.1108/00012530810887953

Russell, J. A. (1980). A circumplex model of affect. *Journal of Personality and Social Psychology, 39*(6), 1161–1178. doi:10.1037/h0077714

Schacter, J., Chung, G. K. W. K., & Dorr, A. (1998). Children's internet searching on complex problems: Performance and process analyses. *Journal of the American Society for Information Science American Society for Information Science, 49*(9), 840–849. doi:10.1002/(SICI)1097-4571(199807)49:9<840::AID-ASI9>3.0.CO;2-D

Serenko, A. (2007). Are interface agents scapegoats? Attributions of responsibility in human-agent interaction. *Interacting with Computers, 19*(2), 293–303. doi:10.1016/j.intcom.2006.07.005

Sim, G., MacFarlane, S., & Read, J. (2006). All work and no play: Measuring fun, usability, and learning in software for children. *Computers & Education, 46*(3), 235–248. doi:10.1016/j.compedu.2005.11.021

Snijders, T., & Bosker, R. (2012). *Multilevel analysis: An introduction to basic and advanced multilevel modeling* (2nd ed.). London: Sage Publishers.

Sweller, J., van Merrienboer, J. J. G., & Paas, G. W. C. (1998). Cognitive architecture and instructional design. *Educational Psychology Review, 10*(3), 251–296. doi:10.1023/A:1022193728205

Thuring, M., & Mahlke, S. (2007). Usability, aesthetics and emotions in human-technology interaction. *International Journal of Psychology, 42*(4), 253–264. doi:10.1080/00207590701396674

Tractinsky, N., Katz, A. S., & Ikar, D. (2000). What is beautiful is usable. *Interacting with Computers, 13*(2), 127–145. doi:10.1016/S0953-5438(00)00031-X

Tuch, A. N., Roth, S. P., Hornbæk, K., Opwis, K., & Bargas-Avila, J. A. (2012). Is beautiful really usable? Toward understanding the relation between usability, aesthetics, and affect in HCI. *Computers in Human Behavior, 28*(5), 1596–1607. doi:10.1016/j.chb.2012.03.024

van Schaik, P., & Ling, J. (2008). Modelling user experience with websites: Usability, hedonic value, beauty and goodness. *Interacting with Computers, 20*(3), 419–432. doi:10.1016/j.intcom.2008.03.001

Xiang, Z., & Gretzel, U. (2010). Role of social media in online travel information search. *Tourism Management, 31*(2), 179–188. doi:10.1016/j.tourman.2009.02.016

Yarosh, S., Radu, I., Hunter, S., & Rosenbaum, E. (2011). *Examining values: An analysis of nine years of IDC research.* Paper presented at the 10th International Conference on Interaction Design and Children. Ann Arbor, MI.

## KEY TERMS AND DEFINITIONS

**Browsing:** Browsing is a search method in which the user selects a relevant subject category from a menu. The user can 'recognize' a relevant category from the provided categories in the menu.

**Classic Interface Design:** Classic interface design aims at simplicity, consistency and focus. The layout of classic interfaces is kept minimal with little graphic elements; key elements of the interfaces are the center of attention and different pages have the same layout. Page components are located on conventional locations. The navigation is a basic, textual menu of categories presented in a horizontally or vertically presented list.

**Emotional Arousal:** The extent to which the user gets exited (by interacting with an interface).

**Emotional Valence:** The extent to which the user's feelings (towards an interface) are positive or negative.

**Keyword Search:** Keyword search is a search method in which a search engine is used to search for information in a vast information space by submitting a search query. The search engine matches this query to information elements in the information space and presents search results from which the user can select a result that is relevant for his search task. The user has to 'recall' and formulate a search query from his memory.

**Perception of Hedonic Quality:** The user's perception of the extent to which interacting with an interface is stimulating for the user and the extent to which the user can identify with the interface (i.e. pleasure-producing quality of an interface).

**Perception of Pragmatic Quality:** The user's perception of how user-friendly an interface is and how effective and efficient search performance is when using this interface (i.e. user-perceived usability).

**Playful Interface Design:** Interface design can be made playful both in design of navigation as in visual design. With a playful navigation approach, category labels are integrated in a screen filling image, often without textual labels. Users have to 'explore' the screen image in search of categories, which makes interacting with the interface a playful experience. Visual design can be made playful by adding many different colors, images and animations to the interface and by playfully arranging visual elements on the screen.

**Search Performance:** The effectiveness and efficiency (for example in amount of time and clicks needed) with which a user can search and find relevant information by interacting with a digital interface.

**User Experience:** The research field of User Experience (UX) argues for a broader perspective for evaluation of systems or interfaces than usability. Besides instrumental qualities (i.e. pragmatic quality / usability), also non-instrumental qualities are important, such as visual aesthetics, hedonic quality or haptic qualities.

## ENDNOTES

[1] Six of the AttractDiff 2 items were not used in our study, because these verbal anchors were too difficult to translate in a picture that we thought could be well-interpreted by children: isolating – integrating, gaudy – classy, takes me distant from people – brings me closer to people, typical – original, conservative – innovative, commonplace – new.

[2] Jiske Naber and Marjolein Makkinga (students of the Master Communication studies) assisted the authors by analyzing verbal utterances of 25 children that conducted search tasks on the Image map Website.

[3] Aafke Ariaans (MA student) assisted the authors by analyzing the reliability and validity of the data.

[4] Yvonne Joosten (MA student) assisted the authors by conducting qualitative analyses of search engine use.

[5] Amy Mooij (MA student) assisted the authors by conducting qualitative analyses of the children's navigation paths.

## APPENDIX 1

"How interface design and search strategy influence children's search performance and evaluation"

## Task Descriptions Translated from the Original Dutch Versions with the Optimum Navigation Path Presented for Each Task

## Task 1

You've seen a chameleon in the zoo and you saw that he was moving very slowly.
Now you wonder how a chameleon captures its prey, because he seems far too lazy for that.
Can you find out how a chameleon catches its prey at Junior Winkler Prins online?
*Optimum Navigation Path Task 1:*

- **Correct Main Category:** Nature
- **Correct Subcategory:** Reptiles and amphibians
- **Correct Content Page:** Chameleon

## Task 2

You would like to become an astronaut and explore space in search of alien planets, like in the movies. Can you find out who was actually the first living creature that traveled through space at Junior Winkler Prins online ?
*Optimum Navigation Path Task 2:*

- **Correct Main Category:** Science and technology
- **Correct Subcategory:** Space and Space travel
- **Correct Content Pages:** Space/ Astronaut

## Task 3

You spend your holiday in Friesland with your parents and your father told you that he participated in the famous Dutch skating tour named 'Elfstedentocht' once.
He also told you that he met the Dutch crown prince Willem-Alexander during the tour.
Can you find out under what name Willem-Alexander participated in the scating tour that day?
*Optimum Navigation Path Task 3:*

- **Correct Main Category:** Sports and exercise
- **Correct Subcategory:** Stadiums & Tournaments
- **Correct Content Page:** "Elfstedentocht"

## Task 4

It is often said that Christopher Columbus discovered America. Some say that this is not true. They say that another nation discovered America 500 years before Columbus did.

Can you find out what people discovered America before Columbus did at Junior Winkler Prins online?
*Optimum Navigation Path Task 4:*

- **Correct Main Category:** History
- **Correct Subcategories:** Time of cities and states/ Time of discoverers and reformers/ Time of monks and knights.
- **Correct Content Pages:** Vikings/ Discoveries.

## Task 5

Isaac Newton invented a device to be able to see the stars better. Can you find out what the name of that device is at Junior Winkler Prins online?
*Optimum Navigation Path Task 5:*

- **Correct Main Category:** Famous people / Science and technology.
- **Correct Subcategories:** Inventors and scientists/ Space and space travel/ Measuring, weighing or counting/ How it works.
- **Correct Content Pages:** Isaac Newton/ Star/ Telescope.

## APPENDIX 2

## Bipolar Picture Anchors for Pragmatic and Hedonic Quality from the AttracDiff 2 Questionnaire

Pragmatic Quality (PQ)

*Figure 14. Technical – human*

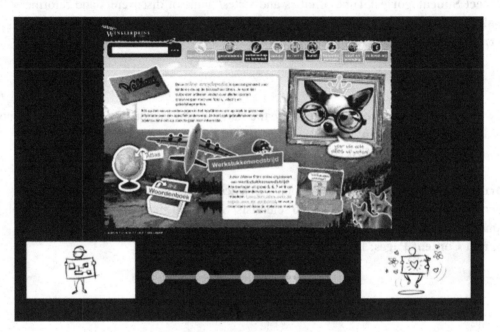

*Figure 15. Complicated – simple*

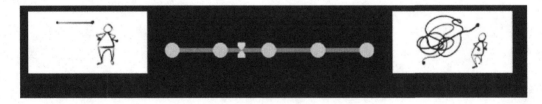

*Figure 16. Impractical – practical*

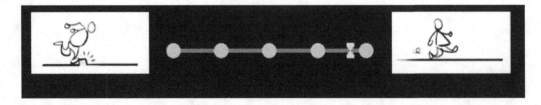

*Figure 17. Cumbersome – direct*

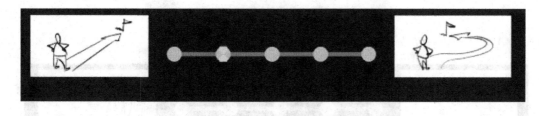

*Figure 18. Unpredictable – predictable\**

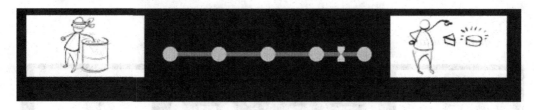

*Figure 19. Confusing – clear*

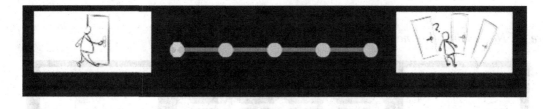

*Figure 20. Unruly – manageable*

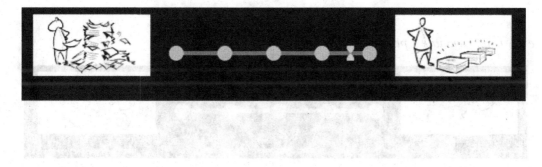

## Hedonic Quality – Identification (HQI)

*Figure 21. Amateurish – professional*

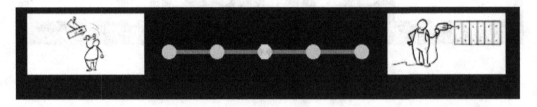

*Figure 22. Cheap – valuable*

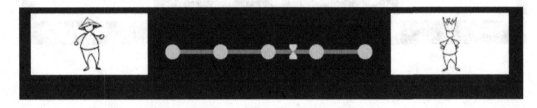

*Figure 23. Non-inclusive – inclusive\**

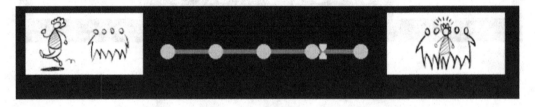

*Figure 24. Unpresentable – presentable*

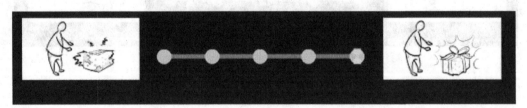

## Hedonic Quality – Stimulation (HQS)

*Figure 25. Standard – creative\**

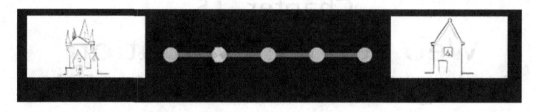

*Figure 26. Cautious – courageous\**

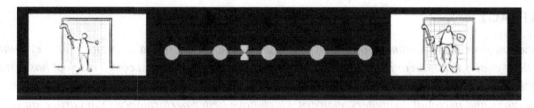

*Figure 27. Lame – exciting*

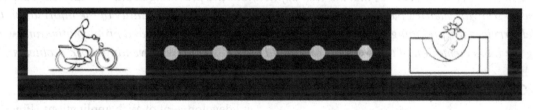

*Figure 28. Easy – challenging*

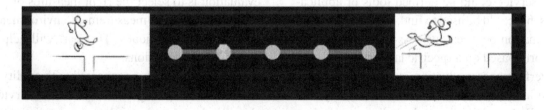

\* Picture anchors that were left out of the final experiment based on the results of the pilot study.

# Chapter 15
# Web Service Evaluation Using Probabilistic Models

**S. Zimeras**
*University of the Aegean, Greece*

## ABSTRACT

*Information system users, administrators, and designers are all interested in performance evaluation since their goal is to obtain or provide the highest performance at the lowest cost. This goal has resulted in continuing evolution of higher performance and lower cost systems leading to today's proliferation of workstations and personal computers, many of which have better performance than earlier supercomputers. As the variety of Web services applications (Websites) increases, it gets more important to have a set of evaluation criteria that should evaluate the performance of their effectiveness. Based on those criteria, the quality of the services that the Web applications are providing could be analysed. This work represents software metrics that could (or need) be used to quantify the quality of the information that the Web services are providing. These measures could be useful to understand problematic frameworks during the implementation of the Websites and could lead to solutions preventing those problems.*

## INTRODUCTION

During the last decade, the Web services (websites) are into the centre of managing information. As Web service could be defined tools or applications that could be used to find, manage and share information between business and science via a platform based on a specific language

Performance evaluation is required at every stage in the life cycle of an information system (like Web applications), including its design, manufacturing, sales/purchase, use, upgrade, and so on. Web applications include product, usage and development characteristics and are subjected to continuous evolution. It is needed to focus on

various aspects aiming to contribute in the design and development of Web applications (Figure 1) (Kastania and Zimeras, 2010)

In general the important goal in performance evaluation is to select the right measures of performance, the right measurement environments, and the right techniques. This part will help in making these selections.

Evaluation is close connected with quality of services. The quality measurement of services should be based on the product characteristics that contribute to user satisfaction and on the product functions that can be present or absent. In order to measure quality the user view, the developer view (models to assure the quality of the process,

DOI: 10.4018/978-1-4666-5129-6.ch015

*Figure 1. Design and development of Web applications (Kastania and Zimeras, 2010)*

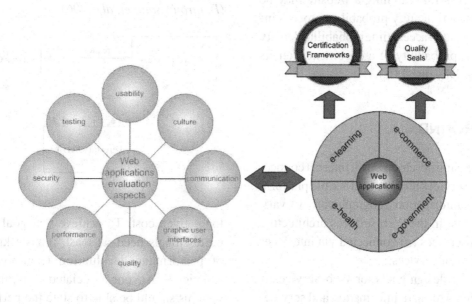

quality requirements for teleservices), the product view and the value-based view should be considered (Figure 2)

Very different measures are necessary for measuring the effectiveness of an information system. Related to the information systems effectiveness is the DeLone and McLean (1992) work. Cameron and Whetten (1983) have proposed a useful framework for selecting appropriate measures for future information systems research focused on organizational performance. Seddon

et al. (1999) propose that the diversity of information systems effectiveness measures is to be encouraged.

This work introduced the reader to software metrics that are used to provide insight about different elements of information systems software. It presented internal metrics that can be applied prior to the release of the product to provide indications relating to quality characteristics, and external metrics applied after product delivery to give information about user perception of product quality (Dhyani, Keong and Bhowmick, 2002).

Software metrics can be used to measure various factors related to software product development. These factors include estimation, early detection and prevention of problems, product assessment, etc. Their utilization within a measurements framework in combination to the use of automated tools can aid towards development process control and higher quality software systems

From probabilistic point of view, in the Web graph properties could be apply random graph models considering the theory of random networks where statistical distributions could be explain the interactions between different elements. Also

*Figure 2. Web metric characteristics*

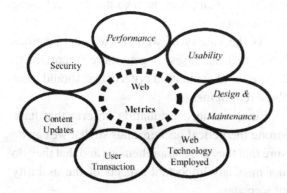

the time access for searching a website may be illustrated as a reliability probability process introducing the inter-access time probability density (time access probability of a document after its last access) (Dhyani, 2001).

## BACKGROUND

Due to increasing development of internet connectivity, Web services provide a reflexible platform distributing information geographically to various directions. In the Web services architecture clients and services are connected via interfaces and locations of services.

One of the design goals for Web Services is to allow clients to share information and services each other in a simple way over the internet.

Web services are built over XML and their framework is divided into three areas (communication protocol, service description, and service discovery) and specifications are being developed for each one (Haddad et al. 2004): 1. The Simple Object Access Protocol (SOAP) (Gudgin et. al., 2000), which enables communication among Web Services, 2. The Universal Description, Discovery and Integration (UDDI) (Bellwood et. al., 2002), which is a registry of Web Services descriptions, 3. The Web Services Description Language (WSDL) (Christensen et. al., 2001), which provides a formal, computer-readable description of Web services. Web services collaboration relies on an interaction model where the different components, service provider, directory service, and service consumer ensures the following roles (Figure 3) (Boutrous-Saab et. al. 2006):

## MAIN FOCUS OF THE CHAPTER

Performance is a key criterion in the design, procurement, and use of these web service systems. As such, the goal of systems engineers, scientists, analysts, and users is to get the highest performance

*Figure 3. Interaction between different components (Boutrous-Saab et. al. 2006)*

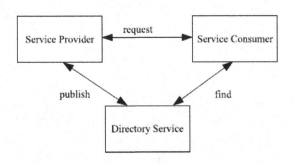

for a given cost. To achieve that goal, systems professionals need, at least, a basic knowledge of performance evaluation terminology and techniques. Anyone associated with information systems should be able to state the performance requirements of their systems and should be able to compare different alternatives to find the one that best meets their requirements. The evaluation is applied when designer wants to compare a number of alternative designs and find the best design. It is required when a system administrator wants to compare a number of systems and wants to decide which system is best for a given set of applications. Even if there are no alternatives, performance evaluation of the current system helps in determining how well it is performing and whether any improvements need to be made. Unfortunately, the types of applications are so numerous that it is not possible to have a standard measure of performance, a standard measurement environment (application), or a standard technique for all cases.

As the variety of web services applications (websites) increases, it gets more important to have a set of evaluation criteria that should meet three requirements.

First, we need evaluation criteria that have strong theoretical backgrounds so that we can be sure that they are comprehensive and that they do not miss any important aspects of the usability of websites.

Second, we need empirical validation for the evaluation criteria in order to be sure that they are relevant to what they intended to, and they produce a reliable result regarding the outcomes of the websites.

Evaluation of a system's performance and user satisfaction are important for the information's extraction about the availability and connectivity between different sources under similar tasks (business trust). Evaluation models are used to understand users' needs and identify important dimensions and factors in the development of systems in order to overcome problematic behave of the system performance (Schumaker and Chen, 2007; Schumaker et. al., 2007; Schumaker et. al. 2007; Wacholder et. al., 2007; Yu et. al., 2007). Evaluation of information systems can focus on a variety of technical properties, including data transmission speed or bandwidth, data quality (e.g., resolution), system functions and features, ease of use, reliability, and service or maintenance requirements. Technical properties such as bandwidth and resolution are steadily improving, while the costs to achieve given levels of technical performance are decreasing. Modelling all the previous technical properties, a SERVQUAL type model could be introduced for the quality evaluation of the Web services. Customer satisfaction is considered as a multifunctional (dimensional) construct which has been described by three main dimensions (which they defined the service quality of the systems): 1. Satisfactory interactions with personnel, 2. Satisfaction with the product, 3. Satisfaction with the organisation. For the system evaluation performance the most common approach is the construction of a target questionnaire which measures the quality characteristics of the systems. Criteria based on the user's response could be introduced (Javeau, 1992): 1. The capability of the user, 2. The understand ability of the user, 3. The honesty of the user, 4. The reliability of the user. In order to analyse the opinions via the questionnaires results an evaluation statistical measure must be introduced where the form $C_jO_i$

measures the opinion of a single user i based on a quality characteristic j with form (Rigou et. al., 2007):

$$C_jO_i = \frac{\sum_{k=1}^{m} Q_k V_k}{\sum_{k=1}^{m} Q_k}$$

where m is the number of questions, $Q_k$ is the weight given to the question k and $V_k$ is the value of the response of the selected user.

Also the opinion of a single user i, is measured by the form $O_i$ with (Rigou et. al., 2007):

$$O_i = \frac{\sum_{j=1}^{n} (C_j * C_jO_i)}{\sum_{j=1}^{n} C_j}$$

where n is the number of different characteristics for measure, $C_j$ is the weight of the characteristic j and $C_jO_i$ is the opinion of a single user i based on a quality characteristic j.

Web metrics is a quality measure for measuring the efficiency of the important parts of the Web services. Technical properties like

- Data transmission speed or bandwidth.
- Data quality (e.g., resolution.)
- System functions and features.
- Ease of use, reliability.
- Service or maintenance requirements.

could be used as important web metrics to evaluate the Web service SERQUAL model. Also Web graph structure could be introduced and analysed to specify the connections between the various parts of the Web service application. From probabilistic point of view, in the Web graph properties could be apply random graph models considering the theory of random networks where statistical distributions could be explain the interactions between different elements. Also the time access for searching a website may be illustrated as a reliability probability process introducing the inter-access time probability density (time access probability of a document after its last access) (Dhyani, 2001).

The random graph modelling is applied when a large amount of data (here the Web services information) must be evaluated via the connectivity between nodes (elements). This is the simplest connectivity model introduced by Barabasi et. al., (1999) where introducing a fixed graph with N connections (vertices) by p-probability. The probability P(k) for vertices (v) with k-edges (Erdos-Renyi random graph) follows the Poisson distribution with (when $N > \lambda\kappa$)

$$P(k) = \frac{1}{k!}e^{-\lambda}\lambda^k$$

and mean $\lambda$ with

$$\lambda = N \binom{N-1}{k} p^k (1-p)^{N-1-k}$$

The expectation of the local clustering clustering coefficient is p. The local clustering coefficient is defined as:

$$local-cluster(v) = \frac{pair-of-neighbours(v)-connected-by-edges}{total-pair(v)}$$

Evaluation of the parameters for the Erdos-Renyi random graph based on the probability P(k) could be considered using Monte Carlo Markov Chains techniques like Metropolis algorithm. Metropolis algorithm is a sampling technique where the main goal is to construct an aperiodic, irreducible Markov chain tending to a desired stationary distribution (where in our case is the P(k)). The algorithm is constructed by two steps:

1. A symmetric proposal process: the probability to move from state Ei to state Ej is equal to the probability to move from state $E_j$ to state Ei ($p_{ij} = p_{ji}$).
2. Acceptance of a move with probability min(1, Pr($E_j$)/Pr($E_i$)) or min(1, P($k_j$)/P($k_i$))

The algorithm works like this:

The probability of moving to state Ej from state Ei is the product of the transition probability from Ei to Ej and the probability of accepting a move from Ei to Ej or

$$q(k_j|k_i) = p_{ij} \cdot min(1, P(k_j)/P(k_i))$$

The impact factor of a web site introduces a statistical measure for the estimation of the site significance based on the information. If the influence of the j site is defined as $w_j$ and the connection strength between the site i and site j is defined as $S_{ij}$, then the influence of the site j is given by:

$$w_j = \sum_i w_i S_{ij}$$

Instead of evaluating the web sites considering graphical models, an alternatively proposed way is the use of Principal Components Analysis (PCA), where m web sites provide the same characteristics (similar information), which described by a quality of service (QoS) matrix Q with

$$Q = \begin{bmatrix} q_{11} & q_{12} & & q_{1m} \\ q_{21} & q_{22} & & q_{2m} \\ & & & \\ q_{m1} & q_{m2} & & q_{mm} \end{bmatrix}$$

*Figure 4. (a) Random graph; (b) Clustered random graph*

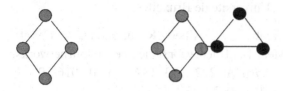

and scores $\sum_{i=1}^{m} w_i q_{ij}$ where $w_{ij}$ is the weight metrics. For the PCA calculation, the Q matrix must be standardised with elements $ST_i = \dfrac{q_i - E(q_i)}{\sqrt{\mathrm{var}(q_i)}}$,

then the calculation of the correlation matrix R is taking place with elements $r_{ij} = \dfrac{1}{m}\sum_{k=1}^{m} st_{ki} * st_{kj}$

with i=1,2,...,m and j=1,2,...,n. Finally the eigenvalues of the correlation matrix $\left| R - \lambda I \right| = 0$ can be computed and the k-th principal component is given by $P_k = \sum_{j=1}^{n} \lambda_{jk} ST_j$ (Haibo et. al. 2007).

## CONCLUSION

During the last years, the use of the web services (especially the web sites) involves the sharing vital information between different sources which they are located in various geographical sites.

The use of these services introduces the investigation of the performance of them leading us to the definition of the quality of the services (QoS). Performance of the evaluation could be achieved by introducing statistical measures based on the questionnaires of the users opinions.

Evaluation of the quality of the web services includes the introduction of web metrics, measures that are check the performance of specific parts of the system for example data transmission speed or bandwidth. For the implementation of the web

metrics application of random graph models is taking place where statistical distributions could be explain the interactions between different elements (Dhyani, 2001).

## REFERENCES

Kastania, A., & Zimeras, S. (2010). Web-based applications in healthcare and biomedicine. *Annals of Information Systems, 7*, 157–166. doi:10.1007/978-1-4419-1274-9_10

Dhyani, D. (2001). *Measuring the web: Metrics, models and methods*. (Master Thesis). Singapore: School of Computer Engineering, Nanyang Technological University.

Dhyani, D., Keong, W., & Bhowmick, S. (2002). A survey of Web metrics. *ACM Computing Surveys, 34*(4), 469–503. doi:10.1145/592642.592645

DeLone, W. H., & McLean, E. R. (1992). Information systems success: The quest for the dependent variable. *Information Systems Research, 3*(1), 60–95. doi:10.1287/isre.3.1.60

Seddon, P.B., Staples, D.S., Patnayakuni, R., & Bowtell, M.J. (1999). The dimensions of information systems success. *Communications of the Association for Information Systems, 2*, 20. Cameron, K.S., & Whetten, D.A. (1983). *Organizational effectiveness: A comparison of multiple models*. Academic Press.

Haddad, S., Melliti, T., Moreaux, P., & Rampacek, S. (2004). Modelling web services interoperability. In *Proceedings of the 6th Int. Conf. on Entreprise Information Systems* (ICEI04), (pp. 14–17). ICEI.

Gudgin, M., Hadley, M., Mendelsohn, N., Moreau, J., & Nielsen, H. (2000). *Simple object access protocol (SOAP)* (Technical Report). World Wide Web Consortium. Retrieved from http://www.w3.org/TR/SOAP/

Bellwood, T., Clment, L., & von Riegen, C. (2002). *Universal description, discovery and integration* (Technical Report). OASIS UDDI Specification Technical Committee. Retrieved from http://www.oasisopen.org/cover/uddi.html

Christensen, E., Curbera, F., Meredith, G., & Weerawarana, S. (2001). *Web services description language (WSDL) 1.1* (Technical Report). World Wide Web Consortium. Retrieved from http://www.w3.org/TR/wsdl

Boutrous-Saab, C., Melliti, T., & Mokdad, L. (2006). Performance evaluation for mobile access to composite web services. In *Proceedings of AICT/ICIW* (pp. 154-159). AICT/ICIW.

Schumaker, R. P., & Chen, H. (2007). Leveraging question answer technology to address terrorism inquiry. *Decision Support Systems*, *43*, 1419–1430. doi:10.1016/j.dss.2006.04.007

Schumaker, R. P., Ginsburg, M., Chen, H. C., & Liu, Y. (2007). An evaluation of the chat and knowledge delivery components of a low-level dialog system: The AZ-ALICE experiment. *Decision Support Systems*, *42*, 2236–2246. doi:10.1016/j.dss.2006.07.001

Schumaker, R. P., Liu, Y., Ginsburg, M., & Chen, H. C. (2007). Evaluating the efficacy of - A terrorism question/answer system. *Communications of the ACM*, *50*, 74–80. doi:10.1145/1272516.1272517

Wacholder, N., Kelly, D., Kantor, P., Rittman, R., Sun, Y., & Bai, B. et al. (2007). A model for quantitative evaluation of an end-to-end question-answering system. *Journal of the American Society for Information Science and Technology*, *58*, 1082–1099. doi:10.1002/asi.20560

Yu, H., Lee, M., Kaufman, D., Ely, J., Osheroff, J. A., Hripcsak, G., & Cimino, J. (2007). Development, implementation, and a cognitive evaluation of a definitional question answering system for physicians. *Journal of Biomedical Informatics*, *40*, 236–251. doi:10.1016/j.jbi.2007.03.002 PMID:17462961

Javeau, C. (1992). L' enquete par questionnaire: Manuel a l'usage du praticien. Bruxelles: Ed. de L' Universite de Bruxelles.

Barabasi, A., Albert, R., & Jeong, A. (1999). Mean field theory for scale free random networks. *Physica A*, *272*, 173–187. doi:10.1016/S0378-4371(99)00291-5

Gao, H., Hong, W., Cui, J., & Xu, Y. (2007). Optimization of principal component analysis in feature extraction. In *Proceedings of the 2007 IEEE International Conference on Mechatronics and Automation*. Harbin, China: IEEE.

Rigou, M., Sirmakessis, S., Stavrinoudis, D., & Xenos, M. (2007). Tools and methods for supporting e-learning communities and their evaluation. In *User-centered design of online learning communities*. Hershey, PA: IGI Global.

## KEY TERMS AND DEFINITIONS

**Evaluation Models:** It is the proposed models that are used to model the effectiveness of the web metrics.

**Probabilistic Models:** Stochastic models which can be expressed by using probabilistic techniques like Bayesian analysis. Estimation of the models could be achieved by applying Monte Carlo Markov Chains (MCMC) techniques.

**Web Graphs:** The term describes the connections of the different levels of the web services using graph theory analysis.

**Web Metrics:** The term web metrics describes a propose measures that used to evaluate the effectiveness of the web service product (web applications, web pages).

**Web Services:** The term *Web services* describes a standardized way of integrating Web-based applications using the XML, SOAP, WSDL and UDDI open standards over an Internet protocol backbone.

# Compilation of References

Aaberge, T., Grøtte, I. P., Haugen, O., Skogseid, I., & Ølnes, S. (2004). Evaluation of tourism websites: A theoretical framework. In A. Frew (Ed.), *Information and communication technologies in tourism 2004* (pp. 305–317). New York: Springer- Wien. doi:10.1007/978-3-7091-0594-8_29

Aaker, D. A. (1991). *Managing brand equity: Capitalizing on the value of a brand name*. New York: The Free Press.

Abanumy, A., Al-Badi, A., & Mayhew, P. (2005). e-Government website accessibility: In-depth evaluation of Saudi Arabia and Oman. *The Electronic. Journal of E-Government*, *3*(3), 99–106.

Abdous, M. (2009). E-learning quality assurance: A process-oriented lifecycle model. *Quality Assurance in Education*, *17*(3), 281–295. doi:10.1108/09684880910970678

Accenture. (2001, April). *eGovernment leadership: Rhetoric vs. reality - Closing the gap*. Retrieved from http://www.epractice.eu/files/media/media_846.pdf

Accenture. (2003). *eGovernment leadership: Engaging the customer*. Retrieved from http://www.accenture.com/us-en/Pages/insight-egovernment-2003-summary.aspx

ACM. (2008). *ACM computer science curriculum 2008: An interim revision of CS 2001*. Retrieved from http://www.acm.org/education/curricula/ComputerScience2008.pdf/view

Adam, S., & Featherstone, M. D. (2007). A comparison of web use in marketing by local government in the United States and Australia. *Database Marketing & Customer Strategy Management*, *14*(4), 297–310. doi:10.1057/palgrave.dbm.3250057

Age UK. (2012). *Aging consumers: Lifestyle and preferences in the current marketplace 2012*. Unpublished.

Agile Alliance. (2013). *Agile alliance: The alliance*. Retrieved April 10th, 2013 from http://www.agilealliance.org/

Akinci, S., Atilgan-Ina, E., & Aksoy, S. (2010). Reassessment of E-S-Qual and E-RecS-QUAL in a pure service setting. *Journal of Business Research*, *63*, 232–240. doi:10.1016/j.jbusres.2009.02.018

Akin, E. (2012). Literature review and discussion on customer loyalty and consciousness. *European Journal of Economics, Finance, and Administrative Sciences*, *51*, 158–173.

Al-adawi, Z., Yousafzai, S., & Pallister, J. (2005). Conceptual model of citizen adoption of e-government. In *Proceedings of the Second International Conference on Innovations in Information Technology*. Retrieved April 10, 2013, from http://www.it-innovations.ae/iit005/proceedings/articles/G_6_IIT05-Al-Adawi.pdf

Al-Hawari, M., & Ward, T. (2006). The effect of automated service quality on Australian banks' financial performance and the mediating role of customer satisfaction. *Marketing Intelligence & Planning*, *24*(2), 127–147. doi:10.1108/02634500610653991

Almarabeh, T., & Abu Ali, A. (2010). A general framework for e-government: Definition, maturity, challenges, opportunities and success. *European Journal of Scientific Research*, *39*, 29–42.

Alptekin, S. E., & Karsak, E. E. (2011). An integrated decision framework for evaluating and selecting e-learning products. *Applied Soft Computing*, *11*, 2990–2998. doi:10.1016/j.asoc.2010.11.023

Alt, J. E., Lassen, D. D., & Skilling, D. (2008, Fall). Fiscal transparency, gubernatorial approval, and the scale of government: Evidence from the states. *State Politics & Policy Quarterly*, 230.

Anderson, R. E., & Srinivasan, S. S. (2003). E-satisfaction and e-loyalty: A contingency framework. *Psychology and Marketing*, 20(2), 123–138. doi:10.1002/mar.10063

Ardito, C., de Marsico, M., Lanzilotti, R., Levialdi, S., Roselli, T., Rossano, V., & Tersigni, M. (2004). Usability of e-learning tools. In *Proceedings of the Working Conference on Advanced Visual Interfaces*, (pp. 80-84). AVI.

Arnesen & Danielsson. (2007). *Protecting citizen privacy in digital government*. Hershey, PA: Idea Group Reference.

Asiimwe, E. N., & Lim, N. (2010). Usability of government websites in Uganda. *Electronic. Journal of E-Government*, 8(1), 1–12.

Au Yeung, T., & Law, R. (2006). Evaluation of usability: A study of hotel websites in Hong Kong. *Journal of Hospitality & Tourism Research (Washington, D.C.)*, 30(4), 452–473. doi:10.1177/1096348006290115

Aula, A. (2005). User study on older adults' use of the web and search engines. *Universal Access Information Society*, 4, 67–81. doi:10.1007/s10209-004-0097-7

Baker, D. L. (2009). Advancing e-government performance in the United States through enhanced usability benchmarks. *Government Information Quarterly*, 26(1), 82–88. doi:10.1016/j.giq.2008.01.004

Baker, L. (1989). Metacognition, comprehension monitoring, and the adult reader. *Educational Psychology Review*, 1, 3–38. doi:10.1007/BF01326548

Bannister, F. (2007). The curse of the benchmark: An assessment of the validity and value of e-government comparisons. *International Review of Administrative Sciences*, 73(2), 171–188. doi:10.1177/0020852307077959

Baowaly, M., Hossain, M., & Bhuiyan, M. (2012). Accessibility analysis and evaluation for government-websites in developing countries: Case study Bangladesh. *Computer Engineering and Intelligent Systems, 3*(4).

Barabasi, A., Albert, R., & Jeong, A. (1999). Mean field theory for scale free random networks. *Physica A, 272*, 173–187. doi:10.1016/S0378-4371(99)00291-5

Barbour, R. S. (2005). Making sense of focus groups. *Medical Education*, 39, 742–750. doi:10.1111/j.1365-2929.2005.02200.x PMID:15960795

Bar-Ilan, J., & Belous, Y. (2007). Children as architects of web directories: An exploratory study. *Journal of the American Society for Information Science and Technology*, 58(6), 895–907. doi:10.1002/asi.20566

Barkas-Avila, J. A., Oberholzer, G., Schmutz, G., de Vito, M., & Opwis, K. (2007). Usable error message presentation in the world wide web: Do not show errors right away. *Interacting with Computers*, 19, 330–341. doi:10.1016/j.intcom.2007.01.003

Barnes, S. J., & Vidgen, R. T. (2003). An integrative approach to the assessment of e-commerce quality. *Journal of Electronic Commerce Research*, 3(3), 114–127.

Barry, B. K., & Carson, R. G. (2004). The consequences of resistance training for movement control in older adults. *Journal of Gerontology*, 59(7), 730–754. PMID:15304540

Bartikowski, B., & Llosa, S. (2004). Customer satisfaction measurement: Comparing four methods of attribute categorizations. *The Service Industries Journal*, 24, 67–72. doi:10.1080/0264206042000275190

Bass, F. M. (1974). The theory of stochastic preference and brand switching. *JMR, Journal of Marketing Research*, 11(1), 1–20. doi:10.2307/3150989

Bauer, H. H., Falk, T., & Hammerschmidt, M. (2006). eTransQual: A transaction process-based approach for capturing service quality in online shopping. *Journal of Business Research*, 59(7), 866–875. doi:10.1016/j.jbusres.2006.01.021

Bauernfeind, U., & Mitsche, N. (2008). The application of the data envelopment analysis for tourism website evaluation. *Information Technology & Tourism*, 10(3), 245–257. doi:10.3727/109830508787157317

Baum, C., & Di Maio, A. (2000). *Gartner's four phases of e-government model*. Retrieved April 15, 2013, from http://www.gartner.com

Bawden, P. (1998). Nortel's practical path to customer loyalty. *Measuring Business Excellence*, 2(1), 8–13. doi:10.1108/eb025513

Bean, L., Carstens, D., & Barlow, J. (2008). E-government knowledge management (KM) and data mining challenges: Past, present and future. In H. Rahman (Ed.), *Social and political implications of data mining: Knowledge management in e-government*. Hershey, PA: IGI Global.

Bearden, W. O., & Teel, J. E. (1983). Selected determinants of consumer satisfaction and complaint reports. *JMR, Journal of Marketing Research*, *20*(1), 21–28. doi:10.2307/3151408

Beatty, S. E., Kahle, L. R., & Homer, P. (1988). The involvement-commitment model: Theory and implications. *Journal of Business Research*, *16*(2), 149–167. doi:10.1016/0148-2963(88)90039-2

Becker, S. A. (2004). E-government visual accessibility for older adults users. *Social Science Computer Review*, *22*(1), 11–23. doi:10.1177/0894439303259876

Becker, S. A., Carstens, D. S., & Linton, T. M. (2010). Heuristic evaluation of state electronic government to promote usability for citizens of all age. *Journal of Management & Engineering Integration*, *3*(2), 24–31.

Beldona, S., & Cai, L. A. (2006). An exploratory evaluation of rural tourism websites. *Journal of Convention & Event Tourism*, *8*(1), 69–80. doi:10.1300/J452v08n01_04

Bellwood, T., Clment, L., & von Riegen, C. (2002). *Universal description, discovery and integration* (Technical Report). OASIS UDDI Specification Technical Committee. Retrieved from http://www.oasisopen.org/cover/uddi.html

Belzile, J. A., & Öberg, G. (2012). Where to begin? Grappling with how to user participant interaction in focus group design. *Qualitative Research*, *12*(4), 459–472. doi:10.1177/1468794111433089

Benbya, H., Passiante, G., & Belbaly, N. A. (2004). Corporate portal: A tool for knowledge management synchronization. *International Journal of Information Management*, *24*(3), 201–220. doi:10.1016/j.ijinfomgt.2003.12.012

Berman, E. (1997). Dealing with cynical citizens. *Public Administration Review*, *57*(2), 105–112. doi:10.2307/977058

Bertot, J. C., Jaeger, P. T., & Grimes, J. M. (2012). Promoting transparency and accountability through ITC's, social media, and collaborative e-government. *Transforming Government: People. Process and Policy*, *6*(1), 78–91.

Beynon-Davies, P. (2007). Models for e-government. *Transforming Government: People. Process and Policy*, *1*(1), 7–28.

Bigné, E., Ruiz, C., & Sanz, S. (2005). The impact of internet user shopping patterns and demographics on consumer mobile buying behaviour. *Journal of Electronic Commerce Research*, *6*(3).

Bilal, D., & Watson, J. S. (1998*). Children's paperless projects: Inspiring research via the web*. Paper presented at the 64th General Conference of the International Federation of Library Associations & Institutions. Amsterdam, the Netherlands.

Bilal, D. (2000). Children's use of the yahooligans web search engine: I. cognitive, physical, and affective behaviors on fact-based search tasks. *Journal of the American Society for Information Science American Society for Information Science*, *51*(7), 646–665. doi:10.1002/(SICI)1097-4571(2000)51:7<646::AID-ASI7>3.0.CO;2-A

Bilal, D. (2001). Children's use of the yahooligans! web search engine: II. cognitive and physical behaviors on research tasks. *Journal of the American Society for Information Science and Technology*, *52*(2), 118–136. doi:10.1002/1097-4571(2000)9999:9999<::AID-ASI1038>3.0.CO;2-R

Bilal, D. (2002). Children's use of the yahooligans! web search engine. III. cognitive and physical behaviors on fully self-generated search tasks. *Journal of the American Society for Information Science and Technology*, *53*(13), 1170–1183. doi:10.1002/asi.10145

Bilal, D., & Kirby, J. (2002). Differences and similarities in information seeking: Children and adults as web users. *Information Processing & Management*, *38*(5), 649–670. doi:10.1016/S0306-4573(01)00057-7

Blake, M. (1993). Internet access for older people. *Aslib Proceedings*, *50*(10), 308–315. doi:10.1108/eb051509

Blass, E., & Davis, A. (2003). Building on solid foundations: Establishing criteria for e-learning development. *Journal of Further and Higher Education*, *27*(3), 227–245. doi:10.1080/0309877032000098662

Blythe, M. A., Monk, A. F., & Doughty, K. (2005). Socially dependable design: The challenge of ageing populations for HCI. *Interacting with Computers*, *17*, 672–689. doi:10.1016/j.intcom.2005.09.005

Bonson-Ponte, E., Escobar-Rodriguez, T., & Flores-Munoz, F. (2008). Navigation quality as a key value for the webpage of a financial entity. *Online Information Review*, *32*(5), 623–634. doi:10.1108/14684520810914007

Bontis, N., Booker, L. D., & Serenko, A. (2007). The mediating effect of organizational reputation on customer loyalty and service recommendation in the banking industry. *Management Decision*, *45*(9), 1426–1445. doi:10.1108/00251740710828681

Boren, M. T., & Ramey, J. (2000). Thinking aloud: Reconciling theory and practice. *IEEE Transactions on Professional Communication*, *43*, 261–278. doi:10.1109/47.867942

Borgman, C. L., Hirsh, S. G., Walter, V. A., & Gallagher, A. L. (1995). Children's searching behavior on browsing and keyword online catalogs: The science library catalog project. *Journal of the American Society for Information Science American Society for Information Science*, *46*(9), 663–684. doi:10.1002/(SICI)1097-4571(199510)46:9<663::AID-ASI4>3.0.CO;2-2

Bose, R. (2002). Customer relationship management: Key components for IT success. *Industrial Management & Data Systems*, *102*(2), 89–97. doi:10.1108/02635570210419636

Boutrous-Saab, C., Melliti, T., & Mokdad, L. (2006). Performance evaluation for mobile access to composite web services. In *Proceedings of AICT/ICIW* (pp. 154-159). AICT/ICIW.

Boyd, D. M., & Ellison, N. B. (2008). Social network sites: Definition, history, and scholarship. *Journal of Computer-Mediated Communication*, *13*(1), 210–230. doi:10.1111/j.1083-6101.2007.00393.x

Bradley, M. M., & Lang, P. J. (1994). Measuring emotion: The self-assessment manikin and the semantic differential. *Journal of Behavior Therapy and Experimental Psychiatry*, *25*(1), 49–59. doi:10.1016/0005-7916(94)90063-9 PMID:7962581

Brajnik, G. (2000). Automatic web usability evaluation: What needs to be done? In *Proceedings of the 6th Conference on Human Factors & the Web*. IEEE.

Brajnik, G. (2001). Towards valid quality models for websites. In *Proceedings of Human Factors and the Web*. Retrieved from www.dimi.uniud.it/~giorgio/papers/hfweb01.html

Brajnik, G. (2002). *Quality models based on automatic webtesting*. Paper presented at CHI2002 Workshop - Automatically Evaluating Usability of Web Sites. Minneapolis, MN. Retrieved from http://www.dimi.uniud.it/~giorgio/papers/quality-models.html

Brereton, E. (2005). Don't neglect usability in the total cost of ownership. *Communications of the ACM*, *47*(7), 10–11.

Bressolles, G., & Nantel, J. (2004). Electronic service quality: A comparison of three measurement scales. In *Proceedings of the 33th EMAC Conference* (pp. 1–7). Murcia: EMAC.

British Standards Institute. (2010). *BS 8878.2010 - Web accessibility code of practice*. Retrieved April 3, 2013, from http://shop.bsigroup.com/en/ProductDetail/?pid=000000000030180388

British Standards. (1998). *ISO 9241-11:1998 - Ergonomic requirements for office work with visual display terminals (VDTs) -- Part 11: Guidance on usability*. Retrieved April 1, 2013, from http://www.iso.org/iso/catalogue_detail.htm?csnumber=16883

British Standards. (2010). *EN ISO 9241-210:2010 - Ergonomics of human-system interaction -- Part 210: Human-centred design for interactive systems*. Retrieved March 28, 2013 from http://www.iso.org/iso/catalogue_detail.htm?csnumber=52075

Brock, J. J. (1984). Competitor analysis: Some practical approaches. *Industrial Marketing Management*, *13*(4), 225–231. doi:10.1016/0019-8501(84)90017-8

Brown, A. L., & DeLoache, J. S. (1978). Skills, plans, and self-regulation. In R. S. Siegler (Ed.), *Children's thinking: What develops?* (pp. 3–35). Hillsdale, NJ: Erlbaum.

Brown, G. H. (1952). Brand loyalty: Fact or fiction? *Advertising Age, 23*, 53–55.

Buhalis, & Schertler. (Eds.). (1999). *Information and communication technologies in tourism 1999.* New York: Springer-Wien.

Buhalis, D. (2003). *eTourism: Information technology for strategic tourism management.* Upper Saddle River, NJ: Pearson - Financial Times/Prentice-Hall.

Buhalis, D. (1994). Information and telecommunications technologies as a strategic tool for small and medium tourism enterprises in the contemporary business environment. In *Tourism--The state of the art.* London: J. Wiley and Sons.

Buhalis, D. (1998). Strategic use of information technologies in the tourism industry. *Tourism Management, 19*(5), 409–421. doi:10.1016/S0261-5177(98)00038-7

Buhalis, D. (2000). Distribution channels in the changing travel industry. *International Journal of Tourism Research, 2*(5), 357–359. doi:10.1002/1522-1970(200009/10)2:5<357::AID-JTR233>3.0.CO;2-B

Buhalis, D., & Costa, C. (2006). *Tourism business frontiers.* Oxford, UK: Elsevier.

Buhalis, D., & Spada, A. (2000). Destination management systems: Criteria for success – An exploratory research. In D. R. Fesenmaier, S. Klein, & D. Buhalis (Eds.), *Information and communication technologies in tourism 2000* (pp. 473–484). New York: Springer-Wien. doi:10.1007/978-3-7091-6291-0_43

Burmeister, O. K. (2010). Websites for seniors: Cognitive accessibility. *International Journal of Emerging Technologies and Society, 8*(2), 99–113.

Burn, J., & Robins, G. (2003). Moving towards egovernment: A case study of organisational change processes. *Logistics Information Management, 16*(1), 25–35. doi:10.1108/09576050310453714

Büyüközkan, G., Arsenyan, J., & Ertek, G. (2010). Evaluation of e-learning web sites using fuzzy axiomatic design based approach. *International Journal of Computational Intelligence Systems, 3*(1), 28–42.

Caemmerer, B., & Wilson, A. (2010). Customer feedback mechanisms and organisational learning in service operations. *International Journal of Operations & Production Management, 30*(3), 288–311. doi:10.1108/01443571011024638

Cai, S., & Jun, M. (2003). Internet users' perceptions of online service quality: A comparison of online buyers and information searchers. *Managing Service Quality, 13*(6), 504–519. doi:10.1108/09604520310506568

Calero, R. C., & Piattini, M. (2005). Classifying web metrics using the web quality model. *Online Information Review, 29*(3), 227–248. doi:10.1108/14684520510607560

Capgemini. (2010). *Digitizing public services in Europe: Putting ambition into action - 9th benchmark measurement* (Technical Report by European Commission). Directorate General for Information Society and Media. Retrieved April 12, 2013, from http://ec.europa.eu/information_society/newsroom/cf/document.cfm?action=display&doc_id=747

Cappel, J., & Huang, Z. (2007). A usability analysis of company websites. *Journal of Computer Information Systems, 48*(1), 117–123.

Carmeli, E., Patish, H., & Coleman, R. (2003). The aging hand. *Journal of Gerontology: Medical Sciences, 58A*(2), 146–152. doi:10.1093/gerona/58.2.M146 PMID:12586852

Carme, S., & Germà, C. (2002). *Predicting overall service quality: A structural equation modelling approach.* Developments in Social Science Methodology.

Carmichael, A., Newell, A. F., & Morgan, M. (2007). The efficacy of narrative video for raising awareness in ICT designers about older users' requirements. *Interacting with Computers, 19*, 587–596. doi:10.1016/j.intcom.2007.06.001

Carmines, E. G., & Zeller, R. A. (1979). *Reliability and validity assessment (Stage university paper series on quantitative applications in the social sciences, no. 7010).* Beverly Hills, CA: Sage.

Carroll, J. (1997). Human-computer interaction: Psychology as a science of design. *International Journal of Human-Computer Studies, 46,* 501–522.

Carstens, D. S. (2005). Cultural barriers to human-computer interaction. In S. Marshall, W. Taylor, & X. Yu (Eds.), *Encyclopedia of developing regional communities with information and communication technology.* Hershey, PA: IDEA Group Inc. doi:10.4018/978-1-59140-575-7.ch026

Carstens, D. S., & Becker, S. A. (2009). A heuristic study on the usability of state government performance data web sites. *Issues in Innovation, 4*(1), 15–44.

Carstens, D. S., & Patterson, P. (2005). Usability study of travel websites. *Journal of Usability Studies, 1*(1), 47–61.

Carter, L., & Belanger, F. (2004). Citizen adoption of electronic government initiatives. In *Proceedings of 37th Annual Hawaii International Conference on System Sciences.* IEEE.

Carter, L., & Belanger, F. (2005). The utilization of e-government services: Citizen trust, innovation and acceptance factors. *Information Systems Journal, 15*(1), 5–25. doi:10.1111/j.1365-2575.2005.00183.x

Casaló, L., Flavián, C., & Guinaliú, M. (2005). The role of accessibility and commitment in the development of an e-government strategy. In *Proceedings of eGovernment Workshop '05 (eGOV05).* Brunel University.

Cassel, C. M., Hackl, P., & Westlund, A. H. (2000). On measurement of intangible assets: A study of robustness of partial least squares. *Total Quality Management, 11*(7), S897–S907. doi:10.1080/09544120050135443

Castillo, J. C., Hartson, H. R., & Hix, D. (1998). Remote usability evaluation: Can users report their own critical incidents? In *Proceedings of the Conference on Human Factors on Computing Systems* (CHI '98), (pp. 253-254). New York: ACM Press.

Cebi, S. (2013). Determining importance degrees of website design parameters based on interactions and types of websites. *Decision Support Systems, 54,* 1030–1043. doi:10.1016/j.dss.2012.10.036

Centre for HCI Design. (2005). *The web access and inclusion for disabled people: A formal investigation conducted by the disability rights commission.* Retrieved June 27, 2013, from http://hcid.soi.city.ac.uk/research/DRC_Report.pdf, http://hcid.soi.city.ac.uk/research/Drc.html

Chadwick-Dias A., McNulty, & Tullis. (2003). Web usability and age: How design changes can improve performance. *CUU, 30*–37.

Chadwick-Dias, A., Tedesco, D., & Tullis, T. (2004). Older adults and web usability: Is web experience the same as web expertise? In *Proceedings of CHI 2004,* (pp. 1391-1394). ACM.

Chaffey, D. (2004). *E-business and e-commerce management* (2nd ed.). Upper Saddle River, NJ: Prentice Hall.

Chambers, C. T., & Johnston, C. (2002). Developmental differences in children's use of rating scales. *Journal of Pediatric Psychology, 27*(1), 27–36. doi:10.1093/jpepsy/27.1.27 PMID:11726677

Chandler, H. E. (1998). Towards opend government: Official information on the web. *New Library World, 99,* 230–237. doi:10.1108/03074809810236784

Charness, N., & Czaja, S. J. (2005). Adaptation to new technologies. In *The Cambridge handbook of age and ageing.* New York: Cambridge University Press.

Chase, B. W., Taylor, R. L., & Phillips, R. H. (2008). Government-wide information and operational accountability. *The Journal of Government Financial Management, 57*(3), 48.

Chen, C. (2006). *Information visualization: Beyond the horizon.* London: Springer.

Chevalier, A., Dommes, A., & Martins, D. (2012). The effects of ageing and website ergonomic quality on the internet information searching. *Ageing and Society,* 1–27.

Chevalier, A., & Kicka, M. (2006). Web designers and web users: Influence of the ergonomic quality of the web site on the information search. *International Journal of Human-Computer Studies, 64,* 1031–1048. doi:10.1016/j.ijhcs.2006.06.002

Chisnell, D. E., Redish, J., & Lee, A. (2006). New heuristics for understanding older adults as web users. *Technical Communication, 53,* 39–59.

Choenni, R., Kalidien, S. N., Ariel, A., & Moolenaar, D. E. G. (2011). A framework to monitor public safety based on a data space approach. In *Electronic government and electronic participation: Joint proceedings of ongoing research and projects, EGOV and ePart 2011* (pp. 196–202). Linz, Germany: Trauner Verlag.

Choudrie, J., Weerakkody, V., & Jones, S. (2005). Realising e-government in the UK: Rural and urban challenges. *The Journal of Enterprise Information Management, 18*(5), 568–585. doi:10.1108/17410390510624016

Christensen, E., Curbera, F., Meredith, G., & Weerawarana, S. (2001). *Web services description language (WSDL) 1.1* (Technical Report). World Wide Web Consortium. Retrieved from http://www.w3.org/TR/wsdl

Chua, A., Goh, D., & Ang, R. (2012). Web 2.0 applications in government websites: Prevalence, use and correlations with perceived website quality. *Online Information Review, 36.*

Churchill, G. A., & Surprenant. (1982). An investigation into the determinants of customer satisfaction. *JMR, Journal of Marketing Research, 19*(4), 491–504. doi:10.2307/3151722

Clark, D. R. (2009). *Bloom's taxonomy of learning domains - The three types of learning.* Retrieved from http://www.nwlink.com/~Donclark/hrd/bloom.html.

Clarkson, J., Coleman, R., Hosking, I., & Waller, S. (Eds.). (2007). *Inclusive design toolkit.* Cambridge, UK: University of Cambridge.

Clemons, E.K., Hann, I., & Hitt, L.M. (2002). Price dispersion and differentiation in online travel: An empirical investigation management science, *48*(4), 534–549.

Clemons, E., Hann, I., & Hitt, L. (2002). The nature of competition in electronic markets: An empirical investigation of on-line travel agent offerings. *Management Science, 48*(4), 534–549. doi:10.1287/mnsc.48.4.534

Coleman, R. (2004). Foreword. In *Countering design exclusion: An introduction to inclusive design.* London: Springer-Verlag.

Coleman, S. (2005). The lonely citizen: Indirect representation in an age of networks. *Political Communication, 22*(2), 197–214. doi:10.1080/10584600590933197

Collier, G., Norris, D. M., Mason, J., Robson, R., & Lefrere, P. (2003). A revolution in knowledge sharing. *EDUCAUSE Review, 38*(5).

Cooke, L. (2010). Assessing concurrent think-aloud protocol as a usability test method: A technical communication approach. *IEEE Transactions on Professional Communication, 35*, 202–215. doi:10.1109/TPC.2010.2052859

Costabile, M. F., Roselli, T., Lanzilotti, R., Ardito, C., & Rossano, V. (2007). A holistic approach to the evaluation of e-learning systems. In *Universal Access in Human-Computer Interaction (LNCS)* (Vol. 4556, pp. 530–538). Berlin: Springer. doi:10.1007/978-3-540-73283-9_59

Coursaris, C. K., & Kim, D. J. (2011). A meta-analytical review of empirical mobile usability studies. *Journal of Usability Studies, 6*(3), 117–171.

Coursey, D., & Norris, D. F. (2008). Models of e-government: Are they correct? An empirical assessment. *Public Administration Review, 68*(3), 523–536. doi:10.1111/j.1540-6210.2008.00888.x

Court of Audit. (2012). *Prestaties in de strafrechtsketen.* The Hague, The Netherlands: Author.

Craven, J., & Booth, H. (2006). Putting awareness into practice: Practical steps for conducting usability tests. *Library Review, 55*(3), 179–194. doi:10.1108/00242530610655984

Crisp, A. M., & Executive, P. S. A. (1999). *Impact of electronic commerce on the european pharmaceutical sector.* Efpia.

Cristobal, E., Flavián, C., & Guinalíu, M. (2007). Perceived e-service quality (PeSQ): Measurement validation and effects on consumer satisfaction and web site loyalty. *Managing Service Quality, 17*(3), 317–340. doi:10.1108/09604520710744326

Cronin, J. J., & Taylor, S. A. (1992). Measuring service quality: a re-examination and extension. *Journal of Marketing, 56*(3), 125–131. doi:10.2307/1252296

Crosby, L. A., & Taylor, J. R. (1983). Psychological commitment and its effects on post-decision evaluation and preference stability among voters. *The Journal of Consumer Research, 9*(4), 413–431. doi:10.1086/208935

Cunliffe, D. (2000). Developing usable web sites: A review and model. *Internet Research, 10*, 295–307. doi:10.1108/10662240010342577

Curran, J. M., Meuter, M. L., & Surprenant, C. F. (2003). Intentions to use self-service technologies: A confluence of multiple attitudes. *Journal of Service Research, 5*(3), 209–224. doi:10.1177/1094670502238916

Curtin, J. I. (2010, February 17). Current government financial reporting leaves taxpayers dissatisfied and distrustful. *Business Wire.*

Czaja, S. J., & Lee, C. C. (2003). Designing computer systems for older adults. In *The human-computer interaction handbook: Fundamentals, evolving technologies and emerging applications.* Hoboken, NJ: Lawrence Erlbaum Associates Publishers.

Czepiel, J. A., & Gilmore, R. (1987). Exploring the concept of loyalty in services. In J. A. Czepiel, C. Congram, & J. Shanahan (Eds.), *The services challenge: Integrating for competitive advantage* (pp. 91–94). Chicago: American Marketing Association.

Dabholkar, P. A., Shepherd, C. D., & Thorpe, D. I. (2000). A comprehensive framework for service quality: An investigation of critical conceptual and measurement issues through a longitudinal study. *Journal of Retailing, 76*(2), 131–139. doi:10.1016/S0022-4359(00)00029-4

Dadashzadeh, M. (2010). Social media in government: From egovernment to egovernance. *Journal of Business & Economics Research, 8*(11), 81–86.

Danielson, D. R. (2002). Web navigation and the behavioural effects of constantly visible site maps. *Interacting with Computers, 14*, 601–618. doi:10.1016/S0953-5438(02)00024-3

Davison, R. M., Wagner, C., & Ma, L. C. (2005). From government to e-government: A transition model. *Information Technology & People, 18*(3), 280–299. doi:10.1108/09593840510615888

Day, E. (2002). The role of value in consumer satisfaction. *Journal of Consumer Satisfaction. Dissatisfaction and Complaining Behavior, 15*, 22–32.

De Jong, M. (1998). *Reader feedback in text design: Validity of the plus-minus method for the pretesting of public information brochures.* Atlanta, GA: Rodopi.

De Jong, M., & Lentz, L. (1996). Expert judgments versus reader feedback: A comparison of text evaluation techniques. *Journal of Technical Writing and Communication, 26*, 507–519.

De Jong, M., & Lentz, L. (2001). Focus: Design and evaluation of a software tool for collecting reader feedback. *Technical Communication Quarterly, 10*, 387–401. doi:10.1207/s15427625tcq1004_2

De Jong, M., & Lentz, L. (2006). Scenario evaluation of municipal web sites: Development and use of an expert-focused evaluation tool. *Government Information Quarterly, 23*, 191–206. doi:10.1016/j.giq.2005.11.007

De Jong, M., & Schellens, P. J. (2001). Readers' background characteristics and their feedback on documents: The influence of gender and educational level on evaluation results. *Journal of Technical Writing and Communication, 31*, 267–281. doi:10.2190/0XJ7-4044-G7LC-AT8Y

De Ruyter, K., Wetzels, M., & Kleijnen, M. (2000). Customer adoption of e-service: An experimental study. *International Journal of Service Industry Management, 12*(2), 184–207. doi:10.1108/09564230110387542

Delias, P., Matsatsinis, N. F., & Karagounakis, A. (2007). Towards a multi-criterion web-based tool for evaluation of an e-learning system. In Innovations in E-learning, Instruction Technology, Assessment, and Engineering Education 2007, (pp. 289-293). IEEE.

DeLone, W. H., & McLean, E. R. (1992). Information systems success: The quest for the dependent variable. *Information Systems Research, 3*(1), 60–95. doi:10.1287/isre.3.1.60

Department for Work and Pensions. (2005). Focus on older people. In *The freetirement generation.* SIRC. Retrieved on March 27, 2013 from http://www.sirc.org/publik/freetirement_generation.shtml

Devaney, E. E. (2009, May 5). *Testimony of the honorable Earl E. Devaney.* Retrieved from http://gop.science.house.gov/media/hearings/oversight09/may5/devaney.pdf

Dhyani, D. (2001). *Measuring the web: Metrics, models and methods*. (Master Thesis). Singapore: School of Computer Engineering, Nanyang Technological University.

Dhyani, D., Keong, W., & Bhowmick, S. (2002). A survey of Web metrics. *ACM Computing Surveys, 34*(4), 469–503. doi:10.1145/592642.592645

Dick, A., & Basu, K. (1994). Customer loyalty: Toward an integrated conceptual framework. *Journal of the Academy of Marketing Science, 22*(2), 99–113. doi:10.1177/0092070394222001

Dickenson, A., Eisma, R., & Gregor, P. (2011). The barriers that older novices encounter to computer use. *Universal Access Information Society, 10*, 261–266. doi:10.1007/s10209-010-0208-6

Dickinson, A., Arnott, J., & Prior, S. (2007). Methods for human–computer interaction research with older people. *Behaviour & Information Technology, 26*, 343–352. doi:10.1080/01449290601176948

Dimitriadis, S., & Baltas, G. (2005). *E-business and marketing*. Athens, Greece: Rosili Publications.

Dingsøyra, T., Nerurc, S., Balijepally, V., & Moea, N. B. (2012). A decade of agile methodologies: Towards explaining agile software development. *Journal of Systems and Software, 85*, 1213–1221. doi:10.1016/j.jss.2012.02.033

Docampo Rama, M., Ridder, H., & Bouma, H. (2001). Technology generation and age in using layered user interfaces. *Technology Generation, 1*(1), 1–16.

Donthu, N., & Garcia, A. (1999). The internet shopper. *Journal of Advertising Research, 39*(3), 52–58.

Doolin, B., Burgess, L., & Cooper, J. (2002). Evaluating the use of the web for tourism marketing: A case study from New Zealand. *Tourism Management, 23*(5), 557–561. doi:10.1016/S0261-5177(02)00014-6

Douglas, A., & Mills, J. E. (2005). Staying afloat in the tropics: Applying a structural equation model approach to evaluating national tourism organization websites in the Caribbean. *Journal of Travel & Tourism Marketing, 17*(2), 269–293.

Doumpos, M., & Zopounidis, C. (2002). *Multicriteria decision aid classification methods*. Dordrecht, The Netherlands: Kluwer Academic Publishers.

Druin, A., Hutchinson, H., Foss, E., Hatley, L., Golub, E., Leigh Guha, M., & Fails, J. (2009). *How children search the internet with keyword interfaces*. Paper presented at the 8th International Conference on Interaction Design and Children. Como, Italy.

Druin, A. (2003). What children can teach us: Developing digital libraries for children with children. *The Library Quarterly, 75*(1), 20–41. doi:10.1086/428691

Duarte, D. L., & Snyder, N. T. (1999). *Mastering virtual teams*. San Francisco: Jossey-Bass.

Duncan, J., & Holliday, W. (2008). The role of information architecture in designing a third-generation library web site. *College & Research Libraries*, 301–318.

Dutch Government. (2012, October). *Rutte II: Coalition agreement: Building bridges*. The Hague, The Netherlands: Author.

Dutka, A. (1995). *AMA handbook of customer satisfaction: A complete guide to research, planning and implementation*. Chicago: NTC Business Books.

Dutton, W. H., & Shepherd, A. (2006). Trust in the Internet as an experience technology information. *Communicatio Socialis, 9*(4), 433–451.

Earl, M. (1996). *Information management: The organizational dimension*. Oxford, UK: Oxford University Press.

Eastman, J. K., & Iyer, R. (2004). The elderly's uses and attitudes towards the Internet. *Journal of Consumer Marketing, 21*(3), 208–220. doi:10.1108/07363760410534759

E-Business Watch / European Commission. (2003b). *ICT & e-business in the tourism sector*. No.13 II/July 2003.

E-Business Watch / European Commission. (2004a). *Electronic business in tourism - The quantitative picture: Diffusion of ICT and e-business in 2003/04*. Sector Report No. 07-I, May 2004.

E-Business Watch / European Commission. (2004b). *Electronic business in tourism - Key issues, case studies, conclusions*. Sector Report No. 07-II, August 2004.

E-Business Watch / European Commission. (2006). *ICT & e-business in the tourism sector - ICT adoption and e-business activity in 2006.* Sector Report No. 8, July 2006.

Edosomwan, J. A. (1993). *Customer and market-driven quality management.* Milwaukee, WI: ASQC Quality Press.

Ehlers, U.-D. (2004). Quality in e-learning from a learner's perspective. *EURODL European Journal of Open, Distance and E-learning.* Retrieved from http://www.eurodl.org/index.php?tag=120&article=230&article=101

Ehlers, U.-D., & Pawlowski, J. (2006). Quality in European e-learning: An introduction. In *Handbook on quality and standardisation in e-learning* (pp. 1–13). Berlin: Springer. doi:10.1007/3-540-32788-6_1

Elling, S. (2012). *Evaluating website quality: Five studies on user-focused evaluation methods.* (Dissertation). Utrecht University, Utrecht, The Netherlands.

Elling, S., Lentz, L., & De Jong, M. (2012a). Users' abilities to review website pages. *Journal of Business and Technical Communication, 26,* 171–201. doi:10.1177/1050651911429920

Elling, S., Lentz, L., & De Jong, M. (2012b). Combining concurrent think-aloud protocols and eye tracking observations: An analysis of verbalizations and silences. *IEEE Transactions on Professional Communication, 55,* 206–220. doi:10.1109/TPC.2012.2206190

Ellis, R. D., & Kurniawan, S. H. (2000). Increasing the usability of online information for older users: A case study in participatory design. *International Journal of Human-Computer Interaction, 12*(2), 263–276. doi:10.1207/S15327590IJHC1202_6

Elrod, T. (1988). A management science assessment of a behavioral measure of brand loyalty. In M. J. Houston (Ed.), *Advances in consumer research* (pp. 481–486). Provo, UT: Association for Consumer Research.

Equality Commission for Northern Ireland. (2004). *Disability discrimination law in Northern Ireland - A short guide.* Retrieved from http://www.equalityni.org/archive/pdf/disabilitysgfinal04.pdf

Ertl, B., Ebner, K., & Kikis-Papadakis, K. (2010). An infrastructure approach for the evaluation of e-learning. *Communications in Computer and Information Science, 111,* 98–104. doi:10.1007/978-3-642-16318-0_11

Eschenfelder, K. R., & Miller, C. (2005). *The openness of government websites: Toward a socio-technical government website evaluation toolkit.* Seattle, WA: MacArthur Foundation/ALA Office of Information Technology Policy Internet Credibility and the User Symposium.

Fairweather, N., & Rogerson, S. (2006). Towards morally defensible e-government interactions with citizens. *Journal of Information. Communication and Ethics in Society, 4*(4), 173–180. doi:10.1108/14779960680000290

Fang, Z. (2002). E-government in the digital era: Concept, practice and development. *International Journal of The computer. The Internet and Management, 10*(20), 1–22.

Fassnacht, M., & Koese, I. (2006). Quality of electronic services: Conceptualizing and testing a hierarchical model. *Journal of Service Research, 9*(1), 19–37. doi:10.1177/1094670506289531

Feng, R., Morrison, A. M., & Ismail, J. A. (2003). East versus west: A comparison of online destination marketing in China and the U.S. *Journal of Vacation Marketing, 10*(1), 43–56. doi:10.1177/135676670301000105

Flavian, C., Guinaliu, M., & Gurrea, R. (2006). The role played by perceived usability, satisfaction and consumer trust on website loyalty. *Information & Management, 43,* 1–14. doi:10.1016/j.im.2005.01.002

Fornell, C., & Cha, J. (1994). Partial least squares. In *Advanced methods of marketing research.* Oxford, UK: Blackwell.

Fornell, C., & Larcker, D. F. (1981). Evaluating structural equation models with unobservable variables and measurement error. *JMR, Journal of Marketing Research, 28*(1), 39–50. doi:10.2307/3151312

Fowler, F. J. Jr. (1993). *Survey research methods.* Newbury Park, CA: Sage Publications.

Frew, D. A. (1999). Destination marketing system strategies: Refining and extending an assessment framework. In D. Buhalis, & W. Schertler (Eds.), *Information and communication technologies in tourism 1999* (pp. 398–407). New York: Springer-Wien. doi:10.1007/978-3-7091-6373-3_39

Fuentes-Blasco, M., Gil-Saura, I., Berenguer-Contrí, G., & Moliner-Velázquez, B. (2010). Measuring the antecedents of e-loyalty and the effect of switching costs on website. *The Service Industries Journal, 30*(11), 1837–1852. doi:10.1080/02642060802626774

Ganesan-Lim, C., Russell-Bennett, R., & Dagger, T. (2008). The impact of service contact type and demographic characteristics on service quality perceptions. *Journal of Services Marketing, 22*(7). doi:10.1108/08876040810909677

Gao, H., Hong, W., Cui, J., & Xu, Y. (2007). Optimization of principal component analysis in feature extraction. In *Proceedings of the 2007 IEEE International Conference on Mechatronics and Automation*. Harbin, China: IEEE.

Gao, Q., Sato, H., Rau, P.-L. P., & Asano, Y. (2007). Design effective navigation tools for older web users. *Human-Computer Interaction, 1*, 765–773.

Gasson, S., & Shelfer, K. M. (2007). IT-based knowledge management to support organizational learning Visa application screening at the INS. *Information Technology & People, 20*(4), 376–399. doi:10.1108/09593840710839806

Gatto, S. L., & Tak, S. H. (2008). Computer, internet, and e-mail use among older adults: Benefits and barriers. *Educational Gerontology, 34*(9), 800–811. doi:10.1080/03601270802243697

Gerson, R. F. (1993). *Measuring customer satisfaction: A guide to managing quality service*. Menlo Park, CA: Crisp Publications.

Gilbert, J., Morton, S., & Rowley, J. (2007). *e*-Learning: The student experience. *British Journal of Educational Technology, 38*(4), 560–573. doi:10.1111/j.1467-8535.2007.00723.x

Gilroy, R. (2005). Meeting the information needs of older people: A challenge for local governance. *Local Government Studies, 31*(1), 39–51. doi:10.1080/0300393042000332846

Go On, U. K. (2013). *Go on UK – Improving digital skills in the UK for people & businesses*. Retrieved on March 3, 2013 from http://www.go-on.co.uk/

Gogus, A. (2012). Bloom's taxonomy of learning objectives. In Encyclopedia of the sciences of learning. Berlin: Springer Science+Business Media, LLC.

Goodman-Deane, J., Langdon, P., & Clarkson, J. (2009). Key influences on the user-centred design process. *Journal of Engineering Design, 21*(2-3), 345–373.

Government Financial Officers Association. (2003). *Using websites to improve access to budget documents and financial reports*. Retrieved from http://www.gfoa.org/downloads/caafr-budgets-to-websites.pdf

Greenbaum, P. E., Turner, C., Cook, E. W. III, & Melamed, B. G. (1990). Dentists' voice control: Effects on children's disruptive and affective behavior. *Health Psychology, 9*(5), 546–558. doi:10.1037/0278-6133.9.5.546 PMID:2226384

Griffin, J. (1995). *Customer loyalty*. Lexington, MA: Lexington Books.

Grigoroudis, E., & Siskos, Y. (2002). Preference disaggregation for measuring and analysing customer satisfaction: The MUSA method. *European Journal of Operational Research, 143*, 148–170. doi:10.1016/S0377-2217(01)00332-0

Grigoroudis, E., & Siskos, Y. (2010). *Customer satisfaction evaluation: Methods for measuring and implementing service quality*. New York: Springer. doi:10.1007/978-1-4419-1640-2

Grönroos, C., Heinonen, F., Isoniemi, K., & Lindholm, M. (2000). The NetOffer model: A case example from the virtual marketspace. *Management Decision, 38*(4), 243–252. doi:10.1108/00251740010326252

Gudgin, M., Hadley, M., Mendelsohn, N., Moreau, J., & Nielsen, H. (2000). *Simple object access protocol (SOAP)* (Technical Report). World Wide Web Consortium. Retrieved from http://www.w3.org/TR/SOAP/

Gummerus, J., Liljander, V., Pura, M., & Van Riel, A. (2004). Customer loyalty to content-based websites: The case of an online health-care service. *Journal of Services Marketing, 18*(3), 175–186. doi:10.1108/08876040410536486

Gupta, H., Jones, E., & Coleman, P. (2004). How do Welsh tourism-SME websites approach customer relationship management? In *Information and communication technologies in tourism 2004*. New York: Springer-Wien. doi:10.1007/978-3-7091-0594-8_49

Gupta, M. P., & Jana, D. (2003). E-government evaluation: A framework and case study. *Government Information Quarterly*, 20, 365–387. doi:10.1016/j.giq.2003.08.002

Gu, R., Oh, L., & Wang, K. (2010). Determinants of customer loyalty for social networking sites. In R. Sharman, T. S. Raghu, & H. R. Rao (Eds.), *Exploring the grand challenges for next generation e-business (LNBIP)* (Vol. 52, pp. 206–212). Berlin: Springer. doi:10.1007/978-3-642-17449-0_21

Haddad, S., Melliti, T., Moreaux, P., & Rampacek, S. (2004). Modelling web services interoperability. In *Proceedings of the 6th Int. Conf. on Entreprise Information Systems* (ICEI04), (pp. 14–17). ICEI.

Hair, J. F., Anderson, R. E., Tatham, R. L., & Black, W. C. (1998). *Multivariate data analysis* (5th ed.). Upper Saddle River, NJ: Prentice Hall International, Inc.

Halaris, C., Magoutas, B., Papadomichelaki, X., & Mentzas, G. (2007). Classification and synthesis of quality approaches in e-government services. *Internet Research: Electronic Networking Applications and Policy*, 17(4), 378–401. doi:10.1108/10662240710828058

Han, J. H., & Mills, J. E. (2005). Use of problematic integration theory in destination online promotional activities: The case of Australia.com in the United States market. In *Information and communication technologies in tourism*. New York: Springer-Verlag. doi:10.1007/3-211-27283-6_23

Han, J.-H., & Mills, J. E. (2006). Zero acquaintance benchmarking at travel destination websites: What is the first impression that national tourism organizations try to make? *International Journal of Tourism Research*, 8(6), 405–430. doi:10.1002/jtr.581

Harris, J. A., McKenzie, K. S., & Rentfro, R. W. (2011). Performance reporting: Assessing citizen access to performance measures on state government websites. *Journal of Public Budgeting, Accounting &. Financial Management*, 23(1), 117–138.

Hartmann, J., Sutcliffe, A., & Angeli, A. D. (2008). Towards a theory of user judgment of aesthetics and user interface quality. *ACM Transactions on Computer-Human Interaction*, 15(4), 15:1-15:30.

Harun, A. (2012). Thailand tourism industry: The impact of tourism sector to Thai's gross domestic product (GDP). In *Proceedings of 2nd International Conference on Business, Economics, Management and Behavioral Sciences* (BEMBS'2012). BEMBS.

Hassanein, K., & Head, M. (2003). Ubiquitous usability: Exploring mobile interfaces within the context of a theoretical model. In *Proceedings of the Ubiquitous Mobile Information and Collaboration Systems Workshop* (UMICS 2003). Velden, Austria: CAiSE.

Hassenzahl, M. (2000). Prioritizing usability problems: Data-driven and judgement-driven severity estimates. *Behaviour & Information Technology*, 19, 29–42. doi:10.1080/014492900118777

Hassenzahl, M. (2004). The interplay of beauty, goodness, and usability in interactive products. *Human-Computer Interaction*, 19(4), 319–349. doi:10.1207/s15327051hci1904_2

Hassenzahl, M., Burmester, M., & Koller, F. (2003). AttrakDiff: Ein fragebogen zur messung wahrgenommener hedonischer und pragmatischer qualitat. In J. Ziegler, & G. Szwillus (Eds.), *Mensch & computer: Interaktion in bewegung* (pp. 187–196). Stuttgart, Germany: B.G. Teubner. doi:10.1007/978-3-322-80058-9_19

Hassenzahl, M., & Tractinsky, N. (2006). User experience – A research agenda. *Behaviour & Information Technology*, 25(2), 91–97. doi:10.1080/01449290500330331

Hawthorn, D. (2007). Interface design and engagement with older people. *Behaviour & Information Technology*, 26(4), 333–341. doi:10.1080/01449290601176930

Hayes, B. E. (1992). *Measuring customer satisfaction: Development and use of questionnaire*. Milwaukee, WI: ASQC Quality Press.

Hellemans, K., & Govers, R. (2005). European tourism online: Comparative content analysis of the ETC website and corresponding national NTO websites. In *Information and communication technologies in tourism 2005*. New York: Springer-Verlag. doi:10.1007/3-211-27283-6_19

Herington, C., & Weaven, S. (2009). E-retailing by banks: E-service quality and its importance to customer satisfaction. *European Journal of Marketing*, *43*(9/10), 1220–1231. doi:10.1108/03090560910976456

Hertzum, M., Hansen, K. D., & Andersen, H. H. K. (2009). Scrutinising usability evaluation: Does thinking aloud affect behaviour and mental workload? *Behaviour & Information Technology*, *28*, 165–181. doi:10.1080/01449290701773842

Hessler, R. M. (1992). *Social research methods*. St. Paul, MN: West Publishing Company.

Hill, N. (1996). *Handbook of customer satisfaction measurement*. Hampshire, UK: Gower Publishing.

Hill, N., & Alexander, J. (2006). *Handbook of customer satisfaction and loyalty measurement*. Aldershot, UK: Gower.

Ho, A. T.-K. (2002). Reinventing local governments and the e-government initiative. *Public Administration Review*, *62*(4), 434–444. doi:10.1111/0033-3352.00197

Hodgkinson, S. (2002). Managing an e-government transformation program. In *Proceedings of Working Towards Whole-of-Government Online Conference*. Canberra, Australia: Academic Press.

Høegh, R. T., Nielsen, C. M., Overgaard, M., Pedersen, M. B., & Stage, J. (2006). The impact of usability reports and user test observations on developers' understanding of usability data: An exploratory study. *International Journal of Human-Computer Interaction*, *21*(2), 173–196. doi:10.1207/s15327590ijhc2102_4

Hogo, M. A. (2010). Evaluation of e-learning systems based on fuzzy clustering models and statistical tools. *Expert Systems with Applications*, *37*, 6891–6903. doi:10.1016/j.eswa.2010.03.032

Holloway, C. (1998). *The business of tourism* (5th ed.). London: Addison Wesley Longman.

Holmes, D. (2001). *E-gov: E-business strategies for government*. London: Nicholas Brealey Publishing.

Homburg, C., & Giering, A. (2001). Personal characteristics as moderators of the relationship between customer satisfaction and loyalty—An empirical analysis. *Psychology and Marketing*, *18*(1), 43–66. doi:10.1002/1520-6793(200101)18:1<43::AID-MAR3>3.0.CO;2-I

Hong, S., Katerattanakul, P., & Lee, D.-H. (2008). Evaluating government website accessibility. *Management Research News*, *31*(1), 27–40. doi:10.1108/01409170810845930

Hong, W., Thong, J. Y. L., Chasalow, L. C., & Dhillon, G. (2011). User acceptance of agile information systems: A model and empirical test. *Journal of Management Information Systems*, *28*(1), 235–272. doi:10.2753/MIS0742-1222280108

Hornbæk, K. (2010). Dogmas in the assessment of usability evaluation methods. *Behaviour & Information Technology*, *29*, 97–111. doi:10.1080/01449290801939400

Hornbaek, K., Bederson, B., & Plaisant, C. (2003). Navigation patterns & usability of zoomable user interfaces with and without an overview. *ACM Transactions on Computer-Human Interaction*, *9*(4), 362–389.

Horngren, C., Sundem, G., Elliot, J., & Philbrick, D. (2009). *Introduction to financial accounting* (9th ed.). Upper Saddle River, NJ: Pearson Education International.

Horton, M., Read, J. C., & Sim, G. (2011). Making your mind up? The reliability of children's survey responses. In L. Little & L. Coventry (Eds.), *25th BCS Conference on Human-Computer Interaction* (pp. 437-438). Swinton, UK: British Computer Society.

Howard, J. A. (1977). *Consumer behavior: Application of theory*. New York: McGraw-Hill.

Huang, J. C. (2003). Usability of e-government web-sites for people with disabilities. In *Proceedings of the 36th Hawaii International Conference on System Sciences*. IEEE.

Huang, C.-K., & Huang, C.-H. (2010). An integrated decision model for evaluating educational web sites from the fuzzy subjective and objective perspectives. *Computers & Education*, *55*, 616–629. doi:10.1016/j.compedu.2010.02.022

Huang, Z., & Brooks, L. (2011). Credibility and usability evaluation of e-governments: Heuristic evaluation approach. In *Proceedings of tGov 2011*. Brunel University.

Hugh, M. G. (2004). Exploring elders interaction with information technology. *Journal of Business and Economic Research*, 2(6), 62–66.

Hu, L., & Bentler, P. (1999). Cut-off criteria for fit indexes in covariance structure analysis: Conventional criteria versus new alternatives. *Structural Equation Modeling*, 6(1), 1–55. doi:10.1080/10705519909540118

Hutchinson, H. B., Bederson, B. B., & Druin, A. (2006). *The evolution of the international children's digital library searching and browsing interface.* Paper presented at the 2006 Conference on Interaction Design for Children. Tampere, Finland.

Hutchinson, H., Druin, A., Bederson, B. B., Reuter, K., Rose, A., & Weeks, A. C. (2005). *How do I find blue books about dogs? The errors and frustrations of young digital library users.* Paper presented at the International Conference on Human-Computer Interaction (HCI). Las Vegas, NV.

Hwang, G.-J., Huang, T. C. K., & Tseng, J. C. R. (2004). A group-decision approach for evaluating educational web sites. *Computers & Education*, 42, 65–86. doi:10.1016/S0360-1315(03)00065-4

Information Society Development Committee under the Ministry of Transport of the Republic of Lithuania (2012). *Pagrindinių elektroninių viešųjų ir administracinių paslaugų vertinimas: 2011 m. tyrimo ataskaita.* Retrieved February 11, 2013, from http://www.ivpk.lt/uploads/Leidiniai/Pagrindiniu%20ePaslaugu%20vertinimas_2012%20tyrimo%20ataskaita.pdf

Inglis, A. (2008). Approaches to the validation of quality frameworks for e-learning. *Quality Assurance in Education*, 16(4), 347–362. doi:10.1108/09684880810906490

International Standards Organisation. (2008). *Ergonomics of human-system interaction -- Part 171: Guidance on software accessibility.* Retrieved from http://www.iso.org/iso/home/store/catalogue_ics/catalogue_detail_ics.htm?csnumber=39080

IOBE. (2007). *The pharmaceutical market in Greece.* Athens, Greece: IOBE.

Irtel, H. (2007). PXLab: The psychological experiments laboratory (2.1.11 ed.). Mannheim, Germany: University of Mannheim.

IS. (2010). Curriculum guidelines for undergraduate degree programs in information systems. New York: Association for Computing Machinery (ACM), Association for Information Systems (AIS).

ISO/IEC 40500. (2012). *Information technology – W3C web content accessibility guidelines (WCAG) 2.0.*

ISO-9241. (1998). *Ergonomic requirements for office work with visual display terminals (VDTs) -- Part 11: Guidance on usability.*

Jacoby, J. (1975). A brand loyalty concept: Comments on a comment. *JMR, Journal of Marketing Research*, 12(4), 484–487. doi:10.2307/3151103

Jacoby, J., & Chestnut, R. W. (1978). *Brand loyalty: Measurement and management.* New York: Wiley.

Jacquet-Lagreze, E., & Siskos, J. (1982). Assessing a set of additive utility functions for multicriteria decision-making: The UTA method. *Journal of Operational Research*, 10(2), 151–164. doi:10.1016/0377-2217(82)90155-2

Jain, S. K., Spinelli, G., Garaj, V., & Dong, H. (2012). *The use of the internet by older people: A behavioural study.* Paper presented at the Universal Design Conference 2012. Fukuoka, Japan.

Jansen, A., & lnes, S. (2004). Quality assessment and benchmarking of Norwegian public web sites. In *Proceeding from European Conference on E-Government*. Retrieved March 15, 2013, from http://www.afin.uio.no/english/research/ arild/QualityAssessment.pdf

Jansen, C., & Balijon, S. (2002). How do people use instruction guides? Confirming and disconfirming patterns of use. *Document Design (Amsterdam)*, 3, 195–204. doi:10.1075/dd.3.3.01jan

Javeau, C. (1992). L' enquete par questionnaire: Manuel a l'usage du praticien. Bruxelles: Ed. de L' Universite de Bruxelles.

Jeong Chun Hai @Ibrahim. (2007). *Fundamental of development administration.* Selangor: Scholar Press.

Jeong, H.-Y., & Yeo, S.-S. (2013, April). The quality model for e-learning system with multimedia contents: A pairwise comparison approach. *Multimedia Tools and Applications.* doi:10.1007/s11042-013-1445-5

Jochmann-Mannak, H., Huibers, T., Lentz, L., & Sanders, T. (2010). *Children searching information on the internet: Performance on children's interfaces compared to Google.* Paper presented at the 33rd Annual International ACM SIGIR Conference on Research and Development in Information Retrieval at the Workshop Towards Accessible Search Systems. Geneva, Switzerland.

Jochmann-Mannak, H., Lentz, L., Huibers, T., & Sanders, T. (2012). Three types of children's informational websites: An inventory of design conventions. *Technical Communication, 59*(4), 302–323.

Joly, K. (2012). One design to rule them all? Responsive web design in higher education. *Internet Technology,* 498-500.

Jones, T., & Sasser, E. Jr. (1995). Why satisfied customers defect. *Harvard Business Review, 73*(6), 88–91.

Jorgenson, D., & Cable, S. (2002, Summer). Facing the challenges of e-government: A case study of the city of Corpus Christi, Texas. *SAM Advanced Management Journal.*

Jung, H.-S., & Baker, M. (1998). Assessing the market effectiveness of the world wide web in national tourism offices. In D. Buhalis, A. M. Tjoa, & J. Jafari (Eds.), *Information and communication technologies in tourism 1998* (pp. 93–102). New York: Springer-Wien. doi:10.1007/978-3-7091-7504-0_11

Jung, I. (2011). The dimensions of e-learning quality: from the learner's perspective. *Educational Technology Research and Development, 59,* 445–464. doi:10.1007/s11423-010-9171-4

Kalakota, R., & Robinson, M. (1999). e-Business, roadmap for success. Reading, MA: Addison-Wesley.

Kalidien, S. N., Choenni, R., & Meijer, R. (2009). Towards a monitoring tool for crime and law enforcement. In *Proceedings of ECIME 2009, 3rd European Conf. on Information Management and Evaluation.* Gothenburg, Sweden: Academic Publishing Limited.

Kalidien, S. N., Choenni, R., & Meijer, R. F. (2010). Crime statistics online: potentials and challenges. In *Proceedings of 11th Annual International Digital Government Research Conference on Public Administration Online: Challenges and Opportunities* (pp. 131-137). Puebla, Mexico: Digital Government Society of North America.

Kalogerou, V. (2007). *Communicational evaluation of websites, national & capodestrian.* Athens, Greece: University of Athens.

Kaplanidou, K., & Vogt, C. (2004). Destination marketing organization websites (DMOs). In *Evaluation and design: What you need to know.* Retrieved from http://www.travelmichigannews.org/research.htm

Kappel, G., Proll, B., Reich, S., & Retschitzegger, W. (2006). *Web engineering: The discipline of systematic development of web applications.* London: John Wiley & Sons Ltd.

Karagiorgoudi, S. (2004). *Systems of websites quality assessment.* Patras, Greece: University of Patras.

Karahasanovíc, A., & Nyhamar Hinkel, U., Sjøberg, D. I. K., & Thomas, R. (2009). Comparing of feedback-collection and think-aloud methods in program comprehension studies. *Behaviour & Information Technology, 28,* 139–164. doi:10.1080/01449290701682761

Karavidas, M., Lim, N. K., & Katsikas, S. L. (2005). The effects of computers on older adult users. *Computers in Human Behavior, 21,* 697–711. doi:10.1016/j.chb.2004.03.012

Kastania, A., & Zimeras, S. (2010). Web-based applications in healthcare and biomedicine. *Annals of Information Systems, 7,* 157–166. doi:10.1007/978-1-4419-1274-9_10

Kašubienė, L., & Vanagas, P. (2007). Assumptions of e-government services quality evaluation. *The Engineering Economist, 5*(55), 68–74.

Katre, D. S., & Gupta, M. (2011). Expert usability evaluation of 28 state government web portals of India. *International Journal of Public Information Systems,* (3), 115-130.

Kaynama, S. A., & Black, C. I. (2000). A proposal to assess the service quality of online travel agencies: An exploratory study. *Journal of Professional Services Marketing, 21*(1), 63–88. doi:10.1300/J090v21n01_05

Kay, R. (2011). Evaluating learning, design, and engagement in web-based learning tools (WBLTs): The WBLT evaluation scale. *Computers in Human Behavior, 27,* 1849–1856. doi:10.1016/j.chb.2011.04.007

Keaveney, S. M. (1995). Customer switching behavior in service industries: An exploratory study. *Journal of Marketing, 59*(2), 71–82. doi:10.2307/1252074

Kekre, S., Mukhopadhyay, T., & Kalathur, S. (1995). Business value of information technology: A study of electronic data interchange. *Management Information Systems Quarterly, 19*(2), 137–156. doi:10.2307/249685

Khan, B. (2005). *Managing e-learning strategies design, delivery, implementation and evaluation.* Hershey, PA: Information Science Publishing. doi:10.4018/978-1-59140-634-1

Kim, D., Kim, & Han. (2007). A perceptual mapping of online travel agencies and preference attributes. *Tourism Management, 28*(2), 591–603. doi:10.1016/j.tourman.2006.04.022

Kim, H. (2005). Developing an index of online customer satisfaction. *Journal of Financial Services Marketing, 10,* 49–64. doi:10.1057/palgrave.fsm.4770173

Kim, S.-E., Shaw, T., & Schneider, H. (2003). Web site design benchmarking within industry groups. *Internet Research, 13*(1), 19–26. doi:10.1108/10662240310458341

King, D., Lee, J., & Viehland, D. (2004). *Electronic commerce: A managerial perspective.* Upper Saddle River, NJ: Prentice Hall.

Kitajima, M., Blackmon, M. H., & Polson, P. G. (2000). *A comprehension-based model of web navigation and its application to web usability analysis.* Paper presented at the 14th Annual Conference of the British HCI Group (HCI 2000), People and Computers XIV: Usability Or Else! Sunderland, UK.

Kolsaker, A., & Lee-Kelley, L. (2008). Citizens' attitudes towards e-government and e-governance: A UK study. *International Journal of Public Sector, 21*(7), 723–738. doi:10.1108/09513550810904532

Koltay, Z., & Tancheva, K. (2010). Personas and a user-centred visioning process. *Performance Measurement and Metrics, 11*(2), 172–183. doi:10.1108/14678041011064089

Kotler, P., & Armstrong, G. (2010). *Principles of marketing* (13th ed.). London: Pearson.

Krahmer, E., & Ummelen, N. (2004). Thinking about thinking aloud: A comparison of two verbal protocols for usability testing. *IEEE Transactions on Professional Communication, 47,* 105–117. doi:10.1109/TPC.2004.828205

Kramer, A. F., Hahn, S., & Gopher, D. (1999). Task coordination and aging: Explorations of executive control processes in the task switching paradigm. *Acta Psychologica, 101,* 339–378. doi:10.1016/S0001-6918(99)00011-6 PMID:10344190

Krathwohl, D. R. (2002). A revision of Bloom's taxonomy: An overview. *Theory into Practice, 41*(4), 212–218. doi:10.1207/s15430421tip4104_2

Kuhl, J. (1986). Motivation and information processing. In R. M. Sorrentino, & E. T. Higgins (Eds.), *Handbook of motivation and cognition* (pp. 404–434). New York: Guilford Press.

Kumar, A., & Kumar, P. (2010). Managing privacy of user generated information in a web 2.0 world. *Journal of Information Privacy & Security,* 3-16.

Kumza, J. M. (2010). Accessibility design issues with UK e-government sites. *Government Information Quarterly, 27,* 141–146. doi:10.1016/j.giq.2009.10.004

Kurilovas, E., & Dagiene, V. (2010). Multiple criteria evaluation of quality and optimisation of e-learning system components. *Electronic Journal of e-Learning, 8*(2), 141 151.

Küster, I., & Vila, N. (2011). Successful SME web design through consumer focus groups. *International Journal of Quality & Reliability Management, 28*(2), 132–154. doi:10.1108/02656711111101728

Laarni, J. (2004). *Aesthetic and emotional evaluations of computer interfaces*. Paper presented at the Nordi CHI 2004 Workshop: Aesthetic Approaches to Human–Computer Interaction. Aarhus, Denmark.

LaBarbera, P. A., & Mazursky, D. (1983). A longitudinal assessment of consumer satisfaction dissatisfaction: The dynamic aspect of the cognitive process. *JMR, Journal of Marketing Research*, *20*(4), 393–404. doi:10.2307/3151443

Lam, S. Y., Shankar, V., Erramilli, M. K., & Murthy, B. (2004). Customer value, satisfaction, loyalty, and switching costs: An illustration from a business-to-business service context. *Journal of the Academy of Marketing Science*, *32*(3), 293–311. doi:10.1177/0092070304263330

Lang, P. J. (1980). Behavioral treatment and bio-behavioral assessment: Computer applications. In J. B. Sidowski, J. H. Johnson, & T. A. Williams (Eds.), *Technology in mental health care delivery systems* (pp. 119–137). Norwood, NJ: Ablex Publishing.

Lanzilotti, R., Ardito, C., Costabile, M. F., & De Angeli, A. (2006). eLSE methodology: A systematic approach to the e-learning systems evaluation. *Journal of Educational Technology & Society*, *9*(4), 42–53.

Large, A., Beheshti, J., & Moukdad, H. (1999). *Information seeking on the web: Navigational skills of grade-six primary school students*. Paper presented at the ASIS Annual Meeting. Washington, DC.

Large, A., & Beheshti, J. (2000). The web as a classroom resource: Reactions from the users. *Journal of the American Society for Information Science American Society for Information Science*, *51*(12), 1069–1080. doi:10.1002/1097-4571(2000)9999:9999<::AID-ASI1017>3.0.CO;2-W

Large, A., Beheshti, J., Tabatabaei, N., & Nesset, V. (2009). Developing a visual taxonomy: Children's views on aesthetics. *Journal of the American Society for Information Science and Technology*, *60*(9), 1808–1822. doi:10.1002/asi.21095

Large, A., Nesset, V., Beheshti, J., & Bowler, L. (2006). Bonded design: A novel approach to the design of new technologies. *Library & Information Science Research*, *28*(1), 64–82. doi:10.1016/j.lisr.2005.11.014

Larson, T., & Ankomah, P. (2004). Evaluating tourism web site complexity: The case of international tourism in the U.S. *Services Marketing Quarterly*, *26*(2), 23–37. doi:10.1300/J396v26n02_02

Law, R., & Jogaratnam, G. (2005). A study of hotel information technology applications. *International Journal of Contemporary Hospitality Management*, *17*(2), 170–180. doi:10.1108/09596110510582369

Law, R., Qi, S., & Buhalis, D. (2010). Progress in tourism management: A review of website evaluation in tourism research. *Tourism Management*, *31*(3), 297–313. doi:10.1016/j.tourman.2009.11.007

Layne, K., & Lee, J. (2001). Developing fully functional e-government: A four stage model. *Government Information Quarterly*, *18*(2), 122–136. doi:10.1016/S0740-624X(01)00066-1

Lee, J.-W. (2010). Online support service quality, online learning acceptance, and student satisfaction. *The Internet and Higher Education*, *13*, 277–283. doi:10.1016/j.iheduc.2010.08.002

Lee, M. (2001). *Comprehensive model of internet satisfaction*. Kowloon, Hong Kong: City University of Hong Kong.

Lee, W., & Benbasat, I. (2003). Designing an electronic commerce interface: Attention and product memory as elicited by web design. *Electronic Commerce Research and Applications*, *2*(3), 240–253. doi:10.1016/S1567-4223(03)00026-7

Legris, P., Ingham, J., & Collerette, P. (2003). Why do people use information technology? A critical review of the technology acceptance model. *Information & Management*, *40*(3), 191–204. doi:10.1016/S0378-7206(01)00143-4

Lentz, L., & Pander Maat, H. (2007). Reading aloud and the delay of feedback: Explanations for the effectiveness of reader protocols. *Information Design Journal*, *15*, 266–281. doi:10.1075/idj.15.3.09len

Lewis, K. M., & Hepburn, P. (2010). Open card sorting and factor analysis: A usability case study. *The Electronic Library*, *28*(3), 401–416. doi:10.1108/02640471011051981

Liang, T., Lai, H., & Ku, Y. (2006-2007). Personalization content recommendation and user satisfaction: Theoretical synthesis and empirical findings. *Journal of Management Information Systems, 23*(3), 45–70. doi:10.2753/MIS0742-1222230303

Lidwell, W., Holden, K., & Butler, J. (2003). *Universal principles of design: 125 ways to enhance usability, perception, increase appeal, make better design decisions and teach through design.* Rockport, MA: Rockport Publishers Inc.

Li, H., Rau, P.-L. P., Fujimura, K., Gao, Q., & Wang, L. (2012). Designing effective web forums for older web users. *Educational Gerontology, 38*, 271–281. doi:10.1080/03601277.2010.544578

Lin, Ch.-T. (2010). Examining e-travel sites: An empirical study in Taiwan. *Online Information Review, 34*(2), 205–228. doi:10.1108/14684521011036954

Lin, H.-F. (2010). An application of fuzzy AHP for evaluating course website quality. *Computers & Education, 54*, 877–888. doi:10.1016/j.compedu.2009.09.017

Liu, G.-Z., Liu, Z.-H., & Hwang, G.-J. (2011). Developing multi-dimensional evaluation criteria for English learning websites with university students and professors. *Computers & Education, 56*, 65–79. doi:10.1016/j.compedu.2010.08.019

Liu, J., Derzsi, Z., Raus, M., & Kipp, A. (2008). eGovernment project evaluation: An integrated framework. *Lecture Notes in Computer Science, 5184*, 85–97. doi:10.1007/978-3-540-85204-9_8

Loiacono, E., Watson, R. T., & Goodhue, D. (2000). *WebQual: A web site quality instrument* (Working Paper). Worcester Polytechnic Institute.

Luckin, R. (2003). Between the lines: Documenting the multiple dimensions of computer-supported collaborations. *Computers & Education, 41*, 379–396. doi:10.1016/j.compedu.2003.06.002

Luftman, J. (2000). Addressing business-IT alignment maturity. *Communications of the Association for Information Systems, 4*(14), 1–51.

Luostarinen, R., Manner, J., Määttä, J., & Järvinen, R. (2010). User-centered design of graphical user interfaces. In *Proceedings of the 2010 Military Communications Conference – Unclassified Program – Cyber Security and Network Management.* IEEE.

Lu, Z., Lu, J., & Zhang, J. C. (2002). Website development and evaluation in the Chinese tourism industry. *Networks and Communication Studies, 16*(3/4), 191–208.

Lynch, P., & Horton, S. (1999). *Web style guide.* New Haven, CT: Yale University.

Madu, C. N., & Madu, A. A. (2002). Dimensions of e-quality. *International Journal of Quality & Reliability Management, 19*(3), 246–258. doi:10.1108/02656710210415668

Malhotra, Y. (2005). Integrating knowledge management technologies in organizational business processes: Getting real time enterprises to deliver real business performance. *Journal of Knowledge Management, 9*(1), 7–28. doi:10.1108/13673270510582938

Malone, T. W. (1980). *What makes things fun to learn? A study of intrinsically motivating computer games* (Technical Report No. CIS-7 SSL-80-11). Palo Alto, CA: Xerox Palo Alto Research Center.

Malone, T. W. (1984). Heuristics for designing enjoyable user interfaces: Lessons from computer games. In J. C. Thomas, & M. L. Schneider (Eds.), *Human factors in computer systems* (pp. 1–12). Norwood, NJ: Ablex Publishing.

*Manila Declaration on World Tourism.* (1980). World tourism conference. Retrieved 2013-04-09, from http://www.univeur.org

Marche, S., & McNiven, J. (2003). E-government and e-governance: The future isn't what it used to be. *Canadian Journal of Administrative Sciences, 20*(1), 74–86. doi:10.1111/j.1936-4490.2003.tb00306.x

Marchionini, G. (1989). Information-seeking strategies of novices using a full-text electronic encyclopedia. *Journal of the American Society for Information Science American Society for Information Science, 40*(1), 54–66. doi:10.1002/(SICI)1097-4571(198901)40:1<54::AID-ASI6>3.0.CO;2-R

Marimon, F., Petnji, Y. L. H., & Casadesus, M. (2012). Impact of e-quality and service recovery on loyalty: A study of e-banking in Spain. *Total Quality Management & Business Excellence*, 23(7), 769–787. doi:10.1080/14783363.2011.637795

Markopoulos, P., Read, J., MacFarlane, S., & Hoysniemi, J. (2008). *Evaluating children's interactive products*. Burlington, UK: Elsevier.

Marques, C. G., Noivo, J., & Veríssimo, M. (2008). e-QUAL: e-Learning with quality: Proposal for an evaluation model on the quality of e-learning courses. *Computers & Education*, 83–90. doi:10.1007/978-1-84628-929-3_9

Martınez-Ruiz, M. P., Jimenez-Zarco, A. I., & Izquierdo-Yusta, A. (2012). The effects of the current economic situation on customer satisfaction and retail patronage behaviour. *Total Quality Management & Business Excellence*, 23(11), 1207–1225. doi:10.1080/14783363.2012.661133

Massanari, A. L. (2010). Designing for imaginary friends: Information architecture, personas and the politics of user-centered design. *New Media & Society*, 12(3), 401–416.

Matsatsinis, N. F., Grigoroudis, E., & Delias, P. (2003). User satisfaction and e-learning systems: Towards a multi-criteria evaluation methodology. *Operations Research*, 3(3), 249–259.

Mayhew, D. J., & Tremaine, M. M. (2005). A basic framework. In *Cost-justifying usability: An update for the internet age*. San Francisco: Morgan Kaufmann Publishers. doi:10.1016/B978-012095811-5/50003-1

McCloskey, D. W. (2006). The importance of ease of use, usefulness, and trust to online consumers: An examination of the technology acceptance model with older consumers. *Journal of Organizational and End User Computing*, 18(3), 47–65. doi:10.4018/joeuc.2006070103

McDonald, S., Edwards, H. M., & Zhao, T. (2012). Exploring think-alouds in usability testing: An international survey. *IEEE Transactions on Professional Communication*, 55(1), 2–19. doi:10.1109/TPC.2011.2182569

McDonald, W. J. (1993). The roles of demographics, purchase histories, and shopper decision-making styles in predicting consumer catalog loyalty. *Journal of Direct Marketing*, 7(3), 55–65. doi:10.1002/dir.4000070308

McIntosh, R. W., Goeldner, C. R., & Ritchie, J. R. (1995). *Tourism principles, practices, philosophies* (7th ed.). New York: Wiley.

McKinney, V., Yoon, K., & Zahedi, F. (2002). The measurement of web-customer satisfaction: An expectation and disconfirmation approach. *Information Systems Research*, 13(3), 296–315. doi:10.1287/isre.13.3.296.76

McQuarrie, E. F. (1988). An alternative to purchase intentions: The role of prior behaviour in consumer expenditures on computers. *Journal of the Market Research Society. Market Research Society*, 16(3), 203–226.

Melitski, J., Holzer, M., Kim, S.-T., Kim, C.-G., & Rho, S.-Y. (2005). Digital government worldwide: An e-government assessment of municipal web sites. *International Journal of Electronic Government Research*, 1(1), 1–19. doi:10.4018/jegr.2005010101

Meloncon, L., Haynes, E., Varelmann, M., & Groh, L. (2010). Building a playground: General guidelines for creating educational websites for children. *Technical Communication*, 57(4), 398–415.

Meng, J., Summey, J., Herndon, N., & Kwong, K. (2009). Some retail service quality expectations of Chinese shoppers. *International Journal of Market Research*, 51(6), 773–796. doi:10.2501/S1470785309200967

Miaskiewicz, T., & Kozar, K. A. (2011). Personas and user-centered design: How can personas benefit the product design processes? *Design Studies*, 32, 417–430. doi:10.1016/j.destud.2011.03.003

Microsoft Corporation. (1999). e-Commerce development: Business to consumer. Microsoft Corporation.

Middleton, M. R. (2007). Approaches to evaluation of websites for public sector services. In *Proceedings IADIS Conference on e-Society*, (pp. 279-284). Lisbon, Portugal: IADIS.

Mihelis, G., Grigoroudis, Siskos, Politis, & Malandrakis. (2001). Customer satisfaction measurement in the private bank sector. *European Journal of Operational Research*, 130(2), 347–360. doi:10.1016/S0377-2217(00)00036-9

Milliman, R. E. (2002). Website accessibility and the private sector: Disability stakeholders cannot tolerate 2% access!. *Information Technology and Disabilities*, 8(1).

Mills, J. E., & Morrison, A. M. (2003). Measuring customer satisfaction with online travel. In A. J. Frew, M. Hitz, & P. O'Connor (Eds.), *Information and communication technologies in tourism* (pp. 11–28). New York: Springer-Wien.

Mintel Group. (2009). *European leisure travel industry - Europe - September 2009*. Online Travel Groups.

Mittal, V., & Kamakura, W. A. (2001). Satisfaction, repurchase intent, and repurchase behavior: Investigating the moderating effect of customer characteristics. *JMR, Journal of Marketing Research*, *38*(1), 131–142. doi:10.1509/jmkr.38.1.131.18832

Monsell, S. (2003). Task switching. *Trends in Cognitive Sciences*, *7*, 134–140. doi:10.1016/S1364-6613(03)00028-7 PMID:12639695

Moon, M., & Welch, E. (2005). Same bed, different dreams? A comparative analysis of citizen and bureaucrat perspectives on e-government. *Review of Public Personnel Administration*, *25*(3), 243–264. doi:10.1177/0734371X05275508

Moon, Y. (2003). Don't blame the computer: When self-disclosure moderates the self-serving bias. *Journal of Consumer Psychology*, *13*, 125–137.

Morgan, M. S., & Dev, C. S. (1994). An empirical study of brand switching for a retail service. *Journal of Retailing*, *70*(3), 267–282. doi:10.1016/0022-4359(94)90036-1

Morgeson, F. V. III, & Mithas, S. (2009). Does e-government measure up to e-business? Comparing end-user perceptions of U.S. federal government and e-business websites. *Public Administration Review*, *69*, 740–752. doi:10.1111/j.1540-6210.2009.02021.x

Morris, M. H., & Holman, J. L. (1988). Source loyalty in organizational markets: A dyadic perspective. *Journal of Business Research*, *16*(2), 117–131. doi:10.1016/0148-2963(88)90037-9

Naumann, E., & Giel, K. (1995). *Customer satisfaction measurement and management: Using the voice of the customer*. Cincinnati, OH: Thomson Executive Press.

Neerincx, M. A., Lindenberg, J., & Pemberton, S. (2001). Support concepts for web navigation: A cognitive engineering approach. In *Proceedings of the 10th International Conference on World Wide Web*, (pp. 119-128). Hong Kong: ACM.

Neilsen, J., & Landauer, T. K. (1993). A mathematical model of the finding of usability problems. In *Proceedings of INTERCHI '93*. ACM.

Newman, J. W., & Werbel, R. A. (1973). Multivariate analysis of brand loyalty for major household appliances. *JMR, Journal of Marketing Research*, *10*(4), 404–409. doi:10.2307/3149388

Nichols, D. M., McKay, D., & Twidale, M. B. (2003). Participatory usability: Supporting proactive users. In *Proceedings of 4th ACM SIGCHI NZ, Symposium on Computer-Human Interaction* (CHINZ '03), (pp. 63-68). Dunedin, New Zealand: ACM.

Nielsen, J. (1995). *Ten usability heuristics*. Retrieved on March 26, 2013 from http://www.nngroup.com/articles/ten-usability-heuristics/

Nielsen, J. (1996, October 1). *Accessible design for users with disabilities*. Retrieved from http://www.nngroup.com/articles/accessible-design-for-users-with-disabilities/

Nielsen, J. (2000). *Why you only need to test with 5 users*. Retrieved March 25, 2013 from http://www.nngroup.com/articles/why-you-only-need-to-test-with-5-users/

Nielsen, J. (2001). *Alertbox: First rule of usability? Don't listen to users*. Retrieved September 13, 2012, from http://www.useit.com/alertbox/20010805.html

Nielsen, J. (2003, August 25). *Usability 101: Introduction to usability*. Retrieved from http://www.nngroup.com/articles/usability-101-introduction-to-usability/

Nielsen, J. (2004). *Card sorting: How many users to test*. Retrieved on March 25, 2013 from http://www.nngroup.com/articles/card-sorting-how-many-users-to-test/

Nielsen, J. (1993). Iterative user-interface design. *Computer*, *26*(11), 32–41. doi:10.1109/2.241424

Nielsen, J. (1994). Heuristic evaluation. In *Usability inspection methods*. New York: John Wiley & Sons.

Nielsen, J. (2000). *Designing web usability: The practice of simplicity*. New Riders Publishing.

Nielsen, J. (2003). *Usability engineering*. Academic Press.

Nielsen, J., & Gilutz, S. (2002). *Usability of websites for children: 70 design guidelines based on usability studies with kids*. Nielsen Norman Group.

Nilsson, R. M., & Mayer, R. E. (2002). The effects of graphic organisers giving cues to the structure of a hypertext document on users' navigation, strategies and performance. *International Journal of Human-Computer Studies, 57*, 1–26. doi:10.1006/ijhc.2002.1011

Noordzij, M., Scholten, P., & Laroy-Noordzij, M. (2012). *Measuring electrodermal activity of both individuals with severe mental disabilities and their caretakers during episodes of challenging behavior*. Paper presented at the 8th International Conference on Methods and Techniques in Behavioral Research: Measuring Behavior. Utrecht, The Netherlands.

Northern Ireland Assembly. (2001, September 20). *E-government*. Retrieved from http://archive.niassembly.gov.uk/research_papers/research/0901.pdf

Nunnally, J. C., & Bernstein, I. H. (1994). *Psychometric theory*. New York: McGraw-Hill.

OECD. (2001). *Citizens as partners OECD handbook on information, consultation, and public participation in policy-making*. Paris: OECD Publishing.

OECD. (2012). *Health data 2012*. Paris: OECD.

Oertel, B., Thio, S. L., & Feil, T. (2001). Benchmarking tourism destinations in the European Union. In P. J. Sheldon, K. W. Wober, & D. R. Fesenmaier (Eds.), *Information and communication technologies in tourism 2001* (pp. 473–484). New York: Springer-Wien. doi:10.1007/978-3-7091-6177-7_25

Ofcom. (2012). *Communications market report*. Retrieved on March 21, 2013 from http://stakeholders.ofcom.org.uk/market-data-research/market-data/communications-market-reports/cmr12/downloads/

Oliva, T. A., Oliver, P. L., & Bearden, W. O. (1995). The relationships among consumer satisfaction, involvement, and product performance: A catastrophe theory application. *Behavioral Science, 40*, 104–132. doi:10.1002/bs.3830400203

Oliva, T. A., Oliver, P. L., & McMillan, I. C. (1992). A catastrophe model for developing service satisfaction strategies. *Journal of Marketing, 56*(2), 83–95. doi:10.2307/1252298

Oliver, R. L. (1996). *Satisfaction: A behavioural perspective on the customer*. New York: McGraw-Hill.

Oliver, R. L. (1997). *Satisfaction: A behavioral perspective on the customer*. New York: McGraw-Hill.

Oliver, R. L. (2010). *Satisfaction: A behavioral perspective on the consumer* (2nd ed.). Armonk, NY: M.E. Shape.

Oliver, R. L., & DeSarbo, W. S. (1988). Response determinants in satisfaction judgments. *The Journal of Consumer Research, 14*(4), 495–507. doi:10.1086/209131

Olmsted-Hawala, E. L., Murphy, E. D., Hawala, S., & Ashenfelter, K. T. (2010). Think-aloud protocols: A comparison of three think-aloud protocols for use in testing data-dissemination web sites for usability. In *Proceedings of the 28th International Conference on Human Factors in Computing Systems*, (pp. 2381-2390). ACM.

Olsen, K. E., O'Brien, M. A., Rodgers, W. A., & Charness, N. (2011). Diffusion of technology: Frequency of use for younger and older adults. *Ageing International, 36*, 123–145. doi:10.1007/s12126-010-9077-9 PMID:22685360

ONS. (2012). *Internet access quarterly update, Q4 2012*. Retrieved on March 19, 2013 from http://www.ons.gov.uk/ons/dcp171778_300874.pdf

Ormrod, J. E. (2006). *Educational psychology: Developing learners* (5th ed.). Upper Saddle River, NJ: Pearson Education.

Osbourne, D., & Gaebler, T. (1992). *Reinventing government: How the entrepreneurial spirit is transforming the public sector*. Reading, MA: Addison Wesley.

Oxford University Press. (2013). *In-depth definition*. Retrieved on March 26, 2013 from http://oxforddictionaries.com/

Pak, R., & Price, M. M. (2008). Designing an information search interface for younger and older adults. *Human Factors: The Journal of the Human Factors and Ergonomics Society*, *50*(4), 614–628. doi:10.1518/001872008X312314 PMID:18767521

Palvia, S. C. J., & Sharma, S. S. (2007). E-government and e-governance: Definitions/domain framework and status around the world. In *Foundation of e-government*. ICEG.

Panopoulou, E., Tambouris, E., & Tarabanis, K. (2008). A framework for evaluating web sites of public authorities. *ASLIB Proceedings: New Information Perspectives, 60*(5), 517-546.

Papadakis, M. (2006). Applications of informatics in services. In *Health policy and economics*. Athens, Greece: Papazisis Publications.

Papadomichelaki, X., Magoutas, B., Halaris, C., Apostolou, D., & Mentzas, G. (2006). A review of quality dimensions in e-government services. In M. Wimmer et al. (Eds.), *EGOV 2006 (LNCS)* (Vol. 4084, pp. 128–138). Berlin: Springer. doi:10.1007/11823100_12

Parasuraman, A., Berry, L. L., & Zeithaml, V. A. (1988). SERVQUAL: A multiple-item scale for measuring customer perceptions of service quality. *Journal of Retailing, 64*(1), 12–40.

Parasuraman, A., Berry, L. L., & Zeithaml, V. A. (1991). Refinement and reassessment of the SERVQUAL scale. *Journal of Retailing, 67*(4), 420–450.

Parasuraman, A., & Grewal, D. (2000). The impact of technology on the quality-value-loyalty chain: A research agenda. *Journal of the Academy of Marketing Science, 28*(1), 168–174. doi:10.1177/0092070300281015

Parasuraman, A., Zeithaml, V. A., & Berry, L. L. (1985). A conceptual model of service quality and its implications for future research. *Journal of Marketing, 49*(4), 41–50. doi:10.2307/1251430

Parasuraman, A., Zeithaml, V. A., & Berry, L. L. (1988). SERVQUAL: A multiple-item scale for measuring consumer perceptions of service quality. *Journal of Retailing, 64*(1), 12–40.

Parasuraman, A., Zeithaml, V. A., & Malhotra, A. (2005). E-S-QUAL: A multiple-item scale for assessing electronic service quality. *Journal of Service Research, 7*(3), 213–233. doi:10.1177/1094670504271156

Paris, M. (2006). Website accessibility: A survey of local e-government websites and legislation in Northern Ireland. Universal Access in the Information Society, 292-299.

Park, Y. A., & Gretzel, U. (2007). Success factors for destination marketing web sites: A qualitative meta-analysis. *Journal of Travel Research, 46*(1), 46–63. doi:10.1177/0047287507302381

Pawlowski, J. M. (2007). The quality adaptation model: Adaptation and adoption of the quality standard ISO/IEC 19796-1 for learning, education, and training. *Journal of Educational Technology & Society, 10*(2), 3–16.

Pearson, J., Pearson, A., & Green, D. (2007). Determining the importance of key criteria in web usability. *Management Research News, 30*(11), 816–828. doi:10.1108/01409170710832250

Petnji Yaya, L. H., Marimon, F., & Casadesus Fa, M. (2012). Assessing e-service quality: The current state of E-S-QUAL. *Total Quality Management & Business Excellence, 23*(12), 1363–1378. doi:10.1080/1478336 3.2012.728850

Petnji Yaya, L. H., Marimon, F., & Casadesus, M. (2011). Customer's loyalty and perception of ISO 9001 in online banking. *Industrial Management & Data Systems, 111*(8), 1194–1213. doi:10.1108/02635571111170767

Petnji Yaya, L. H., Marimon, F., & Casadesus, M. (2013). Can ISO 9001 improve service recovery. *Industrial Management & Data Systems, 113*(8).

Pijpers, R., Marteijn, T., Bosman, M., & Berg, V. D. W., & Dijkerman, E. (2008). Klik en klaar: Een onderzoek naar surfgedrag en usability bij kinderen (No. 111). Den Haag, The Netherlands: Stichting Mijn Kind Online.

Pine, J. B., & Gilmore, J. H. (2011). *The experience economy*. Cambridge, MA: Harvard Business Review Press.

Poh, M., Swenson, N. C., & Picard, R. W. (2010). A wearable sensor for unobtrusive, long-term assessment of electrodermal activity. *IEEE Transactions on Bio-Medical Engineering*, 1243–1252. PMID:20172811

Poon, A. (1993). *Tourism, technology and competitive strategies*. Oxford, UK: CAB.

Posey, W. J. (2006). *Activity based total accountability*. Retrieved from http://billposey.com/abta/

Prakash, V., & Gopalakrishnan, S. (2011). Testing efficiency exploited: Scripted versus exploratory testing. *Electronics Computer Technology*, 168-172.

Preacher, K. J., & Hayes, A. F. (2004). SPSS and SAS procedures for estimating indirect effects in simple mediation models. *Behavior Research Methods, Instruments, & Computers*, 36, 717–731. doi:10.3758/BF03206553 PMID:15641418

Preece, J., Rogers, Y., & Sharp, H. (2002). *Interaction design: Beyond human-computer interaction*. New York: John Wiley & Sons.

Pruitt, J., & Adline, T. (2006). *The persona lifecycle: Keeping people in mind throughout product design*. San Francisco: Morgan Kaufmann Publishers.

Przybyszewski, K. (2006). A new evaluation method for e-learning systems. In *Artificial intelligence and soft computing (LNCS)* (Vol. 4029, pp. 1209–1216). Berlin: Springer. doi:10.1007/11785231_126

PublicTechnology.net. (2007, November 22). *HMRC fall-out: 85 per cent of public now lack confidence in council web services*. Retrieved from http://www.publictechnol-ogy.net/sector/hmrc-fallout-85-cent-public-now-lack-confidence-council-web-services

Qi, S. S., Buhalis, D., & Law, R. (2007). Evaluation of the usability on Chinese destination management organisation websites. In *Information and communication technologies in tourism 2007*. New York: Springer-Verlag.

Qi, S. S., Law, R., & Buhalis, D. (2008). Usability of Chinese destination management organization websites. *Journal of Travel & Tourism Marketing*, 25(2), 182–198. doi:10.1080/10548400802402933

Qi, S. S., Leung, R., Law, R., & Buhalis, D. (2008). A study of information richness and downloading time for hotel websites in Hong Kong. In P. O'Connor, H. Wolfram, & G. Ulrike (Eds.), *Information and communication technologies 2008* (pp. 256–267). New York: Springer-Wien. doi:10.1007/978-3-211-77280-5_24

Rahman, Z. (2004). E-commerce solution for services. *European Business Review*, 16(6), 564–576. doi:10.1108/09555340410565396

Rajput, W. E. (2000). *E-commerce, systems, architecture and applications*. Artech House.

Ray, S., & Mukherjee, A. (2007). Development of a framework towards successful implementation of e-governance initiatives in health sector in India. *International Journal of Health Care Quality Assurance*, 20(6), 464–483. doi:10.1108/09526860710819413 PMID:18030965

Read, J. C., & MacFarlane, S. (2006). *Using the fun toolkit and other survey methods to gather opinions in child computer interaction*. Paper presented at the International Conference on Interaction Design and Children. Tampere, Finland.

Read, J. C., MacFarlane, S. J., & Casey, C. (2002). *Endurability, engagement and expectations: Measuring children's fun*. Paper presented at the International Conference on Interaction Design and Children. Eindhoven, The Netherlands.

Read, J. C. (2008). Validating the fun toolkit: An instrument for measuring children's opinions of technology. *Cognition Technology and Work*, 10(2), 119–128. doi:10.1007/s10111-007-0069-9

Reddick, C. (2011). Citizen interaction and e-government: Evidence for the managerial, consultative, and participatory models. *Transforming Government: People. Process and Policy*, 5(2), 167–184.

Redish, J., & Chisnell, D. (2004). *Designing web sites for older adults: A review of recent research*. Retrieved on April 8, 2013 from http://assets.aarp.org/www.aarp.org_/articles/research/oww/AARP-LitReview2004.pdf

Reichheld, F. F. (1993). Loyalty-based management. *Harvard Business Review*, 71(2), 64–73. PMID:10124634

Reichheld, F. F., & Sasser, W. E. (1990). Zero defections: Quality comes to services. *Harvard Business Review, 68*(5), 105–111. PMID:10107082

Reichheld, F. F., & Schefter, P. (2000). E-loyalty: Your secret weapon on the web. *Harvard Business Review, 87*(4), 105–113.

Revelle, G., Druin, A., Platner, M., Bederson, B. B., & Sherman, L. (2002). A visual search tool for early elementary science students. *Journal of Science Education and Technology, 11*(1), 49–57. doi:10.1023/A:1013947430933

Reynolds, J. (2000). e-Commerce: A critical review. *International Journal of Retail and Distribution Management, 28*(10), 417–444. doi:10.1108/09590550010349253

Ribbink, D., van Riel, A., Liljander, V., & Streukens, S. (2004). Comfort your online customer: Quality, trust and loyalty on the internet. *Managing Service Quality, 14*(6), 446–456. doi:10.1108/09604520410569784

Rigou, M., Sirmakessis, S., Stavrinoudis, D., & Xenos, M. (2007). Tools and methods for supporting e-learning communities and their evaluation. In *User-centered design of online learning communities*. Hershey, PA: IGI Global.

Rintamaki, T., Kuusela, H., & Mitronen, L. (2007). Identifying competitive customer value propositions in retailing. *Managing Service Quality, 17*(6), 621–634. doi:10.1108/09604520710834975

Roberts, R., & Goodwin, P. (2002). Weight approximations in multi-attribute decision models. *J. Multi-Crit. Decision Analysis, 11*, 291–303. doi:10.1002/mcda.320

Roupa, Z., Nikas, M., Gerasimou, E., Zafeiri, V., Giasyrani, L., Kazitori, E., & Sotiropoulou, P. (2010). The use of technology by the elderly. *Health Science Journal, 4*(2), 118–126.

Rowlands, I. (2008). *Information behaviour of the researcher of the future*. British Library JISC. doi:10.1108/00012530810887953

Roy, B. (1996). *Multicriteria methodology for decision aiding*. Dordrecht, The Netherlands: Kluwer. doi:10.1007/978-1-4757-2500-1

Rudall, B. H., & Mann, C. J. H. (2007). Smart systems and environments. *Kybernetes, 36*.

Russell, J. A. (1980). A circumplex model of affect. *Journal of Personality and Social Psychology, 39*(6), 1161–1178. doi:10.1037/h0077714

Rust, R. T., & Lemon, K. N. (2001). E-service and the consumer. *International Journal of Electronic Commerce, 5*(3), 85–101.

Rust, R. T., & Oliver, R. L. (1994). Service quality – Insights and managerial implications from the frontier. In *Service quality: New directions in theory and practice*. Thousand Oaks, CA: Sage. doi:10.4135/9781452229102.n1

Santos, J. (2003). E-service quality: A model of virtual service quality dimensions. *Managing Service Quality, 13*(3), 233–246. doi:10.1108/09604520310476490

Sanzo, M.J., Santos, M.L., & Va'zquez, R., & A´lvarez, L.I. (2003). The effect of market orientation on buyer–seller relationship satisfaction. *Industrial Marketing Management, 32*(4), 327–345. doi:10.1016/S0019-8501(01)00200-0

Sauro, J. (2010). *Can users self-report usability problems?* Retrieved September 13, 2012, from http://www.measuringusability.com/blog/self-reporting.php

Saxena, K. B. C. (2005). Towards excellence in e-governance. *International Journal of Public Sector Management, 18*(6), 498–513. doi:10.1108/09513550510616733

Sayago, S., & Blat, J. (2011). An ethnographical study of the accessibility barriers in the everyday interaction of older people with the web. *Universal Access Information Society, 10*(4), 359–371. doi:10.1007/s10209-011-0221-4

Schacter, J., Chung, G. K. W. K., & Dorr, A. (1998). Children's internet searching on complex problems: Performance and process analyses. *Journal of the American Society for Information Science American Society for Information Science, 49*(9), 840–849. doi:10.1002/(SICI)1097-4571(199807)49:9<840::AID-ASI9>3.0.CO;2-D

Schaik, P. V., & Ling, J. (2004). The effects of graphical display and screen ratio on information retrieval in web pages. *Computers in Human Behavior*. PMID:14983895

Scholl, H. J., Barzilai-Nahon, K., Jin-Hyuk, A., Popova, O. H., & Re, B. (2009). E-commerce and e-government: How do they compare? What can they learn from each other? In *Proceedings of System Sciences, 42nd Hawaii International Conference on system Sciences*. IEEE.

Schriver, K. A. (1997). *Dynamics in document design: Creating text for readers*. New York, NY: Wiley.

Schumaker, R. P., & Chen, H. (2007). Leveraging question answer technology to address terrorism inquiry. *Decision Support Systems, 43*, 1419–1430. doi:10.1016/j.dss.2006.04.007

Schumaker, R. P., Ginsburg, M., Chen, H. C., & Liu, Y. (2007). An evaluation of the chat and knowledge delivery components of a low-level dialog system: The AZ-ALICE experiment. *Decision Support Systems, 42*, 2236–2246. doi:10.1016/j.dss.2006.07.001

Schumaker, R. P., Liu, Y., Ginsburg, M., & Chen, H. C. (2007). Evaluating the efficacy of - A terrorism question/answer system. *Communications of the ACM, 50*, 74–80. doi:10.1145/1272516.1272517

Scott, J. K. (2005). Assessing the quality of municipal government websites. *State & Local Government Review, 37*(2), 151–165. doi:10.1177/0160323X0503700206

Seddon, P.B., Staples, D.S., Patnayakuni, R., & Bowtell, M.J. (1999). The dimensions of information systems success. *Communications of the Association for Information Systems, 2*, 20. Cameron, K.S., & Whetten, D.A. (1983). *Organizational effectiveness: A comparison of multiple models*. Academic Press.

Seidel, D., Richardson, K., Crilly, N., Matthews, F. E., Clarkson, J. P., & Brayne, C. (2010). Design for independent living: Activity demands and capabilities of older people. *Ageing and Society, 30*(7), 1239–1255. doi:10.1017/S0144686X10000310

Serenko, A. (2007). Are interface agents scapegoats? Attributions of responsibility in human-agent interaction. *Interacting with Computers, 19*, 293–303. doi:10.1016/j.intcom.2006.07.005

SFEE. (2003). *The pharmaceutical market in Greece: Facts and figures*. Athens, Greece: SFEE.

Shackel, B. (2009). Usability – Context, framework, definition, design and evaluation. *Interacting with Computers, 21*, 339–345. doi:10.1016/j.intcom.2009.04.007

Shapira, A., Barak, A., & Gal, I. (2007). Promoting older adults' well-being through internet training and use. *Aging & Mental Health, 11*(5), 477–484. doi:10.1080/13607860601086546 PMID:17882585

Shee, D. Y., & Wang, Y.-S. (2008). Multi-criteria evaluation of the web-based e-learning system: A methodology based on learner satisfaction and its applications. *Computers & Education, 50*, 894–905. doi:10.1016/j.compedu.2006.09.005

Siddall, E., Baibarac, C., Byrne, A., Byme, N., Deasy, A., & Flood, N. et al. (2011). Personas as a user-centred design tool for the built environment. *Engineering Sustainability, 164*(ES1), 59–69. doi:10.1680/ensu.1000015

Sienot, M. (1997). Pretesting web sites: A comparison between the plus-minus method and the think-aloud method for the world wide web. *Journal of Business and Technical Communication, 11*, 469–482. doi:10.1177/1050651997011004006

Silcock, R. (2001). What is e-government? *Parliamentary Affairs, 54*, 88–101. doi:10.1093/pa/54.1.88

Sim, G., MacFarlane, S., & Read, J. (2006). All work and no play: Measuring fun, usability, and learning in software for children. *Computers & Education, 46*(3), 235–248. doi:10.1016/j.compedu.2005.11.021

Siskos, J., & Yannacopoulos, D. (1985). Utastar: An ordinal regression method for building additive value functions. *Investigacao Operacional, 5*(1), 39–53.

Siskos, Y., & Grigoroudis, E. (2002). Measuring customer satisfaction for various services using multicriteria analysis. In *Aiding decisions with multiple criteria: Essays in honor of Bernard Roy*. Dordrecht, The Netherlands: Kluwer Academic Publishers. doi:10.1007/978-1-4615-0843-4_20

Siskos, Y., Grigoroudis, E., & Matsatsinis, N. F. (2005). Outranking theory and the UTA methods. In J. Figueira, S. Greco, & M. Ehrgott (Eds.), *Multiple criteria decision analysis – State of the art – Surveys* (pp. 297–344). Berlin: Springer.

Slatin, J., & Rush, S. (2003). *Maximum accessibility: Making your web site more usable for everyone.* Boston, MA: Addison-Wesley Longman.

Snijders, T., & Bosker, R. (2012). *Multilevel analysis: An introduction to basic and advanced multilevel modeling* (2nd ed.). London: Sage Publishers.

Solomon, M. R. (2004). *Consumer behavior.* Upper Saddle River, NJ: Prentice-Hall.

So, S. I., & Morrison, A. M. (2004). Internet marketing in tourism in Asia: An evaluation of the performance of East Asian national tourism organization websites. *Journal of Hospitality & Leisure Marketing, 11*(4), 93–118. doi:10.1300/J150v11n04_07

Soufi, B., & Maguire, B. (2007). Achieving usability within e-government web sites illustrated by a case study evaluation. In *Human interface and the management of information: Interacting in information environments (LNCS)* (Vol. 4558, pp. 777–784). Berlin: Springer. doi:10.1007/978-3-540-73354-6_85

Souza, R., Manning, H., & Dorsey, M. (2001). *Designing accessible sites now.* Forrester Research.

Spathis, C., Petridou, E., & Glaveli, N. (2004). Managing service quality in banks: customers' gender effects. *Managing Service Quality, 14*(1), 90–102. doi:10.1108/09604520410513695

Spiteri, J. M., & Dion, P. A. (2004). Customer value, overall satisfaction, end-user loyalty, and market performance in detail intensive industries. *Industrial Marketing Management, 33*(8), 675–687. doi:10.1016/j.indmarman.2004.03.005

Sproles, G. B., & Kendall, E. L. (1986). A methodology for profiling consumers' decision-making styles. *The Journal of Consumer Affairs, 20*(2), 267–279. doi:10.1111/j.1745-6606.1986.tb00382.x

Spyridakis, J. H., Wei, C., Barrick, J., Cuddihy, E., & Maust, B. (2005). Internet-based research: Providing a foundation for web design guidelines. *IEEE Transactions on Professional Communication, 48*, 242–260. doi:10.1109/TPC.2005.853927

Stahl, B. C. (2005). The paradigm of e-commerce in e-government and e-democracy. *Electronic Government Strategies and Implementation,* 1-19.

Stewart, M. (1995). *Keep the right customers.* New York: McGraw Hill.

Stickdorn, M., & Schneider, J. (2011). *This is service design thinking: Basics-tools-cases.* Amsterdam: BIS Publishers.

Stronge, A. J., Rodgers, W. A., & Fisk, A. D. (2006). Web-based information search and retrieval: Effects of strategy use and age on search success. *The Journal of Human Factors and Ergonomic Society, 48*(3), 434–446. doi:10.1518/001872006778606804 PMID:17063960

Sum, C., & Hui, C. (2009). Academic paper sales persons' service quality and customer loyalty in fashion chain stores A study in Hong Kong retail stores. *Journal of Fashion Marketing and Management, 13*(1), 98–108. doi:10.1108/13612020910939905

Sun, P.-C., Cheng, H.-K., & Finger, G. (2009). Critical functionalities of a successful e-learning system — An analysis from instructors' cognitive structure toward system usage. *Decision Support Systems, 48*, 293–302. doi:10.1016/j.dss.2009.08.007

Surjadjaja, H., Ghosh, S., & Antony, F. (2003). Determining and assessing the determinants of e-service operations. *Managing Service Quality, 13*(1), 39–53. doi:10.1108/09604520310456708

Sweller, J., van Merrienboer, J. J. G., & Paas, G. W. C. (1998). Cognitive architecture and instructional design. *Educational Psychology Review, 10*(3), 251–296. doi:10.1023/A:1022193728205

Swierenga, S. J., Sung, J. E., Pierce, G. L., & Propst, D. B. (2011). Website design and usability assessment implications from a usability study with visually impaired and sighted users. In *Universal access in HCI (LNCS)* (Vol. 6766, pp. 382–389). Berlin: Springer-Verlag.

Syrros, J. (2005). *ICT projects implementation in health sector: Success factors*. Athens, Greece: SEPE.

Szymanski, D., & Hise, R. (2000). E-satisfaction: An initial examination. *Journal of Retailing, 76*(3), 309–322. doi:10.1016/S0022-4359(00)00035-X

Tarafdar, M., & Zhang, J. (2005). Analyzing the influence of web site design parameters on web site usability. *Information Resources Management Journal, 18*(4), 62–80. doi:10.4018/irmj.2005100104

Tarpey, L. X. (1975). Brand loyalty revisited: A commentary. *JMR, Journal of Marketing Research, 12*(4), 488–491. doi:10.2307/3151104

Tedesco, D., Schade, A., Pernice, K., & Nielsen, J. (2008). *Site map usability: 47 guidelines based on usability studies with people using site maps*. Retrieved on April 12, 2013 from http://www.nngroup.com/reports/sitemaps/

Tenenhaus, M., Amato, S., & Esposito, V. (2004). A global goodness-of-fit index for PLS structural equation modeling. In *Proceedings of the XLII SIS Scientific Meeting*, (pp. 739-742). SIS.

Thatcher, J., Bohman, P., Burks, M., Henry, S. L., Regan, B., & Swierenga, S. J. ... Waddell, C. D. (2003). Constructing accessible web sites. Birmingham, UK: Glasshaus.

Thimbleby, H., Cairns, P., & Jones, M. (2001). Usability analysis with Markov models. *ACM Transactions on Computer-Human Interaction, 8*(2), 99–132.

Thomas, P., & Macredie, R. (2002). Introduction to the new usability. *ACM Transactions on Computer-Human Interaction, 9*(2), 69–73.

Thornton, J. B., & Thornton, E. (2013). *Assessing state government financial transparency websites* (Vol. 41). London: Emerald Group Publishing Limited.

Thuring, M., & Mahlke, S. (2007). Usability, aesthetics and emotions in human-technology interaction. *International Journal of Psychology, 42*(4), 253–264. doi:10.1080/00207590701396674

Tierney, P. (2000). Internet-based evaluation of tourism web site effectiveness: Methodological issues and survey results. *Journal of Travel Research, 39*(2), 212–219. doi:10.1177/004728750003900211

Tractinsky, N., Katz, A. S., & Ikar, D. (2000). What is beautiful is usable. *Interacting with Computers, 13*(2), 127–145. doi:10.1016/S0953-5438(00)00031-X

Tranberg, H., & Hansen, F. (1986). Patterns of brand loyalty: Their determinants and their role for leading brands. *European Journal of Marketing, 20*(3), 81–109. doi:10.1108/EUM0000000004642

Tremblay, M. C., Hevner, A. R., & Berndt, D. J. (2010). Focus groups for artifact refinement and evaluation in design research. *Communications of the Association for Information Systems, 26*(27), 599–618.

Truch, E. (2006). Lean consumption and its influence on brand. *Journal of Consumer Behaviour, 5*, 157–165. doi:10.1002/cb.42

Tse, D. K., & Wilton, P. C. (1988). Models of consumer satisfaction: An extension. *JMR, Journal of Marketing Research, 25*(2), 204–212. doi:10.2307/3172652

Tuch, A. N., Roth, S. P., Hornbæk, K., Opwis, K., & Bargas-Avila, J. A. (2012). Is beautiful really usable? Toward understanding the relation between usability, aesthetics, and affect in HCI. *Computers in Human Behavior, 28*(5), 1596–1607. doi:10.1016/j.chb.2012.03.024

Tullis, T., & Albert, B. (2008). *Measuring the user experience: Collecting, analyzing, and presenting usability metrics*. San Francisco, CA: Morgan Kaufmann Publishers Inc.

Turnbow, D., Kasianovitz, K., Snyder, L., Gilbert, D., & Yamamoto, D. (2005). Usability testing for web redesign: A UCLA case study. *OCLC Systems & Services, 21*(3), 226–234.

Tzeng, G.-H., Chiang, C.-H., & Li, C.-W. (2007). Evaluating intertwined effects in e-learning programs: A novel hybrid MCDM model based on factor analysis and DEMATEL. *Expert Systems with Applications, 32*, 1028–1044. doi:10.1016/j.eswa.2006.02.004

Ummelen, N., & Neutelings, R. (2002). Measuring reading behavior in policy documents: A comparison of two instruments. *IEEE Transactions on Professional Communication, 43*, 292–301. doi:10.1109/47.867945

United Nations. (2008). *UN e-government survey 2008: From e-government to connected governance.* Retrieved May 12, 2013, from http://www.ansa-africa.net/uploads/documents/publications/UN_e-government_survey_2008.pdf

United Nations. (2011). *E-government.* Retrieved March 10, 2013, from http://unpan1.un.org

University of Cambridge. (2013). *Inclusive design toolkit.* Retrieved on April 8, 2013, from http://www.inclusive-designtoolkit.com

UNWTO Technical Manual. (1995). *Collection of tourism expenditure statistics.* World Tourism Organization. Retrieved 2013-04-09, from http://www2.unwto.org

*UNWTO World Tourism Barometer.* (2013). Retrieved 2013-04-09 from http://www2.unwto.org

USDA-FNS. (2000). *Dietary intake and dietary attitudes among food stamp participants and other low-income individuals.* U.S. Department of Agriculture – Food and Nutrition Services. Retrieved on June 27, 2013, from http://www.fns.usda.gov/fsp/nutrition_education/research.htm

Van den Haak, M. J., De Jong, M. D. T., & Schellens, P. J. (2003). Retrospective vs. concurrent think-aloud protocols: Testing the usability of an online library catalogue. *Behaviour & Information Technology, 22,* 339–251. doi:10.1080/0044929031000

van der Veer, G. C., & Meguizo, C. P. (2003). Mental models. In *The human–computer interaction handbook: Fundamentals, evolving technologies and emerging applications.* London: Lawrence Erlbaum Associates Publishers.

Van Dijk, J., Pieterson, W., Van Deursen, A., & Ebbers, W. (2007). E-services for citizens: The Dutch usage case. *Lecture Notes in Computer Science, 4656,* 155–166. doi:10.1007/978-3-540-74444-3_14

van Riel, A. C. R., Liljander, V., & Jurriens, P. (2001). Exploring consumer evaluations of e- services: A portal site. *International Journal of Service Industry Management, 12*(4), 359–377. doi:10.1108/09564230110405280

van Rosmalen, M. M., Kalidien, S. N., & de Heer-de Lange, N. E. (Eds.). (2010). Criminaliteit en rechtshandhaving 2010: Ontwikkelingen en samenhangen. Justitie in Statistiek, 1.

Van Schaik, P., & Ling, J. (2008). Modelling user experience with web sites: Usability, hedonic value, beauty and goodness. *Interacting with Computers, 20,* 419–432. doi:10.1016/j.intcom.2008.03.001

Vandermerwe, S. (1996). Becoming a customer owing corporation. *Long Range Planning, 23*(6), 770–782. doi:10.1016/S0024-6301(97)82815-4

Vavra, T. G. (1997). *Improving your measurement of customer satisfaction: A guide to creating, conducting, analyzing, and reporting customer satisfaction measurement programs.* Milwaukee, WI: ASQC Quality Press.

Venkatesh, V., Morris, M. G., Davis, G. B., & Davis, F. D. (2003). User acceptance of information technology: Toward a unified view. *Management Information Systems Quarterly, 27*(3), 425–478.

Viscusi, G. (2009). The eGovQual methodology: Information systems planning as research intervention. *Working Papers on Information Systems, 9*(15).

W3C. (2013). *A little history of the world wide web.* Retrieved on March 22, 2013 from http://www.w3.org/History.html

W3C. (2013). *Accessibility — W3C.* Retrieved April 20, 2013, from, http://www.w3.org/standards/webdesign/accessibility

Wacholder, N., Kelly, D., Kantor, P., Rittman, R., Sun, Y., & Bai, B. et al. (2007). A model for quantitative evaluation of an end-to-end question-answering system. *Journal of the American Society for Information Science and Technology, 58,* 1082–1099. doi:10.1002/asi.20560

Wagner, C., Cheung, K., Lee, F., & Ip, R. (2003). Enhancing e-government in developing countries: Managing knowledge through virtual communities. *The Electronic Journal on Information Systems in Developing Countries, 14*(4), 1–20.

Wagner, N., Hassanein, K., & Head, M. (2010). Computer use by older adults: A multi-disciplinary review. *Computers in Human Behavior, 26,* 870–882. doi:10.1016/j.chb.2010.03.029

WAI. (1998). *Web accessibility initiative 2.0.* Retrieved on March 22, 2013 from http://www.w3.org/WAI/intro/wcag.php

Wäljas, M., Segerståh, K., Väänänen-Vainio-Mattila, K., & Oinas-Kukkonen, H. (2010). Cross-platform service user experience: A field study and an initial framework. In *Proceedings of Mobile HCI'10*. Lisboa, Portugal: HCI. doi:10.1145/1851600.1851637

Wang, L., Bretschneider, S., & Gant, J. (2005). Evaluating web-based e-government services with a citizen-centric approach. In *Proceedings of the 38th Hawaii International Conference on System Sciences*, (pp. 129-137). IEEE.

Wang, Y. S., & Liao, Y. W. (2008). Assessing egovernment systems success: A validation of the DeLone and McLean model of information systems success. *Government Information Quarterly*, 25(4), 717–733. doi:10.1016/j.giq.2007.06.002

Warkentin, M., Gefen, D., Pavlou, P. A., & Rose, G. M. (2002). Encouraging citizen adoption of e-governement by building trust. *Electronic Markets*, 72(3), 157–162. doi:10.1080/101967802320245929

WCAG. (2008). *Web content accessibility guidelines*. Retrieved on March 23, 2013 from http://www.w3.org/WAI/intro/wcag

Webb, H. W., & Webb, L. A. (2004). SiteQual: An integrated measure of web site quality. *Journal of Enterprise Information Management*, 17(6), 430–440. doi:10.1108/17410390410566724

Welle Donker-Kuijer, M., De Jong, M., & Lentz, L. (2008). Heuristic web site evaluation: Exploring the effects of guidelines on experts' detection of usability problems. *Technical Communication*, 55, 392–404.

Wheeler, S. (2012). E-learning. In *Encyclopedia of the sciences of learning 2012* (pp. 1108–1109). Berlin: Springer.

Witt, S. F., & Moutinho, L. (Eds.). (1995). *Tourism marketing and management handbook*. London: Prentice Hall.

Wolkerstorfer, P., Tscheligi, M., Sefelin, R., Milchrahm, H., Hussain, Z., Lechner, M., & Shahzad, S. (2008). Probing an agile usability process. In *Proceedings of CHI 2008*. Florence, Italy: ACM.

Wood, E., Willoughby, T., Rushing, A., Bechtel, L., & Gilbert, J. (2005). Use of computer input devices by older adults. *Journal of Applied Gerontology*, 24(5), 419–438. doi:10.1177/0733464805278378

Wood, F. B., Siegel, E. R., LaCroix, E., & Lyon, B. (2003). A practical approach to e-government web evaluation. In *IT professional human interface and the management of information: Interacting in information environments (LNCS)* (Vol. 4558, pp. 777–784). Berlin: Springer. doi:10.1109/MITP.2003.1202231

Woodruff, R. B., & Flint, D. J. (2006). Marketing's service-dominant logic and customer value. In *The service-dominant logic of marketing: Dialog, debate, and directions* (pp. 183–195). Academic Press.

World Bank. (2013). *Defining e-government*. Retrieved March 10, 2013 from http://web.worldbank.org

Xiang, Z., & Gretzel, U. (2010). Role of social media in online travel information search. *Tourism Management*, 31(2), 179–188. doi:10.1016/j.tourman.2009.02.016

Yang, Z., & Fang, X. (2004). Online service quality dimensions and their relationships with satisfaction: A content analysis of customer reviews of securities brokerage services. *International Journal of Service Industry Management*, 15(3), 302–326. doi:10.1108/09564230410540953

Yannou, B., Yvars, P.-A., Hoyle, C., & Chen, W. (2013). Set-based design by simulation of usage scenario coverage. *Journal of Engineering Design*, 1–29.

Yarosh, S., Radu, I., Hunter, S., & Rosenbaum, E. (2011). *Examining values: An analysis of nine years of IDC research*. Paper presented at the 10th International Conference on Interaction Design and Children. Ann Arbor, MI.

Yen, B., Hu, P. J.-H., & Wang, M. (2007). Toward an analytical approach for effective web site design: A framework for modeling, evaluation and enhancement. *Electronic Commerce Research and Applications*, 6, 159–170. doi:10.1016/j.elerap.2006.11.004

Yoo, B., & Donthu, N. (2001). Developing a scale to measure the perceived quality of an internet shopping site (sitequal). *Quarterly Journal of Electronic Commerce*, 2(1), 31–46.

Youngblood, N., & Mackiewicz, J. (2012, June). A usability analysis of municipal government website home pages in Alabama. *Government Information Quarterly*, 582–588. doi:10.1016/j.giq.2011.12.010

Yu, H., Lee, M., Kaufman, D., Ely, J., Osheroff, J. A., Hripcsak, G., & Cimino, J. (2007). Development, implementation, and a cognitive evaluation of a definitional question answering system for physicians. *Journal of Biomedical Informatics*, *40*, 236–251. doi:10.1016/j.jbi.2007.03.002 PMID:17462961

Zack, M. (1999). Developing a knowledge strategy. *California Management Review*, *41*(3), 125–145. doi:10.2307/41166000

Zajicek, M. (2006). Aspects of HCI research for older people. *Universal Access Information Society*, *5*, 279–286. doi:10.1007/s10209-006-0046-8

Zaphiris, P., Kurniawan, S., & Ghiawadwala, M. (2007). A systematic approach to the development of research-based web design guidelines for older people. *Universal Access Information Society*, *6*, 59–75. doi:10.1007/s10209-006-0054-8

Zeithaml, V. A. (1988). Consumer perceptions of price, quality, and value: A means-end model and synthesis of evidence. *Journal of Marketing*, 2–22. doi:10.2307/1251446

Zeithaml, V. A., Parasuraman, A., & Malhotra, A. (2002). Service quality delivery through web sites: A critical review of extant knowledge. *Journal of the Academy of Marketing Science*, *30*(4), 362–375. doi:10.1177/009207002236911

Zhou, L., Dai, & Zhang. (2007). Online shopping acceptance model - A Critical survey of consumer factors in online shopping. *Journal of Electronic Commerce Research*, *8*(1), 41–62.

Zopounidis, C., & Doumpos, M. (1999). A multicriteria decision aid methodology for sorting decision problems: The case of financial distress. *Computational Economics*, *14*(3), 197–218. doi:10.1023/A:1008713823812

Zwick, D., & Dholakia, N. (2004). Consumer subjectivity in the age of internet: The radical concept of marketing control through customer relationship management. *Information and Organization.* doi:10.1016/j.infoandorg.2004.01.002

# About the Contributors

**Denis Yannacopoulos** is a Professor of Management Information Systems at the Technological and Educational Institute of Pireaus, Greece. He is a proposal and structure evaluator of Continual Professional Training in the Ministry of Labor of Greece, since 1998. He received his PhD degree on the application and experimentation of a multicriteria decision support system from the University of Paris, France, in 1985. He has published many papers in national and international papers, and has participated in many research and consultative committees.

**Panagiotis Manolitzas** is a PhD student at the Decision Support Systems of Technical University of Crete. He holds a Bachelor in Public Administration (specialization in Management Science) from the University of Athens and a MSc in Public Management (specialization in Management Science) from the University of Athens. He taught Management Information Systems, Health Management at University of Athens, Management Information Systems at Technological Educational institute of Piraeus, and Decision Support Systems at Technical University of Crete. He has over 40 publications in international and national scientific conferences and scientific journals. He is a Member of Hellenic Operational Research Society. His research interests lie in the areas of Simulation, Decision Support Systems for the health care organizations, health services research, process mining, multiple criteria analysis, and e-government.

**Nikolaos Matsatsinis** is a full Professor of Information and Decision Support Systems at the Department of Production Engineering and Management of the Technical University of Crete, Greece. He is Director of Decision Support Systems Lab and former President of the Hellenic Operational Research Society (HELORS) from 2009-2012. He received his B.A. in Physics from Aristotle University of Thessaloniki (1980) and his PhD in Intelligence Decision Support Systems for Marketing Decisions from Technical University of Crete (1995). He also has over 30 years of experience in Information and Decision Systems development. He has contribute as scientific or project coordinator on over of 48 national and international projects. He is chief editor in two international scientific journals and member of the international advisory board of three scientific journals. He is the author or co-author of 18 books and over of 90 articles in international scientific journals and books. He has over of 165 presentations in international and national scientific conferences. His research interests fall into the areas of Decision Support Systems, Artificial Intelligent and Multi-Agent Systems, Multicriteria Decision Analysis, Electronic Business, e-Marketing, Consumer Behaviour Analysis, Group Decision Support Systems, Workflow Management Systems. Prof. Matsatsinis is member of the Institute of Electrical and Electronics Engineers (IEEE); member of the American Association for Artificial Intelligence (AAAI); Member of IFIP, CEPIS; International Consortium for Electronic Business; member of INFORMS, EURO, HELORS, Euro Working Group on Multicriteria Decision Aid; Euro Working Group on Decision Support Systems; European Federation for Information Technology in Agriculture, Food, and the Environment – EFITA.

**Evangelos Grigoroudis** is Assistant Professor at the Department of Production Engineering and Management, Technical University of Crete, Chania, Greece. He received the diploma in production and management engineering from the Technical University of Crete, in 1991, and M.S. and Ph.D. degrees from the same university in 1996 and 1999, respectively. His research interests are in service quality, operational research, and customer behavioral analysis. He acts as reviewer for more than 50 scientific journals and he is an Assistant Editor of *Operational Research: An International Journal* and *International Journal of Decision Support Systems*, and a member of the Editorial Board *International Journal of Information and Decision Sciences, International Journal of Information Systems in the Service Sector*, and *International Journal of Multicriteria Decision Making*.

\* \* \*

**Deborah Carstens** joined the Florida Institute of Technology in 2003 and is an Associate Professor of Management Information Systems. She holds a Ph.D. in Industrial Engineering from the University of Central Florida (UCF), MBA from Florida Tech, and B.S. in Business Administration also from UCF. She is a Project Management Professional (PMP). Previously, she worked for NASA Kennedy Space Center (KSC) from 1992 through 2003. She instructs courses in MIS, human-computer interaction, project management, and product development. Her research is in human error analysis resulting in the optimization of systems, safety, processes, and human performance.

**Fa Martı Casadesus**, Prof; is an Associate Professor at the Universitat de Girona in Spain as well as director of l'Agència per a la Qualitat del Sistema Universitari de Catalunya, AQU Catalunya. He studied Industrial Engineering at the Polytechnic University of Catalonia in Barcelona. Later on, he studied his doctoral courses at the University of Girona in Spain. His doctoral thesis is about the ISO 9000 implementation in the industrial companies of the Catalonia Autonomous Region (Spain). He has published several articles in both national and international academic journals (i.e. *Journal of Cleaner Production, Industrial Management & Data Systems, CEDE, TQM & Business Excellence, Economia Industrial, TQM Magazine, International Journal of Quality & Reliability Management, European Business Review, Management Auditing Journal*). He has collaborated in many projects financed by the CCQ (Catalonian Quality Center) of the Catalonian Administration. He is too, the co-leader of the GREPP (Research group on Product, Process, and Planning).

**Sunil Choenni** holds a PhD in database technology from the University of Twente and a MSc in theoretical computer science from Delft University of Technology. Currently, he is heading the department of Statistical Information Management and Policy Analysis of the Research and Documentation Centre (WODC) of the Dutch Ministry of Justice and is a professor of human-centered ICT at Rotterdam University of Applied Sciences in Rotterdam. His research interests include data warehouses and data mining, databases, e-government, and human centered design. He publishes frequently papers in these fields and acts as PC member for various conferences.

**Constantinos K. Coursaris** is an Assistant Professor in the Department of Telecommunication, Information Studies, and Media. He is also Faculty Researcher in Usability/Accessibility Research and Consulting. His formal training consists of a B.Eng. in Aerospace, an MBA in e-Business, and a Ph.D.

in Information Systems with a concentration on electronic business (e-Business) and mobile commerce (m-Commerce). "Dr. C" studies user motivations, expectations, and experiences with new media and the consequent design implications with a focus on social systems. He supplements his research expertise with consulting on social media for governance and/or marketing, and has trained diverse organizations in North America, Europe, the Middle East and North Africa (MENA).

**Charoula Drosopoulou**, post-graduate student in information systems, University of Macedonia. Her thesis is titled: "Mobile Business / Marketing in Tourist Sector." She holds a Bachelor degree in Applied Informatics and working experience in businesses IT Department.

**Dimitrios Drosos** is a lecturer at Technological Education Institute of Piraeus – Business School. He has presented a number of papers at national and international level conferences. He has also authored numerous publications in national and international journals. His principal research interests are in the area of Management Information System, E-Business, Multicriteria Analysis, Customer Satisfaction, and Total Quality Management. During the last years, he has been involved in various projects related to E-Business, Business Strategy, Reengineering, Planning, Management and Implementation of IT projects. He has worked for several years as Director and Project Manager in multinational companies in Greece. From 2009 to date, he has been a member of the Board of the Hellenic Operational Research Society (HELORS).

**Sanne Elling** is a usability specialist at FirMM in Utrecht, The Netherlands. She has done extensive research into different methods for evaluating Websites. She published a dissertation on Website evaluation methodology and was awarded together with Leo Lentz and Menno de Jong with the 2012 best paper award for *IEEE Transactions on Professional Communication*.

**Vassilios Fortsas** is a Ph.D. candidate at the Decision Support Systems Laboratory of the Technical University of Crete. He received his diploma in production and management engineering and M.S. degree from the Technical University of Crete. He has worked as a researcher in several national and EU-funded research programmes, as well as a teaching assistant in a number of courses in the School of Production Engineering and Management, Technical University of Crete, Chania, Greece. He has published papers and book chapters in the fields of multicriteria decision analysis and customer satisfaction.

**Rimantas Gatautis** is the Director of Electronic Business Research Center, at the Kaunas University of Technology where he is also a professor of electronic business. Prof. Dr. R. Gatautis has a wide-ranging experience in European Commission projects in the Leonardo da Vinci, EUREKA, COST, and 6th Framework programs. He is also member of several scientific and advisory committees responsible for evaluating national government programs in the domains of electronic business and electronic government. He currently works as an expert in Lithuania National Study and Science Fund, Information Society Development Committee under Lithuania Government, Education Studies Quality Assessment Center, and as a reviewer of projects in eTen programme. His currently research concentrates on IST influence on enterprises transformation in the transition economies, e-business models in transition economies, socio-economic aspects of IST adaptation, IST influence on governance and democracy processes, knowledge role in value creation, knowledge driven innovations.

**Theo Huibers** is Professor of Information Retrieval at the Human Media Interaction Group of the University of Twente, a position he has held since 2002. As managing partner of a strategy consulting firm, Huibers is also a well-known senior strategy advisor in the media and technology segment. He has published over 60 academic papers in the areas of information theory, XML, information retrieval tasks for children, social media and citizen participation, business strategies, and different aspects of information retrieval.

**Seema Jain** received a BDes and MDes degrees in Product Design from the University of Leeds in 2010. Since 2011, she has worked at Brunel University and Age UK on a Knowledge Transfer Partnership funded by the Technology Strategy Board. Her position as a Multimedia Designer and Researcher allows her to carry out research and channel this through Age UK. Seema specialises in Web usability, ageing population, and User Experience Design and Research. Seema's research interests are in User Experience Design and Research, inclusive design, technology, and communication.

**Hanna Jochmann-Mannak** is a PhD student on Child-Computer Interaction. She studies children's information-seeking behavior in digital environments. More specifically, she studies the effects of playful interface design on children's search performance and affective response. Her interdisciplinary PhD-research project is a collaboration between researchers of the Human Media Interaction Group at the University of Twente and the Language and Communication Group at Utrecht University.

**Sandra Kalidien** studied Psychology at Leiden University where she graduated in methods and techniques and child psychology. She has several years of research experience in different areas, ranging from biotechnology and mental health care to the field of justice. Currently, she holds a research position at the Statistical Information Management and Policy Analysis division of the Research and Documentation Centre of the Dutch Ministry of Security and Justice. Here she leads a project that monitors criminal developments in The Netherlands. Sandra's further interests are related to e-government.

**Mr. Stephen Kies** is a Nathan M. Bisk College of Business student at Florida Institute of Technology studying both Information Systems and Business Administration: Leadership & Social Responsibility majors with a minor in Sustainability. He has been on the Dean's list every college term with an expected graduation in May 2015. Mr. Kies holds several leadership positions in student organizations on campus. He has been working as a student researcher in the areas of government accountability and usability for the University for two-years. After he graduates, he will pursue his Master's degree in Corporate Social Responsibility.

**Georgia Kyriakaki** is a Researcher and PhD Candidate in the Department of Production Engineering and Management, Technical University of Crete in the area of Intelligent Tutoring Systems. She received a Masters of Engineering Diploma from the Department of Electronics and Computer Engineering of the Technical University of Crete and the Diploma of Electronics and Computer Engineering from the Technical University of Crete. Her research interests include Decision Support Systems, Multicriteria Information Systems, Cultural Heritage Information Systems, Learning Management Systems, and Intelligent Tutoring Systems.

**Leo Lentz** is a professor of document design and communication at Utrecht University, The Netherlands. Web usability and text evaluation is the main focus of his research. He has published internationally in several journals and was awarded as a Landmark Author for *IEEE Transactions on Professional Communication* and has been awarded two times for Technical Communication with the Frank R. Smith Outstanding Journal Article Award.

**Eleonora-Ioulia Malama**, Postdoctoral Researcher, holds a bachelor degree in Business Economics, a MSc in Marketing, University of Strathclyde, Scotland, UK. She finished her PhD in Applied Informatics, University of Macedonia, Greece, in 2007. Her academic interests are marketing, e-marketing, advertising, e-commerce, e-business, e-government, marketing information systems, Website evaluation.

**Frederic Marimon**, PhD in Business Administration, is professor at the Universitat Internacional de Catalunya (Spain) and at the Universitat de Girona (Spain). He studied Industrial Engineering at the Polytechnic University of Catalonia in Barcelona, and Master in Business and Administration at the IESE in Barcelona. He is focused on production area, mainly in quality, e-quality measurement and services in companies. He has published several articles in both national and international academic journals, most of them in the quality management issue and also some papers that analyze the diffusion phenomenon of management standards (i.e. ISO 9000, ISO 14000, etc.). At the same time, he is involved in some consultancy projects, most of them related with the implementation of quality systems, although he has also been implicated in other fields such as logistics.

**Petros Pallis** graduated with a degree in Production Engineering and Management from the Technical University of Crete, where he was exposed to a full range of courses, which provided him with a firm foundation in engineering. The areas covered by Production Systems, Decision Support Systems—where he completed his Thesis in Multicriteria Decision Analysis—as well as Product Design and Development fascinated him the most. He took part in different projects as a student employee and an intern later on. His keen interest in design gave him the opportunity to input his ideas and enriched his understanding of the integrated relationships between engineering and the dynamics of aesthetics and style. He has been offered a place to join Product Design Engineering and study for his MSc at the University of Glasgow and the Glasgow School of Art in September 2013.

**Fotini Patsioura** holds a BSc in Applied Informatics from University of Macedonia of Thessaloniki and a MSc degree in E-Commerce from University of Sunderland, UK. Received her PhD in 2007. Her research introduced a conceptual model for measuring the effectiveness of Corporate Advertising Web Sites. Currently, she works at the Department of Informatics and Computerisation of the Municipality of Evosmos, and she is involved with the development and management of e-government applications financed by the Operational Programme "Information Society," such as Municipalities Portals and Geographical Information Systems. She is the employee in charge for the operational planning of "Syzefxis" project of the "Ministry for the Interior, Public Administration and Decentralization" and the management of the municipality's Website and Web-based services. She continues her academic research in analysing and examining qualitative factors and evaluating their impact on the effectiveness of e-commerce B2C, e-government and advertising Websites.

**Ted Sanders** is a full Professor of Discourse Studies and Language use in the department of Dutch of the Faculty of Humanities at Utrecht University. He is also Head of Department of Languages, Literature and Communication. Sanders' research concentrates on discourse structure and coherence. His research is embedded in the "Discourse Representation and Processing" and "Readability and Comprehension" projects of the Utrecht Institute of Linguistics OTS, and includes text linguistics, discourse analysis, cognitive processes of discourse production and understanding, and text evaluation and document design.

**Gabriella Spinelli** is a Senior Lecturer in System Design and Innovation at Brunel University (London). She has 15 years' experience in designing interaction, technologies, and communication, starting from the users. Her recent research interests locate Gabriella's expertise at the interface between design and marketing where most of her work now resides. Prior to her doctoral studies, Gabriella worked at the research centre of Domus Academy (Italy), the Human Factors and Ergonomic Lab at Eastman Kodak (NY), and the Appliance Studio (UK). Throughout her academic career, Gabriella has received considerable research funds to apply user-centred approaches to product/service/system design and commercialization. Lately, she is has been leading a multidisciplinary research group investigating the effects of ageing on decision-making and consumer behaviour. She continues her work as consultant to make her research socially and commercially relevant. Gabriella is the Director for Business Strategy and Innovation at the Brunel Institute for Ageing Studies (BIAS).

**Randy Stockman** is a Computer Engineer with ERC Incorporated at the Kennedy Space Center and a Nathan M. Bisk College of Business student at Florida Institute of Technology in the field of Information Systems. He has been on the Dean's list every semester while at Florida Tech and has been working as a student researcher in the areas of government accountability, information technology, and usability for the university for the past two years. Mr. Stockman has also held many IT jobs around the Space Coast in the past, including a Computer Science/MIS internship with NASA.

**Sarah J. Swierenga** is the Director of Usability/Accessibility Research and Consulting at Michigan State University. A researcher and a practitioner with over 25 years of experience in the scientific study of users in commercial, military, and academic environments, she possesses extensive skills in user interface design and evaluation methodologies. She co-authored *Constructing Accessible Web Sites,* and wrote a chapter for *The User-Centered Design Casebook*. Swierenga served on the U.S. Access Board 508/255 refresh committee, the UPA Voting and Usability Project, and the W3C WCAG2.0 Evaluation Methodology Task Force. She is a Certified Professional Ergonomist.

**Nikolaos Tsotsolas** holds a Diploma in Production Engineering and Management from the Technical University of Crete, Greece (1997), a M.Sc. in Operational Research (2001) from the same university, and a PhD in Statistical Science (2009) from University of Piraeus. He had received a 3-year scholarship from Greek Ministry of Education for performing field research on Post-Optimality Analysis (multiple and near-optimal solutions) in Linear Systems. From 2006 to date, he is member of the Board of the Hellenic Operational Research Society (HELORS). For the last four years, he is a temporary lecturer in Technological Educational Institute of Piraeus. His research interests fall into the areas of multi-criteria analysis, decision support systems, service quality, and post-optimality analysis in mathematical programming.

**Elena Vitkauskaite** is Research Associate in Electronic Business Research Centre and lecturer in department of Marketing in faculty of Economics and Management of Kaunas University of Technology. Presented Masters thesis on "Quality Measurement of Electronic Business: Case of Public Services" at Kaunas University of Technology in year 2006. PhD student since 2008. Preliminary dissertation topic "Localisation of Marketing Decisions in Social Network Sites." Current research issues related to modelling of business processes, quality measurement of electronic services, cross-cultural issues on Web, social network sites. Elena Vitkauskaitė takes part in national and international scientific projects (including special European Commission programs, 6th Framework programs, etc.).

**Maro Vlachopoulou**, Professor of e-Marketing /e-Business, Department of Applied Informatics, University of Macedonia. Her professional expertise, research, and teaching interests include: marketing information systems, e-business/e-marketing models, e-marketplaces, internet marketing plan, new technologies and information systems in marketing, mobile business / marketing, social media / networks and marketing, ERP (Enterprise Resource Planning), CRM (Customer Relationship Management) systems, Supply Chain Management (SCM) Systems, knowledge marketing management systems, e-supply chain management, e-logistics, with particular emphasis on specific applications (e.g. agrifood, environment, health). She has participated in numerous research programs and has published a wide number of papers in International journal and Conferences. Her role at the project as principal investigator is quite important as her expertise and experience at the specific domain is crucial for managing and coordinating the tasks and the team members within the project.

**Athanassios Vozikis** is Assistant Professor at the Department of Economics of the University of Piraeus. He holds a degree in Public Administration from the Panteion University, a M.Sc. in Health Informatics from National Kapodistriako University of Athens, and a Ph.D. in Health Economics and Information Systems from the University of Piraeus. He has been an I.K.Y. (State Scholarships Foundation) scholar for his M.SC. and Ph.D. studies. He is member of the National Council of Public Health, member of several scientific associations and organizations and reviewer of academic journals. He has participated in several research projects related to the analysis–development and implementation of information systems, business and economic re-engineering processes in the health care sector, as well as in various other sectors in public and private organizations. He has participated in several conferences and a number of his articles have been published in academic journals, academic issues and scientific conferences proceedings. He teaches Health Economics, Healthcare Management, Environmental Economics, Information Systems, and Digital Economy courses at an undergraduate level and Health Economics, Health Information Systems, and Strategic Information Systems courses at a postgraduate level. He has been supervisor and referee of several dissertations of postgraduate students. His research interests are in the field of Health Economics, Healthcare Management, Public Health, E.R.P. Systems, Health Information Systems, and Digital Economy.

**Pamela Whitten** is recognized internationally for research in telemedicine and its applications to improve patient care, delivery of health care services and education. Her funded research has enabled her to test innovative telemedicine interventions in a wide array of community settings. In addition to assessing outcomes and impacts of telemedicine, she also conducts research examining technology-based mediated communication to reach underserved populations, such as the creation of health Websites. Her most recent work addresses the role of social media as a health communication intervention strategy. Since 2009, Dr. Whitten has also served as Dean and Professor, College of Communication Arts and Sciences, Michigan State University.

**Richard van Witzenburg** is a geologist and historian, holding a Masters degree in International Relations. He worked for several ICT companies, gaining years of experience with Web design and development, and worked as a researcher for Non-Governmental Organisations in the field of human rights. Richard joined the WODC as a researcher in 2012 and is involved in designing and building interfaces for WODC projects.

**Luc Honore Petnji Yaya** holds a PhD in Quality Management. He is assistant professor at the Universitat Internacional de Catalunya (Spain) Faculty of Economics and Social Sciences. He has a Master in Business Innovation and Technology Management at the Universitat de Girona (Spain), a degree in Mathematics and Computer Science, as well as in Accounting and Finance in Leeds (UK). He participated in various research projects from different universities, and his work has been published in refereed journals such as *Industrial Management & Data Systems, Total Quality Management and Business Excellence, International Journal for Quality Research, Review of International Comparative Management*, etc. He has presented several papers at national and international conferences. His current research interests include quality management as a whole, service operations and e-services quality. In addition, his research interests include business innovation, integration management system, customer satisfaction, customer loyalty, etc.

**Stelios Zimeras** holds a BSc. (Hons) on Statistics and Insurance Sciences from University of Piraeus (5th in the rank) and Ph.D. on Statistics from the University of Leeds, U.K. He had received a full scholarship (fees and maintenance) during his research studies (1993-1997) from the University of Leeds. Since 2008, he is a full time staff member (Assistant Prof) on statistics and probabilities at the Department of Statistics and Financial-Actuarial Mathematics, University of the Aegean, Samos, Greece.

# Index

## A

Accessibility 10, 12-13, 15-16, 20-24, 27-28, 36-37, 41, 46, 68-69, 72, 121-122, 177-178, 180, 188, 192, 196, 198, 200-201, 204-208, 217-223, 225, 230

Accountability 14, 19-26, 28-31, 34-35, 37, 39-41

Annual Income 52-53, 55-57, 144, 154

## B

Bloom's Taxonomy of Learning Objectives 232, 237, 240

## C

Classic Interface Design 281

Cognitive Domain of Bloom's Taxonomy 240

Cognitive Lockup 100, 117

Computer Reservation System's (CRSs) 122, 137

Concurrent Think Aloud Protocols 117

Context of Use 186-187, 205, 221-222

Criminal Justice System 61-63, 69-70

Customer Loyalty 13, 58, 81, 139, 151, 153, 155-159, 162, 170-172, 175

Customer Perceived Service Quality 150, 154

Customer Perceived Value 139, 141, 150, 154

Customer Satisfaction 11, 13, 15, 29-30, 119-120, 122-127, 131-143, 148-152, 154-156, 159-160, 168, 171-175, 230, 237, 291

## D

Data 12, 35, 40, 47, 53, 55, 64, 70, 86, 143, 153, 182, 208, 252, 257, 291

Data Hierarchy 70

Delivery Quality 42, 48, 54-55, 57, 59

Demographic Characteristics 138-139, 142-144, 149-152, 154, 181

Destination Marketing Organizations 72-73, 84

## E

E-Business 4-5, 16-17, 30, 39, 85, 93-94, 120-121, 123, 133, 137, 149, 172, 220

E-Government 1-22, 24-31, 33-39, 41-42, 60, 70, 196-198

E-Government Business Models 1, 4-5, 18

E-Government Web Site Evaluation 18

E-Government Web Site Typology 18

E-Learning 224-234, 236-240, 294

Electronic Service 42-43, 45-47, 49, 51-52, 54-59, 124, 135, 141, 153

E-Marketing 41, 72

Emotional Arousal 251, 255, 258-259, 261, 265, 274, 281

Emotional Valence 241, 249, 258, 261, 264, 266, 274, 281

Environment Quality 42, 48, 52-54, 57, 59

E-Services Quality Evaluation 12, 18

Evaluation Models 15, 49, 81, 291, 294

## G

G2C -Government-to-Citizens (G2C) 41

Global Distribution System's (GDSs) 122, 137

## I

ICTRT Model 72-73, 76-77, 79, 81, 84

Information Processing 173, 181, 202, 277

Information Technology 13, 15-16, 20, 36, 76-77, 82, 115-117, 120-121, 133-134, 136-137, 197-198, 220-222, 278

## K

Keyword Search 243-245, 281